second edition

Social Change

Steven Vago
Saint Louis University

PRENTICE HALL, *Englewood Cliffs, NJ 07632*

Library of Congress
Library of Congress Cataloging-in-Publication Data

Vago, Steven.
   Social change / Steven Vago.—2nd ed.
     p. cm.
  Bibliography:
  Includes index.
  ISBN 0-13-815507-0
  1. Sociology. 2. Social change. I. Title.
HM51.V27 1989
303.4—dc19

Editorial/production supervision and
interior design: **Susan E. Rowan**
Cover design: **Lundgren Graphics, Ltd.**
Manufacturing buyer: **Peter Havens**

For Kathe

Printed in the United States of America
10 9 8 7 6 5 4 3

ISBN 0-13-815507-0

PRENTICE-HALL INTERNATIONAL (UK) LIMITED, *London*
PRENTICE-HALL OF AUSTRALIA PTY. LIMITED, *Sydney*
PRENTICE-HALL CANADA INC., *Toronto*
PRENTICE-HALL HISPANOAMERICANA, S.A., *Mexico*
PRENTICE-HALL OF INDIA PRIVATE LIMITED, *New Delhi*
PRENTICE-HALL OF JAPAN, INC., *Tokyo*
SIMON & SCHUSTER ASIA PTE. LTD., *Singapore*
EDITORA PRENTICE-HALL DO BRASIL, LTDA., *Rio de Janeiro*

Contents

3

Directions of Change   62

4

Sources of Change   85

5

Patterns of Change   114

6

Spheres of Change   150

7

Duration of Change   198

8

Reactions to Change   235

Preface

The second edition of this book is a result of the first edition's wide acceptance and utility in courses on social change. It retains the basic features of the first edition and remains scholarly, comprehensive, and readable.

The objective of the text is to provide a clear, up-to-date analysis of the various theoretical perspectives, directions, sources, processes, patterns, and consequences of social change. It considers factors that stimulate or hinder the acceptance of change in a cross-cultural context, and it emphasizes unintended consequences and costs of both planned and unplanned change. It dwells on the ways of creating and on the methods of assessing change. Unlike other books on the topic, this text highlights those aspects of theory and research that have immediate practical implications for students of social change. Although the orientation of the book is sociological, I did not hesitate to incorporate theoretical and empirical work from anthropology, social psychology, economics, political science, and history.

This edition reflects the many comments and recommendations made by students and colleagues who have used the book in their classrooms and research. Whereas the basic plan of the text remains unchanged, there is much that is new. The novel features include discussions on terrorism, the abortion debate, and the economic and social costs of environmental changes. Most chapters have been restructured, and all have been updated to reflect theoretical and empirical advances since the first edition. A unique aspect of the book is its extensive coverage of cross-cultural material.

Although any errors, inaccuracies, omissions, and commissions are accepted—and regretted—as my own responsibility, much of the book derives from many persons, mostly colleagues and students, whose help and wisdom I gratefully acknowledge. Special thanks go to Professor Clement S. Mihanovich and to my students in courses on social change who patiently endured the earlier drafts and offered many valuable suggestions. Of the many students who read portions of the manuscript, I want to thank Bart A. Mantia, Jim Rinderknecht, Candace L. Rollins, Valerie Traiteur, and Miguel A. Virella, who went beyond the call of duty in helping me with the final preparation of the book. I also wish to express my thanks to the anonymous reviewers whose comments facilitated the development of this book. At Prentice Hall, I extend my gratitude to Nancy Roberts, Acquisitions Editor; Susan Rowan, Production Editor; and James Tully, Copy Editor; for their outstanding processing of the manuscript and to Steele/Katigbak, Indexers, for expertly preparing the index.

S.V.

Introduction: Dimensions of Change

1

This book is about *social change*, which is one of the most important, challenging, and exciting topics in sociology. From the beginnings, social change has been an integral part of the human condition. Since the earliest times, there has been a fascination with change, a constant preoccupation with its ramifications, and prolonged agitation about its consequences.

The science of sociology began in the quest for explanations for social change. The advent of this new science marked the beginning of a long and sinuous road toward making "sense" of change. Yet, in spite of the multitude of efforts since its inception, the discipline of sociology is still confronted with the questions of how society changes, in what direction, why, what specific ways, and by what forces these changes are created. Considering the fact that social change has been ubiquitous and at times a dramatic feature of society, there is still a great deal to learn about its nature and scope. Today social change is a central concern of sociology, and it is likely to remain one of the most intriguing and difficult problems in the discipline.

The intention of this book is to draw attention to the complexities and concerns inherent in the understanding of social change. It will concentrate on the more salient features, characteristics, processes, and perspectives of change in the United States and cross-culturally. The purpose

is to try to make "sense" of change, and to consider what is changing—
and where, why, and how.

The primary mission of the book is to serve as a text in undergraduate
courses on social change. The comprehensiveness and the relatively large
number of references included also make the book a valuable resource for
both graduate students interested in social change and instructors who may
be teaching a course on the subject for the first time. Because the book has
been written with the undergraduate student in mind, no one particular
perspective or approach to change has been taken, nor has a specific ideology or theoretical perspective been embraced. To have done so would
have been too limiting for the scope of this book, since important contributions to social change would have had to be excluded or would be subject
to criticism as being out of context. As a result, the book does not propound
a single thesis; instead, it exposes the reader to a variety of theoretical
perspectives proposed to account for social change in the social science
literature.

THE ORGANIZATION OF THE BOOK

The book examines the principal theoretical, empirical, analytical, and
evaluative aspects in the study of social change. To make the text more
comprehensive and interesting, the sociological perspectives are supplemented with other social science views and an abundance of cross-cultural
and historical illustrations. The following comments on chapter contents
will provide a schematic orientation for the reader.

This chapter examines the nature and the basic concepts of the subject
matter and presents an approach for the conceptualization of social change.
Next, the discussion centers on the inevitability of social change in human
societies with specific examples of what has changed in the United States
during the past century. The chapter concludes by noting the distinction
between social change and cultural change.

Sociological explanations of *why* social change occurs are as old as the
discipline itself. To introduce the reader to the diverse theoretical orientations, Chapter 2 reviews the most influential and important classical and
contemporary *theories* of social change. They are discussed by principal
perspectives and proponents. The review concentrates on evolutionary,
conflict, structural-functional, systems, and social-psychological explanations of social change.

Because some of these theories allude to the directionality of change
whereas others treat it explicitly, Chapter 3 is devoted to an examination
of the more prevalent *directions* and trajectories of social change.

Once we have discussed the predominant explanations of change and
the directions it takes, it is appropriate to turn to the *sources* of change in

Chapter 4. The sources of change encompass the impetus for change, the driving force behind change, and the conditions that are sufficient to produce it. The principal sources of change chosen for analysis are technology, ideology, competition, conflict, political and economic forces, and structural strains.

After the identification and analysis of forces that produce change, we need to consider the question of how and in what form change takes place. In Chapter 5 the discussion focuses on such *patterns* of change as evolution, diffusion, acculturation, revolution, modernization, industrialization, urbanization, and bureaucratization.

One might comment at this stage of the discourse: "So far, so good, but what has really changed in our contemporary world?" In response to this question, Chapter 6 examines trends in such specific social arrangements and *spheres* as family, population, stratification, power relations, education, and economy.

Once a change is accepted at any level of the social system, it is appropriate to ask how long it is likely to be sustained. Thus, the question of *duration* becomes important; this is discussed in Chapter 7 in terms of long-term and transitory (fads, fashions, life-styles, and cults) change phenomena.

Social change contains varying dialectical modes. It is neither automatic nor unopposed. It affects individuals and groups in society in different ways, for whom change may mean different things. Chapter 8, on the *reactions* to change, looks at the social, psychological, cultural, and economic forces and conditions that facilitate or hinder the acceptance of change.

How to bring about social change is among the most crucial and timely questions in the book. Thus, an analysis of *strategies* to create "desired" change is paramount. The aim of Chapter 9 is to analyze a series of social change strategies and tactics used in a variety of change efforts.

The question of what new social arrangements must be made, once change is brought about, has seldom been considered adequately in the literature on social change. The purpose of Chapter 10 is to examine the *impacts* and effects of change, its unanticipated consequences, and the methods of coping with change.

Any alteration of the social system and all forms of social engineering carry a price tag. But the price we pay for it is rarely mentioned. In Chapter 11, the discussion is concerned with the issues of the economics of change and the social and psychological *costs* of "progress."

The last chapter is devoted to the current *methodologies* used in the assessment of the viability of change on social arrangements. Emphasis is placed on technology and environment assessment, techniques of change evaluation, and methodologies for forecasting change with applicable policy implications.

The study of social change is naturally eclectic. Knowledge about it has accumulated in shreds and patches. In attempting to explain social change—whether on the scale of major transformations in society or of a more specialized, localized kind—one is tempted to look for "prime movers" analogous to the *forces* of Newtonian physics. But there are no "laws" in sociology comparable to the laws of physics. At best, we have some good generalizations. Our investigations are guided by a number of theoretical perspectives resulting in a variety of strands of thought and research. In pulling them together, we will be guided by the following concerns:

1. What do we need to know about social change? What are the principal issues in the study of change?
2. What do we really know? What are the major theories and findings in the field? How much confidence can we have in them?
3. What remains to be known? What are the major "unknowns" or lacunae in theory and research?

In a sense, more problems are raised than can be solved in this volume. One of the fascinating aspects of the study of social change is that there are so many loose ends, so many ways of considering the subject, and so much yet to be learned. It is hoped that this book will serve as a useful point of departure for further study of change.

ON THE NATURE OF SOCIAL CHANGE

One of the central issues of our time is change. Everywhere change has become central to people's awareness, and there is a commitment to change that is irreversible, irresistible, and irrevocable. In every society there is technological change, demographic change, rapid ecological change, and change induced by internal incongruities in economic and political patterns and by conflicting ideologies. The fundamental questions relate to what is changing, at what level, and how fast. Moreover, we want to know what type of change is taking place—and what its magnitude, scope, and direction are.

An obvious first question in considering the nature of social change is, "What is changing?" For the layperson, it could be everything or nothing. The question as it is phrased is just too broad, too general to be meaningful. In the United States, the standard form of greeting someone is usually followed by the question, "What's new?" Invariably, we are at a loss to come up with a coherent and cogent response to this habitual but ridiculous question. Still, it is an everyday occurrence. As a rule, we fire back an equally ridiculous and meaningless response saying, "not much," "nothing," or similar remarks in that vein. To avoid this dilemma of uncomfortable ambiguity, we need to go beyond the original question and specify *what* it is that is assertedly changing. Change, when it exists, is change of something with a specific identity—whether this be a norm, a relationship, or the divorce rate. Failure to specify the identity or *what* is changing can easily lead to confusion.

Once we have established the identity of what is changing, the next consideration is the *level* at which change takes place. Even though the concept of social change is inclusive of all social phenomena, in reality, we cannot study and comprehend change without knowing where it takes place. Thus, we need to identify the location in the social system in which a particular change is occurring. We can establish several units of study and focus our attention, for example, on the following levels: individuals, groups, organizations, institutions, and society.

Thus, change is becoming "social" and we are also becoming a bit more specific with our question. We might now pose the question, "What is changing and at what *level*?" We are now talking about the scope of change in relation to the number of persons or groups whose norms or social arrangement change; that is, the location of a particular change in a social system as well as the type of norm, attribute, or relationship that has changed. For example, on the *individual* level we can talk about changes in attitudes, beliefs, aspirations, and motivations. On the *group* level we might consider changes in the types of interaction patterns—in communication, methods of conflict resolution, cohesion, unity, competition, and acceptance and rejection patterns. At the level of *organizations,* the scope of change would include alterations in the structure and function of organizations and changes in hierarchy, communication, role relationship, productivity, recruitment, and socialization patterns. At the *institutional* level, change may include alterations in marriage and family patterns, education, and religious practices. At the level of *society,* change may be seen as the modification of the stratification, economic; and political systems. In the context of the discussion, the level at which change takes place will be easily discernible to the reader.

Now we are getting closer. We know roughly what is changing and at what level. So we might as well be a bit more specific and raise the question, "How long does it take for a certain type of change to come about?" In other words, we are referring to the *rate* of change. That is, at what rate does a specific change take place? The rate of change can be measured by a specific set of time intervals such as days, months, years, decades, or centuries; or it can be designated as slow and rapid. Obviously, rate—that is, time in a comparative sense—enters into the study of social change through the use of words such as long-term or short-term, and will be an important consideration in discussing the duration of change.

The *magnitude* of change is somewhat more difficult to delineate. As an illustration, the three-part scheme proposed by Robert Dahl (1967) for measuring the magnitude of political change—incremental or marginal, comprehensive, and revolutionary—is suggested. Incremental or marginal changes would be those that expand, reduce, or otherwise modify the contours of a particular norm or behavior without altering or repudiating its basic substance or structure. There is consensus in the literature that incremental change is the most common and "normal" pattern of change in the United States. Comprehensive changes might represent the culmination of related incremental changes or, in Dahl's terms, "sweeping innovations or decisive reversals of established" (1967:264) norms or behavior patterns. Changes of revolutionary magnitude would involve wholesale substitution of one type of norm or behavior for another, and decisive rejection of the original behavior as well.

The next concern is the *direction* of change. Direction in this context simply refers to some future position of the entity in relation to its initial position. Direction may be seen as linear or cyclical, or described in general terms such as "higher," "lower," "backward," or "forward" in respect to some scale. It can be analyzed on a value axis using concepts such as progress, improvement, decline, zigzag, or betterment. We can consider it quantitatively in terms of fluctuations in volume, size, or simply in sheer numbers. The three approaches are not mutually exclusive. In any case, we need to specify the type of change before we can talk about its directionality.

To round off our contemplations about the nature of change, we need to ask whether a particular change at a particular level is deliberate or unplanned. Deliberate or *planned* social change refers to inventing or developing social technologies consistent with existing social and behavioral knowledge and adequate to the practical and moral requirements of contemporary change situations. At the individual level, for example, it might be changing attitudes and behavior toward minorities. On the organizational level, it may entail attempts to increase efficiency and productivity. At the institutional level, the object may be to create more educational opportunities for disadvantaged students. The *unplanned* consequences of change include the unanticipated and the dysfunctional results of a planned change. For example, the minimum wage law was intended to provide unskilled laborers with an income slightly above the poverty level. Unintentionally, however, this provision has contributed to the increase in teenage unemployment, particularly among black youth and reduced job prospects for low wage earners. When the minimum wage increased, employers tended to hire more part-time than full-time workers and the overall level of hiring was lower (*The Wall Street Journal*, 1987:60).

In sum, when considering social change, it is helpful to specify its identity (what is changing), and to determine its level, its rate, magnitude, direction, and causes and consequences. With this in mind, let us turn to the definitions of social change.

DEFINITIONS OF SOCIAL CHANGE

There are as many ways of describing social change as there are ways of studying societies (Chirot, 1986:2). Economists, demographers, anthropologists, political scientists, historians, and sociologists bring their own special disciplines to the diverse conceptualizations of change. Even among sociologists, discussions of social change often begin with complaints about the lack of uniformity concerning the definition of change. The point is well taken, for practically every book on social change has a section on definitions, conditioned by the author's theoretical and ideological orientation, in an attempt to narrow the concept down. There is a multiplicity of such ventures with few features in common. Perhaps Thurman Arnold (1937:180) was correct, over two generations ago, in suggesting that a "Definition is ordinarily supposed to produce clarity in thinking. It is not generally recognized that the more we define our terms the less descriptive they become and the more difficulty we have in using them." His admonition is well taken and will be illustrated by a sample of different social change definitions. Then I will propose a way of trying to get out of the definitional quagmire. I do this in light of Karl Popper's (1959:55) caution that "definitions are dogmas, only the conclusions drawn from them can afford us any new insights."

Different Group Activities

In its most concrete sense, social change means that large numbers of people are engaging in group activities and relationships that are different from those in which they or their parents engaged in some time before. As stated by Hans Gerth and C. Wright Mills: "By social change we refer to whatever may happen in the course of time to the roles, the institutions, or the orders comprising a social structure, their emergence, growth and decline" (1953:398). Society is a complex network of patterns of relationships in which all the members participate in varying degrees. These relationships change, and behavior changes at the same time. Individuals are faced with new situations to which they must respond. These situations reflect such factors as the introduction of new techniques, new ways of making a living, changes in place of residence, and new innovations, ideas, and social values. Thus, social change means modifications of the way people work, rear a family, educate their children, govern themselves, and seek ultimate meaning in life.

Change in the Structure of Society

Many sociologists view social change as a change in the structure of society or alteration of the social structure. For instance, Morris Ginsberg (1958:205) writes: "By social change I understand a change in the social structure, for example, the size of a society, the composition or balance of its parts or the type of its organizations. Examples of such changes are the contraction in the size of the family . . . the breaking up of the domainal economy with the rise of the cities, the transition from 'estates' to social classes. . . ." Viewed from a somewhat different perspective, "Social change is the significant alteration of social structures (that is, of patterns of social action and interaction), including consequences and manifestations of such structures embodied in norms (rules of conduct), values and cultural products and symbols" (Moore, 1968:366).

It is understandable why social structure (patterns of social behavior that include statuses, roles, groups, and institutions such as the family, religion, politics, and the economic system) is being emphasized in change. Social structures are not stable, tightly integrated, or harmonious, but are unstable, loosely put together, and torn by dissension. To ignore this profound phenomenon and process is to miss a central fact about societies. Increasingly we accept a Heraclitean view of the world as flux rather than as composed of solid building blocks.

Change in the Structure and Functioning of Society

Others stress that social change is not only a change in the structure, but also in the functioning of society. "Social change comprises modifications in social systems or subsystems in structure, functioning, or process over some period of time" (Allen, 1971:39). Similarly, "By 'social change' is meant only such alterations as occur in social organization—that is, the structure and functions of society" (Davis, 1949:622). Harry M. Johnson (1960:626, 628) goes into some detail in observing that: "Social change is change in the structure of a social system; what has been stable or relatively unchanging changes. Moreover, of structural changes the most important are those that have consequences for the functioning of the system—for attaining its goals more (or less) efficiently or for fulfilling more (or less) efficiently the conditions that must be met if the system is to survive at all."

Change in Social Relationships

Some authors consider social change principally in terms of a specific change in social relationships. For example, "By social change is meant changes in social relationships . . . the changing ways in which human beings relate to one another" (MacIver & Page, 1949:511). A generation later, in the same vein, Judson R. Landis (1974:229) writes: "Social change refers to change in the structure and functioning of the social relationships of a society."

Change in Social Structure and Social Relationships

Ronald Edari (1976:2) combines both elements, social structure and social relationships, in his definition: "When we talk of social change, we mean, at the very minimum, two things: a) the change in the constitution of social entities over time, and b) the change in the relations among entities over time." Taking a somewhat broader and more inclusive view, Robert A. Nisbet (1969:168) views social change as "a succession of differences in time within a persisting identity." And Robert H. Lauer (1982:4) considers change as ". . . an inclusive concept that refers to alterations in social phenomena at various levels of human life from the individual to the global."

A Working Definition of Social Change

A common difficulty with these definitions of social change is the problem of reification, the tendency to equate conceptual abstractions of reality with an actual piece of reality. We can isolate the elements emphasized in the definitions, which include the social structure, the functioning of society, social relationships, forms of social processes, and time. But we still have difficulties in understanding what is changing. The term "change" is often used loosely, and as it has been illustrated, attempts at definitions are sufficiently numerous and conflicting as to be of much help.

At this point, I propose a different approach toward a workable definition of social change. For the present purpose, social change is conceptualized as the process of planned or unplanned qualitative or quantitative alterations in social phenomena that can be depicted on a six-part continuum composed of interrelated analytic components. For the sake of simplicity, these components are called identity, level, duration, direction, magnitude, and rate of change.

> *Identity* of change refers to a specific social phenomenon undergoing transformation such as a definite practice, behavior, attitude, interaction pattern, authority structure, productivity rate, voting pattern, prestige, and stratification system.
>
> *Level* of change delineates the location in a social system where a particular change takes place. Several levels may be designated such as individual, group, organization, institution, and society.
>
> *Duration* refers to the question of how long a particular change form endures after it has been accepted. It may refer to the life span of long-term or short-term (transitory) change phenomena.
>
> *Direction* of change may indicate development or decay, progress, or decline. The pattern can also be linear or evolutionary, occur in cycles or stages, or correspond to some other pattern. It may also be a simple fluctuation or variation on a particular theme.
>
> *Magnitude* may be based on the three-part scheme of incremental or marginal, comprehensive, and revolutionary changes, as discussed in the preceding section.
>
> *Rate* of change may be based on any arbitrary scale such as fast or slow, continuous or spasmodic, orderly or erratic.

Figure 1.1 depicts the elements of this conceptualization of social change. The dimensions of it are arbitrary and may be construed differently

FIG 1.1   Elements of social change definiton.

by those who are experiencing it or experimenting with it. However, when specific meanings are assigned to these dimensions, this conceptualization of social change can become a useful point of departure for empirical and theoretical endeavors in social change.

THE INEVITABILITY OF CHANGE

Why is social change inevitable? What is there in the nature of humans, society, and culture that demands and produces change? What are the reasons for the massive social changes we are facing today? Many different factors interact to generate changes in people's behavior and in the culture and structure of their society. Many of these factors are critical in making change inevitable. Several of them will be considered briefly in the following pages. But one should be careful *not* to assign the position of prime mover to any one of them in isolation. They affect each other, they are interdependent, and we cannot make generalizations about what parts of the social structure "cause" change in others. The impact of these factors differs with the situation, the time, and the place.

Population

Changes in the size, composition, and distribution of a population influence social changes. When there is adequate food supply, populations tend to increase in size. As they grow, they need to find more efficient ways to produce more food. This may result in agricultural innovations and new forms of social organizations. If population growth exceeds available food supplies, one of three changes is likely to occur. Large numbers will starve; there will be conflict and even war to obtain food; or large segments of the population will migrate to other lands to eke out an existence. These responses to food shortages in recent years occurred in several countries such as Cambodia, Haiti, and Ethiopia.

An important population characteristic is its age composition. In the United States, many current changes are due to the large "bulge" of persons born after World War II that is now making its way through the age groups. Between 1946 and 1961, some 64 million infants were born. In the 1950s, the baby boom generation made the country a child-oriented society of new schools and suburbs. In the 1960s and early 1970s, baby boomers fueled the student, civil rights, peace, and alternative life-style movements. Many of the schools that were built to accomodate them in the 1960s are now closed or half-empty. Colleges are fighting to maintain enrollments. Today, we have a "graying" of the American population with important ramifications. Social Security, Medicaid, and health costs are soaring. Within 40 years, one out of five Americans will be 65 or older. In 1965, there were five workers supporting a Social Security recipient. By the time today's college student qualifies, there will be only two workers. The graying of the society generate other changes. More and more people are lining up for promotion at the workplace, but there are fewer openings. This is a factor in midlife career changes, early retirements, underemployment, and unemployment (Peterson, 1987:62–64).

The profound changes that were created by large-scale migration are evident in the history of the United States. The several waves of immigrants in the nineteenth and early twentieth century from western, southern, and eastern Europe brought their own customs, ideas, and life-styles. In the 1980s, Cubans, Mexicans, and Southeast Asians with different languages and cultures generated changes in food habits, music, employment, and education, to name just a few areas.

Conflict

It is a truism in the social sciences that *conflict* is inevitable in any society because of opposed interests or incompatible claims to scarce values such as money or power. Whether or not conflict is destructive or constructive, it can be seen as an omnipresent, creative source of change—a way of possibly renewing, revitalizing, or destroying society. Much change is produced by conflicts among groups within societies. Conflicts are present among classes, residents of different regions, and racial and ethnic groups. For example, the civil rights movement of the 1950s and 1960s not only removed many barriers to black participation in the mainstream of American society but also changed many other aspects of society. Indeed, the end of official southern racism may have been essential to the rapid economic growth now taking place in the South.

Economic Determinism

Closely intertwined with the idea of the inevitability of conflict in society is the Marxian notion of *economic determinism*. Karl Marx began with an assumption: Economic organization, especially the ownership of property, determines the organization of the rest of a society. The class structure and institutional arrangements, as well as cultural values, beliefs, religious dogmas, and other idea systems, are ultimately a reflection of the economic base of a society. He then added an additional assumption. Inherent in the economic organization of any society (with the exception of communistic societies) are forces inevitably generating revolutionary class conflict. Such revolutionary class conflict is seen as dialectical and is conceptualized as occurring in epochs, with successive bases of economic organization sowing the seeds of their own destruction through the pluralization of their own classes and subsequent overthrow of the dominant by the subjugated class. Hence a third assumption: Conflict is bipolar, with exploited classes under the conditions created by the economy becoming aware of their true "interests" and eventually forming a revolutionary political organization that stands against the dominant property-holding class. (Turner, 1974:79) Thus change is built into the nature of the social structure in the tension and conflict between classes, and it is directed toward a vague, wonderful, and presumably ideal utopia.

Innovation

Innovation refers to a new way of doing something. A *discovery* represents an addition to knowledge on the basis of some existing phenomenon such as Einstein's theory of relativity. *Invention*, by contrast, uses existing knowledge in some novel form, for example, steam engine, plastic, or the automobile. Innovations—both discoveries and inventions—are not single acts but the results of cumulative technological and social knowledge. From the beginning of the study of astronomy and physics several thousand years ago in the eastern Mediterranean, astronomical and physical ideas have accumulated, have gradually built up into astronomy and physics we study in school and college. The process of building up has not been regular, but on the whole it has been steady. Although some of the ideas or theories of the early scholars are still acceptable, such as the ideas of the ancient Greek Archimedes on specific gravity, many, many others have been added to the original stock. All innovators, except for some who make purely accidental discoveries, have only the existing "storehouse of knowledge" with which to work. Thomas Edison might have been a great man if he had lived 300 years earlier, but he certainly would not have invented the electric light or the phonograph, because the steps that laid the groundwork for these inventions had not been taken. Leonardo DaVinci, for all his fascination with flight and the amazing draftsmanship for his models for flying machines, could never have succeeded in inventing the airplane. Because such necessary preliminary inventions as the gasoline engine were still far in the future, he had to be satisfied with the invention of the bicycle.

Three basic types of innovations frequently cause social change. The first is **new technology**. The automobile, for example, revolutionized the structure of cities and the character of urban life. More specifically, William F. Ogburn (1922) traced direct connections between the invention of the automobile self-starter and the emancipation of women. When it became easy for them to drive cars, they entered the business world and thus changed their role and the nature of their family relationships.

The second type of innovation is **new culture**. New beliefs, values, and ideologies can and do produce dramatic changes. Robert Nisbet (1980), for example, contends that rapid technological changes in Europe during the seventeenth and eighteenth centuries were stimulated by the idea of progress. People accepted the idea that progress was not only possible but inevitable. This confidence in progress motivated them to achieve scientific and technological progress, and as they succeeded, their confidence and efforts further increased. Likewise, new beliefs, values, and ideologies are often sources of revolutions and subsequent large-scale changes (Brinton, 1959; Goldstone, 1986; Shils, 1972).

The third type of innovation consists of **new forms of social structure**. For example, the modern bureaucratic organization is a new mode of social structure designed to cope with complex administrative demands created by contemporary society.

Diffusion

Although innovations are major sources of change, more often than not they are imported from other societies rather than developed independently within a society. *Diffusion* is the process by which innovations, and other culture traits, spread from one society to another. More rapid progress is possible because societies borrow from each other. Advances in communication and transportation have greatly facilitated contact among societies and among diverse groups within societies. Travelers learn new ways; for example, Marco Polo's Chinese cook introduced spaghetti to Italy, and centuries later Italian immigrants brought it to America. Today's youth culture is a mixture of many influences, including British punk and American rural clothing, folk, soul, rock, and oriental music, and philosophy and hip argot from the drug, jail, and lower-class subcultures. All over the world missionaries have introduced new moral codes, new religious beliefs, and new customs in dress, hygiene, and schooling. Untold millions of inexpensive radios and close to that many TV sets reach people all over the world. The increasing use of communications satellites may turn the world into what Marshall McLuhan called "a global village," in which everyone knows the news almost as soon as it happens. Along with movies, advances in communication technology have created among the poor a desire for change and may have set the grounds for the "revolution of rising expectations" not only in our own society, but all around the world.

The Legal System

Finally, every human society has some type of *legal system*. In the modern world, legislatures, courts, and administrative bodies grind out new rules every day. Many of these laws have an effect on a given segment of society by altering power relationships, redistributing rights and obligations and modifying social relationships. Laws bring changes in behavior and influence life-styles, values, modes of adaptation, and institutional membership patterns and practices. Through the continuous process of regulation, deregulation, and selective enforcement, the legal system is an omnipresent instrument of social change (Vago, 1988).

The list of reasons why social change is inevitable is, indeed, incomplete. We could talk further about *Homo sapiens'* innate curiosity, their eternal desire for new experiences, their willingness to explore new territories, their desire to overcome the problems they created for themselves, their willingness to explore the realm of the unknown. All these conditions make change a ubiquitous feature of human society. Thus, humankind seems to be under the spell of the old Chinese curse: "May your life be an interesting one." And, as the rest of the book will show, it is.

WHAT IS CHANGING?

The reality and ubiquity of social change can be illustrated in several ways. In watching an old film, for example, no one would fail to notice how much is different from that of a couple of generations ago—styles of dress, modes of transportation, style of humor, vocabulary, customs, design of buildings, and the nature of human relations at home, at work, or on the streets. One may listen to the reminiscences of grandparents about the "good old days," although some maintain that they were terrible (Bettman, 1974), or visit a town or city after a prolonged absence to discover changes in life-styles, physical patterns, and forms of communication.

Although the preceding illustrations provide a general notion of what is changing in impressionistic terms, a consideration of certain indicators of change is essential to the realization of what is happening in the domain of social change. Thus, on the following pages, I will briefly describe changes in selected areas that will be explained subsequently. My objective is simply to document the reality and magnitude of change. Because of space limitations, the review of changes will be arbitrarily limited to two periods in the United States: the 1880s and 1950s. These two time periods will be sufficient to illustrate in a general way the vast changes that have taken place in America.

The United States a Century Ago

Some hundred years ago, the rapid growth of cities had yet to begin. Of the 47 million people living in the United States, three-fourths lived in rural areas. The birthrate was high (39.8 per 1,000 inhabitants per year), and infant mortality reached 157 per 1,000 newborns. Less than half of the population was in the labor force, but they spent more than 65 hours a week working. Obviously, no one had ever driven a car, put food in a refrigerator, turned down a thermostat, traveled in an airplane, gone to a movie, listened to a radio, opened a beer can in front of the television set, or wore synthetic fabrics. Industry relied on the steam engine for power, and the principal source of energy available to most families was the horse. The division of labor was elementary by comparison to today's standards. Most Americans worked on their own farms, where responsibilities were allocated primarily on the basis of age and sex.

Very few Americans had been to high school (less than 4 percent of the population), and even fewer of them had ever seen college. A century ago higher learning was not very high. Faculties were often undistinguished, and course offerings were scanty. Students were trained for the ministry, the law, or simply the acquiring of a genteel ability to read Greek and Latin (Collins, 1979). Advanced education for women was still widely regarded as a dangerous experiment. Females were seen as delicate creatures, and just like children and lunatics, they lacked full legal rights (Friedman, 1984:238).

The prevailing norms of society disapproved of outspoken women and of children who did not unquestionably obey their parents. Any public mention of sexual matters was an outrageous breach of etiquette. Spiritually and morally, women had been placed on a pedestal. A girl who indulged in premarital sex relations was marked for life, and her illegitimate child, if she had one, was stigmatized for life. To a single woman, loss of virginity was "a fate worse than death." Most husbands and wives never saw each other nude. Divorce was frowned upon and the rate was low, 0.3 percent. There was little sense of public responsibility for social welfare. Although private charities and philanthropies were common and private citizens struggled to help the less fortunate, there were no old age pensions and no retirement plans, no minimum wage laws, and no federal laws against child labor.

Americans a hundred years ago could not, in their wildest dreams, imagine Eskimos whizzing around the Arctic on snowmobiles. They would never have assumed that drinking water may cause cancer, and it would have been unthinkable to suspect that the sun would not set on the British empire, not to mention the presence of the London Bridge in Arizona. For them, birth control was abstinence and the rhythm method, and they would never have conceived that oral contraceptives could raise theological questions. They would never have believed that carefully built political organizations could be undermined by the introduction of voting machines. In short, life in "the good old days" was very different from life as we know it today. The number of changes that have occurred since the last century—although at varying rates—is almost beyond comprehension. In

Kenneth Boulding's words: "I was born in the middle of human history, to date, roughly. Almost as much has happened since I was born as happened before" (quoted by Toffler, 1970:15). Alvin Toffler (1970:14) illustrates this startling statement by suggesting

> ... if the last 50,000 years of man's existence were divided into lifetimes of approximately sixty-two years each, there have about 800 such lifetimes. Of these 800, fully 650 were spent in caves.
>
> Only during the last seventy lifetimes has it been possible to communicate effectively from one lifetime to another—as writing made it possible to do. Only during the last six lifetimes did masses of men ever see a printed word. Only during the last four has it been possible to measure time with any precision. Only in the last two has anyone anywhere used an electric motor. And the overwhelming majority of all the material goods we use in daily life today have been developed within the present, the 800th, lifetime.

Let us now narrow the time span to roughly "half a lifetime" and take a brief look at the United States in the 1950s.

A Glimpse At The 1950s.

In the 1950s, there were some 90 million fewer people living in the United States than today. The birthrate was almost twice as high, and so were infant mortality rates. Illegitimacy rates were less than half of what they are today. Teenagers started to date at a later age, and they married in their early twenties. By age 30, close to 90 percent of all women were married. A similar pattern existed for males, and they were expected to be several years older than their wives. Premarital cohabitation was considered immoral, and a student living with a member of the opposite sex without the benefit of marriage could be expelled for the offense. Students who lived on campus had strictly segregated and supervised dormitories. Inside the dorm, visiting privileges with members of the opposite sex were greatly curtailed. Visitors were allowed usually during the weekends, and only for a few hours in the afternoon—with the door open. Colleges and universities acted *in loco parentis* (in the place of parents) and required that students be in their dormitories by a certain time, generally by nine or ten on weeknights and by midnight on weekends—unless someone "signed out" (had a very good reason to stay out). Some even required dress codes for the students. Even the academic year was longer; students attended classes on the average of 174 days as compared to about 150 days today (*St. Louis Post-Dispatch,* 1987:1C).

Few women saw divorce as a viable option in the 1950s. Most women did not work, and they had limited ability to provide an income for themselves and their children outside marriage. Children were also a liability in finding a new partner after divorce. In most cases, marital dissatisfaction required adjustments within the marriage, particularly by wives. Men, in contrast, had a greater opportunity to terminate a marriage because of their financial independence.

Children were a major goal of marriage, and many couples started having children soon after they wed. Marriage and having a family were central to women's lives, and through children they viewed themselves as useful and contributing members of society. In the 1950s, the marital division of labor was rather simple; most men worked outside of the home and earned almost all the money while women did most of the housework and took care of children. Quite often, unlike today, couples began their families before they had accumulated such things as a house, a second car, or a washing machine. Not surprisingly, the average number of children was just over three.

The 1950s were also a time when the economy moved into a new age of television, jet planes, lasers, and computers, and American industries became conglomerates and multinationals operating all over the globe. The shift from a predominantly industrial society to an information and service-oriented society had just begun (Naisbitt, 1982). Proportionately, half as many women were in the labor force in the 1950s as today. Most wives went to work either to finance large families or to escape them. Americans allocated a smaller proportion of their income to housing but spent more on food. Suburban living had just begun in earnest. Overseas travel was limited to the affluent, and television was still a luxury. Life expectancy was lower, and people were shorter and weighed less (Issel, 1985).

In the 1950s, acceptance of premarital sex, abortion, homosexuality, and extramarital relations was confined to a small minority (Yankelovich, 1981). The socialization of females so estranged them from their sexuality that in order for males to have intercourse with a "nice girl," the prospect of marriage had to exist. Abortion was illegal and contraceptive technology was in its infancy. Single women confronted with an unwanted pregnancy had few choices: marriage, illegal and usually dangerous termination of pregnancy, giving up the child for adoption, or keeping the child. When they opted for the last alternative, they were usually stigmatized and faced the moral outrage of the community. Homosexuality was both illegal and immoral, and male and female homosexuals kept very quiet about their sexual preferences. The infamous double standard concerning both pre- and extramarital sexual relations was faithfully observed; it was all right for males to engage in intercourse, but not for females who were sensitive about their reputation. Particularly for married women, adultery was considered a significant breach of mores, although it was more or less tolerated for married men—until it became public. In fact, in several states adultery was the only grounds for divorce.

The national mood was conservative, and there was little criticism of the major institutions such as political parties, big business, and the military. There was little effort to change the status of racial and minority groups in society, and segregated facilities—from educational institutions to restaurants and rest rooms—prevailed. Blacks, for the most part, were excluded from the mainstream of American life; they lived in black areas, they went to school with other blacks, sat in the back of the bus, and were in general relegated to an inferior position in society. This was perhaps most pronounced in the South in the 1950s. Women, just like blacks, faced a variety of discriminatory practices at school, in politics, and at the workplace. They were significantly underrepresented in the professions, and they were essentially limited to traditional "female" jobs such as secretaries, nurses, and teachers at the grade school and high school levels.

If one compares life today with what it was a century ago or in the 1950s, the reality and the immensity of change becomes obvious. At this point, I will not offer an explanation or analysis of the reasons for these rapid and intense changes. That will be the topic of Chapter 4.

SOCIAL CHANGE DISTINGUISHED
FROM CULTURAL CHANGE

Although the concepts "social change" and "cultural change" are not always clearly separated in the social science literature, the two terms are distinct. As A.L. Kroeber and Talcott Parsons (1958:582) note, society and culture constitute two independent systems. In their words:

> They are distinct systems in that they abstract or select two analytically distinct sets of components from the same concrete phenomena. Statements made about relationships within a cultural pattern are thus of a different order from those within a system of societal relationships. . . . (W)e feel that the analytical discrimination should be consistently maintained without prejudice to the question of which is more "important," "correct" or "fundamental," if indeed such questions turn out to be meaningful at all.

I share Kingsley Davis's (1949:622) position that social change represents only a part of a broader category called "cultural change." "The latter embraces all changes occurring in any branch of culture, as art, science, technology, philosophy, etc., as well as changes in the forms and rules of social organization." The word "culture" in its social, intellectual, and artistic senses is a metaphorical term derived from the act of cultivating the soil (Latin *cultura*). The cultivation of the mind was seen as a process comparable to the cultivation of the soil; hence, the early meanings of culture in this metaphorical sense centered on a process, "the *culture of* the mind," rather than on an achieved state. A development from this metaphorical use of the word "culture" was a description of certain persons as "cultivated" or "cultured." The first use of "culture" in English as a precise and scientific term is generally credited to E. B. Tylor (1958:1), who said,

"Culture is a complex whole which includes knowledge, belief, art, morals, law, custom and any other capabilities acquired by man as a member of society.'

The word "culture" is the most general in the vocabulary of anthropologists as the term "society" is the most general in the vocabulary of the sociologists. The two concepts are interrelated, but they need to be distinguished from each other. Melville J. Herskovitz (1948:29) formulates the differences as follows: "A culture is the way of life of a people, while a society is the organized aggregate of individuals who follow a given way of life. In simple terms, a society is composed of people, the way they behave is their culture." Sociologists, in studying what people are, also are interested in how they behave. Anthropologists, in studying how people behave, also need a term of the actual systems of activity where culture is present. From the standpoint of the anthropologists, the modes of interhuman behavior (society) are only one aspect of culture, which includes many other things. From the standpoint of sociology, culture is a mere abstraction until it is manifested in some specific system of activity. Yet, many sociologists and anthropologists would probably agree with A.L. Kroeber's (1948:9) characterization of the relationship as that of "two intimately intertwined aspects of a complex phenomenon that regularly occur only in association." The manner in which someone views "culture" and "society" and how he or she portrays their relationship is often indicative of the individual's basic theoretical approach to the studies of changes in society. For example, we shall see in the following chapter on theories that some theorists conceive of culture as an analyzable entity in itself, whereas others stress conflict, structural-functional, systems or social-psychological theories.

In addition to theoretical interests, understanding the idea of culture also has practical applications. Culture affects behavior, morals, role relationships, punctuality, productivity at work, motivation, what people eat and how, mate selection, marriage forms, divorce, the role of women, conversation distance, privacy, child-rearing patterns—the list is practically endless. Corporate culture affects how an organization copes with competition and change, whether in terms of technology, economics, or people. Culture defines negotiation styles, the treatment of subordinates, and gift-giving practices. Not surprisingly, there is a growing emphasis, for example, in the international business arena on understanding and managing cultural differences (Harris & Moran, 1987; Terpstra & David, 1985). There is a growing realization that the cultural environment influences the business environment, and that American companies doing business abroad cannot operate under the same assumptions as they do at home. As an example, consider the issue of sexuality across cultures—the relationship between males and females and the latter's place in society. If one is insensitive to it, it can result in a business fiasco (Vago, 1982). In many countries, male chauvinism is still the dominant norm. In several parts of the world, male and female roles at the workplace are segregated, and it is unlikely for women to hold key executive, managerial, and professional positions in which males report to them. This is not limited to only third world nations. Even in an advanced society like Japan, cultural traditions tend to exclude women from leadership positions in business. As a result, Japanese males often find it demeaning, awkward, and difficult to negotiate with female executives from the United States. But even this bit of cultural intelligence is lacking in some corporations who send women to places such as the Middle East or the Orient in anticipation of doing business.

The concept of culture refers essentially to *knowledge* that is shared by members of a society. It gives people a *sense* of who they are, of belonging, of how they should behave, and of what they should be doing. As an analyzable entity, culture is composed of shared knowledge in a society about norms, symbols, technology, roles, ideologies, values, and social structure, including such institutions as the family and religion. These same elements that make up culture are also found in sociological analyses. They are used both by sociologists and anthropologists, and depending on one's perspective, they may be considered more "cultural" or more "social." At this point, it is worth noting that: "Intellectually, sociology has no claim to a separate existence from anthropology. The distinction between the two is largely a historical accident traceable to racism in late 19th century Europe and North America: dark-skinned colonials were studied by anthropologists; light-skinned colonizers by sociologists" (Van den Berghe, 1977:76). In either case, they are useful concepts, found in both the "cultural" and "social" change literature, and since there will be references to them in the text, a brief discussion of the terms are warranted.

Norms are rules or patterns of behavior defining what is *expected,* customary, right, or proper in a given situation. They are behavioral expectations transmitted from generation to generation that members of a particular group collectively share. They are enforced by sanctions or rewards for correct behavior and punishments for incorrect behavior. The principal types of norms are folkways, mores, and laws. They are differentiated by the degree of legitimation and the severity of negative sanction imposed upon those who violate them.

Folkways are patterns that govern most of our daily life and ordinary interactions with other people. They define what is socially acceptable and correct and are enforced informally and nondeliberately. They may be purely arbitrary conveniences, such as monetary systems, measures, or weights. Others are ritualistic, such as patterns of eating or celebrating birthdays. Still others deal with the proper form of greeting and other special rituals for behavior that we call convention and etiquette. Other folkways define proper behavior for certain social roles. For example, they distinguish between man's work and woman's work and set up the ideals for ladylike and gentlemanlike conduct. Folkways also deal with the styles of dressing, recreation, childbearing, and dating patterns. They compose the backbone of tradition and they are by no means superficial or transitory. Nonetheless, they change. Women, for example, now do many things that were once "men's work." They are physicians, professors, lawyers, and bricklayers. Folkways are effectively enforced by rewards such as praise, approval, and acceptance in a social situation and by such punishments as ridicule, gossip, and nonacceptance.

Mores consist of major rules of conduct deemed essential by society. They are not simply proper like folkways; they are obligatory, and the sanctions that enforce them are invested with greater emotional content than those of folkways. They are supported by the dominant values of the culture and define right and wrong, moral and immoral actions, thoughts, and feelings. In the American culture, examples of mores include having only one husband or wife at a time, being loyal to the country, and rules of incest taboo. The negative sanctions imposed upon those who violate mores include ostracism, demotion, physical punishment, excommunication, or in some cases, imprisonment.

Mores, like folkways, are subject to change, but somewhat more painfully and slowly. Slavery and child labor, once considered moral, are now considered highly immoral. Periods of strictness regarding sexual relations have alternated with periods of permissiveness over the centuries in Western history.

Some social norms considered so important that their enforcement cannot be left to chance are made into *law*. Laws are norms with several specific characteristics. They are formally enacted by the state. They are codified into written documents that are precise and subject to legal interpretations. They have special enforcement agents, such as police, judges, district attorneys, and lawyers, and have definite written institutionalized sanctions. Whereas the penalty or reward for less serious norms may vary considerably, the penalty for disobeying a specific law is clearly stated in the law itself.

The second component of culture under consideration consists of *symbols*. A symbol is defined as any gesture, object, thing, or behavior that is used by members of a society to stand for or represent something else. A symbol communicates information in shorthand form, and it can evoke feelings associated with what it represents. Symbols standing for concrete objects would include "house," "car," and "typewriter." Symbols standing for ideas would include "loyalty," "flag," and "freedom." Symbols standing for imaginary objects would include "racial superiority," "witches," and "angels." The most obvious form of symbolic communication is language, in which each word is a symbol standing for something else, and in which certain sounds are given arbitrary meanings that are shared and accepted by the members of a society. Language symbols are learned through the process of socialization and are used throughout life.

The third element in culture, *technology*, refers to the information, techniques, and tools used by persons to satisfy their diverse needs and desires. For analytical purposes, usually a distinction is made between material and social technology. The former refers to knowledge of how to make and use things. It should be noted that the things produced are not part of the culture but represent, rather, the knowledge that people share and that make it possible to build and use the object. The knowledge is culture, not the object. Social technology is the knowledge about how to establish, maintain and operate the technical aspects of society. Examples of these are procedures for running a university, municipality, or a corporation through such operations as Robert's Rules of Order, bookkeeping, or the kind of specialized knowledge citizens must acquire to function in society such as knowing the laws, how to complete the income tax form, how to vote in elections, and how to use credit cards.

The fourth element of culture, *role*, is crucial in the analysis and understanding of human behavior. It refers to a set of social norms that govern a person's behavior in a society and determines his or her relationship to others. In other words, it is an expected pattern of behavior associated with a given social status. In Ralph Linton's (1936:113–114) words:

> A *status*, as distinct from the individual who may occupy it is simply a collection of rights and duties. . . . A *role* represents the dynamic aspect of a status. The individual is socially assigned to a status and occupies it with relation to other statuses. When he puts the rights and duties which constitute the status into effect, he is performing a role.

University professor, for instance, is a social status. With this status comes a professorial role, defined by social norms prescribing how the person should behave. The status of the professor is fixed in society, whereas the role is more flexible, because different occupants of the status play their roles in somewhat different ways. This is because a single status may involve several roles. The status of university professor incorporates the roles of teacher, adviser, researcher, colleague to other professors, committee member, and even writer of scholarly books. Generally, behavioral expectations differ markedly in American society for age, sex, and occupational roles. To be a male in American society, for example, is still quite different from being a female in the behaviors expected. The larger society also expects certain behaviors from one's occupational category that it does not from others. Compare, for example, what is expected from professional people to what is expected of blue-collar workers in etiquette, speech, and manners.

The fifth, *ideologies*, are shared beliefs about the physical, social, and metaphysical worlds. They may, for example, be statements about the existence of supernatural beings, the best form of government, or racial pride. They help individuals interpret events. They also provide the rationale for particular forms of action. They can justify the *status quo* or demand revolution. Clearly, ideology unites as well as divides and is, therefore, a powerful cultural force within societies.

Values, the sixth component of culture, are the underlying standards or principles by which social and individual goals are chosen and the criteria by which ends and means are judged and evaluated. They determine what is considered desirable, important, and worthwhile, and they explain and justify behavior. People are valuing beings. They continually evaluate themselves and others: What objects are worth owning? What makes a person successful? What activities are rewarding? What is beauty? Of course, different societies have distinctive criteria (values) for evaluating. People are considered successful in the United States, for example, if they accumulate many material things as a result of hard work. In other societies, they might be considered successful if they attain total mastery of their emotions or if they totally reject materialism.

Finally, the last aspect of every culture is its *social structure*, the web of organized relationships among individuals and groups that defines their mutual rights and responsibilities. Most of the social structure of a society is found in its major institutions, which are clusters of norms organized and established for the pursuit of some need or activity of a social group and supported by the groups' knowledge, beliefs, and values, and by appropriate aspects of the material culture. The pivotal institutions that are found in culture are the economic system, the government, religion, the family, education, and the expressional and aesthetic institutions including recreation and the arts. Each of these institutions is an established way of meeting a central and universal need that arises out of humans' biological, psychological, and social makeup.

As an example, consider the cultural pattern of the family as a pivotal institution, a cluster of folkways, mores, and laws that fulfills basic biological, psychological, and social needs. The functions of mating, reproduction, and child rearing are essential to the perpetuation of society, as are orderly gratification of the individual's sexual drives and need for security and affection. The norms of courtship, marriage, and parenthood are designed to meet those needs in socially acceptable ways. In American culture, dates, weddings, and homes apart from the in-laws are among the folkways associated with marriage. Long-standing mores include monogamy, postmarital fidelity, and the rights and duties of husband and wife with regard to each other and their children. A complex legal framework has developed to support these mores, such as licenses and legal ceremonies. There are now laws against bigamy and nonsupport, laws providing for divorce under certain conditions, and laws against marriage before a certain age without parental consent.

From the above discussion of the components of culture, it is by now clear that society and culture are different elements of the same complex and ongoing whole. They are obviously related, but they are not synonymous. Changes in culture bring changes in society, and vice versa. For example, the industrial revolution came about as a result of changes in the techniques of producing power and manufacturing commodities. These (cultural) changes affected the way of life of subsequent generations living in Europe, and the chain reaction is still going on today throughout the underdeveloped parts of the world.

Societies also differ widely in the degree to which change is favorably perceived. At one extreme, new practices, products, or processes may be considered as an undesirable disruption—or even evil. Among Marxist-Leninist politicians and scholars, it is a serious charge to be labeled as a revisionist of the Marxist-Leninist worldview and vision of society. Many followers of Islam accept Muhammad's view that "All innovation is the work of the devil" (Patai, 1983). At the other extreme, change is held to be identical with progress. This is most pronounced in the United States where there is a continuous preoccupation with innovation, with new or improved ways of doing things or selling goods.

In practice, it is not always possible to distinguish between cultural and social change. What one conceives as change is partly dependent upon the phenomenon and level of abstraction chosen for study in the context of a particular theoretical orientation. But one should be aware of the varying usages of change as well as of the varying explanations for change ranging from the cultural to the social and social-psychological, which will be reviewed in the next chapter.

SUMMARY

Social change occurs constantly—although at varying rates—in society. An awareness of the components of change is essential to the understanding and explanation of change. Thus, attention must be paid to what is changing, at what level in a social system, at what rate and magnitude, and in which direction. A distinction needs to be made also between planned and unplanned change and their consequences.

Social change may be defined a number of ways. For the present purpose, it is conceptualized as the process of planned or unplanned qualitative or quantitative alterations in social phenomena, which can be depicted on a six-part continuum composed of interrelated analytic components of identity, level, duration, direction, magnitude, and rate of change. This conceptualization of social change is proposed as a heuristic device for the empirical and theoretical study of social change.

Several forces, processes, and institutions are present in every society that make social change inevitable. They include population changes, conflict, economic determinism, innovation, diffusion, and the legal system. These and other factors in various combinations and to varying degrees produce different types of changes at various levels in society.

Both the reality and the immensity of change in the United States were illustrated by considering selected areas of social life a century ago and in the 1950s. They vividly documented the vast changes that have taken place in America.

For the sake of specificity, a distinction was made between the terms "social" and "cultural" change. A number of concepts—such as norms, symbols, technology, roles, ideology, and social structure—are used in the study of both social change and cultural change.

SUGGESTED FURTHER READINGS

BORDA, ORLANDO FALS, ed. *The Challenge of Social Change*. London: Sage Publications Ltd., 1985. A provocative collection of six articles by noted writers on various facets of social change.

HAMILTON, RICHARD F., and JAMES D. WRIGHT. *The State of the Masses*. New York: Aldine Publishing Co., 1986. A critical analysis of some of the major changes in the United States in the 1970s.

HARRIS, LOUIS. *Inside America*. New York: Vintage, 1987. A good source for a variety of major and many minor changes in the United States. Material is based on public-opinion surveys.

ISSEL, WILLIAM. *Social Change in the United States, 1945–1983*. New York: Schocken Books, 1985. A useful catalogue of changes and the reasons behind them in America since World War II.

LENSKI, GERHARD, and JEAN LENSKI. *Human Societies: An Introduction to Macrosociology*, 5th ed. New York: McGraw-Hill Book Company, 1987. An outstanding resource for the study of social change. The emphasis is on the evolution of social systems from a macrosociological perspective with abundant cross-cultural and historical material.

OGBURN, WILLIAM F. *Social Change*. New York: Viking, 1922. The classic study of social change.

REFERENCES

ALLEN, FRANCIS B. *Socio-Cultural Dynamics: An Introduction to Social Change*. New York: Macmillan, 1971.

ARNOLD, THURMAN. *The Folklore of Capitalism*. New Haven: Yale University Press, 1937.

BETTMAN, OTTO L. *The Good Old Days—They Were Terrible*. New York: Random House, 1974.

BRINTON, CRANE. *The Anatomy of Revolution*. New York: Vintage, 1959.

CHIROT, DANIEL. *Social Change in the Modern Era*. San Diego: Harcourt Brace Jovanovich, 1986.

COLLINS, RANDALL. *The Credential Society: An Historical Sociology of Education and Stratification*. New York: Academic Press, 1979.

DAHL, ROBERT. *Pluralist Democracy in the United States: Conflict and Consent*. Chicago: Rand McNally, 1967.

DAVIS, KINGSLEY. *Human Society*. New York: Macmillan, 1949.

DAVIS, KINGSLEY. "The Myth of Functional Analysis as a Special Method in Sociology and Anthropology." *American Sociological Review*, 24, 1959, pp. 757–772.

EDARI, RONALD. *Social Change*. Dubuque, Iowa: William C. Brown, 1976.

FRIEDMAN, LAWRENCE M. *American Law: An Introduction*. New York: W.W. Norton & Company Inc. 1984.

GERTH, HANS, and C. WRIGHT MILLS. *Character and Social Structure*. New York: Harcourt, 1953.

GINSBERG, MORRIS. "Social Change." *British Journal of Sociology*, 4, 1958, pp. 205–229.

GOLDSTONE, JACK A., ed. *Revolutions: Theoretical, Comparative, and Historical Studies*. San Diego: Harcourt Brace Jovanovich, 1986.

HARRIS, PHILIP R., and ROBERT T. MORAN. *Managing Cultural Differences*, 2nd ed. Houston: Gulf Publishing Company, 1987.

HERSKOVITZ, MELVILLE J. *Man and His Works*. New York: Knopf, 1948.

ISSEL, WILLIAM. *Social Change in the United States, 1945–1983*. New York: Schocken Books, 1985.

JOHNSON, HARRY M. *Sociology: A Systematic Introduction*. New York: Harcourt, 1960.

KROEBER, A.L., ed. *Anthropology*. New York: Harcourt, 1948.'

KROEBER, A.L., and TALCOTT PARSONS. "The Concepts of Culture and of Social System." *American Sociological Review*, 23(5), 1958, pp. 582–583.

LANDIS, JUDSON R. *Sociology: Concepts and Characteristics*. Belmont, Calif.: Wadsworth, 1974.

LAUER, ROBERT H. *Perspectives on Social Change*, 3rd ed. Boston: Allyn & Bacon, 1982.

LINTON, RALPH. *The Study of Culture*. New York: Appleton, 1936.

MacIVER, ROBERT M., and CHARLES H. PAGE. *Society: An Introductory Analysis*. New York: Holt, Rinehart & Winston, 1949.

MOORE, WILBERT E. "Social Change." In David J. Sills' (ed.), *International Encyclopedia of the Social Sciences*. Vol. 14. New York: Macmillan, 1968. Pp. 365–375.

MOORE, WILBERT E. *Social Change*. Englewood Cliffs, N.J. Prentice-Hall, 1974.

NAISBITT, JOHN. *Megatrends: Ten New Directions Transforming Our Lives*. New York: Warner Books, 1982.

NISBET, ROBERT A. *Social Change and History*. New York: Oxford, 1969.

NISBERT, ROBERT A. *History of the Idea of Progress*. New York: Basic Books, 1980.

OGBURN, WILLIAM F. *Social Change with Respect to Culture and Original Nature*. New York: Viking, 1922.

PATAI, RAPHAEL. *The Arab Mind*, rev. ed. New York: Charles Scribner's Sons, 1983.

PETERSON, PETER G. "The Morning After." *The Atlantic*. (October):1987, pp. 43–69.

POPPER, KARL R. *The Logic of Scientific Discovery*. New York: Harper & Row, 1959.

SHILS, EDWARD. "Intellectuals, Tradition, and the Traditions of Intellectuals: Some Preliminary Considerations." *Daedalus*, 101(2), 1972, pp. 21–33.

St. Louis Post-Dispatch. "Educators Weigh Idea to Lengthen College Year." August, 23, 1987, pp. 1C, 4C.

TERPSTRA, VERN, and KENNETH DAVID. *The Cultural Environment of International Business*, 2nd ed. Cincinnati: South-Western Publishing Co. 1985.

TOFFLER, ALVIN. *Future Shock*. New York: Random House, 1970.

TURNER, JONATHAN H. *The Structure of Sociological Theory*. Homewood, IL: The Dorsey Press, 1974.

TYLOR, EDWARD B. *The Origins of Culture*. New York: Harper & Row, 1958.

VAGO, STEVEN. "Blowing the Overseas Business Deal." *St. Louis Commerce*. May 1982, pp. 35–39.

VAGO, STEVEN. *Law and Society*, 2nd ed. Englewood Cliffs, NJ: Prentice-Hall, 1988.

VAN DEN BERGHE, PIERRE. "Response to Lee Ellis' 'The Decline and Fall of Sociology'." *American Sociologist*, 12, 1977, pp. 75–76.

YANKELOVICH, DANIEL. *New Rules: Searching for Self-Fulfillment in a World Turned Upside Down*. New York: Random House, 1981.

Wall Street Journal. "Hill Democrats Plan Efforts to Increase Minimum Wage Amid Employer Protests." March, 25, 1987, p. 60.

2 Theories of Change

As the noted sociologist S.N. Eisenstadt remarks, "tendencies to change are inherent in all human societies, because they face basic problems to which no overall continuous solutions exist." (1982:534). Attempts at a sociological explanation of these "tendencies" and of social change are as old as the discipline itself. This chapter shall draw on the rich literature of sociological theory to examine the specific and complementary contributions of influential "classic" and contemporary theorists to social change. We will consider their contributions to social change from the evolutionary, conflict, structural-functional, systems, and social-psychological perspectives.

The chapter deals with only a few of the important classical and contemporary theories of social change in a rather brief fashion. This approach serves certain goals. It provides the reader with some conception of the content of the different theories and how the various theories relate to one another. The discussion of these theories clearly shows the complex and multifaceted nature of social change and also serves to provide, through classification and examination of the various theories, a way of differentiating, organizing, and understanding a great mass of material. Thus, although the concern is to suggest the magnitude of the field, an attempt is made also to lend order to that magnitude.

Wilbert E. Moore (1969:810) points out that "The mention of 'theory of social change' will make most social scientists appear defensive, furtive, guilt ridden, or frightened. Yet the source of this unease may be in part an unduly awe-stricken regard for the explicitly singular, and implicitly capitalized word 'Theory.' " But the word "theory" in itself should not be that frightening. *It is simply a network of interrelated hypotheses* (statements of probable relationships between two or more variables—actions or attributes that can be measured or categorized) *or propositions* (statements of relationships between two or more facts or concepts) *concerning a phenomenon* (an observed or observable fact, occurrence or circumstance) *or set of phenomena.* Sociological theories are attempted models (abstractions of reality that are used for analytical purposes) of social reality. Some theories approach closer to this reality, but they are never an entirely accurate picture of it. What is essential to this conception is that theories are never true or false, right or wrong, but always *more* or *less* adequate.

At this point it will be useful to sketch out some of the major purposes served by theory. First of all, theory is a convenient way of organizing experience. It allows one to handle large amounts of empirical data with relatively few propositions. It also enables one to go beyond the empirical data and to see implications and relationships that are not evident from any datum taken alone. Furthermore, a theory also provides a stimulus and a guide for further empirical investigation. Theory leads to predictions about events not yet observed and encourages the researcher to examine the consequences of these predictions. These, in turn, either may lead to further empirical data in support of the theory or may suggest needed modifications or possible rejection of the theory.

Consequently, we cannot ignore theory; instead, we can only choose among alternative theories. All theories purport to say something about actual events and phenomena and are not merely fictitious representations of imaginary situations. As a result, one can choose among many theories or explanations of reality as kinds of models. According to Jay Forrester (1971:53):

> Each of us uses models constantly. Every person in his private life and in his business life instinctively uses models for decision making. The mental image of the world around you which you carry in your head is a model. One does not have a city or a government or a country in his head. He has only selected concepts and relationships which he uses to represent the real system. A mental image is a model. All of our decisions are taken on the basis of models. The question is not to use or ignore models. The question is only a choice among alternatives.

Prior to the discussion of specific theoretical approaches, a cautionary note is in order regarding the procedures followed in this chapter for classifying various theories. It will become clear that many theories of social change tend to overlap and, for all practical purposes, may fall under several different headings. For example, the reader may find that a theory that has been placed under the heading of "Structural-functional" will contain similar elements to those embodied in "Evolutionary theories." Any such effort at classification of theories should be viewed essentially as a heuristic device to facilitate discussion rather than to reflect the final status of the theories considered.

Any attempt to group or categorize theories under particular labels is open to question. The present effort should not be an exception. The categories used are in some ways arbitrary; the number of categories can be increased or decreased depending upon one's objectives. These categorizations simply provide some semblance of order for the principal theoretical approaches to social change. In the schema employed, theories are presented in a chronological order and are classified under the general headings of *Evolutionary* theories, based on assumptions of predictable, cumulative change from one stage to another, usually more complex, and in the direction of increasing adaptability; *Conflict* theories, based on the assumption that conflict is endemic to all societies and delineating the conditions that as a result tend toward instability; *Structural-functional* theories, devoted to the explanation of the function that a given structure performs in the maintenance of the stability of a social system or its subsystems; *Systems* theories, which provide some contemporary "options" to the evolutionary and structural-functional theories; and *Social-psychological* theories, focusing on individuals and their personality.

EVOLUTIONARY THEORIES

In the latter half of the nineteenth century, the concept of evolution assumed a central place in explanations of all forms of human development in both the social and biological sciences. The most influential among the biological evolutionists was Charles Darwin (1809–1882), whose theory of natural selection provided a solid base for the explanation of biological evolution. Just as biologists traced stages in the development of the organisms, sociologists envisioned society as proceeding inevitably through a fixed set of stages—for example, from savagery through barbarism to civilization. This evolution was believed to occur in response to a set of "natural laws" that explained each stage in the organization of a society in terms of the stage that preceded it (Timasheff, 1961:23). Moreover, the idea of evolution was tied with ideas of progress, development, and advancement; each stage represented a "higher" stage than the one before it, with the final stage in the series approximating societal perfection.

But Robert A. Nisbet (1969:161) warns us that it is a popular misconception to assume that nineteenth-century social evolutionism was just an adaptation of the ideas of biological evolutionism, as advocated by Darwin, to the investigation of social institutions. Many of the major works on social evolution appeared or were begun before the publication of Darwin's book, notably those of Comte, Spencer, and Morgan. Nisbet points out that there is a substantial difference between the theory of biological evolution and the theory of social evolution. Although the two approaches have some common features, the methodologies used in the biological and social sciences are different. The biological theory is mostly a statistical theory and deals with statistical abstractions of biological organisms.

By contrast, in evolutionary theories, typologies (ways of grouping or classifying data and ideas) are dominant. Nisbet (1969:162) notes that the object of inquiry in any theory of social evolution seems to be invariably social class, kinship, culture, law, society as a whole, or other classifications of institutionalized and structured behavior. The early sociologists all believed in social evolution, the progressive development of social patterns over long periods of time. Among others, Auguste Comte (1798–1857), Lewis Henry Morgan (1818–1881), and Herbert Spencer (1820–1903) were particularly concerned with the identification of the types of stages through which they assumed all societies must pass. I will describe their theories in some detail.

Auguste Comte

The theories of progress that developed broadly and loosely in the eighteenth century, particularly by Condorcet, and advanced in the early nineteenth century, particularly by Saint-Simon, formed the starting point for Comte's thinking, which centered in the explicit search for a law of progress. Comte (1915), like many of the philosophers of his period in France, believed in progress toward a perfect society. He insisted, however, that it would come about not by political revolution, but by the proper application of a new moral science, which he named "sociology" in 1839. Comte thus became known as the "founder of sociology." The highest of all sciences, it would use the "positivist" scientific method of observation, experimentation, and comparison to understand order and promote progress.

The road to perfect society involved the human intellect passing through three historical phases of sophistication: the theological, the metaphysical, and the positive. The progress of knowledge, which is the underlying basis for his theory of evolution through the "law of the three stages," is not only inevitable but also irreversible. It is, in addition, asymptotic; that is, we always approach, but never attain, perfect positive knowledge.

Comte's description of each of the three stages is as follows: In the *theological* stage, people think inanimate objects are alive. This general view itself goes through three phases: animism or fetishism, which views each object as having its own will; polytheism, which believes that many divine wills impose themselves on objects; and monotheism, which conceives the will of one god as imposing itself on objects. The second, or *metaphysical*, stage is a period when causality is explained in terms of abstract forces; causes and forces replace desires, and one great entity, nature, prevails. The third, or *positive*, stage is the scientific period when people develop explanations in terms of natural processes and scientific laws. At this point in a society's development it becomes possible to control human events. Comte contended that Western civilization had already reached the positive stage in control of the physical environment and was on the verge of the positive stage with respect to social relations.

Each stage not only exhibits a particular form of mental development but also has a corresponding material development. In the theological state, military life predominates; in the metaphysical state, legal forms achieve dominance; and the positive stage is the stage of industrial society. Thus, Comte held that historical development shows a matching movement of ideas and institutions.

Lewis Henry Morgan

Another nineteenth-century proponent of uniform evolutionary stages was Lewis Henry Morgan. After graduating from Union College in 1840, he practiced law in upstate New York for a few years, but he devoted much of his time to anthropological research, which eventually became his chief interest. His best-known work, *Ancient Society*, was published in 1877.

Morgan postulated that the stages of technological developments and kinship systems were associated with different social and political institutions. On the basis of historical data, he concluded that culture evolves in successive stages that are essentially the same in all parts of the world. The order of stages is inevitable and their content is limited because mental processes are similar among all peoples under similar conditions in various societies.

He described the progress of humankind through three main stages of evolution: savagery, barbarism, and civilization. But he also subdivided savagery and barbarism into upper, middle, and lower segments. He distinguished these stages in terms of technological achievements. The seven stages are in his words:

I. Lower Status of Savagery, From the Infancy of the Human Race to the commencement of the next Period.

II. Middle Status of Savagery, From the acquisition of a fish subsistence and a knowledge of the use of fire, to etc.

III. Upper Status of Savagery, From the Invention of the Bow and Arrow, to etc.

IV. Lower Status of Barbarism, From the Invention of the Art of Pottery, to etc.

V. Middle Status of Barbarism, From the Domestication of animals on the Eastern Hemisphere, and in the Western from the cultivation of maize and plants by Irrigation, with the use of adobe-brick and stone, to etc.

VI. Upper Status of Barbarism, From the Invention of the process of Smelting Iron Ore, with the use of iron tools, to etc.
VII. Status of Civilization, From the Invention of a Phonetic Alphabet, with the use of writing, to the present time. (L.H. Morgan, 1964:18)

Morgan contended that each stage and substage was initiated by a major technological invention. For example, he considered pottery to be characteristic of lower barbarism, domestication of plants and animals to be characteristic of middle barbarism, and iron tools to be characteristic of upper barbarism. Civilization was heralded by the invention of the phonetic alphabet, and the organization of political society on a territorial basis was the line of demarcation where modern civilization began. Each of these stages of technological evolution, Morgan maintained, was correlated with characteristic developments in the family, religion, political organization, and property arrangements. For example, he speculated that the family evolved through six stages. Human society began with indiscriminate promiscuity and without a real family structure. It was followed by cohabitation of brothers and sisters. In the third stage, group marriage prevailed, but brothers and sisters were not allowed to mate. Then came marriage between single pairs, followed by the patriarchal family in which the husband could have more than one wife. Finally, the stage of civilization was characterized by monogamous family with a degree of equality between husband and wife.

Morgan's ideas of evolution made a strong impression on Marx and his co-worker, Engels. The latter, following the advice of Marx, in 1884 published *The Origins of the Family, Private Property and the State*, a volume making extensive use of Morgan's theories and of his illustrations, taken largely from observations of American Indian tribes.

Herbert Spencer

Herbert Spencer was an English railroad engineer who became "the second founding father of sociology" (Timasheff, 1961:30). Spencer saw evolution as an unilinear development, that is, as a steadily continuing accumulative process by which everything in the cosmos was continually being synthesized at ever higher levels of complexity. He maintained that human society had followed a course of natural development, from relatively simple patterns of organization to more complex structures, characterized by an increasing specialization of parts.

Spencer held that the process of societal evolution followed inexorable laws of nature in that it led inevitably toward progress, toward the development of increasingly desirable and just forms of society. But Spencer also posited that there is an equilibrium between population and food supply. Should the population growth exceed the needed resources for survival, a struggle for existence will occur. Those individuals who are best able to adapt to the new conditions will manage to survive. Crucial to an understanding of Spencer's evolutionary model is the basic analogy between change in both biological and social organisms. He suggested that an increase in mass or size in either of these organisms corresponds to an "increase in structure from a few like parts to numerous interrelated parts" (Applebaum, 1970:30).

He also argued that although a particular stage of societal evolution might seem oppressive or undesirable, it was absurd to believe that society could be improved by legislation. The state should play the smallest possible role in regulation of society in order not to interfere with natural evolutionary processes.

Spencer had a strong influence on the young science of sociology. For example, in the United States at the turn of the century, William Graham Sumner (1840–1910), one of the most important American sociologists, became an outspoken theorist of social evolution. In a famous dictum, Sumner (1896:87–88) argued that stateways could not change folkways. That is, social improvement could only come about through natural evolution of society and not by legislation. His arguments are still echoed today by those who oppose laws providing for more equitable treatment of minorities on the ground that morality cannot be legislated. But to equate his ideas wholly with right-wing ideology is a mistake largely due to sociologists' misunderstanding of his work. That would be too simple a portrayal of Spencer's genius (Turner, 1986:412).

Other vanguards of American sociology accepted part of the evolutionary theory of social change while embracing the notion that society could be improved by deliberate effort. Lester Frank Ward (1841–1913), a paleontologist who became the first president of the American Sociological Society in 1906, for instance, believed that both human beings and human society had developed through eons of evolution, but he maintained that once intellect has evolved in humans, they gained the ability to help shape the subsequent evolution of social forms (Ward, 1911:451). Through the application of intelligence, people could effect desired changes in society (although desired changes to some may not be desired by others). In this respect Ward was following in the tradition of Auguste Comte, who maintained that human intelligence had reached the point where society could be reconstructed through application of the scientific method.

Several other sociologists have taken an evolutionary approach to social change. In Germany, Ferdinand Toennies (1855–1936) described the trend from what he calls *Gemeinschaft* to *Gesellschaft* as one in which small, primitive, traditional, homogeneous, closely knit communities are eradicated and replaced by a large, urbanized, industrial society where human relations are impersonal, formal, contractual, utilitarian, realistic, and specialized. The *Gemeinschaft* relationship is an intimate one, not unlike that found in primary groups such as the family. The close interpersonal ties that bind lifelong friends and neighbors in a rural village provides one familiar example. Because members of the community are concerned with each other's well-being, they do things for each other without consideration of repayment or personal gain. The *Gesellschaft* relationship, on the other hand, is based on individualistic and mutual distrust. In Toennies' (1957:65) words:

> Here everybody is by himself and isolated, and there exists a condition of tension against all others. Their spheres of activity and power are sharply separated, so that everybody refuses to everyone else contacts with and admittance to his sphere, i.e., intrusions are regarded as hostile acts.

In the *Gesellschaft* relationships people are competitive and struggle with each other to gain a personal advantage. There is no common sentiment that generates trust or concern for one another. Contract becomes instrumental in defining relationships: "For everything pleasant which someone does for someone else, he expects, even demands, at least an equivalent" (Toennies, 1957:78). Urbanization of society is considered as the main reason for the increase in *Gesellschaft* relationships.

Similarly, Howard P. Becker (1899–1960) saw the transition as being from a sacred, traditionally oriented society to a secular society that evaluates customs and practices in terms of their pragmatic outcomes (1950). In anthropology, Robert Redfield (1897–1958) put the transition as being from folk to urban (folk-urban continuum). He described folk society as

> small, isolated and homogeneous with a strong sense of group solidarity. The ways of living are conventionalized into that coherent system which we call a "culture." Behavior is traditional, spontaneous, uncritical and personal. There is no legislation or habit of experiment and reflection for intellectual ends. Kinship, its relationships and institutions are the type categories of experience and the familial group is the unit of action, the sacred prevails over the secular, the economy is one of status rather than of market. (Redfield, 1947:294)

Change for Redfield is the consequence of an "increase of contacts bringing about heterogeneity and disorganization of culture" (1941:369).

Judging from this representative sample of evolutionary theories, there seems to be agreement among theorists that change is natural, directional, imminent, continuous, and necessary and proceeds from uniform causes (Nisbet, 1969:159–189). These theories also contained, as all theories do, an implicit ideological component. The general evolutionary approach, because of its emphasis upon natural laws and its fixed series of stages, perhaps had a special appeal to political conservatives. Sumner, for example, used it to justify the social class system of the time, maintaining that the operation of natural selection had placed the most able groups at the top of the structure. He also believed that people should not interfere with the operation of natural laws and the evolution of society, and thus he opposed all ideas of the possibility of guided social change.

By the early part of the twentieth century, enough information had been gathered by social scientists on societies throughout the world to make it appear unlikely that societies everywhere had passed through the same series of stages. Thus, the idea of a unilinear evolution was generally discarded. Furthermore, both the general idea that present societies represent the highest stage in any evolutionary sequence and that there is a necessary link between social change and progress were discredited.

The evolutionary approach is, however, still with us in more contemporary forms. The renewed interest in evolutionary theory is evidenced, for example, by Gerhard and Jean Lenski's analysis of the evolution of societies. They maintain that continuity, innovation, and extinction are basic aspects of the evolutionary process and that evolution is fundamentally cumulative change because it involves a gradual addition of new elements to an already established base (Lenski & Lenski, 1987:66–77). But the idea of unilinear evolution—that is, all societies inevitably passing through the same set of fixed stages—has given way to the idea of a multilinear evolution (Stewart, 1953:313–336). Those who hold this view reason that, because societies were often very different to begin with, they may have appropriately undergone varying patterns of change and that the same patterns of change may produce slightly varying products in a society that started from different beginnings.

Remnants of the classical, evolutionary theories of social change can still be found in some of the contemporary anthropological theories such as those of Leslie White and Julian Steward (Lauer, 1982:120–123) and theories dealing with economic development or societal modernization. An illustration of the latter point would be the notion of Rostow (1961) who distinguished among five stages (the traditional setting, preconditions for "takeoff," takeoff, drive toward maturity, and high mass consumption) of economic development, which all developing societies, he argued, have to go through in their process of modernization. Rostow gained the distinction of having originated virtually the only stage theory of history since they evolved in the nineteenth century. His stages will be elaborated in some detail in the next chapter.

In sum, we may turn to the main assumptions to which, according to Smith (1973:27–28), evolutionists subscribed:

1. *Holism*—studying the whole unit rather than its parts
2. *Universalism*—change is natural, universal, perpetual and ubiquitous, and requires no explanation
3. *Potentiality*—change is inherent and endogenous in the unit undergoing change
4. *Directionality*—change is progressive
5. *Determinism*—change is inevitable and irreversible for all units

6. *Gradualism*— change is continuous, cumulative growth
7. *Reductionism*— "laws of succession" are uniform and the basic topic of change is everywhere the same.

CONFLICT THEORIES

Conflict theory assumes that social behavior can best be understood in terms of tension and conflict between groups and individuals. It suggests that society is an arena in which struggles over scarce commodities take place. Conflict theorists consider change, rather than order, as the essential element of social life. Change is viewed as an intrinsic process in society, not merely the outcome of some improperly functioning or imbalanced part of the social system. Structural differentiation is felt to be the source of conflict, and social change occurs only through this conflict. A number of social theorists have espoused this approach, and in this section we shall focus on the main ideas of three important conflict theorists: Karl Marx, Lewis Coser, and Ralf Dahrendorf.

Karl Marx

Of all the social theorists, few were as important, brilliant, original, or influential as Karl Marx (1818–1883). Part philosopher, part economist, part sociologist, and part historian, Marx combined political partisanship with deep scholarship in his work. His writings are generally considered among the most basic and most crucial in the study of conflict theory with regard to social change. In his words: "Without conflict, no progress: this is the law which civilization has followed to the present day" (Marx, quoted by Dahrendorf, 1959:27).

Marx postulated that every society, whatever its stage of historical development, rests on an economic foundation. He called this the "mode of production" of commodities. The mode of production in turn has two elements. The first is "the forces of production" or the physical or technological arrangement of economic activity. The second is "the social relations of production" or the indispensable human attachments that people must form with one another in carrying out this economic activity. In Marx's words:

> The sum total of these relations of production constitutes the economic structure of society—the real foundation, on which rise legal and political superstructures and to which correspond definite forms of social consciousness. The mode of production in material life determines the general character of the social, political, and spiritual processes of life. It is not the consciousness of men that determines their existence, but, on the contrary, their social existence determines their consciousness. At a certain stage of their development the material forces of production in society come into conflict with

the existing relations of production, or—what is but a legal expression for the same thing—with the property relations within which they had been at work before. From forms of development of the forces of production these relations turn into their fetters. Then comes the period of social revolution. With the change of the economic foundation the entire immense superstructure is more or less rapidly transformed. (Marx, 1959:43–44)

The determinant or independent variable for Marx is the mode of production. Changes in this produce changes in the relations of production, that is, changes in the way in which groups of people are attached to this production technology. To illustrate this point, Marx divided history into five major stages, each characterized by a type of economic production. These stages are: (1) tribal ownership, a type of primitive communism; (2) ancient communal and state ownership accompanied by slavery; (3) feudalism; (4) capitalism; and (5) communism, which is divided into a dictatorship of the proletariat and "pure" communism. With the exception of pure communism, each stage is characterized by economic and other conflicts between two or more opposing economic groups with the separate and opposing economic interests. The economic conflict between these groups inevitably leads to further social and political conflicts as each group seeks to further its own interests at the expense of other groups. This is epitomized in the opening lines of the famous *Communist Manifesto* of 1848:

> The history of all hitherto existing society is the history of class struggles. Freeman and slave, patrician and plebian, lord and serf, guild-master and journeyman, in a word, oppressor and oppressed, stood in constant opposition to one another, carried on an uninterrupted, now hidden, now open, fight, a fight that each time ended, either in a revolutionary reconstitution of society at large, or in the common ruin of the contending classes. (Marx & Engels, 1955:1)

For Marx, conflict is a normal condition of social life whose nature and variations are some of the most important things to be described and analyzed by social science. Conflict and change for him are inseparable. The economic production is the substructure upon which the rest of society, the superstructure, is built. Social institutions—such as the government, the family, education, and religion—are dependent upon the mode of economic production in a given society. Variations and changes in economic production give rise to variations and changes in other social institutions with their associated values, attitudes, and norms.

In a capitalistic society all individuals will move from intermediate groups to become either proletarians (workers) or bourgeoisie (property owners). The struggle is inevitable between these two classes and will result, as class consciousness and militant class action develop, in the overthrow of the existing system. It will culminate in the establishment of a new form of economic production—communistic production—and the new historical stage, communism. The proletariat, having won the revolution, will become the dominant group in this final historical stage.

In brief, the series of events leading to an ultimate proletariat revolution is as follows: "(1) the need for production; (2) the expansion of the division of labor; (3) the development of private property; (4) increasing social inequality; (5) class struggle; (6) creation of political structures to represent each class's interests, and finally, (7) revolution. Each event leads inevitably to the next event" (Duke, 1976:28). And, according to Marx, no person or group of people can stop the revolution from occurring.

The Marxian approach to social change has been attacked on a number of grounds. One group of criticisms deals with the fact that it overemphasized economic determination and ignored ideological, political, and other factors that influence social change. Others maintain that it insisted upon the dialectical model of change through thesis, antithesis, and synthesis (action, reaction, and combination) and did not allow for regressive change or for change to occur in other ways. Some sociologists have criticized Marx as placing too much emphasis on conflict and economically based power and rank. They argue, instead, that conflict is often integrative, as we shall see in the writings of Coser, and that consensus, integration, and cooperation are much more frequently in evidence than conflict. These critics argue that shared values are common to normative systems, and functional and economic interdependence all tend to gloss over or reduce class conflict to a minimum. Finally, many critics have challenged his formulations regarding revolution. They have stressed that most revolutions, especially those in the twentieth century, have been middle-class revolutions. They argue that, aside from Marx's inadequate predictions of the place of revolution, he misjudged the depth of alienation and frustration of the average worker. Marx also failed to see the tendency of workers to identify with national, community, religious, racial, sexual, and occupational groups.

Notwithstanding these limitations, scholars felt compelled to develop and expand his ideas and, in so doing, often produced some of their most important work. Each succeeding generation has had sociologists working directly in the Marxian tradition. Consequently, his approach remains an important and influential one in contemporary sociology.

Lewis A. Coser

The conflict approach to social change gained additional momentum during the middle of the twentieth century, prompted by race conflicts, class struggles, and the warring of interests. Undoubtedly, the best-known conflict theorist among contemporary American sociologists is Lewis A. Coser. In his widely read book, *The Functions of Social Conflict*, Coser (1956) holds that conflict has both positive and negative effects. He explains that conflict is part of the socialization process and that no social group can be completely harmonious. Conflict in society is inevitable because individuals have a predisposition for hate as well as love. Thus, conflict is part of the human condition. But conflict can be constructive as well as destructive because it frequently resolves disagreements and leads eventually to unity. He believes that conflict makes for an increase in adjustment and adaptation as groups learn to live side by side. Moreover, conflict encourages "in-group" cohesion because the members of the group have a common enemy and a common cause.

Coser views conflict as a means of promoting social change. People who feel that their society satisfies their needs are not likely to want to alter anything in it. Those whose needs are not satisfied will attempt to change the situation by confronting the dominant group that has suppressed their goals. An obvious example is the civil rights movement in the United States. But Coser maintains that conflict can lead to change in a number of ways, including the establishment of new group boundaries, the drawing off of hostility and tension, the development of more complex group structures to deal with conflict and its accompaniments, and the creation of alliances with other parties. Each of these can result in a new distribution of social values, with the concomitant formation of a new social order. Therefore, conflict is seen as a creative force that stimulates change in society (Coser, 1956:153).

Ralf Dahrendorf

Another influential contemporary conflict theorist is Ralf Dahrendorf. He rejects the Marxian notion of social class as determined by the relations to the means of production and defines it in terms of the unequal distribution of authority. All groups in society are seen as divided into those who have authority and those who do not. He maintains that social conflict has a structural origin and is to be "understood as a conflict about the legitimacy of relations of authority" (Dahrendorf, 1959:176). In any organization, roles and positions can be dichotomized into two "quasi-groups" whose members have opposed "latent interests." The group in position of power or authority is interested in preserving the status quo, whereas the subordinated group is interested in change. These two "quasi-groups" are potential antagonists in that their members share common experiences, roles, and interests, whether or not they are aware of them.

Under proper "conditions of organization," interest groups emerge out of quasi-groups as the members develop a leadership cadre, effective intragroup communication, a consistent ideology, and an awareness of their common interests. Dahrendorf suggests that the more the subordinate interest groups become organized, the more likely they will be in conflict with the dominant group. The "conditions of conflict," such as opportunities for social mobility and the responses of the agents of social control, will determine the intensity and violence of conflict. By "intensity" he refers to the emotional involvement and animosity felt by the participants. He proposes that the more organized the interest groups and the more regulated their conflict, the less violent the conflict will be. Conflict, in turn, leads to structural change as a result of a change in dominance relations. The type, speed, and magnitude of change depends on the "conditions of structural change." These conditions include the capacity of those in power to stay in power and the pressure potential of the dominated interest group. Conflict between workers and management, the unionization process, and the changes brought about by the unions are used by Dahrendorf to illustrate his theory.

He concluded that "the great creative force" that leads to change in society is social conflict. "The notion that wherever there is social life there is conflict may be unpleasant and disturbing." But ". . . societies and social organizations are held together not by consensus but by constraint, not by universal agreement but by the coercion of some by others . . . and as conflict generates change, so constraint may be thought of as generating conflict. We assume that conflict is ubiquitous, since constraint is ubiquitous wherever human beings set up social organizations" (Dahrendorf, 1967:479–480).

Dahrendorf altered Marx's theory in several ways. He saw conflict as a problem of unequal authority in all sectors of society as contrasted to the strict Marxian notion of classes. Then, he suggested the importance of dealing with external conflict while, in the Marxian conception, conflict is identified as its primary source in the internal workings of society. Furthermore, Dahrendorf pointed out that conflict in a given society results not from internal contradictions arising in historical development but from pressures exerted by other societies. Finally, Dahrendorf contended that many of the conflicts are not capable of resolution as Marx has suggested, but most frequently are controlled through "compromise."

Unlike other conflict theorists, Dahrendorf argued that ". . . it is the task of sociology to derive conflicts from special social structures and not to relegate these conflicts to psychological variables (agressiveness) or to descriptive historical ones (the influx of Negroes into the United States) or to chance" (Dahrendorf, 1973:102).

The past decade or so witnessed the rise of a series of conflict theories that are variously referred to in the sociological literature as "radical," "activist," "critical," "humanist," and the like. These theoretical approaches are greatly influenced by the writings of C. Wright Mills, whose polemic attacks on "the power elite" gave direction to a whole group of generally younger sociologists who reject the concept of value-free science and use their research and teaching to promote what they believe to be desirable, and what some define as radical social change (Mills, 1956). These radical sociologists argue that directed social change should be the primary goal of all scientific endeavors.

STRUCTURAL-FUNCTIONAL THEORIES

Although many scholars now accept the theory that all industrialized societies eventually develop cultures with certain similarities, controversy rages over the way in which these changes come about. In sociological theorizing there is a group of thinkers who emphasize the so-called functionalist, or "structural-functional," approach. The word "structure" generally refers to a set of relatively stable and patterned relationships of social units, and "function" refers to those consequences of any social activity that make for the adaptation or adjustment of a given structure or its component parts. In other words, "structure" refers to a system with relatively enduring patterns, and "function" refers to the dynamic process within the structure. The structures are the various parts of the social system. In the case of society, the principal structures are usually considered to be the societies' institutions—family, government, economic system, religion, and education—and the analysis focuses upon the interrelations among these institutions. Each structure and each part within the larger structure is conceived to have a function in assisting the society to operate and preserving it intact.

Historically, structural-functional theorizing was brought into sociology by borrowing directly, and developing analogies for, concepts in the biological sciences. Biology, since the middle of the nineteenth century, frequently referred to the "structure" of an organism, meaning a relatively stable arrangement of relationships between the different cells, and to the "function" of the organism, which considered the consequences of the activity of the various organs in the life process. The principal consideration of this organic analogy was how each part of the organism contributes to the survival and maintenance of the whole.

Sociologists of the structural-functional school usually distinguish between the latent function and the manifest functions of social relationship (Merton, 1957:19–84). *Manifest* functions are those that are built into a social system by design; like manifest goals, they are well understood by group members. *Latent* functions are, by contrast, unintentional and often unrecognized. They are unanticipated consequences of the system that has been set up to achieve other ends. For example, the system of free public education in the United States has the manifest function of opening educational opportunities to all citizens and thereby increasing their ability to participate equally in a democratic society. In practice, however, the system has had the unintended effect of opening opportunity for some and closing it for others based on financial considerations.

Despite Spencer's adoption of the word "function," the first systematic formulation of the logic of a structural-functional approach in sociology can be found in the works of Emile Durkheim (1858–1917). In the sociological classic, *The Division of Labor in Society* (which will be examined further in Chapter 3), Durkheim (1947) makes a clear distinction between the function of the division of labor and its efficient cause. Its basic function is the integration of society; its cause was the increase in "moral density" induced by population pressure. Function, for Durkheim, is a contribution to the maintenance of social life and society, as it can be seen further in his discussions on the social significance of religion, punishment, and ceremony.

In addition to Durkheim, structural-functional analysis in the United States was greatly influenced by the works of two British anthropologists, A.R. Radcliffe-Brown and Bronislaw Malinowski. Function was seen by Radcliffe-Brown (1956:189) as a contribution to the continuing existence of the social structure. Institutions and individuals alike worked toward this goal. "The continuity of structure is maintained by the process of social life, which consists of the activities and interaction of the individual human beings and of the organized groups into which they are united. The social life of the community is here defined as the *functioning* of the social structure. The *function* of any recurrent activity, such as the punishment of a crime, or a funeral ceremony, is the part it plays in the social life as a whole and therefore the contribution it makes to the maintenance of the structure continuity." Maintenance of the structure, for him, entails harmonious relationships between groups, social continuity or the nurturing of tradition and the existence of those institutions necessary for survival.

Malinowski's (1926) theoretical perspective was built around the assertion that cultural items exist to fulfill basic human and cultural needs: "The functional view of culture insists therefore upon the principle that every type of civilization, every custom, material object, idea and belief fulfills some vital function, has some task to accomplish, represents an indispensable part within a working whole." Such a theory, by its very nature "aims at the explanation of anthropological facts at all levels of development by their function, by the part which they play within the integral system of culture, by the manner in which they are related to each other within the system . . ." (1926:132–133).

The early structural-functional theorists viewed the world in systematic terms. For them such systems were considered to have needs and prerequisites that had to be met to assure survival. They tended to view such systems with needs and requisites as having normal and pathological states, thus connoting a system of equilibrium and homeostasis. The social world was seen as composed of mutually interrelated parts, and the analysis of these interrelated parts focused on how they fulfilled the requisites of the systems as a whole and how, therefore, system equilibrium was maintained.

Some of these ideas are incorporated in contemporary structural functional analysis, especially the notion of systems of interrelated parts. To account for social change in a structural functional context, let us now look at some of the principal tenets of this approach:

(1) Societies must be analyzed "holistically as systems of interrelated parts"; (2) Cause and effect relations are "multiple and reciprocal"; (3) Social systems are in a state of "dynamic equilibrium" such that adjustment to forces affecting the system is made with minimal change within the system; (4) Perfect integration is never attained so that every social system has strains and deviations, but the latter tend to be neutralized through institutionalization; (5) Change is fundamentally a slow, adaptive process, rather than a revolutionary shift; (6) Change is the consequence of the adjustment of changes outside the system, growth by differentiation and internal innovations; and (7) The system is integrated through shared values. (Van den Berghe, 1967:294–295)

One way to examine the structural functional approach to social change is in terms of the negative or unintended or, as Merton would say, dysfunctional elements. Merton (1968:40) is suggesting that the dysfunctional elements that tend normally to be a part of any social system may themselves, in their accumulation, culminate in the more overt types of change that affect the structure itself. Accordingly, "By focusing on dysfunctions as well as functions, this approach can assess not only the bases of social stability but the potential sources of change. . . . The stresses and strains in a social structure which accumulate as dysfunctional consequences of existing elements . . . will, in due course, lead to institutional breakdown and basic social change. When this change has passed beyond a given and not easily identifiable point, it is customary to say that a new social system has emerged."

Stability and change in society are basically complementary processes. Parsons (1966:21) argues that "At the most general theoretical levels, there is no difference between processes which serve to maintain a system and those which serve to change it." Or, as Kingsley Davis (1949:634) put it, "It is only in terms of equilibrium that most sociological concepts make sense. Either tacitly or explicitly anyone who thinks about society tends to use the notion. The functional structural approach to sociological analysis is basically an equilibrium theory." The widespread use of equilibrium approaches is characteristic not only of sociology but of other social sciences as well.

In essence, equilibrium theory seeks to uncover the general conditions for the maintenance of a social system in stable equilibrium and specify the mechanisms by which that stability is preserved or reestablished after the occurence of internal or external disturbances.

Talcott Parsons

The most influential and best-known representative of contemporary American sociologists embracing this approach is Talcott Parson (1902–

1979). Detailed examination of Parsons's complex ideas concerning social change that appeared in a number of this publications over time [for example, *The Social System* (1951); *Societies: Evolutionary and Comparative Perspectives* (1966); *The System of Modern Societies* (1971); and *The Evolution of Societies* (1977)] is beyond the scope of this discussion. The ensuing analysis will only consider some of his ideas of change in the context of equilibrium theory.

He considers stability" . . . as a defining characteristic of structure . . . equivalent to the more specific concept of stable equilibrium—which in another reference may be either 'static' or 'moving.'" For him "a system then is stable or (relatively) in equilibrium when the relation between its structure and the processes which go on within it and between it and its environment are such as to maintain those properties and relations, which for the purposes in hand have been called its structure, relatively unchanged. Very generally, always in 'dynamic' systems, this maintenance is dependent on continually varying processes, which 'neutralize' either endogenous or exogenous sources of variability which, if they went far enough, would change the structure." By analogy, "A classic example of equilibrium . . . is the maintenance of nearly constant body temperature by mammals and birds—in the face of continuing variation in environmental temperature and through mechanisms which operate either to produce heat, including slowing up its loss, or to slow down the rate of heat production or accelerate its dissipation." Therefore, "Contrasted then with stability or equilibrating processes are those processes which operate to bring about structural change. That such processes exist and that they are of fundamental scientific importance is nowhere in question" (Parsons, 1973:73).

In "An Outline of the Social System," which succinctly summarizes functionalism, Parsons (1961) views society as a system surrounded by three other systems (personality, the organism, and culture). He considers a society in equilibrium when its boundaries with the other three systems are not breached. Social equilibrium consists in "boundary maintenance"; social change consists in boundary breaking. "If a subboundary is broken, resources within the larger system counteract the implicit tendency to structural change" (Parsons, 1961:71).

Social change considered as boundary destruction and equilibrium restoration has two sources: endogenous (that is, affecting boundaries within the system) and exogenous (that is, initiated from one of the systems outside the social system). The external (exogenous) forces of social change are internal to the other systems (personality, the organism, culture), which are said to delineate society. "The exogenous sources of social change consist in endogenous tendencies to change in the organisms, personalities, and cultural systems articulated with social systems in question" (Parsons, 1961:71). Many kinds of exogenous changes affect the social system—for example, genetic changes in the population, changes in the technique of exploiting nature, and the impact of other social systems, as in war or in the form of cultural influences. These changes are external to the social system, but they have an impact on it.

Endogenous changes are caused by "strains" within the system itself. In Parsons' (1961:71) words: "The most general, commonly used term for an endogenous tendency to change is a 'strain." *Strain* here refers to a condition in the *relation* between two or more structured units (i.e., subsystems of the system) that constitute a tendency or pressure toward changing that relation to one incompatible with the equilibrium of the relevant parts of the system." In other words, these strains result from certain disequilibria between inputs and outputs across the boundaries of subsystems. Several things can happen to these stresses and strains; they can be resolved, they can be arrested, they can be isolated, or they can be compensated for by changes in the structure of the system.

There are two main types of changes, depending on the source (exogenous or endogenous) of the model for reequilibrium once the forces to repair boundary destruction are underway. "The first . . . is the one where the principal model component comes from outside the society. This has been true of the contemporary underdeveloped societies. . . . The second . . . is that occurring when the cultural model cannot be supplied from a socially exogenous source, but must . . . be evolved from within the society" (Parsons, 1961:78).

Adjustments within the system will generally be associated with the reorganization of roles. This can take several forms, involving the disappearance, the creation, or the modification of roles. Changes of this kind tend to be more complex and continuous than changes where roles are not affected. Based on Parsons's theoretical framework, Neil J. Smelser (1959) recognizes a sevenfold sequence where the reorganization of roles leads to other kinds of structural differentiation within the social system. In his famous study of the British cotton industry, Smelser characterized advanced societies as differing from underdeveloped or traditional societies in their degree of complexity and structural differentiation of basic institutional roles.

The process of structural differentiation is seen as a sequence of steps or stages, including the following:

1. Dissatisfaction with the goal-achievement of the social system or subsystem in question and a sense of opportunity for change in terms of the potential availability of facilities.
2. Symptoms of disturbance in the form of "unjustified" negative emotional reactions and "unrealistic" aspirations on the part of various elements in the social system.
3. A covert handling of these tensions and mobilization of motivational resources for new attempts to realize the implications of the existing value system.
4. Encouragement of the resulting proliferation of "new ideas" without imposing

specific responsibility for their implementation or for "taking the consequences."

5. Positive attempts to reach specification of the new ideas and institutional patterns which will become the objects of commitments.

6. Responsible implementation of innovations carried out by persons or collectives which are either rewarded or punished, depending on their acceptability or responsibility in terms of existing value systems.

7. If the implementations of Step 6 are received favorably, they are gradually routinized into the usual patterns of performance and sanction; their extraordinary character thereby diminishes. (Smelser, 1959:15–16)

William F. Ogburn

William F. Ogburn's (1886–1959) cultural lag theory may be considered a kind of equilibrium theory. As Appelbaum (1970:73) notes, however, this is the case only "With respect to nonmaterial culture. With respect to material culture—i.e., technology—cultural lag theory is closer to evolutionary theory in positing smooth, cumulative change in the direction of ever increasing complexity." Ogburn's theory reasons that societies operate as homeostatic mechanisms in that changes that upset equilibrium in one part tend to produce compensating changes to restore that equilibrium. In this situation, however, the new equilibrium condition differs from the old one and there is a lag between the two equilibrium states. The unequal rates of change produce a strain or maladjustment, which in turn produces a "lag," until the more slowly changing, usually nonmaterial, culture catches up. For example, if technology changes, the curriculum may be out of date, and students will be less able to get jobs. Unemployment may then be a problem until education is modernized. In Ogburn's words (1964:86): "A cultural lag occurs when one of two parts of culture which are correlated changes before or in greater degree than the other part does, thereby causing less adjustment between the two parts than existed previously."

In essence, Ogburn argues that material culture and nonmaterial culture change in different ways. Change in material culture is considered to have a marked directional or progressive character. This is because there are generally agreed-upon standards of efficiency that are used to evaluate material inventions. To use airplanes as an example, designers keep working to develop planes that will fly higher and faster and carry more payload at a lower unit cost; and because airplanes can be measured against these standards, inventions in this area appear both rapidly and predictably.

In the area of nonmaterial culture (knowledge and beliefs, norms and values), on the other hand, there are often no generally accepted standards. The obvious directional character of change in material culture is lacking in many areas of nonmaterial cultures.

In addition to the differences in the directional character of change, Ogburn believes that material culture tends to change faster than nonmaterial culture. This difference in rate of culture change gives the basis for the concept of cultural lag. Material inventions bring changes that require adjustments to be made in various areas of nonmaterial culture. The invention of the automobile, for instance, freed young, unmarried men and women from direct parental observation, made it possible for people to work at great distances from their homes, and among other things facilitated crime by making escape easier.

In sum, the structural-functional approach and its ramifications really became dominant in American sociology in the second half of the twentieth century. Indeed, as Kingsley Davis (1959) pointed out, functionalism became almost synonymous with sociological theory. Almost from the beginning, however, the functionalist approach was attacked both for alleged theoretical shortcomings and on ideological grounds. Questions such as "Functional for whom?" were raised—valid questions in that the interests and needs of different groups in society are often in conflict, and what may be functional for one group may be dysfunctional for another. Thus, the model is unable to explain social conflicts and social change because it assumes consensus on basic societal values and goals and it minimizes the importance of power and coercion as a mechanism of social integration (Eisenstadt, 1985:13).

Others argue that functional analysis deals far more adequately with the problem of social order than with the problem of social change; that it is a static, antihistorical mode of analysis with a bias toward conservatism. Some sociologists even suggest that there is an implicit teleology in functional analysis in that this mode of analysis inappropriately attributes purposes to social institutions as if they were conscious beings. As expected, a sizable literature in the field has been devoted to both making and refuting these charges (Gouldner, 1970).

Irving Zeitlin (1973:15) has recapitulated some of the major critiques of this approach as follows:

1. It exaggerates the unity, stability and harmony of social systems;
2. It imputes a positive character to all social institutions;
3. It is ahistorical;
4. It tends to regard existing institutions as necessary and indispensable, and therefore entails a conservative bias.

SYSTEMS THEORIES

One of the limitations of structural-functional theories of social change is the undue emphasis placed on equilibrium and stability (Eisenstadt, 1985:13–14). As Wilbert E. Moore (1974:10) points out, "The fact that sociologists have directed their attention primarily to orderly characteristics

of social systems has had the unnecessary but real consequence of distract-
ing their interests from intrinsic sources of change." The idea that society
is comprised of functionally interdependent units provides a good basis
for an orderly and coherent analysis of change, but it does not provide an
"adequate basis for predicting change, or even for explaining it in a general
or 'lawful' and not simply historical or unique way" (Moore, 1974: 10).

General systems theory takes the emphasis off stability and equilibrium
and looks at the notion of function from a different perspective (Tominaga,
1985: 178). In a sense, this approach provides the concept of "options" to
structural-functional analysis.

From the perspective of general systems theory, a system is viewed
as an organized whole or unit that includes the interactions of its interdependent component parts and its relationships to the environment (Buckley,
1967:41). It is more or less continuous, more or less stable, and more or
less clearly defined by boundaries. It may be visualized as an entity in itself
or as a set of interrelated subsystems. The system functions with something
other than the mere sum of its component parts; its organization and the
relationship of its components to one another must be recognized. "When
we say that 'the whole is more than the sum of its parts' . . . the 'more than'
points to the fact of *organization* which imparts to the aggregate characteristics that are not only *different* from, but often *not found in* the components
alone" (Buckley, 1967:42).

Systems theory distinguishes various levels of system from the simplest
to the most complex and relatively rare. Kenneth E. Boulding (1956), for
example, distinguishes nine levels:

1. static structure;
2. simple dynamic systems, like a clock;
3. cybernetic or self-adjusting system, like a thermostat;
4. self-maintaining open system, as in organisms which take in various kinds of
   food and information;
5. genetic-societal system, as in the division of labor between cells in a plant to
   form a cell-society with "blueprinted" growth;
6. the animal system, characterized by mobility, enormous information intake,
   goal-seeking and self-awareness;
7. the human system, at which there is self-consciousness and symbolic language;
8. social systems; and
9. transcendental systems, of which we have as yet little knowledge.

For most theorists, however, human social behavior is seen as occuring in
a field of five groupings of systems, all of which are simultaneously present
and interacting. They are: the ecosystem, which is the physical and biological environment; the human organism itself; the personality, which
embraces psychological systems; cultural systems; and social systems. In a

way, every social act is seen as simultaneously being physical, biological, psychological, cultural, and social.

General systems theory emphasizes information and communication because "whereas the relations of parts of an organism are physiological, involving complex physio-chemical *energy* interchanges, the relations of parts of society are primarily psychic, involving complex communicative processes of *information* exchange and . . . this difference makes all the difference" (Buckley, 1967:43). For information exchange the word *feedback* is utilized, which is the core concept of cybernetics. Feedback refers to information return and may be either positive or negative. If a system sends out information and receives back information of the same sign, it receives a *positive* feedback. If it receives back information of a different sign, it is *negative* feedback. Feedback processes activate corrective behavior in a system. For example, in learning or decision-making situations, individuals benefit from positive feedback, which reinforces correct choices, and from negative feedback, which penalizes incorrect ones, or at least signals them, that their action is not leading to the appropriate objective. Feedback is, therefore, a way of checking and guiding goal-directed action. In contemporary societies, for example, illustrations of feedback would include voting, protests, and consumer choices.

Society is viewed from the general systems perspective as an adaptive system, which can persist or develop by changing its own structure at times in fundamental ways. The adaptive system depends on:

1. a source for the continuous introduction of "variety" into the system to refine or revitalize the pool of usable information;
2. the maintenance of an optimum level of tension in the system simultaneously with a relatively high level of satisfaction of members' needs;
3. a full, two-way communication network, extending throughout all parts of the system;
4. a selective, or decision-making, system that is sensitive to changes both within and outside of its environment; and
5. effective mechanisms for preserving and propagating those meanings and informations on which the next adaptive process will be based (Buckley, 1967:206–207).

The adaptive systems are considered open systems. Open systems are "open" with respect to their environment. They exchange information, materials, and energies with their environments. They continually process information from within and without in an attempt to adapt. Complex adaptive systems constitute a very general framework within which "many current conceptualizations of the genesis, maintenance, or change of social structure may be organized" (Buckley, 1967:128). A sociocultural system is to be conceived as a complex adaptive organization of components. It continually attempts to "map" the variety of its external environment through science, technology, magic, and religion, and its internal milieu through common understanding, symbols, expectations, norms and values. A constant flow of potentially usable variety is provided by social differentiation, individual and subgroup differences, experience, exploration, turnover of components, and cultural diffusion. The internal source of dynamics for the ongoing process is the continuous generation of varying degrees of tension, stress or strain, within and between the interacting components; such tension is now being recognized as an inherent and essential characteristic of such systems. (Buckley, 1967:128–129).

The closed systems, on the other hand, are subject to entropy, that is, decay or disorganization, although society rarely goes to an entropic state. "A society is often considered closed if it has no communications or transactions with other societies and no migration" (Kuhn, 1974:441). For open systems, conflict, stress, and disturbance are the sources of change. Such systems grow more complex and elaborate as a result of their reciprocal relations with the environment and adapt to strains and pressures from within.

However, social systems are not infinitely adaptive. They operate under constraints, including the coercive power of other social systems, the demands and limitations placed on them by the ecosystem and the nature of the human nature, the scarcity of resources such as the means of subsistence, and the limited energies and capacities of individuals. Moreover, not all elements in a social structure are compatible with each other.

The general systems approach is useful in relating to variables in their total context and assessing their importance more satisfactorily than it is possible when only two or three variables are taken out of context. For example, Jay Forrester (1969) performed computer simulations of what would happen to cities viewed as total social systems on the basis of certain programs. He found that piecemeal planning would only exaggerate current urban problems, that some proposed reforms would have unintended side effects, and that many assumptions about trends are invalid.

In summarizing the potential uses of general systems approach, Buckley (1967:80) emphatically argues that

> only the modern systems approach promises to get at the full complexity of the interacting phenomena—to see not only the *causes* acting on the phenomena under study, the possible *consequences* of the phenomena, and the possible *mutual interactions* of some of these factors, but also to see the *total emergent processes* as a function of possible positive and/or negative *feedbacks*, mediated by the *selective decisions*, or "choices," of the individuals and groups directly or indirectly involved.

But the systems approach also has certain limitations. Most systems analyzed by sociologists are partial representations of reality and consist, fundamentally, of abstractions considered pertinent for a particular study. It is always possible that important components and relationships are not included in the analysis. Most systems analyses are limited to specific topics, and thus it is to be expected that there will be a number of relationships to other systems that cannot be studied in depth because this would involve the analysis of these other systems. It is also plausible that important components of the social phenomena under investigation are not included, for a variety of reasons. The consequence of such omission may be incorrect or distorted analysis. The testing of predictions derived from systems analysis in the area of social change is likely to be a complicated and drawn-out process. Not only are the required data often difficult to assemble, but the changes that may be predicted are usually long term and thus difficult to ascertain in the short run. Systems theory is still in its infancy, and in spite of these and other limitations, it promises to provide a better understanding of the intricacies of social change.

SOCIAL-PSYCHOLOGICAL THEORIES

In a changing society it is important to remember that it is, after all, people who change. It is not surprising, therefore, that the social-psychological approach gained much attention in recent years due primarily to the contributions of David McClelland and Everett E. Hagen to the study of change and, in particular, development. The underlying assumption is that societies develop as a result of the workings of certain psychological factors. Where such factors are present, change will take place; where they are absent, stagnation will prevail. Instead of concentrating on technological and environmental factors, ideas, structural conditions, or social conflict, this approach focuses on individuals with unique personality attributes. It deals with psychological determinants that drive people to act, to push forward, to invent, to discover, create, acquire, build, or expand. The German sociologist Max Weber (1864–1920), who had a stronger influence on Western sociology than any other single individual, was among the first to use this approach in his study of the Protestant ethic and capitalism. Hagen's theory of status withdrawal and McClelland's theory on achievement motivation are examples of the modern social-psychological approach to change and development.

Max Weber

In *The Protestant Ethic and the Spirit of Capitalism*, Weber's theme is that the development of modern industrial capitalism was possible because of specific psychological states occurring after the sixteenth century in Western Europe prompted by the spread of the Protestant ethic. He pays much attention to the spirit of capitalism, stating that "development of the spirit of capitalism is best understood as part of the development of rationalism as a whole, and could be deduced from the fundamental position of rationalism on the basic problems of life" (Weber, 1958:76). The spirit of capitalism is characteristic of situations in which people are preoccupied by the idea of making money, and the acquisition of goods becomes the ultimate purpose in life. Idleness, wastefulness, or continuous enjoyment of life is not tolerated. Life is to be devoted to achieving. In the relentless pursuit of acquisitions, greater efficiency is advocated because this leads to more results. We are under a constant pressure to rationalize our activities and to organize our lives so that credibility, punctuality, honesty, inventiveness, and adaptability to new circumstances become integral parts of our behavior. Because such qualities are instrumental in efforts of achieving, "Capitalism is identical with the pursuit of profit and forever *renewed* profit by means of continous rational capitalistic enterprise" (Weber, 1958:17).

Weber emphatically argues that people, dominated by the capitalist spirit, have little regard for traditions that would impede their climb to greater and greater wealth. "The most important opponent with which the spirit of capitalism . . . has had to struggle was the type of attitude and reaction to new situations which we may designate as traditionalism" (Weber, 1958:58–59). Therefore, the capitalist, the acquisition seeker, is an innovator by nature. Acquisition and profit making become a preoccupation. But greed is not the motivation. The capitalist spirit requires that both the acquisition and the spending of money be strictly rational, calculated, and directed toward the goal of progressive, optimal accumulation.

Weber asserts that modern Western civilization is a product of the Protestant ethic. There is a strong attitude of respect for work in the Protestant ethic. Weber points out that "the god of Calvinism demanded of his believers not single good works, but a life of good works combined into a unified system" (Weber, 1958:117). From this perspective, instead of being punishment for sin, work was worshipful activity through which man glorified God. Rationality and calculation were means to salvation in the next world as well as to success in this one. The world was a place of sin, and the individual must not be trapped by its pleasures. These beliefs constitute the core of what Weber called the *doctrine of wordly asceticism*, a crucial prerequisite of capitalism.

When people work hard, they may accumulate wealth. When they are prohibited from indulging in worldly pleasures, they do not spend it. They save, and savings are one of the foundations of capitalism. Simply by embracing the Protestant ethic, postfeudal citizens began acting in ways that made them more successful members of the rising capitalistic economy. Merchants and manufacturers, ill at ease with the conflict between their traditional beliefs and business behavior, found comfort and reinforcement in the Protestant ethic. It also generated the right atmosphere for the spread of the spirit of capitalism.

Max Weber, as most great and provocative thinkers usually are, is challenged and criticized on a number of grounds. A number of questions centered around the alleged direct causal connection between the Protestant ethic on the one hand and the development of capitalism on the other. "Others have cast doubt on the specific 'mechanism' through which, according to Weber, Calvinist belief became transformed into or linked to motivation for this—worldly economic activities, namely, the psychological derivatives of the idea of predestination, the great anxiety which this idea created among believers, urging them to undertake in a compulsive way this-worldly activities to prove their being of the elect" (Eisenstadt, 1973:215).

On the other hand, in the past three decades or so, with the surge of the great interest in development and modernization, interest in his thesis has arisen once more. Inspired by Weber's contentions, for example, Robert N. Bellah (1957) finds that the Japanese religion's promotion of diligence and frugality made it instrumental in generating the spirit of entrepreneurship and the activity fruitful in Japan's industrialization.

Everett E. Hagen

Everett E. Hagen's (1962) theory is concerned, just like that of Weber's, with the *beginnings* of economic development. He asserts that change from traditional to modern society will not come about without a change in personalities. He develops his ideas within a framework of contrast between traditional and modern societies positing that each of these societies is a product of a different type of personality.

In Hagen's view, traditional societies are characterized by fixed status levels (such as peasants and elites) and the personalities in such social groupings are authoritarian, uncreative, and noninnovational. A member of a traditional society is uncreative because he or she sees the world as an arbitrary place rather than one that is subject to analysis and control. A person's unconscious processes are both inaccessible and uncreative. Interpersonal relations are solved on the basis of "ascriptive authority"; and people avoid anxiety by resorting to authority. Such type of society has a great degree of stability in its institutions and there may be no social change for centuries, for "the interrelationships between personality and social structure are such as to make it clear that social change will not occur without change in personalities" (Hagen, 1962:86).

Modern society is a product of what Hagen calls "innovational" personality. It is characterized by attributes such as creativity, curiosity, and openness to experience. A person with this type of personality persistently looks for new solutions and does not take generally accepted evaluations for granted. Such a person sees the world as having a logical and coherent order that can be understood and explained. In spite of sporadic doubts, individuals such as these are confident that they can evaluate the order of things by themselves and solve the problems they are confronted with. Such people are not necessarily happy and may be driven to creativity by a continual anxiety that causes them to feel satisfaction only when they are striving and achieving and when their accomplishments are acknowledged and favorably evaluated.

Following this discussion of the two personality types, Hagen poses the key question: How can a stable traditional society dominated by authoritarian personalities be transformed into a modern society characterized by innovational personalities? Hagen's answer is that change comes about if and when members of one particular social group perceive that their purposes and values are not respected by other groups in the society whom they respect and whose esteem they value. The phrase he uses for this is *withdrawal of status respect* (Hagen, 1962:185). He considers several situations of status withdrawal: for example, when a traditional elite group is replaced by another group; when symbols and beliefs that a subordinate group considers vital are depreciated or even prohibited by a superior group; inconsistency of economic and other statuses; nonacceptance of a migrant group in a new place of residence; and the delegation of institutional activity without change in the power structure.

Status withdrawal for Hagen means disregard for one's role in society or for one's beliefs and aspirations. He argues that it is painful to be disregarded. People without a role in society become alienated and frustrated. Groups with a low status, or groups that are forced to accept a lower status, become disenchanted with the established order. Their accumulated resentment is then transferred to their children. As a result, frustration and rage continue to be accumulated from one generation to another. Following Merton's typology of modes of individual adaptation, retreatism, he believes, is the typical reaction to withdrawal of status. The retreatist person, he says, "is not free of rage." On the contrary, the rage is intense, but held in leash, with occasional outbursts. But

> retreatism is not a dead end. As retreatism deepens in successive generations, it creates circumstances of home life and social environment that are conducive to the development of innovational personality. The historical sequence seems to be: authoritarianism, withdrawal of status respect, retreatism, creativity." (Hagen, 1962:217)

Hagen considers child-rearing practices in developing countries a decisive factor in the transformation of societies. Following Freud, he assumes that childhood determines what people will become and how they will react to values and events. Values inculcated in a person's mind in early childhood remain for life. Assuming that, he argues, there is reason to expect that the males in a group suffer more from loss of status than females. Thus, because of loss of status, men will despair, become weak, and adopt an attitude of retreatism. Women, on the other hand, resenting the weakness of their husbands, will do everything to instill in the minds of their sons a desire to be better off than their parents. Hagen posits that the mothers will bring up their sons in a spirit of self-reliance in a yearning for achievement and ardent aspiration to prove their worth to others. The innovational personality characterized by creative imagination is likely to come into being if the boy's

> experiences of infancy and early childhood give him a firm and satisfying impression of the loving nurturance of his mother, but that repeatedly he is unable to achieve as she seems to wish him to. He may then feel that the fault must lie in him, and there may become built into him anxiety that he may not accomplish enough, anxiety that drives him all his life to achieve in order to regain fleetingly that temporary feeling of security conveyed by his mother's praise and caresses. In this case, little rage and hatred may be provoked in him, and his unconscious processes will remain accessible to him. (Hagen, 1962:94)

Hagen assumes that the home environment and the lessons of the mother should, in due time, inspire their sons to become innovators and reformers. They will acquire and establish new roles challenging the actual elite. This will come about in Hagen's (1962:242) view when two conditions are fulfilled; "a requisite for economic growth in a traditional society is not merely that upward social mobility by new means is possible, but also that upward social mobility by traditional channels is not possible."

He illustrates his theory with case studies of Japan, Burma, and Colombia, with sporadic reference to the situation of the blacks in the United States. His attempts to account for the importance of personality in development are ambitious and revealing. There are, nevertheless, problems with his theory.

Some of the criticisms deal with the fact that he paid little attention to social structure features that changed the fashion in which socialization impinges upon different members of the same society. Others question his appraisement of the authoritarian personality in traditional society and the innovational personality in modern society. His description of authoritarian personality could easily fit any Prussian Army officer, members of the prewar Japanese military, or any typical bureaucrat who avoids the anxiety of independent, creative, innovative thinking. Still, in spite of some of these criticisms, Hagen is right in telling us that psychological factors and the rearing of a new generation, in general, are important elements in promoting change and development.

David C. McClelland

David C. McClelland, like Hagen, has been primarily concerned with a specific kind of change—economic development. He focused his interest on the investigation of what he called achievement motivation, which subsequently was changed to need for achievement (symbolized by n Achievement). He asserts that economic development, both in historical and contemporary societies, results from a preceding development of n Achievement. And the greater the development of the n Achievement, the more likely that economic development will be intense. He and his colleagues developed several methods of analyzing and measuring the n Achievement in historical societies and for cross-cultural purposes in existing societies. His results led him to suggest that "a society with a generally high level of n Achievement will produce more rapid economic development" (McClelland, 1961:205). The lesson is obvious, for rapid economic growth helps to ". . . encourage and develop those . . . who have a vigorous entrepreneurial spirit or a strong drive for achievement. In other words: *invest in a man, not just in a plan*" (McClelland, 1973:16).

His n Achievement means individual economic achievement that produces economic growth. It is similar to what Max Weber emphasized many times. It is not greed for riches, it is action ". . . on the basis of rigorous calculation, directed with foresight and caution toward the economic success which is in sharp contrast to the hand-to-mouth existence of the peasant, and to the privileged traditionalism of the guild craftsman and too of the adventurers' capitalism, oriented to the exploitation of political opportunites and irrational speculation" (Weber, 1958:76). Similarly, McClelland is talking about accumulation of money, but not about money for its own sake. Accumulation of money is but one measure of success for the n Achievement seekers: ". . . it is *not* profit per se that makes the businessman tick but a strong desire for achievement, for doing a good job. Profit is simply one measure among several of how well the job has been done, but it is not necessarily the goal itself" (McClelland, 1973:162). More specifically, the n Achievement is manifested in behavior characterized by preferences for tasks with moderate difficulties for moderate calculated risks, and energetic innovative activity, especially when it results in personal achievement. Also exhibited are a degree of individualism manifested in a high degree of responsibility and a tendency for prospective planning of individual actions, combined with a better performance if there is a knowledge of the results of the action and an evident probability of success.

Most of McClelland's work and that of his associates was devoted to the analysis of ethnographic accounts of numerous cultures in an attempt to determine the percentage of adult males engaged in entrepreneurial activity. They analyzed the content of folktales and children's stories of 23 nations for content and conditions of n Achievement, and correlated them with subsequent indicators of economic growth. Ancient Greek literature in different periods was analyzed. The finding suggested that such literature written prior to periods considered prosperous in Greece, as a rule, contained stimulation toward entrepreneurial activity. They also established that persons with a high *n* Achievement have a tendency to doodle in multiple or diagonal waves and "S" shapes. Thus, the ceramic patterns of different cultures at different times were compared from that angle. A number of other examinations were made, special psychological tests were constructed to evaluate *n* Achievement, and people in various countries were tested.

Having established the pattern of *n* Achievement, the question is raised: How can achievement motivation be induced? The answer is simple, by *learning*. In the classic Freudian tradition, McClelland and his colleagues believed that motives are learned in reference to both external and internal stimuli. Because most of the motivations are learned in early childhood, the kind of motivations learned at that time and the stimuli experienced in childhood are of crucial importance for subsequent behavior. In other words, the desired motives may be elicited by properly selected stimuli. Achievement motivation could be inculcated in training of self-reliance, high praise for hard work, persistence in goal attainment, and interest in excellence for its own sake. Education and child-rearing practices that emphasize such values are instrumental in creating a foundation for a strong *n* Achievement. "Studies of the family have shown, for instance, that for a boy three factors are important in producing high *n* Achievement—parents' high standards of achievement, warmth and encouragement, and a father who is not dominating and authoritarian" (McClelland, 1973:172).

The work of McClelland and his associates generated much subsequent research on *n* Achievement. Some of these studies revealed positive associations between measures of the achievement motive and various indices such as plans for education for younger children, the extent of planning ahead and the like (J. N. Morgan, 1964). On the other hand, the formulations of McClelland have been severely criticized as historically incorrect, theoretically oversimplified, and methodologically flawed. "In fact, motivational theories have recently fallen into relative disfavor and investigators have turned to other questions concerning the supply of entrepreneurship" (Smelser, 1976:128).

In a later publication, *Motivating Economic Achievement* (McClelland, Winter & Winter 1969), however, he reiterates his belief that achievement motivation is the major stimulant of economic growth. He provides evidence that even adults who were educated in a traditional setting can acquire a strong desire for modernity and can achieve in economic undertakings if they are properly induced in the direction by external agencies. The key is to change their attitude. This can be accomplished when they are put under special training that rewards their prowess and stimulates their desire for acquisition. McClelland argues that they soon start to behave as modern entrepreneurs—that is, they promote economic activities that cumulatively will produce the effect of economic growth, creating more jobs, and subsequently raising the general standard of living.

The book deals with activities and the results of special courses in raising achievement motivation organized in India. In his conclusion he repeats his earlier advice: "sow achievement motivation to harvest economic development."

SUMMARY

In the history of sociology, few theories have been so passionately pursued as that of social change. These efforts of explaining social change should be seen in the context of intellectual, political, and social climates of the particular theorists. In each historical epoch every interpretation of social reality posits certain questions and provides certain answers, thereby effectively excluding the possibility of other questions and other answers. According to S.N. Eisenstadt (1972), tension is inherent in intellectual life because of the tendency to challenge the intellectual construction of social reality. If a theory of society is developed by one group of intellectuals, this will provide an incentive for others to view the matter in another way. Eisenstadt's insight accounts, in part, for the diverse explanations of social change.

Some of the principal theories attempting explanation have been reviewed, and their weaknesses have been noted. Evolutionary theories tried to show that all societies in all spheres of social life pass through similar stages of development, moving from less complex, less differentiated stages to more complex and differentiated stages—culminating in the modern industrial, secular society.

Conflict theorists view change as the outgrowth of inescapable competition for scarce resources among groups in society. Conflict is considered inevitable in social systems and is seen by some as a creative source of change and by others as the only possible means of change.

The structural-functional theorists have sought in various ways to account for change within the overall framework of their theory that society consists of interrelated parts that work together for the purpose of maintaining internal balance.

The systems theory conceives of society as a complex adaptive system and stresses interaction, variety, and change, and the use of information and communication to adapt to external and internal constraints, demands, and disturbances. The concepts of feedback and decision making suggest that social change in society is not subject to blind forces but can be guided.

Social-psychological theories posit that activities of people constitute the essence of change in society and modifications in the behavior can facilitate change and play an essential role in societal development.

Although the study of social change has been the focus of attention of sociologists since the beginning of the discipline, agreement on a general theory is not yet in sight. A satisfactory theory of social change should indicate what elements are changing, what direction the change is taking, and how and why it is occurring. Such a theory should also provide an explanation for both the internal dynamics of society and the relationship between the society and its external environment. In the literature on social change, no theory realizes these objectives.

The quest for such comprehensive theory may well be futile. A concentration on narrower theories of change that seek to explain transformations in particular domains, such as economic or family life, may be more productive in the future.

SUGGESTED FURTHER READINGS

APPELBAUM, RICHARD P. *Theories of Social Change*. Chicago: Markham, 1970. A concise review of evolutionary, equilibrium, conflict, and rise-and-fall theories of social change.

BUCKLEY, WALTER. *Sociology and Modern Systems Theory*. Englewood Cliffs, N.J.: Prentice-Hall, 1967. Depicts the sociocultural system as complex and adaptive.

COSER, LEWIS. *The Functions of Social Conflict*. New York: Free Press, 1956. Building on the earlier work of Georg Simmel, Coser elaborates the many ways in which conflict strengthens rather than weakens group life.

ETZIONI-HALEVY, EVA. *Social Change: The Advent and Maturation of Modern Society*. London: Routledge & Kegan Paul, 1981. An application of the "mainstream" and Marxist theories of social change to modernization.

JANOS, ANDREW C. *Politics and Paradigms: Changing Theories of Social Change in Social Science*. Stanford, Calif: Stanford University Press, 1986. A critical evaluation of the major theoretical perspectives on social change with special emphasis on the Marxist model.

NISBET, ROBERT A. *Social Change and History*. New York: Oxford, 1969. A lucid and highly readable analysis of many of the influential theories of social change.

SMELSER, NEIL. *Social Change in the Industrial Revolution*. Chicago: University of Chicago Press, 1959. One of the more definitive studies of change from a structural-functional perspective.

STRASSER, HERMANN, and SUSAN C. RANDALL. *An Introduction to the Theories of Social Change*. London: Routledge & Kegan Paul, 1981. The authors combine theoretical approaches with major issues of social change to demonstrate how change may be analyzed at different levels of society.

TURNER, JONATHAN H. *The Structure of Sociological Theory*, 4th ed. Chicago: Dorsey Press, 1986. A good overview of the major classical and contemporary sociological theories with many applications to social change.

REFERENCES

APPELBAUM , RICHARD P. *Theories of Social Change*. Chicago: Markham, 1970.

BECKER, HOWARD P., *Through Values to Social Interpretation: Essays on Social Context, Actions and Prospects*. Durham, N.C.: Duke University Press, 1950.

BELLAH, ROBERT N. *Tokugawa Religion: The Values of Pre-Industrial Japan*. New York: Free Press, 1975.

BOULDING, KENNETH E. "General Systems Theory: The Skeleton of Science." *Management Science*, 2, 1956, pp. 197–208.

BUCKLEY, WALTER. *Sociology and Modern Systems Theory*. Englewood Cliffs, N.J.: Prentice-Hall, 1967.

COMTE, AUGUSTE. *The Positive Philosophy*, Harriet Martineau, trans. and ed. London: George Bell, 1915.

COSER, LEWIS A. *The Functions of Social Conflict*. Glencoe, Ill.: Free Press, 1956.

DAHRENDORF, RALF. *Class and Class Conflict in Industrial Society*. Stanford, Calif.: Stanford University Press, 1959.

DAHRENDORF, RALF. "Out of Utopia: Toward a Reorientation of Sociological Analysis." In N.J. Demerath, III, and Richard A. Peterson (eds.), *System, Change, and Conflict: A Reader on Contemporary Sociological Theory and the Debate over Functionalism*. New York: Free Press, 1967, pp. 465–480.

DAHRENDORF, RALF. "Towards a Theory of Social Conflict." In A. Etzioni and Eva Etzioni-Halevy (eds.), *Social Change: Sources, Patterns, and Consequences*, 2nd ed. New York: Basic Books, 1973, pp. 100–113.

DAVIS, KINGSLEY. *Human Society*. New York: Macmillan, 1949.

DAVIS, KINGSLEY. "The Myth of Functional Analysis as a Special Method in Sociology and Anthropology." *American Sociological Review*, 24, 1959, pp. 757–772.

DUKE, JAMES T. *Conflict and Power in Social Life*. Provo, Utah: Brigham Young University Press, 1976.

DURKHEIM, EMILE. *The Division of Labor in Society*, George Simpson, trans. New York: Free Press, 1947.

EISENSTADT, S.N. "Intellectuals and Tradition." *Daedelus* 101(2), 1972, pp. 1–19.

EISENSTADT, S.N. *Tradition, Change and Modernity*. New York: Wiley, 1973.

EISENSTADT, S.N. "Social Change, Differentiation and Evolution." In Lewis A. Coser and Bernard Rosenberg (eds.), *Sociological Theory: A Book of Readings*, 5th ed. New York: Macmillan, 1982, pp. 533–550.

EISENSTADT, S.N. "Macro-Societal Analysis—Background, Development and Indication." In S.N. Eisenstadt and H.J. Helle (eds.), *Macro-Sociological Theory: Perspectives on Sociological Theory*, Volume I. London: Sage Publications Ltd., 1985, pp. 7–24.

FORRESTER, JAY. *Urban Dynamics*. Cambridge, Mass.: MIT Press, 1969.

FORRESTER, JAY. "Counter-Intuitive Behavior of Social Systems." *Technological Review*, 73, 1971, pp. 52–68.

GOULDNER, ALVIN W. *The Coming Crisis of Western Sociology*. New York: Basic Books, 1970.

HAGEN, EVERETT E. *On the Theory of Social Change: How Economic Growth Begins*. Homewood, Ill.: Dorsey Press, 1962.

KUHN, ALFRED. *The Logic of Social Systems*. San Francisco: Jossey-Bass, 1974.

LAUER, ROBERT H. *Perspectives on Social Change*, 3rd. ed. Boston: Allyn & Bacon, 1982.

LENSKI, GERHARD, and JEAN LENSKI. *Human Societies: An Introduction to Macrosociology*, 5th ed. New York: McGraw-Hill Book Company, 1987.

MALINOWSKI, BRONISLAW. "Anthropology." *Encyclopaedia Britannica*, 1st supplementary volume. Chicago: Encyclopaedia Britannica, 1926, pp. 132–133.

MARX, KARL. "A Contribution to the Critique of Political Economy." In L.S. Feuer (ed.), *Marx and Engels: Basic Writings on Politics and Philosophy*. New York: Doubleday, Anchor Books, 1959, pp. 42–46.

MARX, KARL, and FRIEDRICH ENGELS. *The Communist Manifesto*. New York: Appleton, 1955. (Originally published in 1848.)

MCCLELLAND, DAVID C. *The Achieving Society*. Princeton, N.J.: Van Nostrand, 1961.

MCCLELLAND, DAVID C. "Business Drive and National Achievement." In A. Etzioni and Eva Etzioni-Halevy (eds.), *Social Change: Sources, Patterns and Consequences*, 2nd ed. New York: Basic Books, 1973, pp. 161–174.

MCCLELLAND, DAVID C., DAVID G. WINTER, and SARAH K. WINTER, *Motivating Economic Achievement*. New York: Free Press, 1969.

MERTON, ROBERT K. *Social Theory and Social Structure*. New York: Free Press, 1957.

MERTON, ROBERT K. *Social Theory and Social Structure*, revised and enlarged edition. New York: Free Press, 1968.

MILLS, C. WRIGHT. *The Power Elite*. New York: Oxford, 1956.

MOORE, WILBERT E. "A Reconsideration of Theories of Social Change." *American Sociological Review*, 25(6), 1969, pp. 810–818.

MOORE, WILBERT E. *Social Change*, 2nd ed. Englewood Cliffs, N.J.: Prentice-Hall, 1974.

MORGAN, JAMES N. "The Achievement Motive and Economic Behavior." *Economic Development and Cultural Change*, 12(3), 1964, pp. 243–267.

MORGAN, LEWIS HENRY. *Ancient Society*. Cambridge, Mass.: Harvard University Press, 1964. (Originally published in 1877.)

NISBET, ROBERT A. *Social Change and History*. New York: Oxford, 1969.

OGBURN, WILLIAM F. *On Culture and Social Change*. Chicago: University of Chicago Press, 1964.

PARSONS, TALCOTT. *The Social System*. New York: Free Press, 1951.

PARSONS, TALCOTT. "An Outline of the Social System." In Talcott Parsons, Edward A. Shils, Kaspar D. Naegele, and Jesse R. Pitts (eds.), *Theories of Society*, vol. 1. New York: Free Press, 1961, pp. 30–79.

PARSONS, TALCOTT. *Societies: Evolutionary and Comparative Perspectives*. Englewood Cliffs, N.J.: Prentice-Hall, 1966.

PARSONS, TALCOTT. *The System of Modern Societies*. Englewood Cliffs, N.J.: Prentice-Hall, 1971.

PARSONS, TALCOTT. "A Functional Theory of Change." In A. Etzioni and Eva Etzioni-Halevy (eds.), *Social Change: Sources, Patterns and Consequences*, 2nd ed. New York: Basic Books, 1973, pp. 72–86.

PARSONS, TALCOTT. *The Evolution of Societies*. Englewood Cliffs, N.J.: Prentice-Hall, 1977.

RADCLIFFE-BROWN, A.R. *Structure and Function in Primitive Society*. New York: Free Press, 1956.

REDFIELD, ROBERT. *The Folk Culture of Yucatan*. Chicago: University of Chicago Press, 1941.

REDFIELD, ROBERT. "The Folk Society." *American Journal of Sociology*, 52, 1947, pp. 293–308.

ROSTOW, WALT W. *The Stages of Economic Growth. A Non-Communist Manifesto*. New York: Cambridge, 1961.

SMELSER, NEIL J. *Social Change in the Industrial Revolution*. London: Routledge, 1959.

SMELSER, NEIL J. *The Sociology of Economic Life*, 2nd ed. Englewood Cliffs, N.J.: Prentice-Hall, 1976.

SMITH, ANTHONY D. *The Concept of Social Change: A Critique of the Functionalist Theory of Social Change*. London: Routledge, 1973.

STEWART, JULIAN. "Evolution and Progress." In A.L. Kroeber (ed.), *Anthropology Today*. Chicago: University of Chicago Press, 1953, pp. 313–326.

SUMNER, WILLIAM GRAHAM. *Folkways*. Boston: Ginn, 1896.

TIMASHEFF, NICHOLAS S. *Sociological Theory: Its Nature and Growth*, rev. ed. New York: Random House, 1961.

TOENNIES, FERDINAND. *Community and Society: Gemeinschaft und Gesellschaft*, Charles P. Loomis, trans. and ed. East Lansing: Michigan State University Press, 1957.

TOMINAGA, KEN'ICHI. "Typology in the Methodological Approach to the Study of Social Change." In S.N. Eisenstadt and H.J. Helle (eds.), *Macro-Sociological Theory: Perspectives on Sociological Theory*. London: Sage Publications Ltd., 1985, pp. 168–196.

TURNER, JONATHAN H. *The Structure of Sociological Theory*, 4th ed. Chicago: Dorsey Press, 1986.

VAN DEN BERGHE, PIERRE L. "Dialectic and Functionalism: Towards a Synthesis." In N. Demerath and R.A. Peterson (eds.), *System, Change, and Conflict: A Reader on Contemporary Sociological Theory and the Debate over Functionalism*. New York: Free Press, 1967, pp. 294–310.

WARD, LESTER FRANK. *Dynamic Sociology*, 2nd ed. New York: Appleton, 1911.

WEBER, MAX. *The Protestant Ethic and the Spirit of Capitalism*. Talcott Parsons, trans., with a foreword by R.H. Tawney. New York: Scribner's, 1958.

ZEITLIN, IRVING. *Rethinking Sociology*. New York: Appleton, 1973.

3 Directions of Change

Nineteenth-century intellectuals were proud of the achievements of natural sciences and confident in the omnipotence of methods. Regarding society, it was widely believed that the new science of sociology should aim at the discovery of laws, similar to those established in the natural sciences, governing progress and development. As shown in Chapter 2, several of the early sociologists responded to this demand by postulating "social laws" of the inevitable development of human societies toward higher and what they considered "better" stages. Subsequently, as a response to the optimists emphasizing progress, some sociologists developed cyclical theories with the impending final stage of decay and decline. Both groups of theorists used stages to describe the direction of change. Still others used dichotomies from simple to complex in their endeavors to indicate directions. Many of these early attempts to describe the transformation of society in these various ways have been disparaged. Yet, there is still a trend in contemporary sociology toward the acceptance of certain general notions of the earlier attempts to account for direction.

The term *direction* refers to some future position of a social phenomenon under consideration relative to its initial or former position. Most studies of social change presuppose the existence of an entity at a particular level and ask: How does it change, why, and in what direction? The question of the directions of change can be approached from several perspectives. In this chapter, we shall examine:

1. Some of the nineteenth-century assumptions underlying the transformation of societies from simple to complex.
2. Linear theories, based on the notion of social change advancing toward a definite goal.
3. Cyclical theories postulating that societies follow a cyclical course.
4. Models of change describing alternative patterns of direction.
5. Contemporary developments concerning the direction of diffusion of innovations.

In addition to theoretical insight, these perspectives have pragmatic applications and can be helpful in ascertaining the direction of social change in a number of areas. For example, they can be used in the study of macrolevel (large-scale) changes; changes in child-rearing practices; the use of birth-control technology; the dissemination of ideas, fads, and new forms of agricultural production; the spread of cults and religions; and a variety of other social phenomena. Directionality also plays an important role in planned social change, which is a conscious and deliberate intervention to change a specific situation or process (Kettner, Daley, & Nichols, 1985:7).

FROM SIMPLE TO COMPLEX SOCIETIES

One of the prominent arguments in contemporary sociology that has survived from the nineteenth century is that human society has advanced from simple (hunting and gathering, horticultural, or agrarian) to more complex (industrialized, urbanized) forms, and this development has been accompanied by certain qualitative and quantitative changes in the nature of social life and social institutions (see, for example, Chirot, 1986; Lenski, 1976; Lenski & Lenski, 1987; Nisbet, 1969; Parsons, 1977; Wallerstein, 1974). In the past, this view was based on two assumptions: (1) that social evolution is a continuation of biological evolution and (2) that the mechanisms of social evolution are the same as the mechanisms of biological evolution.

In the context of the directions of change, Percy S. Cohen's (1968:208–235) examination of these assumptions is most illuminating. He notes that the first assumption is either meaningless or erroneous. There is no law of biological evolution describing and explaining the actual process of increasing differentiation, specialization, and adaptability. In reality, "most cases of biological mutation were evolutionary failures and the 'story' of biological evolution is a 'success story' only insofar as it is a deliberate selection of the facts of increasing adaptability" (1968:222). In any case, the time period involved in the analysis of social evolution is minuscule as compared with that of biological evolution. This is not to mean that knowledge of biological evolution is not applicable to the understanding of human society. Primatology, for example, sheds some light on the origins of human society and on the psychobiological and, in some cases, even social characteristics of *Homo sapiens*, which have survived the last half-million years of social and cultural development; "but it does not follow from this that social and cultural evolution can be treated as a continuation of biological evolution, unless one assumes that there are similar mechanisms at work in biological evolution" (Cohen, 1968:222) as in social evolution concerning increased differentiation and adaptability to the environment.

Theorists of biological evolution evidently make general assumptions about such mechanisms of evolution. They hypothesize that mutations may occur and are genetically transmissible and transmitted; "though they recognize that although the processes of mutation are lawlike, the actual occurrence of any particular mutation is *very* much a matter of chance" (Cohen, 1968:222). There also are assumptions of laws concerning genetic inheritance and transmission as well as principles of natural selection.

How valid and applicable to social change are these assumptions? The notion of mutation is obviously not applicable in any meaningful sense. The second notion—that genetic inheritance is a factor in evolution—is equally unnecessary. Admittedly, procreation is affected by genetic laws, but the transmission of social characteristics takes place through the process of socialization through social interaction. This is the way members in a society transmit acquired characteristics. To some extent the notion of natural selection does have validity. The argument seems to be that "the more complex and differentiated forms of social structure have a better chance of surviving than the simpler ones because they are either better adapted or more adaptable to their environments and are therefore able to compete favorably with simpler societies" (Cohen, 1968:223).

However, the argument that complex societies are better adapted to their natural and social environment than simple ones is rather doubtful at best. They may be more dependent on it, but not necessarily better adapted to it. Moreover, there are no criteria estimating the implied fit between social structure and its environment. On the contrary, one would argue intuitively that simple societies are, indeed, better adapted. To illustrate, there is practically no tendency for population growth in simple societies to outstrip the means of subsistence, "if only because natural conditions are supplemented by cultural practices such as infanticide, to ensure a high infant mortality rate" (Cohen, 1968:223).

It may also be posited that complex societies are more adaptable than simple ones in the sense that their technology enables them to survive in a greater variety of environments. It is also true that different parts of complex systems are more flexibly interrelated with one another than those of simple systems. As a result, complex systems can adapt more successfully to the introduction of new elements in society. Nevertheless, the argument of greater adaptability (natural selection) to account for the greater survival value of complex social systems is clearly untenable.

A tenable proposition that can be supported is that "the more complex social systems become the more likely they are to develop in the direction of general complexity" (Cohen, 1968:224). Increased complexity brings about increased interdependency, with a concomitant increase in the number of social processes and a similar increase in the number of influences and consequently of outcomes. The more complex a system becomes, the greater will be the degree of autonomy achieved by its parts. This increases the possible number of sources of social change, which, in turn, increases the likelihood of greater complexity.

To illustrate the process of increasing social complexity, let us turn to Emile Durkheim's (1947) widely cited argument in *The Division of Labor in Society*. He notes that primitive societies have little division of labor. They consist of a number of homogeneous units such as families or clans and have what he calls a "segmental" structure. These societies are bound together primarily by their uniformity of practices and beliefs, which Durkheim calls "mechanical solidarity." It is based on similarity among a society's members. An important measure of this form of solidarity is a type of social control that is basically punitive, and there is a great reliance on repressive law. As the size of the population increases and the division of labor becomes more complex, a number of developments take place. The segmentary structure of homogeneous social units is replaced by an increasingly heterogeneous set of units that are interdependent. In addition, the uniformity of ideas, including moral ideas, decreases. This gives rise to a new form of solidarity—an organic solidarity—based on a moral foundation of interdependence involving the acceptance of differences. Repressive law is replaced by restitutive law—that is, laws and methods of enforcement that moved beyond mere punishment toward efforts to redress the consequences of illegal acts. It should be fairly evident that a society characterized by organic solidarity would have greater functional need for a restitutive system of social controls that would serve to maintain equilibrium between functionally disparate individuals and groups rather than simply mete out punishments that would, to be sure, affect the wrongdoer, but would contribute little to the task of maintaining equilibrium in a complex, functionally differentiated system.

In brief, Durkheim's argument is that the growth of the division of labor brings with it a new form of social solidarity to replace the older form, which disappears with the breakdown of the segmentary structure of society. In the more complex society, organic solidarity meets certain needs and fulfills certain functions that were previously met by the mechanical form. Change from simple to more complex forms of society brought with it many changes in the quality of social relationships, in the structure of personality, and in the nature of the relationship between the personality as a system and the social system.

A number of social theorists have suggested similar linear developments in a particular direction. They have further assumed that such developments represent general tendencies in societies. The next section examines these trends in detail.

LINEAR THEORIES OF CHANGE

Through comparative analysis of societies, customs, or institutions, proponents of linear theories of change tried to show both the nature of modern society and what they considered to be the universal trend of its development. The directionality of change was conceived of as stages that would lead to the final stage combining both higher levels of technology and social developments and the extension of rationality, liberty, and progress (Eisenstadt, 1985:10). Notions have persisted since the time of classical Greece and Rome that recognized the historical developments of civilization from precivilized beginnings and acknowledged the possibility of dividing this development into stages and periods for closer scrutiny. Directionality in the context of the stage concept reemerged during the enlightenment, as seen, for example, in the ideas of Giambattista Vico, who postulated that each nation evolves through three stages: the ages of the gods, heroes, and men—ages distinguished by the characteristic relationship between people and the supernatural (Harris, 1968:27).

For the nineteenth-century social theorists, it was also essential that they specify the direction for whatever entity development was claimed. "And it is in this specification that we are given the sequence of stages which for most of us today remains the single most distinctive aspect of the theory of social evolution" (Nisbet, 1969:168).

Morris Ginsberg (1961:200–210) notes that there have been several ways in which the notion of stages have been used to give linear direction to change. One involves the concept of "unilinear recurrence." Here, stages are used to depict regular sequences of some element or form of culture such as forms of the family or economic organization, which were assumed to recur in the same order among different peoples and to describe a sort of evolutionary tendency. Sequences such as "hunting, pastoral, agricultural" were often put forward by earlier theorists. Edward B. Tylor, for example, argued that there was a particular scheme of the forms of the family, and everywhere "The institutions of men . . . succeed each other in series substantially uniform over the globe, independent of what seem the comparatively superficial differences of race and language, but shaped by similar human nature acting through successively changed conditions in savage, barbaric, and civilized life" (Tylor, quoted by Harris, 1968:172).

Other stage theorists describe general trends of social development in the culture of humanity taken as a whole. Their goal is to formulate general trends in societal evolution. To this end, they establish interrelationships among the various elements of culture and related growth processes, and they suggest a theory of the causes underlying such processes. For Auguste Comte, as we have seen in Chapter 2, change progressed through three stages—theological metaphysical, and positive—instigated by intellectual development. Marx divided the evolution of society into a series of stages determined on the basis of different forms of property. The first stage was that of tribal property, found among small groups whose subsistence was based on hunting, fishing, herding, and, later, agriculture. This was followed, depending on locality, by either the Oriental form or the communal and state property of antiquity (the ancient form), and later the Germanic form. From the latter emerged feudalism, which was eventually replaced by capitalism. In the future, socialism, then communism, would overwhelm capitalism.

Sir Henry Maine, restricting himself to legal institutions, saw the direction of evolution progressing from status to contract. "The movement of the progressive societies," he said in his grand dictum, "has hitherto been a movement from Status to Contract" (Maine, 1870:170). Lewis H. Morgan set out a sequence of "ethical periods" and formulated criteria by which the provision of any observable society in the sequence could be recognized. Three periods, which were discussed in the preceding chapter, were designated as savagery, barbarism, and civilization with subdivisions of lower, middle, and upper status.

Another version of the second group of stage theories is the attempt by Lewis Mumford to interpret the history of technology and the development of social organization. The four stages are described as follows:

1. The *eotechnic* stage was based on the use of wind, water, and wood as power, with wood as the principal material for construction. It dominated Western Europe from the tenth to the eighteenth centuries.

2. The *paleotechnic* stage was based on the use of coal and iron, which became important in the eigthteenth century and dominant by the end of the nineteenth and is equivalent to the early industrial revolution. It is marked by key inventions such as the steam engine, railroad, steamship, various automatic devices, and spinning and weaving.

3. The *neotechnic* stage refers to the new economy, which began to emerge in the 1880s based on the use of electricity, the lighter metals like aluminum and copper, and certain rare metals such as tungsten and platinum. The key inventions include the electric motor, electric light, and communication by telephone, telegraph, and radio. This stage is now the dominant one.

4. The *biotechnic* stage "refers to an emergent economy already separating out more clearly from the neotechnic (purely mechanical) complex, and pointing to a civilization in which the biological sciences will be freely applied to technology, and in which technology itself will be oriented toward the culture of life. . . . In the biotechnic order the biological and social arts become dominant: agriculture, medicine, and education take precedence over engineering. Improvements, instead of depending solely upon mechanical manipulations of matter and energy, will rest upon a more organic utilization of the entire environment, in response to the needs of organisms and groups considered in their manifold relations: physical, social, esthetic, psychological" (Mumford 1938:495–96).

A more recent example of this type of stage theory is Walt W. Rostow's (1961) rather controversial sketch of the stages of economic growth, which is also illustrative of the duration of change (Chapter 7). His basic assumption is that the lengthy process of economic development can be depicted according to various stages and that uniformities tend to occur in the sequence of development. Rostow postulates that the overall process of economic growth proceeds through the following five stages:

ROSTOW'S STAGES OF ECONOMIC GROWTH

1. *The Traditional Society.* Agriculture is predominant, there is little capital accumulation, savings are practically nonexistent, and the traditional mentality and attitudes of people hamper development.

2. *The Preconditions for Takeoff.* They include a population increase, the existence of entrepreneurs, an increase in agricultural production, and "reactive nationalism." The idea spreads that economic progress is not only possible but necessary. Education is geared to substantiate the new economic outlook. Banks and other economic institutions are formed, and the state is becoming more centralized.

3. *The Takeoff.* Economic growth becomes the normal condition. The main features of the takeoff are: (a) an increase in the ratio of savings and investment to national income from perhaps 5 to 10 percent or more; (b) the development of one or more substantial manufacturing sectors with high rates of growth; and (c) the existence or quick emergence of a political, social, and institutional framework to exploit the impulses to expansion in the modern sector. The takeoff period began in Britain after 1783, in France and the United States around 1840, and in India around 1950.

4. *The Drive to Maturity.* The application of modern technology becomes evident in all sectors of the economy. From 10 to 20 percent of the national income is steadily reinvested, permitting output regularly to outstrip the increase in population. It takes about 60 years to reach this stage "in which an economy demonstrates the capacity to move beyond the original industries which powered its take-off and to absorb and to apply ef-

ficiently over a very wide range of its resources—if not the whole range—the most advanced fruits of (then) modern technology" (Rostow, 1961:10).

5. *The Age of High Mass Consumption.* The economy shifts toward the production of consumer goods and services. More and more funds are allocated to welfare in the society, and there is a striving for power in the international arena. Rostow thinks that the United States entered this stage of high mass consumption around 1920, followed by Western Europe and Japan in the 1950s.

Other stage theories are relatively recent in origin. They usually consist of attempts by contemporary anthropologists to indicate in more or less specific ways the direction or directional patterns that may be considered a "modern" approach to the classic evolutionary theory. In 1960, Marshall Sahlins distinguished between *specific* and *general* evolution. The evolution of culture is "general" evolution, a development of successive forms (hunting and gathering bands, agriculturists, Industrial Revolution, Atomic Age) through long periods of time. "Specific" evolution, by contrast, is a development of local cultures or groups of cultures through relatively short periods of time. The underlying feature of specific evolution is cultural diversity, induced by a variety of localized factors such as environment, diffusion, and invention. In the general evolutionary view, all the diversity becomes merged into larger patterns that unfold in a progressive fashion. The key feature of the general evolution is "progress," as measured in an objective, empirical fashion.

The same type of general-specific dichotomy can be used in the investigation of cultural subunits as well as cultures. For example, one could trace the *general* evolution of kinship structure or religion or concentrate on the *specific* diversity of kinship or religion as conditioned by a series of localized factors. Among contemporary anthropologists, Elman Service and Morton Fried have undertaken general evolutionary studies of social organization and political systems respectively.

In revitalizing the nineteenth-century stage notion, Fried describes a sequence of political forms from "Egalitarian Societies" through "Rank Societies" and "Stratified Societies" to "The State." In addition to technology, he uses a number of other variables in accounting for the transition from one stage to another, such as population pressure, changes in residence patterns after marriage, development of market economy, and the emergence of new managerial roles (Fried, 1967:196).

Elman Service traces social organization from the level of "Bands" through "Tribes" to "Chiefdoms." To supplement technological and environmental factors, he uses variables such as competition and social inventions to account for the transition process from one stage to another. In the change from the band stage to another, the impact of food production and population increase is crucial (Service, 1962:110). He argues that these two factors alone make possible, but do not cause, a new level of evolution, the tribe. The important causal factor is competition with other groups, and tribal organization is one effective way of organizing a mass of people into an efficiently competitive group. Thus, tribal organization arises in favorable production areas, from a need to compete effectively. In the transition from the tribal level to the next higher one, the chiefdom, increasing food productivity plays an important role. However, the crucial causal variable is specialization, either by locality (as where local groups each produce a different sort of goods, which are then redistributed within a region) or by individual specialization (for example, in the case of farmers, fishermen, etc., contributing their special products to society) (Service, 1962:145).

Julian H. Steward attempts to account for the directionality of change in the context of multilinear evolution, which is based on the assumption that "certain basic types of culture may develop in similar ways under similar conditions but that few concrete aspects of culture will appear among all groups of mankind in a regular sequence" (Steward, 1955:4). This is contrary to the notion of "unilinear evolution," which postulates that all societies pass through similar developmental stages. In the framework of multilinear evolution he describes the evolution of civilizations based on irrigation agriculture. Without explaining why village farming, the first stage in his sequence, might have developed, Steward describes what social organization was necessary to make the technological system work. Improvements in technology and increases in productivity led to larger populations and involved the development of irrigation works of increasing complexity and sophistication. During this continuous process of improvement and increase, there were corresponding changes in social organization, because the components of sociocultural systems are functionally interrelated. When the productive limits of the irrigation technology were reached, further expansion was possible only through warfare. Warfare had the effect of producing temporary expansion, then led to retrogression, with a declining population and lower productivity, aggravated by both the unmet demands of population pressure and the abuses of people by militaristic elites. The abuse of the people, however, was not a recurrent theme at each evolutionary level. In Steward's view of process, the independent variables were environment, technology, and population growth. The functional relationship between these three variables and the rest of the culture—basic religious, social, political, and scientific patterns—were clearly and plausibly elaborated (Steward, 1955:179–209).

The common element in the schemes described is the argument that technological productivity and population density must increase if successive stages of evolution are to emerge. The anthropologists mentioned were not particularly concerned with explanations for the increases themselves. In other words, in the discussion of the processes of evolution, certain crucial factors received analytical attention.' This has not changed since the nineteenth century. Contemporary explanations remain speculative because of the nature of the data that support them. Similarly, from the perspective of sociological analysis, the older evolutionary models broke down for several reasons. One was the assumption that the development of human societies is relatively cumulative and unilinear. It was assumed that the major stages of development were universal—even though there were numerous differences in detail and not all societies reached every stage of evolution.

There was also a failure to specify fully the systematic characteristics of evolving societies or institutions as well as the mechanisms and processes of change through which the transition from one stage to another was effected. The classical evolutionary theories of change tended to point out general causes of change—economic, technological, and so on—or some general trends, such as the trend to complexity, as inherent in the development of societies. They often confused such general tendencies with the causes of change or hypothesized that these general tendencies account for specific instances of change (Wolf, 1977:33–45). Early theorists also indulged in hypothetical reconstructions of the "first stages" of social institutions which provided the first step in their theory.

Finally, as Robert A. Nisbet (1969) asserts, evolutionary theory, as applied to sociocultural phenomena, is based essentially on a foundation of metaphor and analogy: the metaphor of growth and the analogy between the life cycle of organisms and the development of human societies and cultures. In his criticism of evolutionary theory, Nisbet also contends that change lacks directionality: ". . . philosophers of history and social evolutionists to the contrary, long-run directionality tends to be in the beholder's eye, not in the materials themselves" (1969:284). He considers social trends and patterns "inescapably subjective" and any direction assigned to them would be influenced by interests and values, thus making the direction void of objective validity. Gerhard Lenski (1976:554), while acknowledging that some changes are nondirectional and random, points to a variety of long-term historical trends with specific directionality (that is, growth of urban population, increased bureaucratization) in his rebuttal of Nisbet's criticisms.

S.N. Eisenstadt (1970:13–14) suggests that there are four crucial problems to be taken into consideration in an attempt to reappraise the evolutionary perspective. The first one is the extent to which change from one type of society to another is not accidental or random but indicates overall evolutionary trends. The second is the degree to which such changes are cumulative in a particular society. Next is the question of whether such changes really enhance a society's adaptation to its environment. And finally, to what extent is it feasible to talk about the evolution of human society or culture as a whole? Any serious attempt to use linear models to indicate the direction of change in society or of society should be carried out with attention to these problems.

CYCLICAL THEORIES OF CHANGE

Perhaps the oldest notion of social change is that which views society as following a cyclical course. This generalization, which "essentially argues that all human experience has happened before—a kind of sense of *déjà vu* on the grand scale, the disturbing sensation that we have been along this way before—does not deny change, but it does deny that it is leading anywhere over the long term" (Moore, 1974:44). Rhythmic regularity is the underlying factor in life. It is exhibited in human physiology as heartbeat, breathing, hunger, and satiation, and finally as a process of organic growth and decline. The life of every species is a closed cycle of birth and death, forever repeated until the extinction of the species. Among *Homo sapiens*, one of the most universal observations concerning history is that in many respects it often repeats itself. Speculations have ranged from depictions of history as exactly reproducing itself in time, through ideas of statistical, regular recurrences of phenomena, to notions of random recurrences.

The German historian Oswald Spengler (1880–1936) suggested that societies were like people, each with its childhood, youth, adulthood, and old age. They were born, grew up rapidly, reached full maturity—which he called the "golden age"—declined, and died. Spengler's (1932) suggestion that Western civilization was in the process of declining and that nothing could be done to halt the inevitable process is still being referred to in certain pessimistic circles as the inevitable fate of the decadent and hedonistic Western civilization.

Arnold Toynbee (1889–1975), the renowned British historian, saw the development of society as a cyclical process. He proposed that each cycle begins with some sort of "challenge"—initially to make a living from the land, later to make social adjustments. Each challenge is met by a "response": If the response is successful, the society survives and the process continues on to the next challenge; if the response is not successful, the society is destroyed by the unmet challenge. At a certain time and in a certain place a civilization emerges. Under particular conditions, the civilization grows. This growth ultimately brings with it a "breakdown," followed by a decline. Unlike Spengler, Toynbee does not use the rather poetic images of the four ages of humanity to depict the cycle (Toynbee, 1962).

The sociologist most widely associated with the cyclical view of social change is Pitirim A. Sorokin (1889–1968), although he has never explicitly referred to his complex theory as "cyclic." His theory is based on a classification of "sociocultural systems." His most provocative and most neglected book, *Social and Cultural Dynamics* (1937), is a detailed study of the Greek, Roman, and Western cultures from about 600 B.C. to A.D. 1920, with sporadic references to Egyptian, Hindu, and Chinese cultures. He describes three main types of sociocultural supersystems with distinct patterns, each capable of surviving for several centuries. These are the "ideational" system, the "sensate" system, and an intermediate or mixed system, referred to as "idealistic." The ideational system is characterized as one in which the elements are based on faith (sacred). The sensate system is composed of elements based on empirical science and rationality (secular). The idealistic system is a combining of these two forms and is characterized by more emphasis on the creative activity of the human mind, in art, literature, and thought.

Sorokin draws upon the fields of music, literature, painting, science, technology and invention, philosophy, and law, deriving from them a series of statistics that provided the basis for a number of graphs. Using these graphs, he demonstrates that cyclical fluctuations have occured in the creative achievements of Western people from the dawn of history. He then relates these cultural activities to the ideational, idealistic, and sensate systems and charts growth and decline. This leads him to the question: Does the total culture of a given area change altogether as one system or do its various elements change independently from one another?

He asserts that cycles of total culture and the various elements of culture are interrelated and directed by a sort of logical principle residing in the total culture. In his words: "From the moment of its emergence, any empirical, socio-cultural system is a self-changing and self-directing unit that bears in itself the reason for its change, the nature of its functions, the phase of its unfolding, and the essentials of its destiny. As such, it has always a margin of autonomy from all the force external to it" (Sorokin, 1937: vol. 4:73).

He considers the direction of these systems as "variable recurrence" (Sorokin, 1937: vol. 1:186). Cultural change may initially conform to a linear form and then, because of internal changes, alter its direction, and a new form appears. The new form may be again linear, cyclical, or perhaps oscillatory. In the process of several irregular fluctuations, culture may partially return to a condition approaching, but never identical with, a former state. Thus, the culture completes the nearest approximation to a cycle that is possible in the history of human society.

F. Stuart Chapin, in *Cultural Change* (1928:201–223), posits that cycles of national growth and decay may be established. The cycles belong in three orders: the order of material culture, the order of nonmaterial culture, and the order of larger cultural composites. Each cycle is to be understood as the product of a complex of forces, consisting of individual phases of culture, such as the economic, political, religious, and intellectual. These individual components of culture are themselves characterized by a cycle of growth and decline. When the cycles of several cultural forms are chronologically correlated, when they grow together and reach a high point of development at the same time, the result is an era of maturity of the nation or group.

From this, Chapin (1928:210–211) proposes the following hypotheses:

1. Every cultural form has its own law of change with the qualification that for certain groups of social phenomena there may be some basic and common law of change.
2. The law of each cultural form is more likely cyclical in nature and may be rhythmic.
3. It is possible to describe quantitatively the law of its life cycle or periodic function.
4. When the cycles or periods of a number of cultural forms of the first and second order are synchronous, there is an era of maturity of the nation or groups in which the culture traits are found.

In brief, his idea is that certain categories of cultural and social phenomena fluctuate together and that a cyclical form emerges.

The question of synchronous fluctuation has been also investigated by anthropologist A.L. Kroeber (1876–1960), who analyzed a number of cultural fields such as philosophy, science, sculpture, painting, drama, literature, and music (1944). He noted that those individuals who were evaluated by subsequent periods as being great tended to appear in clusters. He assumed that such clusters indicated periods of the greatest cultural creativity and quality. Using a panel of judges to identify the "great" names in the diverse cultural areas, Kroeber noted the periods when they appeared to cluster and then attempted to ascertain the importance of the cultural phenomena they expressed. His analysis covered a period ranging from the early Greek civilization to the 1940s and included all European nations and many Asiatic countries. He found that clusters of "great" individuals did indicate the flourishing of some culture patterns and that intervals without such individuals occur. He posited that these periods of culture defined certain directions of cultural activity or "opportunity."

In opposition to the views of Spengler and Toynbee, Kroeber argues that the same culture may flourish many times. He finds no strict correlation between the growth of different aspects of a culture, although he concedes that periods of a high level of cultural creativity may be established in which several cultural strains show mature development at the same time. Furthermore, he argues that the determination of cultural growth or decline cannot be attributed to any specific single factor or set of factors except perhaps to the general tendency of movements to exhaust themselves.

At first impression, cyclical theories of social change may seem attractive because they deal with observable historical facts: the rise and fall of civilizations. But the models are simplistic, for they assume that history repeats itself. Changes in human societies are not necessarily cyclical, nor are they subject to inexorable laws. Cyclical theorists cannot attribute the same degree of significance to the emergence of modern societies as the evolutionary theorists (Etzioni-Halevy, 1981:18–19). Although there seems to be an element of truth in their contentions, few cyclical models have been developed over the last few decades. In their place, alternative models have been increasingly substituted.

MODELS OF SOCIAL CHANGE

The discussion thus far has concentrated on linear and cyclical theories of social change. The former sees a linear progression from one type of society or characteristic of social life to another. Most of these theories representing this perspective have been evolutionary in that they suggest that "higher" social forms (such as civilization) evolved from "lower" ones (such as barbarism). The latter point of view suggests that social change occurs in cycles or repetitive patterns, rather than proceeding in a linear direction.

It is now recognized that social change does not occur in a smooth unfolding of ultimate forms. As Wilbert E. Moore (1974:34) succinctly states, "If we accept the position that the question, 'What is changing?' is antecedent to all others in making verifiable propositions about social change, the search for a single course or direction of change becomes as dubious an enterprise as the quest for a unique 'prime mover.' The course of change may be gradual or rapid, peaceful or violent, continuous or spasmodic, orderly or erratic."

In spite of the number of possible directions change may take, certain generalizations have been established. "These are worthy of attention . . . as having some validity if their pretentions to unique generality are suitably downgraded" (Moore, 1974:35). A most comprehensive analysis of the directions of change is presented by Moore (1974:34–46), who diagramed various models (abstractions of reality that are used for analytical purposes) of change, as shown in Figure 3.1. We shall examine each one briefly.

Model 1 is the representation of the simplest model of growth—a straight line moving upward over time. It has been widely and naively used to depict a kind of gradual and continuous growth of human civilization. In reality, however, very few processes conform to this pattern without fluctuating. It is seldom accurate as a representation of observed changes that take place over several intervals of time. It can, nevertheless, provide a rough approximation of the direction of change for certain types of phenomena over shorter periods. It could be used as a crude indication, for example, of the average increase of productivity for an entire economy.

Model 2 is evolution by stages. This is a rather traditional way of

MOORE'S
MODELS

FIG 3.1   Directions of Social Change.
(*Source:* Redrawn from Wilbert E. Moore, *Social Change*, 2nd ed. Englewood Cliffs, N.J.: Prentice-Hall, 1974, p. 36.)

viewing history based on the recognition that progress is not continuous; rather, a "breakthrough" occurs at times, bringing about changes followed by extended periods of stability. As we have seen in a preceding section, such stage theories were popular with a number of early theorists. They described the progress of humanity as being divided into a distinctive series of epochs, each markedly more advanced than the previous one in a kind of stairstep fashion. Even now, civilizations are often classified in terms of the quality of tools used, such as "Old Stone Age," "New Stone Age," "Bronze Age," and "Iron Age." Another way of referring to this stairstep stage is in terms of prevailing economic production. A current illustration of this approach is the stages of economic growth suggested by Walt Rostow (1961), which was discussed earlier.

Model 3 represents evolution at unequal rates. It differs from earlier models by recognizing that changes are not necessarily as abrupt as the stairsteps of Model 2. For example, the history of the Western world is marked by irregular and gradual developments and not by sharply differentiated stages. The first peak in Model 3 might represent the Greco-Roman civilization, the second, the Renaissance, and the third, the industrial revolution. It can also be applied to briefer developmental processes to depict the sequence of innovation and accommodation. The growth of an industry, for example, over several decades, may look like Model 3. When a new product is introduced, growth may become quite rapid, but then it levels off after adjustments have been made to this innovation.

Model 4 depicts evolution by cycles and short-term reversals. This model considers the possibility that trends that are generally progressive may be interrupted by temporary retrogressions. For example, business cycles are often described in this fashion, with alternating periods of prosperity and depression. Also, "One may derive a faint bit of wry amusement by applying the same theory of change to the Marxist theory of history. As this is a 'dialectic' theory of change arising from conflict between classes as representatives of inconsistent interests, the top of any cycle might represent the 'thesis,' and the bottom the 'antithesis,' and the transitory periods when the society is on the intermediate trend line the 'synthesis' " (Moore, 1974:39).

Model 5 attempts to bring together unity and diversity within a single notion of "branching evolution." The previous models presented have been deceptively simple. There is always the possibility that one will become committed to one or another of these and assume that all societies inevitably follow that pattern in their evolution. Obviously, this is an erroneous assumption. Some civilizations regress or even die out, others remain stable for long periods, and still others make astonishingly rapid advances. Model 5 combines these different trends in which the branching lines represent the diverse evolutionary courses of various distinct societies. Certain lines extend upward over time, representing progress, whereas others flatten out, turn downward, or even break off. Such lines represent stability, decline, or extinction, as the case may be. It is more a question of detail rather than incompatibility that distinguishes Model 5 from the previous ones in describing the general evolution of humankind.

Model 6 represents trendless cycles. As discussed in the section on cyclical theories, theorists such as Spengler and Sorokin have depicted human civilizations as going through high and low periods in a regular, trendless cycle, not making any progress in the long run, but simply repeating previous periods. It should be observed that, in this model, the peaks and valleys do not show any general upward trend, as in Models 3 and 4. It should be noted also that for a number of social phenomena, changes may be basically cyclical if only rates but not absolute numbers are indicated and used on a graph. For instance, short-term marriage and birthrates in modern societies fluctuate without an obvious trend. A trend could be established in this case by indicating the number of married persons or the size of the population.

Model 7, the logistic curve of growth, was first applied to social phenomena in the context of population growth. Moore (1974:39) cites Raymond Perl, who suggested that human populations grow according to this pattern when they are initially sparse, and then enter a hospitable but limited environment. The model presumes that there are no abrupt changes in the population's control over the environment. Cells grown in a laboratory dish multiply in the same way. At first they increase very fast, but growth levels off as the population approaches the maximum that can be supported by the environment. Hornell Hart (1959:217) raised the possibility that human culture develops through a series of growth surges and that such surges are often inaugurated, disrupted, or terminated by crises such as basic inventions (for example, steamship, atomic bomb), discoveries (the Western Hemisphere), wars, and major economic depressions. He also suggested that obsolete culture complexes such as sailing ships, horsedrawn vehicles, farm machines, and lynching often decline along logistic trends.

Model 8 represents a reverse logistic curve. Once in a while progress is represented by a downward, rather than an upward slope—as, for example, in the decline in mortality rates prompted by improvements in food supply and medical technology. At first mortality declines rapidly. If it continued to drop fast, most members of the society would soon become immortal. However, when mortality declines below a certain minimum, further decline cannot be expected, as shown in this model.

Model 9 is the exponential rate of growth. Occasionally a social phenomenon accelerates in the same way that compound interest increases the balance in one's savings account. This model has been used in connection with innovations or technological changes based on the assumption that the more things that are available to be combined, the greater the number of possible combinations. But it can have broader implications. For example, unrestricted population growth can be depicted by this model.

Model 10 is referred to as *primitivism*. Thus far, all of the models have delineated at least some degree of progress. On the other hand, not everyone is so optimistic about the fate of humankind. Some people consider our epoch as a kind of retrogression from some past golden age. Many see our time as "decadent" and as a first step toward deterioration. This model shows a decline of civilization.

Obviously, these models are not exhaustive of the directions of social change. One may also look at the course of social change as being both cumulative and directional. This is an approach used in the study of industrialization and economic modernization. It is something akin to "once-to-a-system transformation," and Neil J Smelser's observations are illustrative of this process:

> For purposes of analyzing the relationships between economic growth and the social structure, it is possible to isolate the effects of several interrelated technical, economic, and ecological processes that frequently accompany development. These may be listed as follows:
>
> 1. In the realm of technology, the change *from* simple and traditionalized techniques *toward* the application of scientific knowledge.
> 2. In agriculture, the evolution *from* subsistence farming *toward* commercial production of agricultural goods. This means specialization in cash crops, purchase of non-agricultural products in the market, and often agricultural wage-labor.
> 3. In industry, the transition *from* the use of human and animal power *toward* industrialization proper. . . .
> 4. In ecological arrangements, the movement *from* the farm and village *toward* urban centers. These several processes often, but not necessarily, occur simultaneously. (Smelser, 1968:126)

A somewhat similar "once-to-a-system" transformation for the United States is advanced by John Naisbitt (1982) in his highly acclaimed and controversial book, *Megatrends*. He discusses several trends that he claims indicate the direction the country is moving in. They include a shift from a predominantly industrial society to an information society; a trend toward deinstitutionalization; growing decentralization and increased emphasis on self-help; and an increase in the number of options for Americans in many areas of life.

We have seen a number of different theories of the direction of change. They should be considered not as competing generalizations but as suitable to the study of the different aspects of social systems. At a later date, perhaps more complex models will be developed by social scientists. "For the moment, partial theories appear to be the best that can be expected, whether in terms of the sources of changes or the directions of their course through time" (Moore, 1974:46).

CENTER-PERIPHERY
AND PROLIFERATION-OF-CENTERS MODELS

A different approach to directionality of change is taken in the diffusion of ideas, discoveries, and inventions. The concept of *diffusion* is used to describe the spread of cultural elements from one society to another or from one group to another within society. Diffusion may be brought about by many factors, such as travel, migration, trade, or conquest. Much of the content of every culture has been acquired from other societies, and diffusion is a major source of social change. The various processes and components of diffusion will be discussed in greater detail in Chapter 5. The concern here is to show how some aspects of directionality may be incorporated in the spread of discoveries and inventions.

In a well-received book, *Beyond the Stable State*, Donald A Schon (1971) describes two models of diffusion of innovation. The first he calls the "center-periphery" model, which is characterized by one source of innovation and multiple receivers of that innovation. The second is referred to as the "proliferation-of-centers" model, which describes the situation in which the receivers of innovations become innovators in their own right. These two models can be used also to indicate the direction of diffusion and the subsequent change produced by the acceptance of certain innovations. In other words, social change occurs as inventions come into use and disseminate in society. This is a more pragmatic view of change advocated primarily by policymakers and others involved in planned social change (Bennis, Benne, & Chin, 1985). Schon contends that the various systems of diffusion evolve simultaneously with the technological infrastructure in society.

The *center-periphery model*, as Schon (1971:81) points out, rests on three basic elements:

1. The innovation to be diffused exists, fully realized in its essentials, prior to its diffusion.
2. Diffusion is the movement of an innovation from a center out to its ultimate users.
3. Directed diffusion is a centrally managed process of dissemination, training, and provision of resources and incentives.

Proponents of the center-periphery model view diffusion as a form of interaction where one person transmits a new idea to another person. At the most fundamental level of conceptualization, "the diffusion process consists of 1) a new idea, 2) individual 'A' who knows about the innovation, and 3) individual 'B' who does not yet know about the innovation" (Rogers, 1962:12–13). Examples of "diffusers" would be agricultural extension agents (see below), those who introduce new pharmaceuticals to physicians, doctors and nurses, and college professors. Studies on diffusion deal with the spread of, for example, public health practices, drugs, and insecticides.

Schon argues that "The effectiveness of a center-periphery system depends first upon the level of resources and energy at the center, then upon the number of points at the periphery, the length of the radii or spokes through which diffusion takes place, and the energy required to gain a new adoption" (1971:82). He uses as an illustration the diffusion capability of an agricultural extension agent, which depends upon the agent's own energies, the number of location of farmers served, and the time and effort devoted to each farmer.

The scope of the model "varies directly with the level of technology governing the flows of men, materials, money and information" (Schon, 1971:82). The scope of the model also depends on its capacity for generating and managing feedback. He suggests that there are two important variants to this model. The first he calls "Johnny Appleseed":

> Here the primary center is a kind of bard who roams his territory spreading a new message. Into this category fall the traveling scholars, saints and artisans of the Middle Ages; Voltaire and Thomas Paine; and contemporary bards of radical activism like Saul Alinsky. (Schon, 1971:83)

The second variant he calls "the magnet model." For this he gives the illustration of nineteenth-century universities in Germany where students came from all parts of the world and returned to their own country to teach and practice what they had learned. In technology and economics, the United States and Great Britain play magnet, especially to developing nations.

The Johnny Appleseed model allows the innovation to be adapted to the special conditions of the recipient's locality. The magnet model may establish new centers.

Schon warns us, however, that "When the center-periphery system exceeds the resources or the energy at the center, overloads the capacity of the radii, or mishandles feedback from the periphery, it fails. Failure takes the form of simple ineffectiveness in diffusion, distortion of the message, or disintegration of the system as a whole" (Schon, 1971:84).

An elaboration of the center-periphery model is the *proliferation-of-centers approach*. Although it retains the basic center-periphery structure, it tends to differentiate the primary from the secondary centers. The primary centers manage and support the secondary centers, which in turn engage in the diffusion of innovations. Schon uses the illustration of the activities of the Roman army for this model. Regiments of the Roman army moved out from Rome to occupy new territories, subjugated their occupants, and established colonies. The task of these advanced guards was war and government. Once an area was occupied, the military established an approximation to the Roman way of life. "There was a centrally established doctrine and a centrally established method for diffusing it" (Schon, 1971:85). Similarly, missionaries followed the proliferation-of-centers model in disseminating their message.

Schon argues that industrial expansion came about on a worldwide scale through a form of specialization resembling that of the Roman army. "The central message now took the form of technology both for production and for the management of the business firm. These spread throughout the world as industrial centers established decentralized networks of distribution, marketing, production, manpower and financial control" (Schon, 1971:86–87).

Even though there are many variants of this model, "there is a dominant pattern in the primary center's relationship to secondary centers" (Schon, 1971:87). The primary center oversees policies and methodology. It selects territories for expansion, develops methodologies for diffusion, trains new agents for diffusion, sustains decentralized outposts through finances, information, and know-how, monitors decentralized operations, and maintains information throughout the network of outposts.

In varying degrees the spread of colonialism, Christianity, Coca-Cola, and communism all followed this model. It is currently used as a technique of business expansion, and the unfolding of the various multinational corporations (large corporations that operate in many nations) would be a good illustration (Barnet & Muller, 1974; Madsen, 1980).

In collaboration with other information, these two models of diffusion are useful in plotting the direction of a variety of change phenomena. For example, they have been used in agricultural development programs in Africa and Latin America, in the field of medicine and health care, and in a cluster of interrelated movements for civil rights, peace, disarmament, and student revolt.

SUMMARY

This chapter has considered the principal modes of thought on the directionality of social change. The aim of early evolutionary studies was a reconstruction of the patterns of past societal developments. Some theorists posited that the mechanisms of social evolution are the same as biological evolution and, just like biological organisms, societies progress from simple to more complex states.

Such a progression may follow a linear pattern or may go through a series of steps or stages as a result of increased division of labor, societal complexity, and differentiation. Other theorists suggested that society follows a cyclical course of change, in many cases leading to eventual decay and decline. It is now recognized that societies do not develop in a single linear pattern, nor do they follow a cyclical course. Social change is the result of a multitude of causes and can proceed in a given society in several directions and can take on several forms.

Efforts to seek out uniformities and continuities to describe the directionality of change are shifting from entire societies and cultures to specific processes and properties within a society or among societies. Models of diffusion of innovation are illustrative of this trend. Directionality of change is seen also as an outcome of a particular change effort and therefore is an important aspect of planned social change where the objects of change are clearly delineated.

SUGGESTED FURTHER READINGS

ETZIONI, AMITAI. "The American Way of Economic Development." In Orlando Fals Borda (ed.), *The Challenge of Social Change*. London: Sage Publications Ltd., 1985, pp. 57–74. A thought-provoking model for the direction of economic development in America.

MEADOWS, PAUL. *The Many Faces of Change: Explorations in the Theory of Social Change*. Cambridge, Mass.: Schenkman, 1971. An eminently well-written analysis of the principal themes, rhetorics, and situations of change.

NAISBITT, JOHN. *Megatrends: Ten New Directions Transforming Our Lives*. New York: Warner Books, 1982. A popular and controversial book on the trends that indicate the direction the United States is moving in.

ROSTOW, WALT W. *The Stages of Economic Growth, A Non-Communist Manifesto*. New York: Cambridge, 1961. A controversial but good illustration of the use of stages for economic development.

SMELSER, NEIL. *Essays in Sociological Explanation*. Englewood Cliffs, N.J.: Prentice-Hall, 1968. Chapter 8, "Toward a General Theory of Social Change" (pp. 192–280), deals with direction of social adjustment and change in an advanced and comprehensive fashion.

SOROKIN, PITIRIM A. *Social and Cultural Dynamics*, one-volume ed. Boston: Porter Sargent, 1957. An abridgement of his famous four-volume work dealing with temporal "fluctuations" among three predominant cultural systems.

REFERENCES

BARNET, RICHARD J., and RONALD E. MULLER. *Global Reach—The Power of Multinational Corporations*. New York: Simon & Schuster, 1974.

BENNIS, WARREN G., KENNETH D. BENNE, and ROBERT CHIN, eds. *The Planning of Change*, 4th ed., New York: Holt, Rinehart & Winston, 1985.

CHAPIN, F. STUART. *Cultural Change*. New York: Century, 1928.

CHIROT, DANIEL. *Social Change in the Modern Era*. San Diego: Harcourt Brace Jovanovich, 1986.

COHEN, PERCY S. *Modern Social Theory*. New York: Basic Books, 1968.

DURKHEIM, EMILE. *The Division of Labor in Society*, George Simpson, trans. New York: Free Press, 1947.

EISENSTADT, S. N., ed.   *Readings in Social Evolution and Development.* New York: Pergamon, 1970.

EISENSTADT, S. N.   "Cultural Traditions, Power Relations and Modes of Change." In Orlando Fals Borda (ed.),   *The Challenge of Social Change.* London: Sage Publications Ltd., 1985, pp. 9–37.

ETZIONI-HALEVY, EVA.   *Social Change: The Advent and Maturation of Modern Society.* London: Routledge & Kegan Paul, 1981.

FRIED, MORTON.   *The Evolution of Political Society.* New York: Random House, 1967.

GINSBERG, MORRIS.   *Essays in Sociology and Social Philosophy, Vol. 1: On the Diversity of Morals.* London: Heinemann, 1961.

HARRIS, MARVIN.   *The Rise of Anthropological Theory—A History of Theories of Culture.* New York: Crowell, 1968.

HART, HORNELL,   "Social Theory and Social Change." In Llewllyn Gross (ed.), *Symposium of Sociological Theory.* New York: Harper & Row, 1959, pp. 196–238.

KETTNER, PETER, JOHN M. DALEY, and ANN WEAVER NICHOLS.   *Initiating Change in Organizations and Communities.* Monterey, Calif.: Brooks/Cole, 1985.

KROEBER, A. L.   *Configurations of Cultural Growth.* Berkeley: University of California Press, 1944.

LENSKI, GERHARD.   "History and Social Change." *American Journal of Sociology,* 82, November 1976, pp. 548–564.

LENSKI, GERHARD, and JEAN LENSKI.   *Human Societies: An Introduction to Macrosociology,* 5th ed. McGraw-Hill Book Company, 1987.

MADSEN, AXEL.   *Private Power: Multinational Corporations for the Survival of Our Planet.* New York: William Morrow, 1980.

MAINE, SIR HENRY.   *Ancient Society.* London: John Murray, 1870.

MOORE, WILBERT E.   *Social Change,* 2nd ed. Englewood Cliffs, N.J.: Prentice-Hall, 1974.

MUMFORD, LEWIS.   *The Culture of Cities.* New York: Harcourt, 1938.

NAISBITT, JOHN.   *Megatrends: Ten New Directions Transforming Our Lives.* New York: Warner Books, 1982.

NISBET, ROBERT A.   *Social Change and History.* New York: Oxford, 1969.

PARSONS, TALCOTT.   *The Evolution of Societies.* (Jackson Toby, ed.) Englewood Cliffs, N.J.: Prentice-Hall, 1977.

ROGERS, EVERETT M.   *Diffusion of Innovations.* New York: Free Press, 1962.

ROSTOW, WALT W.   *The Stages of Economic Growth: A Non-Communist Manifesto.* New York: Cambridge, 1961.

SAHLINS, MARSHALL D.   "Evolution: Specific and General." In M.D. Sahlins and E. R. Service (eds.), *Evolution and Culture.* Ann Arbor: University of Michigan Press, 1960, pp. 12–44.

SCHON, DONALD A.   *Beyond the Stable State.* New York: W.W. Norton & Co., Inc., 1971.

SERVICE, ELMAN R.   *Primitive Social Organization.* New York: Random House, 1962.

SMELSER, NEIL J.   *Essays in Sociological Explanation.* Englewood Cliffs, N.J.: Prentice-Hall, 1968.

SOROKIN, PITIRIM A.   *Social and Cultural Dynamics,* 4 vols. New York: American Book, 1937.

SPENGLER, OSWALD.   *The Decline of the West.* New York: Knopf, 1932.

STEWARD, JULIAN H.   *Theory of Culture Change: The Methodology of Multilinear Evolution.* Urbana: University of Illinois Press, 1955.

TOYNBEE, ARNOLD.   *A Study of History.* New York: Oxford, 1962.

WALLERSTEIN, IMMANUEL.   *The Modern World-System: Capitalist Agriculture and the Origins of the European World-Economy in the Sixteenth Century.* New York: Academic Press, 1974.

WOLF, ERIC R.   "The Study of Evolution." In Sol Tax and Leslie G. Freeman (eds.), *Horizons of Anthropology,* 2nd ed. Chicago: Aldine Publishing Co., 1977, pp. 33–45.

4 Sources of Change

The goal of this chapter is to analyze several specific factors that generate changes in society. These factors, considered important in the sociological literature, include technology, ideology, competition, conflict, political and economic factors, and structural strains. All these sources of change are in many ways interrelated. Economic, political, and technological factors go hand in hand with ideology, competition, conflict, and structural strains. Consequently, one should be careful *not* to assign undue weight to any particular one of these causes of change. Admittedly, it is often tempting and convenient to single out one "prime mover," one factor, one cause, one explanation, and use it indiscriminately in a number of situations. But this can result in an incomplete and possibly erroneous explanation of the phenomenon under consideration. With this in mind, let us turn to the examination of the sources of change.

TECHNOLOGY

David M. Freeman (1974:12) describes the impact of technology (systematic knowledge, tools, and machines involved in the production of goods and services) by compressing it into a time frame. If we consider the approximately 5-billion-year lifetime of the earth scaled down to the past 80 days, then:

1. Life appeared 60 days ago.
2. Humans in their earliest forms appeared one hour ago.
3. The Stone Age started six minutes ago.
4. Modern humans appeared less than a minute ago.
5. The agricultural revolution occurred 15 seconds ago.
6. Metals were utilized ten seconds ago.
7. The industrial revolution began three-tenths of one second ago.

Technology's capacity to change both the circumstances of human life and the character of social institutions is quite recent and, as the time frame indicates, occurring at an increasingly rapid rate worldwide.

A noted characteristic of technology is exponential growth, as illustrated by the curve in Figure 4.1. It can be applied to such diverse phenomena as the number of books written, energy consumption, and population growth. Exponential growth is growth that doubles within equal periods of time. Many aspects of modern development exceed this minimum requirement and are doubling in decreasing intervals of time, such as the consumption of energy or the depletion of certain natural resources, such as fossil fuels.

Positive and Negative Aspects of Technology

It is easy to demonstrate that throughout history technological innovations have often been a moving force in social change. For example, changes in agricultural technology resulted in food surpluses necessary for

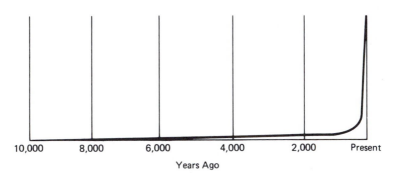

10,000   8,000   6,000   4,000   2,000   Present

Years Ago

FIG 4.1 An exponential growth curve. This curve can be roughly applied to growth in several areas—for example, inventions, energy consumption, or population. For instance, world population growth clearly exhibits exponentiality. At the beginning of the Christian era, there were only 200 to 300 million persons on earth. By 1650 humankind totaled about 500 million. Three hundred years later, in 1950, the figure was more than 2,500 million, and in 1970 it was over 3,600 million. In the year 2000, the world population is expected to be close to 6,000 million.

the growth of cities. The introduction of steam power pushed the world into the Industrial Revolution, changes in weapon technology often upset empires and nations (the long bow in Europe and the atomic bomb in Japan), and the discovery of the cotton gin revitalized a dying slave trade and helped to plant the seeds for the American Civil War.

The influence of technology reverberates on the lives of individuals in society, on social values, on the structure and functions of social institutions, and on the political organizations of society. Technology creates not only new alternatives and opportunities but also new problems for humans (Mesthene, 1986). It has both positive and negative effects that often occur at the same time. These ramifications can be seen even as a result of minor technological innovations such as the introduction of the snowmobile into northern areas such as Alaska and Lapland. The snowmobile drastically changed patterns of reindeer herding and hunting. It shortened the workweek of the hunters and trappers dramatically, increased their leisure time, increased their earnings, established a new basis for stratification in the community (who owns and who does not own a snowmobile), and it generated a serious ecological imbalance as populations of snowbound game animals were wiped out (Pelto & Muller-Willie, 1987).

The Steel Ax Among the Yir Yoront

Even the introduction of less sophisticated technology—such as, for example, the steel ax—can create far-reaching and unforeseen effects in other aspects of the social system. Consider the example of the Yir Yoront tribe of southeastern Australia, who depended on the stone ax as their most basic and essential tool for many centuries (Sharp, 1952). For them the stone ax was more than a tool; it was a symbol of status, of male dominance, and of basic rights of ownership. It played a role in religious ceremonies and was considered as one of the tribe's most valued objects. When a person needed an ax, he would approach one of the leaders to ask permission to use it. Only if the leader considered him worthy would permission be granted. The very scarcity of this valuable tool made access to it a considerable privilege; thus, it served as a means of social control.

Then came the Caucasians, bringing modern technology in the form of steel axes. But instead of progress, the introduction of the steel ax resulted in a drastic upheaval of the social structure of the tribe. It had the following effects:

1. In order to get a steel ax, it was necessary to go to the mission or to a trader and act "deserving, industrious, and dependent." That resulted in a decrease in self-reliance.
2. Possession of the ax had been considered a status symbol and a sign of manhood, but the Caucasians at times gave them directly to young men and children, resulting in the upset of status relations between the young and the old.

3. Similarly, in the past no woman could own an ax. Europeans often gave axes to women to use as their own, thereby upsetting the status relations between males and females.

4. Prior to the introduction of the ax, there was no overall leader or chief of the tribe. However, when dealing with the whites, it was necessary to appoint one or two spokesmen, who gradually acquired more power than they were entitled to traditionally, creating a leader group form of organization in the tribe.

5. Easy access to axes diluted the entire notion of ownership and upset the norms of ownership, thus resulting in an increase in the incidence of stealing and trespassing.

6. Members of the tribe had explained the origins of every major artifact they possessed with some myth showing how the article was given to them by a distant mythical ancestor. Because they had very few artifacts and their technology was virtually stagnant, it was quite easy for them to believe in these stories. However, there was no mythical explanation for the origins of steel axes; the source was obvious. The result was to cast suspicion on the other myths and on the very structure of their religion.

In contemporary society, it is hard to find such dramatic changes in the social systems produced by one single piece of technology such as the steel ax among the Yir Yoront tribe. The closest we could come would be the number of changes followed by the series of technological innovations known as the industrial revolution. The basis of one's livelihood moved from the farm to the factory and from the country to the city. The size of individual enterprise changed as new methods of operation and financing became necessary to exploit technological innovation, resulting in the establishment of entirely new industries. The twentieth century has seen the rise of such mass complexes as the automobile, steel, rubber, glass, petroleum, and textile industries and, more recently, the chemical, aviation, and electronics industries. In a society increasingly dominated by mass industries, new social classes reflect the different productive functions. The big industrial unions are playing an important role in bringing about new power relations between labor and management.

Technology and Work

The spread of technological and scientific developments in the workplace has been accompanied by a variety of changes. In analyzing how technological forces ramify human activities, Neil J. Smelser (1976:96) suggests the following:

1. The technical arrangements of work determine in large part the amount of physical exertion required from the human organism.

2. The technical features of the job influence the degree to which work is paced and human activities are structured.

3. The technical arrangements of production influence the level of skills required of workers.

4. Technical aspects determine in part the degree of specialization of the division of labor and the structuring of authority.

5. Technological features of work influence the character of social interaction. . . . This influence often extends to off-the-job interaction as well.

The change from human to machine technology has transformed work in the industrial era. It resulted in the imposition of a steady pace or rhythm for work, bringing with it an increase in the discipline imposed on workers. This was the result of the need for the uninterrupted flow of material and the fact that workers must be organized around the machines' schedule. Because of the imposition of a steady pace and discipline, workers and work became increasingly time-oriented, which in turn affected other aspects of nonwork time (Linder, 1970).

When the technical aspects of work are highly routinized, monotonous, and devoid of much personal interaction, such as on the assembly lines in an automobile factory, Robert Blauner (1964:15–34) notes that workers become *alienated* to the extent that they are *powerless* at carrying out their work (that is, they have no control over quantity, quality, direction, and pace of work) or to the extent that their work is *meaningless* (that is, it has no clear relation to a broader life program or production program) or to the extent that they are *self-estranged* (they do not identify with their work or enjoy it or find it challenging) or to the extent that they are socially isolated from their supervisors and co-workers.

Technological developments can also bring about alterations in the composition of the work force. Of the 19 million new jobs created in the United States during the 1970s, only a small percentage was in the manufacturing sector. Almost 90 percent of the jobs—some 17 million new openings—were in the service and information sectors (Naisbitt, 1982:17). Many of the new jobs that were created in the nonmanufacturing sector are attributable to the significant advances made in computer technology in recent years. An example of this is the increased utilization of microcomputers in the work force, which requires specially trained workers (Evans & Bernard, 1987).

In addition to changes in the labor force, countless social effects can be attributed directly or indirectly to innovations in technology, many of which will be discussed in detail in Chapter 10. Technology's capacity to contribute to social change is increasing worldwide, with a much more rapid rate of growth in developing countries (Bernard & Pelto, 1987). In the following section, another important source of change, ideology, will be examined.

IDEOLOGY

An *ideology* is a complex belief system that explains social arrangements and relationships (Feuer, 1975; Gouldner, 1976). The functions of ideology are the legitimization and rationalization of behavior and social relationships; the provision of a basis for solidarity in a group or society; and the motivation of individuals for certain types of action. In social change the role of ideology can be analyzed different ways. It can promote stability and support the status quo, or it can contribute to change. It may be either a dependent or independent variable in accounting for any process of stability or change. In this section, ideology will be examined only as a source of change.

Ideology and Change

Max Weber's study of the development of capitalism represents one of the most thorough efforts yet made to establish a relationship between ideology and social change. As discussed in the section on social-psychological theories of change, Weber wanted to establish the principle that ideas as well as technological developments and economic structures could be determining factors in bringing about change. To do this, in the *Protestant Ethic and the Spirit of Capitalism,* he set out to identify the major factors responsible for the rise of capitalism as it had developed in Western societies—the type of capitalism characterized by double-entry bookkeeping, uniform pricing, systematic planning, and bureaucratic social organization.

Weber acknowledged that the development of industrial technology increased agricultural productivity, and improvements in sanitation, preventive medicine, and better methods of transportation had all been necessary to the development of capitalism, but he found the determining factor not in science or technology but in what he called "the Protestant ethic." Calvinism, Weber maintained, made possible the emergence of capitalism by providing people in Western societies with a new "this-wordly" orientation. In focusing their attention on such values as individualism, hard work, and frugality, it paved the way for a major restructuring of economic life.

More than a century ago Karl Marx argued that the ruling ideas of any society are the ideas of its ruling classes. His point was that ideologies do not fall from the sky, nor are they "things" that have a life of their own. Ideologies must be developed and maintained; an ideology must be transmitted to new generations or it will soon perish; and the implications of an ideology for specific issues and events must be determined and communicated because powerful groups and institutions are better able to succeed in this process than are less powerful groups. It is often their ideologies that are propagated.

Perhaps the best case for demonstrating the independent role of ideologies in social change at the macrolevel is Marxism.

> As an ideology, as an active critic of established "capitalist" values and norms, and as the active propagator of "socialist" values and norms, Marxism may have caused more social change than any other force in the modern world. In both industrial and would-be industrial societies, its consequences have been very great. Only nationalist ideology, which is also a powerful and independent type of ideological system in the modern world and which the universalist values expressed in Marxism have consistently neglected or underrated, might be said to have had an influence on modern social change of the same magnitude as Marxism. It can be argued that Marxist and nationalist ideologies together have caused as much social change as changes arising in the economy or polity. (Barber, 1971:260)

The Ideology of the Conjugal Family

At a somewhat lesser degree of comprehensiveness in social systems, in the structure of family systems "we can again see the independent influence of ideology on social change, in the case of the worldwide change toward prevalence of the conjugal family" (Barber, 1971:260). William J. Goode (1963:19) provides a great deal of evidence both for the change and for the influence of ideology.

> One important source of change is the *ideology* of "economic progress" and technological development, as well as the ideology of the conjugal family, and spokesmen for both appear in non-Western countries before any great changes are observable either in industrial or family areas of life.
>
> Elders may deplore both ideologies, but both appeal to the intellectuals, often trained in Western schools, and to the young, to women, and generally, to the disadvantaged. The ideology of the conjugal family is a radical one, destructive of the older traditions in almost every society. It grows from a set of more general radical principles which also arouse these groups *politically* in perhaps every underdeveloped country. Its appeal is almost as universal as that of "redistribution of the land." It asserts the equality of individuals as against class, caste, or sex barriers.
>
> The ideology of the conjugal family proclaims the right of the individual to choose his or her own spouse, place to live, and even which kin obligations to accept, as against the acceptance of others' decisions. It asserts the worth of the *individual* as against the inherited elements of wealth or ethnic group. The *individual* is to be evaluated, not his lineage. A strong theme of "democracy" runs through this ideology. It encourages love, which in every major civilization has been given a prominent place in fantasy, poetry, art, and legend, as a wonderful, perhaps even exalted, experience, even when its reality was guarded against. Finally, it asserts that if one's family life is unpleasant, one has the right to change it.

Utopian Ideologies

Sir Thomas More's famous book *Utopia* was published in 1516. It described an ideal society. Since that time, thousands of utopian schemes have been proposed on the basis of ideologies that "justify or criticize an imagined social system in which new values and norms prevail in a way that *seems* to current common sense knowledge or social science knowledge to be impossible" (Barber, 1971:262).

An example of utopian ideology is the Platonic ideology criticizing the conjugal family as a bastion of social inequality and recommending a familyless society. This system of sexual sharing has been tried repeatedly in contemporary communes. Among the several American communities that attempted to do away with sexual exclusiveness, only the Oneida community (we shall examine it in detail in Chapter 7), which flourished in upper New York State in the mid-nineteenth century, persisted for any length of time. Even though this Platonic ideology for a familyless society may not bring about the abolition of the conjugal family, it may aid in changes that could reduce the inegalitarian effects of the family, changes such as making property inheritance or access to education more equal.

A utopian ideology may still have considerable effects for social change, short of full realization of the utopia itself. "Utopian ideologies are exceptionally dramatic and often powerful systems of ideas that at least tell us the social directions our values and norms do or do not prefer" (Barber, 1971:262). Historically, several utopian ideologies contributed to major changes. The early ideology of Christianity is still with us; the anabaptist ideology that preceded the Reformation in Germany generated a tradition that has survived to this day among pietist communities like the Amish and the Hutterites (Rise & Steinmetz, 1956). The Zionist ideology in the early twentieth century fostered the formation of a type of utopian community called the kibbutz, and there are more than 200 of these communities in modern Israel (Spiro, 1956). Finally, in recent years, utopian ideologies resulted in the formation of utopian communities in the United States for such diverse purposes as sexual sharing, political indoctrination, the practice of Buddhism, and the rehabilitation of drug addicts.

Utopian ideology also plays an important part in the strategy of social change; ". . . inventing and designing the shape of the future by extrapolating what we know of in the present is to envision a direction for planning and action in the present. If the image of a potential future is convincing and rationally persuasive to men in the present, the image may become part of the dynamics and motivation of present action" (Chin & Benne, 1985:30). We shall return to this point in the discussion of strategies of social change.

Political Ideologies

Of all types of ideologies, and there are many, political ideologies have an impact on the principal institutions of society. They are the source for action and, as such, perhaps the most important source of social change. The degree to which individuals ascribe to any political ideology affects their perception of the social structure and their notion of reality, which in turn guides their behavior. Political ideologies are also the most prominent in contemporary American society. D. Stanley Eitzen (1974:402–409) examines several types of ideologies and their implications for social change as represented in Figure 4.2.

5 Political Ideologies of the U.S.

1. *The Orthodox Ideology: Capitalism-Liberalism.* This is the dominant ideology in the United States since about the beginning of the twentieth century. It accepts the status quo, the stratification system, the economic and political systems for they have created an affluent society characterized by: freedom, individualism, civil liberties, due process of law, and democracy. Social change is brought about through working within the existing social institutions, and change occurs most often through compromise and bargaining between legitimate interest groups.

2. *Reform Ideology I: Conservatism.* Although there are several versions of conservatism, they have a number of points in common, such as respect for tradition, belief in the Constitution, the Bible, and other sources that provide a set of guiding principles such as emphasis on private property and freedom and respect for authority. Adherence to these principles favors laissez-faire capitalism, accepts social inequality as a result of compe-

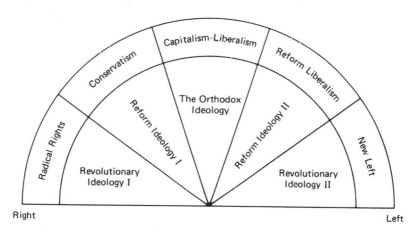

FIG 4.2 The Ideological Spectrum of the United States. (This Spectrum Does Not Indicate Proportions of Political Strength.)

tition and hard work, and opposes socialism and communism. Social change is advocated through conservative reform-oriented government programs that are consonant with conservative views.

3. *Reform Ideology II: Reform Liberalism.* This ideology is impatient with the status quo and with compromise. It emphasizes equality, in which human rights supersede property rights. Social change entails new governmental programs for social improvement and for the reduction of inequality through the elimination of such social ills as poverty, racism, pollution, and war.

4. *Revolutionary Ideology I: The Radical Right.* Since the early 1950s, there has been a resurgence of extremist conservative organizations in the United States, such as the John Birch Society, the Christian Crusade, the Christian Nationalist Crusade, the Minutemen, and the American Nazi Party. These and similar organizations reject the present political system and the government's use of compromise. They continuously question the integrity of government leaders as well as the leaders of principal institutions, and they warn that the moral fiber of America is rapidly breaking down as witnessed by the permissive climate where almost anything goes. Each group has its own specific enemy: intellectuals, communists, foreigners, corrupt government, blacks, or Catholics. Regardless of the enemy, the collapse of the country is imminent. Such groups also oppose a number of things on the sole basis that they are unpatriotic, communist inspired, immoral, socialistic, or may undermine or bring about the downfall of the republic. Their list of opposition would include the union shop, civil liberties, Supreme Court, collective bargaining, the FBI, CIA, National Council of Churches, fluoridation of water, urban renewal, the revised standard version of the Bible, and sex education in the schools. For them, social change is the return to their notion of the "good old days" and the reaffirmation of their ideas and ideals.

5. *Revolutionary Ideology II: The New Left.* There are many versions of the New Left ideology, but they have certain distinctive features in common. The source of major social ills such as racism, poverty, and materialism is in the structure and in social institutions, and therefore the system itself must be restructured. The New Leftists have a hierarchical conception of society—a place for everyone and everyone in his or her place. As a result, they see the system as dehumanizing and alienating to its members. The profit motive is dominant and supersedes humanitarian concerns at all levels. The object of the New Left is to change society, to restructure it so that everyone is free to pursue his or her desires. This new society is to be organized on the basis of cooperation and brotherhood rather than on the basis of competition, conflict, and struggle. This would require the return of the institutions of society to the control of the people—a kind of par-

ticipatory democracy. In addition to the polity, other social arrangements such as the economy, family, education, and religion should also be restructured to meet the criteria of participatory democracy.

These are the dominant political ideologies in the United States. In various forms and to various degrees, they provide the fuel for social change. Each of these positions views change differently, and each emphasizes different types of change. In spite of the conflicting perspectives, they represent important sources of change. Let us now turn to another source of change: competition.

COMPETITION

Competition in society arises from the scarcity of goods, statuses, and services that are universally desired. In the struggle for scarce commodities, competition is usually restrained by tradition, custom, or law. Because these limiting factors keep it within bounds, unrestricted competition is seldom found in actual behavior. Competition is an impersonal struggle for limited ends in accordance with socially prescribed rules. The goals of competition are likewise socially defined. Competition is both an effect and a cause of social change. It is an effect in that a changing society has more goals open to competition than a static society. It causes social change by forcing individuals to adopt new forms of behavior to attain desired goals.

Competition for scarce resources has been an ever-present feature of human societies. Marx and the socialistic philosophers condemned competition—in particular, capitalistic competition—as a means for exploiting the worker. On the other hand, evolutionists such as William Graham Sumner and Herbert Spencer have lauded competition as the means whereby selection and progress were achieved. Georg Simmel believed that "competition is endemic in any organization, and seriously doubted the ability of either capitalistic or socialistic organizations to reduce competition significantly" (Duke, 1976:107).

Competition is present in a number of social arrangements. It is most easily seen among business firms that compete for the customer's dollar. It is also evident among government agencies as they compete for a share of the tax dollar or among religious organizations as they compete for members and their support. (Religious and other voluntary organizations must also compete with alternative organizations for membership and money.) Competition to a great extent controls the organization's "choice of goals" in that its energies must be turned to their competitive activity.

Thus, competition can result in changes within the competing organizations. When there are competitors in the environment who could reduce the security, prestige, and profit of an organization, it can be expected that the organization will take action to overcome the threat from the competition (Hall, 1987:110–112). Such action would entail a greater emphasis on the security of the organization as evidenced in a variety of ways such as greater stress on employee loyalty, efficiency in the work process, and added emphasis on protecting confidential material. There is also a greater tendency to monitor the environment, especially the competing segments of that environment, that can produce changes in the principal activities and the internal normative structure (policies, rules, departmentalization, positions) of the organization. It can also result in increased manipulation of the environment, which may be seen in the form of lobbying, political sabotage, or even in such efforts as contributing time and money to such civic efforts as the United Way campaign. It can also result in attempts to either absorb or banish the competition (Hetzler, 1969:250). Thus, competition can force an organization to change its character to become more complex and more dynamic, thereby influencing the internal structure of organizations.

Competition is also considered as a "potent incentive when mutually desirable rewards are allocated on the basis of performance. In such situations it is productive not only of increased effort but also of distinctly new kinds of effort to achieve greater shares of the reward" (Barnett, 1953:72). Competition is viewed as an important factor in stimulating innovation, and H.G. Barnett outlines several ways of how it may inspire innovation. If nothing else, "it always accentuates the rivalry situation by polarizing the differences between the contestants. It sets them apart and prepares the way for reciprocally interacting withdrawal mechanisms that are characterized by greater or less novelty in their conception" (1953:72–73). The differences that are developed in such situations may be qualitatively distinct and often have as their main purpose the further differentiation of rivals. The differences among the various religions or fraternal organizations would be an illustration of this point. Competition has also given direction to the efforts behind modern technological development, and the same efforts are evident in research institutions, economic institutions, universities, regional and city planning, and advertising. Competition is a factor in prestige and can also lead to imitation. Several remarkable techniques have been created in the United States, for example, to accentuate prestige and class distinctions. They include imported clothes, exotic food and drinks, bizarre and costly entertainments, custom-built automobiles, indoor-outdoor swimming pools, and many other "in" things.

The motivational aspect of competition has also been recognized in developmental programs. For example, Charles Erasmus (1954:152) concluded that in Latin American 4-H programs, results were better when young people worked separate garden spots in competition with each other rather than working the same land cooperatively in such a way that they could not compare results. Afif Tannous (1944:8) suggests that in the Near

East competition between families or parties in a community can be effectively employed to promote social change. He noticed that in one village two groups tried for several years to outdo each other in play production and welfare work. "In most cases it was found that when one family adopted a new agricultural technique successfully, the other families felt challenged to do the same." In Nigeria, when direct appeals for progress and development failed, "apathy could often be broken down by arousing a spirit of competition or emulation between neighboring communities by playing up local rivalries" (Hill, 1957:21). Finally, the same situation is present in India where S.C. Dube (1958:8) found that the desire to build up the reputation of one's village is often instrumental in causing acceptance of developmental projects. "A village which built a new school, constructed a public building, or paved all its lanes could earn a reputation in the vicinity for being 'progressive.' Competition between individuals, families, kin-groups, castes, and villages was also at the back of many programmes." In developing countries the competitive motivation often seems to rise to the national level, where it takes the familiar form of nationalism, which is obviously a potent force in bringing about social change.

In sum, when competition is carried out legitimately for the allocation of scarce resources, it can be seen as an effective instrument of social change with positive results: ". . . a regenerative force that introjects new vitality into a social structure and becomes the basis of social reorganization" (Blau, 1967:301). In the next section we examine a form of competition called conflict.

CONFLICT

Both competition and conflict are characterized by an attempt of two or more parties to reach certain objectives. But the two terms are not identical. Parties in a competition are seeking the same goal, and they must abide by the rules. Parties in a conflict believe they have incompatible goals, and often it involves attempts by adversaries to threaten, injure, or otherwise coerce each other (Kriesberg, 1982:17). Unlike competition, which is continuous and impersonal, conflict is always conscious, intermittent, and personal (Park & Burgess, 1924:574). The emotions of distrust, hatred, suspicion, and fear are accentuated in conflict. Conflict emphasizes the differences between parties and minimizes their similarities.

Conflict is omnipresent in human societies. "The inevitability of conflict derives from mankind's innumerable and changing needs: if starvation is ended, men will fight for prestige; if one power system is destroyed, another emerges; if authority is eradicated, men will compete for precedence. There will be always a scarcity of 'commodities'—whether it be money, prestige, power, love—that will continue to set man against man. Therefore, all men will experience some form of conflict during their lifetime" (McCord & McCord, 1977:4). Conflict may occur among individuals in organizations, in institutions, in communities, in societies, or among nations. It is considered to be endemic to all social relations.

According to John Howard (1974:3–4), *substantive conflict* centers around the distribution of highly valued and scarce resources. He identifies three other bases of conflict: conflict over *symbolic issues,* as in the refusal to pledge alliance to the national flag; the *conflict of ideologies,* such as sexism and racism, which have been created to justify the advantages of various groups; and *cultural conflict,* resulting from differences in lifestyles and values, such as the repudiation of middle-class life-styles by many American youth in the 1960s.

As discussed in the section on theories of conflict in Chapter 2, conflict should not be construed solely as having negative connotations. It can have many other consequences. For example, groups in conflict are likely to increase their internal solidarity and minimize intragroup disagreements. Conflict may also be a factor in the creation of innovative or creative strategies of benevolent intentions, and conflicting situations may result in various forms of accommodation or adjustment or other efforts to compromise or to alleviate tensions and underlying causes.

Conflicts are of primary significance in social change *of* and *within* a system (Coser, 1974). But the relationships between conflict and social change are neither simple nor always direct. Although conflict is an important source of change, change may occur without conflict. When conflict does result in change, that particular change may not be seen as desirable by those who are affected by it. "The exact conditions under which conflict impels or impedes change, and those under which it impels change in a socially desirable direction, have yet to be specific" (Lauer, 1982:216). But "What is important for us is the idea that conflict prevents the ossification of the social system by exerting pressure for innovation and creativity" (Coser, 1974:458). Conflict can generate new social norms and institutions and it may be directly stimulating in the economic and technologic realm. In the Marxian framework, total social systems undergo transformation through conflict.

In some conflict-laden situations, however, a relationship may be established between certain types of conflict conditions and the specific changes they have produced. Louis Kriesberg (1982:246–258), who systematically gathered evidence on the emergence of social conflicts and the processes of their escalation and de-escalation, gives some illustrative outcomes for conflict situations between workers and managers, university students and administrators, blacks and whites, females and males, and in the international arena.

Workers Versus Managers

The principal objective of trade unions has been to improve the working conditions and raise the wages of their members. The turbulent years of the unionization movement have produced a series of changes. There has been a general increase in the material well-being of the workers in an absolute sense: Working conditions have improved; fringe benefits have increased; the number of hours at work has decreased; and, in general, the prestige of blue-collar workers has gone up over the years. However, "More fundamental changes in the structure of the economy, the role of workers in it, and income differentials between workers and managers, were not sought by most trade unions and did not occur" (Kriesberg, 1982:247).

University Students Versus Administrators

Although university students have been engaged in conflict over community, national, and international issues ever since the 1960s, there are also more recent conflicts about the role of the university in international, national, and community affairs. These include university investment policies, such as those involving South Africa; research activities that have military implications, such as the Strategic Defense Initiative (the so-called Star Wars program aimed at developing a space-based defense against ballistic missiles); and certain types of university expansions involving the relocation of impoverished local residents. Other conflicts are related to academic matters, such as the relevance of certain courses or programs, methods of teaching, grading, student involvement in promotion and tenure decisions, dormitory rules, censorship of student publications, control over university organizations, and the treatment of students from minority groups.

By the end of the 1960s, major changes had occurred on campuses. Dormitory rules were relaxed so that in many places members of the opposite sex were permitted not only to visit but to stay overnight; consumption of alcoholic beverages was allowed; administrative control over student publications declined (Vago, 1988:207–208); and important changes took place in curriculum and grading procedures. Special programs in black studies, women's studies, and environmental studies had been added to the curriculum on many campuses. Grading has been relaxed, language requirements for doctoral programs have been eliminated, and new options such as the pass-or-fail system or credit for "real-life" experience have been introduced. Some universities have terminated their contracts with the federal government or with private industries because of activities considered undesirable by students.

In general, students have gained more direct control of university affairs, particularly as they relate to internal matters. They serve on various committees, in some cases as voting members. In some instances, they also participate in faculty recruitment, promotion, and tenure procedures. Kriesberg (1982:249) warns, however, that "It would be an error . . . to regard all these changes as the product of a simple conflict between students and administrators and faculty in which coercion was the sole or even dominant way of changing the other side's position." To a considerable extent, these changes have reflected the dominant ideas in society, ideas that students have helped to formulate. Some of these changes also reflect nonconflicting forces, such as the change in the economy and in the population of students, who then instigated changes in the curriculum as a form of market response.

Blacks Versus Whites

As a consequence of the racial conflict of the 1960s, there have been important collective gains for blacks (Kriesberg, 1982:250–252). Examples of these aggregate gains include the increase in educational opportunities and attainment; a reduction of income differences between blacks and whites; and a drop in the proportion of blacks below the poverty level. There has also been an increase in the collective political power of blacks, especially in the South and in major urban areas. Although it is true that the day-to-day life of many blacks has not changed, or has improved only marginally in spite of the massive efforts and major legislation, commentators maintain that many "genuinely important and historical changes had occurred" (Howard, 1974:28).

Females Versus Males

Kriesberg (1982:252–255) contends that the collective status of women in recent decades has changed in many ways as a result of their struggle for equality. Women for the most part have moved from the role of wife and mother into a dazzling array of formerly male-dominated professions. Today, close to a fifth of all lawyers and physicians are women, as are nearly a fourth of all managers and administrators. Women undergraduate students outnumber their male counterparts. For the first time in American history, a woman appeared on the presidential ticket of a major political party. As the Democratic vice-presidential candidate, Geraldine Ferraro heralded new opportunities for women in the political process. Of course, not all of the changes have been positive. Women are still at a pay disadvantage, and on the average, they earn 69 percent of what men earn (*U.S. News & World Report*, 1987:10). Women's overall physical health has deteriorated relative to men's in recent years. Women are suffering from more ulcers and respiratory ailments than ever before. They also experience a higher incidence of stress and stress-related illnesses. In a sense, they are "adopting life-styles which bode ill for their longevity" (Murphy, 1982:79).

International Conflicts

The most obvious manifestation of conflict at the international level is war. The twentieth century has already had more than 200 wars resulting in a loss of almost 80 million lives. The two world wars alone took over 50 million lives. Two-thirds of the countries of the world, some 97 percent of the global population, have been involved in at least one war in this century (Sivard, 1987:9). There are many causes of such conflict: War may be triggered by a dispute over a soccer match as was the case between Honduras and El Salvador. On the other hand, it could be the result of economic expansion; of scarcity of land or resources; or a series of other factors. The consequences of such hostilities are too well known to catalogue here. However, some of the major change-producing effects of war can be seen in the development of new technologies, in the formation of new political systems, in the reorganization of existing institutions, in the redistribution of wealth, in the redrawing of political boundaries, and in the changes in the composition of the labor force.

In sum, conflict is an endemic and omnipresent feature of human societies. It is a crucial impetus for innovation and change for groups that are driven to seek a competitive advantage in conflict. Conflict can also provide the impetus for change by producing loyalty, solidarity, and cohesiveness in social groups that unite in the face of an antagonist. In the next section a potentially conflict-laden mechanism of change—polity—will be considered.

POLITY

Politics is basically a process of authoritatively deciding who gets what, when, and how (Lasswell, 1958). Those with political power have the ability to control or influence the allocation of resources—which affect people's life chances—through the political process (Etzioni-Halevy, 1981:151). In the United States, polity is organized at three levels—federal, state, and local—and each consists of executive, legislative, and judicial branches. At a given time any branch of government at any level may be actively seeking to maintain stability or to foster change in particular areas of American life. For the moment, only the latter will be considered.

Polity has traditionally played an important part in fostering change in the United States. At times the goals were specific and often were those being advocated by local or regional interests. They involved, among other things, land acquisition and suppression of the Indians; the building of roads and railroads; the encouragement of manufacturing; the irrigation of the land; the development of land grant colleges; the exploration of new lands; and the education of children. More recently there have been attempts to provide financial security for the elderly and adequate health care for all. Attempts have been made also to alter long-standing patterns of inequality between whites and blacks, males and females, and to improve the economic status of recent immigrants (Issel, 1985).

The volume of activities undertaken by modern governments is greater, and the range of such activities is broader, than it ever was before. Governments bring about change through the processes of distribution, regulation, and redistribution (Lowi, 1964). This classification depends upon the number of people affected and their relationships with one another. *Distribution* may involve relatively small numbers of people; it may include government contracts, public works projects, and industries that will bring new wealth to an area. *Regulation* deals with the restriction or limitation of the actions of others; it may include issues such as labor management relations and protection of the consumer and the environment. *Redistribution* calls for the transfer of resources among or between large groups or classes in society. Illustrations of this include graduated income taxes and other public policies intended to transfer resources from one group to another, from the "haves" to the "have-nots." There is, however, a tendency in political systems and subsystems to develop a "mobilization of bias" (Bachrach & Baratz, 1970)—that is, a set of predominant values, beliefs, rituals, and formal and informal institutional procedures that operate systematically and consistently to benefit some people and groups at the expense of others. Those who benefit most can defend and promote their vested interests. Usually, the status quo defenders are also the group with the most power. For example, the history of blacks' demands for access to effective problem-solving apparatus by polity validates this perspective.

It should also be noted that "The structures of power in which the political process takes place offer an explanation not only of how change originates and what direction it takes, but also why it is necessary. Power always implies non-power and therefore resistance. The dialectic of power and resistance is the motive force of history. From the interests of those in power at a given time we can infer the interests of the powerless, and with them the direction of change" (Dahrendorf, 1973:502). In the United States this has been illustrated by several developments, such as the war or attempted war on poverty, the conflict that is intensifying among the haves and have-nots, and the existing contradictions among racial and ethnic groups.

At all levels and branches of polity, new programs and activities are initiated on a regular basis. The impetus for these may come from within the polity or from without. There are specific demands, such as hot lunch programs in school or increased regulation of insurance companies, or general demands requesting the polity to get moving to earn its keep, to work for the common good. In the United States, "Government is supposed to have *programs*. Agencies are supposed to do something, to advance toward some goals. A government with no program is a bad government. An agency without a program is a bad or stagnant agency. Government then takes great pains to show what it is doing. A flock of new programs are announced each year, guaranteed to help the nation or the world. When a new government takes office or when a new man takes the helm at an agency, program-mongering becomes more acute" (Friedman, 1975:190).

These activities may result in a series of palliative or placating measures, or they may produce creative incremental measures that may "breed new possibilities for subsequent radical change, although at the moment of adoption they appear quite modest" (Goulet, 1973:295).

The polity continuously fosters change in society at various levels. Its role obviously varies from situation to situation. On the institutional level, in the context of economic development, Szymon Chodak identifies three ways in which polity can induce change:

1. It can create conditions supportive of economic development without interfering in the actual course of economic activities. This would mean support of trade, business, entrepreneurial and other activities while safeguarding private capital, investments, and the rights of ownership. This takes place during the early stages of capitalism.

2. The polity can regulate some economic activities such as the protection of workers and farmers, but the market retains its competitive character. This is illustrative of advanced capitalism.

3. The polity engages directly in the planning and implementing of economic development by becoming owners of economic enterprises. This is the case in the Soviet Union and Eastern European countries. (Chodak, 1973:247)

In addition to these activities, the polity can stimulate change in developing countries by regulating incentives, controlling prices and trade, and by helping individuals to liberate themselves from traditional kinship, village, or tribal ties. In essence, it entails the provision of welfare and related services that were traditionally provided by one's extended family. Finally, it facilitates integration of society through conflict regulation and accommodation of diverse demands.

In sum, some of the most far-reaching changes have occurred in recent decades in societies that are in the process of development. In modern industrial societies, changes instigated by the polity are principally distributive, regulative, and redistributive in nature.

THE ECONOMY

Economic systems have long been considered as principal initiating forces of social change. Their importance varies from theorist to theorist, but in general there seems to be agreement that, indeed, economic forces shape and guide our lives. As discussed in Chapter 2, Marx argued that the manner in which people obtain their livelihood determines the way they establish their programs of justice, religion, kinship, education, and other social institutions. He pointed to the mode of production and stated that it determines the general character of the social, political, and spiritual processes in society. His idea of economic determinism is still an influential one with a substantial number of followers. However, economic forces are only one of the several factors that seem central in initiating and directing social change. Therefore, instead of describing how economic conditions are seen as "prime movers," the emphasis on the following pages will be on illustrating how economic factors foster change in specific walks of life rather than contributing to the transformation of entire societies.

In the United States, business, industry, and finance are considered to be the great sources of change and progress. They are supported by a strong ideology of free enterprise, which is evident throughout the economic institutions. In many ways change is built into the daily life as part of the economic system.

An important aspect of the economy is the division of labor. One's occupation, particularly in the middle class, is decisive for it provides the person with a certain level of monetary reward, power, and prestige. Increased demand for products and increased specialization to meet those demands have greatly contributed to the growth in the division of labor and the number of occupations. The *1977 Dictionary of Occupational Titles* and its 1986 *Supplement,* for example, include comprehensive descriptions of job duties and related information for over 20,000 occupations in the United States. The degree of specialization is almost as infinite as is shown in the following illustration:

> In the baking industry one can make a living as a cracker breaker, meringue spreader, a pie stripper, or pan dumper. In the slaughter or meat-packing industry one can specialize as: a large stock scalper, belly shaver, crotch buster, gut snatcher, gut sorter, snout puller, ear cutter, eyelid remover, stomach washer (sometimes called belly pumper), hindleg toenail puller, frontleg toenail puller, and oxtail washer. (Wilensky, 1967:78–79)

Increased differentiation in the economic sphere in turn brings about increased differentiation in stratification patterns. One's class position, in turn, determines one's life-style, values, interaction patterns, power, mobility—in short, one's life chances. Economic factors thus condition the distribution of rewards and the allocation of status and prestige. They also contribute to the differentiation between the haves and the have-nots (that is, inequality).

Economic factors contribute to inequality, which in turn begets other forms of inequality that are likely to increase further economic inequality. Economic surpluses have long been considered as a basis for stratification and in the creation of inequality (Lenski, 1966). Jonathan H. Turner and Charles Starnes (1976:3), using the United States as an example, note that economic surplus creates distribution problems, which lead people to compete for the surplus. Those who win in this competition are able to buy power that can be used to maintain or increase their advantage. Once power is bought, there is a decrease of reliance on force, and the emphasis switches to the legitimation of inequality by the use of ideas in order to mitigate inherent conflicts of interests between the privileged and those who are less privileged. Because those who are better off need not expend their resources on forcing acceptance of their privilege, they can now use their increased power to gather more of the economic surplus.

In addition to changes in the division of labor and stratification patterns, economic factors can literally make or break communities through the creation of markets, industries, employment opportunities, or through their manipulation. In a classic study, W. Fred Cottrell (1974) examines one change in the basic economic institution of a community and traces the effects of it throughout the social structure. He has chosen a one-industry town where other economic considerations would not enter to complicate the case.

Caliente, as Cottrell called the town, came into existence in order to service the steam locomotive, which, in the beginning, required frequent stops. The city grew and prospered with the railroad. People built homes, put in a water system using cast iron pipes, established businesses, and built a 27-bed hospital, school buildings, a theater, and even a park. They also established a number of civic organizations such as the Chamber of Commerce and the Masonic lodge. The town was solid, growing, and optimistic.

The town was suddenly threatened with extinction in the mid-1940s when the railroad announced that it would no longer maintain its facilities there. "The location of Caliente, as far as the railroad was concerned, was a function of boiler temperature and pressure and the resultant service requirements of the locomotive" (Cottrell, 1974:683). The replacement of steam engines by diesel engines made the city obsolete from the perspective of the railroad.

Everyone in the town experienced some loss. The railroad company owned 39 homes, a clubhouse, and a hotel in town that became virtually worthless. Workers who had seniority only in the local union had lost even more. A fourth of the workers had to look for new jobs as the diesel engine reduced overall labor needs. The local merchants also lost badly. The younger ones could move out, but even they lost because their property became worthless. Friendship patterns rapidly changed, and the community structure, built on a seemingly solid foundation, began to disintegrate. Attempts to attract new industry failed, and residents found it difficult to justify the cold-blooded profit motive decision of the railroad. But the town was dead, the victim of economic forces beyond the control of the community.

Other economic forces also exert pressure on social life. John Kenneth Galbraith (1973) contends that large corporations, by virtue of their size and power, can create and control the market. Large corporations, he suggests, constitute a "planning system" in the American economy. They determine what customers shall eat, drink, wear, and smoke and how their homes shall look and within broad limits, what price they shall pay for what they buy. The concentration of economic power in large corporations also involves the decline of countervailing power. When a firm buys its former competitors, it is removing checks on its power. An example of this is the beer industry (Currie & Skolnick, 1984:30–32). Over half of the domestic beer market is controlled by giant corporations such as Anheuser-Busch and Miller. Thousands of small breweries either went out of business or were bought up by a few large corporations. Local brands were taken over, the taste of beer became more standardized, and prices rose sharply. At the same time, production costs were reduced as a result of mass production and relocation to parts of the country with cheaper labor. Although some new jobs were created, many people became unemployed because of the buy-outs and relocations.

Large corporations also have a tendency to go "multinational." For example, ITT employs over 400,000 workers in 68 countries. Exxon operates in almost a hundred countries, and its fleet of oil tankers constitutes a navy the size of Great Britain's. General Motors has facilities in 39 countries and sells over $80 billion worth of products annually. Multinationals account for more than a fourth of total world economic production, and their share is increasing.

Critics argue that the globalization of business contributes to the decline of the power of labor as well as to the decline of small business as a result of its inability to compete on the marketplace (Harrison, 1984). It makes it difficult for the U.S. government to keep up with the activities of such corporations, thus making regulatory agencies highly ineffective. It reduces employment opportunities for American workers and undermines "the power of the nation-state to maintain economic and political stability within its territory" (Barnet & Muller, 1974:302).

Defenders of multinationals contend that they introduce great wealth and create jobs in poor countries. They contribute to the economic development of third-world nations by introducing the latest manufacturing techniques, by paying taxes and relatively high wages, and by providing jobs in the manufacturing and service sectors. Thus, the presence of multinationals is seen as a catalyst for modernization because the economies of the host societies will grow from wages and taxes paid by the corporations.

Economic problems can also create a chain of events that can set off changes in a number of ways. Examples of such problems include fluctuating currencies, foreign debts, and trade deficits (Silk, 1987). The almost 40 percent drop in the value of the United States dollar since 1986 in relation to Western European and Japanese currencies significantly increased the price of imported goods and brought in huge amounts of foreign investments. At the same time, the increase in the export of American goods remained negligible. Because of domestic economic problems, several third-world debtor nations, such as Brazil and Argentina, suspended payment of the interest on $68 billion worth of debts. This shocked the financial world, and many American banks raised their prime interest rates in response. This brought about an increase in home mortgage loans, which, in turn, slowed down the housing industry. A decrease in new home construction, in turn, reverberated on other aspects of the economy. As a result of its huge trade deficit, the United States has become the world's largest debtor nation, and its net foreign debt is growing rapidly. Among other things, this trade deficit has resulted in a tighter domestic budget with major reductions in many areas such as education, health care, and programs for the disadvantaged. As one economist warns, America's unprecedented budget and trade deficits threaten "to create enormous disruption in the short run and will produce a fundamentally different global structure for the 1990's" (Silk, 1987).

Economic factors foster change in society in many other ways. They play a role in the reduction of geographical and entrepreneurial frontier opportunities. They sharpen the dichotomy between the employed and the unemployed and contribute to the rise in higher expectations and keener perception of the gap between actualities and potentialities. Current economic conditions also play a role in the transition from a basic condition of labor scarcity to one of job scarcity, and the expanded power of the labor force induces wages to follow increasing productivity, which results in an inflationary force (Harman, 1974:749). These in turn produce further changes in economic, political, and other institutional domains.

In sum, economic forces permeate all aspects of life in society. They are considered to be among the most potent inducements for social change.

STRUCTURAL STRAINS

The concept of *strain* refers to a discrepancy between two or more elements of the social system. It is based on the assumption that the social system is made up of interrelated components. As long as the components are compatible and fulfill positive functions for each other, the social system is relatively stable. In situations where two or more components become in-compatible, the equilibrium of the social system is upset and this may result in social change. Several types of strains can be identified that produce incompatibility among the components of the social system and thus con-tribute to change of that system. They include population imbalances, an-omie, certain forms of scarcity, role conflicts, inconsistencies between the ideal and the real, conflict of values, and status anguish.

Demographic imbalances are inherent in social systems, and they are likely to be manifested in change-producing strains (Moore, 1970:131). Trends in birthrates, for example, may be out of phase with respect to plans for building and improving schools. Migration trends may be out of phase with the receiving area's ability to accommodate new arrivals. Changes in population composition can have an effect on labor force characteristics such as increasing or decreasing the size of nonworking or working pop-ulations. Population growth creates imbalances in food supply and distri-bution. It adversely affects resource utilization and depletion, contributes to large concentrations in urban areas where the resulting strains may be seen in an overload of transportation facilities and traffic congestions. The circadian rhythm impels nearly everyone to go to work at the same time, to take a break at the same time, and to impose demands on energy sources at the same time.

Change-producing strains are created in a society also by anomie, a condition of normative confusion in which the individual has few socially validated guides to behavior. According to Robert K. Merton's (1957:140) often-debated hypothesis, the source of this strain is the discrepancy be-tween goals and means in a society. Individuals are uniformly committed to the *goals* society tells them to desire, but they encounter unequal access to the *means* socially defined as legitimate for achieving these goals. Many people in society are thus subject to intense frustration of their socially legitimate desires—for instance, to be successful, popular, and happy. By being poor, black, or otherwise disadvantaged, many individuals are se-verely handicapped in the race toward the goals society tells them they ought to value and pursue. Because of this frustration in finding access to legitimate means for achieving goals, individuals sometimes turn to ille-gitimate means, that is, deviance, to achieve them. Such deviance may include crime, alcoholism, drug addiction, or even suicide by those who cannot cope with the pressure; or rebellion by those who try to solve the problem by undermining the social order and establishing a new one.

Rebellion as a reaction to strain is considered an important source of social change. This kind of adjustment is characteristic of individuals who start social movements, and it has been used as an explanation for the student unrest in the late 1960s. This pattern also helps to understand why individuals form communes, occupy buildings, destroy property, and for-mulate new ideologies in attempts to substitute new goals and norms for the dominant ones in society.

The presence of universal scarcities in society is another ubiquitous source of change-producing strains. "Any viable social system requires norms that determine allocation of these scarcities, but the latter remain omnipresent sources of potential strain in individual behavior in the relations between and among groups and social categories" (Moore, 1970:132). The allocation of scarce goods is always subject to challenge in society. If the challenge is successful and brings about alterations in the distribution of scarce resources such as in the Marxian perspective, it can have far-ranging consequences on all aspects of life. In modern societies, even time is considered as a scarce resource. "We are all of us compelled to read for profit, party for contacts, lunch for contracts, bowl for unity, drive for mileage, gamble for charity, go out for the evening for the greater glory of the municipality, and stay home for the weekend to rebuild the house" (Kerr, quoted by Linder, 1970:4).

Ambiguity in role expectations and conflict among social roles can also result in change-producing strains. A typical illustration of role ambiguity is the case of the modern American woman whose traditional domestic duties have become uncertain. A commonly used illustration for role conflict is the situation of a black physician whose occupational role calls for deference from others but whose racial role traditionally has called for deference to others.

Moore (1974:20–21) suggests that a "ubiquitous source of change-producing strain arises from the inherent fact that social order is a moral order and from the associated fact that non-conformity to the moral order occurs in all societies." As a result, "the inconsistency between the ideal and the actual is tension producing and hospitable to change." For example, recent manifestations of changing moral standards among youth are indicative of changes in ideal patterns. In addition to discrepancies between expectations and actual situations, conflict in values can also result in strains, culminating in changes. Differences in values among social classes and among ethnic or religious groups often instigate changes, as evidenced by the consequences of recent efforts in school busing.

Finally, strains in a society can be produced by what Robert H. Lauer (1982:238) calls status anguish, which includes marginality, status inconsistency, status withdrawal, and relative deprivation. Marginality is "existence in two or more social worlds without being fully a part of any of them." Illustrations of this would be the foreman, the black psychiatrist, and supervisor in industry. Status inconsistency refers to occupying statuses that have different implications for one's location in a system of stratification, as, for example, the unemployed Ph.D. Status withdrawal was discussed in connection with Hagen's notion of economic development in Chapter 2. Relative deprivation is some kind of perceived or subjective deprivation in regard to some specific standards. Lauer suggests that these four types of status anguish have, in various degrees, contributed to change in society.

SUMMARY

Change in society is produced by a number of factors, and it is important *not* to assign undue weight to any one of these factors in isolation. It is always tempting to have a "pet" theory or a unitary "prime mover," but to account for broad social changes such an exercise would be meaningless.

Among the mechanisms of change analyzed in this chapter, it was noted that technology creates new alternatives, but it also generates new problems, as evidenced by the introduction of the steel ax among Australian Aborigines and the snowmobile among Eskimos. In modern society, technology is associated with changes at work and is considered a factor in alienation.

There are several types of ideologies. Max Weber contended that the Protestant ethic was instrumental in the rise of capitalism. On the other hand, Marxism is associated with large-scale societal transformations. The ideology of the conjugal family contributed to greater equality and freedom of family members. Some of the utopian ideologies are important instigators of change. One way or another, these ideologies all challenge existing social arrangements.

Competition is an endemic aspect of society. It contributes to social change in both ecological and organization contexts. It stimulates innovation and has been effectively used as a motivating force for social change in development programs. When competitors do not abide by rules and regulations, the relationship turns into conflict. It may be substantive, or over ideological, symbolic, or cultural issues. Conflict should not be viewed as having only negative connotations. It plays an important role in social change, as illustrated by the outcomes of conflict between workers and management; university students and administrators; blacks and whites; females and males; and in the international arena.

The polity has traditionally played a role in social change through its activities of distribution, regulation, and redistribution. Government is expected to "do something," and the result is often change at the various levels within society as well as among societies.

Economic factors have contributed to the increase in the division of labor with concomitant changes in the stratification system. In small communities, change in the basic economic institution can have disastrous results, as illustrated by the case of the town of Caliente. Finally, structural strains produced by population imbalances, anomie, scarcity, role and value conflicts, inconsistencies, and status anguish are also ubiquitous sources of change. In the following chapter a series of specific patterns of change will be examined.

SUGGESTED FURTHER READINGS

BERNARD, RUSSELL H., and PERTTI PELTO, eds. *Technology and Social Change*, 2nd ed. Prospect Heights, Ill.: Waveland Press, 1987. A compendium of insightful articles on the interplay between technology and social change.

DOWNES, BRYAN T. *Politics, Change, and the Urban Crisis*. North Scituate, Mass.: Duxbury Press, 1976. A provocative book on the role of polity in urban affairs.

FEUER, LEWIS S. *Ideology and the Ideologists*. New York: Harper & Row, 1975. An exploration of the social and emotional sources of ideological thought and their implications for change.

KRIESBERG, LOUIS. *Social Conflicts*, 2nd ed. Englewood Cliffs, N.J.: Prentice-Hall, 1982. A comprehensive analysis of all kinds of group conflicts and their role in social change.

MANUEL, FRANK E., ed. *Utopias and Utopian Thought*. Boston: Beacon Press, 1967. Readings on types of utopias and their function in social change.

SMELSER, NEIL J. *The Sociology of Economic Life*, 2nd ed. Englewood Cliffs, N.J.: Prentice-Hall, 1976. A comprehensive review of economic factors from a sociological perspective.

TEICH, ALBERT H., ed. *Technology and Future*, 4th ed. New York: St. Martin's Press, 1986. A collection of articles devoted to the various facets of technology.

REFERENCES

BACHRACH, PETER, and MORTON S. BARATZ. *Power and Poverty: Theory and Practice*. New York: Oxford, 1970.

BARBER, BERNARD. "Function, Variability, and Change in Ideological Systems." In Bernard Barber and Alex Inkeles (eds.), *Stability and Social Change*. Boston: Little, Brown, 1971, pp. 244–265.

BARNET, RICHARD J., and RONALD E. MULLER. *Global Reach—The Power of the Multinational Corporations*. New York: Simon & Schuster, 1974.

BARNETT, HOMER G. *Innovation: The Basis of Cultural Change*. New York: McGraw-Hill Book Company, 1953.

BERNARD, H. RUSSELL and PERTTI PELTO (eds.) *Technology and Social Change*, 2nd ed. Prospect Heights, Ill: Waveland Press, 1987.

BLAU, PETER M. *Exchange and Power in Social Life*. New York: Wiley, 1967.

BLAUNER, ROBERT. *Alienation and Freedom*. Chicago: University of Chicago Press, 1964.

CHIN, ROBERT, and KENNETH D. BENNE. "General Strategies for Effecting Changes in Human Systems." In Warren G. Bennis, Kenneth D. Benne, and Robert Chin (eds.), *The Planning of Change*. 4th ed. New York: Holt, Rinehart & Winston, 1985, pp. 22–46.

CHODAK, SZYMON. *Societal Development: Five Approaches with Conclusions from Comparative Analysis*. New York: Oxford, 1973.

COSER, LEWIS A. "Social Conflict and the Theory of Social Change." In Phillip Brickman (ed.), *Social Conflict: Readings in Rule Structures and Conflict Relationships*. Lexington, Mass.: Heath, 1974, pp. 458–466.

COTTRELL, W. FRED. "Death by Dieselization: A Case Study in the Reaction to Technological Change." In Edgar A. Schuler, Thomas Ford Hoult, Duane L. Gibson, and Wilbur B. Brookover (eds.), *Readings in Sociology*, 5th ed. New York: Crowell, 1974, pp. 681–689.

CURRIE, ELLIOTT, and JEROME H. SKOLNICK. *America's Problems: Social Issues and Public Policy*. Boston: Little, Brown, 1984.

DAHRENDORF, RALF. "Market and Plan." In Amitai Etzioni and Eva Etzioni-Halevy (eds.), *Social Change: Sources, Patterns, and Consequences*, 2nd ed. New York: Basic Books, 1973, pp. 500–504.

DUBE, S.C. *India's Changing Villages: Human Factors in Community Development*. London: Routledge, 1958.

DUKE, JAMES T.   *Conflict and Power in Social Life.* Provo, Utah: Brigham Young University Press, 1976.

EITZEN, D. STANLEY.   *Social Structure and Social Problems in America.* Boston: Allyn & Bacon, 1974.

ERASMUS, CHARLES G.   "An Anthropologist Views Technical Assistance." *Scientific Monthly,* 78, 1954, pp. 147–158.

ETZIONI-HALEVY, EVA.   *Social Change: The Advent and Maturation of Modern Society.* London: Routledge & Kegan Paul, 1981

EVANS, MICHAEL, and H. RUSSELL BERNARD.   "Word Processing, Office Drudgery, and the Microcomputer Revolution." In H. Russell Bernard and Pertti J. Pelto (eds.), *Technology and Social Change,* 2nd ed. Prospect Heights, Ill.: Waveland Press, 1987, pp. 359–376.

FEUER, LEWIS S.   *Ideology and the Ideologists.* New York: Harper & Row, 1975.

FREEMAN, DAVID M.   *Technology and Society: Issues in Assessment, Conflict, and Choice.* Chicago: Rand McNally, 1974.

FRIEDMAN, LAWRENCE M.   *The Legal System, A Social Science Perspective.* New York: Russell Sage, 1975.

GALBRAITH, JOHN KENNETH.   *Economics and the Public Purpose.* Boston: Houghton Mifflin, 1973.

GOODE, WILLIAM J.   *World Revolution and Family Patterns.* New York: Free Press, 1963.

GOULDNER, ALVIN W.   *The Dialectic of Ideology and Technology: The Origins, Grammar and Future of Ideology.* New York: Seabury, 1976.

GOULET, DENIS A.   *The Cruel Choice: A New Concept in the Theory of Development.* New York: Atheneum, 1973.

HALL, RICHARD H.   *Organizations: Structures, Processes, and Outcomes,* 4th ed., Englewood Cliffs, N.J.: Prentice-Hall, 1987.

HARMAN, WILLIS W.   "Key Choices of the Next Two Decades." In Edgar A. Schuler, Thomas Ford Hoult, Duane L. Gibson, and Wilbur B. Brookover (eds.), *Readings in Sociology,* 5th ed. New York: Crowell, 1974, pp. 749–759.

HARRISON, PAUL.   *Inside the Third World: The Anatomy of Poverty,* 2nd ed. New York: Penguin Books, 1984.

HETZLER, STANLEY A.   *Technological Growth and Social Change, Achieving Modernization.* New York: Praeger, 1969.

HILL, COLIN.   "Some Notes on Experience of Community Development in Southeast Nigeria." *Community Development Review,* 7, 1957, pp. 18–23. Washington, D.C.: International Cooperation Administration.

HOWARD, JOHN R.   *The Cutting Edge: Social Movements and Social Change in America.* New York: Lippincott, 1974.

ISSEL, WILLIAM.   *Social Change in the United States, 1945–1983.* New York: Schocken Books, 1985.

KRIESBERG, LOUIS.   *Social Conflicts,* 2nd ed. Englewood Cliffs, N.J.: Prentice-Hall, 1982.

LADD, EVERETT C., Jr.   *Ideology in America: Change and Response in a City, a Suburb, and a Small Town.* New York: W.W. Norton & Co., Inc., 1972.

LASSWELL, HAROLD.   *Politics: Who Gets What, When, How.* New York: Harcourt, 1958.

LAUER, ROBERT H.   *Perspectives on Social Change,* 3rd ed. Boston: Allyn & Bacon, 1982.

LENSKI, GERHARD E.   *Power and Privilege: A Theory of Social Stratification.* New York: McGraw-Hill Book Company, 1966.

LINDER, STAFFAN B.   *The Harried Leisure Class.* New York: Columbia University Press, 1970.

LOWI, THEODORE J.   "American Business, Public Policy, Case Studies, and Political Theory." *World Politics,* 16, 1964, pp. 677–715.

McCORD, ARLINE, and WILLIAM MCORD.   *Urban Social Conflict.* St. Louis: Mosby, 1977.

MERTON, ROBERT K.   *Social Theory and Social Structure.* New York: Free Press, 1957.

MESTHENE, EMMANUEL G.   "The Role of Technology in Society." In Albert H. Teich (ed.), *Technology and the Future,* 4th ed. New York: St. Martin's Press, 1986, pp. 72–94.

MOORE, WILBERT E.   "A Reconstruction of Theories of Social Change." In S.N. Eisenstadt (ed.), *Readings in Social Evolution and Development.* New York: Pergamon, 1970, pp. 123–139.

MOORE, WILBERT E.   *Social Change,* 2nd ed. Englewood Cliffs, N.J.: Prentice-Hall, 1974

MURPHY, CULLEN.   "Men and Women: A Survey of the Research." *The Wilson Quarterly.* Winter, 1982, pp. 63–79.

NAISBITT, JOHN. *Megatrends: Ten New Directions Transforming Our Lives.* New York: Warner Books, 1982

PARK, ROBERT E., and ERNEST W. BURGESS. *Introduction to the Science of Sociology.* Chicago: University of Chicago Press, 1924.

PELTO, PERTTI J., and LUDGER MULLER-WILLIE. "Snowmobiles: Technological Revolution in the Arctic." In H. Russell Bernard and Pertti J. Pelto (eds.), *Technology and Social Change,* 2nd ed. Prospect Heights, Ill.: Waveland Press, 1987, pp. 208–241.

RISE, CHARLES S., and ROLLIN C. STEINMETZ. *The Amish Year.* New Brunswick, N.J.: Rutgers University Press, 1956.

SHARP, R.L. "Steel Axes for Stone Age Australians." *Human Organization,* 11, 1952, 17–22.

SILK, LEONARD. "The Global Financial Circus: Everyone Is Growing Frantic." *The New York Times,* April 5, 1987, p. 3.

SIVARD, RUTH LEGER. *World Military and Social Expenditures, 1987–1988.* Washington, D.C.: World Priorities, 1987.

SMELSER, NEIL J. *Sociology of Economic Life,* 2nd ed. Englewood Cliffs, N.J.: Prentice-Hall, 1976.

SPIRO, MELFORD E. *Kibbutz: Venture in Utopia.* Cambridge, Mass.: Harvard University Press, 1956.

TANNOUS, AFIF. "Extension Work Among the Arab Fellahin." *Applied Anthropology,* 3(3), 1944, pp. 1–12.

TURNER, JONATHAN H., and CHARLES E. STARNES. *Inequality: Privilege and Poverty in America.* Pacific Palisades, Calif.: Goodyear, 1976.

U.S. News & World Report. "Women's Pay: The Catch-up Game Quickens." September, 14, 1987, p. 10.

VAGO, STEVEN. *Law and Society,* 2nd ed. Englewood Cliffs, N.J.: Prentice-Hall, 1988.

WILENSKY, HAROLD. "The Early Impact of Industrialization on Society." In William A. Faunce (ed.), *Readings in Industrial Sociology.* New York: Appleton, 1967, pp. 78–79.

5 Patterns of Change

The preceding chapters have been devoted to the principal theories, directions, and causes of change. Thus far the discussion has been guided by the questions of why and in what direction change takes place, and what the driving forces are behind change. In this chapter, the question of *how* change occurs will be considered. The objective is to examine the major processes and dimensions of change, not as "causes" but as "intermediaries" or "carriers" of change, and to analyze the various forms or patterns by which change comes about.

In the sociological literature there have been many attempts to analyze, both qualitatively and quantitatively, the emergence of change patterns in societies. This chapter will describe, compare, and contrast several of the major patterns. In this discussion, the emphasis will be on both cultural and societal forms. Among the former, three seem to be of particular importance: evolution, diffusion, and acculturation. Among the latter, the major ones considered are revolution, modernization, industrialization, urbanization, and bureaucratization.

EVOLUTION

In Chapter 2 the various evolutionary theories of change were discussed in some detail. It was noted that many of the earlier theories were based on the idea that it was possible to improve society through deliberate human effort and that society, especially Western society, was moving inexorably from one stage or phase toward another, usually a better and more desirable one. For example, for Marx and Engels, evolution was to make manifest destiny of the *Communist Manifesto*. Others, in a similar vein, also saw the evolution of societies toward greater complexity, which, they believed, inevitably produces greater human happiness.

Contemporary anthropologists, in an attempt to revitalize evolutionary theory, have focused on culture and technology to show how evolutionary changes take place in society. They have tried to demonstrate that the major source of change is a shift in a society's basic means of subsistence, for instance, from agricultural to industrial. Because each subsistence level is more productive than its predecessor, the result is a greater economic surplus. That makes possible larger populations, more affluence, greater cultural diversity, the emergence of new statuses and roles, faster economic development, and an ever-increasing complexity and efficiency (see, for example, Lenski & Lenski, 1987). In all evolutionary approaches, a recurrent theme is the search for a universal "law" of change. The orientation of this section is different. Instead of considering broad theories of evolutionary change, the emphasis will be on specific evolutionary forms or patterns. These can be characterized by directionality in time, which in its course generates greater variety and complexity.

Directionality, novelty, variety, and increased complexity are key aspects of evolutionary patterns. Some of the so-called revolutions with the "r" removed could be illustrative of this. Consider the agricultural revolution, for example, which could be more appropriately termed as agricultural evolution. Similarly, we can talk about the industrial revolution as industrial evolution. In both instances, there are discernible evolutionary patterns in the use of energy, technology, work skills, and materials. Of course, their emergence was based on already established foundations in the cumulative sequence. Each improvement required novelty, directionality, and variety, and each resulted in increased complexity.

It is plausible and possible to isolate individual change forms and talk about their evolution. For example, Richard Schwartz and James C. Miller (1970) used anthropological data to try to draw a pattern of legal evolution. They posited that legal organization seems to develop with a degree of regularity, and elements of such organization emerge in a sequence such that each constitutes a necessary condition for the next. The preliminary findings show "a rather startling consistency in the pattern of legal evolution. In a sample of fifty-one societies, compensatory damages and mediation of disputes were found in every society having specialized legal counsel. In addition, a large majority (85 percent) of societies that develop specialized police also employ damages and mediation" (Schwartz & Miller, 1970:157). The findings of the study lend support to the belief that "an evolutionary sequence occurs in the development of legal institutions" (p. 171).

A similar sequence of evolution was discussed by Robert N. Bellah (1970) in his paper, "Religious Evolution." He views evolution "as a process of increasing differentiation and complexity of organization which endows the organism, social system, or whatever the unit in question may be, with greater capacity to adapt to its environment so that it is in some sense more autonomous relative to its environment than were its less complex ancestors" (Bellah, 1970:213). In light of this conceptualization of evolution, he traced the emergence of religion in terms of the evolution of religious symbol systems, which moved from "compact" to "differentiated"; religious collectivities, which became more differentiated from other social structures; and increased consciousness of the self as a religious subject. On these grounds he delineated five stages, which he referred to as the primitive, archaic, historic, early modern, and modern religious stages. Bellah noted, however, that these ideal typical stages are not inevitable, and that actual cases may include features that cannot be neatly characterized in terms of any one stage.

But evolution is not characterized merely by qualitative changes in organizations, as was illustrated in the case of legal systems and religion; it is also characterized by quantitative cumulation. The quantitative approach in the study of evolutionary patterns implies that the emergence of certain forms can be ranked along some scale ranging from small to large numbers. Such quantitative scaling is implied, for example, in the study by Morton Fried (1976) of the evolution of stratification. He used two measures: (1) a ratio between positions of prestige available for any given age-sex grade and the number of persons capable of filling them and (2) a ratio between strategic resources and persons possessing impeded or unimpeded access to them. In another study, Raoul Naroll (1964) used the number of people in the most populous building cluster of the ethnic unit study as an index of social development, and showed that this measure can be related systematically in a mathematical formula to the number of occupational specialties and to the number of organizational types.

In his classic study, *The Science of Culture*, Leslie White (1949) proposed a potentially quantifiable measure of the emergence of energy utilization and posited that culture evolved as the amount of energy harnessed per capita per year is increased or as the efficiency of the instrumental means of putting the energy to work is increased. From a different perspective, Marshall Sahlins (1958) used surplus production of food commodities and the degree of their redistribution as a measure of technological efficiency in his stratification study in Polynesia. He demonstrated that the amount of stratification was directly correlated with the size of the group involved in the redistribution of the surplus and with how frequently the food was distributed.

Thus, it is possible to study the evolutionary change forms or patterns in societies both qualitatively and quantitatively. Change patterns such as those of legal systems, religion, stratification, energy utilization, food production, and the like can be isolated and looked upon in an evolutionary or emerging context. These change patterns tend to evolve in a cumulative and incremental fashion, usually with directionality, increased variability, and complexity as a result of the incorporation of novel features.

DIFFUSION

Diffusion refers to the process "by which elements or systems of culture are spread; by which an invention or a new institution adopted in one place is adopted in neighboring areas, and in some cases continues to be adopted in adjacent ones, until it may spread over the whole earth" (Kroeber, 1973:140). Diffusion theory emerged as an alternative to evolution. It is based on the idea of culturally dominant centers, which was made into a theory of social change by G. Elliot Smith (Kroeber, 1973:143). According to Smith, an unusual constellation of circumstances resulted in a great spurt in cultural development in Egypt. Around 3000 B.C., agricultural technology was rapidly improved, geometry was invented, metal-working and tool-making processes were developed, and a new and effective political order was devised. From that center of cultural innovation, cultural elements were carried throughout the Mediterranean and to all peoples of the world. Smith argued that the inventiveness of the Egyptians of that period was the "cause" of social change in various parts of the world, and what the Egyptians invented was diffused to and adopted by most societies.

To document his theory, Smith attempted to locate cultural similarities between the early Egyptians and societies far removed in space and time, such as the Incas of Peru and the people of India and Mexico. He convincingly argued that the bone fishhook in Melanesia was based on a bronze spear developed by the Egyptians, and the Mayan practice of building pyramids out of stone derived from the Egyptian practice of mummifying the dead and burying them in great pyramids. This theory provided an alternative to evolutionary theories in positing that social change was the result of contact and diffusion among societies.

In the United States the anthropologists of the mid-1940s "laid great stress on the importance of diffusion as the pattern of change" (Lauer, 1982:165). In Kroeber's words, "whatever else diffusion does or does not involve, it does always involve change for the receiving culture. The total part played by diffusion in human culture is almost incredibly great" (Kroeber, quoted by Lauer, 1982:165). Kroeber posited that the development of cultural complexes is inversely related to the distance from "high centers" of civilizations. That is, the more isolated and the farther away societies are from such centers, the more retarded or marginal will they be in their development.

George Murdock (1934) estimated that about 90 percent of every culture known to history has acquired its elements from other peoples. Ralph Linton (1936:326–327) provides a now classic illustration of this point by describing the beginning of the day for a typical American in terms of the origins of the objects he or she uses. Among other things, the bed came from the Near East via northern Europe, the cotton from India, the silk from China, the pajamas from India, and the shaving ritual for men originated in Egypt. The custom of wearing a necktie came from seventeenth-century Croatia, the umbrella was invented in southeastern Asia, coins originated in ancient Lydia. While eating breakfast, a typical American uses plates invented in China, a knife from southern India, a fork from Italy, and a spoon derived from Roman society. The orange came from the eastern Mediterranean, cantaloupe from Persia, and coffee from Abyssinia. Wafers are derived from a Scandinavian technique from wheat domesticated in Asia Minor. The after-breakfast cigarette comes from Mexico, from a tobacco plant that originated in Brazil. The newspaper that is being read was imprinted in characters invented in Germany, and "As he absorbs the accounts of foreign troubles he will, if he is a good conservative citizen, thank a Hebrew deity in an Indo-European language that he is 100 percent American" (Linton, 1936:327). And the same 100-percent American that Linton talked about over 50 years ago is surrounded today by products that originated elsewhere (Baker, 1987). Some examples: This text is being composed on a typewriter made in Japan while the author is listening to a radio built in Hong Kong. The paper clips on the Danish desk came from Taiwan, and the stapler was assembled in Korea. And I have not even looked at the labels in my shirt or shoes.

Anthropologists estimate that in the past and the present there have been some 4,000 different human societies (Murdock, 1957). A considerable amount of borrowing goes on among these societies. The processes of diffusion, reinterpretation of borrowed or introduced elements, innovation, and synthesis of the old and new are ongoing and are present in all of them to varying degrees. Diffusion is not always a one-way process, as was implied by Linton's illustration; it can be reciprocal as well. In the United States one might assume that the borrowing between Indians and Caucasians has been a one-way process, but this is not the case. "Our borrowings from the American Indian have been numerous and can be found in many different areas and segments of our culture, and, perhaps, even in our personalities" (Spindler, 1984:23). Many of the things borrowed from American Indians are evident throughout the world. The plants domesticated by American Indians provide close to half of the world's food supply today. They include "Irish" potatoes, corn, beans, squash, and sweet potatoes. A number of drugs can be traced back to them, such as coca in cocaine and novocaine, curare in anesthetics, and cascara in laxatives. Other examples include the woolen poncho, the parka, moccasins, and the commercial cottons used today, all of which had their origins in American Indian culture.

Diffusion is evident also within complex societies. Many of the cultural items can be traced back to specialized groups in society as a component of a specific subculture, which are later taken over by other groups. To illustrate, jazz was developed by American blacks in the South, but as blacks moved north to Chicago and to other urban centers, they carried their music along, and today jazz is an important part of the American cultural heritage. Similarly, attributes of popular culture such as hairstyles, clothes, dance forms, and slang spread from distinct subcultures to society at large.

Over the years a sizable body of literature has developed on diffusion. In addition to anthropologists concerned with how new ideas and practices spread from one society to another, sociologists have studied the diffusion of new values and styles within societies. In particular, rural sociologists have studied the spread of new agricultural technology among farmers' (Cernea, 1985), and medical sociologists have been concerned with the spread of drugs, vaccinations, and family-planning methods. Educationalists have studied school adoption of new teaching methods and equipment. Economists have been concerned with the imitation process by which firms adopt new technological and production processes. Communication researchers have focused on the diffusion process to better understand the dynamics of persuasion and propaganda. Marketeers have studied diffusion implicitly for many years as they attempted to guide and control the spread of new products.

In his book *Diffusion of Innovations*, Everett M. Rogers (1983) reports on over 500 diffusion studies that suggest some remarkably similar findings. Based on this enormous body of research, Rogers developed a theoretical framework on the diffusion of innovations, which has been widely adopted. For Rogers, the crucial elements in diffusion are (1) the *innovation* (which may be a technological development, a fad, a social movement, or a new product), (2) which is *communicated* through certain *channels* (word of mouth, advertising), (3) over *time*, and (4) among members of a *social system*. On the basis of research evidence, he then identifies five stages of the adoption process. They are:

1. *Awareness Stage.* The individual knows of the new idea but lacks sufficient information about it.
2. *Interest Stage.* The individual becomes interested in the idea and seeks more information.

3. *Evaluation Stage*. The individual makes a mental application of the new idea to his or her present and anticipated future situation and makes the decision either to try it or not.
4. *Trial Stage*. The individual uses the innovation on a small scale to determine its utility.
5. *Adoption Stage*. The individual accepts the innovation and commits oneself to its use.

One of the major factors affecting the rate of adoption of an innovation is the characteristics of the innovation itself. Rogers suggests five characteristics that have a major influence on the rate of adoption of an innovation. They are:

1. *Relative advantage* refers to the degree to which an innovation is considered superior to the ideas or products it supersedes. It is determined in terms of efficiency, cost, novelty, or perceived advantage. An example of a product with a high perceived relative advantage is the transistor radio as opposed to the tube-type radio.
2. *Compatibility* is the degree to which an innovation is seen as consistent with the existing values, past experiences, and the needs of the recipients. For example, Eskimo hunters can readily grasp the advantages of the steel blade over the slate knife, but they are very uncertain of the alleged advantages of Christianity over their own religion. Similarly, birth-control practices may be seen as incompatible with existing traditions, values, and beliefs.
3. *Complexity* refers to the extent to which an innovation is seen as relatively difficult to understand and use. The rate of adoption may be put on a complexity-simplicity continuum, and as a rule the adoption rate of an innovation will be slower when it is perceived as complex by members of a social system.
4. *Tryability* is the degree to which an innovation may be experimented with on a limited basis. Certain things can be tried on a small scale; others cannot. Certain inventions, such as the automobile or television, have to be accepted as they are. It is considered advantageous for the adoption rate if an item can be tried out first.
5. *Observability* refers to the extent to which the results of an innovation are visible to others. The fact that certain items such as clothes or durable goods are highly observable facilitates the rate of adoption. The crucial point, according to Rogers, is how these characteristics are *perceived* by members of a social system, for this is what governs their response.

Rogers suggests that the type of innovation decision is related to an innovation's rate of adoption. He outlines three types; (1) *optional*, whereby an individual in a social system has a choice whether or not to adopt an innovation; (2) *collective*, where a majority of a social system's members need to be convinced about an innovation; and (3) *authoritarian*, whereby a decision has been superimposed upon a social system, such as in the case of water fluoridation. Communication channels are also considered as affecting the rate of adoption, and interpersonal channels are considered more effective with more complex innovations than mass media channels.

Finally, both the nature of the social system, whether or not it is modern or traditional, and the extent of the change agents' promotional efforts influence the rate of adoption.

As ideal types, Rogers identifies five adopter categories. They are:

1. *Innovators*, who are eager to try out new ideas. They are daring, risking, and willing to take the consequences for their actions.
2. *Early adopters*, who are more integrated in the social system than innovators and tend to be more prominent, successful, and respected.
3. *Early majority*, who adopt new ideas just before the average in a social system. They tend to be deliberate and they aid in legitimizing innovations, although they are seldom leaders.
4. *Late majority*, who follow after the average social system members; at times, adoption results from social pressures or economic necessity.
5. *Laggards,* who are suspicious of innovators and change agents and have traditional values. They are the last to accept an invention.

The derivative effects of diffusion may be illustrated by the changes in the United States resulting from the invention and adoption of the automobile. These changes were first apparent in the economic institutions directly related to the manufacture of automobiles, such as the steel, rubber, glass, and petroleum industries. Government institutions were affected in a variety of ways, ranging from the revenues from the sale of gasoline to the detection and control of crime. Religion has felt the impact of the automobile in a number of ways, with the automobile often competing with the church for time and energies of the people. Moreover, the family has seen the automobile bring about new patterns of recreation, social control, and economic expenditure, not to mention sexual morality and adolescent discipline.

Finally, the concept of planned diffusion became an important one in recent years in the context of modernization, economic development, and aid to third-world countries. The Peace Corps program would be a good illustration of planned diffusion. In the area of marketing, in particular, a series of new models have been developed dealing with the spread of products, repeat purchase patterns, and the like (Robertson, 1971). Among demographers the diffusion of contraceptive technology in underdeveloped countries is receiving growing attention. Understanding diffusion is an important consideration in planned social change. It is a fruitful subject of investigation that barely has been sampled thus far.

ACCULTURATION

Acculturation refers to taking on material and nonmaterial attributes from another culture as a result of prolonged contact. Such contact can come about in several ways. It can be the result of war, conquest, military oc-

cupation, colonization, or it may be through missionaries or cultural exchanges. It may be produced by migration or the transportation of labor
such as through slavery or penal deportations. Voluntary labor movement
is another factor in creating contact, as is the case in Europe where "guest
workers" from less developed European countries move to France, Germany, and Switzerland. Trade, technical exchange, and the spread of ideas
and institutions represent other sources of contact. Contacts of shorter
duration have been brought about by travel and tourism in recent years.
Indirect forms of contact include mass communication and the transfer of
knowledge.

Diffusion is considered as only one aspect of acculturation. Even though
diffusion occurs in all cases of acculturation, since attributes and ideas have
to be transmitted before they can have an impact on recipient cultures, it
is usually considered as a component of the broader process of acculturation. Diffusion usually deals with one or a small number of attributes,
whereas acculturation provides the group with many possible new ways of
behaving, which might be quite different from those dictated by their own
cultures, traditional norms, and beliefs. In most cases, acculturation is also
more rapid and more observable than diffusion. Acculturation is produced
by contact, whereas contact may not be required in diffusion. Acculturation
brings about greater similarities between two cultures, whereas diffusion
usually refers to a lesser influence or impact.

In general, two cultures that are in contact rarely acculturate reciprocally and to the same degree. Rather, the politically subordinate or technologically inferior group adopts cultural attributes from the dominant
group. Acculturation, in a sense, is cultural borrowing in the context of
subordinate-superordinate relations (Bodley, 1982:14,43). Often status enhancement is considered an inducement to accept new ideas or elements.
Those groups that are considered "inferior" in society feel that by assuming
the characteristics of a "superior" group they will, in consequence, also
become superior and receive the same respect that is given to members of
that superior group. In situations where neither group is clearly "superior"
there may be a standoff in the adoption of attributes, and thus each group
tends to retain its identity (DeVos, 1976:4).

Acculturation may be voluntary or involuntary. The former occurs
when members of a group in contact with another group accept some of
their attributes, characteristics, norms, and values without force or pressure
for compliance by the other group. This situation happens when neither
group is superior to the other. Involuntary acculturation, on the other
hand, seems to be much more widespread. Let us now examine some of
its ramifications.

In the United States, most Indian tribes have made adjustments through
acculturation. A few have been assimilated and others have suffered an-
nihilation as a result of social and cultural contact with whites. It should

be noted, though, that the early contacts were the kind that led to diffusion; trappers, traders, and missionaries carried new traits to the Indians and borrowed in return such things as buckskin clothes, kennels, snowshoes, tobacco, corn, and maple syrup. Diffusion was stimulated but there was not yet acculturation. Acculturation began in earnest with the arrival of white settlers, soldiers, and administrators. The result was the disorganization of the ecological, economic, and political bases of Indian life. The whites continued to borrow ideas and attributes from Indians, but by virtue of the whites' dominant position, there was no reciprocal acculturation. Instead, the dictum seemed to have been: "Acculturate—or else!"

At times, acculturation can be both forced and planned. Consider the attempts of the British colonial office to "civilize" the backward native Africans. This attempt to civilize entailed the teaching of the English language and the transmission of rudimentary skills and technologies. Provisions for medium-level opportunities to encourage limited mobility were made; at the same time, however, colonizers continued to maintain strict boundaries between themselves and the "inferior" groups. Similarly, the Portuguese and Spanish conquerors of Latin America were successful in undermining the native Indian cultures and, with a few exceptions, in imposing their Iberian cultures on these people. Through violence, disease, overwork, and forced migration they succeeded in weakening the native social structures that might have preserved the traditional cultures. This is similar to what happened to slaves in the New World. Even though the measures are less dramatic, the current acculturation process taking place between the Soviet Union and the Eastern European countries is indicative also of planned and forced acculturation. In Eastern European countries the instruction of the Russian language is mandatory. In many cases the history of Russian takes precedence over their native histories. The study of political philosophy and Marxism is required both at the high school and university levels. The dominant Soviet group attempts also to "encourage" the acceptance of a series of other cultural attributes and traits as well.

Acculturation can also be seen as the interaction between a constant and a variable—that is, between an essentially stable receiving culture and an adapting immigrant group (Petersen, 1965:220). The acculturation of immigrants can be depicted on a continuum ranging from total assimilation to total nonassimilation, with most cases falling someplace in between. This continuum may be analyzed in terms of a tripartite typology devised by Ralph Linton (1936:271–287). He considered social roles in any culture under three categories: universals, specialties, and alternatives. *Universals* include attributes that are common to all members of a society. *Specialties* are shared by the members of certain socially recognized categories but not shared by the total population. *Alternatives* include roles shared by certain individuals that are not common to all members of the society or even to all members of any one of the socially recognized categories (Linton, 1936:272–273). Conformity is expected of immigrants only with respect to those ideas and behavior patterns to which all members of society must conform. In the United States, this includes the learning of the English language, self-support, and political alliance. Alternatives refer to the selective acceptance of attributes and the simultaneous retention of certain old country habits. Food preferences among the various immigrant groups in America are illustrative of this. Specialties pertain to the kind of work an individual does, which in turn is a factor in his or her social class position. Thus, total acculturation for immigrants is seen only in terms of Linton's "universals" category, whereas social roles in the "specialties" and "alternatives" categories retain a degree of uniqueness and flexibility.

The most famous case of acculturation at the level of society discussed in the literature is perhaps the transformation of Manus society as a consequence of the occupation of the island by American troops during World War II. The Manus community of the Admiralty Islands in the South Pacific was revisited by Margaret Mead after 25 years. The first time she studied the community, it constituted people with no contact with the outside world and no known writing. The problems of social interaction and reciprocal obligation were handled in terms of kinship. The natives wore G-strings and grass skirts and had a very primitive economic system. When she returned 25 years later, she was "greeted by a man in carefully ironed white clothes, wearing a tie and shoes, who explained that he was the 'counsel,' one of the elected officials of the community" (Mead, quoted by Spindler, 1984:35). A few days after her return, she was asked by another elected official to make up a list of rules for modern child care—feeding, discipline, sleeping, and so forth. "When she explained that her comments would be based on the latest thinking of the International Seminar on Mental Health and Infant Development, held at Chichester, England, in 1952, under the auspices of the United Nations, this man, who was born into what was then a primitive 'stone age' society, *understood what she was saying*" (Spindler, 1984:35).

When she left the island 25 years earlier, she left a primitive isolated nonliterate "stone age" society. When she returned, she found them moving rapidly into the mainstream of the modern world, with concerns that would allow them to accelerate this process even more. Why did it take place? During World War II more than a million Americans managed to reshape the island completely. The Manus natives worked for them and were treated as equals. The Americans furnished a kind of model for the Manus in addition to providing them with a vision of American technological and material culture. Using the "American model" the Manus rapidly threw away their own culture and modeled their life after that one. Contrary to traditional anthropological thinking, the change took place without disruptive effects on the society. This is accounted for by the fact that the change was desired by the entire society.

In sum, acculturation is a form of change that is conditioned by various degrees of convergence among cultures. Acculturation is not necessarily disruptive and painful. On the contrary, because it is more rapid than other forms of change, it may well be less upsetting than gradual change. At times, as Mead suggested, it is easier to embrace a new culture in its entirety—since it is a meaningful, integrated whole—than to try to splice two cultures together. Substituting clothes for grass skirts (to use Mead's own example) without introducing soap produces dirt and disease; without sewing machines, starch, and irons, it creates a society of ragamuffins; without closets, it produces huts that are cluttered with hanging clothes, and so on. As Mead (1961:374–377) points out, it is easier for a Samoan to become a New Yorker than to become a half-acculturated, or perhaps "deculturated" Samoan.

REVOLUTION

By definition, *revolution* is a fundamental, rapid, and violent change in political organization, power relationships, stratification, economic property control, and the predominant myth of a social order within a society (Goldstone, 1986:1–17; Neumann, 1971:122). Revolution is thus the most radical form of social change. Before we proceed further with the patterns of revolutionary change, it should be noted that not all such change can be equated with force or violence, nor does it always entail initiation by antiestablishment forces or radical alteration in social structure or political organization. For example, many of the revolutions in Latin America prior to World War II consisted of overthrowing Colonel A by General Y and his followers, but nothing after the overthrow changed in the basic structure of society. Similarly, Max Gluckman studied what he calls "rebellion cycles" in a number of precolonial African kingdoms. He found that periodic rebellions and replacement by one clan over another served to strengthen rather than weaken the established political and economic structures. Their social systems persisted for generations with minor modifications until truly radical changes were introduced by Western colonial powers (Gluckman, in Gerlach & Hine, 1973:19).

Similarly, there have been what may be designated as "revolutionary" changes in science. "A change in the thought-system, or world view, is revolutionary in the extreme and has wide ramifications in technological, economic, political, and religious spheres of life" (Gerlach & Hine, 1973:20). For example, when Nicholas Copernicus (1473–1543), the Polish astronomer, described the sun as the center of a great system with the earth revolving around it, revolutionary changes in astronomy resulted. Johann Gutenberg (1397–1468) invented movable printing type in 1437, thus revolutionizing the technique of disseminating knowledge. The names of Isaac Newton or Albert Einstein do not require commentaries in terms of their revolutionary contributions to science. In medicine, we need only consider some examples such as Louis Pasteur (1822–1895); Conrad Wilhelm Roentgen, who discovered X-rays (1845–1923); or Ignaz Philipp Semmelweis (1818–1865), a Hungarian physician who through the use of antiseptic methods in obstetrics significantly reduced deaths from puerperal fever. These are just a few illustrations to show that revolutionary and radical forms of social change need not always be violent or involve the basic structures in society. For the remainder of the discussion, the term "revolution" will be used in the context of the original definition.

The patterns of revolution, according to Chalmers Johnson (1964), can be analyzed in terms of (1) the targets selected for attack—government personnel, political regime, the community as a social unit; (2) the nature of the carriers of the revolution—mass or an elite; and (3) its goals and ideologies—reformist, nostalgic, nation-forming, elitist, or nationalist. On the basis of these, he identified six patterns.

1. *The Jacquerie.* A spontaneous mass peasant rising, generally carried out in the name of the traditional authorities, church, and king, and with the limited objectives of purging local or national elites. Examples would include the peasant revolt of 1381, Ket's Rebellion of 1549, and the Pugachev Rebellion in Russia from 1773–1775.

2. *The Millenarian Rebellion.* Similar to the first one but with the extra feature of a utopian dream fostered by a living messiah. This pattern is rather widespread and found in all parts of the world. Illustrations of this would include the Florentine Revolution led by Savonarola in 1494, the Anabaptist Rebellion in Munster, the Sioux Ghost-Dance Rebellion, the Tai P'ing Rebellion, and the Mau Mau Rebellion. In more recent times, Hitler offered overwhelming proof of the significance of a living messiah and a charismatic leader.

3. *The Anarchistic Rebellion.* A nostalgic reaction to progressive change involving a romantic idealization of the previous order. Illustrations of this would include the Vendee, the Boxer Revolt, and the Pilgrimage of Grace.

4. *The Jacobin Communist Revolution.* A rather rare phenomenon, which has been defined as "a sweeping fundamental change in political organization, social structure, economic property control, and the predominate myth of a social order, thus indicating a major break in the continuity of development" (Neumann, quoted by Johnson, 1964:2). This pattern of revolution can occur only in a highly centralized state with good communications and a large capital city, and its target is the government or the regime. Revolutions of this nature serve to increase national consciousness and to create a more rational and stronger state and social structure. Such revolutionary patterns occurred in France, Turkey, Russia and China.

5. *The Conspiratorial Coup d'Etat.* The planned work of a small elite fired by an oligarchic sectarian ideology. It is considered a revolutionary pattern only if it in fact anticipates a social movement and inaugurates social change. Examples include the Nasser revolution in Egypt or the Castro revolution in Cuba. Johnson contends that this pattern of revolution must be distinguished from palace revolts, banditry, assassination, strike, dynastic succession-conflict, and other forms of violence, none of which would entail social change.

6. *The Militarized Mass Insurrection.* A deliberately planned mass revolutionary war guided by a dedicated elite. The outcome of guerrilla warfare is determined by political attitudes, not by military strategy or material, and the rebels are wholly dependent on broad popular support. In the examples found in Yugoslavia, Algeria, Vietnam, and China, the ideology that attracted mass following has been a combination of xenophobic nationalism and Marxism, with a somewhat heavier emphasis on the former.

Like any categorization of historical processes, Johnson's typology of patterns of revolution is concerned with ideal types. In reality, individual revolutions may, at times, display characteristics of several different patterns conditioned by the targets, carriers, and ideologies of the revolution. A difficulty with Johnson's schema is his distinction between rebellion and revolution. The former tends to concentrate on individuals, rather than institutions, with a retrospective outlook, whereas the latter seeks to change institutions and social structures and is innovative. To simplify the distinction between rebellion and revolution, Smith (1973:113) proposed a four-fold typology:

1. *Simple rebellion*, such as the *Jacquerie*, which is nonideological and attempts changes only in the personnel.
2. *Ideological rebellion*, such as anarchism, which attempts to restore the old order as well as change the present elite.
3. *Simple revolution*, such as the early American Revolution, where the ideology attempts alterations in some values, such as governmental or economic, while leaving others intact.
4. *Total revolution*, such as in France in 1789, Russia in 1917, or China in 1949, which attempts to restructure the entire society.

For each revolutionary pattern, it is possible also to establish quantitative changes in several domains. Basically, all revolutionary patterns deal with the class, status, and power systems. Mark N. Hagopian (1974) suggests, as shown in Table 5.1, that the intensity of a revolution pattern on the class, status, and power systems can be ascertained as ranging from negligible to moderate and radical changes to total abolition. Thus, a revolution could include only a moderate change in one aspect of the strati-

TABLE 5.1   A Scale for Measuring the Intensity of Revolution

	NEGLIGIBLE CHANGE	MODERATE CHANGE	RADICAL CHANGE	TOTAL ABOLITION
Class system				
Status system				
Power system				

Source: Mark N. Hagopian, *The Phenomenon of Revolution.* New York: Dodd, Mead, 1974, p. 100.

Negligible change = 0   Radical change = 2
Moderate change = 1   Total abolition = 3

fication system (Score 1) to a revolution that would succeed in abolishing all three aspects (Score 9). For illustrative purposes, the English Revolution may be classified toward the lower end of the scale and the Russian and Chinese revolutions toward the upper end.

Although revolution is seen as affecting all three components of the stratification system (class, status, and power), the transfer of power from one social group to another is usually considered the most crucial. Various significant factors have been considered to precede such transfer of power on a wide scale, but there seems to be a substantial disagreement in the literature about which of these are of paramount importance. Marx, Crane Brinton, and others see economic fluctuations and the increasing nonlegitimacy of the existing government as necessary preconditions for revolution. Even among these theorists, however, there is some disagreement. The Marxists argue that economic conflict between classes plays the primary causal role in revolution. Brinton (1959) advocates the argument of "relative deprivation" or rising expectations. Others argue that economic decline and status crises bring about revolution, and still other observers suggest that military pressures, large-scale corruption, and conflict among the elites are the primary sources of major social upheavals (Close & Bridge, 1985; Goldstone, 1986).

In sum, revolutions are best studied in retrospect. Although the objectives of revolutions are generally clearly stated and couched in emotional and ideological terms, it is very difficult to predict their outcomes accurately. There will always be a discrepancy between ideals and reality. In Mao Zedong's words, "Anything can grow out of the barrel of a gun." As Jack A. Goldstone (1986:207) notes, revolutions have many accomplishments. They include redistribution of land, and elimination of oppressive systems of land tenure and of hereditary privileges of traditional aristocracy. Revolutions have also brought about increases in literacy, improvements in education and medical care, greater equality and economic opportunities, and independence to hundreds of millions of people. But revolutions generally did not deliver their main promises: greater freedom, equality for all, and significantly improved material well-being. In fact, revolutions in many countries resulted in more powerful and authoritarian regimes than the ones they replaced, such as Iran in the 1980s. And let us remember the high price of wars and severe economic dislocations that are often part of revolutionary changes. Some examples from this century include: Internal strife and efforts to collectivize agriculture in Russia and China resulted in the deaths of tens of millions of people; the revolution in Nicaragua caused over 50,000 deaths in a population of 2.5 million; and the bodies are still being counted in the Iran-Iraq war, which followed Iran's revolution.

MODERNIZATION

Modernization is the process by which agrarian societies are transformed into industrial societies. This transition entails the development of advanced industrial technology and the political, cultural, and social arrangements appropriate to sustaining, directing, and utilizing that technology. The aim of modernization is to approximate the characteristics of economically developed and relatively stable nations (Chirot, 1985; Germani, 1981:10–14; Moore, 1974:94). This transition seldom, if ever, takes place smoothly or evenly. Still, it affects every social institution, touches every community, and is felt in all walks of life. Modernization is a comprehensive term that describes many simultaneous changes at several levels. Industrialization, urbanization, and bureaucratization are closely related to modernization. For the purpose of analysis, however, these interrelated change patterns will be discussed separately.

Modernization in a sense is a form of imitation, emulation, and transplantation of patterns, products, and technologies from Western countries to less developed countries. Thus, a prerequisite of modernization is communication and contact among the various cultures and societies. It is usually the leaders of developing countries who set the plans and policies for changing a particular society in motion in the direction of contemporary societies. Industrialization is not always a crucial factor in modernization. For example, African and Asian nations usually start the process of modernization with nation building and the development of modern political systems. The object is the transformation of their social structure and the dissemination of new norms and values through education. The development of industry usually follows later.

By contrast, in Europe in the eighteenth and nineteenth centuries, industrialization gave birth to modernization (Chodak, 1973:259; Kerr, 1983). For some theorists, modernization is seen in terms of humans' increased knowledge and mastery of the environment. Cyril E. Black (1967) suggests that modern societies are characterized by the growth of new knowledge, and this presumes the existence of an individual with an increasing capacity to understand the secrets of nature and to apply this new knowledge to human affairs. Robert N. Bellah (1965) regards modernization as the ability of "learning to learn" and the increased capacity of a social system to process information in a society and to respond to it appropriately. From a different perspective, Marion Levy, Jr. (1966:35) considers modernization as gradable because it appears in different forms. "A society will be considered more or less modernized to the extent that its members use inanimate sources of power and/or use tools to multiply the effects of their efforts. Neither of these elements is either totally absent from or exclusively present in any society." Even though a continuum of modernization may not be established, Levy suggests that one can safely distinguish between relatively modernized countries, such as the United States and England, and relatively nonmodernized countries, such as India and some of the Latin American countries.

In *The Politics of Modernization*, David E. Apter (1965:67) considers modernization as a particular case of development. In his words:

> Modernization implies three conditions—a social system that can constantly innovate without falling apart (and that includes among its essential beliefs the acceptability of change); differentiated, flexible social structures; and a social framework to provide the skills and knowledge necessary for living in a technologically advanced world. Industrialization, a special aspect of modernization, may be defined as the period in a society in which the strategic functional roles are related to manufacturing. It is possible to attempt the modernization of a given country without much industry, but it is not possible to industrialize without modernization.

Based on historical phenomena and modernization processes in developing countries, it is possible, according to Szymon Chodak (1973:261), to generalize that modernization occurred in one of three ways: (1) as a result of *industrialization* of a country, which in turn generates changes in attitudes and behavior, producing a new value orientation, which sets the motivation to generate further industrialization; (2) *spontaneously*, as a result of contact between the more developed and less developed societies and cultures; and (3) as a consequence of purposeful *planned* governmental activity to modernize the economy. On the basis of these generalizations, Chodak (1973:263–271) identified three patterns of modernization that occurred in sub-Saharan Africa: industrial, acculturative, and induced.

1. *Industrial Modernization.* The process of industrialization creates new material conditions and needs, contributes to the formation of new attitudes and value orientations, and increases the division of labor. It increases interdependence in society and new roles, organizations, and systems of activity become more differentiated. Chodak states that "Modernization of

this type arises out of the necessity to adapt the social organization to the requirements of industry" (1973:263).

2. *Acculturative Modernization*. This process is based on the convergence of two different cultures and is manifested through the acceptance of behavior patterns, information about life-styles, and educational practices of a different culture. The selective transplantation of cultural elements does not lead to the replacement of traditional institutions but "very often it leads to its impoverishment, deformation and, in some instances, to all kinds of cultural and social abnormalities" (1973:263). Chodak suggests that during the process of colonialization of Africa, acculturative modernization was typical.

3. *Induced Modernization*. The third pattern of modernization entails modeling a country's organizations, institutions, and value orientations after those of Western countries. "Induced modernization consists of introducing modern forms of government and administration, education, universities, research institutes, universal suffrage, and communications media into an industrially underdeveloped country, without having previously industrialized the country. Induced modernization arises primarily out of the desire to catch up with the more developed societies, especially in the spheres of political organization and education, and partly because of the desire to have easy accessibility to the products of modern technical progress" (1973:267). In modern African countries, in a sense, induced modernization can be equated with nation building through the processes of educational, administrative, and governmental reforms. In all cases of induced modernization, however, it should be noted that the government, the ruling political party, and the elite are the principal organizers and implementers (Chirot, 1985).

Each of these forms of modernization develops through a differentiation of roles, the establishment of specialized institutions, and the generation of specific kinds of interdependencies. For example, the key roles in industrial modernization are those of entrepreneur, worker, inventor, and innovator; in acculturative modernization, the roles of the tradesman, migrant, student, and liberated members of the tribal society; in induced modernization, the roles of politician, intellectual, and the bureaucrat (Chodak, 1973:269–270).

As modernization gains momentum, new characteristics accompany it. They include the "development of a high extent of differentiation; the development of free resources which are not committed to any fixed, ascriptive (kinship, territorial, etc.) groups; the development of specialized and diversified types of social organization; the development of wide nontraditional, 'national', or even supernational group identification; and the concomitant development, in all major institutional spheres of specialized roles and of special wider regulative and allocative mechanisms and organizations, such as market mechanisms in economic life, voting and party activities in politics, and diverse bureaucratic organizations and mechanisms in most institutional spheres" (Eisenstadt, 1973:23).

These have developed concomitantly with basic changes in all major institutions. In the economic sphere these developments were characterized by a greater specialization of economic activities and the growth of scope and complexity of the principal markets—markets for goods, labor, and money. In social organization it resulted in the growth of the population in urban areas in which the more specialized types of economic, professional, and civic activities and enterprises became concentrated and expanded. This gave rise to a change from traditional ascriptive status to the development of a more open form of stratification, with greater opportunities for upward social mobility through economic, occupational, and educational channels (Germani, 1981:173–195).

In the political sphere, modernization is characterized by a development of a more differentiated political structure; by a growing extension of the scope of central legal, administrative, and political activities; by the continuous spread of potential political power to wider groups in society; and by the weakening of traditional elites.

In the cultural sphere, modernization is characterized by a greater differentiation between principal aspects of major cultural and value systems such as religion, philosophy, ideology; by an increased secularization and, concomitantly, the weakening of traditional, cultural elites; by an increase in literacy and secular education; and by the rise of a new secular intelligentsia.

These developments have been closely related to an extension in communication media with a growing permeation into the various local groups, and the resulting growing awareness among the various strata of the population created greater participation in social life and increased consumption of "culture" (Eisenstadt, 1973:23–25).

These institutional changes are accompanied by marked transformations in attitudes and personality, which have been characterized as "modern" in the literature. "The modern man is not just a construct in the mind of sociological theorists. He exists and he can be identified. . . ." (Inkeles & Smith, 1974:290). According to Alex Inkeles and David H. Smith (1974:290), the modern individual's character may be summed up under four major headings:

1. He or she is an informed participant citizen,
2. Has a marked sense of personal efficacy,

3. Is highly independent and autonomous of his or her relations to traditional sources of influence,
4. Is ready for new experiences and ideas; that is, the individual is relatively open-minded and cognitively flexible.

As an informed participating citizen, the individual identifies with newer, larger aspects of regions and state, partakes in public affairs, joins local and national organizations, votes, and keeps informed through the mass media about major events. A sense of efficacy is seen in the conviction that the individual can take actions that affect his or her life and that of the community. One knows that an individual can improve one's conditions in life and, as a result, rejects passivity, resignation, and fatalism. The advice of public officials and trade-union leaders concerning public issues is followed rather than that of the priests or village elders. One's openness to new experience is reflected in the exploration of formerly sacred objects and the individual's willingness to meet strangers and to allow women to take advantage of opportunities outside of the home.

In addition, as evidenced by the writings of Max Weber, Hagen, and McClelland in Chapter 2, the modern individual is also efficient, diligent, orderly, punctual, and frugal. One is rational in decisions on action, and is prepared for change and alert to opportunities as they arise in a changing world. One finds that scrupulous honesty pays in the long run and is a condition for raising efficiency in all social and economic relations (Myrdal, 1968:61). One is also energetic and cooperative; one also accepts responsibility for the welfare of both the community and the nation and is willing to take the long view and forego short-term profiteering. One favors the subordination of speculation to investment and of commerce and finance to production. In a sense, *"the hallmark of modernity is an existential conviction that man can select and can achieve his own future*; that he has indeed many futures, that all he must do—to begin with—is to write his own scenario of the future as he himself dreams it and then to live his drama" (Meadows, 1971:21).

In sum, modernization has no end product. To embark on the modernization process is to accept the fact of continual and prolonged change. Its uniqueness lies in the fact that it is based on the assumptions of the possibility of the active creation by humans of a new social and political order, an order based on premises of universalism and equality, and the spread of these assumptions is combined with the development of far-reaching structural and organizational changes, especially in the economic and political fields (Eisenstadt, 1973:209). In the next section, industrialization, which is an important component of modernization, will be examined.

INDUSTRIALIZATION

Industrialization is the process by which technology based on inanimate sources of energy is substituted for manual labor as the basis of production of goods (Lenski & Lenski, 1987:233–245.). The most commonly used index of industrialization is the proportion of the nation's labor force engaged in agriculture. As the proportion declines, a nation can be considered as becoming more industrial. Clark Kerr (1983:5), for example, considers industrialized nations as those with 25 percent or less of the labor force engaged in agriculture. It should be noted, however, that this is an *index* and not a *measure* of industrialization. The reduction in the agricultural labor force can be seen more appropriately as a consequence of technological, economic, and organizational changes accompanying industrialization. As indicated in the preceding section, the concept of modernization is a more comprehensive term that subsumes industrialization and other concepts such as economic growth or development and the political, social, religious, educational, and other institutional changes that accompany industrialization.

Great Britain is considered the first and the classic case of industrialization (Kerr, Dunlop, Harbison, & Myers, 1964:14). By 1830 it had seen the development of workers who were acclimatized to factory conditions and were able to move from place to place, from employment to employment, as required. Prior to World War I, industrialization had spread widely from England to the Western world and to Japan. It spread largely by diffusion rather than by independent social inventions. Nowadays, much of the interest in industrialization is focused on the changes taking place in economically underdeveloped areas.

There are many descriptions in the literature of the various patterns of industrialization (See, for example, Kerr, 1983; Lenski & Lenski, 1987). Perhaps the most widely known is W.W. Rostow's study of the stages of economic development, which was discussed in Chapter 3. The most commonly used distinctions entail the differences among preindustrial, early industrial, and mature industrial societies, with occasionally the term "postindustrial" added to account for highly advanced societies such as the United States or certain Western European countries. They all have in common very developed international commodity, capital, and labor markets; a disciplined industrial labor force; a highly developed technology; and sophisticated professional, technical, and managerial personnel.

Industrialization is accompanied by a growing degree of complexity in the division of labor and the concomitant distribution of the labor force among occupations. At the most general level, industrialization involves a shift from labor force concentration in agricultural employment to manufacturing employment and eventually to employment in service industries. Wilbert Moore (1969) describes some of the factors that result in increased division of labor. One of these considerations is the growth in size of economic organizations, which encourages the efficiencies that result from occupational specialization. Another is technological change, which brings about new occupational specialties, such as computer programmer, and can also result in the further subdivision of skills as is the case of specialized machine operators who replaced the skilled dressmaker. A third consideration is the development of new products and services, resulting in occupations that previously did not exist. The changes in the size and complexity of the labor force engaged in manufacturing and service are usually accompanied by a growth of unions and management power and a growth of class consciousness among workers. The division of labor is also related to occupational and geographic mobility as well as to higher levels of educational attainment that is more closely related to industrial functions.

Change in population patterns (birth, death, marriages, migration) is also closely linked with industrialization. The sequence of events, often referred to as the "demographic transition," first occurred and proceeded to the greatest degree during the industrialization of Europe. The essence of the demographic transition is a move from a situation where both birth and death rates are high to a situation where both of these are low. Thus, many of the first European countries to industrialize (for example, England and France) have been characterized by low population growth for a number of years, where replacement through fertility equals population losses through deaths. Contemporary developing societies, however, present a different picture. Demographic changes are taking a very different—and highly problematic—form. This is due to the fact that reduction in death rates has been brought about relatively rapidly, whereas a corresponding drop in birthrates lags far behind (Kammeyer & Ginn, 1986).

Rapid reductions in death rates can be achieved through such relatively simple procedures as using insecticides to control mosquitoes, flies, and other disease-transmitting insects. For example, dramatic reductions in world deaths from malaria have been achieved in this fashion. Widespread immunization programs and the greater availability of antibiotic drugs also contributed to the lowering of mortality rates. Birth control, however, is a different matter. In many societies, high fertility is a source of social prestige. In the industrializing context, traditional attitudes may remain a strong positive sanction for bearing children, possibly in keeping with religious values, possibly for practical considerations, such as the economic value of children, or for other complex interrelated reasons. Such societies are generally characterized by a high fertility rate and low or rapidly falling mortality rates, resulting in a rapid population growth and subsequent changes in the economically dependent or nonproductive segments in the population, such as the very young or the old.

Industrialization is also accompanied by changes in family form. Traditional societies are typically characterized by an extended family system. But the more industrialized a society becomes, the more likely it is to move toward the nuclear family (husband, wife, and their children) (Goode, 1963; Germani, 1981:87–90). The nuclear family form presents numerous advantages from the perspective of geographical mobility and increased urbanization, which are associated with industrialization. Traditional patterns in mate selection and parent-child relationships have been replaced by contemporary forms; and, as the family ceases to be an economically productive unit, the social position of women has changed. There is also some evidence to indicate that the rate of divorce and other indicators of family breakdown increase with industrialization. However, it would be erroneous to talk about "family disorganization" as a concomitant of industrialization. Instead, at least in the United States, the modern family has undergone major changes—changes associated with urbanization and industrialization; however, it would be inaccurate to regard these as signs of deterioration. Parsons (1955) argues that the family has become a more specialized structure; although it has lost some of its functions, such as producing economic goods and services and educating the children, it has also become a more exclusive guardian of other functions, such as socializing the very young and providing a setting for emotional tension management for adults. Furthermore, the roles of the husband-father and wife-mother have become more specialized relative to one another. Parsons contends that these new features of the family signify the opposite of disintegration and concludes that the nuclear family is more effective than its predecessor in socializing children for adult roles in industrial society.

Industrialization is related to the increased need for literacy, for education is a determining factor in labor force participation and for social mobility. There is a greater reliance on mass communication channels both as a source of information and as a means for breaking down the previous forms of isolation. It also results in the development of a popular culture, replacing some of the traditional forms of recreation. There is also a sharp division between "work" and "leisure," a distinction that did not exist in agrarian or tribal societies. Time becomes a scarce commodity (Szalai, 1972). There is an increased participation in voluntary associations, an increase in secular attitudes, and the rise of clearly differentiated political and administrative structures.

In sum, industrialization is an important pattern of change. In analyzing it, we often find it difficult to determine where best to "draw the line." Any examination of this pattern of change can be almost indefinitely extended in continuing to discover ways in which its presence makes itself known. In the next section a close associate of industrialization, urbanization, will be considered.

URBANIZATION

The term *urbanization* refers to the process by which an increasing proportion of a country's population comes to live in cities, with a concomitant concentration of economic activity, administrative and political organization, and communication networks in these urban areas (Germani, 1981:203, Iverson, 1984). At times, the term *population implosion* is used to describe this increased concentration of world's peoples in urban or metropolitan areas (Hauser, 1973:430). Urbanization also refers to *how* people live, their patterns of behavior and social relationships. These two aspects—*where* people live and *how* they live—are interrelated. Modernization, industrialization, and urbanization often occur in combination. It is clear, however, that the city and the factory systems are separable. Large urban areas existed in antiquity, and many factories are located in otherwise rural areas (Sjoberg, 1960). The world's earliest cities appeared some 5,000 to 6,000 years ago in Sumer, the southern part of Mesopotamia, and various types of ceremonial cities such as Mecca existed long before the advent of modernization and industrialization (Pfeiffer, 1977:149–170). Even today, urbanization is taking place in less developed societies without simultaneous industrialization (Brown, 1987:38–56; Hardoy, 1975:xi). For example, in Latin America, urbanization has not been accompanied by simultaneous industrialization or by better distribution of opportunity, income, and consumption (Germani, 1981:231–261; Linn, 1983). Consequently, most Latin American countries are not in a position to provide the employment opportunities, or even the basic urban infrastructure such as housing, sewer and utility services, medical care, and education necessary to maintain an extremely large urban population.

In 1986 the world's population was almost 5 billion, and 43 percent lived in urban areas (Population Reference Bureau, 1986). "Urban place" is defined somewhat differently from one country to another, with the bottom limit usually in the range of 2,500 to 5,000 people. Still, the fraction in urban places would not change by more than 5 percent even if the bottom limit were 10,000 (Davis, 1972:31). Urbanization as a process clearly has a beginning and an end. For example, three-quarters of the United States' population of 250 million is now urban, and the maximum level of urbanization is probably around 90 percent. Even after a nation achieves a high level of urbanization, its cities and metropolitan areas can continue to grow. This is the situation in North America and Western Europe. Although there is a limit to the percentage of urbanization possible, there is not yet agreement on the practical limit concerning the size of metropolitan areas.

Historically, it seems that the urbanization of *Homo sapiens* has occurred almost overnight. As recently as 1850 no country in the world was as urbanized (43 percent) as the world as a whole is now. Only about 2 percent of the world's population lived in cities of more than 100,000 inhabitants. The most rapid urbanization of both England and the United States occurred in the nineteenth century, and the twentieth century has witnessed an acceleration of this process in many other countries. (Arango, 1970:9). It is possible to depict both the level and rates of urbanization on a continuum. At the lower end of an urbanization level are the countries that have less than 10 percent of their population located in cities, countries such as Yemen, Saudi Arabia, Afghanistan, Chad, and Uganda. On the other end of the continuum there are countries such as Belgium, Australia, and Uruguay with more than 80 percent of the population in urban areas. In terms of the rate of urbanization, the highest rates are found in Japan, Uruguay, and Yugoslavia, whereas the lowest rates are in Israel, the United Kingdom, and Ceylon (Gist & Fava, 1974:108–112).

Urbanization has been highly significant in both modernization and industrialization, and the three, different as they are, contain a number of parallel features, many of which have already been discussed under the headings of modernization and industrialization. For the present purposes, the emphasis will be on how people live in urban areas and the question is this: Is there something inherent in the settlement patterns of cities and the various areas that produces a distinctive "urban way of life"?

Some 50 years ago, Louis Wirth (1938:9) answered affirmatively. He started by assuming that "the larger, the more densely populated, and the more heterogeneous a community, the more accentuated the characteristics associated with urbanism will be." For him, a city is a permanent settlement, characterized by large size, density, and heterogeneity leading to correspondingly more transitory, anonymous, formalized, and specialized interrelationships—that is, to a more urbanized way of life. He reasoned that the greater the number of people interacting, the greater the potential for differentiation, bringing about lesser dependence on particular persons, less intimate relations, more freedom from the personal and emotional control of intimate groups, and no individual alliance to a single group. Density results in further differentiation and specialization, a separation of residence from the workplace, and the functional specialization of areas in the city. The city thus becomes "a mosaic of social worlds." Because of a high degree of heterogeneity, no common set of values exists in the city, and money tends to become the measure of all things. Formal controls replace informal controls, and it becomes necessary to adhere to predictable routines.

As a consequence of these factors, urban dwellers develop characteristic personality attributes and attitudes. Because of the many life-styles and kinds of people, they develop a relativistic perspective. They become secularized and free of intimate ties; they lack a strong sense of integration and participation. Thus, the city is characterized by anomie. In the middle of the crowd, individuals feel lonely, sense friction and irritation, personal frustration, and nervous tension. Because of the mobility and diversity in the city, they accept instability and insecurity in the world at large as a norm because of their segmental roles and alliances. Their personal integrity is constantly threatened, and they are vulnerable to manipulation by the mass media. For these reasons Wirth suggested that the incidence of personal disorganization, mental breakdown, suicide, delinquency, crime, corruption, and disorder tend to be higher in cities than in rural communities.

Obviously, other factors have an impact on social patterns in urban areas in addition to heterogeneity, density, and large size (Rosen, 1986:68–73). However, there is not yet enough evidence to prove or disprove that number, density, and heterogeneity have the social consequences Wirth observed. In fact, social isolation and insularity similar to what has been described above has been found within the cultural and ethnic enclaves of contemporary American cities. Herbert Gans (1962) found that the Italians of Boston's West End formed a tight and homogeneous folk group having minimal contact with the remainder of the metropolitan area. In this traditionally based subculture, primary groups still retain dominant social position. In spite of their cosmopolitan residence, people in this area of the city remain urban villagers. A similar pattern of cultural isolation is portrayed in Elliot Liebow's (1967) study of black street-corner men in Washington, D.C.

Robert Redfield (1941) argues that all occasions of urbanization repeat a particular series of events—that there is a unilinear continuum from a folk to an urban form of organization. He describes folk societies as small, isolated, and homogeneous, with no division of labor except according to sex and age roles. Face-to-face communications prevail and these societies are marked by a high degree of solidarity. Religion is important, and social control is exercised through the sacred. Cultural patterns are based upon sentiment and tradition; there is no writing, no complex technology; status is ascribed at birth; and members of the society follow folkways uncritically and spontaneously. The family is the central social group. Redfield maintains that the transformation of an isolated folk community into an urban society occurs through a transmission of influences from the latter, resulting in cultural heterogeneity, disorganization, secularization, and individuation in the former. Redfield's approach is evolutionary, and for him the transformation of the world is accomplished by the spread of urbanization into more and more backward areas.

Both Redfield and Wirth argue that urbanization initiated a long-term historical process of detaching individuals from the comprehensive and familiar shared network of interrelations embedded in rural folk communities and that urban society is marked by a greater degree of functional interdependence. The nature of these changes and new conditions suggest that urbanization and its associated social changes probably increased the problems of social instability, raised conditions of class interest and conflict, and began to lay the foundations for the appearance of new and competing ideologies.

Currently urbanization is more highly visible in the underdeveloped nations. In fact, many of these nations have a quite large proportion of the world's urban population, although only a small percentage of the societies are predominantly urban. It should be noted that the recent pattern of urbanization in underdeveloped nations contrasts with the earlier experience of Western Europe. The cities of the underdeveloped nations have grown by the transfer of underemployed to the cities, which have offered little more than the countryside in the way of economic opportunities. The European experience was more a phenomenon of urban growth reflecting a general pattern of industrialization, with the cities characterized by expanding economic opportunities (De Vries, 1984).

The rapid rate of urbanization in developing countries gave rise to the concept of "overurbanization" (Graves & Sexton, 1984). It implies the belief that a particular developing country has too high a proportion of its population residing in cities where high densities are considered detrimental to health and general well-being. More important, overurbanization is often indicative of the fact that the urban population of a nation is too large in relation to the extent of its economic development. Egypt, for example, is far more urbanized than its degree of economic development would warrant. It is more urbanized than France and Sweden, both industrial nations (Davis & Golden, 1954). Overurbanization is usually the result of migration from rural areas at a rate higher than the expansion of employment opportunities in the city. This migration is prompted by high rural densities and lack of economic opportunities for peasants. Life seems difficult in the city, and for many of the migrants it is not better than the countryside; at least in the city, however, there is always hope and the possibility of something better. All over the world, peasants are voting with their feet in favor of city life. It may be argued that insofar as urbanization is associated with the development of a modernized mode of life and general economic progress, the problem in much of the developing world is not overurbanization, but possibly underurbanization.

As migrants flock to urban areas in developing countries, the diversity and heterogeneity of urban areas further increase. Ways of life in the city differ enormously in the various areas. Traditional life-styles exist side by side with Western ways, and they often mingle. In Asian countries, at times, there is a clash between occidental technology and oriental mentality. New arrivals often identify more closely with their native villages or with such sociocultural groupings as caste, tribe, race, or religion than with the city and what the city can offer. They have the bare necessities for survival and often not even those. Their culture is primarily a culture of poverty rather than a distinctively urban way of life. This phenomenon is referred to by Joel Halpern (1967:34–35) as the "peasantization of the cities." For example, in Yugoslavian cities rural migrants construct new houses identical to those they left behind, with a garden, a chicken coop, and (despite city ordinances) a pig or two. For at least a couple of generations they retain ties to their villages. If they live in modern apartment buildings, they create maintenance problems, being unfamiliar with plumbing and central heating, and keep domestic animals inside. In most cases the assimilation of migrants into the urban culture and way of life is a long and tedious process.

Kingsley Davis argues that the recent trend in world urbanization "cannot have existed very long in the past and certainly will not endure long in the future." It began somewhat slowly "in the 16th and 17th centuries, with the entire world probably between one and two percent urban. . . The pace picked up some in the 18th century, but really got under way rapidly in the 19th, continuing and perhaps accelerating a bit around the middle of the 20th century. Within another century—certainly by the year 2100—the entire process of world urbanization should be finished" (Davis, 1972:48, 52–53). Chances are that the next change pattern, bureaucratization, which will be examined in the next section, will be here longer than urbanization.

BUREAUCRATIZATION

For some people, the word "bureaucracy" carries strong negative connotations. It conjures up images of officiousness, red tape, and the endless filling out of forms—such as one or more of the 4,987 different kinds used by the federal government (*Time*, 1978). For sociologists, the term "bureaucracy" simply means a hierarchical social structure for administering large-scale organizations rationally, efficiently, effectively, and impersonally. The topic of this section, bureaucratization, refers to changes within an organization, public or private, toward greater rationality in decision making, improved operating efficiency, and more effective attainment of common goals (Lorsch, 1987). As the size and complexity of an organization increases, there is a greater need for coordination if efficiency and effectiveness are to be maintained or improved. Organizational efficiency can be ideally maximized when there is a hierarchical line of authority, with each role in the chain having clearly defined and stated duties and responsibilities; when all decisions are made on the basis of technical knowledge, not personal considerations; when members are judged solely on the basis of technical knowledge, and discipline is impartially enforced; and when the members are recruited on the basis of their abilities and there is a system of assured tenure and promotion based on merit (Weber, 1947:329–341).

In a truly fascinating book, *The Bureaucratization of the World,* Henry Jacoby (1973:9) cites Alfred Weber, who wrote that "the history of all great civilizations begins with the formation of a bureaucracy which supports and shapes men's whole existence." In ancient Egypt and Babylonia it was the priestly, hierarchically organized class of scribes who created and guarded the magic and sacred character of life. "This class, founded on the economic productivity of the canal system, was probably the most totalitarian bureaucracy ever to have existed in history" (Jacoby, 1973:9–10). The early civilizations of China and India also exhibited similar strong bureaucratic tendencies, and the Inca Empire used a bureaucratic system to administer the construction of agricultural terracing and established a rather efficient communication network that was dependent on suspension bridges. When the Spaniards invaded Peru, they discovered a well-organized system of statistical information using differently colored twines to indicate objects and knots in the twines to represent numbers. Record keeping was also present in ancient Egypt and taxation was determined by record offices with centralized information about citizens and their living conditions. Periodically, a census was taken by the government and "all of Egypt was inventoried" (Jacoby, 1973:10). All of this obviously required an experienced administrative bureaucracy whose structure was subjected to various changes.

As early as the thirteenth century in France, a number of functions came under the jurisdiction of the state and gave rise to a class of people whose position in society was determined by office rather than by ascribed status. By the end of the sixteenth century, they became known as the Fourth Estate. The bureaucracy became a separate class, recognizable by special long gowns (Jacoby, 1973:19). At that time, bureaucracy was associated with absolute monarchy. "It is bureaucracy which represents absolute authority, the monarch being the symbol at its head. . . . When powerful political leaders occupy the throne of an absolute monarchy they themselves are the bureaucratic heads" (Frolich, quoted by Jacoby, 1973:25). By that time, the state bureaucracy never doubted that all economic activities were controllable. In 1577, industry and commerce became regulated by a royal decree in France. New industries were created and the quality and quantity of goods produced were controlled. Wage and price controls were introduced and severe sanctions were imposed to maintain them. A new department was created to inspect and supervise these activities.

It is evident from the above historical sketch that the origin of the state and the development of the bureaucracy are closely intertwined. While examining American democracy in 1832, Alexis de Tocqueville also looked into the origin of the bureaucratic state. He concluded that the disappearance of traditional institutions and the development of an economy under which individuals concentrated exclusively on their own affairs led to greater state control of economic and social functions. General apathy toward public affairs "must almost compulsorily concentrate the direction of all men and the management of all things in the hands of the administration" (Tocqueville, quoted by Jacoby, 1973:53). Marx shared Tocqueville's observation that although the forms of government changed, administrations continued uninterruptedly to accumulate more functions and responsibilities.

Not everyone looked upon the growth of bureaucratization favorably. The Revolution of 1917 in Russia brought the entire administrative machine to a standstill and gave rise to an optimistic idea that a new way of organizing society is possible without the hated bureaucracy. Lenin predicted that the principle of sound government would be carried so far in the future that any cook could govern the state. "Since *everyone* was to participate in the government, *everyone* would become a temporary 'bureaucrat,' and thus *no one* would be a real bureaucrat" (Jacoby, 1973:124). Thus he predicted that bureaucracy would die out. But this dream of Lenin never came true. In 1917, approximately 1 million people were employed in administrative offices in Russia. By 1921, this number increased to almost 2.5 million (Jacoby, 1973:126).

Nowadays the Soviet government bureaucracy is characterized by periodic administrative reforms, fluctuating between utmost centralization and decentralization, while duplicating most of the activities. Whether the move is for centralization or for decentralization, governmental activities are part of an all-encompassing hierarchical structure, and there are seldom changes in the principle of central administration. All administrative bodies connected with the economic as well as social life are still subordinated to the same centralized system. As a result of a remarkable address delivered by Soviet leader Mikhail Gorbachev during the January 27, 1986, Central Committee meeting of the Communist Party, there is now a tremendous amount of official criticism of the way in which bureaucratic administration functions. But it is unlikely to be the point of departure for any change in the system, for the criticism never comes to grips with the system's real nature (Kennedy, 1987:29–43).

The will of the highest party authorities in the Soviet Union is absolute in administrative decision making. Reinhard Bendix (1973:317) notes that formal rules and the administrative procedures can be disregarded by the party at a moment's notice and the bureaucracy does not follow a single line of authority. Instead of relying on the enactment of rules and the supervision of their execution from the top, in the Soviet Union the party hierarchy is used to expedite and control the implementation of orders through regular administrative channels. Thus, the government bureaucracy is based on "two interlocking hierarchies of authority. The work of every factory, of every governmental office, of every unit of the army or the secret police, as well as every cultural or social organization, is programmed, coordinated, and supervised by some agency of government. But it is also propagandized, expedited, criticized, spied upon, and incorporated in special campaigns by an agency of the totalitarian party, which is separately responsible to the higher party authorities" (Bendix, 1973:318).

In developing countries, a stable system of taxation is the precondition for the permanent existence of bureaucratic administration. A highly interdependent relationship exists between bureaucracy and taxation. "The efficiency of the bureaucracy depends upon the effectiveness of its taxation system; and the effectiveness of the taxation system depends on the efficiency of the bureaucratic apparatus." (Lockwood, 1976:380). When a taxation system cannot provide adequate support for the bureaucracy in a developing country, members of bureaucratic organizations will rely on graft and other means to supplement their income. This is why the concept of white-collar crime is simply not applicable to many of these societies. Public servants, police, custom officials, and others in general are dependent upon graft and in a sense "the system is tantamount to a labyrinth of informally levied and collected surcharges in substitution of formal taxation and accounting" (Hetzler, 1969:47).

When there is a more or less stable form of taxation system in developing countries, the bureaucracy can facilitate economic development by rendering the needed legal and public service preconditions for development, including law and order, money and banking organizations, and the administrative apparatus essential for economic enterprises. "The bureaucracy can help modify 'the resource-structure of a country, together with its exploitation, as to make it more favorable to economic growth'. . . can form public corporations or other types of enterprises that will furnish the initiative for economic development, [and] . . . can fashion tax, fiscal, and investment policies that will sustain and enhance economic growth" (Spengler, quoted by Lauer, 1982:324).

In contemporary societies bureaucracies represent significant concentrations of resources and power without being directly accountable to the public at large. Even though this concentration of power and resources is essential to the business of modern industrial society, there is also a sense in which such concentrations raise public anxieties. At times there are questions raised as to what extent bureaucracy is compatible with democracy. There is a tendency in bureaucratic organizations for power to be concentrated in the hands of a few, or what Roberto Michel (1949) calls the "iron law of oligarchy." Admittedly, as demonstrated by Seymour M. Lipset and his associates (1956), under some conditions democratic processes can be maintained in large bureaucratic organizations, but still the relationship between bureaucracy and democracy is an uncomfortable one.

In an age of increasing "bigness" of government, business (Meyer, 1985:34–40), and university (indeed, every kind of organization), one may speculate on how the individual and the democratic process fit into the picture. It is a growing concern in the light of increasing bureaucratization, which pervades all aspects of life.

Although the efficiencies of large-scale organizations have made possible the unprecedented material growth of the twentieth century, the scope of their power and influence has come to threaten basic social and political values, particularly individual freedom (Fischer & Sirianni, 1984:3). There is a disturbing growth of centralized bureaucratic control with technological surveillance and centralized data banks resembling what Bertram Gross (1980) characterizes as "friendly fascism."

Bureaucratic organizations in the Soviet Union and other socialist countries have their own unique problems. Bureaucratic methods were used to rapidly industrialize underdeveloped areas of the world, often resulting in impressive material achievements. In the process, however, socialist states have produced an authoritarian form of bureaucratic collectivism under a bureaucratic police state with its "new class" (Djilas, 1957; McAdams, 1987). Moreover, their reliance on centralized planning has impeded economic development, created shortages in consumer goods, and stymied local initiatives.

In sum, as Otto Hintze writes, "Bureaucratic organization is a first-class sociological work of art which has been fashioned over many centuries. It is an illusion to maintain that it could be suppressed and replaced by 'self government'. . . ." Or, in Joseph Schumpeter's words, bureaucracy ". . . grows everywhere, whatever the political method a nation may adopt. Its expansion is the one certain thing about our future" (Hintze & Schumpeter, quoted by Jacoby, 1973:199, 191).

SUMMARY

In this chapter, several change patterns were considered. The object was to describe the principal forms that change can take. Evolution was seen in the context of directionality, novelty, increased variety, and complexity. Such change patterns are cumulative. These patterns can be investigated both qualitatively as illustrated by the evolution of legal systems and religion and quantitatively as in the case of stratification and food production or energy consumption.

Diffusion theory developed as an alternative to evolutionary theories. It deals with the spread of cultural elements. Historically, it was posited that ancient Egypt was the source of civilization, and from there elements spread to all parts of the world. The process of diffusion refers to the acquisition of elements from other cultures or social groups. The diffusion process includes the stages of awareness, interest, evaluation, trial, and the adoption of an innovation. It is conditioned by the perception of relative advantage, compatibility, complexity, tryability, and observability of an element by members of a culture. The adopter categories include innovators, early adopters, early and late majority, and laggards. Diffusion is considered an important component of planned social change.

Diffusion is subsumed under acculturation, which is a result of contact among cultures. However, cultures in contact seldom acculturate reciprocally, as illustrated by the case of American Indians. Acculturation can also be planned and involuntary, as happened in Africa during colonization. Immigrants in the United States undergo selective acculturation. The process of acculturation can be rapid and nondisruptive, as evidenced by the Manus.

Revolution usually entails rapid and fundamental changes, but such changes may or may not be violent. Several patterns were discussed, such as the Jacquerie, the Millenarian and Anarchistic Rebellions, Jacobian Communist Revolution, Conspiratorial Coup d'Etat, and Militarized Mass Insurrection. Most revolutionary forms bring about alterations in the class, status, and power systems, and the intensity of changes can be ascertained on a continuum.

Modernization refers to the transition from traditional to contemporary society and may take place without industrialization. Three types were identified: industrial, acculturative, and induced. Modernization is accompanied by increased differentiation in the economic, organizational, political, and cultural spheres. Modern people are portrayed as informed, efficient, and independent beings willing to experiment.

Industrialization involves the development of a factory system under mechanical power. An index of industrialization is the proportion of the labor force in agriculture. Industrialization is accompanied by a growing division of labor, a shift from agriculture to manufacturing and service industries, the creation of new specialties and occupations, greater literacy, and demographic changes.

As with modernization, urbanization may take place without industrialization. Living in cities produces a distinctive "urban way of life." The process of urbanization can be depicted on the folk-urban continuum. Currently, urbanization is most rapid in developing countries, where it is associated with distinct life-styles and with the concept of overurbanization.

The final change pattern examined in this chapter is bureaucratization. It refers to greater rationality in decision making and increased efficiency in the attainment of organizational goals. The highlights of two forms of bureaucracy—Western and Soviet—were discussed, and the section concluded with a not-too-cheerful note that bureaucracy, regardless of the form of government, is here to stay. In the next chapter a series of specific spheres of change will be considered.

SUGGESTED FURTHER READINGS

GERLACH, LUTHER P., and VIRGINIA H. HINE. *Lifeway Leap: The Dynamics of Change in America.* Minneapolis: University of Minnesota Press, 1973. A highly readable book, with chapters on evolutionary and revolutionary patterns of change.

GERMANI, GINO. *The Sociology of Modernization.* New Brunswick, N.J.: Transaction Books, 1981. Studies on the historical and theoretical aspects of modernization with an emphasis on Latin America.

GOLDSTONE, JACK A., ed. *Revolutions: Theoretical, Comparative, and Historical Studies.* San Diego: Harcourt Brace Jovanovich, 1986. A selection of readings by major thinkers and writers on the various facets of revolution and social change.

HAGOPIAN, MARK N. *The Phenomenon of Revolution.* New York: Dodd, Mead, 1974. An excellent synthesis of the existing concepts and theories of revolution.

IVERSON, NOEL, ed. *Urbanism and Urbanization: Views, Aspects, and Dimensions.* Leiden: E.J. Brill, 1984. A collection of informative and provocative articles on urbanism and urbanization.

KERR, CLARK. *The Future of Industrial Societies.* Cambridge, Mass.: Harvard University Press, 1983. An interesting discussion of the process of industrialization and the prospects for industrial societies.

ROGERS, EVERETT M. *Diffusion of Innovations,* 3rd ed. New York: Free Press, 1983. An authoritative and comprehensive statement on the current status of diffusion research and theory.

SPINDLER, LOUISE S. *Culture Change and Modernization: Mini-Models and Case Studies.* Prospect Heights, Ill.: Waveland Press, 1984. An informative and entertaining discussion on culture change with good illustrations of acculturation and diffusion patterns.

REFERENCES

APTER, DAVID E. *The Politics of Modernization.* Chicago: University of Chicago Press, 1965.

ARANGO, JORGE. *The Urbanization of the Earth.* Boston: Beacon Press, 1970.

BAKER, RUSSELL. "Made Elsewhere." *The New York Times Magazine,* April 26, 1987, p. 18.

BEALS, ALAN R., GEORGE SPINDLER, and LOUISE SPINDLER. *Culture in Process,* 2nd ed. New York: Holt, Rinehart & Winston, 1973.

BELLAH, ROBERT N. *Religion and Progress in Modern Asia.* New York: Free Press, 1965.

BELLAH, ROBERT N. "Religious Evolution." In S. N. Eisenstadt (ed.), *Readings in Social Evolution and Development.* New York: Pergamon, 1970, pp. 211–244.

BENDIX, REINHARD. "Industrialization, Ideologies and Social Structure." In Amitai Etzioni and Eva Etzioni-Halevy (eds.), *Social Change: Sources, Patterns, and Consequences,* 2nd ed. New York: Basic Books, 1973, pp. 310–319.

BLACK, CYRIL E. *The Dynamics of Modernization.* New York: Harper & Row, 1967.

BODLEY, JOHN H. *Victims of Progress,* 2nd ed. Menlo Park, Calif.: Cummings, 1982.

BRINTON, CRANE. *The Anatomy of Revolution.* New York: Vintage, 1959.

BROWN, LESTER R. *State of the World 1987.* New York: W.W. Norton & Co. Inc., 1987.

CERNEA, MICHAEL M., ed. *Putting People First: Sociological Variables in Rural Development.* New York: Oxford, 1985.

CHIROT, DANIEL. "The Rise of the West." *American Sociological Review,* 50, 1985, pp. 181–195.

CHODAK, SZYMON. *Societal Development.* New York: Oxford, 1973.

CLOSE, DAVID, and CARL BRIDGE, eds. *Revolution: A History of the Idea.* Totowa, N.J.: Barnes & Noble, 1985.

DAVIS, KINGSLEY. "World Urbanization 1950–1970: Analysis of Trends, Relationships and Developments." *Population Monograph,* 2(9), 1972. Berkeley: University of California Press.

DAVIS, KINGSLEY, and HILDA HERTZ GOLDEN. "Urbanization and the Development of Preindustrial Areas." *Economic Development and Cultural Change,* 3, October 1954, pp. 6–26.

DJILAS, MILOVAN. *The New Class.* New York: Praeger, 1957.

DEVOS, GEORGE A., ed. *Responses to Change, Society, Culture, and Personality.* New York: Van Nostrand, 1976.

DeVries, Jan. *European Urbanization 1500–1800*. Cambridge, Mass.: Harvard University Press, 1984.

Eisenstadt, S.N. *Tradition, Change, and Modernity*. New York: Wiley, 1973.

Fischer, Frank, and Carmen Sirianni, eds. *Critical Studies in Organization and Bureaucracy*. Philadelphia: Temple University Press, 1984

Fried, Morton. *The Evolution of Political Society*. New York: Random House, 1976.

Gans, Herbert. *The Urban Villagers*. New York: Free Press, 1962.

Gerlach, Luther P., and Virginia H. Hine. *Lifeway Leap: The Dynamics of Change in America*. Minneapolis: University of Minnesota Press, 1973.

Germani, Gino. *The Sociology of Modernization*. New Brunswick, N.J.: Transaction Books, 1981.

Gist, Noel P., and Sylvia F. Fava. *Urban Society*, 6th ed. New York: Crowell, 1974.

Goldstone, Jack A., ed. *Revolutions: Theoretical, Comparative, and Historical Studies*. San Diego: Harcourt Brace Jovanovich, 1986.

Goode, William J. *World Revolution and Family Patterns*. New York: Free Press, 1963.

Graves, Phillip E., and Robert Louis Sexton. "Overurbanization and Its Relation to Economic Growth for Less Developed Countries." In Pradip K. Ghosh (ed.), *Urban Development in the Third World*. Westport, Conn.: Greenwood Press, 1984, pp. 160–166.

Gross, Bertram. *Friendly Fascism*. New York: Evans, 1980.

Hagopian, Mark N. *The Phenomenon of Revolution*. New York: Dodd, Mead, 1974.

Halpern, Joel. *The Changing Village Community*. Englewood Cliffs, N.J.: Prentice-Hall, 1967.

Hardoy, Jorge E., ed. *Urbanization in Latin America: Approaches and Issues*. New York: Doubleday (Anchor Books), 1975.

Hauser, Phillip M. "The Chaotic Society: Product of the Social Morphological Revolution." In Amitai Etzioni and Eva Etzioni-Halevy (eds.), *Social Change: Sources, Patterns, and Consequences*, 2nd ed. New York: Basic Books, 1973, pp. 428–442.

Hetzler, Stanley A. *Technological Growth and Social Change, Achieving Modernization*. New York: Praeger, 1969.

Inkeles, Alex, and David H. Smith. *Becoming Modern: Individual Change in Six Developing Countries*. Cambridge, Mass.: Harvard University Press, 1974.

Iverson, Noel, ed. *Urbanism and Urbanization: Views, Aspects, and Dimensions*. Leiden: E.J. Brill, 1984.

Jacoby, Henry. *The Bureaucratization of the World*, Eveline L. Kanes, trans. Berkeley: University of California Press, 1973.

Johnson, Chalmers. *Revolution and the Social System*. Stanford, Calif.: Hoover International Studies, vol. 3, 1964.

Kammeyer, Kenneth C.W., and Helen L. Ginn. *An Introduction to Population*. Chicago: Dorsey Press, 1986.

Kennedy, Paul. "What Gorbachev Is Up Against." *The Atlantic*, June 1987, pp. 29–43.

Kerr, Clark, John T. Dunlop, Frederick H. Harbison, and Charles A. Myers. *Industrialism and Industrial Man*. New York: Oxford, 1964.

Kerr, Clark. *The Future of Industrial Societies*. Cambridge, Mass.: Harvard University Press, 1983.

Kroeber, A.L. "Diffusionism." In Amitai Etzioni and Eva Etzioni-Halevy (eds.), *Social Change: Sources, Patterns, and Consequences*, 2nd ed. New York: Basic Books, 1973, pp. 140–144.

Lauer, Robert H. *Perspectives of Social Change*, 3rd ed. Boston: Allyn & Bacon, 1982.

Lenski, Gerhard, and Jean Lenski. *Human Societies: An Introduction to Macrosociology*, 5th ed. New York: McGraw-Hill, 1987.

Levy, Marion, Jr. *Modernization and the Structure of Societies*, vol. 1. Princeton, N.J.: Princeton University Press, 1966.

Liebow, Elliot. *Tally's Corner*. Boston: Little, Brown, 1967.

Linn, Johannes F. *Cities in the Developing World*. New York: Oxford, 1983.

Linton, Ralph. *The Study of Man: An Introduction*. New York: Appleton, 1936.

Lipset, Seymour M., Martin Trow, and James Coleman. *Union Democracy*. New York: Free Press, 1956.

Lockwood, David. "Social Integration and System Integration." In George K. Zollschan and Walter Hirsch (eds.), *Social Change: Explorations, Diagnoses, and Conjectures*, 2nd ed. New York: Wiley, 1976, pp. 370–383.

Lorsch, Jay W., ed. *Handbook of Organizational Behavior*. Englewood Cliffs, N.J.: Prentice-Hall, 1987.

McAdams, John. "Testing the Theory of the New Class." *The Sociological Quaterly*, 28(1), 1987, pp. 23–49.

Mead, Margaret. *New Lives for Old*. New York: Mentor, 1961.

Meadows, Paul. *The Many Faces of Change: Explorations in the Theory of Social Change*. Cambridge, Mass.: Schenkman, 1971.

Meyer, Marshall W. *Limits to Bureaucratic Growth*. Berlin: Walter de Gruyter, 1985.

Michel, Roberto. *Political Parties*. New York: Free Press, 1949.

Moore, Wilbert E. "Changes in Occupational Structures." In William A. Faunce and William H. Form (eds.), *Comparative Perspectives on Industrial Society*. Boston: Little, Brown, 1969, pp. 107–125.

Moore, Wilbert E. *Social Change*, 2nd ed. Englewood Cliffs, N.J.: Prentice-Hall, 1974.

Murdock, George P. *Our Primitive Contemporaries*. New York: Macmillan, 1934.

Murdock, George P. "Word Ethnographic Sample." *American Anthropologist*, 59, 1957, pp. 664–687.

Myrdal, Gunnar. *Asian Drama: An Inquiry into the Poverty of Nations*, vol. 1. New York: Pantheon, 1968.

Naroll, Raoul. "On Ethnic Unit Classification." *Current Anthropology*, 5(4), 1964, pp. 283–312.

Neumann, Sigmund. "The International Civil War." In Clifford T. Paynton and Robert Blackey (eds.), *Why Revolution? Theories and Analyses*. Cambridge, Mass.: Schenkman, 1971, pp. 110–123.

Parsons, Talcott. *Family, Socialization and Interaction Process*. New York: Free Press, 1955.

Petersen, William. *The Politics of Population*. New York: Doubleday (Anchor Books), 1965.

Pfeiffer, John E. *The Emergence of Society, A Prehistory of the Establishment*. New York: McGraw-Hill Book Company, 1977.

Population Reference Bureau. *Population Data Sheet*. Washington, D.C.: Population Reference Bureau, Inc., 1986.

Redfield, Robert. *The Folk Culture of Yucatan*. Chicago: University of Chicago Press, 1941.

Robertson, Thomas S. *Innovative Behavior and Communication*. New York: Holt, Rinehart & Winston, 1971.

Rogers, Everett M. *Diffusion of Innovations*, 3rd ed. New York: Free Press, 1983.

Rosen, Christine Meisner. *The Limits of Power*. Cambridge, England: Cambridge University Press, 1986.

Sahlins, Marshall D. *Social Stratification in Polynesia*. Seattle: University of Washington Press, 1958.

Schwartz, Richard, and James C. Miller. "Legal Evolution and Societal Complexity." In S.N. Eisenstadt (ed.), *Readings in Social Evolution and Development*. New York: Pergamon, 1970, pp. 155–172.

Sjoberg, Gideon. *The Preindustrial City: Past and Present*. New York: Free Press, 1960.

Smith, Anthony D. *The Concept of Social Change: A Critique of the Functionalist Theory of Social Change*. London: Routledge, 1973.

Spindler, Louise S. *Culture Change and Modernization: Mini-Models and Case Studies*. Prospect Heights, Ill.: Waveland Press, 1984.

Szalai, Alexander. *The Use of Time*. The Hague: Mouton, 1972.

Time. "Paper Chase, The Battle Against Red Tape." July 10, 1978, p. 26.

Weber, Max. *The Theory of Social and Economic Organization*, A.M. Henderson and Talcott Parsons, trans. New York: Free Press, 1947.

White, Leslie. *The Science of Culture*. New York: Grove Press, 1949.

Wirth, Louis B. "Urbanism as a Way of Life." *American Journal of Sociology*, 44, July 1938, pp. 1–24.

6 Spheres of Change

To say that the modern world is in the throes of dramatic changes is an obvious understatement. The sense and feeling of change permeates social arrangements at all levels of society. The purpose of this chapter is to examine some of the more important changes in society and to show where they are taking place. The specific changes occurring in such spheres as the family, population, stratification, power relations, education, and the economy will be considered. Changes in these spheres are interrelated; they influence each other as well as the course of society; they often occur more or less simultaneously; and they are set in motion by the social forces discussed in the preceding two chapters.

THE FAMILY

Most sociologists trace the major changes in the structure and functions of the family to the Industrial Revolution and the subsequent urbanization, modernization, and economic development of society (Goode, 1968; Leslie & Korman, 1985; Rosen, 1982). They believe that industrialization was instrumental in transforming the traditional large, authoritarian, relatively stable rural family system into a more egalitarian, emotionally freer, and less sexually stratified nuclear family. This is not to say that industrialization had the same immediate effect on family systems in every society. Cultural and social forces determine the rate of family changes under the impact of industrialization, and there is substantial variation from society to society concerning the direction and magnitude of changes in specific family attributes such as the incidence of divorce or age at marriage.

Although at varying rates, there are a number of specific changes occurring worldwide in family patterns (Goode, 1968:59; Leslie & Korman, 1985:61–75). These include an increased freedom of marital choice, where marital bargaining is taken from the hands of elders. Both the dowry and bride price are disappearing in most parts of the world, the former being replaced by, among other things, an increase in the proportion of working wives (Kaplan, 1985). Young couples are more economically independent; the age of females at first marriage is increasing; and great discrepancies between the ages of spouses are becoming rarer. There is also a decrease of marriage between close kin, such as between cousins. Illegitimacy rates are on the increase. There is a significant decline in infanticide. The institutions of concubinage and polygamy are on the decline. Although the divorce rate is on the increase, the *trend* in any given society depends on its prior level. Remarriage after divorce or after the death of one's spouse is becoming more common in areas where it was rare. Let us now consider some of the specific changes in the American family.

The Changing Functions of the American Family

In a classic essay written more than five decades ago, William F. Ogburn (1934) contended that the American family is ill-adapted to modern industrial society as evidenced by the loss of many of its traditional functions to other agencies such as the school, church, and the state. More recently, historian John Demos (1970:193) reached a similar conclusion.

> Broadly speaking, the history of the family in America has been a history of contraction and withdrawal; its central theme is the gradual surrender to other institutions of its functions that once lay very much within the realm of family responsibility.

In the early days of the United States, the family functioned in several spheres—economic, productive, religious, recreational, educational, status conferring, and reproductive. With industrialization, production was taken out of the home and the economic function of the family declined. Prior to industrialization, the family, according to Demos (1970:183), "was first of all a business agency of economic production and exchange. Each household was more or less self-sufficient; and its various members were inextricably united in the work of providing for their fundamental material wants. Work, indeed, was a wholly natural extension of family life and merged imperceptibly with all of its activities." Children were economic assets, and marriage was a kind of business relationship. With the advent of the factory system, the woman's traditional economic contribution declined, her status as wife and mother diminished, and children became liabilities rather than assets. Today, the consumption of goods and services has replaced production, and all members are encouraged to participate. Once they worked together; now they shop together—for food, clothing, sporting goods, TV sets, and the like.

Traditionally, the family was the principal source of protection for the individual. In addition to physical protection, it provided medical care and economic security. These functions have been largely transferred to the state through the operation of such agencies as the police, welfare departments, the medical profession, and insurance companies.

The religious function of the family is also on the decline. Religion once served as an integrating force, one that complemented other institutional controls in the maintenance of a cohesive family system. The home was the center of religious activities. Today, the church is often taking over many of these functions, and even marriage is becoming a secular matter devoid of religious overtones.

In the early American family, education was considered to be a function of the home. Children where likely to follow the footsteps of their parents, and education was usually of short duration and vocational in nature. Now the education of children, both academic and vocational, is more formal and has passed on to the hands of professionals.

The status-conferring function of the family has also declined, and individuals are evaluated on the basis of their own performance rather than on the basis of ascribed status. A family's status is more often than not ascertained in terms of the husband's occupation, and usually the man leaves his status when he leaves his job. Finally, even the reproductive function of the family has not remained a sole exclusivity of the family, as evidenced by illegitimacy rates.

"In the past, stability has been the great value exemplified by the family and that expected of it by society. This was true because the family was the basic institution in a static society (Burgess, 1973:195). Today, the American society is not static but dynamic, and the family is characterized not by its stability but by its adaptability to a rapid tempo of social change. It is becoming a more specialized structure, but the loss of functions should not be construed as signs of deterioration. They are only indicative of changes that have taken place.

Current Trends

In addition to the disappearance of traditional family functions, other changes have occurred in the American family. There is a trend among young people to delay marriage. Between 1960 and 1986, the median age at first marriage increased from 22.8 to 25.7 years for men and from 20.3 to 23.1 years for women. In part, this is prompted by the desire among some, particularly women, to finish their education and start careers prior to marriage. There is also a growing preference among many people to forgo marriage altogether, and the percentage of men and women who have never married almost doubled between 1960 and 1986. During the same time, one-person households as a percent of all households increased from 13 to 24 percent (one in nine adults lives alone in the United States), and the number of unmarried couples living together almost quadrupled to over 2 million (*New York Times,* 1986).

Over time, family size has also decreased. The number of live births for an average American woman declined from eight at the end of the eighteenth century to three in 1970 (Winch, 1970), and to 1.8 in 1986 (*U.S. News & World Report,* 1987a:58). This was accompanied by a drop in the size of the average household to 3.1 in 1970 (Eshleman, 1974:6) and to 2.6 persons in 1986. There is also a growing tendency among American women to postpone childbearing because of their concern with careers, economic security, and personal freedom (Leslie & Korman, 1985:463). The decline in family size and delayed parenthood are accompanied by what may be called "the streamlined family," that is, the nuclear family without children. Planned childlessness is on the increase. The percentage of couples without children has doubled in the last few decades. Nowadays, motherhood is just one of the many options for married women. In 1986, one out of four ever-married women between the ages of 25 and 34 had never had a child—a total of nearly 3.3 million women—compared to one out of ten in 1960 (*Newsweek,* 1986:68). Economic factors play a crucial role in the decision to forgo parenthood. Childlessness has increased as women have moved in record numbers into well-paying careers. Faced with new options, many wives have decided that motherhood is not an essential or even desirable role. And in the absence of widespread governmental or corporate support for working parents, many feel compelled to choose between children and jobs (Campbell, 1986). The fact that childless couples are happier and more satisfied with their lives than are couples with children may also play a role in the decision to forsake parenthood (Leslie & Korman, 1985:463).

The increased work responsibility of women has also tended to bring about changes in the structure of the family. The percentage of working women has almost doubled since 1940. In the mid-1980s, more than half of all adult women were working, and six out of ten of these were married (Williams, 1987:367). In addition, there has been a substantial increase in the number and types of occupations in which women are employed and greater involvement on their part in high-paying, prestigious occupations and professions. Changes in career patterns and employment opportunities for women bring about such adaptations as the commuter, or long-distance, marriage, in which the spouses live some distance from one another. In such families either the wife or husband assumes primary responsibility for the children.

Socialization

In a traditional society, parents socialize their children to take their place in a world where submission to authority at every level—the family, the school, the workplace—is the linchpin that holds the system together. Because parents believe that the future is clear and predictable, they believe their children will generally follow in their roles. In a modern society, however, parents must prepare their children for an unknown future, with very few things taken for granted. Traditional ideas become outmoded, and new technologies render old skills obsolete. New ideologies replace cherished philosophies. Under these conditions, it is no longer feasible to maintain a commitment to traditional ideas, skills, and goals. Parents, to prepare their children for survival in a changing society, must focus on the future, and must try to anticipate it. This is a task not easily accomplished (Rosen, 1982:166–168).

Urie Bronfenbrenner (1970:117) sees some of the changes that are currently taking place in the family as affecting the socialization and development of children. He contends that the typical American child's contact with adults in general, and parents in particular, is diminishing and such lack of contact can be disastrous. He warns that "we can anticipate increased alienation, indifference, antagonism, and violence on the part of the younger generation in all segments of our society—middle-class children as well as the disadvantaged." In support of his contention, he cites research concerned with effects on children of the absence of one or both parents, usually the father. In general, he considers the effects of parental absence negative and "father absence contributes to low motivation for achievement, inability to defer immediate rewards for later benefits, low self-esteem . . . and juvenile delinquency" (1970:104).

Divorce

Until very recently, the long-term trend in divorce in the United States has been upward. The divorce rate is usually expressed as the number of divorces per 1,000 population. In 1867, the divorce rate was 0.3 per 1,000 population. By the turn of the century, it had reached 0.7, and by 1950, 2.6. There was a small drop to 2.2 in 1960, then it started to climb again, reaching 4.8 in 1975, and hit its peak of 5.3 in 1981. The figure of 4.8 is the lowest since 1975, and represents only the second time in 12 years that the rate edged below five per thousand. It should be noted, however, that the numbers are based on per 1,000 population, not just married couples, so the figures do not reflect the pool of couples actually at risk for divorce.

And that risk is quite high. One out of every two marriages ends in divorce in the United States (Williams, 1987:357). Sociologists generally attribute the high divorce rates to changing family functions, casual marriages, shorter courtships, increases in teenage pregnancies with subsequent "shotgun" weddings, increased job opportunities with economic and sexual freedom for women, a decline in moral and religious sanctions, the prevaling philosophy of "happiness," and, of course, more liberal divorce laws.

The Sexual Revolution

The much publicized "sexual revolution" of the 1960s and 1970s has important consequences for the structure of the family. The term has multiple meanings. It refers to a shift toward a higher incidence of all kinds of heterosexual activity and more permissive attitudes toward homosexuality and variety in the sexual act. It alludes to sexual liberation, greater freedom for women, alternatives to marriage, and, at the same time, to trivialized sex, diminished intimacy, and fewer lasting commitments among partners (Williams, 1987:249–253). There is no doubt that major changes in sexual mores and behavior have occurred. But to call these changes "revolutionary" is questionable. Regardless of how it is described, sex today is no longer tied to reproduction or marriage, nor domestic life to a large family of children. Sex is increasingly liberated from the bonds of matrimony and even heterosexuality. For a contemporary young woman, for example, the choices are:

> Have sex or don't. Have it with a man, or a woman. Use the pill, the IUD, the diaphragm. Have an abortion. Marry, or don't. Do have children. Don't have children. Have a career. Have a career and a child. Have a husband, but no child. Have a child, but no husband. (Rivers, 1975:144)

Among unmarried young people, sexual activity is on the increase and they start younger. About half of the women aged 15 to 19 surveyed in 1982 had had intercourse and about a fifth at age 15 had already experienced coitus. Close to half in this age group had more than one sexual partner (Jones, 1986:46–49). Although there is a decline in births among teens, about a million teenagers get pregnant annually. America's yearly teen-pregnancy rate—one teenage girl in every ten—remains the highest of any developed country (and so is the legal abortion rate) (Jones and others, 1986:1). By age 20, nearly 40 percent of young white women and 63 percent of young black women become pregnant.

There are other derivatives of the changes of sexual mores and behavior. They include alternatives to family living such as group marriage and communal living. *Group marriage* is based on the principle of sharing, variety in sexual experience and partners, and interpersonal intimacy. Group marriage involves three or more people. The most common pattern involves four adults, usually the members of two former couples (Leslie & Korman, 1985:129). Members are motivated by personal growth opportunity and by an interest in having multiple sex partners. Because of its egalitarian structure, sex roles are much less differentiated in group marriage than in the average nuclear family (Williams, 1987:363). *Communal living* arrangements are characterized by lack of private property, financial self-sufficiency, and open sharing of sexual partners. Communal living may involve up to 200 or more people (Leslie & Korman, 1985:131). Although their numbers have diminished drastically since the mid-1970s, group marriages and communal living arrangements still exist in the United States.

Another alternative to family life is *cohabitation*. The number of couples sharing a household increased from about 500,000 in 1970 to close to 2 million in 1985 (U.S. Bureau of Census, 1987:42). Cohabitation is gaining legitimacy as a family form in the United States as evidenced by recent court decisions stating that long-term, unmarried partners may have a claim on each other's property. Such decisions make the legal distinction between cohabitation and marriage somewhat blurred.

But the so-called sexual revolution may be over. Several campus surveys reported a renewed interest in virginity as a value. A 1984 study showed a drop to 38 percent among undergraduate women who engage in sexual intercourse at least once a month. Five years earlier the figure was 50 percent (Williams, 1987:253). The decrease could be attributable to a more conservative campus mood, an increase in women's assertiveness in saying no, and the fear of sexually transmitted diseases. The growing incidence of herpes in the early 1980s was instrumental in changing sexual patterns. The concern that casual sex may lead to incurable genital herpes prompted many people to be more cautious about their sexual behavior. Shortly after the herpes scare, a far more serious disease appeared: AIDS. First diagnosed in the United States in 1981, by mid 1988 more than 40,000 cases had been recorded, with half of its victims already dead. It has reached near epidemic proportions, and the fear of catching this incurable, dreaded disease has significantly altered sexual norms and restricted sexual activities to known partners both among heterosexuals and homosexuals (Leishman, 1987).

In sum, the options have indeed increased for the family. Family life is no longer confined to a traditional, approved form of family in the conjugal type. In the real world a wide range of family patterns can be observed from homosexual unions to mothers living with their illegitimate children, from open sex communes to the Shakers' total rejection of sexuality, from living together without any ceremony to living separately in spite of a ceremony; the list is nearly endless. Whether or not these changes now occurring within the family will inaugurate a totally new system of family is just too early to tell. Regardless, changes in the sphere of the family have been and are dramatic. In the next section, changes in population will be examined.

POPULATION

Assuming that the first human being appeared between 1 million and 2 million years ago, it is estimated that between 60 billion and 100 billion representatives of *Homo sapiens* have lived on Planet Earth. On July 11, 1987, the global population reached the 5 billion mark (*New York Times*, 1987a), representing 5 to 8 percent of all the people who have ever lived. It is estimated that the world population in 1650 was half a billion, and it took approximately 200 years to double. In 1850 it was 1 billion, with a doubling time of 80 years. By 1930 it reached 2 billion, with a doubling time of 45 years (Ehrlich & Ehrlich, 1972:5–6). In 1986, the world's population was expected to double in 41 years (Population Reference Bureau, 1986). James E. Harf and B. Thomas Trout (1986:87) did some quick calculations in an attempt to put these numbers in some kind of perspective. For 1982, they showed that the world population increased by 2.5 people every second as a consequence of 4.15 births and 1.65 deaths. For the globe, this adds up to an increase of 150 people per minute, 9,038 people per hour, 216,916 people per day, 6,597,858 per month, for a total of 79,174,297 new people per year. By the time you finish reading this page, 150 additional people have been added to the world population. The daily increase equals roughly the size of Dayton, Ohio. For 1983, the gain was over 82 million, and the absolute figure continues to grow each year.

The world population growth is the result of natural increase—the excess of births over deaths. For individual countries, net migration—the difference between out-migration and in-migration—is also a factor. Rapid population growth is the result of great declines in death rates along with continuing high birthrates. Mortality rates in Europe began to decline in the eighteenth and nineteenth centuries. The great reductions in mortality did not reach two-thirds of humankind in the developing nations in Asia, Latin America, and Africa until after World War II, primarily as a consequence in the rise of the general level of nutrition, improvements in sanitation, and health care delivery. In general, birthrates have remained high and it can be expected that more than 90 percent of the world's population increase that is anticipated by the end of this century will be generated by developing countries, which are doubling their population almost twice as fast as industrialized nations (Brown, 1987:20–37). By contrast, the United States, Canada, and many European countries are experiencing a decline in fertility since the 1960s (Teitelbaum & Winter, 1985:81–87; Wattenberg, 1987). Seven European countries (Denmark, Sweden, Austria, East and West Germany, Luxembourg, and Hungary), about 4 percent of the world population, are actually experiencing a zero or negative population growth (Population Reference Bureau, 1986).

Consequences of Rapid Growth Rates

In many developing countries the rate of population growth is at least half the rate of economic growth and, in some cases, almost equal to the latter. Because of the high birthrate, the ratios of children to adults are very high when compared with industrialized countries, and the number of young people reaching the ages of labor force participation are rapidly increasing. These factors can produce serious economic consequences. Rapid population growth slows down the growth of per capita income in developing countries and tends to perpetuate inequalities of income distribution. Food supplies and agricultural production must be increased to meet the needs of rapidly growing populations, affecting resource allocation to other economic and social sectors. Because of the rapid increase in the size of the labor force, unemployment and underemployment are becoming increasingly serious problems. Large supplies of cheap labor tend to hold back technological improvements, and industrialization is slowed by mass poverty, which in turn reduces the demand for manufactured goods. It is important to note that population growth at a given level tends to require economic growth at some higher level just to maintain a constant per capita income. This is due to the fact that additional population requires additional production, each production addition being, after the point of diminishing returns is reached, more costly than the previous one.

Rapid population growth is also associated with internal migration and urbanization. It places increased demands for government services in the areas of health, education, welfare, among others. It also places heavy burdens upon resources and the environment (Brown, 1987; Harf & Trout, 1986; Kuznets, 1973).

Demographic Transition

As contrasted to trends in developing countries today, over the past 200 years the now-industrialized nations have experienced what demographers refer to as *demographic transition*, moving from high fertility rates to low mortality and low fertility. Death rates started to drop before birthrates did, causing population growth rates to rise rapidly for a time. Gradually, however, birthrates also began to fall, and rates of growth in most industrialized nations seem to be stabilizing at relatively low levels. In 1986, the United States, for example, had a growth rate of 0.7 percent, whereas Western European countries had 0.1 percent, as compared with 2.3 percent in Latin American countries, and 2.8 in Africa and western Asia.

Let us now consider the major variables in population dynamics. They are *mortality* or death rate, that is, the number of deaths per 1,000 population; *fertility*, which refers to the number of births in a population relative to every thousand women of childbearing age (usually between the ages of 15 and 45); *migration*, which indicates the movement of segments of the population from one geographic area to another; and *population composition*, or age-sex composition, that is, a proportion of males and females in various age groups in a given population.

Mortality

In any given group of 1,000 infants, mortality rates are relatively high in the first year of life, rapidly decline in early childhood, reach their minimum around the ages of four to ten, and then rise gradually but steadily until they reach their maximum at old age. In all countries of the world, mortality rates through the life cycle are declining, though at different rates, as evidenced by a decrease in infant mortality and an increase in life expectancy. Since World War II, health programs involving the use of antibiotics, vaccines, and insecticides have contributed to the decline of mortality rates in developing countries. The most noticeable is the drop in *infant mortality* rates—that is, the number of deaths per thousand during the first year of life. The decline in infant mortality is most rapid in industrialized countries. In the United States, for example, it declined from 99.9 in 1915 to 20 in 1970 and to 10.5 per 1,000 births by 1986 (U.S. Bureau of Census, 1987:74; Population Reference Bureau, 1986). The rates are even lower for other developed nations, for example, 6.2 for Japan, 6.4 for Sweden, and 6.6 for Finland. In developing countries, the decline in infant mortality rates is much slower. In Afghanistan, the rate is 194, and it is not unusual to see rates between 160 and 180 per 1,000 births in African countries, such as Mali and Ethiopia. Even in certain industrialized countries, such as Brazil, it is around 71 per 1,000 births. For the world, the rate is 82 (Population Reference Bureau, 1986). *Life expectancy* is increasing, but much more rapidly in the developing countries. For the United States, it increased from 47.3 years at the turn of the century to 75 years in 1986. In the developing countries, an extremely rapid rise in life expectancy occurred during the first two decades after World War II and is still continuing, though probably at a slower rate (Petersen, 1975:220–273).

There are several changes associated with the decline in mortality rates (Heer, 1975:56–58; Teitelbaum & Winter, 1985:88–89). In societies where there is a high mortality rate, the family is more likely to be dependent on some larger kin group. By contrast, in low-mortality societies, such as Western countries, the nuclear family often lives at a great distance from other relatives as there is a smaller likelihood for children to become orphaned and require the support of extended kin. In high-mortality societies, individuals are more likely to have a stronger present orientation than when mortality is low. It may have an effect on the achievement motivation, for achievement is usually associated with a sacrifice of present values for future goals. There is also a decline in the emphasis placed on how religion will benefit one in the next world with the decline in mortality. The concern with afterlife is waning, and the accent is on how religion will help one in this world (Schneider & Dornbusch, 1958). Finally, there are also changes in the institutions of mourning as a result of the decrease in mortality. Geoffrey Gorer (1965) points out that around the turn of the century there were strict rules of etiquette that the bereaved must observe, as well as what others must show toward them. Today, people are unsure of how to confront bereavement, and the general tendency is to try to deny its very existence.

Fertility

There is an extensive body of literature describing fertility among nations at a given time, within a single nation over time, among geographic areas within a single nation, and among such social categories as educational attainment, income, occupation, religion, or ethnic group. In general, the nations with the lowest per capita income have the highest fertility, and vice versa. In developed countries the level of fertility is lower than it was a hundred years ago, but the decline has not been a regular process. In most nations, fertility in general is higher in rural than in urban areas. In developed nations usually it is highest among persons of the lower socio-economic classes and lowest in the middle and upper classes.

In addition to these variations, there is a general downward trend in fertility in most countries, primarily as a result of the operation of a series of economic and social factors. Harvey Leibenstein (1974) notes some of the reasons for this downward transition.

1. The rise in the education of women and the consequent change in their role and values.
2. The increase in female participation in the nonagricultural labor force.
3. Sustained reduction in infant mortality.
4. A decline in traditional religious beliefs that supported high fertility norms.
5. Urbanization and its secularizing influences and options to traditional behavior patterns.
6. The growth in compulsory education and the decline in the use and value of child labor.
7. Increases in the rights of women and changes in their roles outside of the home.
8. The weakening of the extended family system.
9. Availability of effective chemical and mechanical contraceptives.
10. The development of old-age and welfare systems outside the home.
11. Increases in mobility opportunities.

Obviously, this is only a partial list, even though it indicates many of the changes that have been associated with the decrease in fertility. This list could be supplemented by questions of individual motives, such as, "Why do you want to have *x* number of children?" or "Why do you use (or not use) a certain contraceptive method?" In that case one would be led to conclude that the reasons for a given fertility level are as many of the number of individuals who have borne children. Still, on a worldwide basis, literacy, increased wealth, urbanization, economic development, and industrialization have all contributed to the decrease in fertility. Some demographers and social commentators are even complaining that the United States and other Western countries are not reproducing fast enough to replace themselves (Teitelbaum & Winter, 1985; Wattenberg, 1987). In his latest and rather alarmist book, *The Birth Dearth*, Ben J. Wattenberg (1987) fears that the decline in fertility in the West will bring about economic problems, a weakening of the military might of the West, a decline in the productivity of the aging labor force, and an inevitable bankruptcy of social security systems. He also alludes to the eventual overtake of the West by "inferior" races. Time will tell whether Western civilization is endangered by the "birth dearth."

In addition to the decline in actual fertility rates, there are also changes in the *preference system* that affects the decision to have children (Spengler, 1966). The preference system simply describes the value a couple puts on an additional child relative to the value of all other goals they might achieve without having that child. The changes affecting the preference system include the reduction in infant mortality, the decrease in the productive labor of children, changes in the institutions that provide support for the elderly, decline in rewards that could be expected from society at large for bearing large numbers of children, and the shift from allocation of status by ascription to allocation by achievement.

Migration

It is much easier to discuss general trends in mortality and fertility than in migration. Relevant data for migration often are not available. Furthermore, trends in migration vary from nation to nation, and there has been no generalized change such as those occurring in mortality and fertility. For the sake of brevity, the discussion will be confined to trends in the United States.

Since World War II, approximately a fifth of the total population has moved every year, about 6 percent have changed their country of residence, and roughly 3 percent have moved to a new state (Lee, 1964:127).

Immigration statistics for the United States are available since 1920. Between that date and 1985, some 52.5 million immigrants entered the country (U.S. Bureau of the Census, 1987:11). The period up to about the turn of the century corresponds to the wave of "old immigrants," predominantly composed of Irish leaving their native land because of the potato famine. The second large wave of "new immigrants," made up of individuals from Southern Europe and Eastern Europe, occurred roughly between 1900 and 1921, when restrictive legislations greatly reduced the flow of immigrants to the United States. World War II and its aftermath brought some 20 million refugees from Eastern and Central Europe (Harf & Trout, 1986:102). In 1986, more than 570,000 immigrants entered the country. As contrasted to the older waves of immigration, they came primarily from Latin American and Asian countries. In addition to legal immigration, there has been a substantial growth in illegal immigration since the 1970s. It is estimated that there are anywhere from 4 million to 8 million illegal aliens residing in the United States. In 1987, Congress passed legislation authorizing those who entered the country illegally prior to 1982 to remain and obtain citizenship should they so desire. Still, the flow of illegal immigrants continues. The number of people apprehended for entering the country illegally from Mexico jumped substantially in mid-1987 (Applebomer, 1987).

Age-Sex Composition

The final variable of population dynamics is the age-sex composition, which is determined by the population's sex ratio at birth (sex ratio is the number of males divided by the number of females times 100) and the population's past history of births, deaths, and migrations. As a result of the decline in birthrates, the proportion of the population less than 15 years of age has been steadily declining in industrialized countries. In the United States it declined from 41.6 percent in 1850 to 34.4 percent in 1900 to 22 percent in 1986 (Smith & Zopf, 1976:182; Population Reference Bureau, 1986). By contrast, the world population under 15 years of age is 35 percent; Latin America's population under 15 years of age is 42 percent, and it exceeds 50 percent in eastern African countries such as Kenya and Zimbabwe.

The current "aging" of the population has been widely publicized in recent years (Menken, 1986; Wattenberg, 1987). This refers to the increase in the number and proportion of those 65 years of age and over, which is another characteristic of developed countries. In 1986 in the United States, 12 percent of the population was over age 65. In Latin American countries, the figure was 4 percent, and in a number of countries in Asia and Africa it ranged between 1 and 2 percent.

Changes in the sex ratio in the United States are usually attributed to immigration, as more males than females tend to immigrate. Changes in both the age and the sex structures tend to bring about changes in other domains.

Changes in the age structure alter the *dependency ratio*, which is the ratio of persons in dependent ages (that is, ages under 15 and over 65). In general, the lower the ratio, the easier it is for persons in the economically productive ages to support those in the dependent age category. Age structure changes also relate to the age of persons in the labor force, and developed countries generally have an older labor force as compared to underdeveloped countries. This, in turn, is reflected on patterns of consumption and money allotted to education.

Changes in age-sex structure also affect marriage rates. Assuming that men usually marry women a few years younger than themselves, then females in any population in which the age structure has a downward slope will have more difficulty in finding mates than will men. Rapid change in the rate of population growth can also affect the sex ratio at marriageable ages. In the United States, there were somewhat more boys born in 1941 –1943 than girls born in 1944–1946. In contrast, the number of girls born in 1947–1949 was 14 percent greater than the number of boys born in 1944–1946. Thus, girls born right after World War II and reaching marriageable age in the later 1960s had substantially poorer prospects for marriage than girls born during World War II who reached that age in the mid-decade (Heer, 1975:109). To conclude on a more cheerful note, women born in the 1960s will have an excellent chance to marry (statistically) in the 1980s and early 1990s.

In sum, the principal changes in the population include a general upward trend in terms of absolute numbers, accompanied by a slow decline in fertility and a rapid decrease in mortality. This is particularly evident in developing countries. Worldwide, the gap between birthrates and death rates is still wide enough to cause some alarm. In the next section, changes in the sphere of stratification will be examined.

STRATIFICATION

Stratification refers to a system of ranking individuals and families into levels (strata or class) that share unequally in the distribution of status, wealth, and power or other scarce and highly valued objects in communities and societies (Gilbert & Kahl, 1987; Rossides, 1976:14–17). In all societies, differences exist between some individuals and others in terms of a number of factors. For example, the chief of a tribal society may be differentiated from tribesmen by receiving a greater degree of deference, living in a larger house, and having more wives. The president of a large university in a modern society is also likely to be differentiated in a number of ways from other members of the academic community—for example, a larger office, a larger income, more secretaries, and a reserved parking place.

Types of Stratification Systems

There are three general types of stratification systems. At one extreme is the *caste system*, in which the strata are hereditary, endogamous (marriage partners must be chosen within the group), and permanent. An individual is born into a caste, marries in it, and dies in it. The best-known caste system is that of traditional India. However, with the introduction of modern forms of technology and economic organization, together with the diffusion of ideologies favorable to social change, the traditionally rigid status system has been undermined, although not necessarily abandoned. Much of this change has occurred in cities, not in rural villages, but the values and life-styles associated with a more flexible status system have filtered into the rural sectors, planting the seeds of a "revolution of rising expectations" (Mandelbaum, 1970).

At the other extreme is the *open class system*, in which only individual achievement matters, and one rises or falls in social class according to his or her own accomplishment. But even in this situation an infant is assigned his or her family's status at birth and thus has an initial advantage or disadvantage in life. The United States is considered to have the most open and mobile class system in the world. In the third, the *estate system*, strata are defined by law and are relatively rigid and permanent. But there is some opportunity to shift one's status. Feudal Europe is the most notable example of an estate system. Changes from estate and caste stratification systems to open systems are indicative of changes *of type*, whereas changes in the open class system are changes *within* the stratification system (Barber, 1973:199–209).

Toward Greater Equality

The economic difference between the top and bottom strata of society is greater in underdeveloped and developing countries than in developed nations. Gerhard Lenski (1966:309) finds that the top 1 or 2 percent of the population in nonindustrial societies as a whole usually receives *not* less than half of the total income of the country. In industrial societies the comparative figure is much less. For example, in Great Britain, the top 2 percent receives 8.5 percent of the total income after taxes and in the United States, the top 2.3 percent receives 11.6 percent *before taxes*.

In many industrialized societies, the long-term trend is toward equalization of rights and privileges for all classes and toward the reduction of the power of the elite. Voting rights were extended to all levels, minimum wage laws were enacted to improve the economic position of the working classes, and graduated income taxes were utilized in an attempt to equalize wealth. Other attempts to equalize opportunities included social security for the unemployed, children, and the physically handicapped; education for the masses; free public recreational facilities; and a judicial system to protect the rights of individuals regardless of their class position.

Industrialization and urbanization have profoundly altered the economic basis of stratification. As a result of economic and technological changes, many Western countries have experienced a general improvement in income for the masses, both urban and rural, and a significant increase in the standard of living. The emphasis shifted to consumption, and there is considerable preoccupation with both what and how to consume and under what circumstances. In the United States large-scale changes in major patterns of stratification have been associated with industrialization, creating a large urban working class. Well into the twentieth century, the urban proletariat was generally underpaid and overworked, and the life-style imposed upon it reflected its underprivileged position in the economy. In recent decades, however, a substantial proportion of the urban working class have adopted a middle-class life-style. The basic change making this possible has been the rise in incomes and the shorter workweek. With higher incomes and more leisure time, many workers acquired consumer "needs" of the middle class, such as modern homes and household equipment, an annual vacation and travel, leisure-time activities, and so on. For a while the American dream became a reality. Workers got used to a rapidly growing standard of living in the 1960s and most of the 1970s, but the gains took a turn in the opposite direction starting in about 1978 (Koten, 1987). Suddenly, a generation raised with great material expectations has discovered there is a big gap between its reach for more satisfaction and what is within its grasp. Some examples:

- Between 1970 and 1985, the 20 percent average down payment on the average-priced new home more than quadrupled, rising from around $5,000 to over $21,000.
- Education at a private, four-year college increased from 30 percent to 40 percent of the median family income.
- Real family income has declined by 6 percent for most of the 25 million families that earn from $15,000 to $35,000 a year, as measured in constant dollars.
- Nearly half of the new jobs created pay less than poverty-level income—$180 a week.

In view of these inflationary trends, it is doubtful that the new urban working class can maintain the highly cherished middle-class style of life. And it is little consolation for them that their "real" middle-class counterparts are not faring much better.

Social Mobility

The United States is frequently described as a "mobile society." Because stratification really involves a series of steps, one can consider mobility

with regard to a number of variables such as income, educational achievement, housing, neighborhood status, occupational prestige, and so forth.
There is consensus in the stratification literature that occupation is the best
single indicator of one's overall stratification position. Changes in a stratification position are brought about by vertical mobility, that is, either the
upward or downward movement on an occupational scale. Moreover, mobility can be plotted across various periods of time, which would include
two possible forms: *intergenerational* and *intragenerational*. Intergenerational
mobility concerns changes in occupational prestige *between* generations and
specifically involves the mobility of the offspring relative to the parent.
Intragenerational mobility has to do with mobility within a single generation
or movement following the individual's first major job (Blau & Duncan,
1967). Such mobility patterns may involve changes from manual to non-
manual occupations or movements into and out of the occupational elite
at the top of some kind of occupational scale.

As the economy changed in the United States in the nineteenth century, so did the nature of the occupational roles to be filled. The rise of
industrialization and the increasing technological development of the society had an enormous impact in creating not only "room at the top" but
actual "demand at the top," requiring a new supply. The greatly increased
need for business executives, research scientists, lawyers, and financial managers exerted a demand on the education system that led in turn to a need
for more teachers at every level. This change considerably altered the ratio
of nonfarm to farm and even the ratio of elite to nonelite jobs.

During the same period, American society was playing host to waves
of immigrants who entered the American stratification system near the
bottom and had the effect of pushing those already in the system toward
the top. Irish, Italian, and Eastern European immigrants were all initially
restricted to the less prestigious slots on the occupational ladder, whereas
those workers already on the ladder were encouraged and even prodded
to move up the rungs and fill the new occupational opportunities that were
developing. Widening educational opportunity acted as the crucial mechanism for the transformation. The rise of public universities with low tuition
made possible a massive surge of occupational mobility on the part of ethnic
immigrants previously at the bottom of the stratification ladder.

Urbanization also contributes to changes in stratification patterns and
to an increase in social mobility. Urbanized societies, or even those moving
in this direction, commonly have expanding economies and thus increased
job opportunities and rising income. Growing cities, in particular large
cities, have a complex division of labor, which involves the creation of new
occupations or more jobs and a need for personnel to fill these positions.
Thus, there are opportunities for upward occupational mobility—or prospects for downward mobility. For the United States and other highly in-

dustrialized societies, however, data indicate that in recent decades the rates of total mobility have not changed all that much (Gilbert & Kahl, 1987:166).

Patterns of social mobility vary from one society to another, with perhaps the most marked differentiation to be made between industrial and nonindustrial societies. Moreover, variations among nations in mobility rates can be interpreted in different ways, depending upon which aspect of mobility one examines. S. M. Miller (1960) suggests that chances for long-term upward mobility from blue collar to elite appear to be greater in the United States and Japan. When all possibilities of entry into the elite from other levels are considered, Sweden and the Netherlands may be more open than the United States or Japan. Australia has a very low inheritance of occupational status and hence the highest general mobility figures. Blue-collar to white-collar moves seem to be most prevalent in France, Switzerland, and Great Britain.

Regardless of the prevalence, frequency, and type of social mobility, movement through the class system, either up or down, is an experience that profoundly affects many aspects of an individual's life. (Tumin, 1967). For many, upward social mobility may be a disruptive experience. Through education or other forms of achievement, they realize occupational attainments that place them into life-styles substantially different from those of their parents. In certain situations, life-style differences stemming from occupational factors may be accentuated by considerations of ethnic culture. To illustrate, the upwardly mobile children of immigrant parents may be under considerable pressure to reject or abandon parental beliefs, values, and way of life in order to become assimilated into their new social class. In some cases upward mobility is associated with guilt and anxiety and may result in the breakdown of relations with the parents. It has also been suggested that those who are upwardly mobile into the middle class are generally more politically conservative than those born into middle-class circumstances (Tumin, 1967:93–95).

The Soviet Union

So far, the discussion has centered on changes *within* the stratification system. Let us now examine an attempt to change the *type of* stratification system. Historically, there have been several such attempts, but the focus here will be on the Soviet system. The Soviet Union is the first nation in the history of the world whose aims were eventually to abolish the class system. As a matter of fact, it is frequently claimed that it has already been done. The Soviets claim that a social class is defined by whether its members are owners or workers, and as everyone in the Soviet Union has the same relations to the means of production—all are workers and there are no individual owners—the class system has already been abolished. In theory, surplus of production belongs to everyone, there is no exploitation, and all decisions are made collectively. The trend toward egalitarianism took place during the first decade after the Russian Revolution. It included the removal of almost all the former elite from their high positions through demotion, exile, imprisonment, or death. Farmers and industrial workers were considered in the highest esteem. A special effort was made to open both high schools and universities to children of workers and peasants, none of whom had previously been given such privilege. Quotas were set to reduce the number of children from families who were considered to be "enemies of the state." Private ownership of land and factories was abolished, along with all external signs of rank, title, and special uniforms.

The regime succeeded in reducing inequality drastically, even though they did not achieve a completely egalitarian society. By the 1930s, however, sharp distinctions were made between "classlessness" and "egalitarianism," and the latter was denounced as a "petty bourgeoisie deviation." Stalin argued that "socialism and egalitarianism have nothing in common," and "This ideological offensive against egalitarianism coincided broadly with the change in policy of the Soviet rulers in the early 1930s, which involved increasing wage and salary differentials, and in particular offering substantial financial incentives to highly skilled workers, scientists and technicians, industrial managers and intellectuals. These policies were continued during and after the war, and as a result the range of incomes in the USSR came to be almost as great as that in the capitalist countries" (Bottomore, 1966:57). Many of the blue-collar workers (as in Western countries) receive wages that are about as high or higher than the wages of white-collar workers. Top-level factory managers in the Soviet Union earn four to five times more than skilled workers (Shipler, 1979:43). By contrast, American executives earn, on the average, 12 times more, and many chief executive officers receive compensation in excess of $1 million a year, including bonuses and stock options (Lane, 1982:52).

In addition, occupational and political elites in the Soviet Union enjoy many privileges that do not appear as wages and are not available to others, such as the use of automobiles and chauffeurs, cheap vacations, and special shopping facilities. It is interesting to note that in the Soviet pattern of stratification certain occupations have much more esteem and prestige and perhaps greater economic privileges than similar occupations in the West. Examples include ballet dancers, chess players, and artists.

Today, class distinctions, contrary to the revolutionary ideal of a classless society, are quite pronounced, and there is a definite hierarchy of social classes. Alex Inkeles (quoted by Rossides, 1976:46) distinguishes ten such classes, which appear to be ranked as follows:

1. Ruling elite
2. Superior intelligentsia

3.   General intelligentsia
4.   Working-class aristocracy
5.5. White collar
5.5. Well-to-do peasants
7.   Average workers
8.5. Average peasants
8.5. Disadvantaged workers
10. Forced labor

The Bolshevik Revolution of 1917 succeeded in changing the fundamental relations of power and property, but it failed to create a society ensuring the equality of its citizens, one in which social stratification is absent. Although the system is more open than before the Revolution, with greater mobility opportunities, inequities still persist. One little reported inequity is the substantial gap between the privileged and the poor. In a well-documented study, *Poverty in the Soviet Union*, Mervyn Matthews (1986) investigated the life-styles of the underprivileged in recent years. He found that in the Soviet Union some two-fifths of the nonagricultural labor force earned less than the minimum state standards. This group involved mostly unskilled manual and service workers. The incidence of poverty among larger families, peasants, and pensioners is even higher. The present leadership under Mikhail Gorbachev initiated large-scale economic reforms in 1987 to be incorporated in the next Five-Year Plan. How effective these reforms will be to alleviate the plight of the poor remains a matter of conjecture.

In sum, during the last 200 years, the productive systems of many societies have undergone a profound change. In this relatively short period of time, techniques of production and patterns of economic organization that had endured for thousands of years had been replaced by new and radically different ones. These developments have laid the foundation for a new and profoundly different system of stratification in modern society. These developments have also drastically altered power relations, which will be examined in the following section.

POWER RELATIONS

Few people would disagree with Olsen (1970) that, like "energy in the physical world, power pervades all dynamic social phenomena." Although power has been variously defined, most sociologists would agree with Max Weber's definition of power as "the chance of a man or a number of men to realize their own will in a communal action even against the resistance of others who are participating in that action" (Gerth & Mills, 1946:180). Implicit in this definition is the notion that power cannot be considered an attribute of any individual or group. Rather, it is defined as a relationship *between* individuals or groups. Invariably, power has at least three components: force, authority, and influence (Bierstedt, 1974:220–241).

Force means the application of sanctions to, or the elimination of alternatives from, one group or individual by another. "Surrender or die," "Your money or your life," "Publish or perish," "Behave or get spanked"; all of these are examples of the elimination of possibilities. In earlier days, for example, force used to be an inherent part of the student–teacher power relation. In one instance, a school teacher tells that during his 51 years of teaching, he administered "911,527 blows with a cane; 124,010 with a rod; 20,989 with a ruler; 136,715 with the hand; 10,295 over the mouth; 7,095 boxes on the ear; [and] 1,115,800 slaps on the head. . . ." (Coleman, quoted by Rogers & Skinner, 1968:335).

Authority is a legitimate power, an established right to make decisions and order the actions of others. Weber (Gerth & Mills, 1946:196–252) identifies three main types of authority:

1. *Charismatic* authority the authority of an extraordinary person who is obeyed because of charisma—his image of wisdom, saintliness, or invincibility—such as Christ, Napoleon, or Hitler.
2. *Traditional* authority, resting on a belief of sacred norms and traditions which one must obey; for example, prince, priest, or chief.
3. *Bureaucratic* or rational legal authority, resting on formal office or rank; for example, a general or a president of a university.

Finally, *influence* is the ability to affect the decisions and actions of others beyond any authority to do so. For example, professors have authority to command certain work assignments and to assign grades, but they do not have the authority to compel students to accept their opinions, even though they can influence students to do so. In brief, power is implied because when challenged, it becomes force; when legalized, it becomes authority; and influence rests on some combination of personality attributes and authority.

Power is a universal phenomenon in human societies, and there is an infinite number of power relations—the power of the parent over the child, the master over the slave, the teacher over the student, the warden over the prisoner, the employer over the employee, the general over the lieutenant. In short, it pervades all social relationships.

The Sources of Power

John French and Bertram Raven (1960) identified five different sources of power. They do not exhaust the possible sources of power, but they do identify the major types of resources brought to bear when people attempt to influence other people. The five sources of power, several of which could be in effect simultaneously, are: reward, coercive, legitimate, referent, and expertise.

Reward power is based on the control of resources that affect the lives of those whom a given individual or group wants to influence, such as money or the ability to confer honors. An illustration of this type of power relationship is the employer–employee relation, in which the employer has the power over financial resources as well as the ability to promote or to confer honors on the employee. Another example would be in the political arena where supporters of a candidate or position receive jobs, contracts, and vital information about upcoming policy issues (Bensman & Vidich, 1987:91–92).

Coercive power is essentially based on eliciting fear, which, in turn, inspires compliance. Such power may be exhibited by an individual or a group's capacity to inflict pain. Totalitarian governments, for example, rely to a considerable extent on this kind of power.

Legitimate power depends on values that establish a person's right to influence by virtue of the person's claim on a particular office or position. The values affecting legitimation can be subsumed under what Max Weber calls rational-legal orientation. This orientation places limitations on power, restricting it to the functioning of a given office—for example, the power of elected officials.

Referent power is based on followers' close identification with their leaders. This kind of power was used in the big-city political machines early in this century. At the base of the organization was a notion that kinship, friendship, and ethnic commonality created a helping system in which votes were exchanged for "jobs, bonuses, turkeys on Thanksgiving, coal in the wintertime" (Greer, 1962). Scott Greer suggested that the increase in the scale of the country—that is, the increase in sheer numbers of people, along with bureaucratization and centralization of power—weakened the big-city machine because it moved the locus of power from the city hall and city government to national governments and corporations. In recent times, black, Chicano, and Indian leaders have used referent power in an attempt to mobilize masses to alter power relations (McClusky, 1976).

Expertise power is based on one's special training or access to special information. As societies and governments become more complex and knowledge becomes more specialized and technical, this type of power is becoming increasingly more prevalent (Freidson, 1986). An example of this would be the growing number of specialists and professionals who testify as expert witnesses, for a fee, in lawsuits and criminal cases. According to a *New York Times* (1987b) article, the business of being an expert itself is exploding, and in recent years individuals with knowledge in scores of obscure fields (such as bottle explosions or hot-air balloon accidents) have joined tens of thousands of doctors, university professors, and engineers in the expert-witness industry.

The Dynamics of Power Relations

In *Power and Privilege*, Gerhard Lenski (1966) contends that the variety of inequality a society exhibits depends upon the existing power relations and upon how the power system distributes material surplus, especially food. Focusing his analysis on the basic techniques of subsistence, he develops a typology of societies, each type having a distinguishable degree of inequality and different power relations. The five types of societies are as follows:

1. *Hunting and gathering* societies are characterized by pronounced equality as a result of universally shared economic scarcity. Any superiority that exists is based on personal skills and abilities, a form of superiority that cannot be transmitted socially to children.

2. In *simple horticultural* societies institutionalized inequality first emerges with farming based on the digging stick, a fundamental tool of a gardening economy. Domestication of plants results in a more dependable supply of food, which in turn is related to the emergence of a division of labor, wherein specialized economic occupations and full-time occupations in politics and religion develop. As a result of functional specialization, new social statuses and power relations emerge.

3. In *advanced horticultural* societies there is a noticeable increase in inequality, which accompanies the development of the hoe, permitting a greater utilization of the soil, and of terracing, irrigation, fertilizers, or metallurgy. The higher level of technology leads to an increase in economic specialization and to the development of political power. There is an elaboration of formal statuses, accompanied by an increase in property rights (including rights over human beings, or slavery) and the availability of transferable assets such as money, cattle, and slaves. From the perspective of power relations, this level of technological and social development sees the emergence of well-defined hereditary strata.

4. In *agrarian societies* there is a significant increase in food production and food surplus that leads to advances in transport, communication, engineering, and military technology. New forms of power relations emerge in the form of a city-state, a bureaucratic empire, or feudalism. In such a society there is a well-developed, superior, hereditary social group, and the causes of inequality are primarily economic.

5. In *industrial societies* the development of an industrial technology represents a significant change in the means of subsistence available to society. As a result, sharp increases take place in production and in specialized economic activity. But the subsequent material surplus, according to Lenski, does not lead, as in the past, to increases in inequality but to a reversal of this historic trend. Although economic prestige and political

inequality is still substantial, it is less marked than in agrarian societies. Economic resources are more equitably distributed and there is an emergence of universal suffrage, representing a diffusion and popularization of political power. The major reason for this trend toward increased equality is that industrial society is too complex to be run personally or arbitrarily. The ruling groups find it in their interests to involve the lower and intermediate groups in economic and political processes.

The contention that industrial society is characterized by a decrease in economic and political inequality as compared to agrarian society is a major theme in Lenski's work. It is important to note that the economic elite in industrial society claims a smaller portion of the economic pie than the economic elite of agrarian society, and there is a greater willingness of the political elite to involve the masses in political processes. Moreover, unlike in agricultural societies, in industrial societies, at least in the West, ownership in corporations has more or less become separated from control: Power has passed into the hands of managers (Zeitlin, 1982).

A similar point is made by Gaetano Mosca, who suggests that while wealth may still facilitate recruitment to the ruling class or political elite, in modern industrial societies access to the political or ruling elite has become open to wider and wider strata of the population. Mosca came to this conclusion by tracing the changes in the relations between the ruling minority and the majority that is being ruled. He pointed out that the structure of the ruling class and the criteria of recruitment into it change with the changes in its predominant societal function. Historically, one change was the shift from military skills, first to land ownership and then to wealth, as a criterion of access to the ruling class. At first, the ruling warrior classes acquired ownership of the land, which is the principal source of production and wealth in premodern societies. As revenue from the land increases, accompanied by the growth of population and the development of urban centers of consumption, an important societal transformation occurs: "Wealth rather than military valor comes to be the characteristic feature of the dominant class: the people who rule are the rich rather than the brave." (Mosca, 1973:214).

He further suggests that "If a new source of wealth develops in a society, if the practical importance of knowledge grows, if an old religion declines or a new one is born, if a new current of ideas spreads, then, simultaneously, far-reaching dislocations occur in the ruling class" (Mosca, 1973:215). The ruling classes inevitably decline when they can no longer render the services they once rendered and when their talents lose in importance in the environment in which they live. This is further facilitated when scattered smaller units become integrated into large-scale tightly knit political entities. This brings an ever-increasing concentration of power in the hands of a state that carries out and regulates more and more functions. This is related to a change in the mode of organization of the political structure, the transition from feudalism to bureaucracy. Political bureaucracy first came into being in seventeenth-century France under the reign of Louis XIV, and then, according to Mosca, evolved into the democratic and totalitarian bureaucratic state where the potential political power of nonpoliticians has increased significantly.

Suzanne Keller (1963) contends that industrialization brought about the development of many "strategic elites" defined as "a minority of individuals designated to serve a collectivity in a socially valued way." (1963:4)

In addition to a political elite, an economic elite, and a military elite, Keller discusses cultural, moral, intellectual, scientific, religious, and diplomatic elites among others. She writes (1963:277–278):

> In highly industrialized societies . . . power has become less arbitrary and personal and is increasingly shared among various groups and institutions. . . . The current strategic elites are not as free to exercise their powers as were the aristocracies and ruling classes of the past because in being functionally specialized they are themselves subordinate in spheres not relating to their specialty, and because they are now far more dependent on the good will of the public. . . . Today, no single strategic elite has absolute power or priority . . . and none determines the patterns of selection and recruitment of the rest . . . their more varied skills and experiences result in the formation of a more complex and many-sided social core, one in which a number of personalities must coexist.

Decentralization of Power

In addition to changes in power relations at the societal level, changes are taking place at the level of community. In most American communities, power is diffused to a considerable degree. Thomas R. Dye (1986:49) contends that the community's most important resource is land, and those who control land use are the community's power elite. They include mortgage bankers, real estate developers, builders, and landowners. Community elites, Dye argues, are different from national elites in their economic function. At the local level, the elites' function is to prepare land for capital investment. But their power is limited, for they cannot control the destinies of their communities. Their power is limited to economic development decisions, and they secure mass support for their policies by emphasizing prospects for more jobs and small business opportunities. There is no single center of power, and Paul E. Mott (1970:85–86) cites the factors or conditions that favor an increase in the number of local centers of power and in the number of power relations. "The number of centers of power is to increase as 1) the population (of the community) increases, 2) the ethnic composition becomes more heterogeneous, 3) functional specialization increases, 4) the number of self-conscious social classes increases, 5) as in-migration increases."

Law and Power

Changes in power relations are also brought about by law. As J.O. Hertzler (1961:421) points out, ". . . the law in effect structures the power (superordinate-subordinate) relationships in the society; it maintains the status quo and protects the various strata against each other, both in governmental and non-governmental organizations and relationships." The law affects power relations by stating who may do what to whom. For example, prior to the passing of the National Labor Relations Act of 1935, employers were legally entitled to fire employees who joined unions. This law established workers' legal right to join unions and prohibited employers from penalizing workers for union activity. Civil rights legislation also changed the power relations between blacks and whites by enabling the former to obtain goals more efficiently, pursue goals that otherwise they would not pursue, and act out values more effectively. It resulted in the acquisition of new opportunities and in the formation of new attitudes such as increased self-esteem, courage, and political awareness (McClusky, 1976:393).

In sum, it should be noted that when talking about political power relations, an organized minority generally can control an unorganized majority. Even though there have been important changes in power relations, indicating a trend toward a more egalitarian distribution of power, it is probably true, contrary to popular myth, that "the people" neither possess nor dispense power. It should also be remembered that "it is quite impossible for the government of a society to be in the hands of any but a few . . . there is government *for* the people; there is no government *by* the people" (Aron, quoted by Bottomore, 1964:120).

EDUCATION

In traditional societies, individuals can acquire the knowledge and skills necessary for the successful performance of adult roles without formal education. In more complex societies, parents are unable to pass on to their children the knowledge and skills they will need as adults. As a society becomes more industrialized, there is an ever-increasing demand for general skills—reading, writing, and arithmetic—and for specialized vocational and technical training for specific occupational roles. Today "An abundant and increasing supply of highly educated people has become the absolute prerequisite of social and economic development in our world" (Drucker, 1973:232).

Schools were invented several thousand years ago to prepare a select few for leadership. They educated only an elite class, which was supposed to "carry" the culture for the whole society. The education provided was theoretical, consisting of the *trivium* (grammar, rhetoric, and logic) and the *quadrivium* (arithmetic, geometry, astronomy, and music). While describing education in medieval Europe, Phillippe Ariés (1962) points out that schools lacked a gradation of subjects according to difficulty. There was a very broad age dispersion of students, ranging from age 9 to 24 in the same class; an absence of standard age for beginning school; instruction from a few to several hundred students by one teacher; and the maintenance of control by corporal punishment, humiliation, and reliance on informers. The notion of schooling as preparation for adulthood was foreign to the medieval tradition. Schooling of this nature, largely consistent with training a clerical elite, endured for a long time.

A century or more ago, public schools were created to teach the three R's to the masses. Today education is a dominant institution that touches almost every member of a society at some time, consumes a large portion of a society's financial resources, and is one of the largest employers of the work force. Universal education became a right, if not a mandate, at least up to age 15 in most countries of the world.

During this century, school enrollments at the primary, secondary, and college levels have increased dramatically. In 1985, more that 56 million Americans between the ages of 3 and 34 were enrolled in education institutions. Some examples of changes: Of those age 25 years and over in 1940, 24.5 percent had completed high school and 4.6 percent college. The median school years completed was 8.6. By 1985, 73.9 percent had completed high school, 19.4 percent college, and the median school years completed grew to 12.6. Between 1970 and 1986, school expenditures rose from $70.4 billion to $260.2 billion for all levels (U.S. Bureau of the Census, 1987:114, 115, 121). For the academic year 1987/88, educational expenses exceeded $308 billion. This figure represents about 6.7 percent of the total value of the nation's annual output of goods and services. Public elementary and secondary schools spent $184 billion, or $4,538 per student. This is an increase of 6.5 percent over the academic year 1986/87. The total expenditure for colleges and universities was $124 billion, an increase of 7 percent from the preceding year. Public institutions spent $81.3 billion, or $12,560 per full-time-equivalent student, while private institutions spent $42.7 billion, or $19,391 per full-time-equivalent student (*Chronicle of Higher Education*, 1987a; *New York Times*, 1987c).

Several reasons account for these phenomenal increases both in the number of students and in expenditures. One explanation is the high birthrate following World War II. Another factor is the lengthening educational span with communities adding kindergarten at one end and community colleges at the other. A third explanation is the rising popularity of college educations. But beyond these, the average cost per pupil at every level has been rising faster than either the price or level of the gross national product. This is due, in part, to a national drive to improve education with the customary prescription being a generous diffusion of money. Let us now consider some specific changes in elementary, secondary, and higher education.

Elementary and Secondary Education

Since about the turn of the century the main change in American elementary and secondary education has been from curriculum-oriented subject matter to an emphasis upon the child as a growing personality. Under the former, most weight was given to content and to the capacity to reproduce what had been read or heard. Today, schools are more and more child-centered, with emphasis on self- and social development. This change has been accompanied by a shift from a rather severe authoritarianism to a more permissive practice in teaching methods in which the child has a larger degree of participation. There is greater emphasis on matters of motivation, cooperative learning, mental hygiene, and the like.

The rapid rise in high school population in recent decades led to a proliferation of separate courses, and to such varied courses of study as liberal or college preparatory, commercial, vocational, and fine arts. The trend has been away from the courses designed to prepare the pupil for higher education toward those that have more practical use in jobs or in the home and that give the future citizen some orientation to his or her public and political rights and duties. Ancient languages, algebra, geometry, trigonometry, and formal political history have tended to give way to modern languages, simplified or "new" mathematics, and social studies that emphasize current issues. These changes have been accompanied by a series of educational innovations, such as the use of teaching machines and closed-circuit television, the creation of open classroom environments, and a growing reliance on computers both as a teaching and learning aid.

As increasingly large proportions of young people attend schools at all levels, concern has grown that the quality of education has been declining. A number of shortcomings have captured the public's attention. Examples of these would include the relatively high rate of functional illiteracy among young adults (as high as 40 percent among minority youths); inadequacies in the teaching of science, mathematics, and foreign languages, and the general decline on tests performances (Ravitch, 1985). Studies indicate that American high school students average lower test scores in mathematics, science, and other subjects when compared to their counterparts in Japan, West Germany, the Soviet Union, and some other industrialized nations (Tharp, 1987; *U.S. News & World Report*, 1987b). Some of the differences may be due to greater emphasis on the hard sciences and languages and to the length of the school year. For example, Soviet students routinely study physics and algebra for five years, chemistry and biology for four years, and calculus for two years. Most American high school students do not take even a year of either physics or chemistry. Only 6 percent study calculus. With a 180-day school schedule, the United States is one of the few countries with classrooms idle over half the year. Japanese schools operate more than 240 days, including half-days on Saturdays. Most Japanese high school students do not date, drive cars, hold part-time jobs, or even do household chores. In the United States, 76 percent of high school seniors spend fewer than five hours per week on homework; in Japan, less than 35 percent do.

The past decade has also witnessed a decline in the Scholastic Aptitude Test (SAT) scores. Between 1967 and 1980, average verbal scores dropped about 40 points, from 466 to 424, and mathematics scores fell 26 points, from 492 to 466 out of a total of 800 possible points in both categories. Between 1980 and 1985, there was a slight increase in test scores (7 points in verbal and 9 in mathematics), but the percentage demonstrating superior performance (scores of 600 and above in either category) continued to decline (U.S. Bureau of the Census, 1987:135).

Several reasons are cited for the decline of SAT scores. They include the fact that more lower-scoring minorities and disadvantaged students have been taking the tests since the mid-1960s; that learning standards in schools are down as evidenced by an increase in absenteeism, grade inflation, and easier textbooks; that changing family structures, notably the increase in one parent or broken homes, have hurt the children's learning ability; and that easier access to colleges along with a growing lack of motivation may have resulted in less preparation by students for college entrance examinations. The decline in scores are further attributed to an increase in disciplinary problems in schools, high rates of truancy, and the substantial amount of time spent viewing television on school days.

Generally, these are the reasons given for the school systems' incapability of teaching the fundamentals to America's poor children. It is interesting to note that "The same school system that had taught the fundamentals to the children of immigrants from provinces in southern Italy where from 67 percent to 79 percent of the adult populations could not read or write Italian, now presumably could not do the same for the children of native-born Americans, all of whom spoke English and most of whom were at least literate" (Armbruster, 1977:11).

Armbruster (1977:54) further points out that over the past decade, the lack of academic climate in high schools, the proliferation of elective courses, less homework, and lax attendance requirements, in many instances, resulted in a discouraging situation in which

> many schools have tended to educate children for a nonexistent world. Certain things in life simply cannot be avoided or blamed on someone else; actions have personal consequences; outside the school environment one normally has to produce to be promoted; work must satisfy the needs of the economy to be profitable to the worker; many trades and professions require work that gives no credit for good intentions or for being nearly accurate—much work,

and advanced study, must be explicit, meticulous and correct every time; it is important to be well informed and logical, not just spontaneous and talkative. To let students believe otherwise is to mislead them dangerously— especially if they are underprivileged.

Higher Education

Today's universities have their origins in the institutions that developed in eleventh- and twelfth-century Europe. They began in Italy, spread to Spain and France, from there to Germany and Scandinavia, then to England, Scotland, and finally America. The contemporary American university is an amalgam borrowed from Western Europe, particularly England and Germany. The assumptions underlying the undergraduate curriculum originally came from England, whereas graduate education is grounded in German scholarship and science. The English influence can be dated from the founding of the first college, Harvard, in 1636. The German influence did not take hold until more than two centuries later. The curriculum was designed to produce a learned clergy and cultivated gentlemen and to impart an aristocratic life-style to the wellborn. In the seventeenth century more than half of the college graduates became ministers, and most college professors were clergymen, or at least were trained in theology. Prior to the Civil War almost all the college presidents were ministers.

In the early American college the principal method of instruction was *recitation*. This is a process in which students repeat from memory, often verbatim, textbook assignments. (Remnants of this method are still found in Eastern European and Soviet universities.) For *disputation*, students defended or attacked a proposition in Latin, the required language of instruction. Later on, the lecture by teachers supplemented student recitations. Because of the limited number of books, students often copied down word for word what the instructor said. As the size of classes increased, the lecture method slowly replaced recitation and disputation. The blackboard was first used at Bowdoin College around 1823. The *seminar method* was imported from Germany in the mid-nineteenth century. Finally, the *discussion class*, designed to supplement lectures, was introduced at Harvard in 1904 (Boyer, 1987:149).

The early colleges were for male students only and higher education did not become a reality for women until the early 1800s. (Now women make up 52 percent of the undergraduate student body.) By 1860 there were 246 colleges and universities in the United States and 17 state universities. In 1862 higher education gained support from the passage of the Morrill Act by Congress. This act granted each state a large area of land for the purpose of endowing at least one agricultural college. These "land-grant colleges" contributed greatly to the expansion of agricultural and engineering education. Further support for higher education came from the passage of the GI Bill by Congress in 1944, and its extension in 1952. The Economic Opportunity Act of 1964 authorized grants for college work-study programs, and in 1972 the Higher Education Act authorized, for the first time, direct all-purpose aid to colleges and universities. The greater financial support by the government resulted in the greater involvement of the government in higher education.

In 1984, there were 3,331 institutions of higher education in the United States: 2,025 were classified as four-year (which includes 159 universities), and the remaining 1,306 as junior colleges (U.S. Bureau of the Census, 1987:138). The number of two- and four-year colleges almost doubled during the last generation. A similar increase took place among the number of college students. By the fall of 1986, total college enrollment in institutions of higher learning amounted to over 12.5 million, and college students nowadays can choose from a list of more than 6,000 different majors (Boyer, 1987:102). The percentage of high school graduates who go to college also grew steadily over the years, reaching almost 55 percent in 1985. This is the highest in the world. But the days of steady growth in the size of the college population may be numbered. As a result of the downturn of fertility since the 1960s, demographers and educators anticipate an overall decrease in the size of the college population for the coming years.

A phenomenal increase has occurred in the number of junior colleges. In 1960 there were 521 such institutions; by 1984, there were 1,306. In 1960, there were 451,000 junior college students; today there are close to 5 million. From 1965 to 1970, there were 194 new junior colleges that opened up in America, about one every nine days for half a decade. The junior college diploma is rapidly replacing the high school diploma as a minimum credential for entrance into the "educated" middle class.

Concomitant with the growth in the number of colleges has been the steady increase in the number and types of degrees conferred. The number of bachelor's degree recipients increased from 839,730 in 1971 to 979,477 in 1985 (*Chronicle of Higher Education*, 1987b:34). But there were some major changes in the field of study. The number of business majors more than doubled and accounted for almost 24 percent of all bachelor's degrees conferred in 1985. There was a tenfold increase in the number of students majoring in computer and information sciences, and a fourfold increase among those in communications. At the same time, the number of education majors declined by half, and there were notable decreases in foreign languages, mathematics, and the social sciences.

Between 1971 and 1978, the number of M.A. degrees conferred increased from 230,509 to 311,620. From 1978, however, there was a gradual decline to 286,251 in 1985. There is an uneven trend among doctoral recipients; their number peaked in 1975 at 34,083, and in 1985, 32,943 degrees were granted (U.S. Bureau of the Census, 1987:147; *Chronicle of*

Higher Education, 1987b:34). In 1985, half of all M.A. degrees were earned by those majoring in business and education (26.5 percent and 23.5 percent, respectively), and over a fifth of Ph.D. recipients were in education.

As the population of the United States became increasingly well educated, women made significant gains (Bianchi & Spain, 1986:137). In terms of enrollment, women represent more than 52 percent of the college population. In 1985, slightly more women (50.7 percent) than men earned bachelor's degrees, and about the same number of women as men received M.A. degrees. But women represented only 34 percent of Ph.D. recipients. Differences still exist between men and women in their major field of study. More than two-thirds of students in majors such as architecture, engineering, physical sciences, and religion are men. Those fields in which over two-thirds are female include education, foreign languages, library sciences, and health professions. But women made significant inroads in traditional "male" areas of study. For example, women recipients of medical and law degrees more than doubled since the 1970s, and women increased substantially in fields such as mathematics and engineering.

Data show that overall minority enrollment has also continued to grow. In 1976 there were approximately 1,691,000 minority students in two- and four-year colleges, representing 15.4 percent of all students. By 1984, the figure had risen to about 2,063,000, or 17 percent of the total. The patterns, however, vary widely by race. Black enrollment as a percentage of enrollment reached a peak in 1976, when 1,032,000 blacks made up 9.4 percent of the college population. By 1984, there were about 1,070,000 black students, or 8.8 percent of the total. Over the same period, Hispanic students gradually increased from 383,000, or 3.5 percent, in 1976, to 529,000, or 4.3 percent of the college population in 1984. Enrollment of American Indian students decreased slightly, from about 84,000 to 83,000, in that same period. The one ethnic minority to show substantial gains was Asian-Americans. Their representation increased to about 382,000, or 3.1 percent of all students in 1984, up from 197,000, or 1.8 percent, in 1976 (Fiske, 1987). In addition to the decline in enrollment, fewer and fewer black college students are graduating. From 1975 to 1985, while the number of whites receiving bachelor's degrees remained steady, the number of blacks getting college diplomas declined about 6 percent. Blacks are also underrepresented among the recipients of advanced degrees. For example, in 1986, eleven were awarded doctorates in engineering and three in computer science (*U.S. News & World Report,* 1987c:75). One factor in the declining number of black and Hispanic students is the cost of college, which has been increasing at twice the rate of inflation in recent years. From 1980 to 1985, college costs rose 64 percent. In 1987, it cost $5,604 a year to attend the average public institution and $10,199 at a typical private one (*Chicago Tribune,* 1987; *Newsweek,* 1987). It is compounded by a substantial decline in federal student assistance: Federal grants and scholarships fell from $13 billion in 1975 to $5 billion in 1985, a drop of 62 percent.

Traditionally, the objectives of higher education were to make available to students the tools of learning, to open up new horizons for them to explore, and to assist them to understand their cultural heritage. Today, by contrast, as a 1987 Carnegie Foundation report succinctly observes, "careerism dominates the campus" (Boyer, 1987:102). Students view general education as an irritating interruption—an annoying detour on their way to their degree. The report finds that most students go to college to pursue a special field of study that leads to a career. A third of undergraduates would drop out if college did not increase their prospects of employment.

Most students (and parents) want to translate their educational dollars into marketable skills. As a result, career-related education has increased dramatically since the mid-1970s. Almost all colleges, in response to the demand and competition for students, added new vocational majors and split up old ones into smaller pieces. New programs were created such as medical technology, computer programming, and police science. Colleges, which in the past had one major in business administration, in response to marketplace demands have a dozen or so business-related majors such as fashion merchandising, foods and nutrition in business, and health services administration. Gerontology, which hardly existed as an academic subject in the early 1970s, has become one of higher education's fastest-growing disciplines, and colleges and universities offer more than 1,300 different programs as growing numbers of elderly people create demands for practitioners (Watkins, 1977:10). The vocationalization of higher education is being promoted both in two- and four-year colleges and universities. The emphasis seems to be on technically competent workers, not on a corps of free-thinking liberal arts graduates. The shift away from liberal arts and toward career-oriented vocational majors is not limited to American campuses. A similar trend prevails in both Western and Eastern European colleges. It has even reached China, where there are "three ways"—black, gold and red—for students to pursue a career. The black way is to leave China to study abroad, to earn a black graduation cap and gown. Gold involves going into business in the hope of becoming rich. And red refers to joining the Communist Party and becoming a government official. In all three cases, students are driven by "blatant opportunism instead of devotion to the socialist ideals" in their academic work (Gargan, 1987).

The Great Training Robbery

Most Americans believe that the more education a person has, the better he or she will do in life. Education seems to be the most popular solution for the individual's desire for success and social mobility. This idea is reflected in the growing trend toward "credentialism." The more society relies on formal education as its basic training device, the more individuals find that educational credentials are essential if they are to have access to jobs and opportunities for promotion. As these credentials become more and more important, mere experience in the labor market is downgraded. An emphasis on educational credentials has been said to be justified in that, because the economy has become more technical and complex, a more highly educated work force is necessary. Ivar Berg (1970) attacks this notion and argues that on every occupational level Americans tend to overestimate the value of education, denying employment opportunities to those with less education and demanding more education than most jobs require. Berg finds no relation between formal education and work productivity, turnover rates, work satisfaction, or promotion. If anything, there is an inverse relation between amount of formal education and occupational perform- ance. He notes that formal education plays one single role for blue-collar, white-collar, and engineer-scientist workers: It determines where one en- ters the occupational system. What is important, in other words, is that employers believe that formal education makes better workers and there- fore use it as a criterion for hiring. But once hired, workers with more or less formal education exhibit no significant difference in work perform- ance. The only apparent difference is in income because workers with more formal education enter the labor force at higher levels and change jobs more often. William Sewell (1971:793) agrees with Berg and criticizes the importance placed on credentials by both colleges and employers. "This criticism is particularly persuasive whenever it can be shown that the ed- ucational requirements for entry into an occupation have little bearing on the activities of that occupation." (Sewell, 1971: 793).

Publish or Perish

Traditionally, the emphasis in colleges was quite clearly on teaching. The goal was to preserve and transmit existing truths rather than to advance knowledge. "Even as late as 1857, a committee of the Columbia College board of trustees attributed the poor quality of the college to the fact that three professors 'wrote books' " (Lewis, 1975:3). However, with the spread of graduate education modeled after German universities, faculty advance- ment and promotion soon became dependent on scholarly research rather than on teaching. A number of universities advocated "productive" work in an attempt to establish a "national reputation" (Lewis, 1975:7). By the turn of the century, many academics in universities lived by the code of "publish or perish," and they were judged only according to the merit of their research, rather than on their teaching. Today this trend is becoming even more pronounced. Evidence of publication and research is a crucial factor both in hiring as well as in retention and promotion. Nowadays, it seems that when the chips are down, it's published research, not classroom skills, that is likely to determine one's professional fate. An important preoccupation on campus is the attempt to determine the proper balance between research and teaching. Ideally, good teaching and quality research should flourish side by side (Boyer, 1987:127).

Publish and Perish

For several decades the shift from unskilled labor to skilled, technical, and professional employment appeared to have created an inexhaustible demand for education. But by the 1970s higher education caught up with the demand, and competent college graduates in many fields were unhappily scanning the help-wanted ads. For example, in 1965 there were two teaching vacancies for each new Ph.D. In 1972, graduates and vacancies were about equal. Two years later the bottom fell out of the academic job market for newly minted Ph.D.s. Those in the humanities and the social sciences were particularly affected by it, and many graduates were unable to find jobs in academia. It was commonplace to have hundreds of qualified applicants for an assistant professorship at a small college in English, history, or even in sociology. Many of the tenured positions were eliminated. For the few lucky ones who obtained an academic appointment, it was more often than not for a specified short time period, ranging from one to five years. At many colleges, it became very difficult (if not impossible) to get tenure. Many qualified graduates became frustrated by the shortage of academic jobs and sought placement outside of academia.

By 1987, the days of glut in a growing number of academic fields were rapidly drawing to a close as professors hired in the 1950s and 1960s started to retire. A major portion of academia's 440,000 full-time and 225,000 part-time faculty members were hired during that period to teach the baby-boom generation. They will start retiring in droves in the mid-1990s—right at the time that the baby-boom's boomlet begins to pour into colleges. It is estimated that between 1985 and 2010, institutions of higher education will have to hire between 450,000 and 500,000 new faculty members (Prokesch, 1987:20). In view of the declining enrollment in Ph.D. programs, the next crisis in higher education may well be the shortage of qualified faculty members.

In sum, education over the years has undergone drastic changes. Universities have been transformed into huge complexes with enormous power, college students now far outnumber farmers in the United States, and there are some 665,000 full- and part-time faculty members. The education level of the American population is steadily growing; more and more graduate from high school; there is a steady decline in the proportion of dropouts; more and more high school graduates go on to college and professional schools, and, ironically, more and more find it harder and harder to find a job after graduation. While the level of education goes up in the United States (not necessarily the quality) there are still 758 million people worldwide who cannot read or write, which represents an estimated illiteracy rate of 18.5 percent. The growth of population in the world still outpaces the advance in literacy rates.

THE ECONOMY

The structure of an economic system is based on production, distribution, and consumption. Production involves the assembling and applying of resources and it requires land, capital, and labor. Land refers to physical territory and resources; capital consists of the means of production—of money, equipment, and tools; and labor pertains to people who produce goods and services. Distribution entails some system of exchange in which goods and services have some equivalent values. Finally consumption refers to the utilization of goods and services produced by the economy.

Production

In traditional societies production is located in family units. Subsistence farming is predominant, and other industry is supplementary—but still attached to the family and village. Neil J. Smelser (1976:151) points out that as the economy develops, many of the production activities are removed from the family–community complex. In agriculture, the introduction of money crops differentiates between the social contexts of production and consumption. The use of agricultural wage labor separates work roles from what previously might have been a family productive unit. In industry there are several levels of differentiation. In the simplest form, household industry, only the workers' own needs are supplied and there is no surplus to enter the market. "Handicraft production" differentiates between production and consumption even though the latter may take place in the local community. On the other hand, "cottage industry" usually involves a differentiation between consumption and community because production is for unknown consumers in the market, usually through wholesalers. In manufacturing and factory systems the worker is segregated from capital and frequently from his or her family. It brings about a structural differentiation in the labor force as a response to the exigencies of production and marketing. More specialized and efficient roles and organizations are required than the one found in traditional family and community structures. Changes in the production process bring about an increase in the division of labor, with concomitant alterations in the composition, size, and variety of the labor force.

Most economies today, whether fully industrialized or not, contain

three basic sectors, with the proportion of labor force in each sector depending on society's technological development. The *primary sector* refers
to that part of the economy that directly generates raw materials from the
natural environment, such as fishing, mining, or agriculture. The primary
sector dominates the economies of preindustrial societies where virtually
the entire population is engaged in hunting, gathering, or agricultural
activities. The *secondary sector* refers to that part of the economy that trans-
forms raw materials into manufactured goods. Examples of this sector
would include the refining of petroleum, the manufacture of wood into
furniture, metals into tools, building materials, and automobiles. Most of
the labor force is engaged in "blue-collar" occupations in this sector. The
tertiary sector refers to that part of the economy that generates services rather
than goods. The United States became the first country in the 1950s to
have more than half of its labor force engaged in the tertiary sector—
providing services and processing information (Naisbitt, 1982:14–15) in
locations such as offices, hospitals, universities, and restaurants. After considering some changes in the labor force of the United States, I will return
to this point.

The civilian labor force has grown from 22 million in 1890 to close
112 million in the first half of 1987 (U.S. Department of Labor, 1987:9).
Although the proportion of the population represented in the labor force
remained relatively constant at about 40 percent, there have been significant
changes in its composition over the years.

The percentage of manual blue-collar workers was a close second to
those employed on farms at the turn of the century. Between World War
I and World War II, because of the growth of industrialization and the
accelerated decline of farm employment, blue-collar workers comprised
almost 40 percent of the labor force. But by the mid-1950s, the percentage
of white-collar workers exceeded those in blue-collar occupations, and this
gap has increased greatly between 1960 and 1987. Technological advances
that increased production also contributed to reducing the number of manual workers. The decline in steel and automobile industries, due primarily
to competition from abroad, cost the country hundreds of thousands of
blue-collar jobs. The shift from producing goods to service industries, to
be discussed shortly, also played a significant role in the decline in the
number of blue-collar workers.

Those in clerical and related occupations represented 3 percent of
the labor force in 1900. By the mid-1980s, they represented almost 20
percent. This category includes such occupations as word processors, clerks,
typists, proofreaders, and office machine operators. Some are in entirely
new fields. For example, in 1960 there were approximately 12,000 "computer specialists" in America. By 1970, the number had grown to 260,000,
and today it exceeds 1.2 million. Contrary to popular belief, the introduction of new technology, such as, for example, computers for office data

application, does not necessarily result in the reduction of employees. When computers were introduced in the mid-1950s, some experts predicted that large numbers of clerical and kindred workers would be displaced and that job opportunities for millions of people, in one of the largest occupational employment categories, would be curtailed. Yet, over the last three decades, employment of clerical workers has continued to increase, and between 1972 and 1986, the number of such workers grew by 40 percent (Mark, 1987:27). Office computerization made possible work that previously had been impractical because it would have been too costly and time-consuming. It gave rise to new kinds of data analyses, extending the scope of activities for many industries, thus creating new jobs. In addition, it created new occupations such as tape librarian and console operator. New industries were also created to manufacture computers and related paraphernalia. As a result, thousands are employed in manufacturing microelectronic devices, advanced communication equipment, and other technologies that are gaining prominence (Perrolle, 1987).

The percentage of people in the professions and related occupations also quadrupled since the turn of the century. One reason for the growth in the number of professionals is the greater sophistication in knowledge, techniques, and machinery, resulting in a growing demand for technically trained people. There is also a growing demand for services from such diverse occupations as accounting, divorce law, and psychiatry. Many occupations are also becoming professionalized (Ritzer & Walczak, 1986). Their members are changing their names to something more prestigious, for example, beauticians to hairstylists and morticians to funeral directors, and developing codes of ethics and rights of passage whereby members may gain access to the occupation as professionals. This trend is accompanied by an increase in licensing requirements for many occupations.

There was also a dramatic increase in the number of women in the labor force since 1900—from about 5 million then to over 50 million today. Around the turn of the century, few married women entered the work force because their wages were much lower than those of single women (Bianchi & Spain, 1986:166). As the wage differential started to narrow, more and more married women increased their participation in the workplace. Rising educational attainment of women, along with economic growth during the 1950s, the increasing divorce rate, the women's movement, changing attitudes about the desirability (and necessity) of working outside the home, and the rising consumption aspirations are among the main factors bringing about the current high level of labor force participation among women.

Since 1950, an increasing proportion of the labor force is found in service-producing jobs. In April 1987, there were over 77.2 million workers in service-producing occupations and 25 million in goods-producing jobs

(U.S. Department of Labor, 1987:59). Within the service sector there are hidden changes, as Daniel Bell (1973:127–128) points out:

> The word "service" disguises different things, and in the transformation of industrial to post-industrial society there are several stages. First, in the very development of industry there is a necessary expansion of transportation and of public utilities as auxiliary services for the movement of goods and the increasing use of energy. . . . Second, in the mass consumption of distribution (wholesale and retail) and finance, real estate and insurance. . . . [A] third sector, that of personal services, begins to grow—restaurants, hotels, auto services, travel, entertainment, sports. . . . Finally the claims for more services and the inadequacy of the market in meeting people's needs for a decent environment as well as for better health and education lead to the growth of government, particularly at the state and local level, where such needs have to be met.

Today there are more than 17 million local, state, and federal government workers. It is worth noting that in 1950 there were 6.4 million; in 1960, 8.8 million; and in 1970, 13 million. The rapid growth in the number of government workers is accompanied by a "quiet explosion in the scope of pervasiveness of federal regulation" (Lilley & Miller, 1977:49). Government regulation of business, industry, and labor is steadily increasing, and today there are 27 major regulatory agencies. Incidentally, their budget was close to $17 billion for fiscal year 1988. Business and industrial firms must abide by laws regulating wages and hours of employment, health and safety measures, and many other matters.

Distribution

In traditional societies, goods and services are exchanged on a non-economic basis without the use of money or a clearly delineated market system. In such a society one does not necessarily exchange scarce goods or labor in order to get what one needs. A self-regulating price market for the exchange of goods and services is brought about by the advent of economic surplus and the introduction of money as a means of exchange. It should be noted, however, that not all exchanges of goods and services take place in a market situation. For example, the redistribution of wealth through charity or progressive taxation is an exchange of potentially marketable commodities outside of the market. Furthermore, "The mobilization of economic resources for public goals—through eminent domain, taxation, direct appropriation, and selective service—involves the transfer of economic goods and services without the intrusion of an economic market" (Smelser, 1976:119).

The economist Karl Polanyi and his associates (1957) suggest that economic activities fall into three main patterns of exchange. The first pattern is called *reciprocative*, which is illustrated by the ritualized gift giving among families, clans, and tribes. Farmers in many societies help each other at harvest. Goods and services are given because it is traditional to do so. The only principle of calculation is the loose principle that the giving and receiving of goods or services should "balance out" in the long run.

The second form of exchange is *redistributive*. This involves bringing economic goods and services to a central source—usually governmental—and then redistributing them throughout the populace. Several examples of this form occurred in ancient Asian and African civilizations. Modern examples are organized charity or progressive taxation. Like reciprocative exchange, redistributive forms are characterized by an absence of economic calculation and price payment. In this situation the principle of calculation seems to be one of justice or equity based on a traditional notion of what the recipients deserve.

The third form of exchange, the one that is most common in the Western world, is simply referred to as *exchange*. In this type of distribution, economic goods and services are brought into a market context. Prices are not standardized on the basis of tradition but result from bargaining for economic advantage. Formal economic analysis is equipped to handle only this type of exchange. In modern societies, distribution can also be seen as a one-way exchange, whereby goods and services are given to individuals without receiving in return an exchangeable market value. Examples of this one-way exchange would include redistribution through taxation, donations, public support of children, welfare, medicaid, and legal aid (Boulding, 1973).

Consumption

"Production not only supplies the need with an object," wrote Marx, "but also supplies the object with the need" (quoted by Anderson, 1976:164). In traditional societies the limited production obviously does not supply the object with too many needs for consumption. By contrast, modern economic systems depend on the sustaining and creating of needs. Growth in the economic domain is based upon the continuous expanding of consumption and . . . "consumption, rather than being the *privilege of the elite*, is becoming *the duty* of the masses" in modern societies (Kando, 1975:14).

Traditional societies often have *sumptuary laws*, or laws that lend the power of the "state" to moral and religious norms governing consumption. Such laws establish differential consumption by, for example, stipulating that only aristocrats can wear fur or silk. In caste, multireligious, or multiethnic societies there are strong normative traditions that define appropriate forms of consumption for each level or segment of society, especially in the areas of food, drink, and clothing.

In the United States a unique feature of consumption is that a large proportion of the American population consumes the same items and services. A tendency of industrial economy is to create a national or international market for products and services and to transform all citizens into equivalent consumers. A mass-production economy obviously does not seek to restrict consumption according to social position or religious or ethnic factors. The only restriction on consumption is income.

Of course, the various economic classes spend different amounts in their overall consumption. Differences in consumption, and the resulting sharp distinctions in prestige, do not exist in the United States to the same degree as in other developed countries. The primary reason is that the majority of the population consumes a wide range of similar products, often brand-name goods with national prestige: food (staples as well as nonstaples); beverages (milk, beer, soft drinks); household products (soap, waxes); household appliances (refrigerators, vacuum cleaners); clothes; and such items as cigarettes, entertainment products, and sporting goods. The important point is that a vast portion of the public consume these goods in common regardless of income.

Personal consumption expenditures more than doubled in the United States in the past ten years, from 1,129 billion to more than 2,601 billion dollars. In addition to inflation, this increase in expenditure is associated with an increase in per capita disposable income; continued improvement of technology generating new products available to be demanded; the shortening of working hours; and the concomitant increase in leisure time, which, of course, increases the capacity to consume various leisure-related products such as travel, TV, and entertainment.

While personal consumption expenditures doubled, personal disposable income increased from 1,142 billion to 2,828 billion for the same time period. In 1987 the average workweek was 38 hours. The average adult in the United States has 2,650 leisure hours per year (Andresen Securities Research, 1973:Table 1). This comes to over 110 days per year. Much of the increase in leisure time is spent on consumption. Needs and desires for new products are constantly being created by advertisements and reinforced by an increased time spent watching television. In the United States 98 percent of all households have TV sets, almost all in color. The average American between the ages of 3 and 16 spends more time in front of the television set than in school. An average adult woman spends more than 30 hours a week, and an average adult man some 25 hours per week watching TV.

John Kenneth Galbraith (1973:33–37) points out that the ideal consumers are women, a group with daylong TV exposure. He sees women as serving a crypto-servant function in household administration and maintenance involving goods, food, child care, social enjoyment, and social displays. He observes that "The servant role of women is critical for the expansion of consumption in modern economy. . . . In few matters has the economic system been so successful in establishing values and moulding resulting behaviour to its needs as in the shaping of a womanly attitude and behaviour. . . . Thus it is women in their crypto-servant role of administrators who make an indefinitely increasing consumption possible." The role of youth and women in maintaining consumption is evident in the manner in which advertising promotion and TV content are fixed. Youth and women are more likely than men to have the time to consume, and consumption does require large amounts of time. For many, consumption becomes an entire way of life.

As disposable income increases in society, consumption patterns undergo drastic alterations. The proportion of income spent on food, housing, and religious and welfare activities diminishes while there is an important increase in expenditures on foreign travel, tourism, recreation, private education, and personal care. For example, expenditures for overseas travel increased from $3.9 billion in 1970 to more than $16.5 billion in 1986.

In addition to the general increase in expenditures by consumers, there seems to be a decline of ostentatious display by the rich in the United States and an increase in what David Caplovitz (1963:13) calls "compensatory consumption." Compensatory consumption refers to the purchase of selected items of the standard middle-class package by the poor, such as an expensive pair of shoes, an expensive hat, or a color TV. This is their way of compensating for lack of other symbols of success and status.

Changes in consumption patterns are accompanied by the growth of consumer-based activities. In the public sphere, Alan Gartner and Frank Riessman (1974:76–78) point out that in 1960 no state had consumer affairs offices. However, 33 did by 1970; and by mid-1973, all 50 states had such offices. Nationally, a number of consumer protection laws have been passed, and 138 public interest groups with over 400,000 dues-paying members were formed to work on consumer issues. Membership in consumer credit unions more than doubled during the course of the 1960s and 1970s.

In sum, these are some of the changes that occurred in the triad of production, consumption, and distribution in the economic sphere. The general trend in developed countries seems to be the continuous increase in production, accompanied by a growing general level of income and an increase in consumption expenditures. There is also a trend toward the reduction of extremes in consumption among the various segments in society.

SUMMARY

This chapter examined changes that have occured in several specific spheres. It should be recalled that social change may originate in any institutional area, bringing about changes in other areas, which in turn make for further adaptations in the initial sphere of change. Changes that have taken place in the various spheres are interrelated; they influence each other as well as the course of society.

Many of the dramatic trends have slowed down or halted in some areas, while in others, new currents have set in. The decline in the functions of the American family has been compensated for by an ascent of its "companionship" function. The trend is toward a nuclear family with egalitarian conjugal roles. The size of the family is decreasing, and there is an increase in childless families. The divorce rates are up and the new morality seems to reverberate in the family structure.

The population of the world is expected to double in 41 years at the present rate of natural increase of 1.7 percent. In developing countries the consequences of this rapid growth rate are felt in economic, social, and political institutions. Mortality rates are declining and life expectancy is on the increase. The trend in fertility is downward, but with little effect on growth rates as a result of more rapid declines in mortality rates. As a result of the demographic transition, modern societies have both low mortality and fertility rates, and seven European countries are experiencing a zero or negative population growth. There is an increase in migration and a change in the place of origin of immigrants into the United States. There has been a pronounced increase in the dependency ratio in developed countries in recent years.

In the sphere of stratification an important change is the opening of opportunities for much higher rates of mobility. The trend is toward equality, but it is questionable whether absolute equality can ever be attained. There was an attempt to establish a classless society in the Soviet Union, but it only resulted in a different type of stratification system. Its unique feature is the lack of "hereditary consideration" for social mobility.

In power relations, important changes have occurred in the ruling elite over time. Access to the political elite has became open to wider and wider strata of the population, and there is a proliferation of "power elites." The political power of nonpoliticians has increased enormously, and it has been accompanied by the decentralization of power. The scope of political participation has been widened, but there is still room for expansion for minorities and ethnic groups.

Education is now separated from the family and, to a great extent, from community life. The development of schools and universities spread education from a monopoly of a few to the property of the masses. This trend was associated with changes in curriculum and the lengthening of the education process for more and more students. Today there seems to be too much emphasis on credentials by employers. Test scores are declining in high schools, and college education is becoming increasingly vocationalized. The marketability of a liberal arts degree is on the decline, and the market for Ph.D.s is tight. For some younger faculty members, the credo of "publish or perish" is slowly changing to "publish *and* perish."

In the economic sphere, changes in production have been associated with alterations in the size and composition of the labor force. Farming has declined dramatically, but there have been important increases in the categories of craftspeople and kindred workers and in professional and technical jobs. The number of women in the labor force is rapidly increasing, and the composition of the labor force changed from predominantly goods-producing to predominantly service-producing workers. With the advent of economic surplus and money, forms of distribution have changed from reciprocative to redistributive and exchange. The trend in consumption is toward more leisure and recreational goods, accompanied by a decline in the proportion of expenditures for the basics such as food or housing. There is an increased concern with the protection of consumers as evidenced by the number of recent laws and organizations. In the next chapter the reactions to change will be examined.

SUGGESTED FURTHER READINGS

GILBERT, DENNIS, and JOSEPH A. KAHL. *The American Class Structure: A New Synthesis*, 3rd ed. Chicago: Dorsey Press, 1987. A synthesis of the most pertinent social science research on stratification patterns and changes.

LESLIE, GERALD R., and SHEILA K. KORMAN. *The Family in Social Context*, 6th ed. New York: Oxford, 1985. A well-written and comprehensive text on the family with many cross-cultural examples.

RAVITCH, DIANE. *The Schools We Deserve: Reflections on the Educational Crisis of Our Times*. New York: Basic Books, 1985. A collection of thought-provoking essays on the swings of the educational pendulum from one extreme to another.

RITZER, GEORGE, and DAVID WALCZAK. *Working: Conflict and Change*, 3rd. ed. Englewood Cliffs, N.J.: Prentice-Hall, 1986. A sociological overview of work in America.

TEITELBAUM, MICHAEL S., and JAY M. WINTER. *The Fear of Population Decline*. Orlando, Fla: Academic Press, 1985. In addition to a good review of the basic demographic trends and concepts, this book raises a number of controversial issues.

WASTE, ROBERT J., ed. *Community Power: Directions for Future Research*. Beverly Hills, Calif.: Sage Publications Inc., 1986. A compendium on the various facets of power relations, particularly at the community level.

REFERENCES

ANDERSON, CHARLES H. *The Sociology of Survival: Social Problems of Growth*. Homewood, Ill.: Dorsey Press, 1976.

Andresen Securities Research. *The Entertainment Industry*. New York: Andresen and Company, 1973, Table 1.

APPLEBOME, PETER. "Aliens Risking Death to Flee Poverty." *The New York Times*, July 5, 1987, p. 9.

ARIÈS, PHILLIPPE. *Centuries of Childhood*, Robert Baldick, trans. New York: Knopf, 1962.

ARMBRUSTER, FRANK E. "The More We Spend, the Less Children Learn." *The New York Times Magazine*, August 28, 1977, pp. 9–11, 53–60.

BARBER, BERNARD. "Change and Stratification Systems." In Amitai Etzioni and Eva Etzioni-Halevy (eds.), *Social Change: Sources, Patterns, and Consequences*, 2nd ed. New York: Basic Books, 1973, pp. 199–209.

BELL, DANIEL. *The Coming of Post-Industrial Society: A Venture in Social Forecasting*. New York: Basic Books, 1973.

BENSMAN, JOSEPH, and ARTHUR VIDICH. *American Society: The Welfare State & Beyond, Revised*. South Hadley, Mass: Bergin & Garvey, 1987.

BERG, IVAR. *Education and Jobs: The Great Training Robbery*. New York: Praeger, 1970.

BIANCHI, SUZANNE M., and DAPHNE SPAIN. *American Women in Transition*. New York: Russell Sage, 1986.

BIERSTEDT, ROBERT. *Power and Progress: Essays on Sociological Theory*. New York: McGraw-Hill Book Company, 1974.

BLAU, PETER, and OTIS DUDLEY DUNCAN. *The American Occupational Structure*. New York: Free Press, 1967.

BOTTOMORE, T.B. *Elites in Society*. New York: Basic Books, 1964.

BOTTOMORE, T.B. *Classes in Modern Society*. New York: Pantheon, 1966.

BOULDING, KENNETH E. "Urbanization and the Grants Economy: An Introduction." In Kenneth E. Boulding, Martin Pfaff, and Anita Pfaff (eds.), *Transfers in an Urbanized Economy*. Belmont, Calif.: Wadsworth, 1973, pp. 1–6.

BOYER, ERNEST L. *College: The Undergraduate Experience in America*. New York: Harper & Row, 1987.

BRONFENBRENNER, URIE. *Two Worlds of Childhood: U.S. and U.S.S.R.* New York: Russell Sage, 1970.

BROWN, LESTER R. *State of the World 1987*. New York: W.W. Norton & Co. Inc., 1987.

BURGESS, ERNEST W. "The Family in a Changing Society." In Amitai Etzioni and Eva Etzioni-Halevy (eds.), *Social Change: Sources, Patterns, and Consequences*, 2nd ed. New York: Basic Books, 1973, pp. 191–198.

CAMPBELL, ELAINE. *The Childless Marriage: An Exploratory Study of Couples Who Do Not Want Children*. New York: Tavistock, 1986.

CAPLOVITZ, DAVID. *The Poor Pay More: Consumer Practices of Low-Income Families*. New York: Free Press, 1963.

Chicago Tribune. "Soaring College Costs Put Parents in a Bind," April 19, 1987, pp. 1, 10.

Chronicle of Higher Education. "Earned Degrees Conferred in 1984–85 by U.S. Colleges and Universities," July 15, 1987b, p. 34.

Chronicle of Higher Education. "Stable Enrollment, Totaling 12.3 Million, Seen This Year," September 2, 1987a, p. A2.

DEMOS, JOHN. *A Little Commonwealth: Family Life in Plymouth*. New York: Oxford, 1970.

DRUCKER, PETER F. "The Educational Revolution." In Amitai Etzioni and Eva Etzioni-Halevy (eds.), *Social Change: Sources, Patterns, and Consequences*, 2nd ed. New York: Basic Books, 1973, pp. 232–238.

DYE, THOMAS R. "Community Power and Public Policy." In Robert J. Waste (ed.), *Community Power: Directions for Future Research*. Beverly Hills, Calif.: Sage Publications Inc., 1986, pp. 29–51.

EHRLICH, PAUL R., and ANNE H. EHRLICH. *Population, Resources, Environment*, 2nd ed. San Francisco: Freeman, 1972.

ESHLEMAN, J. ROSS. *The Family: An Introduction*. Boston: Allyn & Bacon, 1974.

FISKE, EDWARD B. "Enrollment of Minorities in Colleges Stagnating." *The New York Times*, April 19, 1987, pp. 1, 18.

FREIDSON, ELIOT. *Professional Powers: A Study of the Institutionalization of Formal Knowledge*. Chicago: The University of Chicago Press, 1986.

FRENCH, JOHN R.P., and BERTRAM RAVEN. "The Bases of Social Power." In Dorwin Cartwright and Alvin Zander (eds.), *Group Dynamics: Research and Theory*, 2nd ed. New York: Harper & Row, 1960, pp. 607–623.

GALBRAITH, JOHN KENNETH. *Economics and the Public Purpose*. Boston: Houghton Mifflin, 1973.

GARGAN, EDWARD A. "Students in China Turn Cynical and Apathetic." *The New York Times*, July 5, 1987, p. 3E.

GARTNER, ALAN, and FRANK RIESSMAN. *The Service Society and the Consumer Vanguard*. New York: Harper & Row, 1974.

GERTH, HANS H., and C. WRIGHT MILLS, eds. and trans. *From Max Weber, Essays in Sociology*. New York: Oxford, 1946.

GILBERT, DENNIS, and JOSEPH A. KAHL. *The American Class Structure: A New Synthesis*, 3rd ed. Chicago: Dorsey Press, 1987.

GOODE, WILLIAM J. "Industrialization and Family Change." In S.N. Eisenstadt (ed.), *Comparative Perspectives on Social Change*. Boston: Little, Brown, 1968, pp. 47–62.

GORER, GEOFFREY. *Death, Grief, and Mourning*. New York: Doubleday, 1965.

GREER, SCOTT. *The Emerging City*. New York: Free Press, 1962.

HARF, JAMES E., and B. THOMAS TROUT. *The Politics of Global Resources: Population, Food, Energy, and Environment*. Durham, N.C.: Duke University Press, 1986.

HEER, DAVID M. *Society and Population*, 2nd ed. Englewood Cliffs, N.J.: Prentice-Hall, 1975.

HERTZLER, J.O. *American Social Institutions*. Boston: Allyn & Bacon, 1961.

JONES, ELISE F., et al., *Teenage Pregnancy in Industrialized Countries*. New Haven: Yale University Press, 1986.

KANDO, THOMAS M. *Leisure and Popular Culture in Transition*. St. Louis: Mosby, 1975.

KAPLAN, MARION A., ed. *The Marriage Bargain: Women and Dowries in European History*. New York: Harrington Park Press, 1985.

KELLER, SUZANNE. *Beyond the Ruling Class: Strategic Elites in Modern Society*. New York: Random House, 1963.

KOTEN, JOHN. "Steady Progress Disrupted by Turbulence in Economy." *The Wall Street Journal*, March 11, 1987, p. 33.

KUZNETS, SIMON. *Population, Capital, and Growth*. New York: W.W. Norton & Co., Inc., 1973.

LANE, DAVID. *The End of Social Inequality? Class, Status and Power under State Socialism*. London: George Allen & Unwin, 1982.

LEE, EVERETT S. "Internal Migration and Population Redistribution in the United States." In Ronald Freedman (ed.), *Population, The Vital Revolution*. New York: Doubleday, 1964.

LEIBENSTEIN, HARVEY. "An Interpretation of the Economic Theory of Fertility: Promising Path or Blind Alley?" *Journal of Economic Literature*, 12, 1974, pp. 457–479.

LEISHMAN, KATIE. "The Second Stage of the Epidemic: Heterosexuals and AIDS." *The Atlantic*, February 1987, pp 39–58.

LENSKI, GERHARD. *Power and Privilege: A Theory of Social Stratification*. New York: McGraw-Hill Book Company, 1966.

LESLIE, GERALD R., and SHEILA K. KORMAN. *The Family in Social Context*, 6th ed. New York: Oxford, 1985.

LEWIS, LIONEL S. *Scaling the Ivory Tower: Merit and Its Limits in Academic Careers*. Baltimore: The John Hopkins University Press, 1975.

LILLEY, WILLIAM, III, and JAMES C. MILLER, III. "The New 'Social Regulation'." *Public Interest*, Spring 1977, pp. 49–61.

MAEROFF, GENE I. "Colleges Fight Dabbling by U.S." *St. Louis Post-Dispatch*, September 13, 1977, p. 3B.

MANDELBAUM, DAVID G. *Society in India: Continuity and Change*. Berkeley: University of California Press, 1970.

MARK, JEROME A. "Technological Change and Employment: Some Results from BLS Research." *Monthly Labor Review*, 110(4), April 1987, pp. 26–29.

MATTHEWS, MERVYN. *Poverty in the Soviet Union*. Cambridge, England: Cambridge University Press, 1986.

McCLUSKY, JOHN E. "Beyond the Carrot and the Stick: Liberation and Power Without Control." In Warren G. Bennis, Kenneth D. Benne, Robert Chin, and Kenneth E. Corey (eds.), *The Planning of Change*, 3rd ed. New York: Holt, Rinehart & Winston, 1976, pp. 382–403.

MENKEN, JANE. ed. *World Population and U.S. Policy*. New York: W.W. Norton & Co., Inc., 1986.

MILLER, S.M. "A Comparative Social Mobility." *Current Sociology*, 9(1), 1960, pp. 1–66.

MOSCA, GAETANO. "The Varying Structure of the Ruling Class." In Amitai Etzioni and Eva Etzioni-Halevy (eds.), *Social Change: Sources, Patterns, and Consequences*, 2nd ed. New York: Basic Books, 1973, pp. 210–222.

MOTT, PAUL E. "Configurations in Power." In Michael Aiken and Paul E. Mott (eds.), *The Structure of Community Power*. New York: Random House, 1970, pp. 85–86.

NAISBITT, JOHN. *Megatrends: Ten New Directions Transforming Our Lives*. New York: Warner Books, 1982.

New York Times. "Competition for the Nuclear Family," December, 14, 1986, p. 9E.

New York Times. "Zagreb Baby Hailed As 5 Billionth Person," July 12, 1987a, p. 7.

New York Times. "Expert Witnesses: Booming Business for the Specialists," July 5, 1987b, pp. 1, 12.

New York Times. "Education Cost Put at $308 Billion in 1987–1988," August 23, 1987c, p. 10.

Newsweek. "Three's a Crowd," September 1, 1986, pp. 68–76.

Newsweek. "Fuming Over College Costs," May 18, 1987, pp. 66–72.

OGBURN, WILLIAM F., and CLARK TIBBITTS. "The Family and Its Functions, Reports on the President's Research Committee on Social Trends in the United States." In *Recent Social Trends in the United States*. New York: McGraw-Hill Book Company, 1934, pp. 661–708.

OLSEN, MARVIN E., ed. *Power in Societies*. New York: Macmillan, 1970.

PERROLLE, JUDITH A. *Computers and Social Change: Information, Property, and Power*. Belmont, Calif.: Wadsworth, 1987.

PETERSEN, WILLIAM. *Population*, 3rd ed. New York: Macmillan, 1975.

POLANYI, KARL, CONRAD ARENSBERG, and HARRY PEARSON. *Trade and Market in the Early Empires*. New York: Free Press, 1957.

Population Reference Bureau. *Population Data Sheet, 1986*. Washington, D.C.: Population Reference Bureau, Inc., 1986.

PROKESCH, STEVEN. "Mounting Competition for College Teachers." *The New York Times. Educational Life* (Supplement), April 12, 1987, pp. 20, 29, 31.

RAVITCH, DIANE. *The Schools We Deserve: Reflections on the Educational Crisis of Our Times*. New York: Basic Books, 1985.

RITZER, GEORGE, and DAVID WALCZAK. *Working: Conflict and Change*, 3rd ed. Englewood Cliffs, N.J.: Prentice-Hall, 1986.

RIVERS, CARYL. "The New Anxiety of Motherhood." In Uta West (ed.), *Woman in a Changing World*. New York: McGraw-Hill Book Company, 1975, pp. 141–152.

ROGERS, CARL R., and B.F. SKINNER. "Some Issues Concerning the Control of Human Behavior: A Symposium." In Robert Perrucci and Mark Pilisuk (eds.), *Social Problems in Depth*. Boston: Little, Brown, 1968, pp. 331–335.

ROSEN, BERNARD CARL. *The Industrial Connection: Achievement and the Family in Developing Societies*. New York: Aldine Publishing Co., 1982.

ROSSIDES, DANIEL W. *The American Class System: An Introduction to Social Stratification*. Boston: Houghton Mifflin, 1976.

SCHNEIDER, LOUIS, and STANFORD M. DORNBUSCH. *Popular Religion: Inspirational Books in America*. Chicago: University of Chicago Press, 1958.

SEWELL, WILLIAM. "Inequality of Opportunity for Higher Education." *American Sociological Review*, 36(5), 1971, pp. 793–809.

SHIPLER, DAVID U. "Making It—Russian Style." *The New York Times Magazine*, February 11, 1979, pp. 38–46.

SMELSER, NEIL J. *The Sociology of Economic Life*, 2nd ed. Englewood Cliffs, N.J.: Prentice-Hall, 1976.

SMITH, T. LYNN, and PAUL E. ZOPF, Jr. *Demography: Principles and Methods*, 2nd ed. Port Washington, N.Y.: Alfred, 1976.

SPENGLER, JOSEPH J. "Values and Fertility Analysis." *Demography*, 3(1), 1966, 109–130.

TEITELBAUM, MICHAEL S., and JAY M. WINTER. *The Fear of Population Decline*. Orlando, Fla: Academic Press, 1985.

THARP, MIKE. "High Schoolers in U.S. Lack Drive of Japan's But Show Spontaneity." *The Wall Street Journal*, March 10, 1987, pp. 1, 20.

TUMIN, MELVIN M. *Social Stratification: The Forms and Functions of Inequality*. Englewood Cliffs, N.J.: Prentice-Hall, 1967.

U.S. Bureau of the Census. *Statistical Abstracts of the United States: 1987* (107 edition). Washington, D.C., 1987.

U.S. Department of Labor. "Employment and Earnings," 34(5), May 1987.

U.S. News & World Report. "The Birth Dearth: Dangers Ahead?" June 22, 1987a, pp. 56–65.

U.S. News & World Report. "The Brain Battle," January 19, 1987b, pp. 58–64.

U.S. News & World Report. "Why Fewer Blacks Are Graduating," June 8, 1987c, pp. 75–76.

WATKINS, BEVERLY T. "Gerontology Comes of Age as an Academic Field." *Chronicle of Higher Education*, March 21, 1977, p. 10.

WATTENBERG, BEN J. *The Birth Dearth*. New York: Pharos Books, 1987.

WILLIAMS, JUANITA H. *Psychology of Women: Behavior in a Biosocial Context*, 3rd ed. New York: W.W. Norton & Co., Inc., 1987.

WINCH, ROBERT S. "Permanence and Change in the History of the American Family and Some Speculations as to the Future." *Journal of Marriage and Family*, 1970, pp. 173–179.

ZEITLIN, MAURICE. "Corporate Ownership and Control: The Large Corporation and the Capitalist Class." In Anthony Giddens and David Held (eds.), *Classes, Power, and Conflict: Classical and Contemporary Debates*. Berkeley: University of California Press, 1982, pp. 196–223.

7 Duration of Change

The process of social change is directional in time: It has a beginning, a middle, and an end. The term *duration* refers to the life span of a social arrangement or innovation after its introduction. It is concerned with the question of how long will a change be sustained after it is accepted at any level of the social system without major modification or replacement by a functional alternative. The goal of this chapter is to examine the notion of duration, which is a key dimension in social change.

Preoccupation with the duration or temporality of change can be traced back to the nineteenth-century evolutionary thinkers (Ingold, 1986:128–133). They were concerned with spans of time in their study of growth or decay, progression or retrogression. But localizing events *in* time—that is, the study of duration—can be, and often is, a complicated and difficult undertaking. The investigation of the temporal dimension of a phenomenon requires information on its initial point of occurrence, the time frame during which it becomes established, and on its termination. On occasions, changes enter social life so slowly and imperceptibly that we remain unaware of them until they have been fully institutionalized. In other instances, the introduction of an innovation can set off a chain reaction of subsequent changes in a very short time period. For example, at the organizational level, the introduction of a new technology in a factory may alter existing work groups, which in turn leads to worker demands for union control over job assignments, which causes the union to grow in size and strength, which forces management to revise many of its policies and programs, which ultimately changes the structure and functioning of the whole organization.

Notwithstanding the difficulties, it is possible to isolate and study the duration of a variety of change phenomena. Increasingly, social scientists are analyzing social change processes of disparate duration and in a wide range of societies (Boskoff, 1972:245). Such analyses are valuable and have potentially relevant implications for planning and forecasting by providing an approximation of how long and under what circumstances a similar change phenomenon may be sustained in the future. We shall begin this chapter with a brief discussion of the duration of broad historical trends. It is followed by a study of such transitory social changes as fads and fashion, life-styles, social movements, and cults, and a related analysis of the conditions that have contributed to their demise. Table 7.1 provides a synoptic overview of the types of changes that will be considered and an indication of their approximate duration.

DURATION OF CHANGE FROM A HISTORICAL PERSPECTIVE

Social change always occurs in historical settings, and any sociological analysis of change must take account of sequences of events through which change becomes manifest. Moreover, as it was discussed in Chapter 3, most instances of broad-scale social change are directional in nature, and thus

TABLE 7.1   Approximate Duration of Change Phenomena

TYPES OF CHANGE	REPRESENTATIVE CHANGE PHENOMENA		APPROXIMATE DURATION
Broad historical change	Horticultural era		10,000 years
	Agrarian era		4,800 years
Industrial technology	Modern craft age		285 years
	Machine age		85 years
Societal revolutions	Commercial revolution		200 years
	Scientific revolution		100 years
Economic development	"Takeoff" for the United States		60 years
Transitory social changes	Fashion {	Clothing and adornment	6 months–60 years
		"Scientific" theory	2–50 years
		Material objects	1–30 years
	Fads		1 month–1 year
	Life-styles		4–40 years
	Social movements		1–25 years
	Cults		1–15 years

societies are seen as evolving along identifiable lines and evidencing new forms. Social scientists for a long time have identified historical eras with distinct characteristics. Some even assign dates to them. For example, Gerhard and Jean Lenski (1987:85) suggest one way of designating human history:

Hunting and gathering (from the origins of *Homo sapiens* to circa 7000 B.C.)
Horticultural (from circa 7000 B.C. to circa 3000 B.C.)
Agrarian (from circa 3000 B.C. to A.D. 1800)
Industrial (since circa A.D. 1800)

In a similar fashion, one may talk about the duration of technologies in industry or agriculture. In a historical context, Delbert C. Miller (1957a:245–277), for example, identifies four major stages in the evolution of modern technology and calls them the *modern craft age*, the *machine age*, the *power age*, and the *atomic age*. Each age is unique and each age has left a technical heritage that remains in various forms even as the new emerges and becomes dominant. The principal elements in technology that shape a pattern are: power, tools, work skills, material, transportation, and communication.

The modern craft age in industry is dated as beginning with the fifteenth century, "which is often regarded as the threshold of modern civilization" (Miller, 1957a:253). The machine age was inaugurated by Watt's invention of the steam engine in 1785 and its application to the textile industry. The power age is characterized by the widespread use of electricity, which began in 1953 and is still in progress. Miller contends further that the evolution of machines in agricultural technology parallels the four-stage patterns of industrial technology. The dates and duration of each stage are somewhat different. The modern craft age began in the year 1000, the machine age in 1830, the power age in 1920, and the atomic age in 1960 (Miller, 1957b:336–337). It is also possible to ascertain the duration of specific shorter-term technological innovations in the context of the four ages of industrial and agricultural technologies and the reasons for their discontinuities. For example, one could establish how long the steam press for printing books and newspapers was sustained in a particular society and why and under what circumstances it was replaced by a more modern version.

From another perspective, C.P. Wolf (1976:78) attempted to establish the duration of some of the major societal revolutions. He asserts that "Societal revolutions are mass events, not point events . . . the metric of societal change must record . . . *structural* time. . . . Institutional structures have a built-in time scale of 'structural duration.' " Wolf identifies a number of societal revolutions and places their structural duration in a more or less arbitrary time frame. For example, the "commercial revolution" is put between the thirteenth and fifteenth centuries; the "communication revolution" between the fifteenth and sixteenth centuries; and the "scientific revolution" between the sixteenth and seventeenth centuries. The "demographic revolution" started in the eighteenth century and still goes on in some parts of the world.

Finally, let us recall Walt M. Rostow's (1961) idea that the lengthy process of economic development can be depicted by a series of five stages. Each stage, for the analysis of duration, may be considered as representing the acceptance of a unique configuration and constellation of novelties with more or less identifiable and designatable life spans. Rostow estimates that, for example, the mature economy is attained roughly 60 years after the beginning of takeoff (stage three). Thus, for the United States, the takeoff was around 1840, and the mature stage was attained around the turn of the century. It remained in that stage until approximately 1920, when it entered into stage five, the age of high mass consumption. In the Rostowian framework of stages, the duration of each stage or phase of development is indicated. Using a crude analogy, his five stages may be compared to five flights in a staircase, which entail both a continuous progression upward and stops at the intervening floors. The length of the stay at each floor prior to embarking to the next one would be, in this analogy, the duration of change. Let us now turn to the consideration of short-term transitory changes.

TRANSITORY SOCIAL CHANGES

As Richard T. LaPiere (1965:66) points out: "To constitute a socially significant change, the new must be not only adopted by a sufficient number of the members of a social population to give it currency, but so integrated into the social system that it will endure . . . No change may justly be deemed socially significant until the new has been so effectively transmitted from the generation in which it occurs to the next generation that it is thereafter considered as the normal and is taken for granted as an integral part of things as they are." Obviously, not all changes are socially significant and sustained for generations. Many social changes are transitory and of relatively short duration. Often "The new is in many instances adopted with great rapidity until the majority of the members of at least a class of the population have become involved; its appearance and spread are invariably recognized; and, like births and deaths and other events, it is usually the subject of much reporting and comment. At the time of its occurrence the new may have a considerable impact on social life; but it may be abandoned even more rapidly than it came into use, with the result that it never becomes an established part of the social system and rarely leaves any durable imprint" (LaPiere, 1965:59).

In the following pages, several forms of transitory changes will be examined, such as fads and fashion, life-styles, and cults. Although it is argued that any given transitory change generally contributes little, if anything, to changes in the social system, "the occurrence of transitory changes in a society is symptomatic of conditions that are conducive to the appearance of significant changes in that society. In the modern world trying out something new is one way in which individuals attempt to resolve their frustrations or to secure satisfactions that are not otherwise forthcoming; and the occurrence of a great number of transitory changes is thus an indication that the felt needs of many of the members of the society are not being satisfied by the established practices of social life, that for many of the members of society life is in some respects frustrating or inadequate" (LaPiere, 1965:65).

At times transitory changes operate as a substitute for important changes or socially significant changes by reducing tension and discontent and by diverting energies and abilities that might otherwise be applied to something else. It is also possible that "a social population may become so much engrossed in the excitements of transitory changes that it tends to ignore and neglect the inadequacies of the social system itself" (LaPiere, 1965:66).

Transitory changes tend to be of shorter duration than the changes LaPiere calls "socially significant." People are more conscious and more aware of short-term transitions than of long-enduring and continuous patterns of social life. Transitory changes also provide a good opportunity for social scientists to investigate events that influence the course of society and shape our lives. In the following pages, several such events of relatively short duration will be examined in the context of fads and fashion, life-styles, and cults.

FADS AND FASHIONS

Rolf Meyersohn and Elihu Katz (1957:594) point out that "The study of fads and fashions may serve the student of social change much as the study of fruit flies has served geneticists: neither the sociologist nor the geneticist has to wait long for a new generation to arrive." Fads and fashions provide an extraordinary opportunity to study the duration of change, the processes of influence, the diffusion of innovation, and a whole series of other social phenomena. For the present purposes, however, the discussion of fads and fashions will be limited principally to the duration of change.

Can fads be distinguished from fashions? Fashions are of a cyclical nature and typically exhibit a diffusion process resembling an S-shaped pattern, though more pronounced and more condensed in time. Fads, in contrast, tend not to repeat themselves and tend to exhibit much more rapid growth followed by generally complete collapse, although occasionally adoption can stabilize at a lower residual level. Figure 7.1 shows generalized diffusion patterns for fads and fashions. Fashions are culture patterns that are adopted by a given segment of a society for a relatively brief period of time and then abandoned. Fads, on the other hand, are culture patterns of even shorter duration that tend to appear suddenly and disappear as suddenly. An erroneous distinction is made from time to time between fads and fashion by assuming that fashion is usually triggered by affluent trendsetters. Thorstein Veblen (1911) linked fashion to *conspicuous consumption*—the practice of spending money to display one's wealth. Persons lacking the means to buy exactly what the rich can afford obtain less expensive imitations. As a particular fashion trickles downward in society, the rich move on to something else. Thus, fashion originates at the top of the social hierarchy then moves to mass popularity. This contention is not always tenable; for example, Elihu Katz and Paul F. Lazarsfeld (1955:247–270) found in their study of personal influence and fashion behavior that there were as many fashion leaders among women in the middle class as in the upper class, and only low-status women were underrepresented in fashion leadership. Furthermore, in recent decades, some fashions have originated in the lower classes and have been adopted subsequently by the more affluent. Witness, for example, the popularity of blue jeans, which were worn initially by manual laborers. For the purpose of analyzing duration patterns, fads and fashions will be treated separately in the next two sections.

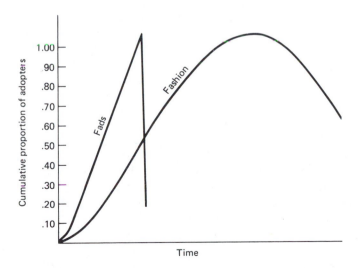

FIG 7.1   Generalized Diffusion Patterns for Fads and Fashions.

Fashion

Fashion operates only in societies with an open class system. According to Georg Simmel (1957:541–558), the elite in such societies are engaged in a prolonged effort to set themselves apart from individuals of lower classes by distinctive customs, mannerisms, and life-styles. But because individuals of slightly lower status who are closest to the elite are eager to raise *their* statuses, they no sooner become aware of a new pattern of elite behavior than they adopt it for themselves. Individuals on the next lower rung of the status ladder are drawn into adopting the new fashion next, for similar reasons, and this process goes on until the new item has spread to all the classes. In the interim, the elite, having observed that the new fashion no longer sets them apart from the rest of the population, abandon it in a hurry to take up some newer fashion, which begins the process of imitation and diffusion all over again.

In a complementary theory to Simmel's, Herbert Blumer (1968) proposed that fashion represents a spontaneous adjustment of large segments of a population in complex societies to a constantly shifting environment. This adjustment takes place in two stages: innovation and selection. In the innovative stage, all kinds of new fashions are proposed for adoption, but most of them are ignored. In the selection stage, the new fashions are selected by prestigeful individuals and groups and are then diffused through the society by way of established channels of influence. This process performs three functions:

> First, it introduces uniformity by selecting from many models one which is to carry the stamp of propriety and thus compel adherence . . . second, fashion provides for an orderly march from the immediate past to the proximate future . . . third, the fashion process nurtures and shapes a common sensitivity and taste, as is suggested by the congeniality and naturalness of current fashion in contrast to the oddness and incongruity of past fashion. (Blumer, 1968:344)

The transitory nature of fashion is evidenced by the intrinsic relationship of two common expressions to the concept of fashion—*in fashion* and *outmoded*. Blumer (1968:341–342) observes that "These terms signify a continuing pattern of change in which certain social forms enjoy temporary acceptance and respectability only to be replaced by others more abreast of the times." Although most pronounced in the area of adornment patterns, fashion changes occur in many other aspects of social life "that are relatively independent and that can therefore change without seriously affecting other aspects of society" (LaPiere, 1965:61).

Changes in fashion are most noticed in clothing and adornment. At times changes in dress and decoration patterns are described in terms of a "fashion cycle." However, the notion of "cycle" is misleading. It implies a repetitive rise and fall, as if a wheel had turned and the fashions that were "in" had to go "out" for a time and then reappear at predictable intervals. Of necessity, there are some recurrent variations of specific elements of style—such as dress length and width, which is cyclical within the limits of practicality and morality. There are revivals of styles from time to time, but the fashions of another day never quite come back in their entirety; neither history nor fashion ever plays itself back completely unchanged. For example, A.L. Kroeber's (1919) studies of fashion have shown that the periodicity of cycles in dress styles during recent centuries is different for different dimensions of the dress.

Fashions are cyclical, however, to the extent that they go through stages of increasing and decreasing popularity. James M. Carman (1966) used mathematical time-series models to study fashion trends in women's clothes from 1786 to 1965. The predictive accuracy of his models is good, based on two cyclical theories. One of these posits three cycles lasting approximately 100 years: a bell, or full-skirt, cycle; a bustle cycle; and a tubular, or sheath, cycle. The other theory suggests shorter cycles of 30 to 50 years. In a study by Dwight E. Robinson (1976:1136–1137) of fashions in shaving and trimming of the beard in England between 1842 and 1972, he found a "most remarkable" correspondence with "Kroeber's width of skirt wave, which rose and fell between 1811 and 1926, and the beard wave, which rose and fell between 1842 (or very possibly 1840) and 1956." The reasons that skirt width and beard frequency fluctuate together are open to speculation.

Marvin Harris (1973) in an article, "What Goes Up May Stay Up," suggests that fashions reflect the dominant interests and values of a society at a particular time. Throughout history, clothing was designed to show the social position of its wearer (Lurie, 1987:193). For example, in the eighteenth century, elaborate clothing reflected an ornate and decorative upper-class culture. The end of the eighteenth century, however, saw some unusual fashions. To illustrate: "The last time well-bred Western women bared their nipples was during that elegant, albeit short-lived, period called the *Directoire*, a time of stylish Graecisms ranging from neo-pagan piety to pseudo-Pompeian household furniture, when women, at least those who could afford to do so, dressed as goddesses and also, for the first time since antiquity, showed their bare feet" (Rudofsky, 1974:44). The fashion of women baring their nipples lasted for four years, from 1795 to 1799. Its demise may have been brought about by the early signs of the upcoming Victorian era and Victorian prudishness.

There are many other instances in fashion where the duration can be more or less specified. The corset, for example, which was fashionable for approximately 60 years, operated on three levels—mechanical, aesthetic, and moral. "The corset," wrote Thorstein Veblen (1911:172), "is in economic theory substantially [an instrument of] mutilation for the purpose of lowering the subject's vitality and rendering her personally and obviously unfit for work. It is true, the corset impairs the personal attractiveness of the wearer [Veblen, of course, refers to the naked woman], but the loss suffered on that score is offset by the gain in reputability which comes of her visibly increased expensiveness and infirmity." The corset was a hallmark of virtue and its use marked an advanced technique of disfigurement. Rustproof summer corsets were advertised as a necessity for summer wear and for swimming, and unbreakable electric corsets guaranteed quick cures for all kinds of diseases such as paralysis, rheumatism, spinal complaints, constipation, liver and kidney troubles, and so forth. According to the 1880s advertisements, the corsets were "constructed on scientific principles, [and their] therapeutic value is unquestioned."

One would never guess what freed women from the corset. What brought about the corset's disappearance was the necessity of conserving steel for armaments during World War I. In view of this patriotic objective, women decided that corsets were nonessential. "Subsequently, a member of the War Industries Board revealed that the American women's sacrifice released 28,000 tons of steel during World War I, enough to build two battleships" (Rudofsky, 1974:189).

After World War I, there are other illustrations of fashion change with more or less specific duration. For example, "Following World War I and until about 1929, the female torso became a flattened tube, and the body was as wide at the waist as at the hips. . . . This was the era of the 'flapper' fashions, and the bust disappeared altogether in an effort to achieve a 'boyish flat appearance'. . . . Women with large breasts were forced to wear correctors or flatteners in an attempt to conform to prevailing fashion" (Morrison & Holden, 1973:571). Prior to attempting to acquire a male front, women enthusiastically accepted a "sweeping homogeneous front bulge, a highly artificial protuberance that I shall call the monobosom, to distinguish it from the double-breasted chest. It embodied a new concept of corporeal modesty—the merger of two pointed secondary sexual characteristics into a singe mass of flesh that has no organic precedent in human history. Apparently, one bulge seemed less immodest than two" (Rudofsky, 1974:44).

In the context of fashion, almost every generation has its own ideas on supporting some part of the human anatomy. For about two decades around the turn of the century, almost everyone went through life ankle-supported. Young and old wore laced boots. A shoe that did not reach well above the ankle was considered disastrous to health. Then ankle-support gave way to arch support. For almost another generation, "Western woman, whom nature forgot to endow with a magnificent rear end, had at times to rely on make-believe to render herself desirable; witness the bustle of the eighteen-seventies, a gross illusion of steatopygia" [extreme accumulation of fat on and around the buttocks] (Rudofsky, 1974:99–100). And the illustrations could go on and on. The important point is that no part of the human anatomy is free of fashion, there is a tendency among people to "accentuate the appropriate" (Green, 1977), and in many instances changes in adornment patterns are documentable with more or less exact life spans.

Although it would be interesting to continue with illustrations of changes in clothes and adornment patterns, fashion is not limited to these aspects of social life. Fashionlike changes in technique, theory, and interests occur in every field of science and in almost any aspect of group life. For example, the publication of *The Principles of Scientific Management* by Frederick W. Taylor (1911) started a fashion that lasted for almost four decades, with a tremendous impact on the entire field of organizational management. Taylor believed that a maximization of efficiency in organizations could be achieved by the segmentation of all tasks involved in production into a series of simple movements and operations. Each worker could be trained to perform a few simple operations, and the combined efforts of all workers laboring for the common good would maximize efficiency and productivity. Taylor also believed that the average workers were interested in doing only what is minimally required by management. Therefore, in addition to the redesigning and simplifying of tasks, increased productivity could be achieved by the creation of incentives to work harder during a specified time period. He suggested that workers could be directed, like robots, to perform at command in a predetermined manner. Adhering to a mandatory schedule of rest pauses and work periods, the worker would be at peak efficiency at all times during the workday. This is basically the idea of scientific management, which was discredited, regretfully, too late.

Certain fashions in science not only are influential but can have serious implications. This is the case with phrenology. It is associated mainly with the work of Franz Joseph Gall (1758–1828), who investigated the bumps and other irregularities of the skulls of inmates of penal institutions and asylums for the insane. The theory of phrenology is based on the notion that the exterior of the skull corresponds to the interior and to the brain's conformation. The brain can be divided into faculties or propensities that are related to the shape of the skull. Furthermore, each proportion in the brain represents a distinct mental or moral disposition and, depending upon the relative concentration of these propensities or faculties, they determine the conformation of the skull, which, in turn, can be detected by touching it (Schafer, 1969:110–115).

Phrenology spread rapidly in Europe. It had its own journal, called *Phrenological Journal*, and "the art of reading bumps," as it was called in the United States, was so successful that an American university established a professorship of phrenology. Observed *The Encyclopedia Americana* (1957:22): "The most necessary thing for a professor of phrenology was a happy faculty for flattering everybody, and the more they flattered, the more people paid to have their heads charted to get information as to other characteristics." As long as phrenology was concerned with squeezing heads in the form of a crude aptitude test, it was relatively harmless. But not so when it was adopted in prisons toward the end of the nineteenth century in the United States. At that time phrenological profiles of inmates were a part of the prison records, and phrenology was used as an important criterion in probation and parole. It was even used in New York's Sing Sing prison until about 1910, when it was finally discredited.

When fashion centers around a material object, one of its most important characteristics is that replacement of that object is made before its life span ends. Quite often such objects are acquired without regard for their durability. In modern societies, the public is ready to accept anything new, anything different; in fact, there is a demand for novelty and for continuous refinement of existing products. The greatly accelerated stylistic changes have been used to create technological obsolescence, which is perhaps most pronounced in the United States in terms of trading automobiles in every couple of years or so.

Fads

"The more trivial, unpredictable, rapidly spreading, and rapidly disappearing changes are those of a faddish character. Changes of this sort occur when the value of the new to the individual who adopts it arises, not from what the new is or does, but from the fact that, being new, it attracts favorable attention from others. As more and more adopt it, its value rapidly diminishes, so that within weeks or months of its initial appearance, the new has become old and uninteresting; and the change has come to an end" (LaPiere, 1965:59–60). In many instances the duration of fads can be determined with a fair degree of accuracy.

Although the terms "fad" and "crazes" are frequently linked and both are instances of culture patterns of very short duration, they can, at times, be distinguished by "the quickness with which they alternate, the utter superficiality of their content, and the irrationality and intensity of the temporary fascination for them" (Davis, 1949:79). Neil J. Smelser (1963) notes that the craze may be superficial (hula hoops, celebrity fan clubs) or serious (war crazes); it may be political (bandwagons), expressive (dance steps), religious (revivals), or economic (speculative boom) just to mention a few types.

A fad often provides a way of ascertaining personal identity (Turner & Killian, 1987:146–148). It is a way of demonstrating that one is different and is worth noticing (observe the popularity of punk attire and hairdo among some teenagers). Fads seem to be more numerous in periods of group crisis, implying that certain recreational fads divert attention from the problems at hand. Many of the fads have little significance for participants beyond identifying them with an in-group and thus giving them prestige. Fears and belief in special formulas (megadoses of vitamin C against the common cold) may also have a faddish character. There are, of course, more serious fads such as war crazes, or those found in the arts and sciences.

For the present purposes of attempting to ascertain the duration of change, economic crazes are of particular interest. They are also unique because they involve a risk that other fads and crazes do not. Individuals are willing to gamble their entire fortunes because of the belief that they will get rich quickly if they only seize the opportunity. The Florida land boom of 1925/1926 is an excellent illustration of economic crazes.

At the turn of the century, the southern part of Florida was rather isolated and thinly populated. With the advent of the railroad and automobiles, it entered a period of steady growth. This growth greatly accelerated during the early 1920s. For example, the population of the city of Miami grew from 30,000 in 1920 to an estimated 75,000 by 1925. It was a general period of prosperity in the United States, where it seemed that everybody could become rich. Plans were announced for grandiose real estate development, and lots were offered for sale. One financier proposed to build a settlement on land dredged up from Tampa Bay. He sold three million dollars' worth the first day, even before the dredging operation had even begun. Rumors of tremendous profits spread, and the demands for lots for resale were so great that realtors could sell land that was still under water. Thousands of people flocked to Florida to participate in the boom, and lots were bought and sold, sight unseen, all over the United States. During the summer of 1925, a race was on to get into the market before prices increased, and eager buyers were easy to find. By January 1926, confidence in the boom began to falter, prices started to decline, and many people defaulted on their promises to buy land. In September 1926, a hurricane hit the Miami area, killing more than 400 people. "Now the rush to unload land began in earnest; buyers defaulted on their binders, and developers and realtors went bankrupt. There was an exodus of forlorn speculators from the state, most of them with scarcely enough money to get home. Promoters who, a few months previously, had been regarded as public servants, showing small investors the route to Eldorado, were now denounced as charlatans. Investors who had been envied by their neighbors as bold, shrewd adventurers were now pitied as gullible fools who had been fleeced" (Turner & Killian, 1987:150–151). The craze lasted for approximately one year, from the summer of 1925 until September 1926.

At times a craze can become an obsession for its followers. For example, the use of LSD became a craze among a small number of college students, with an estimated 5 or 6 percent having tried it at least once at the peak of the craze in 1967 (Meyer, 1969:201). With Timothy Leary as its main prophet, LSD was to bring the world into a new nirvana of peace, love, creativity, and ultimate salvation. However, the growing fear of the hazards of LSD seems to have reduced its users to no more than 1 percent of college students by 1969 (Meyer, 1969:201).

Many other fads are of much shorter duration than the LSD craze. For example, in the popular music industry, the life span of a "hit" is about one month (Meyersohn & Katz, 1957:598). The pet rock craze lasted a couple of months, as did the attempts by college students to set new records by crowding into telephone booths or Volkswagens. Pac Man, Cabbage Patch dolls, and Trivial Pursuit did not fare much better. Rubik's Cube endured a bit longer, possibly due to the challenge it posed. In some instances, fads catch on and become a permanent part of a culture. For example, two decades ago soccer was limited to a handful of devoted aficionados, mostly of European or Latin American origin. Today it is played all over the United States. Some other games caught on, such as Monopoly and backgammon, but many more lasted only for a short period of time. Fads of varying duration are present even in health care. In psychiatry, for example, more than 450 different forms of psychotherapy are now being purveyed in the marketplace (Hunt, 1987:30). How many of these will be around next year or even next month is open to conjecture.

One of the most widely publicized fads of recent years was "streaking" (racing nude through a public place)—practiced by few, but enjoyed by many. It lasted approximately four months in 1974. Let us examine it in the context of the natural history of fads, which "seeks to determine the origin of a given item, the conditions of acceptance by the first participants (the "innovators"), the characteristics of those whom the innovators influence, the shifts from minority to majority acceptance, its waning, and where it goes to die" (Meyersohn & Katz, 1957:597).

Streaking was spearheaded by college students and spread like wildfire to all corners of the country. However, it was not confined to the United States. In the later stages, the fad was also found in Europe and Latin America. The fad cut across various class lines and appealed to diverse age and sex groups. Granted the incidents of nudity on college campuses is nothing new, but the sheer numbers of those who became involved, the publicity they received, and the cycle of unbelief to mild indignation to popularity is unprecedented in modern times.

How, when, and where it all started is difficult to determine. The first mention of streaking in a national magazine appeared in a *Newsweek* (1974a:63) article dated February 4, 1974. By March 18, 1974, the streaking fad was at its peak of heightened popularity. At college campuses around the country, categories of streaking activity were being devised and competition over a totally absurd phenomenon was clearly evident and highly publicized (*Newsweek*, 1974b:41–42). But streaking was no longer limited to the college campus; junior and senior high school students were emulating their elders in greater and greater numbers. En route to New York from London, an adult male streaker jogged up and down the aisles of a Pan American jumbo jet, and a senior citizen was arrested in Lima, Ohio, for taking a bare stroll in the public square, which the participant called "snailing" (*Time*, 1974:58–59).

By April 1974, streaking was on the decline, and altogether the fad lasted roughly four months. The post mortem for streaking in the popular literature endured for another month or so, and then interest rapidly waned. Streaking as an activity became too diffused, too popular, and was no longer differentiated by age, sex, or occupational groups. Because everyone could participate in it, the fad, in its later stages, left no one astounded. Positive rewards and reinforcement for the activity were no longer forthcoming and because of mass participation, its novelty value quickly wore out. In the next section, the duration of various changes in life-styles will be considered.

LIFE-STYLES

The term *life-style* was introduced into the sociological literature by Max Weber. He posited that social status was determined primarily by one's style of life, how one consumed, rather than how one produced. "Certain goods become objects for monopolization by status groups. . . . The decisive role of a 'style of life' . . . means that status groups are the specific bearers of all 'conventions.' In whatever way it may be manifest, all 'stylization' of life either originates in status groups or is at least conserved by them" (Weber, 1966:26). The notion of life-styles, however, goes beyond the differences in consumption patterns. The term also refers to those patterns of conduct over which individuals have options or choices, although they may have the same resources. These options include modes of dressing, utilizing leisure time, spending vacations, using drugs, and joining groups (Bensman & Vidich, 1987:101–151; Gilbert & Kahl, 1987:143–148; Tumin, 1985:99). Life-styles often pervade many aspects of life and imply a central life interest (Feldman & Thielbar, 1975:2).

Social Class and Life-Styles

To a considerable extent, life-styles are determined by one's social class position. "To the extent that the various classes live apart from one another, they develop recognizable subcultures with values that give a special and unique flavor to life" (Kahl, 1957:186). Life-styles based on class position are temporal and tend to be of relatively short duration. The major traditional life-styles of the nineteenth century are now defunct and have been replaced by new sets of living patterns. Consider, for example, the traditional aristocratic life-style of the American South, which emphasized elegance, leisure, *noblesse oblige*, chivalry, and slavery. Over time, this life-style was subjected to a continuous process of dilution and has all but disappeared (Bensman & Vidich, 1987:123–124).

Similarly, class-based life-styles, which were described in the section on stratification in Chapter 6, between the Great Depression and the 1960s are all but passé. The wealthy can no longer be characterized by charity work or elaborate codes of etiquette. For them, there is more to life than selective social ties and memberships in exclusive clubs. They do not follow the pattern of European feudal aristocracy and have their children study liberal arts rather than vocational subjects. By the same token, lower-middle-class life-styles are no longer dominated by respectability, religion, home ownership, and patriotism, nor can the poor be characterized as apathetic or fully resigned to a life of relative misery and deprivation.

The life-styles of professionals and managers, as epitomized by William H. Whyte's (1957) *The Organization Man*, endured about four decades. As Whyte paints the portrait of the organization man, he emerges as a rather frightening character, totally identified with organizational goals, a belief in the group as the source of creativity, rather than the individual, a belief that belongingness is the ultimate need of the individual. He was satisfied to devote his entire life to one organization, with no thought of changing employers and with no concern for family. The problems of society were decidedly secondary. This particular life-style again may have had its beginning during the post-Depression years, climaxing in the 1950s and to a great extent coming to an end by the mid-1960s. Today, it seems that more and more individuals view their work life as one part of a broader life experience, which involves not only job but family, community, social responsibilities, and concern for political and economic issues. In other words, one's commitment to careerism, to an organization, appears to be on the decline.

Since the 1960s, the American class structure has undergone some important changes. Proportionately, the size of the working class has declined while the upper-middle and middle classes, working poor, and underclass have expanded. The distinction between white-collar and blue-collar workers has all but disappeared. Generally, those in the top half of the class structure seem to be gaining privilege and power at the expense of those in the bottom half (Gilber & Kahl, 1987:340). These changes have been accompanied by a decline in the monolithic class-based life-styles. New life-styles, and a much greater variety of them in any one socioeconomic group, have replaced or supplemented older ones. We no longer talk about *the* life-style of, say, the upper middle class. Rather, the emphasis is on several (although overlapping) characteristic life-styles. Today, the life-styles of the upper middle class, for example, include the following (Bensman & Vidich, 1987:145–148):

1. The style of the *Country Gentleman*, where the emphasis is on sports or on nautical activities. An advocate of this life-style spends a considerable amount of his income on his chosen pleasure. He may build his life around a boat, nautical dress styles, and involvement in cup races. This may be combined with elaborate entertainment in country or golf clubs involving

all members of the family. Fresh air, sun, and fun are preferred to books and intellectually demanding activities.

2. The style of the *Culture Vulture* involves intellectual and cultural activities. Books, talk, theater, music, and museum attendance are part of daily activities. Publishers, book and record clubs, dance, theater, and music groups all depend on the cultural demand created by this segment of the upper middle class.

3. The *Cultured Academic*, who may not be a professor, but finds the university community to be an ideal place of residence. Many professionals, business persons, and managers have opted to live in the vicinity of universities such as Cambridge, MIT, or Princeton. They participate in university-sponsored cultural events, maintain old school ties, and tend to blend into the academic environment. The Ph.D. *nouveau riche* (a scientist turned entrepreneur who became rich because of a good idea related to space, electronics, etc.) contributes to this life-style because it offers a compromise between an intellectual past and newly gained economic success.

4. The *Fun-Lover* prefers to be a participant in sports, parties, dancing, safaris, flying, and skiing. In this group, the accent is on "fun" of the jet-set variety. They prefer to be continuously on the move and convey the impression of being "in." They like to think of themselves as being influential in science, technology, and administration. Examples of this life-style would include the world-traveling junior executive, the international consultant, or the youthful college president.

5. The old-upper-middle-class *Vulgarian* who emphasizes conspicuous consumption. For the most part, these are people who own their own businesses and have succeeded beyond their expectations. They have plenty of money but they do not exactly know what to do with it. So they spend it on Cadillacs and Caribbean cruises and other symbols of material success.

Another interesting recent development is the emergence of so-called life-style enclaves that have sprung up around the country and where people who share interests live together—an affluent retirement village, a yuppie neighborhood in a big city, a DINK (double-income, no kids) condominium development, or a community of pilots who build homes around a shared airstrip (Koten, 1987:19). Thus, life-styles are not solely class-based. The term "life-style" essentially implies a focus in life and

various things may be of central interest to a person: work, ethnic heritage, politics, lineage, children, avocational pursuits, and others. A distinctive life style is evident when a single activity or interest prevades a person's other interests or unrelated activities—a drug addict is an extreme example. Avid baseball fans, television enthusiasts, and "professional" San Franciscans also provide examples of life styles based on a central life interest. Some people are interested in astrology; if this interest is central, it too may color their lives. They may wear signs of the zodiac, prefer to interact and marry only those of certain birth signs, and make crucial decisions according to the position of the planets. (Feldman & Thielbar, 1975:2)

There have been several life-styles of relatively short duration in the past two decades in the United States for which it is fairly easy to ascertain temporal dimensions. Of these, the ones under the general label of "counterculture" have received a great deal of scholarly and popular attention.

Counterculture Life-Styles

The term *counterculture* is often used to embrace a cluster of recent life-styles of relatively short duration (Roszak, 1969). These life-styles represent a distinct subculture, and the term counterculture is used because it is "so radically disaffiliated from the mainstream assumptions of our society that it scarcely looks to many like a culture at all, but takes on the alarming appearance of a barbaric intrusion" (Roszak, 1969:42). A well-known spokesman for the merits of this counterculture is Charles Reich (1970), who in his book, *The Greening of America*, analyzes and cites some of the alternatives that are emerging and affecting the overall society. Central themes of Reich's analysis are that America has veered from its original humanistic purpose and that the "corporate state" has become a death-dealing machine. In examining America's earlier "levels of consciousness," he describes the manner in which America has moved off course. He first analyzes the drive that made it a corporate state and led it into becoming a death-dealing, machine-enslaved society. In Reich's terminology, *Consciousness I* involved the enormous promise of America and *Consciousness II* relates to the life-style that emanated from the rise of the corporate state. *Consciousness III*, according to Reich, is the adaptation of the new young revolutionary and dropout. It rests, he asserts, on various premises: respect for each individual, for his or her uniqueness and for his or her privacy; abstention from coercion or violence against any individual; abstention from killing or war; respect for the natural environment; respect for beauty in all its forms; honesty in all personal relations; equality of status between all individuals; genuine democracy in the making of decisions; and freedom of expression and conscience.

"There is a revolution coming," he writes. "It will not be like revolutions of the past. It will originate with the individual and with culture, and it will change the political structure only as its final act." He asserts that "the revolution will not require violence to succeed and it cannot be successfully resisted by violence" (Reich, 1970:2) One characteristic of the revolution, on the part of the young, affluent dropout, is the development of life-styles that are alternatives to the status quo, and is based on opposition to the status quo. Hippies; yippies; Weathermen; committed psychedelic drug trippers; black, brown, and white power advocates, are all characterized by a disenchantment with the dehumanization of the larger society and a subsequent involvement with alternative life-styles which, they believe, are more humanistic (although it should be noted that the Weathermen, yippies, and similar groups could hardly be considered as humanists).

The 1960s witnessed the rise of several alternative life-styles in the context of counterculture. This was a period of turbulence, an era of rapid social change, when many American youth played important roles of challenger and innovator. They viewed the so-called establishment as threatening, and its institutional norms and traditional values were seriously questioned. Many rejected the material values of their parents, and "In phrases redolent of nearly all utopian thought of the past, they proclaim that happiness and a meaningful life are not to be found in things, but in the cultivation of the self and by intensive exploration of inner sensibilities with like-minded others" (Davis, 1971:106).

There were several ways of exploring "inner sensibilities." Many began to experiment with mind-altering substances, such as LSD, peyote, and especially marijuana. Timothy Leary's admonition to "turn on, tune in, and drop out" progressively captured the imagination of millions of young people during this period. An important consequence of these experiments was the evolution and development of alternative life-styles and a different perception of the world. Hippie communal colonies began to emerge in both urban and rural areas. The best known of these is the Haight-Ashbury district in San Francisco, initially populated by the so-called flower children. It lasted about two years and "The Haight, as a youth community, was dead. However, the anti-values expressed and acted out by those in the Haight of 1966 were diffused (even as they were romantically distorted) across America by both under- and overground media" (Lewis, 1974:379). Many hippies later formed tribes and lived in communes, some lived near Indian tribes or in simulated "Indian" styles, others established nonviolent subgroups. However, some groups dedicated to violence developed as the original hippie life-style waned.

In the quest for a new humanistic community, a militant and sometimes violent life-style became, for some, a methodology for change. Unlike the more retreatist classic hippies, such diverse and transient groups as the yippies, white panthers, Weathermen, and various self-labeled "freaks" are more apt to engage in aggressive behavior against a system they find oppressive. In the optimistic words of Abbie Hoffman (1969:77):

> In the past few years our numbers have grown from hundreds to millions of young people. Our conspiracy has grown more militant. Flower children have lost their innocence and grown their thorns. We have recognized that our culture in order to survive must be defended. Furthermore we have realized

that the revolution is more than digging rock or turning on. The revolution is about coming together in a struggle for change. It is about the destruction of a system based on bosses and competition and the building of a new community based on people and cooperation. That old system is dying off all around us and we joyously come out in the streets to dance on its grave. With our free stores, liberated buildings, communes, people's parks, dope, free bodies and our music, we'll build our society in the vacant lots of the old and we'll do it by any means necessary. Right on!

The yippies, perhaps more than the other groups, epitomized this life-style of militancy and violence. The "formal" origin of this life-style is clearly spelled out by Jerry Rubin (1970:86):

We started yippie with an office, a mailing list, three telephone lines, five paid staff organizers, weekly general meetings and weekly Steering Committee meetings. We were the hardest workers and the most disciplined people you ever met, even though we extol sloth and lack of discipline. We are a living contradiction, because we're yippies. Marijuana is compulsory at all yippie meetings.

Yippies take acid at breakfast to bring us closer to reality. Holden Caulfield is a yippie. The Old Nixon was a yippie; the New Nixon is not. Yippies believe every nonyippie is a repressed yippie. We try to bring out the yippie in everybody. Yippies proclaim: Straights of the world, drop out! You have nothing to lose but your starched shirts! . . . America says: DON'T! The yippies say: DO IT.

The goal of the yippies is to turn on everybody who can be turned on and turn off everybody else. In the words of Abbie Hoffman (1968:157):

Our message is always: Do what you want. Take chances. Extend your boundaries. Break the rules. Protest is anything you can get away with. Don't get paranoid. Don't be uptight.

The life-styles of the counterculture persisted for a relatively short time period. Their celebrated prophets are today part of the "establishment," and many former advocates of these life-styles have embraced more pragmatic middle-class values. In general, life-styles endure as long as they serve a set of more or less clearly identifiable needs. These needs may be emotional and personal for the individuals involved, or they may be dictated by utilitarian or ideological principles and objectives. In some cases it may be a combination of both. But regardless of whether a particular life-style is more personal or utilitarian, one is concerned with how long it may be expected to endure. Some life-styles may persist for a period of many years, while others may dissolve in a relatively short time. At the most general level, the duration of a life-style can be ascertained in terms of the functions it performs for the society in which it is a part, the degree to which it provides certain satisfactions to its advocates, and the extent to which new adherents to that life-style can be recruited.

The analysis of the duration of class-based or counterculture-based life-styles is hampered by the lack of reliable data. One can only assign rough temporal dimensions, and even then questions of reliability pop up. Even in the cases of hippie or yippie life-styles, the life span can vary from analyst to analyst. In some instances, however, the duration of life-styles can be approximated with a great degree of accuracy. This is the case with experiments in communal living. There have been several such ventures of discernible duration. The Oneida community is one of the most successful American experiments in communal living to date. It began in the 1840s, its radical family form lasted about 30 years, and at its peak it served 288 persons. It is an excellent sociological example of unique life-styles and will be examined in some detail in the following pages.

The Oneida Community

William M. Kephart (1987:43–92) provides a comprehensive account of the Oneida community. The beginnings are traced back to Putney, Vermont, in 1831, where a fierce religious revival was in progress. One of those deeply affected was John Humphrey Noyes, a young Dartmouth graduate intent upon the practice of law. He gave up law for the ministry, and was licensed to preach after graduation from Yale's Theological Seminary in 1833. He had been a minister only a short time when he announced that he was perfect—sinless. This statement alienated him from the mainstream of Christian orthodoxy, cost him his license, and forced him to reexamine his own principles.

His doctrine of "perfectionism"—the attainability of the sinless or perfect state—attracted a small group of followers. Noyes began to publish Perfectionist literature, and began to develop a complex marriage system —a form of group marriage that was to be the basis of Oneida's social structure. Monogamous marriage was considered as a sign of selfishness.

In 1846 the Putney community was formed, and members followed a "share the wealth" type of economy in which private ownership was condemned. They also practiced group marriage; that is, every adult male had marital privileges with every adult female, and vice versa. As might be expected, the citizens of Vermont were up in arms, and in 1847 Noyes was arrested and charged with adultery. He did not want to stand trial and escaped to New York State, followed by his flock. In 1848, they took up residence on the banks of the Oneida Creek in New York, and the small group had some difficulties surviving the first few winters. Fortunately, one of the members invented a steel trap, which turned out to be a very profitable venture. A substantial part of the Oneida economy came to be based on the manufacture of the steel traps, and the group became free of financial worries.

The entire community was housed under one roof, the famous Mansion House. Although each adult had his or her own small room, the building was designed to encourage a feeling of togetherness, hence the inclusion of a communal dining hall, recreation rooms, library, concert hall, and the like. The community was a close group, with members seldom going very far from home. The system of sustained cultural enclosure served as a solidifying force. They raised their own food, made all their own clothes, did their own laundry, ran their own school, and performed a number of other collective tasks. But their unique social organization was not the only thing that held the Oneida community together. As the membership increased, three basic principles of Noyes' teaching combined to form the very heart of the Perfectionist life-style: (1) economic communism; (2) mutual criticism; and (3) complex marriage.

Economic Communism

A principal feature of the Oneida Community was its adherence to *economic communism.* Throughout their existence, members rejected all forms of individual wealth and private property. They had no concept of private ownership, not even in the realm of personal belongings such as clothes, trinkets, or children's toys. The needs of individual members were taken care of, and they never once had second thoughts about private property.

In addition to the manufacture of steel traps, members of the community found a ready market for their crops, and their prosperity slowly increased. At one point it became necessary to hire outside help, and eventually the Perfectionists were employing several hundred local workers. Beginning in 1877 they embarked on the manufacture of silverware. It proved so successful that when the community dissolved, the silverware component was perpetuated as a joint stock company (Oneida, Ltd.), whose product is still widely used today.

The various jobs within the community were rotated from year to year in order to prevent feelings of discrimination. It was quickly pointed out to members that at one time or another almost everyone took a turn at the necessary menial tasks. Still, although jobs were generally rotated, individual variations in ability were recognized, and members were not placed in positions beyond their capacities. Any kind of social differentiation by occupational status was played down. Plant superintendents and farm laborers, as a result, had the same status.

Members of the community, in their efforts to promote equality, were required to eat the same kind of food, wear the same type of clothing and live in the same home. For both sexes, dress was uniformly simple, and no adornments or jewelry were allowed. It is interesting to note that Noyes was responsible for a genuine innovation in the women's clothing style. Being dissatisfied with ordinary female attire, he set up a committee to work on the problem of designing an appropriate dress. The costume they decided upon—a short, knee-length skirt with loose trousers down to the shoes—became the standard dress of all Oneida women.

Mutual Criticism

The community had neither laws nor law-enforcing officers, but there was little need for them as major infractions were nonexistent. As in any organization, however, problems of human conduct are likely to occur. And even though the Oneidans considered themselves to be Perfectionists, they acknowledged that individual idiosyncracies did exist. *Mutual criticism* was the method by which such problems were handled. When someone deviated from the group norms, whenever there was a manifestation of a personality or character witness, a committee of peers would meet with the offender to discuss the matter. The experience was, at times, traumatic for certain members. Some, in fact, left the community rather than submit to what they considered unwarranted censure. There is no question that mutual criticism served as a measure of social control. The only exception was Noyes, who was never criticized by the community.

Members of the community were so convinced of the effectiveness of mutual criticism that they actually used the technique as a cure for illness. Known as "krinopathy," the criticism cure was applied to both adults and children and was often used for everything from common colds to more serious diseases. According to their organ, the *Circular*:

> It is a common custom here for everyone who may be attacked with any disorder to send for a committee of six or eight persons, in whose faith and spiritual judgment he has confidence, to come and criticize him. The result, when administered sincerely, is almost universally to throw the patient into a sweat, or to bring on a reaction of his life against disease, breaking it up and restoring him soon to usual health. (Kephart, 1987:62)

Even death did not necessarily put a stop to the process. "Deceased members whose diaries or letters were found to be incriminating might find themselves subjected *in absentia* to a 'rousing criticism' " (Kephart, 1987:62).

Complex Marriage

The world remembers the Oneida community not for its social and economic system, but for their practice of *complex marriage*. Just as the term "Mormon" brings to mind polygamy, so the name "Oneida" conjures up thoughts about unique and advanced sex practices. It was the founder,

Noyes, who coined the term "free love," but it was discarded in favor of "complex marriage." Noyes had no time for romantic love or monogamous marriage, and he considered such practices as signs of selfishness and personal possession. Romantic love, or "special love" as it was referred to in the community, was considered to give rise to jealousy and hypocrisy and made spiritual love impossible to attain.

Consequently, the Perfectionists promulgated the idea of complex marriage because it was natural for all men to love all women and women to love all men. It followed that every adult should consider himself or herself married to every other adult of the opposite sex. In extolling the virtues of group marriage, Noyes stated:

> The human heart is capable of loving any number of times and any number of persons. This is the law of nature. There is no occasion to find fault with it. Variety is in the nature of things, as beautiful and as useful in love as in eating and drinking. . . . We need love as much as we need food and clothing, and God knows it; and if we trust Him for these things, why not for love? (Kephart, 1987:68)

It should be pointed out, however, that the members of the community abided by the doctrine of complex marriage, not for reasons of lust, as it was sometimes charged, but because of the conviction that they were following God's word.

The system of complex marriage was relatively uncomplicated. As everyone lived in the Mansion House, sexual relations were easy to arrange. If a man desired sexual intercourse with a certain woman, he simply asked her. If she agreed, he would stay with her overnight in her room. In case of a shortage of single rooms, the couples could use one of the "social" rooms set aside for that purpose.

Even in complex marriage, sex is never a simple matter. And from the very beginning, there were a number of prohibitions and restrictions. Sex was not to be considered as a "wifely duty," that is, something accepted by the female to satisfy the male.

Noyes preached the separation of the "amative" from the "propagative" functions of sex. He believed that only when the two were separated could the true goals of Perfectionism be attained. "In practice, this meant that males could have sexual intercourse up to, but not including, ejaculation. (Females, of course, could achieve sexual climax at any time.) There were two exceptions to the non-ejaculatory rule: (a) when the male was having intercourse with a female who was past menopause, and (b) when a child was desired" (Kephart, 1987:70). As the community grew, men became more enthusiastic than women in the sexual domain, and the practice of having the man ask the woman for sexual relations was replaced by a new system.

Under the new system, if a man desired sexual relations, he would transmit the message to a central committee member, usually an older woman, who would thereupon make his request known to the woman in question. In practice the use of a go-between served a number of purposes, such as sparing women the embarrassment of voicing a refusal or conjuring up an excuse. The use of a go-between also provided a measure of control over the sexual system. It helped to prevent their members from falling in "special love," and when a particular couple were having too-frequent relations, the go-between would simply disallow further meetings between them. The Oneidans were presumed to act like ladies and gentlemen at all times; inappropriate behavior, suggestive language, and overt displays of sexuality were not tolerated. Sexual behavior was not openly discussed within the community, and the subject of "who was having relations with whom" never became common knowledge. A male member who became too inquisitive on this score was literally thrown out of the community. He "found himself, one winter night, suddenly, unceremoniously, and horizontally propelled through an open window, and shot—harmlessly but ignominiously—into the depths of a snowdrift. It was the first and only forcible expulsion in the history of the community" (Kephart, 1987:72).

As may be expected, John Humphrey Noyes also had some "advanced" ideas about the subject of children. He felt that only those who possessed superior physical and mental abilities should have children. In the words of the *Circular*:

> Why should not beauty and noble grace of person and every other desirable quality of men and women, internal and external, be propagated and intensified beyond all former precedent by the application of the same scientific principles of breeding that produce such desirable results in the case of sheep, cattle, and horses? (Kephart, 1987:78)

The term "eugenics" had not yet been coined. However, he proposed, in effect, a eugenic program in which specially chosen adults would be utilized for breeding purposes. A committee would decide on the individuals who could become parents, and there would be no appeal. Noyes called this program *stirpiculture*, and it was not long before the scientific world was discussing the implications of this unique experiment.

For the first two decades, members of the community had largely refrained from bearing children. They reasoned that procreation should be delayed until such time as the group had the facilities for proper child care. Noyes rejected all forms of contraception and advocated the birth control technique of *coitus reservatus*, that is, sexual intercourse up to, but not including, ejaculation on the part of the male. Until they had mastered the necessary coital control, younger men in the community were required to limit their sexual relations to women who had passed menopause.

At the beginning of the eugenics program, 53 women and 38 men were chosen to be parents by the committee. During the decade or so of the program, there were 58 live births. Noyes himself fathered upwards to a dozen children. For the first 15 months, children remained under the care of their mothers. After that they were transferred to a special section of the Mansion House, called the "children's house," where they were raised communally. They would spend most of their childhood in age-graded classes. Although they were treated with kindness by their parents, sentimentalizing was frowned upon, the feeling being that under Perfectionism all adults should love all children, and vice versa. The children were well adjusted, and as a group they were remarkably healthy. Mortality comparisons indicate that the products of stirpiculture had a significantly lower death rate than children born outside the Oneida community.

The Breakup

Outside pressures against the community, as might have been predicted, were becoming irresistible. Professional crusaders and self-appointed watchdogs of American morals complained about such practices as "free love," "lust," and "animal breeding," and were successful in creating a storm of adverse public criticism. As a result of ever-increasing pressure campaigns, the Oneidans were forced to give up their practice of complex marriage. In 1877 Noyes resigned, and in 1879 he left the community for the same reason that he fled Putney 32 years before: to escape the law. No new leader appeared, and during 1880 plans for dissolution were discussed and approved. "And on January 1, 1881, the Oneida community officially ceased to exist" (Kephart, 1987:86).

At that time the community gave up its distinctive style of life, its complex form of marriage, and its stirpiculture children. The members entered into monogamous marriages, retained their accumulated capital, and launched Oneida Company, Ltd., a venture in silversmithing that still continues today. The style of this corporation was much influenced by idealism, and its board of directors and managerial staff frequently took cuts in salary in order to help the company. This practice, along with the habit of generally low wages for executives, has disappeared as the company had to compete in the larger markets for top executives. Today Oneida Ltd. is a worldwide organization with thousands of employees, and its stocks are traded at the New York Stock Exchange.

Explanations for the community's disintegration vary. Internally, the aging Noyes was apparently unable to turn the leadership over to his son. The son was more interested in biology than in experimental communities. Although the power of the community was formally vested in the council of elders, Noyes usually tipped the balance of power in matters that concerned him. He was, however, unable to provide for his succession. The community also outraged official morality, and the worsening community relations may have contributed to the disbanding. Noyes also had a habit of initiating young virgins into the sexual life of the community, and apparently some girls were under the age of consent. As a result, he was charged with rape and fled the community in an attempt to avoid prosecution. There was also conflict between the generations; some younger members objected to the principle of ascendancy, and some preferred monogamous marriage over complex marriage. This conflict between the generations may have contributed to the internal tension. However, any explanation offered must be less than adequate because much of the data—the diaries and the personal accounts of the community—were burned to protect the reputation of those involved after the establishment of the corporation. All that remains are in the recollections of children of members and the published accounts of the community's life. Thus, the case of the community raises questions that must finally remain unanswered.

Still, the case of Oneida is perhaps the best-documented illustration of a life-style of specific duration. Its complex marriage, economic communism, mutual criticism, and unique child-rearing program lasted approximately 30 years. It had a high degree of internal cohesion; it was highly homogeneous, dominated by upper-middle-class literate people; and it drew on the prior organization of Perfectionist circles. The commitment to remain aware of the community's development and one's own progress toward a more perfect being further contributed to social solidarity and to its distinctive character. Although this venture in utopia was not durable, it provided an excellent case study of unconventional life-styles. In the next section, duration of another type of transitory social phenomena, cults, will be examined.

CULTS

Cults and social movements are considered transitory social phenomena because of their relatively short duration (LaPiere, 1965:59–66). In the sociological literature, both cults and social movements are generally subsumed under the heading of *collective behavior* (Smelser, 1963; Turner & Killian, 1987). A cult is a collectivity with the continuity of a social movement and usually makes demands only on the behavior of its members. A social movement, by definition, is a collectivity acting with some continuity to promote or resist change. Leadership in a movement is determined by the informal response of participants rather than by formal procedures legitimizing authority (Turner & Killian, 1987: 223). Often, social movements are expressed through new trends in literature, art, the popular press, and the adoption of novel life-styles. Thus, as a collective activity, successful social movements have an identifiable life span. For example, William A.

Gamson (1975), in a study of 53 "challenge" groups in the United States between 1800 and 1945, in addition to analyzing the strategies and out-comes of these movements, also indicated the approximate duration of each. As we shall discuss in the next chapter, social movements cover an extremely broad spectrum of human activities. Important social movements in the United States have focused on the abolition of slavery, temperance, civil rights, resistance to war, feminism, and environmentalism. But there have been literally hundreds of other social movements in the United States aimed at solving a wide range of problems. Even though in this section the emphasis is on cults, let us for a moment consider the nature of social movements.

There are several types of social movements based on the objectives of participants. Some examples:

> *Revolutionary movements.* Participants in these movements are deeply dissat-isfied with the existing social order and promote change in accordance with their ideology. Such movements can bring about sweeping social changes, as happened, for example, in countries such as Russia, China, Cuba, and Iran.
>
> *Reactionary movements.* These are social movements whose members oppose certain changes and aim to return to the "good old days." Examples include the Moral Majority, the Ku Klux Klan, the John Birch Society, and the Amer-ican Nazi Party. They all oppose social changes advocated by other move-ments.
>
> *Reform movements.* Participants are generally satisfied with the existing social order but feel that certain reforms are necessary in specific areas. Reform movements generally work with the system, often through the legislative process. Examples include the consumer, environment, and anti-nuclear movements.
>
> *Expressive movements.* Instead of changing external conditions in society, fol-lowers of expressive movements are concerned with the modification of the attitudes and behavior to enable them to cope better with the outside world. They accept society as is, and any change must come from within. Many expressive social movements have a religious focus, seeking to transform people's lives radically, as is the case with the various fundamentalist Christian sects. Participants in such movements seek to achieve mastery over their feelings and emotions and search for inner ways to accept current conditions.

Like all transitory social phenomena, cults and social movements have a life cycle, a series of stages in their natural history. Armand L. Mauss (1975:61) noted that social movements pass through five stages, which he calls (1) incipiency, (2) coalescence, (3) institutionalization, (4) fragmenta-tion, and (5) demise. In the *incipient* phase, early advocates of the movement formulate its essential definition and orientations. This is accompanied by a period of popular excitement in which the goals and orientations of innovators gradually spread through relevant segments of the population. The next stage is *coalescence*, in which one or more groups form around leaders and develop patterns of formal organization, specifying goals, norms, a division of labor, social controls, and so forth. As these groups interact with the larger society, *institutionalization*, the process of "strengthening, stabilizing, and perpetuating a pattern of social ordering" (Olsen, 1978:117), gradually occurs through the establishment of definite norms that assign status positions and role functions. The movement becomes a recognized part of society that must somehow be taken into account by the public. But "An irony in the natural history of social movements is that their very success leads to *fragmentation*" (Mauss, 1975:64). Fragmentation in turn leads to the final stage of movements, to their eventual *demise*. A social movement to promote change may reach this final stage for various reasons. Its goals may become official policy, as happened to the Townsend movement of the 1930s, when Social Security provided its goal of old-age pensions (Messinger, 1955).

A movement may become part of the establishment itself; for example, organized labor movements and unions for a long time have been the recognized bargaining agents with management. A movement can also be repressed by the larger society; for example, the New Left, or its leaders, are co-opted or "bought off." Finally, it should be noted that not all movements pass through all stages. A movement may collapse and vanish at any stage, and a large number of movements—because of their objectives, strategies, or internal makeup—never reach the institutionalization stage of stability and recognition and thus fail to exert any effect on the larger society. Figure 7.2 shows the normal pattern for the natural history of a social movement. For movements that pass through these five stages, their life span can be determined with some degree of accuracy.

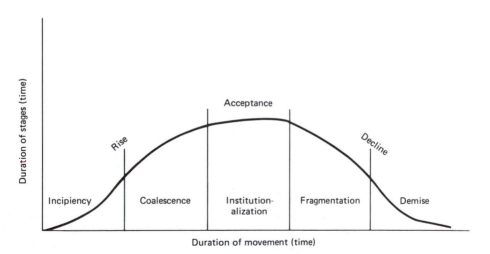

FIG 7.2 Normal Pattern for the Natural History of a Social Movement.
(*Source:* Armand L. Mauss, *Social Problems as Social Movements.* Philadelphia: Lippincott, 1975, p. 66.)

Two cults, the Ghost Dance and the Cargo, which will be considered here, have proved to be objects of intense fascination for students of social movements and social change, and they have received a great deal of attention both from anthropologists and sociologists. Of course, there have been many other examples of cults in the annals of anthropology and sociology. They range from the religious cults at the dawn of human civilization to, for example, the belief in the ultimate salvation through drugs during the Middle Ages to Normal Vincent Peale's "power of positive thinking" in modern times. More recently, the International Society for Krishna Consciousness, a cult of purported Indian origin; Reverend Sun Myung Moon's Unification Church (whose members are called Moonies); and Bhagwan Shree Rajneesh's now defunct communal cult in Oregon attracted many followers (*New York Times*, 1987). Following the grisly events at the People's Temple in Guyana, where more than 900 cult members committed mass suicide in late 1978, many such cults are viewed with skepticism and encounter strong opposition, especially when they start recruiting children from middle-class families.

The Ghost Dance Cult

A cult that has received a great deal of consideration from social scientists is the well-known Ghost Dance religion. This cult, which lasted only a short period of time and involved relatively few Indians, has generated an inordinate amount of interest among sociologists and anthropologists. "The reason seems to be that it now acts as something of a symbol or representational drama of the agony of the American Indian, faced with the inevitability of defeat at the hands of the predatory white and feeling that his old gods had failed him" (Wilson, 1973:48).

By the 1870s the plight of the Plains Indians of North America had reached its lowest ebb. The Indians had been driven into the most barren wastelands as reservations; the white man had killed many of their finest warriors (along with a number of women and children). Venereal disease, tuberculosis, and alcoholism greatly diminished the population, and near-starvation was commonplace.

In 1870 a prophet appeared to the Paiute Indians of Nevada. He called himself Wovoka, the Messiah. When he was 20 years old the sun went into an eclipse and Wovoka fell asleep and was taken into the spirit world.

> After showing him all, God told him he must go back and tell his people they must be good and love one another, have no quarreling, and live in peace with the whites; that they must work, and not lie or steal . . . that if they faithfully obeyed his instructions they would at least be reunited with their friends in this other world, where there would be no more death or sickness or old age. He was then given the dance which he was commanded to bring

back to his people. By performing this dance at intervals, for five consecutive days each time, they would secure this happiness to themselves and hasten the event. (Mooney, 1965:14)

There was a strong belief that the white man and his destructive ways would disappear. How was this to occur? As the Ghost Dance spread from tribe to tribe, different answers were given to this question. Although it originated among the Paiute, the more warlike and proud Sioux gave this belief a more militant interpretation, believing that they themselves must participate in some way in the expulsion of the whites—with the help of "ghost shirts," which would make the wearer invulnerable to the white man's bullets:

> . . . the white man's gunpowder would no longer have power to drive a bullet through the skin of an Indian. The whites themselves would soon be over-whelmed and smothered under a deep landslide, held down by sod and timber, and the few who might escape would become small fishes in the rivers. (Mooney, 1965:29)

There were rumors of increasing belligerence among the Sioux, which caused the white settlers to take precautionary military measures. The conflict between whites and Sioux Indians escalated, and the whites attempted to arrest the leader of the Ghost Dance cult among the Sioux, Sitting Bull. In one of the bloodiest encounters between Indians and whites, the Battle of Wounded Knee on December 29, 1890, more than 350 Indians, including many women and children, were massacred. This massacre was triggered by a tragic misunderstanding. While the Indians were surrendering their weapons to federal troops, a great deal of tension arose in the camp as soldiers overturned teepees, beds, and furniture in their search for guns. A medicine man kept walking among the warriors assuring them that the whites would be helpless against the ghost shirts and, therefore, the Indians should resist the troops. Somehow, a shot was fired at the soldiers. Their retaliation resulted in the well-known massacre.

This defeat signaled the end of the Ghost Dance cult among the Sioux. Prior to the battle with the federal troops at Wounded Knee, the cult had lasted slightly over one year.

The occurrence of the Ghost Dance is explained in the literature as the result of the wholesale disintegration of Indian social organization, which followed the arrival of the white man to the plains (Wilson, 1973:49–50). The loss of their hunting grounds, the influx of settlers, the extension of the railroads, the steady and often illegal takeover of land by federal authorities, and the official encouragement of the decimation of the buffalo herds all contributed to a severe strain on the Indian community. The loss of the buffalo was particularly devastating to the Sioux. It was a source of food, shelter, clothing, and an article of trade. Social status was measured in terms of buffalo-hunting skills. The buffalo also represented a sacred significance in the culture of the Sioux, acting like a totem animal to the tribe. The loss of the sacred aspects of a culture, particularly when it is brought about by outsiders, can be very disturbing to any community, and this particular event further enhanced the receptivity of the Sioux to the Ghost Dance. The Ghost Dance, with its belief in imminent extinction of the white man and its magical belief in the protective powers of the ghost shirt, seems to have met the needs of the Sioux during this stage of disorganization.

After this defeat at Wounded Knee, large numbers of Indians turned to the use of peyote, a carrot-shaped cactus that produces visual and auditory hallucinations. It was no accident that the popularity of the peyote cult followed the demise of the Ghost Dance. "The Ghost Dance promised redemption and liberation at a time when the Indians were ready for rebellion, and provided the motivating force for uprisings such as that of the Sioux; the peyote cult emerged when the Ghost Dance was being snuffed out and the Indians were forced to admit defeat, but when, however, the white man had changed his attitude and substituted assimilation in place of destruction" (Lanternari, 1965:59).

The Cargo Cult

Cargo cult is the designation of a kind of movement, primarily restricted to Melanesia, which is centered around a belief in the coming of a cargo ship, staffed by ancestral spirits, which would contain European goods such as radios, tobacco, steel axes, alcohol, trucks, and occasionally arms. The arrival of the Cargo ship, the natives believed, would initiate a new era of plenty and would release them from their present sufferings. The Cargo cultists devoted their lives to preparations for the arrival of the Cargo; they built piers for the ship and warehouses for the goods; they imitated European ceremonials; and renounced their old life-styles and destroyed the crops and livestock in the belief that these would hasten the coming of the Cargo.

One of the most spectacular of these Cargo cults was the Vailala Madness, which broke out in the Gulf of Papua after World War I. It was supposedly initiated by an old man named Evara. Evara went into a trance at the death of his father and awoke giving forth prophesies.

> He prophesized the coming of a steamer carrying the spirits of dead ancestors on board, who would bring them the "cargo". . . . The spirits had revealed that all the flour, rice, tobacco, and other "trade" belonged to the Papuans, not the whites. The latter would pass into the hands of its rightful owners, the natives. To obtain these goods it was necessary to drive out the whites. (Worsley, 1957:81)

Once started, the cult

involved a kind of mass hysteria, in which numbers of natives were affected by giddiness and reeled about the villages. So infectious was it that almost the whole population of a village might be affected at one time. The leaders of the movement poured forth utterances in "djaman" ("German"), which were in fact a mixture of nonsense of syllables and pidgin English. Sometimes these were incomprehensible, but sometimes the leaders gave intelligible utterances to prophesies and injunctions. The central theme of the former was that the ancestors would soon return to the gulf in a ship, bringing with them a cargo of good things. The leaders of the movement communed with them by means of flag-poles, down which messages were transmitted to the base where they were received by those who had ears to hear—an obvious adaptation of the idea of a wireless mast. Elaborate preparations were made to receive the ancestors, and offerings of food for them were placed in special houses under the control of the leaders. (Piddington, 1957:739)

The leaders of the cult claimed that they were told by their ancestors to have the people abandon the old ceremonial customs and to burn their noisemakers and ceremonial masks. The Vailala Madness, in its intense form, lasted only about three years. It was unrealistic and therefore ineffective in coping with the stressful situation in which the natives found themselves.

Another version of the Cargo cult, the Taro cult, started in about 1914, when a native prophet, Buninia, emerged from a trance in which he had been visited by a Taro or food spirit. The "Taro men" designed dances, singing, and community eating rituals that were followed by trances, seizures, and ecstatic experiences. Followers of the cult were assured that their ancestors would bring them food as well as European garments and tools. The natives were reacting to the relative wealth of their new white neighbors, and the Taro cult was able to offer them what they lacked—that is, hope for material improvement. Whites came into the area around the turn of the century in search of gold. Gold mines were established with the aid of the native labor. The working conditions of the natives were anything but ideal, resulting in the development of hostility toward the white man. The cult helped them to channel this hostility and, at the same time, contributed to the development of some unity among the traditionally antagonistic tribes in the area. By 1930, however, the Taro cult started to decline in importance. Its decline was facilitated by the perception of the British administrators of the Taro cult as an antiwhite, antigovernment organization. However, it was not seen as a great enough threat to the colonial system to be harshly suppressed.

Another New Guinea Cargo cult resulted in unanticipated consequences. The disciples of the cult went to the mission station and presented the missionary with their belief, asking him what he thought of it. In the words of Ward Goodenough (1963:314–315):

> He did not sneer, but expressed approval of its obvious Biblical content, of the aspirations it revealed, and what it was they were trying to conceptualize within the outwardly fantastic myth. Finding that he was not hostile, they asked him if he could show them the road by which they might achieve their aspirations. By agreeing to teach them the way, he came to occupy the position of "prophet" for the revitalization movement, at least in the people's eyes. In this way he acquired considerable control over its adaptation and transformation phases. He succeeded, accordingly, in getting the several villages in the movement to revise a number of their marriage and family customs in the direction endorsed by his religious denomination.

In this particular instance, the missionary had found a way of working from the "inside" to the "out," introducing many changes in the pattern of village life that were in keeping with the aims of his mission. This entailed the cooptation of cult leaders, which in turn resulted in the rapid demise of the original belief system.

There have been a number of other Cargo cults that have made their presence felt in a wide variety of locales throughout Melanesia. The principal theme of the cults is that the returning ancestors will drive out the whites—in some cases with the help of the cultists, in other cases, by themselves (Wilson, 1973:51–52). In the former instance, which marks a more militant interpretation of the Cargo cult, the Cargo is always thought to contain artifacts of war such as weapons, radios, and trucks. All of the Cargo cults were basically anti-European in character, and they rarely lasted for long. "They have succumbed either to the frustrations of repeated failure of the Cargo to arrive or to the antagonism of fearful colonial authorities" (Wilson, 1973:51). In addition to its bizarre manifestations, the Cargo cult has attracted attention because of the fact that it often erupted in a relatively stable and homogeneous community. Just as in the case of American Indians, the coming of the white man meant the loss of land and the disruption of native social organizations. Social disorganization was also brought about by the use of native labor in mines and plantations, which often resulted in a separate residence away from their villages. This, in turn, affected the network of family obligations to which the islanders felt traditionally bound. Finally, the coming of the white man meant the arrival of highly divisive Christianity. There were competing missionaries, but they managed to renounce uniformly many traditional sacred practices as sinful. Simultaneously, they preached the value of obligations and associations that ignored the old tribal and kinship ties. On top of this, the Europeans brought a new life-style and new models of consumption, which the natives were able to envy but not to emulate.

In the words of a frustrated old villager: "When we followed our customs, we lived in peace and honor. Now everything is new and pulls us in different directions. We are confused" (Kristof, 1987:6). At the same time, the unrealistic, bizarre, and fanatic nature of cults greatly contributed to their own demise. One can only wait so long for the Cargo to arrive.

SUMMARY

In this chapter we have considered the question of how long change will be sustained after its introduction and before its demise or drastic alteration in a social system. In a historical context, the study of the duration of change is problematic because of the broad and amorphous time dimensions. Still, it is possible to talk about general longevity patterns for historical periods in terms of distinct eras of considerable life span.

The discussion of the duration of change becomes more concrete and meaningful in the framework of transitory social changes. Here we are dealing with datable, recognizable, and, in many instances, measurable events of relatively short duration.

Fads and fashions provide an extraordinary opportunity to study the life span of changes. Both are culture patterns that are adopted by a given segment of a society for a relatively brief period of time and then abandoned. Of the two, fads are of shorter duration; they tend to appear suddenly and disappear as suddenly. Fashion and faddish changes are present in most aspects of group life, and some, such as phrenology or the Florida land boom, can have serious implications.

The study of life-styles affords another occasion for the analysis of the duration of change. Class-based life-styles tend to endure longer than the so-called counterculture life-styles of hippies or yippies. An excellent sociological example of unique life-styles of discernible duration is found among the members of the Oneida community, which endured approximately three decades.

Cults and social movements are considered as transitory social-change phenomena because of their relatively short duration. Both have a life cycle, a series of stages in their natural history. The Ghost Dance and the Cargo cults, both of short duration, proved to be objects of intense fascination for social scientists. In the next chapter the various strategies of change will be examined.

SUGGESTED FURTHER READINGS

BENSMAN, JOSEPH, and ARTHUR J. VIDICH. *American Society: The Welfare State & Beyond, Revised*. South Hadley, Mass.: Bergin & Garvey Publishers, 1987. See in particular Part III on emerging life-styles and the new classes.

FELDMAN, SAUL D., and GERALD W. THIELBAR, eds. *Life Styles: Diversity in American Society*, 2nd ed. Boston: Little, Brown, 1975. A collection of articles on diverse life-styles in the United States.

KEPHART, WILLIAM M. *Extraordinary Groups: The Sociology of Unconventional Life-Styles*, 3rd ed. New York: St. Martins Press, 1987. A highly readable account of the Old Order Amish, the Oneida community, the Father Divine Movement, the Shakers, the Mormons, the Hutterites, and some of the modern communes.

MEYERSOHN, ROLF, and ELIHU KATZ. "Notes on a Natural History of Fads." *American Journal of Sociology*, 62, May 1957, pp. 594–601. The natural history of fads is told as a succession of chronological stages.

RUDOFSKY, BERNARD. *The Unfashionable Human Body*. New York: Doubleday (Anchor Books), 1974. An entertaining and insightful treatment of fashion changes and the prejudices and inhibitions that entrap the human body.

SIMMEL, GEORG. "Fashion." *American Journal of Sociology*, 62, May 1957, pp. 541–558. A classic statement of the role of fashion in society.

TURNER, RALPH H., and LEWIS M. KILLIAN. *Collective Behavior*, 3rd ed. Englewood Cliffs, N.J.: Prentice-Hall, 1987. See particularly the outstanding sections on cults and social movements.

WORSLEY, PETER. *The Trumpet Shall Sound: A Study of "Cargo" Cults in Melanesia*. London: Macgibbon and Kee, 1957. One of the most comprehensive treatments of cults in print.

REFERENCES

BENSMAN, JOSEPH, and ARTHUR J. VIDICH. *American Society: The Welfare State & Beyond, Revised*. South Hadley, Mass.: Bergin & Garvey Publishers, 1987.

BLUMER, HERBERT. "Fashion." In David L. Sills (ed.), *International Encyclopedia of the Social Sciences*, vol. 5. New York: Macmillan/Free Press, 1968, pp. 341–345.

BOSKOFF, ALVIN. *The Mosaic of Sociological Theory*. New York: Crowell, 1972.

CARMAN, JAMES M. "The Fate of Fashion Cycles in Our Modern Society." In Raymond M. Haas (ed.), *Proceedings of the American Marketing Association*, 1966, Chicago: American Marketing Association, pp. 722–737.

DAVIS, FRED. "Why All of Us May Be Hippies Someday." In Dennis Pirages (ed.), *Seeing Beyond: Personal, Social and Political Alternatives*. Reading, Mass.: Addison-Wesley, 1971, pp. 102–113.

DAVIS, KINGSLEY. *Human Society*. New York: Macmillan, 1949.

Encyclopedia Americana. "Phrenology," vol. 22, p. 22. New York: Americana Corporation, 1957.

FELDMAN, SAUL D., and GERALD W. THIELBAR, eds. *Life Styles: Diversity in American Society*, 2nd ed. Boston: Little, Brown, 1975.

GAMSON, WILLIAM A. *The Strategy of Social Protest*. Homewood, Ill.: Dorsey Press, 1975.

GILBERT, DENNIS, and JOSEPH A. KAHL. *The American Class Structure: A New Synthesis*, 3rd ed. Chicago: Dorsey Press, 1987.

GOODENOUGH, WARD HUNT. *Cooperation in Change*. New York: Russell Sage, 1963.

GREEN, ROBERT L. "Accentuate the Appropriate." *The New York Times Magazine*, September 18, 1977, pp. 40–45.

GREENE, BOB. "Abbie Hoffman Ready to Join 'Heroes' of One-Man Shows." *St. Louis Post-Dispatch*, October 26, 1977, p. 3H.

HARRIS, MARVIN. "What Goes Up May Stay Up." *Natural History*, 81, January 1973, pp. 18–25.

HOFFMAN, ABBIE. *Revolution for the Hell of It*. New York: Dial, 1968.

HOFFMAN, ABBIE. *Woodstock Nation*. New York: Vintage, 1969.

HUNT, MORTON. "Navigating the Therapy Maze: A Consumer's Guide to Mental Health Treatment." *The New York Times Magazine*, August 30, 1987, pp. 28–49.

INGOLD, TIM. *Evolution and Social Life*. Cambridge, England: Cambridge University Press, 1986.

KAHL, JOSEPH A. *The American Class Structure.* New York: Holt, Rinehart & Winston, 1957.

KATZ, ELIHU, and PAUL F. LAZARSFELD. *Personal Influence.* New York: Free Press, 1955.

KEPHART, WILLIAM M. *Extraordinary Groups: The Sociology of Unconventional Life-Styles.* 3rd ed. New York: St. Martin's Press, 1987.

KOTEN, JOHN. "The Shattered Middle Class." *The Wall Street Journal,* March 9, 1987, p.19.

KRISTOF, NICHOLAS D. "Space Age Succeeds Stone Age on Pacific Isle." *The New York Times,* July 19, 1987, pp.1, 6.

KROEBER, A. L. "On the Principle of Order in Civilization as Exemplified by Changes of Fashion." *American Anthropologist,* 21, 1919, pp. 235–263.

LANTERNARI, VITTORIO. *The Religious of the Oppressed: A Study of Modern Messianic Cults.* New York: New American Library (Mentor Books), 1965.

LaPIERE, RICHARD T. *Social Change.* New York: McGraw-Hill Book Company, 1965.

LENSKI, GERHARD, and JEAN LENSKI. *Human Societies: An Introduction to Macrosociology,* 5th ed. New York: McGraw-Hill Book Company, 1987.

LEWIS, GEORGE H. "Capitalism, Contra-Culture, and the Head Shop: Explorations in Structural Change." In Marcello Truzzi (ed.), *Sociology for Pleasure.* Englewood Cliffs, N.J.: Prentice-Hall, 1974, pp. 374–387.

LURIE, ALISON. "Fashion and Status." In John Stimson and Ardyth Stimson (eds.), *Sociology: Contemporary Readings,* 2nd ed. Itasca, Ill.: F.E. Peacock Publishers, 1987, pp. 193–202.

MAUSS, ARMAND L. *Social Problems as Social Movements.* Philadelphia: Lippincott, 1975.

MESSINGER, SHELDON. "Organizational Transformation: A Case Study of a Declining Social Movement." *American Sociological Review,* 20, February 1955, pp. 3–10.

MEYER, ROGER E. "LSD: The Conditions and Consequences of Use and the Treatment of Users." In J. R. Wittenborn et al. (eds.), *Proceedings of the Rutgers Symposium on Drug Abuse,* 1969. Springfield, III.: Charles C. Thomas, pp. 199–208.

MEYERSOHN, ROLF, and ELIHU KATZ. "Notes on a Natural History of Fads." *American Journal of Sociology,* 62, May 1957, pp. 594–601.

MILLER, DELBERT C. "Influence of Technology on Industries." In Francis R. Allen, Hornell Hart, Delbert C. Miller, William F. Ogburn, and Meyer F. Nimkoff (eds.), *Technology and Social Change.* New York: Appleton, 1957a, pp. 245–277.

MILLER, DELBERT C. "Impact of Technology on Agriculture." In Francis R. Allen, Hornell Hart, Delbert C. Miller, William F. Ogburn, and Meyer F. Nimkoff (eds.), *Technology and Social Change.* New York: Appleton, 1957b, pp.324–351.

MOONEY, JAMES. *The Ghost-Dance Religion and the Sioux Outbreak of 1890.* Chicago: University of Chicago Press, 1965.

MORRISON, DENTON E., and CARLIN PAIGE HOLDEN. "The Burning Bra: The American Breast Fetish and Women's Liberation." In Robert R. Evan (ed.), *Social Movements: A Reader and Source Book.* Chicago: Rand McNally, 1973, pp. 564–583.

New York Times. "Guru's City in Desert Sits Nearly Empty," August 9, 1987, p. 11.

Newsweek. "Blue Streak; Streaking," February 4, 1974a p. 63.

Newsweek. "Streaking: One Way to Get a B.A.," March 18, 1974b pp. 41–42.

OLSEN, MARVIN E. *The Process of Social Organization: Power in Social Systems,* 2nd ed. New York: Holt, Rinehart & Winston, 1978.

PIDDINGTON, RALPH. *An Introduction to Social Anthropology,* vol. 2. London: Oliver & Boyd, 1957.

REICH, CHARLES. *The Greening of America.* New York: Random House, 1970.

ROBINSON, DWIGHT E. "Fashions in Shaving and Trimming of the Beard: The Men of the Illustrated London News, 1842–1972." *American Journal of Sociology,* 81(5), 1976, pp. 1133–1141.

ROSTOW, WALT W. *The Stages of Economic Growth: A Non-Communist Manifesto.* New York: Cambridge, 1961.

ROSZAK, THEODORE. *The Making of a Counterculture: Reflections on the Technocratic Society and Its Youthful Opposition.* New York: Doubleday, 1969.

RUBIN, JERRY. *Do It!* New York: Simon & Schuster, 1970.

RUDOFSKY, BERNARD. *The Unfashionable Human Body.* New York: Doubleday (Anchor Books), 1974.

SCHAFER, STEPHEN. *Theories in Criminology.* New York: Random House, 1969.

SIMMEL, GEORG. "Fashion." *American Journal of Sociology,* 62, May 1957, pp. 541–558.

SMELSER, NEIL J.   *Theory of Collective Behavior.* New York: Free Press, 1963.

SUTERMEISTER, ROBERT A.   *People and Productivity,* 3rd ed. New York: McGraw-Hill Book Company, 1976.

TAYLOR, FREDERICK W.   *The Principles of Scientific Management.* New York: Harper & Row, 1911.

Time.   'Streaking, Streaking Everywhere," March 18, 1974, pp. 58–59.

TUMIN, MELVIN M.   *Social Stratification: The Forms and Functions of Inequality,* 2nd ed. Englewood Cliffs, N.J.: Prentice-Hall, 1985.

TURNER, RALPH H., and LEWIS M. KILLIAN.   *Collective Behavior,* 3rd ed. Englewood Cliffs, N.J.: Prentice-Hall, 1987.

VEBLEN, THORSTEIN.   *The Theory of the Leisure Class.* New York: Random House (Modern Library), 1911.

WEBER, MAX.   "Class, Status and Party." In Reinhard Bendix and Seymour Martin Lipset (eds.), *Class, Status, and Power: Social Stratification in Comparative Perspective,* 2nd ed. New York: Free Press, 1966, pp. 21–28.

WHYTE, WILLIAM H., Jr.   *The Organization Man.* New York: Doubleday, 1957.

WILSON, JOHN.   *Introduction to Social Movements.* New York: Basic Books, 1973.

WOLF, C.P.   "The Structure of Societal Revolutions." In George K. Zollschan and Walter Hirsch (eds.), *Social Change: Explorations, Diagnoses, and Conjectures.* New York: Wiley, 1976, pp. 63–99.

WORSLEY, PETER.   *The Trumpet Shall Sound: A Study of the "Cargo" Cults in Melanesia.* London: Macgibbon & Kee, 1957.

8 Reactions to Change

The objective of this chapter is to consider the conditions that facilitate or hinder the acceptance of change. Those involved in social change at the theoretical and practical levels recognize the inclinations of individuals, groups, organizations, institutions, and even entire societies to seek and ward off change at the same time. At every level in society, there are forces that seek to promote change, and there are those that strive to maintain the status quo. Change is both sought and opposed, and in the long run the forces that promote change in society will have an edge over those that strive toward conservatism. Change often involves disruption, the reorganization of behavior patterns, and requires some alterations of values, attitudes, and life-styles. Very few changes of any magnitude can be accomplished without impairing the life situations of some individuals or groups. As Donald Klein (1985:98) aptly notes, "It is probably inevitable that any major change will be a mixed blessing to those undergoing it in those instances when the status quo or situation of gradual change has been acceptable to many or most people. The dynamic interplay of forces in social systems is such that any stable equilibrium must represent at least a partial accommodation to the varying needs and demands of those involved. Under such circumstances, the major change must be desired by those affected if it is to be accepted."

To a great extent the structure of a society dictates whether change will be opposed or advocated. When a society is highly integrated so that each element is tightly interwoven with all the others in a mutually interdependent system, change is difficult and costly. For example, among a number of Nilotic African societies, such as the Pakot and Masai, the culture is integrated around the cattle complex. Cattle are not only a means of subsistence; they are also a necessity for bride purchase, a measure of status, and an object of intense affection (Schneider, 1959). Such a system is strongly resistant to social change. But when the culture is less highly integrated, so that work, play, family, religion, and other activities are less dependent upon one another, change is easier and more frequent. A tightly structured society, where every individual's roles, duties, and privileges are clearly and precisely defined, is less given to changes than a more loosely structured society, where social roles, lines of authority, privileges, and obligations are more open to individual rearrangement. For example, the structure of American society is highly conducive to social change. The prevailing individualism, lack of rigid social stratification, great emphasis on achieved status, high level of educational attainment, and institutionalization of research all tend to encourage rapid social change (Bensman & Vidich, 1987; Naisbitt, 1982; Toffler, 1980).

In the Western world change seems normal, and most people pride themselves on being progressive and up to date. By contrast, the Trobriand Islanders off the coast of New Guinea had no concept of change and did not even have any words in their language to express or describe change. When Western visitors tried to explain the notion of change, the islanders could not understand what they were talking about. Societies obviously differ greatly in their outlook toward change. Those who revere the past, who worship their ancestors, honor and obey their elders, and are preoccupied with tradition and rituals, will change slowly and unwillingly. When a culture has been relatively static for a long period of time, individuals are likely to assume that it should remain so indefinitely. They consider their customs, culture, and technique as correct and everlasting. The accent is on the status quo, and change is never consciously or seriously considered. Still, change occurs in such a society, but in most cases it is too slow and too gradual to be noticed.

Although the rate of change varies from society to society, and within society among its various subgroups, it is possible to identify and analyze factors that inhibit or promote change in a variety of domains and levels. We shall now examine the conditions that play a role in the acceptance or rejection of change. A number of cross-cultural illustrations of actual situations, many drawn from the experience of George M. Foster (1973) in developing countries, will be considered to show the influence of specific factors in concrete change situations.

As a convenient way of organizing the diverse sources, conditions, and causes of acceptance and rejection of change, they will be considered in terms of social, psychological, cultural, and economic factors. Obviously there is a fair amount of overlapping among these factors, and the conditions of acceptance and rejection can only be separated for analytical purposes. They are the opposite sides of the same coin. The factors that are found in the nature of the social structure of the group or society are simply referred to as "social"; those dealing with perception, learning, and motivation are designated as "psychological"; factors that are culture based are called "cultural"; and those with an economic base are termed "economic." Clearly, economic factors set the limit of change in many situations. As it will be shown, individuals are often reluctant to change their ways because of cultural, social, and psychological factors. But equally as often they are aware of the benefits of change and are anxious to alter their traditional ways, but the economic cost is just too great. If the economical potential is not present, attention to the other three factors will be meaningless. With these introductory remarks in mind, let us now turn to the stimulants to change.

SOCIAL STIMULANTS

All societies are constantly changing—some rapidly and some very slowly. A number of factors influence the rate of change and facilitate the acceptance of an innovation. The ones that play an important role in stimulating change include the desire for prestige, contact with other peoples, friendship obligations, social class, authority, problems of "fit," order of presentation, timing, degree of participation in decision making, and competition. In the following paragraphs, these social stimulants to change will be examined.

Desire for Prestige

In every society certain types of behaviors are emulated because they confer prestige and status. The forms of behavior that are considered prestigious obviously differ from society to society. In traditional societies, certain nonmaterial and symbolic achievements are rewarded with high status, such as religious asceticism, chastity, and fulfillment of ritual obligations. In the contemporary world, prestige is increasingly sought through the acquisition of certain visible material symbols such as clothes, food, housing, and automobiles. George M. Foster (1973:155–158) provides a number of illustrations of how the prestige factor is significant in bringing about social change. For example, in modern Indian villages, Western clothes, cigarettes, sunglasses, and tea are popular, both because of utility and because they possess prestige value. In Zambia (formerly Northern Rhodesia) the refrigerator confers a great deal of prestige and is usually placed in the center of the living room. In Melanesia the prestige factor to a great extent accounts for the use of corrugated iron roofs on the better homes, which, although more durable, are less comfortable than the old fashioned sago-palm thatch. In India, mothers of lower socioeconomic groups increasingly spend money on highly advertised, patented, powdered carbohydrate foods, which have prestige value, rather than on milk and other locally produced foods that represent better nutritional value for the same price.

Felix M. Keesing (1958:400) points out that an innovation will be accepted more readily if it will add to the prestige of the acceptors. This is illustrated by the observation of Foster (1973:157) that, in Latin America, latrines frequently are installed not because of an appreciation of the desirability of environmental sanitation, but because they add an extra note of elegance to a man's home and he thereby rises in importance in the eyes of his peers. Similarly, in rural Egypt, modern medicine is making some progress because it is becoming a sign of social prestige to bring a physician into one's home. In the same vein, using a tractor, even though it may not be economical, is a symbol of being modern in many areas. For example, Foster saw in Zimbabwe many tractors whose use was clearly not economic—as a matter of fact, many of them were inoperable—but they were valued and prominently displayed for the prestige they conferred upon the owner.

Contact

It is frequently proposed in the social-change literature that contact with other societies stimulates change (Bochner, 1982; Keesing, 1958:401). Because many new attributes and traits come through diffusion, those societies in closest contact with other societies are likely to change most rapidly. During the period of overland transportation, the land bridge connecting Asia, Africa, and Europe was the center of civilizing change. With the introduction of sailing vessels, the center shifted to the fringes of the Mediterranean Sea and still later to the northwest coast of Europe. Areas of greatest intercultural contact are centers of change. Traditionally, war and trade have always led to intercultural contact, and today travel, tourism, and the mass media are adding to the contact between cultures. Through contacts, behaviors are modified, new practices are introduced, and new symbols of prestige are established. For example, as a result of increased tourism and contact with Westerners, Soviet and Eastern European youth seek to emulate certain Western practices and attires, and oftentimes a pair of faded blue jeans sells on the black market for $80 to $140 (although such transactions carry a heavy penalty). In general, there are certain conditions of contact that facilitate the acceptance of a novelty. They include situations when there is equal status between members of different cultural groups, when the contact is of an intimate rather than casual nature, and when the contact is pleasant and rewarding (Jaspars & Hewstone, 1982:128).

Friendship Obligations

Friendship patterns in much of the world are more carefully worked out and balanced than they are in the United States. In addition to liking and free association with someone of a person's choice, friendship implies mutual obligations and reciprocal favors. Friendship in this context provides the basis for cooperation in many societies. As a result of this type of friendship bond, many changes and innovations are accepted in order to please the proponent or those friends who have already accepted them. For example, authorities on international business emphasize the importance of friendship ties in business ventures in Africa. Friendship comes before business, and trust must be established before Africans enter business deals or consider the acceptance of new products or practices (Harris & Moran, 1987:484–485).

Social Class

Different social classes in a society react to change in different ways. For example, upper classes will be more likely to accept modern medical practices because these people can afford them, are better educated, and are in closer contact with clinics and physicians (Gould, 1957:512). They also have the means to obtain many innovations inaccessible to members of the other classes. "When it is a question of items of material culture, this group is often the most receptive. But frequently these people are basically conservative. They are content with their position, and if major changes in the way of life of their community occur, there is no certainty that they will continue to enjoy their advantage" (Foster, 1973:170).

One would think that the poorest people in a society would be most receptive to change. However, this is not the case, and usually they tend to be the most reluctant to adopt new ways. As pointed out by T. R. Batten:

> This is because they of all people can least afford to take risks. They have no reserves to tide them over failure. They know that they can just make a living by doing as they do, and they need to be very sure before they do anything differently. (Batten, quoted by Foster, 1973:170–171)

The most receptive people to change, in general, are those in the middle class. They have enough that they can take limited risks without threatening their well-being, but their situation is not so secure that the attraction of greater income, and the satisfaction of other felt needs, would not be a strong motivation to action. Moreover, they do not usually represent vested interests that may be threatened by major innovations, nor are they in a state of apathy, believing that no change is possible (Foster, 1973:171).

Authority

There are at least two kinds of authority that can be recognized as influencing receptivity to change. The first is the kind in which a respected leader vouches for, or approves, a proposed change. He or she is not actually forcing the people to change; rather, the person is using the authority inherent in his or her position to reassure others that it is, indeed, safe, advantageous, and desirable. Foster (1973:171) cites an illustration from an Algerian village where an old-fashioned teacher, as a result of his prestige and moral authority, was able to introduce many innovations in all areas of life.

When dealing with the welfare of the majority, at times the use of authority is required over the beliefs of a dissident minority. For example, compulsory vaccination and chlorination of water have brought about important health benefits over the protest of small minorities. Similarly, the introduction of the New World potato into Europe required the initial use of authority for the benefit of all concerned. When the potato was first introduced in Europe in the late eighteenth century, it was opposed and was considered poisonous in that it would cause diarrhea and would otherwise be harmful. But in Germany, the head of the army ordered every soldier to plant potatoes to care for, harvest, and eat. Apparently the length of the military service was sufficiently long to give the soldiers time to learn how to cultivate potatoes and to develop a taste for them. When the men returned to their farms after their military duty, they started to grow potato crops. It soon became a staple food in Germany and later spread to other parts of Europe.

The Problem of "Fit"

Acceptance of change is greatly facilitated when it can be integrated into the existing configuration of culture (Keesing, 1958:398). If a new form can be integrated or associated with traditional patterns, it has a greater chance of being accepted than if there is nothing to tie it to. For example, the horse fitted easily into the hunting culture of the Apaches, as it enabled them to improve their hunting techniques. Also, many non-Western societies have readily accepted the procedures and materials of scientific medicine—inoculations, antibiotics, and even surgery—where these were consistent with their traditional folk medicine. It was easier for the ill Navaho to swallow the doctor's pill while the Navaho's healing dance continued.

The acceptance of an innovation is further facilitated when new tools and techniques can be adapted to preexisting ways of using the body. Traditional and established motor patterns are important, and if a new innovation can fit into this existing framework, the possibilities for successful introduction are multiplied. For example, at times it is easier to modify a tool than the motor pattern. When Mexicans were furnished with modern wheelbarrows at railroad construction sites, they removed the wheel and lifted the barrow proper to their backs, supporting and carrying it with a forehead tumpline. This is owing to the fact that Mexicans for centuries have moved earth by carrying it in a basket supported on their backs in this fashion. As a matter of fact, even today the tourists in Mexico City may see earth from the foundations of new skycrapers being carried out of the ground in the same fashion. "The knack of handling a wheelbarrow is not something an adult picks up easily, so the willing railway workers, not wishing to displease their masters by rejecting their help, solved the problem by changing the tool to conform to their motor patterns" (Foster, 1973:166).

The Order of Presentation

It has been argued that the success of an innovation depends to a great extent on the supporting circumstances that may exist as well as on the recognition by individuals of the need for the innovation (Foster, 1973:167). When an innovation appears at the time when the supporting factors are at a maximum, the chances for acceptance are excellent. In other words, people need to be ready for the introduction of a given innovation. For example, villagers in developing societies do not look upon literacy as an abstract thing that is good by itself. It takes time, hard work, and when it is achieved, there are few, if any, tangible benefits. Consequently, attitudes toward school programs are generally not favorable. However, when there is some concrete benefit accruing from literacy programs, chances are that such campaigns will be successful. For example, in Nigeria during World War II, for a short while adult literacy campaigns were successful for the simple reason that people wanted to communicate with their young men who were away as soldiers. When they returned, there was much less felt need for literacy. In general, literacy becomes important when villagers begin to see that those individuals who are literate have extra advantages, or when they sense that they are less likely to be cheated by city people if they can read. "As standards of living are raised and there is increased travel and contact with the remainder of the nation, conditions become increasingly favorable for presenting adult education programs to rural peoples. But until such time arrives, slight success is the usual rule" (Foster, 1973:169). In the same vein, in those parts of the world where curative facilities for the ill are not available, preventive health programs have little meaning to the people.

Timing

Related to the order of introduction of an innovation is *timing*. In rural areas the acceptance of an innovation is conditioned by the right time within a yearly cycle. This is particularly true when one's pocketbook is involved. In rural communities the amount of available cash fluctuates during the year. During the harvest time people have the most cash available. This is the period for weddings, fiestas, and other activities involving large expenditures. If new material items or practices come to the attention of villagers during this period, they are more likely to spend money on it than a couple of months before or after harvest time. In Batten's words:

> The government officer must not only be prepared to give his time, but also to give it the right time of the year. People are much busier on their farms at some seasons than at others, and they can take on project work more successfully in the slack season when they have the most leisure time. The project which is stimulated too late, so that it is left half-done when the busy season comes round again, may never be completed, and may prejudice the people against attempting other projects in the future. (Batten, quoted by Foster, 1973:169–170).

Participation in Decision Making

In the United States an innovation will be more readily accepted if the people who are to change are involved in planning and execution. In a classic study by Kurt Lewin (1965), conducted during World War II, the object was to change meat consumption patterns to less desirable, but more plentiful, cuts such as kidneys and sweetbreads. In Lewin's study, two experimental conditions were employed. In one, housewives heard a lecture of the benefits of these foods; in the other, a discussion was initiated among women. The same information was relayed in both cases. Results gathered at a later date indicated that 32 percent of the individuals participating in the discussion used the unfamiliar meats, compared to only 3 percent of the individuals who heard the lecture. It has since been repeatedly suggested in the social-science literature that change is effected more readily and with more relative permanence if the mass of the people involved participate in some way in the change program, although it is recognized that the notion of participation is class- and culture-specific.

Similarly in formal organizations, employees' participation in planning and implementing change tend to capture their excitement. It may result in better decisions because of employee input, and it may create more direct communications through personal involvement (Nadler, 1987:365). If employees feel deprived, bringing them into the decision-making process will augment their involvement in the acceptance of the decision that is made. In general, if the decisions are important for the subordinates in terms of their own work, the acceptance of change will be aided through their involvement (Hall, 1987:173).

Competition

As discussed in Chapter 4, Sources of Change, competition often spurs people to make changes. It may take place between individuals, between groups, or between villages. Competition as a stimulant to change is perhaps most pronounced in the contemporary marketplace. Consumers increasingly expect and prefer new products. This point of view is reflected by Gerald Zaltman (1965:3) who states that "today more than ever before the flow of goods and services consists of innovations. Consumers not only expect a constant change in the items available to them, but they have come to consider such change desirable." The continuous production of new automobile models and the growth of the range of household electrical appliances are two simple illustrations. The processes of continuous innovation, invention, and new technologies under the impetus of competition also create new demands for investment and capital. This provides a basis for renewed expansion, thus further promoting change in the economic sphere.

PSYCHOLOGICAL STIMULANTS

When individuals are confronted with new opportunities, acceptance of those opportunities is conditioned by a number of psychological factors. In this section several psychological factors are examined that are considered as facilitative in the acceptance of change. They include motivation, perceived needs, communication patterns, attitudes, and forms of personal influence.

Motivations to Change

Motivation is a purposive or goal-directed behavior that is acquired through experience by learning. It is a way of gratifying needs and desires, and thus there are many different types and levels. Many motives are culture-bound in that their presence or absence is a function of characteristics of a particular culture. To illustrate:

> . . . religious beliefs in some cultures offer motivations to certain kinds of change, but in other cultures these motivations are weak or lacking. In post-Reformation Protestant Europe the desire to find salvation through personal interpretation of the Scriptures placed a great premium on literacy. A religious motivation—the desire to read the Bible—thus helps explain the world's first mass literacy development. . . . In India . . . the desire to be able to read the sacred scriptures of the Gita, and hence to enjoy a more secular place in afterlife, motivated some people to learn to read, in a fashion reminiscent of early Protestantism. (Foster, 1973:152)

Certain kinds of motivations seem to be universal or nearly universal in that they cut across all kinds of societies and cultures and are found in some degree almost everywhere. These motivations for stimulating change are universal in nature and include such things as the desire for prestige, economic gain, and the wish to comply with friendship obligations.

The element of play, the fascination with a novel or unusual toy, has long been recognized as an important factor in invention and also seems to be significant as motivation in change. Foster (1973:172–173) cites an illustration of the effect of the play motive in East Bengal as a stimulant to change. He noticed that nearly 80 percent of all families in a village had built bore-hole latrines, all within the course of several weeks. This kind of success rate was highly unusual for the prevailing environmental sanitation programs in that area. A bit of probing revealed that in that part of East Bengal there is a thick covering of rich alluvial soil, which permits the use of an auger for drilling the latrine pit. Four men can bore through as much as 20 feet of this soil in an hour and the results are little short of miraculous. It turned out that the villagers were enchanted with this marvelous new tool and wanted to try their hand at it. Competition between groups of men were informally organized, and records were set and broken for latrine drilling in rapid succession. Foster concludes this little anecdote by saying that "For several weeks this was undoubtedly the happiest village in the country. And, at the end of the time, a good job of environmental sanitation had been done—but not for the reason the health team thought" (1973:163). Of course, the element of play stimulates the acceptance of innovations in many other ways. For example, the current fad among youngsters playing video games increases their computer literacy and, at the same time, helps their parents to accept and use personal computers.

Perceived Needs

Acceptance of change in a society is greatly affected by how its members perceive their needs. "Needs" are obviously subjective; they are real if people feel that they are real. In many underdeveloped and malnourished parts of the world, individuals not only need *more* food, they also need *different* foods, especially vegetables and legumes. Agricultural changes that bring *more* food are more readily accepted than those bringing *different* foods for which they feel no need (Arensberg & Niehoff, 1971:155).

It is often argued that changing conditions tend to create new needs—genuine objective needs, not just subjectively "felt" needs. For example, urbanization created a need for sanitary engineering; the modern factory system created a need for labor unions; and the high-speed automobile created a need for superhighways. A culture is integrated and therefore any change in one part of the culture creates a need for adaptive changes in related parts of the culture. Individuals can also develop a need when they learn that an improved method, an innovation, exists. "Therefore, innovations *can* lead to needs, as well as vice versa. Some change agents use this approach to change by creating needs among their clients through pointing out the desirable consequences of new ideas" (Rogers & Shoemaker, 1971:105).

Communication Patterns

Communication is a circular interaction that involves a sender, a message, and a receiver. Several characteristics of the sender can promote the acceptance of change. If the person is considered an expert in a particular field, he or she is likely to exert a favorable influence. Closely related to the question of expertise is the source of credibility. In general, the more credible the source, the greater the persuasive impact (Weyant, 1986:83–86). Credibility is often determined by level of education, social status, and professional attainment. Other sender characteristics that are likely to influence the receiver include trustworthiness, power, attraction, likability, and similarity.

Several characteristics of a message may stimulate the acceptance of change. One is the use of fear-arousing as opposed to more rational, less emotional, appeals. For example, the highly emotional and fear-arousing appeals to combat AIDS through what is popularly referred to as "safe sex" seem to be effective in altering sexual practices and behavior.

A second characteristic is the organization of the message. In terms of stimulating acceptance of change, is it more effective to present one side of an argument or both sides? In a classic study by Carl Hovland and his associates it was found that presentation of both sides was more effective in converting the highly educated. The presentation of only one side of the argument was more effective among the poorly educated and those originally favoring the advocated view. Two-sided communications, it has been discovered, appear to be more effective "inoculators" than are one-sided communications. In summarizing the relative merits of one and two-sided communications, they say this:

1. A two-sided presentation is more effective in the long run than a one-sided one (a) when, regardless of initial opinion the audience is *exposed* to subsequent counter-propaganda, or (b) when, regardless of subsequent exposure to counter-propaganda, the audience initially *disagrees* with the commentator's position.
2. A two-sided presentation is *less* effective than a one-sided presentation if the audience initially agrees with the commentator's position and is not exposed to later counter-propaganda. (Hovland, Lumsdaine, & Sheffield, 1949:109)

Finally, there is the question of primacy versus recency effects in the delivery of a message. There are arguments in support of both sides of the question. Those in favor of recency contend that an audience is more likely to recall material presented last. Those in favor of primacy argue that attention span of an audience declines by the time the second speaker presents the argument. The key seems to be the time interval between the presentations. If there is little time between the two, the first speaker will have an advantage. If the time interval is greater, it is more likely (assuming that the speakers are equal in characteristics such as expertise, trust, attractiveness, and so on) that the second speaker will be more effective. It should be noted, however, that these are broad generalizations, and the question of primacy versus recency should be seen as just one of the many variables stimulating the acceptance of a message.

Receiver characteristics also need to be taken into consideration. For example, research shows that many voters do not respond directly to appeals by politicians. These appeals, instead, are evaluated in the context of their memberships in groups and organizations such as social clubs and labor unions. If a person is supported by a group holding similar views, the individual will be more resistant to change than when such support is absent. By contrast, when group ties are weak or lacking, one is more susceptible to persuasive appeals. This explains, to an extent, why new immigrants, who lack family, community, and group ties, are more likely candidates for extremist political and religious organizations. Such organizations provide the individual with a sense of solidarity, identity, and belongingness. Extremist organizations, such as the John Birch Society, capitalize on this through their appeals to the uprooted, and are relatively successful in areas with large migrant populations. Related to this is the idea that when individuals make a public commitment before a group, the probability of their acceptance of a change will increase. For example, Alcoholics Anonymous and the various quit-smoking and weight-reduction groups rely heavily on such public commitments (Albrecht, Chadwick, & Jacobson, 1987:232–237).

Attitudes

In the acceptance of a change, one would tend to think that information must precede attitudes and that favorable attitude toward the change must precede behavior. However, empirical research has not clearly specified these relationships. Leon Festinger (1964) notes that whereas many studies examine attitude change, little research exists to document the relationship of attitude change and behavior change. In fact, the relationship between the two has been subject to considerable debate. Arthur R. Cohen (1964:137–138) pointedly concludes:

> Most of the investigators whose work we have examined make the broad psychological assumption that since attitudes are evaluative predispositions, they have consequences for the way people act toward others, for the programs they actually undertake, and for the manner in which they carry them

out. Thus attitudes are always seen as precursors of behavior, as determinants of how a person will actually behave in his daily affairs. In spite of the wide acceptance of the assumption, however, very little work on attitude change has dealt explicitly with the behavior that may follow a change in attitude.

Festinger, in support of Cohen's conclusion, suggests that when attitudes are changed on the basis of persuasive communication, this change "is inherently unstable and will disappear or remain isolated unless an environmental or behavioral change can be brought about to support and maintain it (1964:415). His main point is that unless environmental change to support the new opinion occurs, "the same factors that produced the initial opinion and the behavior will continue to operate to nullify the effect of the opinion change" (p. 416). Thus attitude change may not serve as a sufficient condition for a behavioral change, and it seems reasonable that the probability of behavioral change would be greater as environmental circumstances also change.

Personal Influence

Personal influence refers to a change in an individual's attitude or behavior as a result of interpersonal communication. A theory of particular importance regarding the acceptance of personal influence is that of Herbert C. Kelman (1961). He elaborates three processes by which individuals respond to personal influence. These are compliance, identification, and internalization. *Compliance* occurs when the person accepts influence in the hope of achieving a favorable reaction from another person or persons. The individual does not accept the influence because he or she believes in its content but because of an anticipated gratifying social effect. Influence based on *identification* occurs when the opinion or behavior accepted is associated with a "satisfying self-defining relationship" to a person or a group. Identification is basically role imitation, whereby influence results from admiration of another person, or role maintenance, whereby acceptance is necessary to maintain a role relationship with another person. The motivational basis for identification is different from that of compliance in that the person is not primarily concerned with pleasing the other individual, but with meeting the other's expectations—or at least perceived expectations—for his or her own role performance. *Internalization* occurs when an individual accepts influence congruent with his or her particular value system. The content of the advocated opinion or behavior is of major concern and becomes integrated with the individual's existing values. Kelman's theory is very helpful in understanding the role of personal influence in facilitating the acceptance of change.

Individuals facing new life experience—such as migrants, newlyweds, or new college students—tend to be more susceptible to personal influence because, in such states of life, habits for handling many situations are not yet established and the individual is open to new information. Similarly, individuals aspiring to membership in certain groups may be inclined to emulate the behavior of persons already in these groups and be susceptible to their influence. Merton (1957:265) calls this "anticipatory socialization"; that is, an individual tends to adopt the attitudinal and behavioral characteristics of group members before he or she actually belongs to the group. For example, the medical student at the first opportunity dons the white coat of the profession and runs to the nearest medical supply store to buy his or her symbolic stethoscope. Among consumers, anticipatory socialization entails the development of expectations regarding product ownership and adaptive patterns of consumer behavior (Moschis, 1987:26–28). Such aspirational behavior might be seen in the social climber, who drives the "right" kind of car, buys the "right" kind of clothes, joins the "right" clubs, and sends his or her children to the "right" schools. In all of these cases, the individual who lacks actual membership acquires the visible symbols of that membership and is more prone and willing to accept changes than those who are already in the group.

These are the more important psychological factors that stimulate the acceptance of change. However, it should be noted that the list is not exhaustive. In the next section we shall consider some of the principal cultural stimulants to change.

CULTURAL STIMULANTS

The term *culture*, which was discussed in some detail in Chapter 1, refers to the totality of learned behavior traits that are manifested and shared by members of a society. In general, the existing culture base largely determines what new traits will be accepted. Different cultures exhibit different degrees of capability and readiness for accepting change. Both the context of culture and the degree of cultural integration not only play a role in the receptivity for the new but also encourage innovation. This section will focus on these cultural conditions to show under what circumstances they facilitate the acceptance of change.

High and Low Context Cultures

Edward T. Hall (1976) has suggested the concept of *high* and *low context* as a way of understanding different cultural orientations. Cultures differ widely in the extent to which unspoken, unformulated, and unexplicit rules govern how information is handled and how people interact and relate to each other. In high-context cultures, much of human behavior is covert or implicit, whereas in low-context cultures much is overt or explicit. The amount of contexting required for understanding everyday life extends from low in some cultures to high in others. Hall, for example, places West Germany, Switzerland, Scandinavia, and the United States at the low end of the continuum; France in the middle; and China, Japan and the Arab countries at the high end of the scale.

In a low-context culture, messages are explicit; words carry most of the information in communication. Bonds between people are often fragile, formal, and legal. Involvement of people with each other is low, and there are fewer distinctions made between insiders and outsiders. In such cultures, Hall contends, change is easy, rapid, and welcomed by most people.

In high-context cultures, less information is contained in the verbal part of the message, as much more information is in the context of communication, which includes the background, associations, and basic values of the communicator. Who you are—that is, your values and position or place in society—is crucial in the high-context culture, such as Japan or the Arab countries. Bonds between people tend to be strong and there is a deep involvement of people with each other. They get along with much less legal paperwork than is deemed essential in low-context cultures such as the United States. In a high-context culture, a person's word is his or her bond. There is less need to anticipate contingencies and provide for external legal sanctions in a culture that emphasizes obligation and trust as important values. In these cultures, shared feelings of obligation and honor take the place of impersonal legal sanctions. Greater distinctions are made also between insiders and outsiders; and cultural patterns are enduring and slow to change. In such cultures, an awareness of the cultural environment is essential to create receptivity for an innovation coming from the outside (Vago, 1982).

Cultural Integration

The degree of integration of a culture is also considered a factor in the acceptance of change. Highly integrated and harmonious cultures tend to produce a sense of security and satisfaction among its members. On the other hand, a culture with a lower degree of integration in which the various themes and patterns are less perfectly coordinated adapts more easily to circumstances that bring about change. In a highly integrated culture, change, even if it begins in only one aspect of culture, may cause the whole culture to disintegrate. For example, when the British abolished headhunting in Melanesia, the results were dramatic. The people lost their interest in living, and the birthrate dropped rapidly; on one island the number of childless marriages increased from about 19 percent to 46 percent, on another from 12 percent to 72 percent. Why? Headhunting was the center of social and religious institutions; it pervaded the whole life of the people. They *needed* to go on headhunting expeditions because they needed heads to appease the ghosts of their ancestors on many occasions, such as making a new canoe, building a house for a chief, or making a sacrifice at the funeral of a chief. Although their headhunting expeditions lasted only a few weeks, and the actual fighting only a few hours, preparations lasted for years. They had to build new canoes and celebrate numerous rites and feasts, which stimulated horticulture and the breeding of pigs. The number of festivities and celebrations increased as the date for the expedition neared. Other activities commenced when the successful hunters returned. With the integrating pattern of their lives denied them, the Melanesians lost interest in their living (Montagu, 1968:94).

In a society in which there is little harmony and integration of cultural norms and understandings, there is usually much conflict, confusion, waste, insecurity, and social unrest. These conditions provide a fertile ground for the acceptance of change. Moreover, such a culture tends to be more rational and more secular, with a high emphasis on achievement orientation and individualism. There is a higher degree of social mobility, high rates of literacy, and strong occupational differentiations. Personal obligations to family and friends are minimal, and contractural relations tend to prevail. Religion is superficial for most people, the nuclear family dominates, the outlook is cosmopolitan, and the emphasis is on innovativeness. In such a climate, novelty is not only encouraged but eagerly sought after.

In highly integrated cultures, it is helpful at times to enlist the aid of prevailing religious beliefs and existing sacred writings of the people. For example, Foster (1973:164) suggests that:

> In working with the *fellahin* of the Middle East good results often can be attained by the use of citations from the Koran, thus adding the supreme religious validation to the lesser authority of the technician. Expressions such as "Allah hath said in His exalted book" and "All those who love the prophet" and "He who is willing among you to honor his religion and Allah's book" seldom fail to arouse active response. In addition, the Koran contains a wealth of statements pertinent to literacy, health, and improvements in agriculture, which can be cited to clinch the truthfulness of an argument for innovation. . . . Examples of such statements, which can be used in health and developmental programs, are given: . . . for personal hygiene, "Cleanliness is a part of Islam"; to encourage dental hygiene, "If it were not hard upon my people I would have asked them to brush their teeth before each prayer" (That is, five times a day); and to stimulate cooperation, "A Moslem to a Moslem are as the walls of a building supporting one another."

Receptivity is evidently stimulated when the change is seen in the context of a religious framework. When the recipients of a change are aware that the proposed innovation has the support of the existing deities, acceptance of it will be greatly enhanced. For example, in development programs in Arab countries it helps to introduce a given innovation with the phrase, "In the name of Allah" (Patai, 1983:143–155).

Different groups in a society may show differing receptivity to change.

Obviously, in every changing society there are liberals and conservatives. In general, literate and educated people tend to accept changes more readily than the illiterate and uneducated. And a group may be highly receptive to change of one kind, but highly resistant to changes of other kinds. For example, there are many churches of strikingly modern architecture where the sermons have remained basically unchanged since the days of Luther.

The characteristics of a social group obviously influence the acceptance of a new idea or practice as has been demonstrated in a now classic study by Saxon Graham (1956), on the acceptance of five innovations in the United States—television, canasta, supermarkets, hospital insurance, and medical service insurance—across social class levels. His research revealed that no single social class was consistently receptive in adopting all five innovations. Television, for example, diffused more quickly among lower social classes, while the card game canasta diffused more quickly among upper social classes. Graham argues that the critical factor in acceptance is the extent to which the attributes of the innovation are compatible with the attributes of the culture of the receiving social system. The "cultural equipment" required for the adoption of television, according to Graham, included an average education, a minimum income, and a desire for passive spectator entertainment. This cultural pattern coincided with a lower social class level.

Finally, the perception of the relative merits of a novelty is considered as influential in facilitating acceptance. On the lighter side, this may be illustrated by the promotion of movies by film distributors. If the movie is good, it usually is placed in a small number of theaters and not distributed on a mass basis for a considerable period of time. This results in a fairly slow process of diffusion, which often relies heavily on personal influence. If the movie is bad, it is shown in multiple runs in neighborhood theaters, with heavy advertising in order to secure as much acceptance as possible before word spreads among moviegoers as to the film's true merits (Katz & Lazarsfeld, 1955:180). Let us now examine some of the economic conditions and factors that stimulate the acceptance of change.

ECONOMIC STIMULANTS

Convincing evidence exists that the desire for economic gain is an important stimulant to change. If something has a purely utilitarian value (that is, if it is valued because of what it will do), change may be accepted quite readily. Frederic C. Fliegel and Joseph E. Kivlin (1966), in a study of the acceptance of new farm practices by American farmers, find that those that are perceived as most profitable and least risky are most readily accepted. However, if some feature of the traditional culture is valued intrinsically aside from what it will do, change is less readily accepted. To illustrate, for the American farmer, cattle are a source of income, to be bred, culled, and butchered whenever most profitable. In contrast, cattle are considered sacred in India, and there is a prohibition on the slaughter and consumption of beef among Hindus (Nair, 1987). For many of the Nilotic peoples of Africa, cattle represent intrinsic values. The owner recognizes and loves each cow. To slaughter one would be like killing one of the family. The average Westerner, who takes a rational and unsentimental view of economic activities, at times finds it hard to accept the sentiments and values of non-Western peoples. (By the same token, many non-Western peoples resent and find hard to accept a great variety of Western sentiments, values, and practices.) Westerners may be irritated by the Biaga of central India, who refused to give up their primitive digging sticks for the far superior moldboard plow. Why? The Biaga loved the earth as a kindly and generous mother; they would gently help her with the digging stick to bring forth her yield; but could not bring themselves to cut her "with knives."

Perception of Economic Advantages

However, economic forces ultimately tend to override many traditional values and practices. Lucy P. Mair, for example, suggests that the modern African's actions increasingly are determined by a perception of economic advantage and not by "an abstract theory of the sacredness of land which inhibits their recognition of its economic potentialities," and she proposes as a generalization of wide application that: "the conservative force of tradition is never proof against the attraction of economic advantage, provided that the advantage is sufficient and is clearly recognized. In the case of land it is abundantly clear that the emotional and religious attitudes towards it which are inculcated by native tradition have not prevented the development of a commercial attitude" (Mair, quoted by Foster, 1973:154–155).

Cost

Change is always costly. In general, the very poor resist all change because they cannot afford to take *any* risk (Arensberg & Niehoff, 1971:149–150). However, cost is a relative judgment. It is generally a function of an individual's economy of preferences:

> The price of a novelty in goods or labor is measured by a prospective acceptor's reference to his total wealth, by his comparison of its cost with the cost of some alternative, and also by his estimate of the pressures of his need for it. The man who can afford a yacht may still find the price of a new lawn mower excessive; yet the sick man considers that any sacrifice is not too great to secure relief. An American mortgages his salary to buy an automobile, whereas the English workingman considers this price too high for him to pay. (Barnett, 1953:361)

H.G. Barnett (1953:360) further suggests that the restraining effect of novelty costs is evident when they are absent. It is fairly easy to get individuals to try something if doing so entails no financial cost to them. Initially they may think that it is worthless or harmful just because it is free, but they are more likely than not to accept it because it is free. The practice of giving away free things is widespread in the United States, and advertising campaigns often include giving away free samples. Only those individuals who are suspicious that there might be some strings attached to such a sample will reject it and fail to give it a trial. Obviously, trying something does not commit them, so what can they lose? Sponsors of TV and radio giveaway shows, box-top contests, and the like capitalize on this appeal and win often enough to make the gamble a sound business practice. Such activities have often resulted in the adoption of a given product.

At the organizational level, cost is one of the most obvious dimensions influencing the acceptance of change. In formal organizations the financial cost can be divided into (1) initial cost and (2) continuing cost. When the outcome of cost-benefit analysis is favorable for the organization in question, the likelihood of accepting a given innovation is enhanced (Hall, 1987:206–208). Social cost is another form of expense and is an important factor in explaining the rate of adoption, particularly in developing countries. Gerald Zaltman and his associates (1973:34–35) cite an international management consulting firm in which it was observed that even seemingly minor management changes (from the consulting viewpoints) in power and status within the organization, resulting from the adoption of more efficient management science techniques, produced sufficient internal conflict to cause a substantial number of medium-size business firms in developing areas to discontinue the newly adopted practices.

Social cost may come in the form of ridicule, isolation, ostracism, or even exclusion or expulsion from some important reference groups. "Social position within a group influences the degree to which such a cost may occur and how serious the individual may perceive this cost. The marginal member of a group may have little to lose by innovating; therefore, even in the presence of considerable disapproval, he may proceed to adopt an innovation. There is always the possibility that the decision might prove to be a wise one, and he may gain stature as a consequence. . . . A high-status member of a group may also adopt, again, even in the presence of potential or actual ridicule. The high-status person can do so because he generally has an inventory of goodwill or social credit upon which he can draw, and he will suffer little if the innovation does not succeed" (Zaltman, Duncan, & Holbek, 1973:35).

In many instances the cost factor is also related to the efficiency of a given product or article. At the time of their initial introduction, most machines and articles are crude. For example, the first airplane barely got off the ground, and the first automobile barely exceeded the speed of a horse-drawn carriage. The first radio was hardly audible and the first television set barely visible. Indeed, imperfections are part of discoveries and are to be expected to exist. If any invention, however, meets a need and persists, it tends to be steadily improved. Today's airplane is a far cry from the Wright Brothers' flying machine of 1903. Similarly, today's automobile, usually a smoothly functioning machine, bears little resemblance to the contraptions of the turn of the century. Mass production usually brings about an increased efficiency and a lowering of the cost. Once the mechanical imperfections are removed, accompanied by a decline in cost of the article, the likelihood of its acceptance will be increased.

Vested Interests

Vested interests also relate often to economic matters and appear as promoters of change whenever they believe the proposed change will be profitable to them. Over time in a society, certain interests tend to be more successful than others. They manage to have their views accepted by the society at large, and they accumulate money, organization, and power. In so doing, they become *vested interests*: interest groups that derive special advantage from maintenance of the status quo, that seek to protect their special advantages, and that oppose all further changes except those favorable to them. The railroads, for example, have opposed the growth of trucking industry and at the same time promoted innovations in engines and passenger cars as well as improvements in organization and delivery of services. In the social-change literature, more emphasis is placed on the opposition than the promotion of change by vested interests, perhaps because, in part, opposition to change is more dramatic and widespread than support of change. The changes that vested interests make are mainly improvements in existing practices, whereas the opposition they show is directed against major, and for them threatening, innovations. More will be said about the role of vested interests in social change in the discussion of social barriers to change in the next section.

In sum, social scientists have placed much more emphasis on the reasons for opposing rather than accepting change (Bennis, 1987:37–39; Germani, 1981:167–172; Hall, 1987:197–211; Zaltman & Duncan, 1977:61–89). Still, by pulling together the social, psychological, cultural, and economic stimulants to change, it is possible to come up with some generalizations concerning the conditions of acceptance. There is sufficient evidence in the social-science literature to indicate that change will be more readily accepted if it is adopted by consensual group decision; when people have an opportunity to empathize with opponents; when there is an opportunity to recognize and discuss valid objections and to take appropriate measures to relieve unnecessary fears or hardships. The likelihood of acceptance is further increased when people feel that the change is not going to threaten their autonomy or security; when it does not clash with pre-vailing values and ideas that have long been cherished; and when it is seen as reducing rather than increasing present burdens. When these conditions are met, readiness to accept change gradually becomes a characteristic of many individuals, groups, or institutions in a society. The good old days are no longer nostalgically cherished; instead, there is an anticipation of a better life in the days to come. The spontaneity of youth is cherished, and innovations are protected until they have had a chance to establish their worth. In such a situation the ideal is more and more seen as possible.

In the contemporary world, however, situations of resistance to change are much more numerous than situations of acceptance. Even within rapidly changing societies, there is considerable resistance to new ideas, new scientific and technological developments, and new patterns of social life. Often change is resisted because it conflicts with traditional values and beliefs, or a particular change may simply cost too much money. Sometimes people resist change because it interferes with their habits or makes them feel frightened or threatened. In the following pages the various conditions of resistance to change will be examined.

RESISTANCE TO CHANGE

One can always find a justification in some more or less practical terms for active resistance to change. The peasant in a developing country will find reasons for refusing to try out a new tool, a new technique, a fertilizer, or a different mode of cultivation. The new, the different, the peasant may insist, will only poison the soil, produce inferior grain, upset God, or cause his wife to bear only girls. A modern businessperson may single out ventures with new things or practices that have failed to produce a profit. Bureaucrats will have a body of rules and precedents to justify their conservatism; a scholar, the whole of history to protect him or her from new ideas. "And for everyone, primitive, peasant, and modern layman and expert alike, there is always as the final and ultimate defense against anything new some version or other of the thesis that what was good enough for father is good enough for son" (LaPiere, 1965:175–176).

Anything new or novel can be the object of resistance. It can be a social or cultural innovation, a scientific discovery, or mechanical or social invention. Regardless of the type of novelty, its unqualified acceptance can in no way be assured regardless of how socially or otherwise beneficial it may be seen. Many things that are new are opposed, and whenever change is attempted, resistance is likely to appear. Although the term *resistance* conjures up a pejorative connotation in general, this is not always the case. In fact, resistance can be a healthy phenomenon. It is a positive force when, from some objective perspective, the proposed change is harmful to society.

In situations where an intended change is subjectively harmful to a person or a group, resistance is justifiable (Zaltman & Duncan, 1977:62). With this in mind, let us now turn to the social, psychological, cultural, and economic barriers to change.

SOCIAL BARRIERS

Many social factors act as barriers to change. The ones that will be examined in the following pages include vested interests, status interests, social class, ideological resistance, group solidarity, authority, fear of the unfamiliar, forms of rationalization, and organized opposition.

Vested Interests

Change may be resisted by individuals or groups that fear a loss of power, wealth, or prestige should an innovation gain acceptance. "A particularly potent obstacle to change is the opposition to innovation by strong, organized groups that stand to lose by the change. . . . Such groups [are] called *vested interests.* . . . A realistic inventory of the sources of resistance to social change needs to give prominence to vested interests" (Nimkoff, 1957:68). There are many different types of vested interests for whom the status quo is profitable and preferable. Students attending state universities have a vested interest in tax-supported higher education. Divorce lawyers constitute a vested interest and for a long time have fought efforts to reform the divorce laws. Physicians opposing various forms of "socialized medicine" constitute a vested interest. In fact, nearly everyone has some vested interests—from the rich with their tax-exempt bonds to the poor with their welfare checks.

Many of the social and economic changes that have been promoted in developing countries threaten the security of some groups or individuals. Witch doctors and midwives resent medical programs because they fear that the competition will be injurious to them. Landlords oppose education of their tenants for fear that it will promote unrest and may result in land redistribution. Moneylenders in villages oppose low-interest government-managed credit programs, and merchants object to consumer cooperatives. In such instances, "untrue rumors are among the most common techniques used by individuals who feel threatened by proposed changes" (Foster, 1973:117). For example, when a census of the inhabitants was taken in Indian villages, there were rumors that anyone who gave his age as over 65 would be killed. In another instance, when an expert appeared in the village, there were rumors that the villagers would be driven out and all the land would be used for setting up an American colony.

Closer to home, residents in a community often develop vested interests in their neighborhood. When zoning changes, they often organize to resist it. Objections are made against new interstate highways or the construction of correctional facilities in one's neighborhood. Parents may resist busing their children, or residents may organize in opposition to landing the supersonic Concorde.

Contrary to popular impressions, the American university is a strong bastion of resistance to change. Curriculum changes may be viewed as trivial matters by many individuals, but the departments that are to be affected adversely by the proposed changes are quite likely to resist as long as they can. For over a hundred years the American Ph.D. program, which was transplanted from Germany, remained unaltered. Only recently have there been some minor modifications in the requirements.

Throughout history new ideas have often met with entrenched resistance by vested interests. The astronomical theories of Copernicus and Galileo were long suppressed because they challenged beliefs about the central position of human beings in the universe. *On the Revolutions of the Celestial Orbs* was published by Nicholas Copernicus in 1543. However, a license to print a book exposing the heleocentric hypothesis was refused until 1822 by the Roman Catholic Church and only then was a decree quietly issued by the Holy Office:

> There is no reason why the present and future Masters of the Sacred Palace should refuse license for printing and publishing works treating of the mobility of the earth and the immobility of the sun, according to the common opinion of the modern astronomers. (Smith, quoted by Bierstedt, 1974:213)

At times there are vested interests in skills and knowledge. Artisans, for example, are usually reluctant to adopt a new tool or material because doing so would render their existing skills obsolete and demand that they learn to utilize new ones. At the organizational level, change can threaten occupational groups (Hall, 1987:200). Resistance is likely to come about when some specialties foresee that they will not be needed if certain changes are implemented. There was a fair amount of resistance to the adoption of the early typewriter because it devalued the skill of handwriting, which had been a prized ability of the educated person. LaPiere (1965:192) suggests that "no man . . . will passively accept a change that destroys the value of hard-won skills and knowledge and that demands that he acquire a complex of new and different skills and knowledge if he is to hold his own." Thus, in many cases, those who must adapt to a new innovation at times find it to be a personal disadvantage to do so.

Status Interests

The acceptance of almost any innovation will adversely affect the status of some individuals in society; and, to the degree that those whose status is threatened consciously recognize the danger, they will resist adopting it. In most societies, through time, individuals made some improvements in their social status, became a known artisan, a tribal elder, a wise old parent, and this rise in social status was a recognition of the person's increased value to society. In rapidly changing societies, past experience often has little bearing on the present, and those who have earned a high status often see that status jeopardized by an innovation, and as a result, they resist its adoption. Nowadays occupational status and age are no longer correlated. The modern business prefers highly educated employees. Not surprisingly, fear of loss of status associated with seniority and not with education may prompt resistance. People who benefited from the existing order are unlikely to welcome anything that will lower their self-esteem (Bennis, 1987:37).

Resistance stemming from the fear of status depreciation can take many forms. For example, Raphael Patai (1983:115–117) calls attention to one of the basic features of the Beduin ethos, which is a contempt for any kind of physical labor with the exception of tending of the livestock and raiding, considered the only proper occupations for a free person. He comments that among the many despised varieties of work, agricultural labor is the one most emphatically rejected. For Beduins, to engage in cultivation would not only result in an irreparable loss of status, but it would also dishonor them. As a result of this disdain for agriculture, attempts in several Arab countries to have the Beduins settle in one place have met with little success. The same fear of loss of status compels young people in many Arab countries to be clerks for inadequate wages rather than helpers at construction sites with considerably more pay.

Social Class

In general, rigid class and caste patterns tend to hinder the acceptance of change. However, different social classes in a society tend to react to and alter the course of change in different ways. In highly stratified societies, individuals are expected to obey and take orders from those in superior positions of authority or power. Those in position of superiority, in turn, dictate to those below them. "This limits the free interplay of ideas and opinions that is so important in so many change situations" (Foster, 1973:127). The prerogatives of the upper strata are jealously guarded, and attempts to infringe upon them by members of lower socio-economic groups are often resented and repulsed. For example, under the traditional Indian and Pakistani rigid caste system, members of different castes could not draw water from the same well, go to the same schools, eat together, or otherwise mingle. The types of work one could do were rigorously prescribed, and any violation of rules was condemned. A somewhat similar situation existed in the United States concerning the position of blacks up to recent years.

Members of the upper classes, in general, are more likely to accept innovations, whereas those in the lower classes or those who are downwardly mobile tend to resist them. Occupation is one of the bases of stratification, and rarely, if ever, have any considerable proportion of the members of an occupational group willingly renounced their established skills and knowledge in favor of some innovation that required the development of new skills and understandings (LaPiere, 1965:191). In most cases there is a tendency to cherish the old ways of doing things and to adhere to the status quo.

Ideological Resistance

Resistance to change on the grounds of ideological traditionalism is quite prevalent (Germani, 1981:169–172; Zaltman & Duncan, 1977:66). For example, many non-Western societies are reluctant to accept innovations that they see as Westernizing influences. This nationalistic fear is very common, and even many Europeans and Canadians worry about the "Americanization" of their societies. For a while, the expression "the co-cacolanization of Europe" was in vogue. These attitudes are not against change as such, but against the perceived political implications of certain changes. To illustrate: In Islamic countries, anti-Western sentiments derive, in part, from a fear that the adoption of Western technology will destroy the ancient faith (Patai, 1983:194–196). Or a nationalistic ideology rationalizes that rapid population growth contributes to the strength of a nation and any attempt at family planning or fertility moderation is a neocolonialist plot.

There are many other types of ideological resistance to change. The Catholic Church opposes birth control and abortion on ideological grounds, and the medical profession uses ideological arguments to resist anything suggesting socialized medicine and fought against the enactment of the Medicare Law of 1965 (Allen, 1971:278–279). Thus, it may be concluded that the basic intellectual and religious assumptions and interpretations regarding existing power relations, morality, welfare, and security tend to be rather consistent and adversely disposed to change.

Group Solidarity

In peasant and folk communities there is a strong sense of solidarity, which is reflected in bonds of mutual obligation within the framework of family and friendship, a preference for small-group identification, and a willingness to criticize anyone who deviates from customary norms (Foster, 1973:106).

When economic well-being is roughly at the same level and individuals have generally the same access to resources, reciprocal obligations are effective in maintaining a society. Conditions of equality and cooperation are incompatible with trends toward individualization, migration, and changes in the division of labor. In villages, those who make economic progress no longer find their relationships in balance. Progressive individuals must be prepared to disregard many of the traditional obligations and ties that their societies expect of them. The prevalence of mutual obligations, the accent on self-esteem and prestige, factors that in part make up solidarity and hold societies together, can effectively curb the acceptance of innovations (Zaltman & Duncan, 1977:72).

Identification with small groups provides a sense of psychological security and satisfaction for most people. Foster (1973:111) points out that frequently innovations that upset such traditional groups meet with strong resistance, and at times people will forgo comfort, convenience, and economic gain in return for more enjoyment in life. For example, in many Latin American villages women wash clothes under conditions that are anything but comfortable. The pleasures of working in the company of others and the discussions and joking compensate for the hardship. They resist efforts to alter this pattern of working regardless of the hardships involved. In a far corner of Africa the village well serves the same function, and women resented the fact of builders putting running water into all houses and rebelled because they were taken away from their only excuse for social contact.

Authority

Whenever an established pattern of authority is threatened by a change, resistance is likely to occur. This is perhaps most pronounced at the level of organizations (Zaltman & Duncan, 1977:75). For example, when two or more departments at a university merge, one of the most difficult problems to overcome is the feeling on the part of individual departments that they are going to lose control over decision making and be subjected to a reduction in influence. Chairpersons, whose authority is likely to diminish, will be the most vocal (and frustrated) opponents of such reorganization.

At the level of community, authority figures play a decisive role in the acceptance or rejection of change (Waste, 1986). However, in many societies leadership and authority patterns as an institution are not fully developed and insufficient to guide group decisions that are needed in order to make major changes (Foster, 1973:122). Often individuals who speak out for a new project or idea or volunteer their services will be criticized rather than praised for their efforts, and their neighbors will suspect that they see opportunity for personal gain at their own expense. Roger M. Keesing (1968) describes the Kwaio of the Solomon Islands who have chiefs only on Tuesdays. Their social organization included no chiefs, but it became necessary to invent some to handle dealings with white officials after World War II. To avoid conflict between these new chiefs and the traditional holders of authority and influence, they simply agreed that the chiefs would "reign" only on Tuesdays when the white officials called.

At times, authority within the family is a deterrent to acceptance of change. For example, among the Navaho the decision to enter the hospital is reached only after a family conference. A wife and husband alone are not free to exercise their discretion in this context. Similarly, among some traditional Spanish-speaking Mexicans in San Jose, California, hospitalization is a grave and serious step and is a family, not an individual, problem (Foster, 1973:119). In such situations, resistance to medical practices, among other types of change, can be anticipated.

Fear of the Unfamiliar

A good deal of the initial resistance to any innovation stems from apprehension, from fear of the unknown. Even today many individuals in Western countries are still afraid of air travel. Although carefully gathered government studies indicate that flying is many times safer than traveling by automobile, these individuals are petrified by the idea of getting into an airplane and taking off. Fear is also a factor in resistance to change that threatens individuals with a loss of status, income, or power. Individual opposition to both the civil rights movement and the women's movement has often reflected the fear of the dominant group members—whites on the one hand, males on the other—that gains for a minority would mean losses for them. In such situations, stereotyped thinking is likely to act as a further barrier to the acceptance of change. Fear has often prevented the use of particular plants as food; for example, in parts of the United States the tomato was considered as poisonous as recently as a century ago. Even such a minor change from the familiar as the use of aluminum in place of iron in cooking pots and pans has aroused considerable apprehension; housewifes were afraid that the new metal would contaminate the food cooked in it and even experts doubted the use of aluminum as kitchenware (LaPiere, 1965:178–179).

Often, even the name of a given product can elicit apprehension among people. Some years ago the Colgate Palmolive Company introduced a new toothpaste called Cue into French-speaking districts in Canada. The product was never accepted, for the word has an obscene connotation in French (it means ass) (Rogers & Shoemaker, 1971:150–151).

Rationalization as a Source of Resistance

At times resistance to change occurs for quite plausible reasons when the proposed change is seen as being possibly deleterious for a social system, or when the outcomes are impractical or highly debatable (Warren, 1977:51). New forms of social organization may also be resisted for a while on the grounds that they do not work, or do not work well enough to justify their cost in time, effort, or money. At times, however, some of the rationales for opposing change are anything but logical and reasonable. When the railroad could not exceed 30 miles per hour, people in opposition to it argued that the speed was more than the human body could endure. Today, possibly, their great grandchildren claim that people cannot endure supersonic speeds. Doctors disapproved of the use of early automobiles because it would lead to atrophy of the human legs (LaPiere, 1965:187). This kind of rationalization is perhaps best epitomized in the popular saying that if "God wanted man to fly, He would have given him wings."

Organized Opposition

At times, widespread individual resistance to change may become mobilized into organized opposition that can assume formal organizational structure (for example, the National Rifle Association (NRA) opposing gun control), or it may be channeled through a social movement (such as the recent pro-life activities).

In traditional societies the existing social organizations are often strong enough to delay, if not prevent, the acceptance of change. Through much of the Middle Ages, family, church, guild, and state cooperated in maintaining the existing order. In modern societies, by contrast, with a multiplicity of informal and formal organizations often in conflict with each other, new organizations have developed to combat particular threats to the status quo. For example, the Ku Klux Klan developed in opposition to the early efforts of reformers to bring the blacks of the South something of that equality with whites that was their constitutional right (LaPiere, 1965:197), and a nativist group, the League of Deliverance, attempted to mobilize West Coast workers to prevent the employment of Chinese labor (Gamson, 1975:148). These and similar organizations have resisted change that was under way, and although most of them have fought a losing battle, their delaying effects have often been considerable.

At times, however, when organized opposition to change is not forthcoming, the consequences can be disastrous. For example, more than 6 million Jews were slaughtered in concentration camps during World War II, in part because they did not organize resistance to the changes beginning in the early 1930s in Nazi Germany. In the next section, the psychological factors in resistance to change will be considered.

PSYCHOLOGICAL BARRIERS

It is suggested in the social-change literature that "All of the forces which contribute to stability in personality or in social systems can be perceived as resisting change" (Watson, 1969:488). Any detailed account of these forces is obviously beyond the scope of this book. For the present purposes the emphasis will be on selected psychological barriers to resistance. They include habit, motivation, ignorance, selective perception, and communication.

Habit

From the psychological perspective, an initial impediment to change is the matter of *habit*. Once a habit is established, its operation often becomes satisfying to the individual. Hugo Munsterberg, while teaching at Harvard University, used the following pedagogical device to drive home to his students the tenacity of habit formation. "He would write the word *habit* on the blackboard, then erase the 'h.' 'Observe,' he would say, 'you still have a bit of it' and you still have a 'bit' of it when you remove the 'a.' Even when you wipe out the 'b' you still have 'it' " (Nimkoff, 1957:62). Habits, once formed, resist change. Individuals become accustomed to behaving in a certain manner and they feel comfortable with it. An individual who is accustomed after dinner to his chair, brandy, and a newspaper, may resist any change in the details of his routine.

In a well-known case of product failure, an American firm attempted to market a new product called Analoze, a combination pain killer and stomach sweetener in the form of a lozenge. Because Americans annually ingest billions of headache pills and aids to acid indigestion, it was felt that a lozenge combining the benefits of both would be a natural winner. But Americans have a deeply established habit of swallowing headache pills with water rather than dissolving them in their mouth or chewing them, and this habit apparently prevented Analoze from becoming a success. After extensive and very expensive efforts to market this pill the company withdrew it from the market; it was a total failure (Rogers & Shoemaker, 1971:136–137).

The customs of a society may be seen as collective habits and especially where sentiment pervades custom, custom is slow to change when challenged by new practices and ideas. Habits of individuals that impede social change are derived from social experience and can often be modified by using a group approach to the problem. For example, new foods are introduced into a diet with great reluctance, but when the individuals have a chance to discuss the relative merits of the proposed substance in the interest of better nutrition, the likelihood of its acceptance is increased (Lewin, 1965).

Motivation

The *motivational* forces stimulating the acceptance of change may be handicapped by the active or potential resistance of different sectors of society. How these different sectors influence motivation has been described by Clark Kerr and his associates (1964) in their study of industrialization processes in developing countries. They identify five such sectors: (1) the family system, (2) class and race, (3) religion and ethical evaluations, (4) legal concepts, and (5) the concept of the nation-state. The manner in which these sectors of society control change and affect motivation may be seen in the following evaluations.

1. The extended family system, they argue, weakens industrial incentives to work, save, and invest, and reserves key managerial positions for family members, regardless of relative competence of insiders and outsiders.
2. A class structure based on traditional social status does not encourage motivation keyed to economic performance.
3. Traditional religious and ethical values, which emphasize "peace" and "duty" unrelated to economic gain or advancement and which oppose change, particularly in science and technology, do not enhance the cause of innovation.
4. Traditional customs and social norms that deny individual and property rights and fail to guarantee contracts do not facilitate the processes of acceptance of novelty.
5. Finally, divisive groups in developing society that hinder or prevent the emergence of a strong nation-state system do not serve the cause of accelerated acceptance of change.

Collectively, these five sectors reinforce the traditional motivational forces in society geared to the preservation of the status quo.

Ignorance

Ignorance is another psychological factor associated with resistance to change. At times ignorance goes hand in hand with fear of the new. This has often been the case with new foods. Not too long ago many individuals assumed that citrus fruit brought an acid condition to the digestive tract. Once it has been proved otherwise, resistance based on the acid matter has faded. Many examples abound of products and procedures that failed to be accepted by people for whom they would seemingly have been beneficial as a result of their misconceptions and ignorance about them. For example, in a rural village in Peru an effort was made to reduce the incidence of typhoid and other water-borne diseases by introducing the hygienic measure of boiling contaminated water. But in spite of efforts to convince the residents of the advantages of the innovation and the great benefits to their health, most refused to take it up. Their beliefs about the origins of disease and their association of boiled water with illness prevented them from accepting this new kind of behavior (Wellin, 1955).

Selective Perception

Once an attitude has been formed, an individual responds to other suggestions within the framework of his or her established outlook. Situations may be perceived as reinforcing the original attitude when they are actually dissonant. In a classic experiment, a common stereotype associating blacks with carrying razors led observers of a cartoon to think they had seen the razor in the hands of a black rather than of a white person (Allport, quoted by Watson, 1969:491). It is a well-known fact in social sciences that individuals prefer news sources, whether in print or broadcast, with which they are already in agreement. "By reading or listening to what accords with their present views; by misunderstanding communications which, if correctly received, would not be consonant with preestablished attitudes; and by conveniently forgetting any learning which would lead to uncongenial conclusions, subjects successfully resist the possible impact of new evidence upon their earlier views. There are relatively few instances in which old prejudices have been changed by better information or persuasive arguments" (Watson, 1969:491).

Perception is to a great extent determined by culture, and individuals in different cultures frequently perceive the same phenomenon in different ways. For example, in rural Mexico, the Indians are reluctant to call the priest for the last rites for a sick relative even though they are Catholics. They have noticed that on entirely too many occasions the patient dies shortly after the priest visits. In another instance, an anthropologist was unable to measure his subjects for his anthropometric records: The only time an Indian was measured was for a coffin, and if they permitted the anthropologist to measure them, they know they would die (Foster, 1973:130).

George Foster (1973:131–141) analyzes a number of situations in which selective perception hinders the acceptance of change. In one instance he describes a case of perceptual misinterpretation. A linguist missionary couple was living in a village in southern Mexico in a native house with stick walls and thatched roof. For decoration, they placed on their wall a picture of the black and white scottie dogs that advertised the whiskey of the same name. The Indians showed enormous interest in the picture; as a matter of fact, their fascination bordered on veneration. It dawned on the couple that the only pictures the Indians had ever seen were of Christ, the Virgin, and the saints. Not wanting to create the belief that Americans worship dogs, they quickly removed the scotties from the wall.

At times the perception of health issues can be problematic. In much of the developing world, hospitals are perceived as places where people go to die, not to get well. As a result, there is much resistance to hospitalization because the patient perceives it as meaning his or her family has lost all hope for the person. Foster (1973:132) cites a famous saying about the largest hospital in Egypt: "He who enters it will be lost (dead) and he who comes out of it is born (as a new man)."

Differential perception has a bearing also on the acceptance of agricultural programs. At times people perceive vegetables as a delicacy rather than as a staple or necessary item. In other instances new food crops are used for animal consumption.

Another aspect of differential perception has to do with gifts. Many aid programs offer commodities and services without cost. However, acceptance of such programs often has been negligible. "The reason is that in many situations people interpret a gift as something without value; if something has value, they reason, no one would be so foolish as to give it away. Hence, the mere act of offering something for nothing is interpreted by potential recipients as meaning that the offering is not worth the trouble to collect or use it" (Foster, 1973:136). For example, when free powdered milk was first distributed in Chilean health centers, very few women would use it. They suspected that it was of poor quality, or downright harmful. A free gift in their experience was suspect. However, when a token charge was made for the milk, they perceived that in the eyes of the clinic personnel the milk had some value and shortly they started to use it in great quantities. Making a nominal charge for goods or services has been found effective to facilitate acceptance.

At times there are misperceptions about the objectives of a given proposal or project for change. For example, contraceptive devices had been rejected by many Indian villagers because they feared that family planning change agents were trying to stop birth completely. Occasionally, similar objects intended for different purposes result in the same use as a consequence of misperception. For instance, one of the earlier forms of birth control that was tried in a village in India was the "foaming tablet" that produced contraceptive effects when placed in a woman's vagina. Unfortunately, these tablets were similar in appearance to aspirin and other pills that the village women had received from public health workers. The similarity of the foaming tablets with a previous innovation led to their eventual rejection, for women simply swallowed the tablets (Rogers & Shoemaker, 1971:150). While on the topic of contraceptives, it is worth noting that in many parts of the world, the condom is associated with prostitution. Its purchase is perceived by others, such as the seller, that the buyer is planning to have an encounter with a prostitute. Strong norms against prostitution, especially in Latin America, carry a negative connotation regarding anything associated with prostitution. As a result, it is difficult to promote condoms among certain groups for the purpose of family planning (Zaltman & Duncan, 1977:74).

Communication

"One of the obvious principles of human communication is that the transfer of ideas occurs most frequently between a source and a receiver who are alike, similar, homophilous. *Homophily* is the degree to which pairs of individuals who interact are similar in certain attributes, such as beliefs, values, education, social status, and the like" (Rogers & Shoemaker, 1971:14). In homophilious situations, communication of ideas is likely to have greater effects in terms of knowledge gained, attitude formation, and change, and overt behavior change. "One of the most distinctive problems in the communication of innovations is that the source is usually quite heterophilious to the receiver." (*Heterophily* is the mirror opposite of homophily and is defined as the degree to which pairs of individuals who interact are different in certain attributes) (Rogers & Shoemaker, 1971:15). Such a situation results in ineffective communication, which in turn hinders the acceptance of change. In other words, they simply do not speak the same language. This also impairs the effectiveness of the mass media as an instrument of social change (Comstock, 1983).

In a large, complex, and heterogeneous society, the language problem is multiplied by the presence of a number of subgroups within societies who in expressing themselves use specialized vocabularies that are not fully comprehensible to nonmembers. At times, for example, American teenage slang is to some degree unintelligible to most parents. Similarly, members of the various professions and occupations, such as physicians, lawyers, and carpenters, all use specialized words and expressions.

"Medical personnel appear to be among the worst offenders with respect to poor communication" (Foster, 1973:143). For example, in a Spanish-speaking community in the United States a physician gave a young mother with limited command of English the following instruction: "Apply a tight pectoral binding and restrict your fluid intake." At a Mother's Club meeting in Temuco in Chile, a physician advised expectant mothers to walk "three kilometers a day." However, this instruction was meaningless, for the women simply were not trained to think in terms of distance as an educated person would (Foster, 1973:143). These two illustrations simply show how communication can be a factor in resistance to change. The problem is further compounded in cross-cultural communication. For instance, many business people abroad assume that, because their counterparts speak good English, they are probably familiar with American business jargon such as "ballpark figures," "front-end money," and "the bottom line." But when someone from France, for example, tries to translate "bottom line," it can have a completely different meaning. (*Une ligne du derriere?*)

At times there are also problems with symbolic communication. The meaning of an action or a gesture often can be quite different from what it was intended to elicit. For example, in New Zealand, a successful health-education poster designed to encourage students to brush their teeth depicted a whale jumping out of the water in pursuit of a tube of toothpaste. The same poster was reproduced for use in Fiji. The response was immediate and overwhelming! Fiji fishermen sent a rush call to New Zealand for large quantities of this wonderful new fishbait (Foster 1973:144)! In another instance, a well-meaning gesture by an American labor-relations expert created a great degree of embarrassment. In Micronesia a few years back, our expert sought to recruit Palauan workers for a mining operation.

He first demanded to see the "chief"—a request that posed a problem because they have no chief in their social structure. Finally, they produced a person with whom the American expert sought to establish rapport by throwing an arm around his shoulders and laughingly tousling his hair. In Palauan culture this little gesture was an indignity comparable in our culture to opening a man's fly in public (Useem, 1952). Needless to say, this expert was not very successful. In the next section, cultural barriers to change will be examined.

CULTURAL BARRIERS

Resistance to change is usually most pronounced when traditional values and beliefs are involved. In India, for example, much of the population is ill fed or even starving, yet over 300 million cows, sacred to the Hindus, are not only exempt from being slaughtered for food, but are also allowed to roam through villages and farmlands, often causing extensive damage to crops. However, it is unlikely that the raising of cattle for food will be acceptable in India in the near future as the eating of beef runs counter to long-held religious beliefs. Many factors influence values and beliefs in a culture. They include fatalism, ethnocentrism, norms of modesty, the degree of cultural integration, notions of incompatibility, prevailing motor patterns, and superstitions.

Fatalism

Fatalism constitutes an important impediment to change. "In many parts of the world we find cultures adhering to the belief that man has no causal effect upon his future or the future of the land; God, not man, can improve man's lot. . . . It is difficult to persuade such people to use fertilizers, or to save the best seed for planting, since man is responsible only for the performance, and the divine for the success of the act" (Mead, 1953:201). Fatalism entails a feeling of a lack of mastery over nature. One has no control over one's life, and everything that happens to a person is caused by gods, evil spirits, or fate. Expressions such as "it was my fate" or it is the "will of Allah" are common reactions to problems such as epidemics and crop failures (Harris & Moran, 1987:418–419; Patai, 1983:147).

Religious beliefs and sacred writings often contribute to fatalistic attitudes. Foster (1973:86) cites some illustrations: In rural Brazil a health officer found it difficult to persuade mothers to seek help for their sick children during the month of May. In Catholic theology, May is the "Month of the Virgin Mary," and in that part of Brazil it is believed that when a child dies in May, it is particularly fortunate because the Virgin is "calling" her child to come to be with her. To obtain medical aid during this time would be contrary to the will of the Virgin. In Egypt, some authorities consider high infant mortality rates related to the perception of that as Allah's will, and no one can extend life because the Koran says: "Wherever you are, death will seek you, even if you are in strongly built castles."

Ethnocentrism

Americans are not the only ones who consider themselves superior, possessing the only "right" way of thinking about the world and of coping with their environment. Similarly, most primitive peoples before extensive contact with the Western world were extremely *ethnocentric,* thinking that they were *the* people, and their ways were the only correct ones dealing with the environment. Foster (1973:86–87) declares: "The real essence of culture, all of us believe, lies in what we think and do, our attitudes, our social forms, and our religious beliefs." Feelings of superiority about one's culture make people unreceptive to the ideas and methods used in other cultures. A version of ethnocentrism is also found in some organizations where one encounters resistance often referred to as NIH, or "Not Invented Here" (Bennis, 1987:37). For example, some faculty members may balk at a new teaching method because it originated outside of their department or school.

Related to ethnocentrism are pride and dignity, which also constitute barriers to change. Quite frequently, adults feel that "they will lose face" if they go back to school. Often older women resist modern maternal and child health care programs on the grounds that if young pregnant women attend clinics, for example, such would reflect on the ability and judgment of the older ones.

Norms of Modesty

Ideas about *modesty,* like ideas about most everything else, are culturally conditioned. Proper behavior in one setting may be highly shocking in another (Bock, 1970). In many parts of the world nudity or seminudity is taken for granted, and modest dress is not always associated with covering the sex organs. For example, in the Amazon Basin, Indian women were observed at close range in a state of nature. When seen by travelers, they were highly embarrassed, but this embarrassment usually disappeared when the women have retired for a moment to reappear wearing a string of beads or some other kind of ornament (Foster, 1973:90).

In many cultures medical examination and treatment may be resisted by native women when it is done by a male physician, and frequently the husband may object to the treatment. Ideally this resistance could be overcome by having it done by female physicians. However, this is not always the case. Women on the island of Yap in Micronesia are resistant to genital examination by a male physician, but they are even more resistant to examination by a female. "Yap women regard all other women, regardless of age, as potential rivals for men's attention; at the same time, they believe their own genitals are their strongest power over men. Exposing their source of power to potential rivals, they believe, weakens their competitive position and threatens them with loss of masculine attention" (Schneider, cited by Foster, 1973:91).

Cultural Integration

Anthropologist R. A. Manners (1952) uses an interesting metaphor by comparing highly integrated cultures with a delicate watchlike mechanism. He suggests that the rapid introduction of new elements into such a culture acts very much like the dropping of a grain of sand into the delicate works of a watch. The watch runs poorly or the culture becomes disorganized and anomic. Thus, he points out, highly integrated cultures tend to be resistant to change, whereas less delicately balanced cultures tend to assimilate change better if the change is not too radical or sudden.

Incompatibility

Resistance is often due to the presence in the recipient cultures of material and systems that are, or considered to be, irreconcilable with the invading traits or systems and as a result tend to block them, checking their further diffusion (Kroeber, 1973:141). When such *incompatibility* exists in a culture, change comes about with difficulty. For example, the contrast between a monotheistic and a polytheistic religion underlines this point. Monotheistic peoples can accept a new deity only by rejecting the previous incumbent, which would be asking a great deal from them (Foster, 1973:93).

Motor Patterns

Motor patterns and customary body positions are conditioned by culture and learned in childhood. "Culture determines the positions in which we sleep, stand, sit, and relax. Culture determines what gestures we use, how we hold and use tools, and how we manipulate our bodies in an unlimited number of situations." (Foster, 1973:101). In many cases unfamiliar muscular activity involved in a new activity may underlie its rejection. To change established motor patterns is difficult and tiring. For example, as part of a community development program in the Cook Islands, a raised cooking stove was devised so that food would be protected from animals and dirt, and women would not have to stoop continually in preparing the meals. However, the raised stove was generally rejected because it was very uncomfortable to have to stand on one's feet while cooking. In another instance an attempt was made to introduce latrines in rural El Salvador (the outhouse version, which was considered an improvement over disposing of bodily wastes in the traditional fashion). A coffee planter built the standard American model, that is, a square wooden structure with a raised seat, perforated by one or more holes, for each house. However, he was quite upset when his employees refused to use them. "Finally, an old man offered a suggestion. 'Patron, don't you realize that here we are squatters?' The planter ripped out the seats, replaced them with a perforated slab floor, and was gratified to find that public acceptance was much greater. He had learned what has had to be learned independently time after time, in many parts of the world: for psychological or physiological reasons, latrines with raised seats seem to cause constipation among people who customarily defecate in a squatting position" (Foster, 1973:103).

Superstitions

Superstition is an uncritical acceptance of a belief that is not substantiated by facts. In many instances superstitions act as important barriers to change. In one instance in Zimbabwe (formerly Southern Rhodesia), nutrition-education efforts were hampered because many women would not eat eggs. According to widespread belief, eggs cause infertility, they make babies bald, and they cause women to be promiscuous. In the Philippines, it is widely believed that eating squash and chicken at the same time produces leprosy. In some places women are not given milk during late pregnancy because of the belief that it produces a fetus too large for easy delivery, and in other places a baby may not be given water for several months after birth because water's "cold" quality is upsetting to the infant's heat equilibrium. Finally, in areas of Ghana, children are not given meat or fish because it is believed that they cause intestinal worms (Foster, 1973:103–104). Obviously, where such superstitious beliefs prevail, the acceptance of novelty, which is contrary to traditional ideas, will be greatly hampered. In the final section, economic barriers to change will be considered.

ECONOMIC BARRIERS

Resistance to change stemming from economic factors mostly relates to technological innovations, machines, and gadgets, although it can apply to social inventions and scientific discoveries as well. At times the cost of an invention can prevent its adoption, at least for a while. A society of limited economic means cannot afford to initiate programs involving nuclear energy nor can the majority of its citizens afford to adopt such modern appliances and conveniences as central heating, refrigerators, or automobiles. Even in the most affluent societies, limited economic resources constitute a barrier to changes that might otherwise be readily adopted. For example, in the United States, most everyone would readily accept the desirability of more effective controls on pollution, cheaper and more convenient systems of public transportation, and adequate health care for all. The fact that improvements in these areas come very slowly is a matter not only of priorities but also of cost. Cost, perceived profitability, and economic resources in a society can act as effective barriers to change, as will be shown on the following pages.

Cost

At times the *cost* of acquiring or using a novelty can be prohibitive as far as some potential acceptors are concerned. This is an important deterrent to the widespread adoption of a variety of modern innovations in both the technological and the ideological domains. A large number of people in the world today are ready to accept—in fact, psychologically they have already accepted—electric lights, television, dishwashers, central heating, sanitation programs, modern house design, and many other changes, but they are simply unable to afford them. The willingness to accept is there, but the economic sacrifice is either too great or completely beyond the scope of realization. In some cases the cost of an innovation is so great that no one can afford it. The idea is acceptable and it has important implications, but the returns to be expected are not commensurate with the investment required to produce it. Such is the present status of an effective and comprehensive health insurance plan for everybody in the United States.

Perceived Profitability

The perception of economic *profitability* is an important consideration involving predisposition toward an innovation. However, profitability alone would not ensure the adoption of an innovation. For example, even if the price of beef were to be reduced by 90 percent in India, Hindus would not begin eating cows. Nevertheless, there are many novelties that do not run so counter to cultural and social norms, and in these cases the rate of acceptance is likely to be more rapid if the innovation is more economically or socially profitable. Even in these instances, however, it should be noted that the increase in profitability needs to be rather spectacular to effect the rate of adoption. "Many students of peasant life feel that the relative economic advantage of a new idea must be at least 25 to 30 percent higher than existing practice for economic factors to affect adoption. When an innovation promises only a 5 to 10 percent advantage, a peasant farmer probably cannot even distinguish that it is advantageous" (Rogers & Shoemaker, 1971:143). His limited skills with figures, elementary accounting ability, and lack of experience with the scientific method of reaching conclusions all act to limit the farmer's comparing ability. In some instances, as noted by Rogers and Shoemaker (1971:143), to induce farmers to change, the potential payoff must be very high—not 5 to 10 percent, but 50 to 100 percent. Occasionally a new practice is accepted because of the financial incentives but is rejected for some other reasons at a later stage. For example, when government agencies introduced hybrid corn to the Spanish-American farmers of the Rio Grande Valley a few years ago, they readily adopted it because of its superior yield and high profitability; but within three years they had all returned to the old corn. The reason was that the hybrid corn did not make good tortillas (Apodaca, 1952).

Limited Economic Resources

In many underdeveloped and developing countries changes are desired but cannot be adequately implemented because of other economic pressures. In such countries, from 70 to 90 percent of the labor force is in agriculture; there is a lack of employment opportunities outside of agriculture; there is very little capital per head, and for most people existence is near the "subsistence" level; and savings practically do no exist for the large mass of the people. Whatever savings do exist are usually achieved by a land-holding class whose values are not conducive to investment in industry or commerce. A major proportion of expenditures is spent on food and basic necessities. There are poor credit facilities and a very low volume of trade per capita (Leibenstein, 1972).

These economic characteristics in underdeveloped countries tend to hinder capital formation, which in turn is considered as a principal obstacle to change. These countries seem to face more difficulties than the now-advanced countries when they began their industrialization. Simon Kuznets (1965) points to six major differences:

1. The present level of per capita product in the underdeveloped countries in their preindustrial phase is much lower than it was in the now-advanced countries, with the single exception of Japan.
2. The supply of land per capita is much smaller in developing countries today than it was in the present advanced countries when they began their industrialization.
3. Agricultural productivity in developing countries today is probably lower than it was in advanced countries in the past.
4. The inequality in the distribution of income is wider today than in the past, but not in a way that favors accumulation of productive capital.
5. The social and political structure of the low-income countries today is a much greater barrier than it was in the past.
6. Most of the present-day underdeveloped countries are launching development after a long period of colonial status, whereas the European countries began industrialization after a long period of political independence.

At times, nations that are scarcely emerging from the stage of feudalism are quite unwilling to go through the stage of laissez-faire capitalism.

They see and emulate social security programs in the advanced nations, along with minimum wage legislation, factory safety and maximum-working-day legislation, trade union movements, and the like. These programs are carried out in the context of an insufficient system of taxation and are usually of relatively short duration. Moreover, expenditures on these types of activities, admirable as they are in principle, take away funds from more essential matters such as basic health care, education, and the like.

In addition, the limited savings and investment patterns are not conducive to national development or large-scale changes. For example, in India too much of the limited savings goes into the hoarding of gold and of jewelry imported legally or illegally into the country, thus using up its scarce foreign exchange. Many underdeveloped countries also suffer from chronic inflation. Hence, there is a natural tendency for people to invest in real estate and in the holding of inventory. Finally, there is the frequent tendency of the rich in underdeveloped countries to pile up their savings abroad, legally or illegally, thereby making it unavailable to the nation for its internal development.

Other change-inhibiting economic factors include the lack of natural resources, such as oil, timber, coal, uranium, gas, and agricultural acreage. Obviously, the natural resources available to a society's economy can vary; some have a plentiful supply, others very few. However, more important than the level or abundance of indigenous resources is the degree of access a society has to natural resources, whether its own or those of another society. When availability of and access to natural resources are limited, in most cases, the economic structure of a society will not be able to support large-scale changes. Related to natural resources is labor, which can be viewed in both quantitative and qualitative senses. The number of people who can participate in the economy (quantity) always affects economic processes, but more important, the level of skill, knowledge, expertise, and motivation (quality) is an equally significant influence on the economy. Both labor and natural resources are closely associated with a society's ability for capital formation, a prerequisite for industrialization and modernization.

In sum, as Foster (1973:78) points out, "Cultural, social and psychological barriers and stimulants to change exist in an economic setting . . . [which] seems to set the absolute limits to change." Quite often people are aware of the value of change and are anxious to modify their traditional ways, but the economic conditions prevent them from doing so. In such situations, economic factors constitute a formidable barrier to change.

SUMMARY

In every society there are factors that promote change, and there are those that strive to maintain the status quo. The former are considered as stimulants to change, whereas the latter are seen as barriers; they can be separated only in an analytical sense. In reality, stimulants and barriers operate simultaneously. In this chapter they were examined in social, psychological, cultural, and economic terms.

One of the principal social stimulants to change is the desire for prestige. Societies in contact with one another are more likely to accept novelty than those in relative isolation. Strong friendship obligations in developing societies are also considered factors in the acceptance of change. Different social classes react to change in different ways, and in general, those in the middle classes are more likely to accept an innovation. Authority influences receptivity to change, and at times it is required over the beliefs of a dissident minority. Acceptance of change is enhanced when it can be integrated into the existing configuration of society. However, both the sequence and the timing of an innovation are important. Under certain circumstances competition acts as a stimulant to change, and in general a novelty will be more readily accepted if the people who are to change are involved in its planning and implementation.

On the other side of the token, social barriers to change are often manifested in the form of vested interests and status interests. In such situations, change is resisted by individuals or groups who fear a loss of power, wealth, or prestige should an innovation gain acceptance. Rigid class and caste patterns also tend to hinder the acceptance of the new. Resistance can also be based on ideology and rational conviction. Societies with a high degree of social solidarity and diffuse authority patterns will be resistant to change. At times individuals are afraid of social dislocation and apprehensive of the unknown. In many occasions prevailing moral sentiments provide a sound basis for resistance. Resistance may also be irrational and covert and, on occasions, change may meet with organized opposition.

Acceptance of or resistance to change is also conditioned by a number of psychological factors. Favorable motivational dispositions, perceived needs, clear-cut lines of communication, positive attitudes, and personal influence tend to facilitate the acceptance of change. By contrast, habit, ignorance, forms of selective perception, and unclear communication hinder change.

As Ralph Linton suggested, "If we know what a society's culture is, including its particular system of values and attitudes, we can predict with a fairly high degree of probability whether the bulk of its members will welcome or resist a particular innovation" (Linton, quoted by Allen, 1971:288). In a society where there is a high degree of emphasis on tradition, a fatalistic outlook on life, a strong sense of ethnocentrism, highly traditional norms of modesty, prevalence of superstitions, and inflexible motor patterns, there will be, in general, resistance to change. By contrast, where these conditions are absent or present to a lesser degree, the culture will be less tightly integrated and more receptive to novelty.

Of the four sources of acceptance or resistance, the economic factors are perhaps the most decisive. Perception of economic advantage and reasonable costs can in most cases facilitate the acceptance of change. On the other hand, regardless of the desirability of a given change, its compatibility with the recipient culture and many other considerations, it will not be accepted if the economic sacrifice is too great. In other words, regardless of how much people in a society want something, if they cannot afford it, the chances are that they will not be able to get it. However, once a novelty is affordable, its perceived profitability will facilitate its acceptance. In the following chapter the strategies of change will be considered.

SUGGESTED FURTHER READINGS

FOSTER, GEORGE M. *Traditional Societies and Technological Change*, 2nd ed. New York: Harper & Row, 1973. Chapters 4 and 9 represent a most comprehensive treatment of the various barriers and stimulants to change. Many of the examples used in the present chapter came from this book.

HARRIS, PHILIP R., and ROBERT T. MORAN. *Managing Cultural Differences*, 2nd ed. Houston: Gulf Publishing Company, 1987. A nontechnical discussion of cultural impacts on international business with many useful and practical hints on various stimulants and barriers to change.

KUSHNER, GILBERT, MICKEY GIBSON, JOHN GULICK, JOHN J. HONIGMANN, and RICHARD NONAS. *What Accounts for Socio-Cultural Change? A Propositional Inventory*. Chapel Hill: University of North Carolina, Institute for Research in Social Science, 1962. A collection of some 400 hypotheses under 13 categories concerning the conditions under which change will be accepted or rejected.

PATAI, RAPHAEL. *The Arab Mind*, rev. ed. New York: Scribner's, 1983. A fascinating and possibly controversial account of the way of life in Arab countries. Helpful in trying to understand current events in the Middle East.

ZALTMAN, GERALD, and ROBERT DUNCAN. *Strategies for Planned Change*. New York: Wiley, 1977. See, in particular, Chapter 3 on the various barriers to change. The discussion is a useful supplement to the material presented in this chapter.

REFERENCES

ALBRECHT, STAN L., BRUCE A. CHADWICK, and CARDELL K. JACOBSON. *Social Psychology*, 2nd ed. Englewood Cliffs, N.J.: Prentice-Hall, 1987.

ALLEN, FRANCIS R. *Socio-Cultural Dynamics: An Introduction to Social Change*. New York: Macmillan, 1971.

APODACA, ANADETO. "Corn and Custom: The Introduction of Hybrid Corn to Spanish American Farmers in New Mexico." In Edward H. Spicer (ed.), *Human Problems in Technological Change*. New York: Russell Sage, 1952, pp. 35–39.

ARENSBERG, CONRAD, and ARTHUR M. NIEHOFF. *Introducing Change: A Manual for Community Development*. Chicago: Aldine-Atherton, 1971.

BARNETT, HOMER G. *Innovation: The Basis of Cultural Change*. New York: McGraw-Hill Book Company, 1953.

BENNIS, WARREN. "Using Our Knowledge of Organizational Behavior: The Improbable Task." In Jay W. Lorsch (ed.), *Handbook of Organizational Behavior*. Englewood Cliffs, N.J.: Prentice-Hall, 1987, pp. 29–49.

BENSMAN, JOSEPH, and ARTHUR J. VIDICH. *American Society: The Welfare State & Beyond, Revised*. South Hadley, Mass: Bergin & Garvey, 1987.

BIERSTEDT, ROBERT. *Power and Progress: Essays on Sociological Theory.* New York: McGraw-Hill Book Company, 1974.

BOCHNER, STEPHEN, ed. *Cultures in Contact: Studies in Cross-Cultural Interaction.* Elmsford, N.Y.: Pergamon, 1982.

BOCK, PHILIP K., ed. *Culture Shock: A Reader in Modern Cultural Anthropology.* New York: Knopf, 1970.

COHEN, ARTHUR R. *Attitude Change and Social Influence.* New York: Basic Books, 1964.

COMSTOCK, GEORGE. "The Mass Media and Social Change." In Edward Seidman (ed.), *Handbook of Social Intervention.* Beverly Hills, Calif.: Sage Publications, Inc., 1983, pp. 268–288.

FESTINGER, LEON. "Behavioral Support for Opinion Change." *Public Opinion Quarterly,* 28, Fall 1964, pp. 404–417.

FLIEGEL, FREDERIC C., and JOSEPH E. KIVLIN. "Attributes of Innovation as Factors in Diffusion." *American Journal of Sociology,* 72, November 1966, pp. 235–248.

FOSTER, GEORGE M. *Traditional Societies in Technological Change,* 2nd ed. New York: Harper & Row, 1973.

GAMSON, WILLIAM A. *The Strategy of Social Protest.* Homewood, Ill.: Dorsey Press, 1975.

GERMANI, GINO. *The Sociology of Modernization.* New Brunswick, N.J.: Transaction Books, 1981.

GOULD, HAROLD A. "The Implications of Technological Change for Folk and Scientific Medicine." *American Anthropologist,* 59, 1957, pp. 507–516.

GRAHAM, SAXON. "Class and Conservatism in the Adoption of Innovations." *Human Relations,* 9, 1956, pp. 91–100.

HALL, EDWARD T. *Beyond Culture.* Garden City, N.Y.: Anchor Press/Doubleday, 1976.

HALL, RICHARD. *Organizations: Structures, Processes, and Outcomes,* 4th ed. Englewood Cliffs, N.J.: Prentice-Hall, 1987.

HARRIS, PHILIP R., and ROBERT T. MORAN. *Managing Cultural Differences,* 2nd ed. Houston: Gulf Publishing Company, 1987.

HOVLAND, CARL I., A.A. LUMSDAINE, and F.D. SHEFFIELD. *Experiments on Mass Communication.* Princeton, N.J.: Princeton University Press, 1949.

JASPARS, JOS, and MILES HEWSTONE. "Cross-Cultural Interaction, Social Attribution and Inter-Group Relations." In Stephen Bochner (ed.), *Cultures in Contact: Studies in Cross-Cultural Interaction.* New York: Pergamon, 1982, pp. 127–156.

KATZ, ELIHU, and PAUL F. LAZARSFELD. *Personal Influence.* New York: Free Press, 1955.

KERR, CLARK, JOHN T. DUNLOP, FEDERICK H. HARBERSON, and CHARLES A. MYERS. *Industrialism and Industrial Man.* New York: Oxford, 1964.

KESSING, FELIX M. *Cultural Anthropology: The Science of Custom.* New York: Holt, Rinehart & Winston, 1958.

KEESING, ROGER M. "Chiefs in a Chiefless Society: The Ideology of Modern Kwaio Politics." *Oceania,* 38, June 1968, pp. 276–280.

KELMAN, HERBERT C. "Processes of Opinion Change." *Public Opinion Quarterly,* 25, Spring 1961, pp. 57–58.

KLAPPER, JOSEPH T. *The Effects of Mass Communication.* New York: Free Press, 1960.

KLEIN, DONALD. "Some Notes on the Dynamics of Resistance to Change: The Defender Role." In Warren G. Bennis, Kenneth D. Benne, and Robert Chin (eds.), *The Planning of Change,* 4th ed. New York: Holt, Rinehart & Winston, 1985, pp. 98–105.

KROEBER, A.L. "Diffusionism." In Amitai Etzioni and Eva Etzioni-Halevy (eds.), *Social Change: Sources, Patterns, and Consequences,* 2nd ed. New York: Basic Books, 1973, pp. 140–144.

KUZNETS, SIMON. S. *Economic Growth and Structure: Selected Essays.* New York: W.W. Norton & Co., Inc., 1965.

LaPIERE, RICHARD T. *Social Change.* New York: McGraw-Hill Book Company, 1965.

LEIBENSTEIN, HARVEY. "Characteristics of Underdeveloped Areas." In Walter L. Johnson and David R. Kamerschen (eds.), *Readings in Economic Development.* Cincinnati: South-Western Publishing Co., 1972, pp. 35–37.

LEWIN, KURT. "Group Decision and Social Change." In H. Proshansky and B. Seidenberg (eds.), *Basic Studies in Social Psychology.* New York: Holt, Rinehart & Winston, 1965, pp. 423–436.

MANNERS, R.A. "Cultural and Personality Factors Affecting Economic Growth." In Bert Hoselitz (ed.), *Progress of Underdeveloped Areas.* Chicago: University of Chicago Press, 1952, pp. 72–88.

MEAD, MARGARET, ed.   *Cultural Patterns and Technical Change*. Paris: UNESCO, 1953.

MERTON, ROBERT K.   *Social Theory and Social Structure*. New York: Basic Books, 1957.

MONTAGU, ASHLEY.   *Man Observed*. New York: Putnam, 1968.

MOSCHIS, GEORGE P.   *Consumer Socialization: A Life-Cycle Perspective*. Lexington, Mass.: Heath, 1987.

NADLER, DAVID A.   "The Effective Management of Organizational Change." In Jay W. Lorsch (ed.), *Handbook of Organizational Behavior*. Englewood Cliffs, N.J.: Prentice-Hall, 1987, pp. 358–369.

NAIR, K.N.   "Animal Protein Consumption and the Sacred Cow Complex in India." In Marvin Harris and Eric B. Ross (eds.), *Food and Evolution: Toward a Theory of Human Food Habits*. Philadelphia: Temple University Press, 1987, pp. 445–454.

NAISBITT, JOHN.   *Megatrends: Ten New Directions Transforming Our Lives*. New York: Warner Books, 1982.

NIMKOFF, MEYER F.   "Obstacles to Innovation." In Francis R. Allen, Hornell Hart, Delbert C. Miller, William F. Ogburn, and Meyer F. Nimkoff (eds.), *Technology and Social Change*. New York: Appleton, 1957, pp. 56–71.

PATAI, RAPHAEL.   *The Arab Mind*, rev. ed. New York: Scribner's, 1983.

QUINT, MALCOLM N.   "The Idea of Progress in an Iraqi Village." *Middle East Journal*, 12, 1958, pp. 369–384.

ROGERS, EVERETT M., and F. FLOYD SHOEMAKER.   *Communication of Innovations: A Cross-Cultural Approach*, 2nd ed. New York: Free Press, 1971.

SCHNEIDER, HAROLD K.   "Pakot Resistance to Change." In William B. Bascom and Melville J. Herskovitz (eds.), *Continuity and Change in African Cultures*. Chicago: University of Chicago Press, 1959, pp. 144–167.

TOFFLER, ALVIN.   *The Third Wave*. New York: William Morrow, 1980.

USEEM, JOHN.   "South Seas Island Strike: Labor-Management Relations in the Carolina Islands, Micronesia." In Edward H. Spicer (ed.), *Human Problems in Technological Change*. New York: Russell Sage, 1952, pp. 149–164.

VAGO, STEVEN.   "Blowing the Overseas Business Deal: Hypothetical Blunderplax Company Shows How Not to Succeed," *St. Louis Commerce*, May, 1982, pp. 35–38.

WARREN, ROLAND S.   *Social Change and Human Purpose: Toward Understanding and Action*. Chicago: Rand McNally, 1977.

WASTE, ROBERT J., ed.   *Community Power: Directions for Future Research*. Beverly Hills, Calif. Sage Publications, Inc., 1986.

WATSON, GOODWIN.   "Resistance to Change." In Warren G. Bennis, Kenneth D. Benne, and Robert Chin (eds.), *The Planning of Change*, 2nd ed. New York: Holt, Rinehart & Winston, 1969, pp. 488–498.

WELLIN, EDWARD.   "Water Boiling in a Peruvian Town." In Benjamin D. Paul (ed.), *Health, Culture, and Community*. New York: Russell Sage, 1955, pp. 71–103.

WEYANT, JAMES M.   *Applied Social Psychology*. New York: Oxford, 1986.

ZALTMAN, GERALD.   *Marketing Contributions from the Behavioral Sciences*. New York: Harcourt, 1965.

ZALTMAN, GERALD, and ROBERT DUNCAN.   *Strategies for Planned Change*. New York: Wiley, 1977.

ZALTMAN, GERALD, ROBERT DUNCAN, and JONNY HOLBEK.   *Innovations and Organizations*. New York: Wiley, 1973.

9

Strategies of Change

This chapter examines the ways of bringing about change at various levels in society. At no other period in history has there been so much preoccupation with social change as today. Accompanying this preoccupation with change is a marked theoretical and practical interest in change strategies and tactics. In many areas of social life where change is not occurring, or taking place too slowly, there is often a great concern about how to stimulate or accelerate change. Demands for social change come from a variety of sources, and there is a growing emphasis on creating, guiding, directing, and managing change. There are also demands to develop new methods, to refine existing ones, and to translate theoretical knowledge into practical applications. At the outset, it should be remembered that strategies and tactics are neutral processes, with value judgments entering into the picture during their applications. The various ways of creating changes in society may be approved or deplored (is revolution "good" or "bad?"), or considered with scientific detachment. But there is no way of denying their importance.

The consequences of a particular change may be beneficial to one party and detrimental to another. The concepts of benefits and detriments are often relative and are also value judgments on someone's part, and "any manipulation of human behavior inherently violates a fundamental value, but that there exists no formula for so structuring an effective change situation that such manipulation is totally absent" (Kelman, 1972:575). People often feel that things are just not quite the way they ought to be and advocate and express a need for change. Invariably there will be others who oppose that advocated change. For example, population control is debated, advocated, and resisted both at the village level in underdeveloped countries and in high government offices. In some areas, court-ordered school desegregation is found to reinforce what it was intended to abolish. Heated and emotional discussions abound on both sides of the abortion issue. At the same time, as a result of purposive, directed change efforts, important strides have occurred in the delivery of health care; there is a noticeable decline in sex discrimination and in infant mortality; and important advancements have been made in reducing racial discrimination, at least in the United States.

This chapter will examine a series of social-change strategies (plans of action of policy) and tactics (specific means or techniques stemming from a strategy) used in a variety of change efforts at several levels. The chapter is designed to provide a greater understanding of the general targets, agents, and methods of planned social change and to analyze the roles of violence and nonviolence, social movements, and the law in creating change.

TARGETS, AGENTS, AND METHODS
OF PLANNED SOCIAL CHANGE

Planned social change refers to deliberate, conscious, and collaborative efforts by change agents to improve the operations of social systems (Bennis, Benne, & Chin, 1985:3). In the social-change literature, planned change has been referred to as social planning, social engineering, change management, or social marketing (Zaltman, Kotler, & Kaufman, 1972:2). Three fundamental issues are involved in the analysis of planned social change. The first has to do with the target of the change, the second with the agents of the change effort, and the third with the methods that will be utilized in the change effort. In the following pages, these three components of planned social change—targets, agents, and methods—will be examined.

Targets of Change

Planned social change usually begins as an effort to solve a problem or to rectify a situation. After the identification of the type of change desired, it is necessary to give attention to the system level on which the change is sought. Change may be sought on the individual level, or, at the other extreme, it may be change of social structural arrangements rather than simply of individuals. There is an infinite number of gradations between the individual and societal levels, and it is therefore helpful to designate the level of the system that is to be changed—that is, to identify the target system. Obviously, the nature of the target system is related to the methods to be used in bringing about change. For example, strategies used to effect change in an organization may be utterly ineffective in producing changes in individual behavior.

Various target systems have been identified for planned social change. Roland L. Warren (1977:56) incorporates four target systems—individuals, organizations, communities, and societies—in his model of purposive change. Harvey H. Hornstein and associates (1971) discuss a number of change targets, including individuals and organizational structures. They have identified five aspects of individual functioning that are frequent targets of change strategies: feelings, values, attitudes, perceptions, and skills, and actions (overt behavior) (1971:15). The target system of organizational structure was broken down into three common targets of change: (1) social characteristics, including group size and composition in terms of identifiable individual features such as intelligence, manual dexterity, and authoritarianism, structure of authority, status hierarchy, incentive systems, and formal channels of communication; (2) environmental characteristics, including spatial relations among group members and other features of physical setting; and (3) task characteristics, such as special task demands (that is, manual skill, knowledge, or creative ability), task difficulty, and the degree to which the task is specific or vague in prescribing behavior necessary for its completion (1971:149).

Gerald Zaltman and Robert Duncan (1977:10–11) in *Strategies for Planned Change* include time dimension in addition to the level of society that is the target of the change. The time dimension is obviously arbitrary, and can range from a short term of a few days or months to a long term of several months or years. Table 9.1 shows the six types of change identified on the basis of these two dimensions.

TABLE 9.1   Time Dimensions and Target Levels

TIME DIMENSION	MICRO (INDIVIDUAL)	INTERMEDIATE (GROUP)	MACRO (SOCIETY)
		LEVEL OF SOCIETY	
Short term	Type 1 (1) Attitude change (2) Behavior change	Type 3 (1) Normative change (2) Administrative change	Type 5 Invention-innovation
Long Term	Type 2 Life-cycle change	Type 4 Organizational change	Type 6 Sociocultural evolution

Source: Gerald Zaltman and Robert Duncan, *Strategies for Planned Change.* New York: Wiley, 1977, p. 11.

At the micro or individual level, there may be short-term changes in attitudes and behavior (Type 1). An illustration of this change would be the use of sensitivity training to alter a person's attitudes. An illustration of a more long-term change at the microlevel (Type 2) is the training and socialization process of new recruits in an institution. Priests, for example, when they start their training program, learn a new set of attitudes and behavior that affects their entire life. At the group or intermediate level of short-term change, normative or administrative change may be brought about. Normative changes take place when a group alters its norms temporarily to experiment with an innovation (Type 3). For example, in a corporation a team sets up a novel computerized information bank. Team members are given freedom to experiment, and they can bend established organizational rules. The change agent (in this case, the manager responsible for the innovation) encourages the team. Once the innovation has been tried and found useful, it is institutionalized (Kanter, 1983:234). At this point, it will become a more long-term change (Type 4) at the organizational level. The original participants in the change effort will be rewarded, this process then providing incentives for others to experiment.

At the societal level of change, short-term (Type 5) change is often the result of innovations or inventions. For example, the introduction of birth-control technology in a receptive society can alter birthrates and population size in a relatively short time period. In the long run, these changes could result in major changes in the social structure of the society. The long-term consequences are (Type 6) sociocultural change—that is, the facilitation of the modernization process in an underdeveloped nation.

In the literature on planned social change, there is also a distinction between change target system and the change client system. The former is seen as the unit in which the change agent is trying to alter the status quo such that the individual, group, or organization must relearn how to perform its activities. The latter is the individual or group requesting assistance from a change agent in altering the status quo. At times they are identical. In other instances, they can be separate entities, such as parents seeking psychiatric help for their child. In this case the parents represent clients, the therapist the change agent, and the child the change target. The important point in distinguishing between the change target system and the change client system is that change agents may try to influence some system in which there is no support or wish for assistance in any change (Zaltman & Duncan, 1977:18).

There is no commonly accepted typology of change targets in the literature. Most typologies, however, include an individual level; an intermediate level dealing with groups, communities, and organizations; and macrolevel target systems. Let us consider each of them separately.

Individuals as Change Targets

There are two ways of looking at individuals as change targets. In the first instance, it can be assumed that individual change is the principal mediator of social and organizational change. Changing of the various aspects of the individual is considered as a stepping-stone to other types of changes—particularly groups and organizations. The assumption is that, because groups and organizations are made up of individuals, it is individuals who can bring about change in the systems in which they are members. Thus, a change on an individual level can be evaluated in terms of its possible benefits and usefulness to the system of which they are members.

When the individuals are the target of planned change, a number of diverse strategies may be deployed. As an extreme illustration; "At Atascadero State Mental Hospital in California, homosexual child molesters are trained to cruise in gay bars so they will not have to resort to children; heterosexual child molesters are taught to pick up women at parties; and rapists are coached in sex techniques to improve their relationships with their wives" (Sage, 1977:79). This strategy of planned change is labeled as behavior modification. Three general techniques are involved in behavior modification: those that work with negative reinforcers (punishments for undesirable behavior); those that use positive reinforcers (rewards for desirable behavior); and those that attempt to undermine the subject's character structure. In addition, behavior-modification programs may include drugs, hypnosis, electroconvulsive shocks, brainwashing, and, in extreme cases, psychosurgery. Behavior modification is being used in a variety of institutional settings, such as schools, mental hospitals, and prisons, to change a large assortment of behavior "with remarkable success" (Albrecht, Chadwick, & Jacobson, 1987:17).

Behavior modification is obviously only one of the many strategies for changing individuals. Depending on the kind of change desired, and whether or not it is to be implemented on a one-to-one basis or in a small-group situation, one may choose from the arsenal of psychoanalytical, social-psychological, or educational strategies. The social sciences can offer a broad spectrum of technologies, stemming from several theoretical assumptions, which can be used with varying effectiveness with individual change targets.

Intermediate Target Systems

The group has come to occupy a strategic place both as a medium and as a target of planned social change in recent years (Benne, 1985:75). The link between the individual and the larger social system is the group. This is particularly true in a formal organization such as the army. The individual's membership in a squad or tank crew is one's link to the larger army. Similarly, students are linked to the larger school system through the classroom, student government, or a varsity sports team. In a less obvious fashion, the same is true of individuals' linkage with less formally organized systems such as the community, racial, and ethnic groupings. Therefore, the group is a medium for influencing both the individuals who are its members and the larger system of which their group is a part.

Kenneth D. Benne (1985:75) points out that larger social systems usually depend on small groups in formulating and shaping their policies and programs, whether it is a committee, cabinet, or board. Change in the composition and functioning of such a group can also produce change in the wider social system that is dependent upon that group for direction and guidance. Consequently, the management of small-group activities and processes is an important target in planned social change.

On the community level, intergroup relations are often the target of planned social change (Kettner, Daley, & Nichols, 1985). In many instances the object is to change the relations between racial, ethnic, and religious groups. These relationships are often marked by strong feelings of fear and hostility and by historically embedded stereotypes. At times, changes can be effective in such intergroup relations by changing the composition of group members. For example, an important study on "Interracial Housing" by Morton Deutsch and Mary Evans Collins (1965) shows that integrated housing projects had a positive impact on relations between the races and on the attitudes of white women toward their black neighbors. White women in the integrated projects were more likely to have contacts with black women, to have black friends, and to engage in neighborhood activities with blacks than were white women in segregated projects. In addition, women in the integrated projects were more likely to express positive attitudes toward blacks and, on the basis of recall, were more likely to report a positive change in attitude since living in the projects. Deutsch and Collins note that the success of such changes is enhanced when supportive attitudes from the wider community are forthcoming.

In many cases the target of planned change is the organization, where attempts are made to improve internal communications, increase efficiency, work satisfaction, and productivity (Hall, 1987). Of course, the various organizations can have specific client systems as change targets. For example, in the case of family planning associations, the mothers and the public at large are seen as the target, and with the various antidrug groups the actual and potential users are the targets. In the case of the American Heart Association, the target includes smokers and overweight people.

It should be pointed out, however, that not all changes can be effected at the group level by making the group the target of change. "Just as it may be necessary to change the group in which an individual functions in order to change the individual, it may be necessary to change the social structure in which the group is embedded in order to change the group.

For example, the students at a particular university may be generally convinced that the grading system impedes learning. It would not be feasible for that university to abolish grades while it continues to function in a competitive social milieu where grades are used for securing employment, gaining admission to graduate school, and maintaining enrollment at a manageable level. For some kinds of change, then, only the social structure itself is an appropriate target" (Lauer, 1982:340–341).

Macrolevel Target Systems

Affecting changes in macrosystems or in the structure of society are obviously much more difficult than in microlevel or intermediate-level target systems. Targets at that level would include attempts to change national policies, cultural patterns, resolving issues between nations, attempts at modernization, industrialization, urbanization, nation building, altering statuses of minority groups, and the like. At the macrolevel, in many instances there are highly complex target systems. In many cases it is very difficult to identify such complex target systems except in the most general terms. This dilemma is epitomized in the popular expression, "Let's change the whole system." In some instances, however, target systems at the macrolevel may be clearly identified. This is the case, for example, of national policies dealing with certain aspects of society such as agriculture, the economy, or formal educational systems. At times, efforts are directed only at a segment of one of these factors, for example, energy policy, aid to unemployed, minimum wage, child health programs, and farm mortgage policies. In other instances, there are efforts to deal with a segment of the society, such as the poor, as evidenced by a multitude of legislative undertakings on poverty. Additional macrolevel target systems will be further discussed under the headings of Social Movements, and Law and Social Change, in this chapter.

Change Agents

In planned social change, *change agents* are professionals who influence innovation decisions in a direction considered desirable by an organization. Change agents may be external or internal to the social system in which change is desired, and the change desired may also be classified as external or internal in origin (Zaltman & Duncan, 1977:187). To achieve change, there must be organization. Ideally, the change effort should be compatible with the values of the target population, and the organization itself should be accepted by society (Hall, 1987:25–27).

Philip Kotler (1972:177–178) points out that change agents fall into two groups: leaders and supporters. The *leaders* include six types of persons: (1) the *directors*, who started or head the organization and wield the power; (2) the *advocates*, who wield the pen rather than the power but are close to those in power; (3) the *backers*, who provide the purse and supply the financial resources to keep the organization going; (4) the *technicians*, who as employees or volunteers provide professional advice or service, for example, public relations specialists, professional fund raisers, advertising practitioners, community organizers, lawyers, and management consultants; (5) the *administrators*, who run the day-to-day affairs of the organization; and finally, (6) the *organizers*, who have effective skills in enlisting supporters and running the programs and campaigns.

The *supporters* include: the *workers,* who are committed enough to the particular change efforts to give their time to it; the *donors*, who make contributions of money rather than time to the cause; and finally, a much larger group of *sympathizers*, who neither work nor give much money to the cause but give it lip service support.

Everett M. Rogers (1972:196–197) identifies several functions of the change agent, including: developing a recognition for need for change among the clients; establishing a change relationship with them; diagnosing the client's problem; examining the client's goals and alternatives, then creating the intent to change in the client; encouraging the client to innovate; stabilizing the change behavior so as to prevent discontinuance; and, finally, achieving a terminal relationship with the client.

In addition, Zaltman and Duncan (1977:185–224) note that in situations where an organization has defined the problems for the change agent and established the objectives of the change effort, the change agent: should be sensitive to the needs and perspectives of the change target system in seeking solutions to change situations; should always seek the simplest solution when working with a change problem; should have administrative capabilities; should strive to maintain good interpersonal relations with persons and the change target system; should be sensitive to and tolerant of constraints; should have self-confidence and a positive self image to accept setbacks; should be able to define the change program in a fashion that is effective to the various participants of the change program; and, finally, should try to maximize cooperation with members of the change target system.

Methods of Planned Social Change

In the literature on planned social change, there is no definitive method for categorizing the various strategies of change. Consequently, various authors on the topic use labels that are somewhat arbitrary and on many occasions overlapping. Moreover, in many change situations, the change agent is likely to utilize multiple change strategies to accomplish the desired objective. It is also conceivable that a change agent may resort to a sequence of strategies over time, again depending on the particular change situation. With this in mind, let us now examine some of the principal change strategies.

A most comprehensive review of change strategies for affecting changes in human systems is presented by Robert Chin and Kenneth D. Benne (1985). They emphasize that a common element in all approaches to planned change is the conscious utilization and application of knowledge as an instrument for altering patterns and institutions of practices. Although their orientation is primarily toward educational change, the strategies they discuss are applicable to many different types of planned change situations. They identify three broad categories of strategies: empirical-rational, normative-reeducative, and power-coercive.

The *empirical-rational* strategies are based on the assumption that people are rational, and they follow their rational self-interests once this is revealed to them. For this strategy, the emphasis is on changing individuals. With regard to educational change, under this category of strategies, they include such activities as basic research and dissemination of knowledge to general education, personal selection and replacement, the use of systems analysts as staff and consultants, and applied research and the development of linkage systems for diffusing its findings. They also include utopian thinking as a strategy of change in the form of future scenarios and an emphasis on more adequate communication on interpersonal relationships.

The *normative-reeducative* strategies are based on the assumption that change will occur only as the individuals involved are brought to change their normative orientations to old patterns and develop commitments to new ones. Such changes involve changes in attitudes, values, skills, and significant relationships. Such approaches to effecting change "bring direct interventions by change agents, interventions based on a consciously worked out theory of change and of changing, into the life of a client system, be that system a person, a small group, an organization, or a community" (Chin & Benne, 1985:32). These change strategies have a number of common elements: The emphasis is on the client system and its perception of its own problem and the need for change; an assumption that such problems are seldom purely technical, having a group dynamic component; the notion of a change agent collaborating with the client who is the change target; the attempt to uncover nonconscious elements, impede problem solution, so that they may be dealt with; and the selective use of knowledge from the behavioral sciences. "These approaches center in the notion that people technology is just as necessary as thing technology in working out desirable changes in human affairs" (Chin & Benne, 1985:33). They are used, for example, at the organizational level to improve problem-solving capabilities, methods of conflict resolution, and communication, and to increase organizational effectiveness and efficiency.

The *power-coercive* strategies are based on the application of economic, political, or moral power. Although the accent is more often on political and economic sanctions, Chin and Benne point out that strategies of non-violence fit this category through the application of moral power. They also include the use of political institutions and law to achieve change. Similarly, they include efforts to manipulate or reconstitute "power elites." It is suggested that this last approach is justified only when it is necessary to remove barriers to accomplishing change through democratically and scientifically oriented methods.

As a refinement of one of the three strategies discussed by Chin and Benne, Ronald Lippitt and his associates (1958) apply the normative-reeducative strategy to four different types of client systems: individuals, small groups, large organizations, and communities. It should be noted that their method of change is limited to situations in which an individual, group, organization, or community engages a consultant as change agent in order to help it change itself. They developed a model to fit this relationship between a client system and a change agent acting as consultant. It is based on five phases: (1) development of a need for change ("unfreezing"); (2) establishment of a change relationship; (3) working toward change ("moving"); (4) generalization and stabilization of change ("freezing"); and (5) achieving a terminal relationship (Lippitt, Watson, & Westley, 1958:130).

From a different perspective, Richard E. Walton (1972) distinguishes between the *power strategy* and the *attitude change strategy*. The power strategy is based on the assumption that the way to bring about change is to build a power base and manipulate that power strategically. The attitude change strategy is based on the notion that the desired behavior change will be best produced through attitude change, based on a growth of trust and goodwill.

In an approach to develop strategies for social action, Philip Kotler (1972:183–184) identifies three basic ways in which a change agent can attempt to influence a change target: by coercion (power), persuasion, or education.

The *power* strategy attempts to bring about change in the target through the use of agent-controlled sanctions. In such situations, change agents are primarily concerned with changing the behavior rather than the beliefs or values of the change target. They seek changes through sanctions such as authority, force, or payment. Change agents in a position of authority (managers over workers, army officers over draftees, judges over defendants) attempt to bring about change by withholding rewards or administering punishment. If the change agent has no authority over the change target, two possibilities exist. If the agent views the target as an enemy, the power strategy may take the form of force or threat of force—demonstration, noncooperation, or violence. The second option entails the use of payment (gifts or bribes) to bring about the desired behavior.

Kotler's second way of bringing about change is through a *persuasion* strategy, which attempts to induce the desired behavior in the target through identifying the social object with the change agent's existing beliefs or values. The change agent seeks to find arguments indicating that the desired behavior serves the natural interests of the change targets. Based on the Aristotelian approach, three persuasive arguments are possible: *logos,* or appeals to logic; *pathos,* or appeals to emotions; and *ethos,* or appeals to values. For example, in television campaigns to discourage smoking all three appeals have been used. "*Logic-laden* commercials attempted to prove that cigarette smoking was harmful to health, *affect-laden* commercials sought to activate smokers' fears of death, and *value-laden* commercials implied that the smoker was immoral or irresponsible to his family because his death would hurt *them*" (Kotler, 1972:184).

The *reeducative* strategy attempts to induce the desired behavior in the change target through the internalization of new beliefs or values. In such a situation the change agent seeks a deep and lasting change in the behavior of the change target that he believes cannot be produced through power or persuasive approaches. It is used by psychotherapists in individual situations or milieu therapists in group situations.

By now, it is obvious that there are many ways to categorize the strategies of planned change. In an influential book, *Strategies for Planned Change,* Gerald Zaltman and Robert Duncan (1977) recapitulate and combine many of the previously discussed approaches. They then suggest that the various strategies can be depicted on a continuum by degree of external pressure exerted on the targets. They identify four general strategies: facilitative, reeducative, persuasive, and power—ranging from minimum to maximum outside pressure.

Facilitative strategies are the ones that make easier the implementation of changes by and/or among the target group. It is based on the assumption that the target group: (1) already recognizes a problem; (2) is in general agreement that remedial action is necessary; and (3) is open to external assistance and willing to engage in self-help (Zaltman & Duncan, 1977:90). The effectiveness of the strategy is enhanced when the target groups are aware of the availability of assistance, committed to seek and accept assistance, and willing to remedy a situation. For example, on Indian reservations, children do poorly in school and have a high dropout rate. The problem is recognized, and funds are made available to rectify the situation by trying to create an environment more conducive to learning.

Reeducative strategies are used when time is not a pressing factor. In such a strategy the relatively objective presentation is intended to provide a rational justification for action. It is based on the assumption that humans are rational beings and capable of modifying their behavior when information is presented to them. Reeducation rather than education is used because at times the strategy involves the unlearning or unfreezing of something prior to the learning of the new attitude and behavior. Such reeducation strategies have been found very effective in third-world countries in a number of areas such as sanitation, increased use of hygiene facilities, and in various public health campaigns.

Persuasive strategies try to bring about change through bias in the way in which a message is structured and presented. Attempts to create change may be based on reasoning, or on rational or emotional appeals. Most advertisers and many nonprofit organizations rely on these strategies. In planned change efforts, persuasive strategies are used frequently in family planning programs and in marketing.

Power strategies involve the use of coercion to secure the target's compliance. Zaltman and Duncan suggest that the ability to exercise power is founded on an obligatory relationship between the change agent and change target. It is indicative of a situation in which the target is dependent on the change agent for satisfaction of its goals. "The strength of power is related to the degree of dependency, which in turn is a function of several factors: (1) the goals controlled by the change agent and the target's motivational investment in those goals, (2) the availability of alternatives to satisfy the target's goals, and (3) the cost of alternative modes of goal attainment" (Zaltman & Duncan, 1977:153). In some instances, the exercise of power has a cost to its user. There may be a cost involved in rewarding the target for compliance or punishing the target for noncompliance. Cost may also incur in the form of retaliation on the part of the target. An illustration of the use of the power strategies would be the various regulatory agencies in the domain of the environment, energy use, advertising, and auto safety. In general, power strategies are desirable when the change sought must be immediate and when the commitment by the target is low to a particular change.

At times the use of *multiple strategies* is desirable. A good illustration of the use of multiple strategies is the case of a massive vasectomy campaign in Kerala, India, in 1970. It lasted for one month and over 15,000 sterilizations were performed. Various persuasive strategies were used in the form of house-to-house visits by family-planning educators, public meetings, press releases, special newspaper supplements, and variety entertainments and cultural performances with particular reference to the campaign. The use of incentives (payment or bribe) can be called a form of power strategy according to Kotler (1972:183). Finally, the location and the physical layout of the camp and the transportation system established to bring in persons for the operation reflect considerable concern with facilitative strategies (Zaltman & Duncan, 1977:179).

VIOLENCE

In the previous section, references were made to the various power strategies of change in the context of legitimate authority manifested through institutional channels. The intent of this section is to examine the use of violence and coercion as extralegal strategies to effect change. Violence is conceptualized as direct or indirect action applied to restrain, injure, or destroy persons or property. The discussion in this section will be limited to those change efforts in which violent methods are deliberately used in the formulation and implementation of social change.

The use of violent strategies of social change is as old as humankind. Samuel P. Huntington (1972:282) points out that in no society do significant social, economic, or political changes take place without violence or the imminent likelihood of violence. At times, as H.L. Nieburg (1972:161) asserts, "The threat of violence and the occasional outbreak of real violence—which gives the threat credibility—are essential elements in peaceful social change not only in international, but also in national communities."

Violent strategies of change include ghetto riots, university confrontations, guerrilla warfare, oppressive measures by the state, various forms of insurrection, terrorism, and, in its ultimate form, revolution. Decentralized and spontaneous violence is a common means through which disadvantaged groups call attention to their grievances and their demands for social change. There appear to be some periods or situations in which violence succeeds more often than nonviolence. As it was noted previously, William A. Gamson (1975) studied 53 American groups and movements that promoted various social changes between 1800 and 1945. He claims that those that gained their goals were generally the ones that used violence (or, more correctly, had violence thrust upon them through police or mob attack), while all the nonviolent victims of attack failed to achieve their goals.

At times, the use of violence is a necessary stimulus for change. For example, "The history of reform in the United States—from the Jeffersonians down through abolitionists, populists, the labor movement, and the civil rights movement—is studded with instances of violence and other forms of disorder which helped to trigger changes in governmental policy" (Huntington, 1972:282). The early 1830s riots and other violence in England played an important role in consolidating Whig support for the Reform Act of 1832. Similarly, in India, middle-class groups in the mid-1950s used violence on occasions to wrest concessions from the government. In the United States, following the Birmingham riots in 1963, President Kennedy declared that passage of his civil rights bill was necessary "to get the struggle off the streets and into the courts." Failure to pass the bill, Kennedy warned, would lead to "continued, if not increased, racial strife—causing the leadership on both sides to pass from the hands of reasonable and responsible men to the purveyors of hate and violence" (Huntington, 1972:283).

The effectiveness of violence as a strategy of social change lies in the willingness of certain segments of the population to go beyond the accepted patterns of action to promote change. The use of violent strategies represents a threat to existing political organization and procedures. However, it should be noted that the repeated use of violent strategies depreciates their value. "In 1963 racial riots in the United States and monkish self-immolation in Vietnam helped to produce significant changes in governmental policy and political leadership. Three years later similar events failed to produce similar consequences" (Huntington, 1972:284).

There are certain common elements in the use of violent strategies for effecting social change. Ted Gurr (1967) outlines the principal strategic steps that are used to induce violent social change. As the first step, the change agent must *increase* the perception of relative deprivation among the potentially violent group. This can be done by minimizing the group's perceptions of the rewards and benefits to be gained at its current social position while enhancing the perceived discrepancy between the group and other segments of society. This perceived discrepancy in turn would lead to feelings of frustration and anger.

The second step entails the maximization of the *intensity* of anger of the group. The change agent, according to Gurr, should argue that: (1) the social goals are desirable, for example, economic benefits, improved well-being, and increased status; (2) the deprivation to which the group is subjected is indeed illegitimate, for example, by underscoring instances of social discrimination; (3) the deprivation is severe, for example, by pointing to the discrepancies between the group and its desired state while minimizing the similarities; and (4) by emphasizing the occurrence of continuous and unjust deprivation.

In the third step, the change agent must emphasize the social facilitation variables and minimize the social control variables that transform anger into violence. The accentuation of social facilitation variables entails: (1) giving examples that society is violent in other spheres, for example, violence is as American as apple pie; (2) amplifying racial, communal, and other in-group ties by emphasizing shared states of deprivation and indicating harassment by other groups; and (3) giving critical incidents that will trigger violence at optimal points in time. Gurr points to two ways for the change agent to minimize social control variables: (1) create conditions that will evoke either no retribution or an overreaction; and (2) create conditions that cut off the availability of mechanisms that discharge anger nonviolently. The first instance is illustrated by overreaction by the police to ghetto and campus violence, thus helping to increase violence. The second might entail the creation of certain incidents that bring about curfews, a temporary cessation on mass gatherings, and similar events.

Obviously, not all of these steps were present in the more than 300 outbursts of collective racial violence that occurred in major central cities between 1963 and 1969 in the United States (Downes, 1970). Many of the participants of these racial riots saw their grievances as rooted in the existing arrangements of power and authority in contemporary society and their action was—on a direct or symbolic level—an attempt at altering these arrangements (Skolnick, 1969:7). However, not all violent activities are aimed at achieving either specific or symbolic objectives. Many individuals participated because food, liquor, clothing, appliances, and other goods could be procured through looting, or to vent their anger against specific merchants and police who had harassed or exploited them.

During the initial stages, racial violence was relatively spontaneous and unorganized. They were black-dominated and property-oriented. By 1968, however, the police were becoming more effective in controlling or repressing violent events. The development of improved control capabilities led to more organized small-scale terrorism or guerrilla warfare by black extremist groups such as the Revolutionary Action Movement and the Black Panthers. This violence took the form of arson and attempts to kill police, firefighters, and merchants in the ghetto. This new pattern of violence was black-dominated but person-oriented, and it also involved more systematic attacks on whites. In many instances the violent outbursts were precipitated by specific incidents that involved the police, and on other occasions were linked to a variety of urban grievances (Wilson, 1968:23).

Martin Oppenheimer (1969) points out that violence can be a successful change strategy in the long run only if those using it have mass support or majority neutrality. After the violent outbursts and turmoil of the 1960s, blacks had neither. This is not to say, however, that their efforts were in vain. The unrest contributed to a series of efforts to improve the plight of blacks and the underprivileged, including model city programs, the war against poverty, black studies programs in universities, and so on.

In addition to riots, there are other forms of violence aimed at bringing about change. They include the various types of revolutions discussed in Chapter 5, such as civil wars, wars of national liberation, *putsch*, and *coup d'états*. Regarding the latter, Edward Luttwak (1979) notes that in the twentieth century, *coups* are more common than elections as a means of changing governments in many countries. There are many more military governments in existence than parliamentary democracies, and between 1946 and 1978, there were close to 300 *coups* worldwide.

Terrorism is a special form of violence to effect radical change. Scholarly interest in terrorists and terrorism has been expanding ever since the late 1960s, when a wave of dramatic incidents—hijackings, kidnappings, bombings, and hostage-takings—began. The term *terrorism* is a politically loaded concept, and scholars trying to define it encounter practical and theoretical dilemmas, perhaps best reflected by the oft-cited adage, "One person's terrorist is another person's freedom fighter." In essence, there is a conflict of different ideologies, and what constitutes terrorism depends on one's political views. To illustrate: President Reagan refers to the U.S.-backed Contra rebels trying to overthrow the Nicaraguan government as "freedom fighters." Others, in particular the Sandinistas, call the rebels terrorists, arguing that Contra violence against civilian population constitutes terrorism. Similarly, in South Africa, where violence is used by both sides, the use of the label "terrorist" for either the black nationalists or the white minority government depends on one's view of apartheid as a just racial policy or as racism, as well as on one's notions on law and order, and civil disobedience, among other concerns.

Part of the lack of consensus also stems from the vast differences among "terrorist" groups themselves. They range from the Irish Republican Army to the various factions of the Palestinian Liberation Organization, and from the Basque nationalists in Spain to the Baader-Meinhof gang in West Germany and the Red Brigades in Italy. The Sunnis, Shiites, Sikhs, and Salvadorans, among many others, have their own peculiar causes and terrorist groups. As a tactic, terrorism has been used by groups on the far right and on the far left. Terrorist acts have been committed by groups that have been vindicated by history, as well as by those that have been condemned by it.

But what is terrorism? It may be defined as a type of surreptitious warfare based on the indiscriminate use or threat of violence where the most important result is not the physical or mental damage of the victims, but the psychological effects produced for the purpose of altering the state of mind or policy of a nation or group whose members are directly assaulted or intimidated (Grosscup, 1987:13; Turner & Killian, 1987:319).

Indiscriminate violence against innocent people is used for a variety of objectives. One is to coerce a nation into taking some specific action to carry out the terrorists' goal. Example: The Arab skyjackers of a TWA plane in 1985 killed one passenger and held 39 American tourists hostage in Lebanon for 17 days while demanding that Israel release over 700 Shiite Muslims. Another objective is to demoralize and intimidate the opposition. Example: Arab terrorist incidents in the Vienna and Rome airports in 1985 and terrorist acts against the United States in 1986 adversely affected the willingness of Americans to live and work in Lebanon, created unrest among Americans working abroad, and discouraged many American tourists from going to Europe. A third objective is to call attention to the terrorist cause. Terrorists create newsworthy events; they mobilize the news media to disseminate a message that otherwise would not capture public attention. This manipulation of the media is often successful: It gives the terrorists publicity and the power to instill fear, which is out of proportion to their real numbers and strength (Turner & Killian, 1987:321–322).

In many parts of the world terrorist activities are highly organized and well financed (Grosscup, 1987). Manuals on terrorist strategies and tactics abound (Marighella, 1985). In a cookbook-like fashion, among other things, they spell out techniques of raids and infiltrations, ambushes, street operations, bomb-making, executions, kidnappings, sabotage, conducting a war of nerves, obtaining weapons, and negotiating for hostages. Terrorists are also getting technologically more sophisticated, and the threat from terrorist groups could escalate dramatically were they to use nuclear weapons or chemical or biological warfare agents. The advances in science and technology could turn modern society into a potential victim of terrorism where there is no immunity for the noncombatant segment of the population or for those who have no direct connection to particular conflicts or grievances that instigate acts of violence.

In most of the literature on planned social change, the use of violent strategies is not considered a desirable means for inducing social change. For example, after examining numerous violent attempts to bring about change, Oppenheimer concludes that the use of violence tends to subvert or inhibit the emergence of a truly democratic and humanistic regime (1969:55–68). The use of violence, Oppenheimer argues, tends to foster the worship of action. Rational thought is denigrated. Moreover, in spite of Franz Fanon's (1968) arguments about the liberating effects of oppressed people engaging in violent acts, Oppenheimer asserts that violence negatively affects individual mental health and personality. The survivors of successful attempts to bring about change are usually incapable of creating a humanistic order because they are conditioned to use violence both to solve problems and against enemies of the new order. This, in turn, further subverts democratic processes and humanistic values. To change society, Oppenheimer argues that the only appropriate strategy is a "protracted nonviolent struggle."

Before examining nonviolent and direct action strategies of change, one should note that violence need not be directed toward other groups. Nieburg (1972:170) describes the Dukhobor Sons of Freedom (of Vancouver, B.C.), who have adopted a novel technique of displaying violence as they conduct their immemorial campaign against compulsory public education. They set fire to their own homes and barns, standing by and watching the blaze. They also parade naked in the middle of city streets. The unusual nature of these demonstrations is plain. Their religion forbids them to threaten or use violence against others. Instead, they demonstrate symbolically their discipline and passionate commitment of their own way of life by inflicting violence upon their own property. The naked marches result in arrests and imprisonment, and the house burnings force welfare authorities to provide temporary shelter. In the process, however, the demonstrations invoke public attention and sympathy for the believers. This may well give the local authorities incentive to ignore their defiance of school attendance laws. As a matter of fact, this is what has happened during the past two generations. The law has been circumvented and there has been no concentrated efforts on the part of authorities to enforce it.

NONVIOLENCE AND DIRECT ACTION

There are many contemporary images of nonviolence as a strategy for social change: consumer boycotts, rent strikes, civil rights demonstrations, labor pickets, or young males refusing to register for the military draft. This strategy has a long history. Socrates practiced civil disobedience as a form of nonviolent resistance over 2,000 years ago. Centuries ago in the Far East creditors fasted on a debtor's doorstep until they were paid. Christ and his disciples practiced many of these techniques. Americans threw English tea into Boston Harbor to protest British taxes. In the nineteenth-century United States, Henry David Thoreau stated his philosophy of civil disobedience, which still serves as an inspiration for nonviolent action (Hornstein and others, 1971:533–534).

Chin and Benne (1985:41) consider nonviolence as one of the power-coercive strategies. It is a way of forcing the change target to give in, to make concessions, and, occasionally, to cooperate with the change effort. It is based on "moral power," and "Part of the ingredients of the power of the civilly disobedient is in the guilt which their demonstration of injustice, unfairness, or cruelty of the existing system of control arouses in those exercising control or in others previously committed to the present system of control" (Chin & Benne, 1985:41). The strategy of nonviolence is likely to be effective, other things being equal, according to the value orientation of the change target and of the pertinent third parties. When the change target, in the form of established authority, is relatively immune to the moral appeal involved, the reaction to nonviolence may be brutal repression. "Unless there are third parties with power to intervene and who are deeply impressed by the moral issues and the brutal repression, the efforts may be ruthlessly squelched" (Warren, 1977:156). On the other hand, in situations in which the target and third parties are susceptible to the moral appeal of the nonviolent action, it may be highly effective.

Hornstein and his associates (1971:537–542) suggest that the choice of nonviolent strategy and tactics can reflect either an indirect or a direct approach to the opponent's power. The indirect approach is based on the decision to meet the violent style of the opponent with nonviolence. The direct approach is based on attempts to upset the opponent's power base, attitudes, availability of resources, public image, and opinion of third parties. In such instances the conflict is external to the opponent, not internal.

The Indirect Approach

In the indirect approach, an important assumption shared by non-violent change agents is that the amount, duration, and intensity of violence is *minimized* by nonviolent change tactics. It is based on the notion that "using nonviolence against a violent attacker acts like a 'moral jujitsu'; the nonviolent behavior throws the attacker off guard, and exhausts him through an internal conflict between his needs to vent aggressive behavior and the situational inappropriateness of attacking a passive other" (Hornstein and others, 1971:538). However, the reality of the situation does not always support this assumption. For example, in many instances, physical harm is present; witness the beatings of student demonstrators by police at Berkeley, Columbia, and other campuses as they protested the war in Vietnam in the late 1960s and early 1970s.

From a related perspective, Gene Sharpe (quoted by Hornstein and others, 1971:538–539) shows that nonviolence is selected as a strategy because it technically disconfirms the opponent's expectations of violence. "The opponent, in his disconfirmed state, will now be responsive to a nonviolent strategy and agree to play the game 'in kind.' " In reality, whether or not the opponent will respond this way, however, depends on a number of factors. Some of these are as follows:

1. If the nonviolent behavior is seen as appropriate.
2. If the nonviolent tactic is new.
3. If the nonviolent action is seen as resulting from a strategy or a way of life.
4. If the opponent can trust the nonviolent actor.
5. If the nonviolent actor is valued as a human being.

It is obvious that the outcome of an indirect approach is highly speculative, particularly in view of the number of factors that could make it fail.

The Direct Approach

In the direct approach there are two factors involved: techniques of *attitude change* and the use of *third parties*. Hornstein and his colleagues suggest that both are used to manipulate the political position of the opponents as well as to change their behavior and/or attitudes toward the issues.

Gene Sharpe (1971:546–577) advocates three mechanisms of *attitude change*: conversion, accommodation, and nonviolent coercion. *Conversion* takes place when the opponents change both their attitudes and their behavior toward the nonviolent actor. It takes place in situations in which the opponents are persuaded by a variety of messages as well as situations of identification with the nonviolent actor. Illustrations of tactics in this category of nonviolent protest would include petitions, pickets, declarations, teach-ins, and marches. *Accommodation*, according to Sharpe, is a mild form of coercion involving a willingness to go along with the nonviolent demonstrators without measurably changing one's attitude. An illustration of this would be the hunger strike, a tactic that is successful when the suffering of the participants becomes intolerable to the opponent or to third-party witnesses. *Nonviolent coercion* is present in situations in which opponents have no choice about their compliance. It is used to force opponents to behave in a certain fashion by the change agent whether or not they like it. However, it will sustain change only when the threat of continued or renewed action is present or when there are new laws to support the change. Strikes, boycotts, occupations, and sit-downs are illustrative tactics of nonviolent coercion.

In the direct approach, *third parties* often have an effect on the success of a nonviolent strategy. Their impact is based on "(1) their own attitudinal position and its correspondence to the attitudes of demonstrators or the opponent; (2) their communication to the opponent about his behavior; and (3) their availability to maintain surveillance over agreed-upon changes by either party" (Hornstein and others, 1971:541). Third parties with high prestige who support the demonstrators are likely to increase the perceived pressures on the opponent to change. By contrast, if they support the opponent's position, it will probably decrease the likelihood of change. Regarding the second point, communication that supports the nonviolent demonstrators is particularly effective when an opponent has responded violently to the nonviolence. The presence of the mass media is especially important here, as witnessed by the events at the 1968 Chicago Democratic Convention. Finally, surveillance is particularly effective in accommodation and coercion strategies. The changes brought about by these approaches require impartial third parties to monitor the future course of events of both sides in the conflict.

After this overview of nonviolent strategies of change, it is appropriate to consider some of the tactics that are used. Incredible as it may seem, there are at least 146 tactics used in nonviolence (Sharpe, 1971:546). Prior to discussing some of the tactics, it should be noted that a change agent should not expect to achieve success with nonviolent tactics unless he or she has made provisions for sufficient training in their use, and planning in their application and execution. An understanding of the tactics alone is not sufficient, they need to be rehearsed extensively with those who will be involved in the action (Hornstein and others, 1971:542).

Direct-Action Tactics

Martin Oppenheimer and George Lakey (1972) discuss some of the more important direct-action tactics used in the recent civil rights struggle in the United States. They list them under three headings: demonstrations, noncooperation, and direct intervention.

Demonstrations are used primarily to express a position, a point of view. They are not so effective as noncooperation or direct intervention. The tactics used here include: marches and parades; picketing and vigils; fraternization; "hounding" (following and reminding officials of the immorality of their behavior); publishing leaflets and renouncing honors.

Noncooperation entails methods of direct action in which campaigners withdraw their usual degree of cooperation with the opponents. Depending upon local laws, the tactics may be legal or illegal and include: strikes; hartal (staying home for a day or so, leaving factories and places of business empty); consumer boycotts or selective buying; rent strikes; school boycotts; and refusal to pay taxes.

Direct nonviolent intervention consists of physical confrontation rather than withdrawal of cooperation or demonstrating. It carries the conflict into the opponent's camp and often alters the status quo abruptly. There are several tactics involved, such as: sit-ins; pray-ins in churches; wade-ins on beaches; fasting; reverse strikes (working longer hours than called for in support of certain demands); and nonviolent interjection and obstruction (such as lying down on sidewalks or in front of bulldozers, or physically occupying a site).

The nonviolent strategy of *satyagraha* involves many of the tactics outlined by Oppenheimer and Lakey. "It is characterized by adherence to a stated truth by means of behavior which is not violent but which includes self-suffering" (Bondurant, 1972:303). This strategy was used during the Nationalist movement in India and involved the various methods of noncooperation and civil disobedience. Joan V. Bondurant (1972:305) outlines the various steps involved in a *satyagraha* campaign.

1. Attempt to resolve the conflict or grievance by negotiation and arbitration.
2. Prepare the group for direct action.
3. Engage in demonstrations and propaganda campaigns.
4. Try to appeal to the opponent for a final time; if there are no concessions, issue an ultimatum.
5. Engage in economic boycott and strikes of various forms.
6. Initiate actions of noncooperation with established authorities and institutions.
7. Engage in civil disobedience, but exercise care in selecting the laws to be violated;
8. Assume some of the functions of the government.
9. Establish a parallel government to handle those functions.

The *satyagraha* strategy is progressive in nature, and it can stop at any stage at which the opponents concede to the demands. In India, various groups have used this strategy and many of the steps were incorporated in civil rights and related activities in the United States.

No discussion of nonviolent tactics (or violent tactics) of social change should be complete without some reference to Saul Alinsky (1972:138–139), a master tactician in community organization. In his words:

> I have emphasized and re-emphasized that tactics means you do what you can with what you've got, and that power in the main has always gravitated towards those who have money and those whom people follow. The resources of the Have-Nots are (1) no money and (2) lots of people. All right, let's start from there. People can show their power by voting. What else? Well, they have physical bodies. How can they use them? Now a melange of ideas begins to appear. Use the power of the law by making the establishment obey its rules. Go outside the experience of the enemy, stay inside the experience of your people. Emphasize tactics that your people will enjoy. The threat is usually more terrifying than the tactic itself. Once all these rules and principles are festering in your imagination they grow into a synthesis . . . [for example] . . . I suggested that we might buy one hundred seats for one of Rochester's symphony concerts. We would select a concert in which the music was relatively quiet. The hundred blacks who would be given the tickets would first be treated to a three-hour pre-concert dinner in the community, in which they would be fed nothing but baked beans, and lots of them; then the people would go to the symphony hall—with obvious consequences. Imagine the scene when the action began! The concert would be over before the first movement! (If this be a Freudian slip—so be it.)

SOCIAL MOVEMENTS

Many of the strategies and tactics discussed thus far are often used by social movements. In Chapter 8, social movements were discussed in a different context, and they were defined as collectivities acting with some continuity to promote or resist change. Several types were identified such as revolutionary, reactionary, reform, and expressive movements. These various types of social movements have a number of common characteristics. Luther P. Gerlach and Virginia H. Hine (1973:169–190) elaborated on five such characteristics: type of organization structure, patterns of recruitment, ideology, personal commitment, and opposition, as follows:

1. The *organizational structure* of social movements is segmentary, composed of semiautonomous cells or segments. The movement organization is decentralized and polycephalous, or "many headed." Movements generally do not have a single paramount leader who controls through a coordinated organization; instead, each cell or unit has its own leader or leaders. The various organizational units are regulated by personal, structural, and ideological ties.

2. *Patterns of recruitment* follow lines of preexisting personal relationships and are based on face-to-face contact with friends, neighbors, associates, or colleagues.

3. Every movement has its *ideology*, which codifies values and goals, provides a conceptual framework for interpreting relevant experiences and events relative to these goals, motivates and provides rationale for the changes sought,

defines the opposition, and conceptually unites the fragmented groups in the movement.

4. A *commitment* is brought about by an act or experience that differentiates a participant in some important way from the established order, or his place in it, identifies him with a new set of values, and commits him to change patterns of behavior.

5. *Opposition*, which may be real or perceived, is essential to promote a movement and to offer a basis for its commitment process. It is a force against which participants of a movement can be united.

Roland L. Warren (1977:267) notes that social movements are not formal organizations, but they generally contain formal organizations that have important implications for the consideration of movement strategies.

> By their very nature, social movements do not act. Rather, within them, specific individuals and specific organizations take various actions . . . movement organizations do not of themselves constitute the entire social movement, since many adherents of the movement are not actually members of any of the movement organizations. Hence, much of the action that takes place on behalf of a social movement is action that is neither planned by nor controllable by any formal inclusive movement organization. One can speak of the strategies employed by these individuals, and by these organizations, but the movement itself, as an amorphous network of individuals and organizations linked in part formally but largely informally, has no strategy, does not plan, and does not act, and—for better or worse—is therefore largely uncontrollable.

A common strategy in a social movement is usually adopted by the numerous coalitions of various organizations formed within the movement. Because movements are multicentered, coordination of the various activities is typically problematic. Warren considers this a weakness of social movements. Lack of coordination results in duplication, wasted effort, inability for concerted action, inconsistent pursuit of intermediate objectives, conflicting loyalties, and internal strife. On the other hand, a movement's strengths are "in its variability, lack of rigidity, action through mutual adjustment and feedback providing resilience and flexibility, difficulty of hostile parties in finding a specific target for recrimination, and in the very redundancy of many of the efforts. These attributes make it difficult to direct and difficult to control, but also difficult to destroy" (Warren, 1977:268).

With these clarifications in mind concerning the composition of a social movement, let us consider the various change strategies used by the various organizations within the social movement. The strategies used in social movements have two fundamental objectives: One is to promote the growth of a social movement as a change-promoting system, and the other is to engage the change target. For the present purpose, the emphasis will be on the strategies used to engage the target.

Change Strategies

Several principal strategies are used by social movements in their attempt to influence the actions of their target systems. The main ones include bargaining, coercion, and persuasion (Turner & Killian, 1987:297–299). *Bargaining* "takes place when the movement has control over some exchangeable value that the target group wants and offers some of that value in return for compliance with its demands." Bargaining may entail the offer of votes or other support to the target group in return for support of the movement. *Coercion* is "the manipulation of the target group's situation in such fashion that the pursuit of any course of action other than that sought by the movement will be met by considerable cost or punishment." It is a form of negative bargaining in which the threat of harm rather than actual harm is considered. When harmful action is used, it is a way of demonstrating tactically that the movement has the real potential of inflicting harm. The extreme form of coercion is the threat of total destruction when the movement has the power to do so. Lesser forms include terrorism, civil disobedience, and assassination. *Persuasion* involves the use of symbolic manipulation without substantial rewards of punishments under the control of the movement. The procedure is to identify the proposed course of action with values held by the target group. It always includes calling attention to rewards and penalties that will ensue for the target group on the basis of various courses of action. It should be noted that these three general types of strategies are not mutually exclusive, and various combinations of the elements in all three may be used by any given movement to engage a target system.

John Wilson (1973:226–227) notes that many social movements are often remembered more for the tactics they used than for their objectives. For example, student movements such as the Free Speech Movement and Students for a Democratic Society have achieved their notoriety through the use of disruptive and violent tactics and not through the enunciated goals and objectives, which were poorly formulated by the leaders and dimly understood by the public at large. There are two reasons, Wilson (1973:227) points out, why tactics contribute to the establishment of the identity of a movement. First, social movements use methods of persuasion and coercion that are, more often than not, novel, dramatic, unorthodox, and of questionable legitimacy. Second, "tactics may be all there is to 'see' in the movement. Many social movements are not much more than tactical machines, having little substance beyond their efforts to bring some cause to the attention of the public or coerce some agent of authority." Again, for example, the Free Speech Movement defined its priorities in terms of tactical actions, and demonstrations of disruptive nature were given priortiy over other "projects such as building up a loyal following or establishing an organization" (p. 227).

Social movements employ a repertoire of strategies and tactics to influence change targets to help build up memberships, raise money, or influence politicians. At this point it should be noted again that there is a distinction between strategy, referring to a general design or plan of action, and tactics, which refer to specific means or methods of carrying out that plan or design. Tactics are specific techniques such as strikes, boycotts, and teach-ins that are deployed to implement strategies.

Change Tactics

The tactics used predominantly by social movements are called the "politics of disorder" by Wilson (1973:229) to "distinguish them from the 'politics of order,' in which reliance is placed on the courtroom, the legislature, and the mass media, and from the 'politics of violence,' in which the accepted rules of bringing about social change are rejected and resort is made to mob demonstrations, bombing, and physical assault." The tactics used in the politics of disorder fall under the heading of "direct action" and involve, among other things, demonstrations, economic boycotts, rent strikes, and sit-ins. It should be noted, however, that social movements also use the politics of order, such as petitions, lobbies, and selective voting, as well as violence, as evidenced by some members of the antibusing movement who tried to physically prevent the passage of school buses and by some members of the antiabortion movement who firebombed abortion clinics.

There are two reasons suggested by Wilson (1973:234) that social movements might select the politics of disorder. "The first is that social movements, usually propagating ideas which find little or no support among established groups, lacking in authority, and finding themselves excluded from the established networks of communication and the centers of power, reason that they must shout to make themselves heard. The second reason is simply that the politics of order have been tried and found wanting and a group which started out using the provided avenues of protest becomes a movement acting outside them."

It is obvious that not all tactics used by social movements are effective in advancing the movement toward its objective and maintaining, at the same time, followers as a united group. There is no way of telling in advance which tactic will be successful since a great deal depends on the movement's circumstances and resources and the opposition it encounters. Still, it is possible to make some general observations "about the qualities which tactics must have to prove of use to social movements" (p. 235). Wilson (1973:236) points out that a tactical program needs to meet three requirements: It must have breadth, simplicity, and flexibility. With regard to *breadth*, activities in which pressure is brought to bear on the target group from a number of fronts simultaneously would tend to be more effective than reliance merely on economic, political, or other measures. *Simplicity* means that the tactics should be manageable, and not too inconvenient and time-consuming for the members. *Flexibility* "means avoiding total and irrevocable commitment to any given set of tactics, and it means foresight and planning for the reactions which a given set of tactics is likely to provoke" (pp. 237–238). A movement should avoid employing all the power at its disposal in any given tactical campaign. In general, the tactics used by social movements work only so long as they contain an element of surprise.

The choice of tactics by a social movement is determined by three factors: opposition, ideology, and public opinion. With regard to *opposition*, Wilson (1973) suggests that "All social movements find themselves in a subordinate position of power relative to the group they are trying to defeat or win over" (p. 239). He distinguishes three degrees of subordination: partial inequality, dependency, and subjugation. In a situation of *partial inequality*, a movement is composed of "minority people who are granted equal status on some grounds but not on others (homosexuals), or consists of people agitating on behalf of a deprived group (students in the South, Pentecostals), or people acting as guardians of the national conscience, attempting to reverse social policies considered immoral (nuclear pacifists, prohibitionists)" (pp. 239–240). In these instances movements are reluctant to resort to tactics of "questionable legitimacy." In a *dependency* situation, the movement is made up of minority people "who feel at the mercy of the target group." They want to improve their position, but they believe they cannot do so without the help of the target group. The object is to win over the target group rather than to defeat it. The movement must use patience to educate, persuade, and set an example. The women's suffrage movement would be indicative of this situation. In the situation of *subjugation*, "the minority group from which the movement draws its following is completely dominated by the majority group to the extent of economic exploitation and the deprivation of civil rights" (p. 241). There is no value consensus with the target group and there is no likelihood of enlisting its help. Any progress to be made will be through the group's own efforts and by means of its own resources. The object of the movement here is to defeat the opponent, and the tactics that are used include harassment, obstruction, personal assault, destruction of property, and so on. The use of illegal tactics is justified because the system itself is considered illegal. An illustration of such a movement would be the Black Panthers.

The second determinant of the choice of tactics is *ideology*. In general, the specific tactics selected will be in accord with the values a movement espouses. Most movements have a set of statements about which means are appropriate for the realization of a given set of objectives. As a result, "social movement tactics show a strain toward symbolic, meaningful consistency with the movement's values, even if this means that opposition to the movement is intensified, the burdens placed upon the membership are increased, or the most pragmatically efficient means of attaining the movement's goals are rejected" (p. 245). Ideological factors are also pronounced when issues of alliances become important.

The final determinant of the selection of tactics is *public opinion*. As Wilson (1973:251) writes: "Social movements, to achieve their goals, and lacking the authoritative means to do so, must establish their credentials with the general public. They must gain the support of public opinion (or at least not alienate it) even though they are seeking, in the long run, to change it. Specifically, this means that tactics must be chosen which will generate public sympathy or at least not deviate from prevailing social attitudes toward appropriate collective acts . . . no social movement will succeed in bringing about large-scale social change unless it wins public sympathy or at least acquiescence for its activities."

In the context of public opinion, the choice of violent tactics is generally detrimental to movements. The public may feel threatened by the use of violent tactics, and at the same time, may also be alienated by movements using them. Public opinion can also be a factor in deciding which movements should be politically active. In such instances, care should be exercised by movements not to use tactics that might confirm the public notion that the group is socially unfit to make political or economic judgments. For example, the feminist movement suffered during the early stages because the tactics used by many groups were contrary to the popular image of ladylike conduct.

In brief, the rationale for choosing a set of tactics is not necessarily reflected in the movement's objectives. The selection of tactics is "a function of a number of social forces impinging on the social movement, among the most important of which are the action of the opposition, the moral constraints implicit in the ideology, and the prevailing social attitudes toward social protest. The combination of these factors provides many configurations" (Wilson, 1973:256).

Accomplishments of Social Movements

Thus far the discussion has centered on the types of social movements, the principal strategies they employ, and the conditions that determine the use of specific tactics. The remainder of this section will address the question: What are some of the specific accomplishments of social movements? As Lewis Killian notes (1964), the significance of any social movement must be found in the consequences that the movement has had for the larger society or for the social order from which it emerged. That is, has the movement led to any significant social or cultural change? Unless this question can be answered affirmatively, Killian asserts that the movement is little more than a passing curiosity or a sidelight of history. In one study of 53 movements between 1800 and 1945, about half of the movements were unsuccessful in bringing about any of the changes they sought (Gamson, 1975). In many other cases, Killian's question can be answered affirmatively. Early labor movements, for example, eventually brought an end to child labor in American factories. Labor movements were also responsible for gaining shorter working hours, safer working conditions, and the right for collective bargaining. Legislation protecting the environment is another area in which social movements have been successful. The product-safety movement resulted in a variety of safety devices, including the installation of automobile seat belts (Turner & Killian, 1987:397). Let us consider briefly two other movements, the civil rights and women's movements, that have attempted to overcome social inequities that existed in the recent past.

Civil rights movements have contributed to a series of legal reforms of considerable importance and impact. Some of the most notable of these reforms were *Brown* vs. *Board of Education of Topeka, Kansas*, a Supreme Court case in 1954; the Civil Rights Acts of 1957, 1960, 1964, and 1968; the Voting Rights Act of 1965; and President Nixon's Executive Order 11478, issued in 1969 (U.S. Commission on Civil Rights, 1975).

In the 1954 decision the Supreme Court reversed the *Plessy* vs. *Ferguson* decision of 1896 (which had allowed separate but equal education facilities for blacks and whites to be imposed by the states), saying that "segregation, with the sanction of the law, therefore has the tendency to retard the education and mental development of Negro children and to deprive them of some of the benefits they would receive in a racially integrated system" (Marden & Meyer, 1968).

The Civil Rights Act of 1957 followed on the heels of the early victories of the civil rights movement and constituted a countermeasure to the strong opposition in the South to the *Brown* vs. *Board of Education* decision of the Supreme Court. It was the first civil rights legislation to be enacted since 1875. Its accomplishments were to establish a Civil Rights Commission, to gather data on voting violations, to empower the Justice Department to initiate action where voting violations occurred in federal elections, and to require nondiscriminatory qualifications for the selection of juries in federal courts. This relatively innocuous legislation was topped by the Civil Rights Act of 1960, which was designed to impede interracial violence without eroding the power and authority of state officials (Blaustein & Zangrando, 1968).

In 1964 and 1968 Congress enacted Civil Rights Acts that were far more extensive than any such preceding laws in American history. They included detailed provisions to ensure equality in the areas of voting, public accommodations and facilities, education, and employment. Desegregation problems of school districts were to be aided by funds and training handled by the Department of Health, Education, and Welfare.

The 1965 march from Selma to Montgomery led to another piece of legislation: the Voting Rights Act of 1965. This assigned federal examiners to register voters and to observe elections in states or counties where discrimination existed. Literacy tests and other discriminatory means of limiting voter participation were outlawed. The act was constructed so as to help the poor, uneducated, or other minority groups as well as blacks. In Executive Order 11478, Nixon went beyond the former, more or less passive federal support of equality of opportunity and employment, and ordered that federal agencies develop affirmative programs in which minority applicants would be actively sought out and specifically trained to perform at their highest potential. The Civil Service Commission was given the power to enforce the executive order and, in particular, to consider all complaints of discrimination in federal employment based on race, color, religion, sex, or national origin (U.S. Commission on Civil Rights, 1975). These are just some of many legislative changes in which civil rights movements played an important role.

Among the civil rights movements, the women's liberation movements have also made important strides against a series of discriminatory practices in legal, financial, political, and educational arenas. The best known of these movements is the National Organization for Women, formed by Betty Friedan in 1966 "to bring women into full participation in the mainstream of the American society *now*" (Gruberg, 1968:105). Others include the American Association of University Women and a series of professional groups and caucuses such as Sociologists for Women in Society.

To meet the demands of feminist movements for equal access of women to all political and economic opportunities, Congress has passed civil rights legislation covering women as well as ethnic minorities, and at least two executive orders (Nos. 11246 and 11375) have been issued intended to prevent discrimination on the basis of sex in government and industry. For the record, it should be pointed out that when Title VII of the proposed Civil Rights Act of 1964 was initially reported out of the House Judiciary Committee, it included prohibitions of employment discrimination based on race, color, religion, or national origin—but not sex. It was only one day before the passage of the act that an amendment was offered to include a ban on sex discrimination in an apparent attempt to kill the bill. But it passed the House and the Senate and the sex discrimination provisions in Title VII remained as a milestone for women seeking equal employment opportunities with men (U.S. Commission on Civil Rights, 1975:20).

In addition to employment and political participation, the feminist movements were instrumental in advancing a concentration of reforms in state and federal laws (Kanowitz, 1969). They include remedial measures to overcome injustice and discrimination in the provisions on marriage, property, support, divorce, health, birth control, abortion, sterilization, finances, taxes, consumer credit, housing, and welfare.

In the realm of sexual behavior there have been some movements aimed at bringing about reform. For prostitutes there is a nationwide movement and an organization named "Call Off Your Old Tired Ethics" (COYOTE), which had its first national convention in San Francisco in June 1974 at the Glide Memorial Methodist Church. Described by its "founding mother," retired prostitute Margo St. James, as a "loose woman's organization," COYOTE works for the legalization of prostitution and for the protection of prostitutes' civil liberties. Until prostitution is legalized in a given area, however, COYOTE advocates the arrest of the customer as well as the prostitutes, not only in the interest of equal justice, but also because, as Ms. St. James has put it, "men won't change the laws unless they get their nuts caught in the cracker, too." Feminist groups such as NOW also regard the antiprostitution laws and ordinances as highly discriminary against women and they would prefer the abolition of such laws on the grounds that a person's sexual behavior is properly her own private affair; they insist that as long as there are laws, they should be made to apply to male customers as well as to female prostitutes (Berman, 1974).

It is still a far stride to NOW's Bill of Rights (Morgan, 1970:512), but the changes wrought by the women's movements are evident in many areas of life. This may have been a reason for the decline in NOW membership: In 1982, it had 250,000 members, but by 1987 it was down to 150,000 (Peirce, 1987:3B). Another reason for the decline is that the women's agenda has ballooned far past the feminist causes that NOW traditionally stressed. Since 1982, women have moved day care, welfare reform, child-support payments, and maternal and child care into the political mainstream of state legislatures. The years of efforts are paying off in more and more bills ensuring equality for women on every front, from insurance to taxes, to salary and pensions. At the same time, there is a growing belief that women's rights are being abandoned in today's conservative climate, and this belief is most pronounced among younger women to whom feminist struggles are seen as past history (Leslie & Korman, 1985:73). The next section will consider law as an instrument of social change.

LAW AND SOCIAL CHANGE

The relationship between law and social change is reciprocal, and law can be seen as both an effect and cause of social change (Champagne & Nagel, 1983:187; Vago, 1988:219). In this section, law will be considered only as an active instrument for guiding and shaping future behavior and social forms—that is, as a strategy of social change.

Many historical examples abound in which laws have been used to create broad changes in society. Since Roman times, laws have been instrumental in effecting changes at all levels in society. There are several illustrations of the idea that law, far from being simply a reflection of social reality, is a powerful means of *accomplishing* reality—that is, fashioning it or making it. In spite of the ideas of Marx, Engels, and Lenin that law is an epiphenomenon of bourgeois class society doomed to vanish with the advent of the Revolution, the Soviet Union succeeded in making enormous changes in society by the use of laws (Dror, 1968). More recently, the attempts by Nazi Germany, and later on by Eastern European countries, to make wholesale social changes through the use of laws—such as income redistribution, nationalization of industry, land reform and introduction of collective farms, provision of free education and health care, and the restructuring of the stratification system—are examples of the effectiveness of law to induce change (Eorsi & Harmathy, 1971). When the Communists seized power in China in 1949, virtually all vices ubiquitous in Western countries—pornography, prostitution, gambling, and usury—were eliminated by government decree along with business operations that were dependent on profits from such activities (Vago, 1988:224).

Recognition of the role of law as a strategy of change is becoming more pronounced in contemporary society (Lempert & Sanders, 1986:352–427). It is now generally accepted that the "law . . . increasingly not only articulates but sets the course for major social changes" (W. Friedmann, 1972:513) and "attempted social change through law is a basic trait of the modern world" (L. Friedman, 1975:277). An almost identical observation is made by Yehezkel Dror (1968:673) in stating: "the growing use of law as a device of organized social action directed toward achieving social change seems to be one of the characteristics of modern society. . . ." In an influential article entitled "Law and Social Change," Dror (1968) distinguishes between the indirect and direct aspects of law in social change.

Dror (1968:673) argues that "law plays an important indirect role in social change by shaping various social institutions, which in turn have a direct impact on society." He uses the illustration of the compulsory education system, which performed an important indirect role in regard to change by fostering the operation of educational institutions, which in turn play a direct role in social change. He points out in the discussion that law interacts in many cases directly with basic social institutions, constituting a direct relationship between law and social change. For example, a law enacted to prohibit polygamy has a great direct influence on social change, having as its main purpose alterations in important patterns of behavior. He warns, however, that "The distinction is not an absolute but a relative one: in some cases the emphasis is more on the direct and less on the indirect impact of social change, while in other cases the opposite is true" (Dror, 1968:674).

Dror contends that law exerts an indirect influence on social change in general by influencing the possibilities of change in various social institutions. For example, the existence of a patent law protecting the rights of inventors encourages inventions and furthers change in the technological institutions that in turn may bring about other types of social change.

For all modern societies, every collection of statutes and delegated legislation is "full of illustrations of the direct use of law as a device for directed social change" (Dror, 1968:676). A good example to induce social change by law directly was the enactment of Prohibition in the United States to shape social behavior. (It was also one of the most conspicuous failures, showing that there are limits to the effective use of law to bring about social change.) Others would include the use of legislative powers to bring about extensive changes in social structure and culture, as evidenced in Japan and Turkey, where large segments of Western law were received with the intention of advancing the Westernization process of these countries.

Another way of looking at the role of law in social change is in terms of Mayhew's (1971:195) notion of the possibility of either redefining the normative order or creating new procedural opportunities within the legal apparatus. He calls the first an "extension of formal rights," illustrated by the pronouncement of the Supreme Court that the defendant accused of serious crimes has the right to professional representation. The second is termed the "extension of formal facilities" and is illustrated by the establishment of a system of public defenders who provide the required professional representation. The extension of formal rights and of formal facilities have definite implications.

A rather different perspective on law in social change is presented by L. Friedman. He refers to change through law in terms of two types: "planning" and "disruption." Planning "refers to architectural construction of new forms of social order and social interaction. Disruption refers to the blocking or amelioration of existing social forms and relations" (L. Friedman, 1973:25). Both operated within the existing legal system and can bring about "positive" or "negative" social change, depending on one's perspective.

Lawrence Friedman (1975:277) infers that revolution is the most distinct and obvious form of disruption. But

> milder forms are everywhere. Judicial review is frequently disruptive. American courts have smashed programs and institutions from the Missouri Compromise to the Alaska pipeline. Activist reformers have played a sensational role in American life in the last decade. Ralph Nader is the most well-known example. . . . He stimulates use of legal processes as a lever of social change. Much of his work is technically disruptive; it focuses on litigation and injunctions, on stopping government dead in its tracks, when it fails to meet his ethical and policy standards. Legal disruption can . . . include lawsuits; particularly after *Brown* v. *Board of Education*, reformers have frequently gone to court to upset many old and established arrangements.

Social change through litigation has always been an important feature in the United States. Whether or not the change brought about by such action is destructive or constructive depends on one's interpretation. The fact remains that law can be highly effective in producing social change. For example, when the California Supreme Court destroyed the legal basis for the system of financing schools in the state, Friedman (1973:27) succinctly observed: "Many a *coup d'état* in small countries have achieved less social change than this quiet *coup d'état* in the courts."

Friedman refers to this as an American phenomenon and raises the question: Will this spread to other countries? His response is that creative disruption of the judicial type presupposes a number of conditions that rarely coincide and are apparently not present in other countries to the same degree. These conditions include an activist legal profession, financial resources, activist judges, a genuine social movement, and what he describes as "the strongest condition," the fact that in the United States "Elites—the power holders—must accept the results of disruptive litigation, like it or not" (L. Friedman, 1975:278). Clearly, no socialist or authoritarian country will tolerate anything like the American form of judicial review. Their legal structures are not designed to accommodate these patterns.

In the context of litigation, the role of the Supreme Court in social change invites attention. While discussing the Supreme Court's ability to influence social change, Grossman (1970:545) suggested that the Court can "offer some limited support to social change by not deciding a case where its refusal to decide upholds or reinforces a lower court decision which itself favors change by legitimizing a governmental change policy, and also by refusing to decide a case in which a lower court decision has gone against forces seeking to preserve the status quo." There are, however, several momentous ways in which the Court, indeed, can influence social change; such as: (1) by a conscious and explicit program of innovation that may specify particular behavior changes, (2) by reinforcement of prior policy decisions seeking change against challenges to their authority or legitimacy, (3) by reinforcement or legitimation of the change-oriented policies of other governmental agencies or of important groups in society, (4) by specific invalidation of symbolic challenges to social change processes or policies (Grossman, 1970:545).

A good illustration of the role of the U.S. Supreme Court in social change is its 1973 decision on abortion, striking down most state laws prohibiting abortion and providing specific guidelines regulating lawmaking in this area. This decision is an important one, not only because of the sweeping consequences it has for most states, and despite the reputed conservatism of the new appointees to the Court, but also because of the role the Court continues to play in social change. It is able to act on controversial questions of law when the legislatures cannot or will not act on controversial social issues. In this manner, it relieves one kind of buildup of political and social pressure through changes in the interpretation of law at times when most legislatures prefer to ignore the problem or heed them much more slowly.

Few sociologists and legal scholars today would accept the notion of Sumner (1906) that folkways and mores change slowly in response to modifications in conditions of social existence and in the interests of various groups. A body of research is accumulating, and theoretical perspectives have been presented that attempt to establish when and under what conditions law can "not only *codify* existing customs, morals, or mores, but also . . . *modify* the behavior and values presently existing in a particular society" (Evan, 1965:286). As William M. Evan (1965:286-287) lucidly articulates this position:

> As an instrument of social change, law entails two interrelated processes: the institutionalization and the internalization of patterns of behavior. In this context, institutionalization of a pattern of behavior means the establishment of a norm with provisions for its enforcement, and internalization of a pattern of behavior means the incorporation of the value or values implicit in a law. . . . Law can affect behavior directly only through the process of institutionalization; if, however, the institutionalization process is successful, it, in turn, facilitates the internalization of attitudes or beliefs.

However, the extent to which the impact of law is felt and the degree to which it can be efficient vary according to the conditions present in a particular situation. The following stipulations can have great bearing on the effectiveness of law as a strategy of social change: (1) The law must emanate from an authoritative and prestigeful source; (2) the law must introduce its rationale in terms that are understandable and compatible with existing values; (3) the advocates of the change should make reference to other communities or countries with which the population identifies and where the law is already in effect; (4) the enforcement of the law must be aimed toward making the change in a relatively short time; (5) those enforcing the law must themselves be very much committed to the change intended by the law; (6) the implementation of the law should include positive as well as negative sanctions; and (7) the enforcement of the law should be reasonable not only in terms of the sanctions used but also in the protection of the rights of those who stand to lose by violation of the law (Evan, 1965:288–291).

Chin and Benne (1985:41–42) justly include law under the power-coercive approaches to effecting social change. Law in society is backed by legitimate authority, which has the mechanisms to enforce compliance in several ways. For example, in the context of analyzing incentives for compliance with environmental law, Stuart S. Nagel (1975:341–356) discussed the following methods: (1) sliding fees that go down as a reward for high compliance and go up for low compliance; (2) contingent injunctions that enjoin certain activities subject to the possibility of jailing for contempt if the noncomplying behavior is not changed; (3) the use of tax deductions, credits, exemptions, and subsidies to encourage compliance; (4) civil penalties whereby private persons can bring lawsuits for damages caused by noncompliance; (5) adversely publicizing wrongdoers; (6) the use of selective government buying power to reward high compliers and thereby punish some noncompliers; (7) fines and jail sentences; and (8) conference persuasion.

Thus far, the discussion highlighted some of the general conditions in which law can be considered as a strategy of social change. Perhaps the best way to illustrate how law can be used as an instrument of change is to turn to a concrete case.

In the mid-1960s the author had undertaken a study of wage garnishment (a process that enables a creditor upon a debtor's default to seize his wages in the hands of his employer prior to being paid to the debtor) on low-income families. The findings indicated that existing wage garnishment laws at that time in Missouri were more counterproductive than functional as a collection device. It was shown, among other things, that a number of employers had immediately dismissed employees upon the receipt of the first garnishment suit and that such an action was detrimental not only to the debtor but also to the creditor, the employer, and society at large. Moreover, in many cases the judgment debtors were often "judgment-proof" in the sense that they had few, if any, tangible assets. Under the former system, garnishment proceedings may be instituted to attach wages due to the debtor by an employer and have the employer pay these wages to the creditor through the court. The objective of the proposed reform was to present a procedure to provide the judgment debtor who is being garnished protection from possible dismissal from his job or from bankruptcy and, at the same time, to enable creditors to maintain an effective collection method.

On the basis of the author's data and recommendations, House Bill 279 was designed and introduced in the 74th General Assembly of the State of Missouri. Under the proposed bill, the service of the writ would be made upon the defendant only, and the employer of the defendant would not be involved in the litigation process. Upon entry of the judgment, the court may order the judgment debtor to make payments to the clerk of the court. The payments would be dispersed in turn by the clerk. In settling the amount of these payments, the court would take into consideration the circumstances of the defendant, including his or her income and other obligations or considerations bearing on the issue. If the judgment debtor fails to obey the order of the court, *then and only then* may the creditor summon the employer as a garnishee. The primary intention of the bill was to prohibit employers from discharging employees upon the receipt of the first garnishment suit, thus saving thousands of jobs for low-income individuals annually in Missouri. It was estimated that on the national level, approximately 500,000 individuals are fired each year as a direct result of the practice of wage garnishment. The societal implications of the proposed change are obvious (Vago, 1968:7–20). Today, wage garnishment is regulated nationally. This is the result of the Consumer Credit Protection Act (P.L. 90–321), passed in 1968. The act protects consumers from being driven into bankruptcy by excessive garnishment of wages by limiting the amount of wages subject to garnishment to 25 percent of the employee's weekly disposable income. It also prohibits an employer from firing an employee solely because of wage garnishment (Vago, 1988:130).

SUMMARY

This chapter considered several social change strategies and tactics used in a variety of change efforts. Three aspects of planned social change were discussed—targets, agents, and methods. The target for planned change may be conceptualized on several levels, and for the present purposes, individual, intermediate, and macrolevel target systems were discussed. Change agents are usually professionals who influence the change effort in a direction deemed desirable by a change agency. There are two broad categories of change agents: leaders and supporters. There are many categorizations in the typologies of planned change strategies, and the principal methods can be subsumed under facilitative, reeducative, persuasive, and power strategies.

The use of violent strategies of social change is as old as humans. Their effectiveness is based on the willingness of certain segments of a society to go beyond the accepted patterns of action to promote change. The use of such a strategy entails the perception of relative deprivation among a potentially violent group, the maximization of the intensity of anger, and the emphasis of social facilitation variables. In most instances in the literature, violent strategies are not considered as desirable means for including social change.

Nonviolent strategies of change also have a long history. They are based, to a great extent, on "moral power," and they are likely to be effective when they are in accord with the value orientation of the change target and pertinent third parties. The choice of nonviolent strategy can reflect either an indirect or direct approach to the opponent's power. The former is based on the decision to meet the violent style of the opponent with nonviolence. The latter is founded on attempts to upset the opponent's power base, alter the opponent's attitudes and public image, and the opinion of third parties. The tactics of nonviolence can be classified under the headings of demonstration, noncooperation, and direct intervention. The nonviolent strategy of *satyagraha* involves many of these tactics.

The various types of social movements discussed have a number of characteristics in common, including an organizational structure, patterns of recruitment, ideology, personal commitment, and an opposition or target system. A common strategy in a social movement is generally adopted by the numerous coalitions of various organizations formed within the movement. The principal strategies used by movements in their attempts to influence the actions of their target systems are bargaining, coercion, and persuasion. Many of the movements are remembered more for the tactics they have deployed rather than for their objectives. The tactics used by social movements have been referred to as the "politics of disorder." A tactical program should have breadth, simplicity, and flexibility. The tactics used in a social movement are determined, to a great extent, by three factors: opposition, ideology, and public opinion.

There is a growing recognition of the role of law as a strategy of social change in contemporary society. Law can play an indirect role in social change by altering various social institutions, which in turn have a direct impact on society. Law can also exert a direct influence by legitimizing certain programs or procedures and delegitimizing traditional practices. In the United States, change through law may originate in one of four arenas: the judiciary, the legislature, the executive, and administrative agencies. Law is classified under power-coercive approaches to social change, and it is backed by legitimate authority, which has the mechanisms to enforce compliance. The chapter concluded with a concrete illustration of how law was used to induce change in the context of wage garnishment.

SUGGESTED FURTHER READINGS

BENNIS, WARREN G., KENNETH D. BENNE, and ROBERT CHIN, eds. *The Planning of Change*, 4th ed. New York: Holt, Rinehart & Winston, 1985. A good collection of articles on the various aspects of planned social change.

HORNSTEIN, HARVEY A., BARBARA BENEDICT BUNKER, W. WARNER BURKE, MARION GINDES, and ROY J. LEWICKI, eds. *Social Intervention, a Behavioral Science Approach*. New York: Free Press, 1971. An anthology of articles on diverse change strategies. The introduction to these various parts and the discussions are all highly comprehensive, and the sections on violent and nonviolent strategies are recommended.

KETTNER, PETER M., JOHN M. DALEY, and ANN WEAVER NICHOLS. *Initiating Change in Organizations and Communities: A Macro Practice Model*. Monterey, Calif.: Brooks/Cole 1985. A presentation of an integrated model for initiating and carrying out changes in organizations and communities.

SEIDMAN, EDWARD, ed. *Handbook of Social Intervention*. Beverly Hills, Calif.: Sage Publications, Inc., 1983. A compendium on the ways of creating change in a variety of settings.

TURNER, RALPH H., and LEWIS M. KILLIAN. *Collective Behavior*, 3rd ed. Englewood Cliffs, N.J.: Prentice-Hall, 1987. See Part Four for an up-to-date comprehensive review of social movements and their change strategies and tactics.

VAGO, STEVEN. *Law and Society*, 2nd ed. Englewood Cliffs, N.J.: Prentice-Hall, 1988. See, in particular, Chapter 7 on the role of law in social change.

WARREN, ROLAND L. *Social Change and Human Purpose: Toward Understanding and Action*. Chicago: Rand McNally, 1977. A systematic discussion of purposive social change at several levels in society.

ZALTMAN, ERALD, and ROBERT DUNCAN. *Strategies for Planned Change*. New York: Wiley, 1977. This book describes in succinct ways the various strategies and tactics available for creating social change.

ZALTMAN, GERALD, PHILIP KOTLER, and IRA KAUFMAN, eds. *Creating Social Change.* New York: Holt, Rinehart & Winston, 1972. A comprehensive reader on the various strategies of social change.

REFERENCES

ALBRECHT, STAN L., BRUCE A. CHADWICK, and CARDEL K. JACOBSON. *Social Psychology,* 2nd ed., Englewood Cliffs, N.J.: Prentice-Hall, 1987.

ALINSKY, SAUL. *Rules for Radicals.* New York: Vintage, 1972.

BENNE, KENNETH D. "The Current State of Planned Changing in Persons, Groups, Communities, and Societies." In Warren G. Bennis, Kenneth D. Benne, and Robert Chin, (eds.), *The Planning of Change,* 4th ed. New York: Holt, Rinehart & Winston, 1985, pp. 68–82.

BENNIS, WARREN G., KENNETH D. BENNE, and ROBERT CHIN, eds. *The Planning of Change,* 4th ed. New York: Holt, Rinehart & Winston, 1985.

BERMAN, HARRIET KATZ. "Quarantine: Policing Prostitution." *Civil Liberties,* 301, March 1974, p. 1.

BLAUSTEIN, ALBERT P., and ROBERT L. ZANGRANDO. *Civil Rights and the Black American: A Documentary History.* New York: Simon & Schuster, 1968.

BLUMER, HERBERT. "Social Movements." In Serge Denisoff (ed.), *The Sociology of Dissent.* New York: Harcourt, 1974, pp. 4–20.

BONDURANT, JOAN V. "Satyagraha as Applied Socio-Political Action." In Gerald Zaltman, Philip Kotler, and Ira Kaufman (eds.), *Creating Social Change.* New York: Holt, Rinehart & Winston, 1972, pp. 303–313.

CHAMPAGNE, ANTHONY, and STUART S. NAGEL. "Law and Social Change." In Edward Seidman (ed.), *Handbook of Social Intervention.* Beverly Hills, Calif.: Sage Publications, Inc., 1983, pp. 187–211.

CHIN, ROBERT, and KENNETH D. BENNE. "General Strategies for Effecting Changes in Human Systems." In Warren G. Bennis, Kenneth D. Benne, and Robert Chin (eds.), *The Planning of Change,* 4th ed. New York: Holt, Rinehart & Winston, 1985, pp. 22–45.

DEUTSCH, MORTON, and MARY EVANS COLLINS. "Interracial Housing." In William Peterson (ed.), *American Social Patterns.* New York: Doubleday, 1965, pp. 7–62.

DOWNES, BRYAN T. "A Critical Reexamination of the Social and Political Characteristics of Riot Cities." *Social Science Quarterly,* 51(2), 1970, pp. 349–360.

DROR, YEHEZKEL. "Law and Social Change." In Rita James Simon (ed.), *The Sociology of Law.* San Francisco: Chandler, 1968, pp. 663–680.

EORSI, GYULA, and ATTILA HARMATHY. *Law and Economic Reform in Socialistic Countries.* Budapest: Akademiai Kiado, 1971.

EVAN, WILLIAM M. "Law as an Instrument of Social Change." In A.W. Gouldner and S.M. Miller (eds.), *Applied Sociology: Opportunities and Problems.* New York: Free Press, 1965, pp. 285–293.

FANON, FRANZ. *The Wretched of the Earth.* New York: Grove Press, 1968.

FRIEDMAN, LAWRENCE M. "General Theory of Law and Social Change." In J.S. Ziegel (ed.), *Law and Social Change.* Toronto: Osgoode Hall Law School/York University, 1973, pp. 17–33.

FRIEDMAN, LAWRENCE M. *The Legal System: A Social Science Perspective.* New York: Russell Sage, 1975.

FRIEDMANN, WOLFGANG G. *Law in a Changing Society,* 2nd ed. New York: Columbia University Press, 1972.

GAMSON, WILLIAM A. *The Strategy of Social Protest.* Homewood, Ill.: Dorsey Press, 1975.

GERLACH, LUTHER P., and VIRGINIA H. HINE. *The Dynamics of Change in America.* Minneapolis: University of Minnesota Press, 1973.

GROSSCUP, BEAU. *The Explosion of Terrorism.* Far Hills, N.J.: New Horizon Press, 1987.

GROSSMAN, JOEL B. "The Supreme Court and Social Change: A Preliminary Inquiry." *American Behavioral Scientist,* 13, 1970, pp. 535–551.

GRUBERG, MARTIN. *Women in American Politics: An Assessment and Sourcebook.* Oshkosh, Wisc.: Academia Press, 1968.

GURR, TED R. *The Conditions of Civil Violence: First Test of a Causal Model.* Monograph 28, Princeton, N.J.: Princeton University Press, 1967. Center for International Studies.

HALL, RICHARD H. *Organizations: Structures, Processes, and Outcomes,* 4th ed. Englewood Cliffs, N.J.: Prentice-Hall, 1987.

HORNSTEIN, HARVEY H., BARBARA BENEDICT BUNKER, W. WARNER BURKE, MARION GINDES, and ROY J. LEWICKI, eds. *Social Intervention: A Behavioral Science Approach.* New York: Free Press, 1971.

HUNTINGTON, SAMUEL P. "Reform and Political Change." In Gerald Zaltman, Philip Kotler, and Ira Kaufman (eds.), *Creating Social Change.* New York: Holt, Rinehart & Winston, 1972, pp. 274–284.

KANOWITZ, LEO. *Women and the Law: The Unfinished Revolution.* Albuquerque: University of New Mexico Press, 1969.

KANTER, ROSABETH MOSS. *The Change Masters: Innovations for Productivity in the American Corporation.* New York: Simon & Schuster, 1983.

KELMAN, HERBERT C. "Manipulation of Human Behavior." In Gerald Zaltman, Philip Kotler, and Ira Kaufman (eds.) *Creating Social Change.* New York: Holt, Rinehart & Winston, 1972, pp. 574–584.

KETTNER, PETER M., JOHN M. DALEY, and ANN WEAVER NICHOLS. *Initiating Change in Organizations and Communities: A Macro Practice Model.* Monterey, Calif.: Brooks/Cole, 1985.

KILLIAN, LEWIS. "Social Movements." In Robert E.L. Faris (ed.), *Handbook of Modern Sociology.* Chicago: Rand McNally, 1964, pp. 426–455.

KOTLER, PHILIP. "The Five C's: Cause, Change Agency, Change Target, Channel, and Change Strategy." In Gerald Zaltman, Philip Kotler, and Ira Kaufman (eds.), *Creating Social Change.* New York: Holt, Rinehart & Winston, 1972, pp. 172–186.

LAUER, ROBERT H. *Perspectives on Social Change,* 3rd ed. Boston: Allyn & Bacon, 1982.

LEMPERT, RICHARD, and JOSEPH SANDERS. *An Invitation to Law and Social Science: Desert, Disputes, and Distribution.* New York: Longman, 1986.

LESLIE, GERALD R., and SHEILA K. KORMAN. *The Family in Social Context,* 6th ed. New York: Oxford, 1985.

LIPPITT, RONALD, JEANNE WATSON, and BRUCE WESTLEY. *The Dynamics of Planned Change.* New York: Harcourt, 1958.

LUTTWAK, EDWARD. *Coup d'Etat: A Practical Handbook.* Cambridge, Mass.: Harvard University Press, 1979.

MARDEN, CHARLES F., and GLADYS MEYER. *Minorities in American Society.* New York: American Book, 1968.

MARIGHELLA, CARLOS. *The Terrorist Classic: Manual of The Urban Guerrilla.* Chapel Hill, N.C.: Documentary Publications, 1985.

MAYHEW, LEON H. "Stability and Change in Legal Systems." In Bernard Barber and Alex Inkeles (eds.), *Stability and Social Change.* Boston: Little, Brown, 1971, pp. 187–210.

MOORE, WILBERT E. *Social Change,* 2nd ed. Englewood Cliffs, N.J.: Prentice-Hall, 1974.

MORGAN, ROBIN. *Sisterhood Is Powerful: An Anthology of Writings from the Women's Liberation Movement.* New York: Random House, 1970.

NAGEL, STUART S. *Improving the Legal Process.* Lexington, Mass.: Heath, 1975.

NIEBURG, H.L. "The Threat of Violence and Social Change." In Gerald Zaltman, Philip Kotler, and Ira Kaufman (eds.), *Creating Social Change.* New York: Holt, Rinehart & Winston, 1972, pp. 161–171.

OPPENHEIMER, MARTIN. *The Urban Guerrilla.* Chicago: Quadrangle Press, 1969.

OPPENHEIMER, MARTIN and GEORGE LAKEY. "Direct Action Tactics." In Gerald Zaltman, Philip Kotler, and Ira Kaufman (eds.), *Creating Social Change.* New York: Holt, Rinehart & Winston, 1972, pp. 313–319.

PEIRCE, NEAL. "Women Advocates Are Now in System." *St. Louis Post-Dispatch,* August 14, 1987, p. 3B.

ROGERS, EVERETT M. "Change Agents, Client, and Change." In Gerald Zaltman, Philip Kotler, and Ira Kaufman (eds.), *Creating Social Change.* New York: Holt, Rinehart & Winston, 1972, pp. 194–213.

SAGE, WAYNE. "Crime and the Clockwork Lemon." In Charles H. Swanson (ed.), *Focus: Unexplored Deviance.* Guilford, Conn.: Dushkin Publishing Group, 1977, pp. 79–84.

SHARPE, GENE. "Mechanisms of Change in Nonviolent Action." In Harvey A. Hornstein, Barbara Benedict Bunker, W. Warner Burke, Marion Gindes, and Roy J. Lewicki (eds.), *Social Intervention: A Behavioral Science Approach.* New York: Free Press, 1971, pp. 546–557.

SKOLNICK, JEROME H. *The Politics of Protest.* New York: Ballantine, 1969.

SUMNER, WILLIAM G. *Folkways.* Boston: Ginn, 1906.

TURNER, RALPH H., and LEWIS M. KILLIAN. *Collective Behavior*, 3rd ed. Englewood Cliffs, N.J.: Prentice-Hall, 1987.

U.S. Commission on Civil Rights. *Twenty Years After Brown: Equality of Economic Opportunity.* Washington, D.C.: Government Printing Office (630–354/396, July 1975).

VAGO, STEVEN. "Wage Garnishment: An Exercise in Futility Under Present Law." *Journal of Consumer Affairs*, 2, 1968, pp. 7–20.

VAGO, STEVEN. *Law and Society*, 2nd ed., Englewood Cliffs, N.J.: Prentice-Hall, 1988.

WALTON, RICHARD E. "Two Strategies of Social Change and Their Dilemmas." In Gerald Zaltman, Philip Kotler, and Ira Kaufman (eds.), *Creating Social Change.* New York: Holt, Rinehart & Winston, 1972, pp. 352–359.

WARREN, ROLAND L. *Social Change and Human Purpose: Toward Understanding and Action.* Chicago: Rand McNally, 1977.

WILSON, JAMES Q. "Why Are We Having a Wave of Violence?" *The New York Times Magazine*, May 19, 1968, p. 23.

WILSON, JOHN. *Introduction to Social Movements.* New York: Basic Books, 1973.

ZALTMAN, GERALD, and ROBERT DUNCAN. *Strategies for Planned Change.* New York: Wiley, 1977.

ZALTMAN, GERALD, PHILIP KOTLER, and IRA KAUFMAN, eds. *Creating Social Change.* New York: Holt, Rinehart & Winston, 1972.

10 Impact of Change

In the 1980s, there has been a growing concern with the impact of change (Brannigan & Goldenberg, 1985; Goldhaber, 1986; Finsterbusch, 1980; Finsterbusch, Llewellyn, & Wolf, 1983). The term "impact" refers essentially to the effect or influence of a particular change or innovation after its introduction. A change may have an impact at any level in society, or it could influence the course of an entire society. The impact of a change may be major or minor, important or insignificant, direct or indirect. Depending on one's particular perception, interpretation, and evaluation, the impact of a particular change may have harmful or beneficial effects, or it may be functional or dysfunctional for a given social system. In this chapter, the impact of change will be examined from the following perspectives: social impact of technology, responses to change, social disorganization, unintended consequences of change, and ways of coping with change.

More often than not, the study of the impact of change is a complicated undertaking. In some instances, it is relatively easy to identify the direct consequences of a change. In most cases, however, complications arise when attention is focused on other impacts or consequences. As an example, let us consider the 1973 Supreme Court decision that declared restrictive state abortion laws to be unconstitutional. According to the guidelines set by the Court, an abortion decision during the first trimester of pregnancy is left to a woman and her physician, free of any regulation by government. Since 1973, an estimated 18 million legal abortions have been performed in the United States; more than one-quarter of all pregnancies now end in abortion, at a rate of roughly 4,000 a day. In some areas, such as New York State, the number of abortions every year nearly equals the number of live births.

Certain effects flow immediately from the content of this change. The direct effect of an abortion is to terminate the life of a fetus. The immediate effect of the Court decision was to enable women to obtain abortions legally. This resulted in an increase in the number of abortions performed; "a decline in birthrates and rates of illegitimate births; a decrease in the number of women with dependent children on welfare; lower maternal-mortality and infant-mortality rates" (Mauss, 1975:473); and a reduction of the cost of abortion (*Newsweek*, 1985).

Another impact of the abortion decision was the revitalization of the various pro-life (antiabortion) movements. Abortion is again a topic of considerable controversy (and some violence in the form of attacks on abortion clinics), and it has been called feticide, "war on the unborn," "baby killing," and "slaughter of the innocent," by its opponents. At the same time, pro-choice proponents emphasize individual rights and the quality of life, and proclaim that abortion is a merciful, humanitarian backup method of birth control that is necessary in population growth. Regardless of one's position on the controversy, the abortion question is at once a moral, medical, legal, sociological, demographic, psychological, and political problem (Callahan, 1970:1–2). Let us consider each of these briefly.

As a *moral* problem, abortion raises the question of the nature and control of incipient human life. Pro-life morality tends to subordinate all other considerations to the fetus's right to life. Pro-choice proponents contend that the mother's rights are prior to all other considerations. In this view, a woman's freedom rests finally on her control of her own reproductive processes. Thus, she alone has the right to decide to abort. A third position tries to balance the relative rights of mother and fetus.

As a *medical* problem, abortion affects the doctor's conscience and medical skills. Should medical technology designed to improve human life be used for this purpose? There are also questions about the viability of the fetus and the unsettled issue of when life begins. From a different perspective, some physicians who perform abortions are beginning to be concerned about harassment, safety, and rising malpractice insurance.

As a *legal* problem, abortion raises the question of the extent to which society should concern itself with the unborn life, with motherhood, with family, and with public control of the medical profession.

Sociologically, abortion touches on the woman's role in society, family organization and disorganization, national demographic policy, and the role of formal and informal sanctions. Pro-choice proponents tend to be highly educated, well-paid careerists with few children, almost no ties to formal religion, and a strong vested interest in their work roles. These women see themselves as equal to their husbands, and the unavailability of abortion would limit their competitive chances in the world. Thus, abortion is perhaps as much an economic issue as a psychological and physical one. By contrast, pro-life advocates generally tend to be practicing Roman Catholic women with large families and low-paying or no outside jobs. They believe in traditional sex roles and see motherhood as the highest mission in life. For the first group, loss of the right to abortion would threaten their place in the world of work; for them motherhood is an option and children a project. For the second, motherhood is a calling and children a gift. These different views are shaped by divergent social and economic expectations (*Newsweek*, 1985).

As a *demographic* problem, abortion raises the question as to whether abortion provides a useful, legitimate, and desirable means of fertility regulation where such regulation is needed.

As a *psychological* problem, abortion involves highly emotional issues such as conception, pregnancy, birth, and child rearing. Some women feel exploited by abortion, and they regret having ended their pregnancies. At times, this feeling may result in depression, or in extreme cases, suicide.

Finally, as a *political* problem, abortion presents the American political system with a unique difficulty. The American political system is built to a great extent on interest-group bargaining, which is well suited to producing compromise. But abortion is among the very few issues that inherently does not admit compromise. Just as a woman cannot be slightly pregnant, neither can her fetus be a little bit aborted. And if one side takes the position that life begins at conception, while the other argues that it is a gradual development achieved by degrees over nine months of gestation, there is no way to compromise between the absolutist and relativist positions. In the political arena, one is either for or against abortion. In an era of single-issue politics, candidates for political office and elected officials are well aware of this dilemma.

Thus, the impact of abortion needs to be considered in all of the domains discussed above. Additional effects, such as the consequences of more frequent abortions on infertility and premature deliveries, the effects of women's ability to exercise greater control over their reproductive lives, and its significance for the changing role of women, need to be entertained. On a global basis, abortion is considered perhaps the most widely used single method to control fertility (Petersen, 1975:205). As such, its long-term consequences need to be viewed in the context of broader population policies. Obviously, in such a context, the consequences of abortion could reverberate on many other aspects of life.

This discussion on the impact of abortion clearly illustrates the complexity of the effects of social change. In most instances, no social change leaves the rest of social life entirely unaffected. In some cases, the impact of change can be shattering. Recall the case of Caliente, which involved the introduction of a new invention in an American community, or the introduction of the steel ax to the Yir Yoront of Australia. The consequences of these innovations are dramatic, but so are the effects of a number of other innovations. Let us briefly consider some of them.

THE SOCIAL IMPACT OF TECHNOLOGY

There are many ways to consider or categorize the social impacts of technology. One common way is simply to examine specific impacts of certain technologies, such as the effect of television on violence or the effects of computers in the office (Goldhaber, 1986:32–33). This approach was taken by William F. Ogburn (1933:153–156) in a now classic article entitled "The Influence of Invention and Discovery." He compiled a list of 150 effects attributable directly to the introduction of the radio. These effects are listed under the following 11 broad headings:

 1. Uniformity and diffusion
 2. Recreation and entertainment
 3. Transportation
 4. Education
 5. Dissemination of information
 6. Religion
 7. Industry and business
 8. Occupations
 9. Government and politics
10. Other inventions
11. Miscellaneous

Ogburn suggests that each one of the 150 items listed under these categories might be broken down into additional, particular, and more detailed effects. For example, the impact of the radio on increasing interest in sports is broken down in detail to show an additional 15 social effects. More than two generations after Ogburn's article, a study conducted in rural Uganda underscores the multiple impacts of the radio (Robbins & Kilbride, 1987:256–259). The radio is given a prominent and visible place in the home. Often, the radio is decorated and proudly shown. Radio ownership enhances one's social position. Among the radio's effects: "It makes a person get more friends than before and the neighbors come for news and announcements. . . . To those who are not married, the radio makes women to love men. . . . It shows that the person is rich. . . . In the old days, men did not respect their wives. They could beat them. The radio has made men change. . . . The radio has given knowledge as to how to care for children and to prevent diseases. . . ." (Robbins & Kilbride, 1987:256–257).

In addition to the radio, Ogburn also analyzed a number of other inventions. For example, for the X-ray machine, he listed 61 influences causing changes in industry, in medicine, in science, and in trade. Similarly, he noted 150 social effects from the use of the automobile. (Forty years later, Gabor Strasser, 1973:926–928, almost doubled Ogburn's figure of social effects attributable to the automobile, and his list may well be incomplete.)

Ogburn has distinguished three general forms of the social effects of invention. The first is *dispersion*, or the multiple effects of a single mechanical invention, as was illustrated in the case of the radio or the automobile. The second general effect is *succession*, or the derivative social effects of a single invention, which means that an invention produces changes, which in turn produce further changes, and so on. "Derivative effects of invention follow one another like ripples after a pebble is thrown in water . . . the invention of the tin can is said to have influenced the movement for woman suffrage. It first led to canning factories, then it reduced the time in preparing meals in the home; it thus gave women more time for activities outside the home, including participation in the movement for woman's rights and the suffrage. In turn, woman's suffrage has had a series of derivative effects" (Ogburn, 1933:124). Another illustration of the derivative social effects would be the invention of the cotton gin, which simplified cotton processing and made cotton more profitable, resulting in the encouragement of planting of more cotton, which in turn required more slaves. The increase in slavery and growing southern dependence upon cotton exports helped to provoke the Civil War, which greatly stimulated the growth of large-scale industry and business monopoly. These in turn encouraged antitrust laws and labor unions, and the chain reaction is still continuing. Obviously, not all these developments are viewed as directly related to the cotton gin, but it helped to produce them all.

The third form of the social effects of invention is called *convergence*, that is, the coming together of several influences of different inventions. For example, the automobile, the electric pump, and the septic tank helped to make the modern suburb possible.

Ogburn further notes that the effects of invention on society are of various degrees and kind. One of the first effects of invention is the change in the *habits* of the individuals using them, as in the case of persons who use typewriters instead of pen and ink. When there is a large number of individuals whose habits are changed, then a *social class* is affected. Thus, there develops a class of women typists and stenographers who have a place in society in relation to other groups and classes. This, in turn, changes certain organizations, and the organization of various businesses is affected by the use of typewriters. At times inventions have far-removed effects on *social institutions*, such as the family, which is affected by the employment of daughters, wives, and single women in offices and factories. Additional influences are those affecting *ethics* and codes of conduct related to these material changes. For example, years ago "it was almost a moral precept that woman's place was in the home. The appearance of women on the streets and in places of business for many years slowly affected manners and customs closely related to ethical codes" (Ogburn, 1933:162). The final influence, he notes, is on systems of thought or *social philosophies* that tend to be influenced by inventions. Thus, the inventions attracting women away from home are related to the social philosophy concerning the equality of sexes and in the resulting greater social justice for women.

Technological innovations also affect wealth, power, culture patterns, gender relationships, and work (Goldhaber, 1986:33–82). Technological innovation is one of the principal ways of creating and redistributing wealth. Examples abound. Toward the end of the nineteenth century, elevators increased already high land values in major cities. Air conditioning has opened up areas in the South with hot and humid climates to modern commerce and industry. Mechanization of farm technology resulted in the growth of agribusiness, causing many farmers with small holdings to go bankrupt. Certain skills also lose their value when a new technology is introduced. For example, the traditional Swiss watch industry declined as a result of the transition to electronic, digital watches. The potential of labor-saving technology also reduces the value of many skills.

Technology at times can extend the power of the already powerful, and at times it can increase the power of the relatively weak. For example, advances in communication technology are useful for augmenting the power of small groups of managers in multinational corporations or governmental bureaucracies. Information technologies allow organizations to have access to a far wider range of information than in the past, and to be able to use it in turn for strengthening themselves even further. By contrast, bicycles can augment the power of large groups to communicate, or to organize to resist centralized authority. Similarly, new information technologies such as video recorders or cable television can lessen the power of those who control the major networks to decide the flow of issues and concerns reaching public attention.

New technologies alter culture patterns and ways of life. A good example is how the bicycle changed mate-selection practices in the French countryside in the late nineteenth century. Young males suddenly had the opportunity to travel longer distances, which extended the number of potential available spouses beyond one's village. This changed traditional courtship practices and a whole set of criteria to select a husband or wife. And what was true for the bicycle is even more the case for cars and airplanes. Technology has had a profound impact on patterns of intimacy, home life, socialization practices, and leisure-time activities, in addition to many other areas.

In virtually all societies, tasks and social roles are divided along gender lines, although the divisions vary from society to society. Gender roles are often tied to particular technologies, often leaving women in a lower-status position. In traditional societies, certain tools are considered feminine, others are masculine. Similarly, in modern societies, certain technologies seem to have gender attached to them. To illustrate: The introduction of type-writers into offices coincided with the introduction of women into clerical roles; the early telephone operator or receptionist came to be identified as female. Computers are often seen as "male" tools, whereas the almost identical word processors are perceived as "female" tools.

One of the most pronounced technological impacts on work is automation. As a result, old skills become obsolete, the character and the composition of the labor force change, and more and more workers who cannot obtain new skills enter into lower paid occupations or join the ranks of the unemployed or early retirees. Technology is also helpful to compensate for a skill that cannot be easily learned. For example, authentic Persian carpets are handmade individual products of particular Iranian villages. The designs are unique to areas and villages. The carpets are hand-knotted and have visible irregularities of symmetry, of color, and of shape. With the help of computers, the basic patterns can be analyzed; variations and irregularities can be programmed. As a result, modern rug-making factories can reproduce the intricate patterns with ever-greater fidelity, making it difficult to distinguish the imitations from the real thing. And the imitation can come from any place where there is a rug factory with state-of-the-art machinery. In the next section, responses to the effects of social change will be examined.

RESPONSES TO CHANGE

The effects of social change are never evenly distributed, and in a differentiated society the impact of a change will tend to differ for individuals, groups, and social strata variously located in the structure. However, it is possible to make some generalizations about the consequences and impacts of large-scale social changes and some of the more typical responses to them. For the first part of the discussion, the emphasis will be on the forms of alienation and their behavioral consequences that may be construed as responses to change.

The analysis will take place in the context of the so-called mass-society "theory," in which, according to Melvin Seeman, the major theme is that the passing of the old community has had powerful and often destructive impacts. It is a theory in the sense that it states three major elements in the transition process. "It becomes a theory—at least in the sense that it can produce testable propositions through a set of independent, intervening, and dependent variables—by combining (1) a historically oriented account of contemporary *social structure*, (2) assertions about the *psychological effects* of that structure, and (3) predictions about the resulting *individual behavior*" (Seeman, 1972:468–469). In this theory, alienation is the principal intervening variable; it is produced by the social structure, and in turn it produces distinctive behavioral responses. Seeman concedes that the theory is highly debatable, and it currently has more critics than adherents. An often remarked shortcoming of the theory is its lack of sufficient articulation of the process by which the various responses come about. It is also plausible that some students in the universities will not see the mass-society thesis as credible because it goes against their own past experience and does not reflect their present circumstances. Some may even see it as a threat to their hopes and aspirations (Hamilton & Wright, 1986:401). Still, in the present context, Seeman's thesis is important and informative.

As Table 10.1 shows, the structural features that are the independent variables are quite standard ones in the sociological literature. They demonstrate what is happening in a broad social change process in a historical perspective. The five trends that constitute the basis of this part of the argument are:

TABLE 10.1   A Schematic Summary of Mass-Society Theory

(A) CONTEMPORARY STRUCTURAL TRENDS	(B) FORMS OF ALIENATION	(C) BEHAVIORAL CONSEQUENCES
1. Kinship to impersonality	1. Powerlessness	1. Political passivity (e.g., nonvoting)
2. Traditional to rational forms	2. Meaninglessness	2. Wildcat strikes
3. Homogeneity to heterogeneity	3. Normlessness	3. Mass movements
4. Stability to mobility	4. Value isolation (cultural estrangement)	4. Ethnic prejudice
5. Enlargement of scale	5. Self-estrangement	5. Mental disorder
	6. Social isolation	6. School absenteeism
		7. Low information level
		8. Suicide

Source: Melvin Seeman, "Alienation and Engagement." In Angus Campbell and Philip Converse (eds.), *The Human Meaning of Social Change.* New York: Russell Sage, 1972, p.. 468.

Note: The figure implies that the factors in column A lead to the development of one or more forms of alienation (column B) with the illustrative behavioral consequences in column C; but the figure is not constructed to be read line by line (e.g., powerlessness is not necessarily tied to kinship–impersonality).

1. The decline of kinship as a major criterion of place and of decision making, and the consequent increase of anonymity and impersonality in social relations.

2. The decline of traditional social forms and the rise of secularized, rationalized forms, which includes (a) the emergence of bureaucracy as an *organizational* form, (b) the growth of mechanization and standardization (in work and elsewhere) as a *technical* form, and (c) the secularization of beliefs and values, an *ideological* form of secularization involving the weakening of "given" standards of behavior.

3. The shift from homogeneity to heterogeneity, which entails increased social differentiation involving an increased specialization of tasks for individuals and institutions with increased division of labor and interdependency. This, of course, entails standardization in other spheres such as in mass culture and consumption.

4. Increased physical and social mobility, which implies the waning of locality ties and immediate interpersonal bonds.

5. Enlargement of scale, meaning that the basis of action (for example, communication, transport, politics, urbanization, etc.) have become massive in the literal sense that big corporations, cities, and nations make decisions that affect large populations. (Seeman, 1972:469–470)

These historical trends, Seeman points out, are guides to measurable variables. However, once the related indices are specified, a number of assumptions may be made between the relationship of social change and alienation. Alienation refers to the fact that there are "six related but distinguishable notions, and that these six varieties of alienation can be rather sharply defined in terms of the person's *expectancies* or his *values*" (1972:472). Therefore, to be alienated means to be characterized by one or more of the following:

1. A sense of *powerlessness*: a low expectancy that an individual's own behavior can control the occurrence of personal and social rewards; for the alienated individual control is located in external forces, powerful others, in luck, or fate.

2. A sense of *meaninglessness*: a sense of the incomprehensibility of social affairs, of events whose dynamics a person does not understand and whose future course the individual cannot predict.

3. A sense of *normlessness*: a high expectancy that socially unapproved means are required to achieve given objectives; the perspective that an individual is not bound by conventional standards in the pursuit of what may be, after all, quite conventional goals, for example, wealth, or high status.

4. *Value isolation* (or cultural estrangement): a person's rejection of commonly held values in the society; the assignment of low reward value to goals or behavior that are highly valued in a given society. An illustration of this would be the highly alienated artist or intellectual who rejects the going standards of success.

5. *Self-estrangement*: it means to be engaged in activities that are not rewarding in themselves. For example, the classic description of a worker carrying out unfulfilling or uncreative work.

6. *Social isolation*: a person's low expectancy for inclusion and social acceptance, typically manifested in feelings of loneliness, rejection, or repudiation. (Seeman, 1972:472–473)

The behavioral consequences of the various forms of alienation are illustrated in Table 10.1. "These consequences in turn become matters that a democratic society would find important in its accounting of the personal meaning of social change" (Seeman, 1972:474). Furthermore, each of the dimensions or forms of alienation is associated with a series of more specific and empirically demonstrated consequences. Let us select just one dimension: powerlessness. It has been associated with membership and participation in organizations that can mediate between the individual and the state or corporation, with a tendency not to engage in planned and instrumentally oriented action and by a readiness to participate in relatively unplanned and/or short-term protest activities, with poor learning, and with a greater sense of powerlessness among minority groups.

The concept of alienation has been used to account for a number of diverse responses to rapid social change. For example, Ted Gurr (1972:134) drew together a sample of incidents in which alienated groups expressed their disenchantment by resorting to violent uprisings. His focus was on discontent resulting not from objective wants but from perceived discrepancies between human needs and opportunities to satisfy those needs. Using as his sample 1,100 occurrences of strife in 114 nations during the period of 1961–1965, he found that 93 percent originated in such discontent. The same conclusion is reiterated in a variety of historical and theoretical studies of revolution (Goldstone, 1986).

Although Seeman's conceptualization of the forms of alienation and their behavioral consequences is a good way of viewing responses to social change, it's not the only way in the literature. For example, the Cargo cult, which was discussed in Chapter 7, can also be considered as a response to, and a way of coping with, accelerated change induced by European contact in Melanesia during the period of colonial rule. The Cargo cult is "one of the basic modes of reaction or adjustment to situations of rapid culture change characteristic of an entire area in a specific historical phase" (Schwartz, 1976:159). The cult responses are comparable to forms of religious responses to rapid culture change, crises, and domination reported throughout the world (Lanternari, 1965). Social movements are also considered as responses to changing social conditions.

Responses to change can also be viewed in the context of Hagen's notion of status withdrawal, which was discussed in Chapter 2 (Hagen, 1962). Hagen applied Merton's typology of modes of individual adaptation to the analysis of individual and group responses to social changes resulting in status withdrawal brought about by conquest, colonialization, or changes within the elite. Status withdrawal was defined as the perception on the part of individuals or groups that "their purposes and values in life are not respected by groups in the society whom they respect and whose esteem they value" (1962:185). Several responses to a situation of status withdrawal are possible. Initially, aggression and rebellion may occur or attempts may be made to ignore the situation and pretend that things have not changed. According to Hagen, the usual response is *retreatism,* in which an attempt is made to maintain the traditional and valued ways of life, clandestinely as necessary. The adult generation experiencing this conflict retreats to a passive "safe" life-style, and although behavior may change, there are no basic personality changes.

Retreatism can also be seen as a response to status withdrawal on the part of groups. As a whole, the American Indians have been forced into a retreatist position in response to a conflict between their values and way of life and their defeat and placement on reservations by the federal government. Traditional avenues to status have been closed off, and the opportunities and means for achievement in the white society are extremely limited. The retreatist response is perpetuated by the children being raised to esteem traditional values but with no clear role model for the future (Hagen, 1962:490).

Retreatism as it has been described by Hagen is one possible response to a particular type of change situation. Other responses, following Merton's typology, could entail innovation, ritualism, and rebellion. Innovation offers a potential for responding in a fashion which is beneficial to the individuals or groups involved. Ritualism may entail the rejection of new cultural goals, and rebellion, a nonacceptance of the change and possible attempts to counteract it.

TABLE 10.2 Responses to Changing Conditions

MODES OF REACTION	GOALS	WAYS TO GOALS
Conformity	+	+
Social reform	−	+
Innovation	+	−
Rebellion	−	−
Ritualism	0	+
Antisocial behavior	0	−
Apathy	0	0
Nonconformity	+	0
Anarchism	−	0

Source: Johannes Ponsioen, *The Analysis of Social Change Reconsidered: A Sociological Study.* The Hague: Mouton, 1969, p. 66.

Keys to Symbols:
(+) = Acceptance of existing standards and values.
(−) = Rejection of existing standards for new ones.
 (0) = Nonattachment.

Johannes A. Ponsioen (1969:65–66) on the basis of three responses —acceptance of standards and values (+), rejection of existing standards for new ones (−), and nonattachment (0)—expands Merton's typology and comes up with nine combinations that are possible when separately applied to goals and institutionalized means as shown in Table 10.2. This approach greatly expands the modes of responses that may be used to change conditions.

SOCIAL CHANGE AND SOCIAL DISORGANIZATION

As Robert E. Park (1975:38–39) gloomily notes:

> We are living in a period . . . of social disorganization. Everything is in a state of agitation—everything seems to be undergoing change. . . . Any form of change that brings any measureable alteration in the routine of social life tends to break up habits; and in breaking up the habits upon which the existing social organization rests, destroys that organization itself. Every new device that affects social life and the social routine is to that extent a disorganizing influence. Every new discovery, every new invention, every new idea, is disturbing. . . . Apparently anything that makes life interesting is dangerous to the existing order.

In many instances, indeed, social change is disruptive, and an underlying condition for social disorganization is change.

A widely accepted definition of social disorganization refers to "inadequacies in a social system that keep people's collective and individual purposes from being as fully realized as they could be." Obviously the concept of social disorganization is relative, "It is not tied to any absolute standard, which would be Utopian, but to a standard of what, so far as we know, could be accomplished under attainable conditions." Quite simply stated, "When we say that a group or organization or community or society is disorganized, we mean that its structure of statuses and roles is not working as effectively as it might to achieve valued purposes" (Merton, 1976:26). Thus, social disorganization entails the breakdown of the organizational structure, the various elements in society become "out of joint," and the influence of social norms on particular groups or individuals is weakened. The result is that the collective purposes of society are less fully realized than they could be under a different, better organized system. Value and norm conflicts, mobility, weak primary relations, lack of group cohesiveness, and other ingredients of social disorganization can also lead to deviance such as mental illness, drug abuse, alcoholism, suicide, and crime (Clinard & Meier, 1985:64–68; Liska, 1987:63–64).

The processes of social change can provide the impetus for social disorganization by creating conditions for conflicting interest and values, conflicting status and role obligations, faulty socialization, and faulty social communication (Merton, 1976:26–27).

Conflicting interests and values are produced by the increased complexity and diversity of social life as illustrated by the different demands and expectations of workers, management, and stockholders. Individuals occupy a variety of statuses in society and these statuses "can pull in different directions by calling for opposed modes of behavior" (Merton, 1976:26). When there is no provision of a shared set of priorities among these competing obligations, the individual's behavior becomes unpredictable and socially disruptive, and regardless how it is judged, it remains disorganizing. For example, "Competition between obligations of home and work, of local mores and national law, of religion and state, of friendship and the 'organization' make for potential conflicts" (1976:27). Social change also brings about faulty socialization by not providing adequate resocialization of individuals involved in these processes. Individuals simply do not know how to behave in their newly acquired statuses or in radically changed social situations. Finally, faulty social communication is produced in situations of change by structural inadequacies or partial breakdown in channels of communication between people in a social system.

Social disorganization is also generated by the fact that change tends to be uneven resulting, as it was discussed in Chapter 2, in what William F. Ogburn (1950) has termed *culture lag*. Some areas of society change faster than others, with the result that the parts of the system no longer mesh as a whole. In general, technological changes take place more rapidly than changes in other institutions and values; humanity accepts new tools more readily than new ideas. For example, industrialization has proceeded much faster than the development of social controls over the pollution that industrialization generates. Similarly, although developments in medical science have contributed to a global population explosion, religious prohibitions against artificial methods of birth control have not been modified, nor in most parts of the world has there been any change in the traditional attitudes and preference systems for large families (Brown, 1987:20–37).

Social disorganization is also produced by what Philip M. Hauser (1973:430) calls the "social morphological revolution" (changes in the size, density, and heterogeneity of population and the impact of these changes on humans and society). This is the result of three developments: (1) the remarkable increase in the rate of population growth itself, often referred to as "the population explosion"; (2) the increasing urbanization and metropolitization of the people, which he calls the "population implosion"; and (3) the increasing heterogeneity of the population composed of different nationalities and racial groups, which he designates "population diversification." These demographic changes have in turn been affected by technological and social changes. These developments are highly interrelated and constitute the elements of the social morphological revolution.

Hauser (1973:435–436) asserts that the combined effects of these developments have profoundly altered human nature and the social order.

> . . . the social morphological revolution has modified the human aggregation as a physical construct and as an economic mechanism; it has transformed human behavior and social organization, including the nature of government; it has generated and aggravated a host of problems—physical, personal, social, institutional and governmental. . . . Examples of the physical problems are given by the problems relating to housing supply and quality, circulation of persons and goods, solid and human waste removal, air and water pollution, recreational facilities, urban design, and the management of natural resources. . . . Examples of personal, social and organizational problems are given by the incidence of delinquency and crime, alcoholism, drug addiction, and mental disorders. . . . It is revealed also in unemployment, poverty, racism, bigotry, intergroup conflict, family disorganization, differential morbidity and mortality, labor-management conflict, the conservative-liberal debate, the maladministration of criminal justice; and in corruption, malapportionment and inertia in government, and the fragmentation and paralysis of local government.

In short, the social morphological revolution has transformed the "little community" (a concept used by Redfield) into the "mass society." Hauser suggests that much of the chaos and disorganization of contemporary society may be understood as frictions in the transition still under way from the little community to the mass society, and he cites governmental, racist, and other "lags" that have taken place. Without a doubt, population growth has affected all social institutions. Judah Matras (1977:251–256) cites a number of instances, in support of Hauser's contentions, in which population growth or changing age, class, or ethnic composition may render political institutions and community decision-making processes ineffective by forcing them to form coalitions, political machines, and political exchange and trade-off routines. These in turn, become disorganized under changing population composition and need to be periodically revamped. Similarly, various forms of population pressures can affect and disorganize educational institutions, churches, voluntary organizations, police forces, business and industry, communications, and recreational institutions.

Social disorganization is often associated with personal demoralization. For example, Vine Deloria, Jr. (1970) notes that the extermination of the buffalo highly demoralized the American Indians of the Great Plains. As it was described earlier, the buffalo provided food, clothing, and shelter, and dozens of parts of the buffalo carcass were used by the Indians. The buffalo hunt provided the principal object of the Indians' religious ceremonials and the avenues to social status and recognition. Other status-conferring activities, such as warfare, were also dependent upon a large supply of dried buffalo meat. The government's attempt to pacify the

Indians through the extermination of the buffalo resulted in their demoralization. The integrating and status-conferring functions of the war party and the buffalo hunt have disappeared. Religious ceremonials became empty and meaningless. The hunting economy was destroyed and the Indians lived, and at times starved, on government handouts. The traditional goals and values that gave meaning to life were now unavailable; the Indians found it extremely difficult to substitute the white man's goals and values for their own. In a few instances where Indians did successfully adopt the white man's economy, this too was soon destroyed by the white man's "need" for the Indian's land. They suffered from the destruction of their own culture, but they were denied full access to the white man's culture. Moreover, they were subjected to unknown diseases and corrupted by alcohol. Thus, it is no surprise that many Indian tribes became deeply demoralized. Depopulation became widespread, and only in recent decades had the Indian population begun to grow again.

Developing countries have perhaps the highest disorganization rate because they are undergoing accelerated changes that are compounded by population pressures, sporadic food shortages, scarcity of resources, and environmental problems (Harf & Trout, 1986). Modernization and "progress" bring new hardships to many in developing countries (Scott & Kerkvliet, 1973). Robert H. Bates (1974) points out that modernization promotes new systems of social stratification and encourages increased ethnic competition within developing countries, thus contributing to disorganization. It should be noted, however, that although modernization is generally associated with social disorganization, there is not empirical evidence that modernization directly contributes to personal disorganization and psychic strain (Inkeles, 1973:358–359).

It is important to note that disorganization under some circumstances can be both the effect and the cause of social change. The notion of disorganization is based on the assumption that at some point in the past a given problem did not exist or was not recognized and that society had a fairly stable equilibrium in which practices and supporting values were in harmonious agreement. Then social change of some kind disrupted this harmonious agreement and brought to the fore new practices or new conditions in which the old practices no longer worked properly, or new knowledge that made old practices obsolete, or new value judgments that declared old practices no longer endurable. This, in turn, created a confusion in which old rules were both debated and ignored, yet no new rules were generally accepted. In other words, change had disorganized and disrupted the organization of the former system of behavior. Eventually, however, new rules and practices will develop, and, at least for a while, a new equilibrium will appear and will be preserved until disrupted by another round of change. In brief, disorganization and reorganization are going on continuously. Moreover, as it was shown in the preceding chapter, willful, purposeful disorganization can be used as a tactic of achieving some desired change. Illustrations of purposeful disorganization would be some of the tactics used in the effort to thwart the Vietnam War or to obtain greater justice for black students through the takeover of university buildings in the late 1960s and early 1970s. Allen (1971:380) suggests that, to some extent, one could say that the use of disruption in order to obtain desired changes amounts to "disorganization for good reasons." In the examples given, "if disorganization was a 'means,' the 'ends' were stopping the Vietnam War, increasing justice for blacks, and so on."

The issue of disorganization for "good reasons" raise some interesting questions. Although individuals generally prefer social order and tend to dislike anarchy and chaos, "nevertheless organization is not inevitably linked with what is 'right' nor disorganization with what is 'wrong.' One can point out that a good example of a *well-organized* nation would be Germany under Hitler. Other sociocultural systems or subsystems may be well organized but open to serious criticisms. Justice is just as important as 'order,' and other values may be of prime consideration" (Allen, 1971:381). Obviously, whether or not disruption and disorganization is the "right" course of action to be followed is a value-laden issue open to considerable debate. The important point to remember for the present purpose is that disorganization can be seen both as an effect and as an instrument of social change. In the next section, the unintended consequences of change will be considered.

UNINTENDED CONSEQUENCES

Any change of a certain magnitude will disturb the prevailing and ever-temporary balance of social forces, and will bring about subsequent changes, some of which can have unintended ramifications throughout the social structure. Technological innovations and attempts to solve social problems are notable examples. Consciously designed changes foster subsequent unplanned and unintended developments—unanticipated consequences that invariably differ in character and scope from the initial planned change. It should be noted, however, that many of the unanticipated consequences are not at all the results of consciously designed change efforts. Instead, as Robert M. MacIver (1942:20) presciently stated many years ago, they "are the social resultants of a great many individual or group actions directed to quite other ends, but together conspiring to bring them about." To illustrate this point, business people, labor unions, and politicians may all pursue a common goal of economic prosperity, but the conjecture of their separate efforts may instead produce an economic slump.

Examples of unanticipated consequences of change efforts are almost bewildering in their abundance. Almost every effort is accompanied by them. Perhaps the best-known example is Prohibition, which was designed to end alcohol consumption in the United States. In fact, it did little to reduce consumption rates. More serious, however, was its consequence—of making potential criminals of millions of citizens and yielding vast profits for organized crime. Similarly, the efforts by the Drug Enforcement Administration to crack down on the importation of marijuana resulted in a phenomenal increase in domestic production. Currently, over 50 percent of marijuana consumed in the United States is produced domestically, and in some states, such as Hawaii, Oregon, and California, it is the biggest cash crop (Vago, 1988:157). Similarly, the quota system imposed in the mid-1980s on imported Japanese cars backfired. Instead of the quota protecting American car manufacturers and workers, the Japanese benefited from it. The trade limits created a shortage of Japanese autos in American showrooms, thus enabling their makers to increase prices and boost their revenues by as much as $2 billion a year. That extra profit, which came out of the pockets of American consumers, gave the Japanese carmakers even more money for research to improve their competitive position against Detroit (*Time*, 1987:59).

There are many other instances of politically sponsored and governmentally enforced changes that have produced unintended consequences. Many people benefited from the federal programs addressed to the alleviation of poverty. Some of these activities, however, have served to perpetuate poverty among the beneficiaries and others have not directly benefited them. In the Seattle-Denver minimum income maintenance experiment, for example, the guaranteed payments were shown to be a disincentive to work and destructive of family bonds. While comparing the rate of marital breakups between those receiving the minimum payment and those in a control group, it was found, unexpectedly, that "those in the benefit group suffered from a higher incidence of breakups" (Institute for Socioeconomic Studies, 1979:4). Several other programs of urban renewal thus far have created further slums. One reason for that unintended result was the practice of demolishing ruined apartment houses whose renovating could not be financed. This in turn displaced slum dwellers, who were forced to move someplace else, where they created new slums. In the same vein, the minimum wage laws have created difficulties for many people in finding employment. Congress last voted in 1977 to increase the minimum wage; the last of four increases occurred in 1981, when it rose to $3.35. Since 1981, the minimum wage has remained the same (while prices have climbed 28 percent), and in 1987, some 3.5 million workers earned $3.35 an hour, and another 1.5 million workers were paid below the minimum. As a result of the last increase, 644,000 jobs were lost (*Wall Street Journal*, 1987:60). Why? The workers are generally unskilled and predominantly young, their jobs are often marginal, and they are among the first to go when increased costs force employers to cut back. This is particularly the case for small businesses in the restaurant and retail fields. The minimum-wage provision contributes to unemployment among young workers, especially among black teenagers, whose unemployment rate is over 40 percent. There is a demonstrated correlation between rises in the minimum wage and teenage unemployment. The act, formally designed to improve the lot of the poor, in fact, priced many of the poor out of the job market. Because of these unintended consequences and strong opposition from business, a bill introduced in Congress in 1987 to increase the minimum wage to $4.65 an hour in three years is likely to encounter difficulties (*New York Times*, 1987:5E).

Closer to home, there are also some unintended consequences of the familiar Buckley amendment, which requires that in institutions with federal support all records (particularly those concerning students) be open to inspection by persons concerned. Warren Bennis (1976) raised an important question in his article "Have We Gone Overboard on 'The Right to Know'?" He admitted that the Buckley amendment is laudable in its intent, but one consequence of it is already clear. College administrators are now reluctant to put any very substantial information into any student's record. "What will be set down will be so bland and general as to be useless, for example, to college-entrance officials who want to make a considered judgment of an applicant's overall merits. If, for example, he had threatened to cut a teacher's throat but had not done so, he could scarcely be described as 'possibly unstable.' The student or his parents might sue" (1976:21). The various "sunshine" laws that have been passed by numerous states prohibiting closed meetings and the Freedom of Information Act, which became effective on February 19, 1975, requiring that most records of federal agencies be provided to anyone upon request, also resulted in fewer written recorded discussions, more private meetings, and greater secrecy with "more winks than signatures ('don't write, send word') if for no other reason than the avoidance of some new capricious lawsuit" (1976:20).

In all of these illustrations, the changes were undoubtedly initiated with the best of intentions on the part of those who proposed them. Few individuals would question, for example, the intentions of sending emergency food supplies to disaster-stricken countries and even fewer would consider the possibility of unintended consequences. But even such an action can have deleterious consequences as evidenced by the donation of emergency food supplies by the United States to Guatemala after the earthquake. According to the *New York Times* (Riding, 1977), it was entirely unnecessary, and had the effect of hurting the very farmers it was intended to help. When the earthquake struck on February 4, 1976, taking 24,000 lives and leaving 1.2 million people homeless, Guatemala had just harvested its largest grain crop in many years. The food was undamaged, and within days was recovered from the rubble of devastated homes. The United States sent thousands of tons of grain to be donated to rural victims of the quake. It knocked the bottom of the grain market in the country, and did considerable damage to the vulnerable economies of the small farmers—Indians living in the highlands north of Guatemala City, who were worst hit by the disaster. Dependent on sales of grain to generate money to rebuild their homes, they found that the aid supplies caused the market price of corn to drop drastically so that they could not sell their own products to obtain sufficient funds for reconstruction. Moreover, with the decline of farm income, the string of small mountain cooperatives suddenly found themselves decapitalized, dangerously weakening a new and important experiment in local organization. The food aid also upset community leadership patterns. Some leaders were more successful than others in obtaining food handouts, and those who were able to produce "free things" suddenly assumed greater positions of power and influence.

On many occasions even seemingly trivial changes forced upon people tend to produce dysfunctional consequences. For example, Christian missionaries to the South Seas were distressed by the near nudity of the natives; to them it was an indication of sexual immorality "for in Western society clothing not only is a protection of the body against the elements, but is also, although perhaps only incidentally, a requisite for virtue. On the assumption that lack of clothing stimulated sexual desire, they attempted to improve the sexual morality of the natives by inducing them to clothe their bodies. It may be doubted that putting clothes on the natives had any significant effects upon their sex conduct; but there is no doubt that it contributed along with newly introduced diseases, alcohol, and Western food practices, to the decimation and sometimes total extermination of native populations. For as is now clear, under the high temperature and humidity conditions of tropical regions, clothing has markedly adverse effects on physical welfare" (LaPiere, 1965:76–77).

It is probably inevitable that in the short run most change efforts will produce some unintended consequences and over the long run even the most successful attempts will have some unplanned by-products. It should be noted, however, that the unintended consequences are not always deleterious. A good illustration of a positive, but unintended, consequence of a change effort has to do with the effects of the liberalization of pornography laws in Denmark on the incidence of child molestation. In the words of Berl Kutchinsky (1973:179), "The unexpected outcome of this analysis is that the high availability of hard-core pornography in Denmark was most probably the very direct cause of a considerable decrease in at least one type of serious sex offense, namely, child molestation. Between 1965 (the first year of the availability of hard-core pornographic pictures) and 1969 (the year of the repeal of the Penal Ban, and of peak production) the number of cases of this type dropped from 220 to 87. The implication of our conclusion is that a large number of such offenses have been avoided since the late 1960s, because potential offenders obtained sufficient sexual satisfaction through the use of pornography, most probably combined with masturbation." In a later study, Kutchinsky found a similar decrease in child molestation in West Germany, which he attributed to an increased availability of pornographic material (U.S. Department of Justice, 1986:974). Bear in mind that the intent of liberalizing pornography laws was not even remotely related to an attempt to reduce sex crimes.

It is easy to go on listing unanticipated consequences of change. The important point to remember is that change has by-products both in the long run and in the short run, and, in most cases, the unintended consequences, both beneficial and deleterious, tend to increase over time. The impact of the automobile, for example, in 1895, when there were less than a dozen such machines on the road, is qualitatively different from today, when there are over 150 million in the United States alone. Consider the following statement from the *Scientific American* published in 1899 (quoted by Ayres, Simon, & Carlson, 1973:738): "The improvement in city conditions by the general adoption of the motor car can hardly be overestimated. Streets clean, dustless and odorless, with light rubber-tired vehicles moving swiftly and noiselessly over their smooth expanse, would eliminate a greater part of the nervousness, distraction, and strain of modern metropolitan life." As this quote illustrates, the determination of the impact of automobile technology has not been notably successful. Its by-products are too well known to warrant further reiteration here. The automobile, in turn, created a series of other changes whose unanticipated consequences could fill another volume. Again, the important point to remember is that most social and technological changes have brought in the wake of their primary intended effect a series of unforeseen effects—some adverse and some beneficial. In the next section, ways of coping with both intended and unintended effects of changes will be examined.

COPING WITH CHANGE

In the eloquent and at times overdramatic words of Alvin Toffler (1970:11): "Western society for the past 300 years has been caught up in a fire storm of change. This storm, far from abating, now appears to be gathering force. Change sweeps through the highly industrialized countries with waves of ever accelerating speed and unprecedented impact." Warren G. Bennis and Philip E. Slater (1968:124) describe modern society as *The Temporary Society*—"of temporary systems, nonpermanent relationships, turbulence, uprootedness, unconnectedness, mobility, and above all, unexampled social change." These writers take the position that in many areas accelerated social change complicates life by shifting standards, updating some behaviors as desirable, outdating others as old-fashioned and out of place. Ways of behaving that at one time may have been effective in establishing individuals' positions and identities became obsolete. Middle-class white parents, proud of their achievements in acquiring material goods and providing their children with the "best" in schooling, travel, recreational opportunities, and living conditions, find these values viewed as unimportant or as evidence of materialistic decadence. Black parents who learn to shelter their children from hostile environments through accommodation find themselves attacked as weaklings or Uncle Toms. Men who learned to behave in protective, although patronizing, ways toward women are called "chauvinist pigs" and women who learned to play seductive and submissive roles toward men are considered "unliberated."

Change further complicates life by increasing the rate of friction between groups and within groups. As established standards of behavior break down, as efforts to develop appropriate standards for dealing with a changing order come to the fore, as underprivileged groups seek changes to improve their situation, and as new notions of appropriate identity emerge, friction increases. Moreover, change is always difficult, and it is especially difficult for those benefiting from the status quo. As it was shown in Chapter 8, it is not surprising that change elicits resistance and resentment among some segments of the population. By the same token, lack or slowness of change will result in anger and protest among other segments. When change comes about in one area, it will reverberate on other aspects of social life, although it should be recalled that some aspects of social life (such as values and thought systems) change more slowly than others (such as technology). Change, in many instances, is disturbing; it upsets the routine and the predictability of everyday life.

In particular, in the domain of technological changes, as Donald Schon (1971:27–28) writes:

> Individuals must somehow confront and negotiate, in their own persons, the transformations which used to be handled by generational change . . . while technological change has been continuing exponentially for the last two hundred years, it has now reached a level of pervasiveness and frequency uniquely threatening to the stable state.

These technological changes cannot be isolated from the social relationships in which they are embedded. Even an apparently minor innovation such as the introduction of hybrid maize may undermine a whole tradition of peasant life, as it did in France by revamping agricultural and dietary practices.

In many instances, change in every level of society is disruptive, can result in a series of unanticipated consequences, and can bring about social disorganization in its wake. When change is especially frustrating or upsetting, the question of coping with it becomes of paramount importance.

On the individual level there is a set of rather versatile psychological defense mechanisms (such as rationalization, repression, projection, denial, reaction formation, and sublimation) that can be relied upon in case of unexpected or threatening developments (Albrecht, Chadwick, & Jacobson, 1987:11). These defense mechanisms can be used to facilitate adjustment and coping. In the case of certain personal problems, for example, it is more a question of learning to live with them than of resolving them. This is particularly true in the case of adjusting to typical "private" problems such as death or divorce. The psychological literature is extensive on this topic and it outlines the various strategies for coping (Bridges, 1980; Coelho, 1972).

Coping is required in situations of fairly drastic change that defies familiar ways of behaving, and which requires the production of new behavior "and very likely gives rise to uncomfortable affects like anxiety, despair, guilt, shame, or grief, the relief which forms part of the needed adaptation. Coping refers to adaptation under relatively difficult conditions" (White, 1974:48–49).

The past few decades have offered many opportunities to observe ways in which people cope in extreme situations. David A. Hamburg and his associates (1974:412–414) describe some instances of coping under extreme stress in the Nazi concentration camps. They cite the work of Eitinger, which was based on direct observations in the camps followed by semistructured interviews and medical examinations over many years. The principal question is: How it was that some people were able to survive this prolonged physical and psychological ordeal? Obviously, a certain physical minimum of survival possibilities were present, and Eitinger has been concerned with patterns of coping behavior that tended not only to foster physical survival but to maintain mental health both during the stay in the camp and after it. One of his major findings was that "identification with the aggressor" was not frequently used by inmates, and when it was used, it tended to have a damaging effect on self-esteem and interpersonal relationships in the long run. Inmates were found to be greatly helped if they felt they had *something to live for*. "The prisoners who fared best in the long run were those who for one reason or another could retain their personality system largely intact—where previous interests, values, and skills could to some extent be carried on during the period of incarceration. Very fortunate in this respect were some members of service professions, such as physicians, nurses, clergymen and social workers" (Hamburg and others, 1974:413).

Another method of coping in this extreme situation that has proved effective in the long run involved *linkages with valued groups*. To illustrate, prisoners who were able to stay together with family members or to remain in contact with some of their prewar friends benefited from such relationships. Moreover, strong identification with ethnic or national groups also proved quite supportive. For example, when Norwegian prisoners were asked several years later what helped them to survive, their response very often conveyed a strong thrust: "Being together with other Norwegians." Basically, the maintenance of self-esteem, a sense of dignity, sense of group belonging, and a feeling of being useful to others all seemed to contribute significantly to survival, both in physical and psychological terms.

By contrast, conditions of high physical and psychological vulnerability are summarized by Eitinger (quoted by Hamburg and others, 1974:413) as follows: "Prisoners who were completely isolated from their family, bereft of all contact with groups to whom they were related before the war, people who very quickly abandoned themselves and their innermost values, people who were completely overwhelmed by the notion that they had nobody and nothing to struggle or live for, all felt completely passive and had lost their ability to retain some sort of self-activity. They were those who most usually succumbed." This work on coping and on survival under extreme conditions underlines the importance of both group support and of individual strategies in coping and adaptation.

Fortunately, not too many change situations result in such extreme hardship and stress threatening the survival of individuals, as in the case of the Nazi concentration camps. In the context of less drastic change on the individual level, a person can develop what David Mechanic (1974:33) calls "coping capabilities." Such capacities entail the ability not only to react to changes, but also to influence and control the demands to which an individual will be exposed. But to do so, Mechanic suggests that the individual must be motivated to meet those demands as they become evident in a change situation. He points out that there is a way of escaping anxiety and discomfort by lowering motivations and aspirations, but there are many social constraints against this mode of reducing stress. For successful coping, the individuals must also have the capabilities to maintain a state of psychological equilibrium "so that they can direct their energies and skills to meeting external, in contrast to internal, needs" (1974:33). Defense mechanisms that may be successful in diminishing pain and discomfort may be catastrophic for personal coping if they retard enactment of behavior directed toward changing conditions. "To put the matter bluntly, such defenses as denial—a persistent and powerful psychological response—will do a drowning man no good!" (Mechanic, 1974:33)

Mechanic points out that people's abilities to cope depend on the efficacy of the solutions that their culture provides, and the skills they develop are dependent on the adequacy of the preparatory institutions to which they have been exposed. "To the extent that schools and informal types of preparation are inadequate to the task men face, social disruption and personal failure will be inevitable no matter how strong the individual's psychological capacities" (1974:33). In the same vein, the kinds of motivations that individuals have, and the directions in which such motivation will be channeled, will depend on the incentive system in a society, that is, the patterns of behavior and activities that are valued and those that are condemned. In this context, social supports are essential in maintaining an individual's psychological comfort for "men depend on others for justification and admiration, and few men can survive without support from some segment of their fellows" (1974:33–34).

The ways in which individuals cope with changing conditions are institutionalized and they tend to be cumulative through the generations. People learn from the experience of others, and mechanisms of coping are taught from one generation to another. "The ability of men and societies to adapt to the conditions of their lives depends in large part on the adequacy of such institutionalized solutions" (Mechanic, 1974:34). But institutionalized solutions to problems must change as the problems themselves change. With rapid technological and social change, "institutionalized solutions to new problems are likely to lag behind, and the probability increases that a larger proportion of the population will have difficulties in accommodating to life problems. . . . Increasingly, it is clear that major stresses on modern man are not amenable to individual solutions, but depend on highly organized cooperative efforts that transcend those of any individual man no matter how well developed his personal resources" (1974:34).

Mechanic advocates a kind of "collective" coping through group organization and cooperation that allow for the development of mastery through specialization of function, pooling of resources and information, developing reciprocal help—giving relationships, and the like. "The effectiveness of individuals in many spheres of action is dependent almost exclusively on the maintenance of viable forms of organization and cooperation that allow important tasks to be mastered" (1974:35). Mechanic also notes that "individuals who may be adaptive and effective persons from a psychological perspective may be unfitted because of their values and individual orientations for the kinds of group cooperation that are necessary in developing solutions to . . . problems. Thus, many effective copers may become impotent in influencing their environment because of their resistance or inability to submerge themselves into cooperative organized relationships with others" (1974:36–37).

Peter Marris (1975) presents a somewhat different perspective on coping with change at the level of individuals from that of David Mechanic. He argues that people assimilate new experiences by placing them in the context of a familiar, reliable construction of reality. This structure, in turn, rests not only on the regularity of events themselves, but on the continuity of their meaning. This is accomplished through what Marris calls the "conservative impulse," which is a tendency of adaptive beings to assimilate reality to their existing structure and to avoid or reorganize parts of the environment that cannot be assimilated. He posits that conservatism and adaptability are interdependent, and the readiness to react to new kinds of experience depends on the ability to assimilate them into familiar principles. Coping with social change in this instance is, in a sense, an ability to interpret new events in light of familiar principles.

Of course, coping with change is not limited to the level of individuals. At the primary group level, for example, coping with change is an essential function of the family (Leslie & Korman, 1985). In a sense, the family is a system of accommodation to social change. At the level of organizations, coping with change, among other things, entails the manipulation of the environment for the purpose of continuously attaining organizational objectives and internal adjustments in structure, procedures, and personnel (Gross & Etzioni, 1985; Hall, 1987).

At the level of society, there have been several historical illustrations of successful coping with change. For example, Everett E. Hagen (1962:350) notes that many of the samurai of Japan turned to business to recover the purpose and prestige they had lost in the disintegration of feudal society. According to Levy (quoted by Greer, 1975:132), others joined the police force because this preexisting social character fitted nicely the requirements of the function, and the dangerous samurai had a job in modern Japan. Similarly, Clifford Geertz (1963) has shown how the Balinese aristocracy exploited old feudal ties to create new large-scale commercial organizations, after Dutch rule and the Populist regime that followed had deprived them of political authority. Both these groups have in common a sense of superiority derived from pride in their social class, their ethnic culture, and a sense of frustration because their superiority could not find recognition through conventional careers. In a way, the revitalization movements, such as the Ghost Dance and Cargo cults that were discussed earlier in this text, are also attempts to cope with dramatic changes. Finally, the more recent movements of national liberation and decolonialization in developing countries also seek, at least in principle, to enable the populace to adjust to changing conditions.

Undoubtedly, ways of coping with social change are an important aspect in the study of change. Thus far much of the research on coping and adaptation has been limited to specific individual strategies in dealing with stress and disaster situations or with extreme hardships such as in prisons or concentration camps or to formal organizations such as hospitals (Powell, 1975). Certainly we need to know more about major cultural differences in coping behavior, how coping strategies may be used under diverse situations and at different levels, and we need to further our understandings about the long-term versus the short-term coping strategies. Additional information about coping patterns under specified conditions could benefit individuals, organizations, and institutions challenged by crises of social change and assist them further in anticipating typical or recurring coping exigencies. In the long run, it should be possible to identify change situations that are especially disruptive and to design coping strategies for various levels by pertinent social criteria such as age, sex, ethnic group, and the like, and to identify the risks, costs, opportunities, and benefits associated with each strategy in each situation, taking into account important considerations such as cultural and subcultural settings. It is not difficult to imagine the utility of such knowledge for educators, planners, and policymakers.

SUMMARY

This chapter considered the impact of change from the following perspectives: social impact of technology; responses to change; social disorganization; unintended consequences of change; and ways of coping with change.

Technology can have a multitude of social impacts. Ogburn, for example, compiled a list of 150 effects that are directly attributable to the introduction of the radio, and it would be safe to assume that the television has brought still more. There are three general forms of social effects of inventions: dispersion, succession, and convergence. In various ways, technology affects habits of individuals, which in turn reverberate on social classes and social institutions. Additional influences are those affecting ethics, codes of conduct, and social philosophies. Technological innovations have important implications on wealth, power, culture patterns, gender relationships, and work.

Responses to change were first considered in the context of the mass-society theory encompassing contemporary structural trends, forms of alienation, and behavioral consequences. The various manifestations of alienation such as powerlessness, meaninglessness, normlessness, value isolation, self-estrangement, and social isolation were seen as responses to change. Other forms of responses discussed included the Cargo cult, religious responses, social movements, status withdrawal in the context of retreatism, and an expansion of Merton's typology of modes of individual adaptation.

Social change is disruptive and underlying much social disorganization is the phenomenon of social change. The processes of change provide the impetus for disorganization by creating conditions for conflicting interests and values, conflicting status and role obligations, faulty socialization, and faulty social communication. Disorganization is also generated by the fact that change tends to be uneven, resulting in culture lag. The social morphological revolution has greatly altered individual behavior and social organization, and generated and aggravated a host of problems. Social disorganization is often associated with personal demoralization as evidenced by the American Indians of the Great Plains as a result of the extinction of the buffalo. The rate of social disorganization is perhaps highest in developing countries for they are undergoing accelerated changes and at the same time they are relatively unfamiliar with change processes.

Disorganization can be both the effect and the cause of social change, and at times it may take place "for good reasons."

Social change entails a series of unintended effects, some adverse and some beneficial. There is an abundance of illustrations of unanticipated consequences of change efforts. In many cases these unanticipated consequences are deleterious for individuals affected by the change. In the short run, most change efforts will result in unintended consequences, and over the long run even the most successful attempts will have some unplanned by-product. At times the unanticipated consequences can be beneficial, as illustrated by the unintended effects of the liberalization of pornography laws in Denmark and West Germany on the incidence of child molestation.

Change has become the prevailing life mode; a life rooted in constants seems a thing of the past. Social change complicates life by shifting standards, values, and behavior patterns. It also increases friction between groups and within groups. When change is especially frustrating or upsetting, the question of coping with it becomes of paramount importance. Coping is required in situations of drastic change that defy familiar ways of behaving and require the production of new behavior or new responses. Under conditions of extreme stress, as in the case of the Nazi concentration camps, individuals were greatly helped if they felt they had something to live for, and when they maintained linkages with valued groups. In less extreme situations, individuals can develop "coping capabilities," which are based on socially conditioned and institutionalized patterns of responses. In many instances, the major stresses on modern people are not amenable to individual solutions, but depend on highly organized cooperative efforts in the form of "collective" coping through group organizations. Coping is also facilitated when new experiences are placed in the context of a familiar, reliable construction of reality. Our knowledge of coping strategies under diverse situations and by diverse groups requires further expansion. In the next chapter the costs of change will be considered.

SUGGESTED FURTHER READINGS

BRANNIGAN, AUGUSTINE, and SHELDON GOLDENBERG eds. *Social Responses to Technological Change.* Westport, Conn.: Greenwood Press, 1985. A collection of papers and comments on the various responses to technological change.

COELHO, GEORGE V., DAVID A. HAMBURG, JOHN E. ADAMS, eds. *Coping and Adaptation.* New York: Basic Books, 1974. A collection of 21 interdisciplinary articles on coping and adaptation.

DEVOS, GEORGE A., ed. *Responses to Change, Society, Culture and Personality.* New York: Van Nostrand, 1976. A reader dealing with cross-cultural responses to social change.

GOLDHABER, MICHAEL. *Reinventing Technology: Policies for Democratic Values.* New York: Routledge & Kegan Paul, 1986. See, in particular, Chapters 3 and 4 on the social impact of technology.

MARRIS, PETER. *Loss and Change.* New York: Doubleday (Anchor Books), 1975. A short, provocative essay on the ways of coping with change.

OGBURN, WILLIAM F., with the assistance of S.C. Gilfillan. "The Influence of Invention and Discovery." In *Recent Social Trends in the United States, Report of the President's Research Committee on Social Trends.* New York: McGraw Hill Book Company, 1933, pp. 122–166. An often-quoted classic essay on the social effects on invention and discovery.

REFERENCES

ALBRECHT, STAN L., BRUCE A. CHADWICK, and CARDELL K. JACOBSON. *Social Psychology*, 2nd ed. Englewood Cliffs, N.J.: Prentice-Hall, 1987.

ALLEN, FRANCIS R. *Socio-Cultural Dynamics: An Introduction to Social Change.* New York: Macmillan, 1971.

AYRES, ROBERT U., SUSAN C. SIMON, and JACK W. CARLSON. "Technology Assessment and Policy-Making in the United States." In Marvin J. Cetron and Bodo Bartocha's (eds.), *Technology Assessment in a Dynamic Environment.* New York: Gordon and Breach, 1973, pp. 733–763.

BATES, ROBERT H. "Ethnic Competition and Modernization in Contemporary Africa." *Comparative Political Studies*, 6, January 1974, pp. 457–484.

BENNIS, WARREN G. "Have We Gone Overboard on 'The Right to Know'?" *Saturday Review*, March 6, 1976, pp. 18–21.

BENNIS, WARREN G., and PHILIP E. SLATER. *The Temporary Society.* New York: Harper & Row, 1968.

BRANNIGAN, AUGUSTINE, and SHELDON GOLDENBERG, eds. *Social Responses to Technological Change.* Westport, Conn.: Greenwood Press, 1985.

BRIDGES, WILLIAM. *Transitions: Making Sense of Life's Changes.* Reading, Mass: Addison-Wesley, 1980.

BROWN, LESTER R. *State of the World 1987.* New York, W.W. Norton & Co., Inc., 1987.

CALLAHAN, DANIEL. *Abortion: Law, Choice and Morality.* New York: Macmillan, 1970.

CLINARD, MARSHALL B., and ROBERT F. MEIER. *Sociology of Deviant Behavior*, 6th ed. New York: Holt, Rinehart & Winston, 1985.

COELHO, GEORGE V. *Coping and Adaptation: A Behavioral Science Bibliography.* Public Health Service Publication No. 2087, National Institute of Mental Health, U.S. Department of Health, Education, and Welfare, 1972. Washington, D.C.: Government Printing Office.

DELORIA, VINE, JR. *Custer Died for Your Sins: An Indian Manifesto.* New York: Macmillan, 1970.

FINSTERBUSCH, KURT. *Understanding Social Impacts: Assessing the Effects of Public Projects.* Beverly Hills, Calif.: Sage Publications, Inc., 1980.

FINSTERBUSCH, KURT, LYNN G. LLEWELLYN, and C.P. WOLF, eds. *Social Impact Assessment Methods.* Beverly Hills, Calif.: Sage Publications, Inc., 1983.

GEERTZ, CLIFFORD. *Peddlers and Princes: Social Development and Economic Change in Two Indonesian Towns.* Chicago: University of Chicago Press, 1963.

GOLDHABER, MICHAEL. *Reinventing Technology: Policies for Democratic Values.* New York: Routledge & Kegan Paul, 1986.

GOLDSTONE, JACK A., ed. *Revolutions: Theoretical, Comparative, and Historical Studies.* San Diego: Harcourt Brace Jovanovich, 1986.

GREER, SCOTT. "Urbanization and Social Character." In James A. Inciardi and Harvey A. Siegal (eds.), *Emerging Social Issues.* New York: Praeger, 1975, pp. 125–156.

GROSS, EDWARD, and AMITAI ETZIONI. *Organizations in Society.* Englewood Cliffs, N.J.: Prentice-Hall, 1985.

GURR, TED. "Sources of Rebellion in Western Societies: Some Qualitative Evidence." In James S. Short, Jr., and Marvin W. Wolfgang (eds.), *Collective Violence.* Chicago: Aldine Publishing Co., 1972, pp. 132–148.

HAGEN, EVERETT E. *On the Theory of Social Change: How Economic Growth Begins.* Homewood, Ill.: Dorsey Press, 1962.

HALL, RICHARD H. *Organizations: Structures, Processes, and Outcomes*, 4th ed. Englewood Cliffs, N.J.: Prentice-Hall, 1987.

HAMBURG, DAVID A. "Coping and Adaptation: Steps Toward a Synthesis of Biological and Social Perspectives." In George V. Coelho, David A. Hamburg, and John E. Adams (eds.), *Coping and Adaptation*. New York: Basic Books, 1974, pp. 403–440.

HAMILTON, RICHARD F., and JAMES D. WRIGHT. *The State of the Masses*. New York: Aldine Publishing Co., 1986.

HARF, JAMES E., and B. THOMAS TROUT. *The Politics of Global Resources: Population, Food, Energy, and Environment*. Durham, N.C.: Duke University Press, 1986.

HAUSER, PHILIP M. "The Chaotic Society: Product of the Social Morphological Revolution." In Amitai Etzioni and Eva Etzioni-Halevy (eds.), *Social Change: Sources, Patterns, and Consequences*, 2nd ed. New York: Basic Books, 1973, pp. 428–442.

INKELES, ALEX. "Making Man Modern: On the Causes and Consequences of Individual Change in Six Developing Countries." In Amitai Etzioni and Eva Etzioni-Halevy (eds.), *Social Change: Sources, Patterns, and Consequences*, 2nd ed. New York: Basic Books, 1973, pp. 342–361.

Institute for Socioeconomic Studies. "Flare-Up on Negative Income Tax." *Socioeconomic Newsletter*, 4(1), January 1979. White Plains, N.Y.: Institute for Socioeconomic Studies.

KUTCHINSKY, BERL. "The Effects of Easy Availability of Pornography on the Incidence of Sex Crimes: The Danish Experience." *Journal of Social Issues*, 29(3), 1973, pp. 163–181.

LANTERNARI, VITTORIO. *The Religions of the Oppressed: A Study of Modern Messianic Cults*. New York: New American Library (Mentor Books), 1965.

LAPIERE, RICHARD T. *Social Change*. New York: McGraw-Hill Book Company, 1965.

LESLIE, GERALD R., and SHEILA K. KORMAN. *The Family in Social Context*, 6th ed. New York: Oxford, 1985.

LISKA, ALLEN E. *Perspectives on Deviance*, 2nd ed. Englewood Cliffs, N.J.: Prentice-Hall, 1987.

MACIVER, ROBERT M. *Social Causation*. Boston: Ginn, 1942.

MARRIS, PETER. *Loss and Change*. New York: Doubleday (Anchor Books), 1975.

MATRAS, JUDAH. *Introduction to Population: A Sociological Approach*. Englewood Cliffs, N.J.: Prentice-Hall, 1977.

MAUSS, ARMAND L. *Social Problems as Social Movements*. Philadelphia: Lippincott, 1975.

MECHANIC, DAVID. "Social Structure and Personal Adaptation: Some Neglected Dimensions." In George V. Coelho, David A. Hamburg and John E. Adams (eds.), *Coping and Adaptation*. New York: Basic Books, 1974, pp. 32–44.

MERTON, ROBERT K. "The Sociology of Social Problems." In Robert K. Merton and Robert Nisbet (eds.), *Contemporary Social Problems*, 4th ed. New York: Harcourt, 1976, pp. 5–43.

New York Times. "Rewriting the Social Contract for America's Have-Nots," April 12, 1987, p. 5E.

Newsweek. "America's Abortion Dilemma," January 14, 1985, pp. 20–29.

OGBURN, WILLIAM F. "The Influence of Invention and Discovery." In *Recent Social Trends in the United States: Report of the President's Research Committee on Social Trends*. New York: McGraw-Hill Book Company, 1933, pp. 122–166.

OGBURN, WILLIAM F. *Social Change*. New York: Viking, 1950.

PARK, ROBERT E. "Social Change and Social Disorganization." In Stuart H. Traub and Craig B. Little (eds.), *Theories of Deviance*. Itasca, Ill.: F. E. Peacock Publishers, 1975, pp. 37–40.

PETERSEN, WILLIAM. *Population*, 3rd ed. New York: Macmillan, 1975.

PONSIOEN, JOHANNES. *The Analysis of Social Change Reconsidered: A Sociological Study*. The Hague: Mouton, 1969.

POWELL, FRANCIS P. *Theory of Coping Systems: Change in Supportive Health Organization*. Cambridge, Mass.: Schenkman, 1975.

RIDING, ALAN. "U.S. Food Aid Seen Hurting Guatemala." *The New York Times*, November 6, 1977, p. 51.

ROBBINS, MICHAEL C., and PHILIP L. KILBRIDE. "Microtechnology in Rural Buganda." In H. Russell Bernard and Pertti Pelto (eds.), *Technology and Social Change*, 2nd ed. Prospects Heights, Ill.: Waveland Press, Inc. 1987, pp. 244–267.

SCHON, DONALD. *Beyond the Stable State*. New York: W.W. Norton & Co., Inc., 1971.

SCHWARTZ, THEODORE. "Cargo Cult: A Melanesian Type—Response to Change." In George A. DeVos (ed.), *Responses to Change: Society, Culture and Personality*. New York: Van Nostrand, 1976, pp. 157–206.

SCOTT, JAMES, and BEN KERKVLIET. "The Politics of Survival: Peasant Response to 'Progress' in Southeast Asia." *Journal of Southeast Asian Studies*, 4, September 1973, pp. 241–267.

SCOTT, JAMES, and BEN KERKVLIET.   "The Politics of Survival: Peasant Response to 'Progress' in Southeast Asia." *Journal of Southeast Asian Studies*, 4, September 1973, pp. 241–267.

SEEMAN, MELVIN.   "Alienation and Engagement." In Angus Campbell and Philip E. Converse (eds.), *The Human Meaning of Social Change*. New York: Russell Sage, 1972, pp. 467–527.

STRASSER, GABOR.   "Methodology for Technology Assessment, Case Study Experience in the United States." In Marvin J. Cetron and Bodo Bartocha (eds.), *Technology Assessment in a Dynamic Environment*. New York: Gordon and Breach, 1973, pp. 905–937.

Time.   "What Am I Bid for This Fine Quota?" March 16, 1987, p. 59.

TOFFLER, ALVIN.   *Future Shock*. New York: Random House, 1970.

U.S. Department of Justice.   *Attorney General's Commission on Pornography. Final Report*. Vols. 1 and 2. Washington, D.C.: U.S. Government Printing Office, July 1986.

VAGO, STEVEN.   *Law and Society*, 2nd ed. Englewood Cliffs, N.J.: Prentice-Hall, 1988.

Wall Street Journal.   "Hill Democrats Plan Efforts to Increase Minimum Wage Amid Employer Protests" March 25, 1987, p. 60.

WHITE, ROBERT W.   "Strategies of Adaptation: An Attempt at Systematic Description." In George V. Coelho, David A. Hamburg, and John E. Adams (eds.), *Coping and Adaptation*. New York: Basic Books, 1974, pp. 47–68.

11 Costs of Change

It is, indeed, a truism that like everything else, change has its costs. There are various types of costs, and this chapter will examine some of the more preponderant economic, social, and psychological costs of change that are taking place at various levels in society. Certain outcomes of change, such as environmental degradation, are in one way or another costly for almost everyone. Other changes affect groups and individuals in different ways; some will find change beneficial and others disadvantageous. As Vilfredo Pareto (1935:1472–1473; Powers, 1987) pointed out, for every choice made or imposed, some other potential good is sacrificed. Pareto was concerned with the price that individuals as members of a collectivity have to pay when conflicting and contradictory benefits are emphasized. For example, an army protects the country from the danger of foreign invasion. At the same time, it endangers the careers and even the lives of many young persons. This is the classic case of Pareto's dilemma of utility *"for* a community" and *"of* a community." The former refers to the various individual and group interests in a community where the emphasis is on divergent personal benefits, advantages, and satisfactions. The latter refers to the interests of a community *as* a collectivity, to its capacity to survive in a hostile environment through collective strength and determination. Essentially, Pareto makes a distinction between what is good for some individuals and groups in a community versus what is good for the community as a whole. Often, the choice is painful.

Many contemporary illustrations abound of Pareto's dilemma of utility "for a community" and "of a community." At times a choice has to be made—for example, between air pollution and employment in a community. Because of the high cost of pollution-abatement devices, a company may be forced to close down. The costs of the resulting unemployment may be juxtaposed with the costs of pollution. Continued employment can be seen as a "utility for a community," while elimination of the source of pollution is a "utility of a community." The choice can be especially difficult in a situation where the polluting industrial firm is the principal employer in a community.

Pareto's notion of conflicting utilities has obvious implications for the study of the costs of change. Different groups or communities in a society are affected by change differently, and the introduction of something new will invariably result in benefits for some and losses for others. As Peter L. Berger (1974:223) points out: "There can be no social change without costs. The questions to be asked with intense seriousness are just what the particular costs are, who is being asked to pay them, and whether the putative gains make these costs acceptable." It is obvious that the costs of social change are never evenly distributed. What is not so obvious in many instances is the answer to the question: Who benefits from the change and who pays for it? Multiple objectives and values of competing social groups are noncommensurable. There is really no calculus for determining "net" pains and pleasures for widely differing groups. Equality, for example, is a uniformly relative and never an absolute condition. When a foundation for a new equality is established, some other inequality by necessity is imposed. The principal question is never equality in the abstract, but *which* equality, at what price of some new equality. As Charles Frankel (1973:57) notes, "The victory of those who say that women cannot have equality so long as marriage, home, and family are perceived as their primary goals puts the young woman who wants just such roles at a psychological and educational disadvantage."

There are, however, several large-scale changes at the level of society that extract a toll from most of us. Table 11.1 provides a rough notion of the potential sources of costs in a number of areas of disruption resulting from rapid economic growth, environmental deterioration, increased pressures on natural resources, and population growth. The costs stemming from these and other changes can, of course, be categorized in a number of different ways. For example, they may be subsumed under the major institutions, or the costs may be analyzed under the headings of "micro" and "macro" changes. For the sake of simplicity and clarity, such costs are classified under the captions of "economic," "social," and "psychological." It should be noted, though, that these three cost categories are separated

TABLE 11.1   Potential Sources of Economic and Social Costs

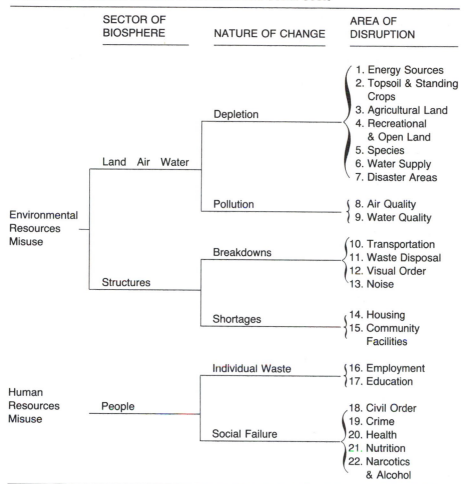

Source: Paul R. Ehrlich and Anne H. Ehrlich, *Population, Resources, Environment, Issues in Human Ecology*, 2nd ed. San Francisco: Freeman, 1972, p. 396.

only for analytical reasons, and, as may be expected, there is a fair amount of overlapping among them. Finally, it should be recalled that the word "cost," in addition to referring to the price of something, also implies a loss or sacrifice. In this sense the term has a negative connotation, which may give an impression that parts of this chapter convey a degree of pessimism. In emphasizing the costs of social change, the discussion will be obviously biased toward material supporting the arguments. But it is not my intention to paint a bleak picture of social change or to belabor the notion that "The history of mankind is a history of pain" (Berger, 1974:137). The purpose is simply to analyze the costs associated with the process of change. Sociology is, at least ideally, value-free, and the interpretation of events is conditioned by evidence and not by notions of "good" or "bad," although it should be recognized that not all sociologists adhere to the notion of a value-free discipline. With this in mind, let us turn to the economic costs of change.

ECONOMIC COSTS

In the traditional credo of the economists, more is better. Indeed, the description of economic growth as a process that "widens the area of choice" would seem to favor an economic system that, over time, produces—among other things—a per capita increase in goods and services. Such an increase presupposes economic growth, a highly debated subject that will be briefly examined in the context of economic costs of change.

Economic Growth

The proponents of accelerated economic development argue that "growth is a necessary condition for social advance, for improving the quality of the total environment . . . it is still demonstrably true that growth in per capita gross national product has been associated with rising levels of human well-being" (Heller, 1972:11, 29). This notion is supported by the view that "The pattern of growth in the United States in the postwar years yielded benefits to individuals far in excess of the costs it required of them. To that extent our material progress has had humane content" (Lampman, 1968:162). The benefits of rapid economic development, its advocates argue, entail an increased range of choices, greater control over the environment, more services and goods, improved status of women, a release from the drudgery of hard physical labor, greater humanitarianism (Hacker, 1970:353–354), and steadily lower prices for foodstuffs and raw materials (Kennedy, 1987:30).

The benefits of economic development are undeniable. It brings about a remarkable improvement in the standard of living for the average person compared with the average individual in preindustrial or early industrial societies (Lenski & Lenski, 1987:278). The concomitants of economic growth include greater educational opportunities, better health care, improved nutrition, increased availability of all types of goods and services, greater material comfort, more leisure opportunities, longer life expectancy, and so on.

The realization of the benefits of economic development is the subject of virtually all of the literature dealing with the problems of underdeveloped societies. The various accounts focus sharply on statistics that show the extent to which progress must be made in order to emerge as the equal of developed nations. Data on birth and death rates, literacy, rate of gross domestic product, per capita income, percent of urbanization, and the like from underdeveloped countries are compared with those of developed nations. But the numbers do not take into account such factors as environmental pollution and dehumanization at the workplace and in the marketplace (Greenhouse, 1987). Furthermore, a large part of the literature on development deals with the strategies of development and concerns itself with whether a broad push is needed to ensure rising per capita income, whether a basic level of investment is the key to emergence, how the generation of capital allows the progress of growth, and so forth.

Unfortunately, too little has been said about the costs of growing pains associated with rapid growth rates and economic development, and these costs can be great (Mishan, 1977). Any society has at all times a number of possible growth rates that it may pursue under different "growthmanship" strategies. For each of these rates there is a different cost involved, with higher and higher rates involving greater sacrifice on the part of the people and on the resources of the society. It may be said that the "proper" rate of growth for a society is the one in which the benefits of increasing the rate of growth slightly are weighed against and balanced with the costs of achieving that rate of increase. Ideally, the goal of a society should be that of optimization of the rate of development and not the maximization of that rate. Humans do not live by GNP alone. For development, the emphasis needs to be on what is the optimal (read "best") and not the maximal (read "largest") volume of goods and services. However, who will determine the optimal versus the maximal rate of development is another question.

A symposium on the developing nations states that "in many countries high growth rates have been accompanied by increasing unemployment, rising disparities in incomes both between groups and between regions, and the deterioration of social and cultural conditions" (*Development and Environment*, 1972:6–7). Aspirations that may have been limited in the absence of development may rise rapidly with the emergence of the first signs of development when the people realize that things are not what they should be. Personal satisfaction may decline, not increase, especially when growth is associated with high rates of inflation and unemployment as happened in many parts of the world in the 1970s and 1980s (Bensman & Vidich, 1987; Hamilton & Wright, 1986). Ezra J. Mishan (1967:171) pointed out over two decades ago that the continued pursuit of economic development in the Western world is more likely "on a balance to reduce rather than increase social welfare." Similar warning was sounded by Barry Commoner (1971:295), who associated much of economic development with ecologically faulty and socially wasteful types of production rather than with an improvement in the actual welfare of individuals. Some authors go so far as to suggest that economic activity, as currently pursued, "could be approaching a level where further growth in the gross world product costs more than it is worth" (Brown & Postel, 1987:6).

Environmental Costs

Intentionally or unintentionally, economic activity has often had a negative effect on the environment. From the beginning of human history, the need for basic resources, such as wood for fire and shelter, ran counter to the preservation of the natural habitat. Overgrazing transformed hundreds of thousands of acres of fertile land into barren deserts. Improper plowing techniques caused fertile soil to wash away during heavy rains. But the threats posed to the environment in earlier years are minuscule compared with the current level of damage and destruction. In this section are presented some examples of economic costs associated with development and change as they affect the environment. The discussion will focus on waste, air and water pollution, and climate modification,

Waste

An inevitable concomitant of economic growth is *waste*. Every step in the production process—whether food, clothing, drugs, cars, or books—creates useless material that is discarded. Growing populations, rising incomes, and changing consumption patterns combine to complicate further waste-generation and management patterns. The volume of waste expands as the size of a community grows, for as people earn more money, they increase their consumption of food, beverages, and durable goods, and they demand more convenience items. As more women enter the labor force, for example, the demand for convenience products grows. Frozen, canned, and vacuum-packed food packages are often used for the preparation of meals at home. In developed countries, packaging contributes roughly 30 percent of the weight and 50 percent of the volume of household waste. In the United States, nearly $1 out of every $10 spent for food and beverages pays for packaging. In 1986, Americans spent more for food packaging than farmers received in income (Pollock, 1987:102–103). Between 1920 and 1970, the volume of waste produced each year by the average American household doubled (Ward & Dubois, 1972:129), and currently each American produces, on the average, one ton of waste per year, and at any given time accounts for 11 tons of steel in personal possessions (car, refrigerator, washing machine, mattress springs, etc.), most of which are designed to become junk as soon as possible. The returnable bottle and recyclable paper had become too costly by the late 1980s, and the economic costs of the "Kleenex mentality" are practically unmeasurable.

Much of household waste also contains hazardous or toxic materials such as mercury from batteries, cadmium from fluorescent lights, and toxic chemicals from cleaning solvents, paints, and wood preservatives. In addition, thousands of businesses produce the equivalent of more than a ton of toxic waste annually for each person in the United States (Shabecoff, 1985:31) in the form of contaminated oil, solvents, acids, and sludges. This does not include wastes from service stations, dry cleaners, photo-processing laboratories, and other "small generators." Electric power plants, hospitals, and industry also produce an estimated 100,000 tons of radioactive waste annually.

Frightening incidents, such as at New York's Love Canal region in 1979 or at Times Beach, Missouri, in 1982, focused attention on a new generation of environmental hazards that defy easy solution: dangerous wastes. Some 800 families had to leave the Love Canal area after unusually high rates of illness and death resulting from chemical leaks from an old industrial dump. The Times Beach area was contaminated with deadly dioxin—one of the most toxic substances made and a suspected cause of cancer. The cost of relocating residents and removing the contamination has already exceeded $70 million.

Only about 10 percent of toxic waste is disposed of properly. In many cases, the deadly materials have been piling up for years in dumps and pits. They have been dumped in sewers, rivers, and oceans. Most toxic waste cannot be disposed of safely because there are no available sites or else the cost of proper disposal is too great. Even for nontoxic waste, it is estimated that by 1990 roughly half of the cities in the United States will have run out of landfill space (Browne, 1987:16E).

Air Pollution

Another costly byproduct of economic growth is *air pollution*. It is worst in big cities, but because of world air currents, it is rapidly becoming a global concern. The major source of pollutants in developed countries is from transport vehicles. Oil, coal, and natural gas used for heating and generating electricity are also major contributors. In addition, chemical plants, paper and steel mills, oil refineries, smelters, and trash burning spew additional tons of pollutants into the air. There is a great deal of variation from area to area in the kind and amount of pollutants. The most common pollutants include carbon monoxide, hydrocarbons, nitrogen and sulfur oxides, ozone, and an assortment of tiny particles of soot, ash, and other industrial by-products.

Some of the more costly forms of air pollution can be seen in the effects of acid rain and ozone depletion. Pollutants from coal-burning plants, automobiles, and other industrial sources include sulfur and nitrogen oxides. They are changed by a chemical process in the atmosphere, then travel great distances and fall as sulfuric and nitric acids in rain, snow, fog, or even dry particles. Acid rain has dramatic effects on the environment. Several countries in Europe have reported significant forest damage (Harf & Trout, 1986:125). Over half of the trees in West Germany and Austria have been damaged during the 1980s. In tens of thousands of lakes on both sides of the Atlantic all aquatic life has been destroyed. As one observer sardonically noted, lacking organic material, "the water of an acidified lake assumed the crystal clarity of a swimming pool—a deceptive beauty indeed" (Hillary, 1984:137). Acid rain is also harmful to exposed metal surfaces, buildings made of limestone or marble, and automobile paint. Drinking water is affected, and acid rain also contributes to soil erosion and deforestation problems. It has even been known to turn blond hair temporarily green. Acid rain also poses a difficult international problem; pollution generated in one country often rains down on another. For example, much of the pollution created in the United States often ends up in Canada where it creates serious environmental damages.

Acid rain represents only one dimension of the pollution problem stemming from the productive process. Another serious concern is ozone depletion, which is created by the release of chlorofluorocarbons into the atmosphere. Used as propellants in aerosol cans, as foam-blowing agents, and as coolants for refrigerators and air conditioners, the gases emitted from these sources contribute to the thinning out of the ozone layer. As this protective layer of ozone diminishes, the amount of ultraviolet and cosmic radiation reaching the earth's surface increases, causing increased rates of skin cancer and destroying the food sources of many marine animals. It also contributes to climatic changes by warming the earth's atmosphere. Although many industrial nations have restricted the use of freon gases contributing to ozone depletion, there is an increased demand for and use of them in third-world countries. As a result, an additional 10 percent depletion of the ozone layer by the middle of the next century is projected. Such a depletion could result in nearly 2 million additional skin cancer cases each year, damage to materials such as plastic and paints worth about $2 billion annually, and incalculable damage to crops and marine life (Postel, 1987:161).

Water Pollution

The economic costs of *water pollution* are also inestimable. With 97 percent of the earth's water in the salty seas, and three-fourths of the remainder locked up in glacial ice, the less than 1 percent of available fresh water appears a very small resource to serve the world's growing industrial and agricultural needs. Thus, it is not surprising that three-fourths of the world's population is without an adequate or safe water supply (McHale, 1970:13). Freshwater supplies take a heavy load of pollution, because the lakes and rivers are the drainage systems into which industry, agriculture, and municipalities dump their wastes. In turn, pollution reduces marine life and fisheries and ruins recreational pleasures in many key urban areas. In addition, Ehrlich and associates (1973:185) point out that rural areas, especially the corn belt and California's agricultural valleys, already confront serious water quality problems as a result of nitrate runoff from the soil in heavily fertilized agricultural areas. The nitrogen content of the Midwest's water drainage system is equal to the sewage of 20 million people, or twice that of the Lake Erie basin population. This, in turn, presents serious health problems. Already physicians in some areas recommend bottled water for infants.

Another kind of water pollution is thermal discharge from factories and power plants. The higher temperature of the discharge decreases the dissolved oxygen in the water, thus increasing metabolic rates while depleting oxygen supplies. As a consequence, small organisms such as fish larvae and plankton are destroyed. This, in turn, will create taste and odor problems in municipal water supplies and will contribute to the reduction of the fish supply.

Marine life is also affected by spills from oil tankers. Accidents involving huge tankers are becoming quite common. This problem was further augmented during 1987 by Iranian attacks on tankers in the Persian Gulf (*U.S. News & World Report*, 1987a:35–36). Dozens of ships were damaged, resulting in massive oil spills. In addition, smaller spills and oil wastes routinely flushed from the tanks of ships contribute significantly to pollution. Commercial fishing fleets each year dump some 50 million pounds of packaging material into the sea and lose some 300 million pounds of indestructible plastic fishing lines and nets. The resulting annual death toll is 1 million to 2 million sea birds, about 100,000 sea mammals, and countless fish. Moreover, about 30 percent of the fish in the world's oceans have tiny pieces of plastic in their stomach that interfere with digestion (Browne, 1987).

Climate Modification

Fluctuation in the earth's temperature is another environmental problem brought about by economic activity. The climate can be affected in three ways: (1) by changing the concentration of substances such as water; (2) by releasing heat into the atmosphere; and (3) by making changes in the physical and biological properties of the earth's surface (Harf & Trout, 1986:129).

The burning of fossil fuels causes a buildup of carbon dioxide in the atmosphere, which produces a "greenhouse effect" by holding heat in and thus raising the earth's temperature. As the consumption of fossil fuel increases, so does the amount of carbon dioxide released into the atmosphere. In this century, close to 140 billion tons of carbon dioxide have been released into the atmosphere, and half of it is still there. Massive deforestation and desertification further compound the problem because there is no vegetation to absorb it. The resulting warming effect can increase the earth's temperature from 1 to 3 degrees centigrade (Postel, 1987).

Increased temperatures could destabilize or melt polar ice caps, raising the level of the oceans. This could result in the flooding of coastal populations and agricultural areas. This, in turn, has implications for rainfall patterns with profound long-term effects on agriculture because if the trend continues, the best weather, for example, for growing food in the United States would shift northward into Canada, while farming in more southerly regions, including the Midwest and California, would require massive additional irrigation (*St. Louis Post-Dispatch*, 1987b). Because of the reduction in rainfall, climate change could carry a global price tag of $200 billion for irrigation adjustments alone (Postel, 1987:164). A decrease in temperature could have the opposite effect, hurting agricultural areas of the temperate zones and requiring substantially higher levels of energy for heating.

There are many other unmeasurable economic costs resulting from development. Soil depletion costs us in the form of lost nutrients and lowered production; deforestation costs us in the form of soil erosion, decline in rainfall and water supply, and loss of beauty and recreational enjoyment; depletion of fish and wildlife costs us in terms of food, ecological balance, and biological richness; pollution costs us in terms of health, recreation, and productivity. The magnitude of the cost is unknown, although we know it is already of extensive proportions.

Dennis Gabor (1970:9) emphatically points out that "*The most important and urgent problems of the technology of today are no longer the satisfaction of primary needs or of archetypal wishes, but the reparation of the evils and damages wrought by the technology of yesterday.*" Barry Commoner (1971:295) estimates that the United States needs to spend at least $40 billion a year on environmental reconstruction if the country is to avoid disaster. "Wealth has been gained by rapid short-term exploitation of the environmental system, but it has blindly accumulated a debt to nature—a debt so large and so pervasive that in the next generation it may, if unpaid, wipe out most of the wealth it has gained us. In effect, the account books of modern society are drastically out of balance, so that, largely unconsciously, a huge fraud has been perpetrated on the people of the world."

Toward Modernity—The Costs of Transition

Economic costs stemming from environmental conditions are not the only ones that incur in the process of economic growth and development. There are other ways in which the costs of economic development might be considered. For example, one may compile a list of costs to the traditional society in moving toward a more modern society or one may consider the trade-offs involved in accepting a higher rate of development.

W. Arthur Lewis (1956:426–435), for instance, has presented a list —cataloging some of the costs of transition to traditional societies in the process of development:

1. The economizing spirit necessary for development may lead directly to materialism.
2. Development and growth promote individualism, but in doing so, tend to break down the social structure. An individual becomes more cognizant of his responsibilities for himself and less aware of his responsibilities to family and tribe.
3. In the development of the new skills necessary for a technologically oriented society, the old handicrafts and skills will die.
4. The economies of scale inherent in development require the mobilization of capital and the separation of ownership from the use of capital. The individual becomes an employee, rather than an independent man, and is thus subjugated to the corporation.
5. Man becomes a slave of the clock and loses independence of action.
6. Large-scale production leads to the growth of cities. Cities become the homes of the slums of a country, and grow at the expense of the villages.
7. Growth and development are dependent on the inequitable distribution of income, and providing the incentives for hard work guarantees that inequalities will persist.

In cataloging the alleged costs of economic development, Lewis is very careful to point out that some of the things listed as costs are not *necessarily* costs at all. A change in social structure is not perforce evil. Development of the new skills, along with the division of labor, does not require that specifications for products be relaxed in mass production or that the older skills are redundant to society. The fact that large-scale production involves large organizations in which some people are employed who do not own the capital of the productive process does not necessarily mean that large industries are inherently bad. He also notes that these costs of modernization can be subjected to other interpretations and that a case may be made for their inherently negative consequences.

Another way of calculating economic costs in transition is by emphasizing the trade-offs involved in growth and development. At least three of these trade-offs are considered to be of prime importance:

1. In attempting to increase the rate of growth, we sacrifice current leisure for current work. "The high productivity and consequent high cost of labor have made people increasingly conscious of the fact that time is money: and this seems to have engendered the belief that time should be fully and efficiently utilized . . ." (Scitovsky, 1964:219).
2. In increasing the growth rate, current consumption is traded for future consumption.
3. The greater the rate of growth and change, the greater is the difficulty in changeover, with resultant temporary underutilization of resources.

The important point to recall is that the incremental cost of each equal addition to the growth rate will be higher as the growth rate increases.

Sacrifice of the first units of consumption for increased growth will not be particularly painful, but further sacrifices begin to strike into "necessities" and may become very painful indeed. As long as the benefits of develop-ment are greater than the costs of achieving those benefits, a transfer to growth is in order; but when the marginal benefits of the increased flow of future goods are just equal to the (rising) marginal costs of achieving them, further shifts can only reduce society's achievements, for the cost of further increases in the growth rate will be greater than the benefits arising from it. In the next section, the social costs will be considered.

SOCIAL COSTS

The preceding section emphasized the economic and environmental costs of change. There are, however, a number of social costs borne by society that do not appear in the calculus of economic costs. Some of the examples of social costs incurred in development and growth are painfully obvious: air that kills plant life and forces eyes to water, streams that will not support life, and the sprawl of the slum. William K. Kapp (1971:viii) is convinced that "the disruption of man's environment and the social costs resulting from productive activities are among the most fundamental and long-term issues mankind has ever faced."

The notion of social costs is essentially a normative concept. It cannot be satisfactorily measured. It is not reducible to single numbers and is difficult to define with any precision. It entails a wide variety of cost ele-ments, and Kapp (1971:13–14) asserts that the term covers all direct and indirect losses suffered by third persons or the general public in the course of private economic activities. These social losses may be seen in damages to human health or in the destruction or deterioration of property values and the premature depletion of natural wealth; or they may be evidenced in the impairment of less tangible values. Some losses can be traced to individual industries, others to particular production processes or business practices. Other social costs, Kapp notes, arise in the operation of the competitive system within a given framework of generally accepted insti-tutions and governmental policies. The notion of social costs is broad enough to include even certain "social opportunity costs"—that is, those social cost elements that take the form of wastes or inefficiencies of certain kinds.

In terms of *social opportunity costs*, Denis Goulet (1973:230) raises the issue of "sacrificed generations." He points out that throughout history people have lived in conditions far below those objectively demanded by human dignity and to this extent, generations have always been "sacrificed." In the early stages of modernization and development, "consumer goods must be rationed so as to build up infrastructure, provide a pedagogy of solidarity, and increase work input even without appreciable rewards. If this happens, generations are 'sacrificed' not in any absolute sense, but in the purely relative sense that their social deprivations are prolonged. . . . Whether he is poor or rich, a man must never be allowed to become a simple object or a pure means for obtaining social goals. Underdevelopment's great misery clearly dehumanizes man; therefore, some efforts to meet minimum needs is required. But the most fundamental sacrifice of generations lies in the radical alienation, whether in abundance or misery."

At times attempts are made to justify social costs, in particular in socialist countries, and to regard them as the short-run price paid for a high level of long-run efficiency and social performance of the economic system. The argument is that social losses are justified by the change, and that not much is to be gained from a detailed consideration of social costs (Berger, 1974:71–103).

The Automobile

In discussing social costs, many authors single out the automobile to illustrate their points. Mishan (1967:173) is convinced that "the invention of the private automobile is one of the great disasters to have befallen the human race," and he calls it society's greatest nightmare. Barry Weisberg (1971:118) writes: "Considered by some to be one of the greatest inventions of American science and technology, in reality the automobile has been responsible for more deaths and human misery than any other single factor in American life." The automobile is the leading cause of death for people between 15 and 34 years of age. There are annually over 60,000 fatal accidents, and some 5 million Americans are injured. Deaths resulting from automobile accidents exceed all the deaths from wars since 1775. The production, distribution, and care of the automobile consumes approximately 16 percent of the labor force and 13 percent of the GNP. This does not include the hospitals, police, courts, and a myriad of other agencies and institutions in its service. Nor does it include traffic congestions.

Traffic tie-ups, of course, are not new. There were probably chariot jams on the streets of ancient Rome. But now traffic congestion is pandemic, affecting hundreds of metropolitan areas and afflicting millions of people. An article, appropriately titled "Jam Sessions" (*U.S. News & World Report*, 1987b), paints a rather dismal picture. North of Beverly Hills, California, nearly a half-million cars per day pass the intersection of the Ventura and San Diego freeways. Afternoon rush hour across San Francisco's Bay Bridge starts at 2 P.M. and ends five hours later. Commuters spend an estimated $150 billion to travel to work and back, and time lost in traffic jams in the Los Angeles Basin amounts to some 84,000 hours each day. Put a bit more graphically, if a worker is tied up in traffic 20 minutes each working day —10 minutes each way to and from work—and stays on the job 45 years, the person will spend nearly two working years tied up in traffic! Traffic congestion costs Americans 1.25 billion vehicle-hours and 1.4 billion gallons of gas each year.

People are beginning to react to traffic jams in strange ways. During the summer of 1987 in Los Angeles, there were some 50 shootings, and four people were murdered in traffic-related assaults. Drivers increasingly vent their frustration by speeding; tailgating; excessive horn honking; pounding the steering wheel; making obscene gestures; and, in extreme cases, shooting other motorists. There is also a new term in the psychiatric jargon: traffic stress. In its ultimate form, it can lead to physical ailments, such as neck pains, high blood pressure, and ulcers. And the road ahead is even more discouraging.

The Quality of Life

The concept of "quality of life" refers to subjective self-reports on such areas as well-being, happiness, satisfaction, fulfillment, fear, worrying, morale, pain and suffering, and the like (Andrews, 1986). On both sides of the Atlantic, pollsters have been regularly measuring both short- and long-term changes in subjective well-being. In the United States, poll data indicate that the proportion of respondents reported to be "very happy" has decreased from 35 percent in 1957 to 22 percent in 1972 (Campbell, Converse, & Rodgers, 1976:26). Similarly in France, for example, half of the respondents polled felt that the quality of life had deteriorated during the same period (Herman & Du Boff, 1974). Since the mid-1970s, the various Euro-Barometer surveys carried out in Europe showed little variation in long-term subjective well-being. The same pattern seems to prevail in the United States (Inglehart & Rabier, 1986). This means that roughly the same proportion of people have been reporting to be "very happy," "happy" or "dissatisfied" with life.

In other indicators, there have been some noticeable changes. For example, fear "grew in waves throughout the 1960s" as a correlate of the rising crime rates (Harris, 1973:168–169). In the early 1960s, there was practically no concern with crime and violence as an important issue, and as late as 1964 only 8 percent mentioned it. By 1968, however, 65 percent did so, and today it is a major preoccupation. The majority of people reportedly live in some fear, even in their own homes. Recent data indicate, for example, that the majority of women in big cities are afraid to walk the streets, roughly the same proportion worry about being raped, and 81 percent of the general population feel that law and order have broken down (McGarrell & Flanagan, 1985:173–178). Whether or not this fear is justifiable is not the essential issue: The *presence* of fear is the reality. Fear, in turn, is a social cost that we unwittingly pay (Lewis & Salem, 1986).

According to an influential report, *Work in America* (1973:26), the quality of life at work is as bad as ever, despite optimistic comments about improvements and safety. In 1969, exposures to industrial pollutants at the workplace caused a million new cases of occupational disease, including

3,600 deaths and some 800,000 cases of burns, lung and eye damage, dermatitis, and brain damage. There were also for the same year some 90,000 permanent impairments, and 2 million temporary disabilities. Between 1980 and 1984, a total of 32,342 Americans died traumatic deaths at work (*St. Louis Post-Dispatch*, 1987b). Mining and construction ranked as the two riskiest occupations. Although men account for 52 percent of the labor force, 95 percent of all on-the-job deaths occurred among males. Among female workers, 42 percent of all on-the-job deaths resulted from homicide, compared to 11 percent for males. In the United States, work-related accidents and illnesses account for twice as many losses as strikes and walkouts. The most significant aspect of work-related accidents is the fact that they are avoidable. "Competent authorities have estimated that from 70 to 90 percent of all work injuries could be prevented by proper safety devices" (Kapp, 1971:65).

In addition, more and more workers are claiming—and getting—compensation for psychological disabilities caused by mental stress on the job. Stress-related compensation cases have risen by at least 50 percent since 1980; and the cost to insurance companies and employers more than doubled in that time to $50 million in 1986. In California, for example, though the absolute number of stress claims remains relatively small, such claims grew 462 percent from 1980 to 1986, to about 7,200 claims (*Forbes*, 1987:12).

Environment and Social Costs

In addition to the decline in the quality of life, there are more specific social costs associated with change. The more disturbing ones include the rising incidence of environmentally induced illnesses, the lengthening list of endangered species, soil erosion, and ecological undermining of the world food economy.

Environmentally Induced Illnesses

Environmentally induced illnesses are the consequences of the introduction of toxic materials into the environment and the creation of conditions conducive to the rapid spread of certain infectious diseases. Air pollution, which is rapidly becoming a global problem, has reached serious levels in many urban areas. School children in Los Angeles are cautioned against vigorous play because of air pollution. In Tokyo, traffic police officers inhale pure oxygen from oxygen tanks every two hours to avoid carbon monoxide poisoning. In many parts of the world, air pollution is a major health problem, contributing to many chronic diseases and killing a substantial number of people each year. In the United States, the current mix of sulfates and particulates in ambient air may cause 50,000 premature deaths annually—about 2 percent of general mortality. As many as four out of ten Americans are exposed to high concentrations of ozone, which is associated with skin cancer. High sulfur dioxide concentration is primarily responsible for a higher rate of lung cancer deaths (Postel, 1987:170).

Another source of concern is the rapidly increasing level of toxic compounds now circulating in the biosphere. Some 70,000 chemicals are presently in everyday use, with some 500 to 1,000 new ones added to the list each year. The estimates of cancer deaths caused by these substances range from 1 percent to 10 percent. There is a lack of information on the toxic effects of an estimated 79 percent of chemicals now used. Less than a fifth have been tested for acute effects, and fewer than a tenth for chronic (that is, cancer-causing), reproductive, or mutagenic effects. "Given how little is known about the extent of people's exposure to these substances, their introduction to the environment is akin to playing Russian roulette with human health" (Postel, 1987:172).

Another serious health hazard is radiation pollution. In large doses, radiation is associated with a high incidence of leukemia and other cancers. One of the long-term effects is genetic mutation. Environmentalists are concerned that nuclear pollution will further increase as the nuclear in-dustry expands. In spite of elaborate safeguards, accidents can occur, as evidenced by the 1979 Three Mile Island and the 1986 Chernobyl nuclear accidents. Although the long-term effects are not known, it is estimated that the Chernobyl accident will cause up to 135,000 extra cancer cases and a maximum of 35,000 deaths (Flavin, 1987:60).

Endangered Species

Humans are not the only species threatened by the deterioration of the environment. "Thus far during this century, an average of one species per year quietly made its exit somewhere in the world" (Brown, 1974:66). It is noted that more than 300 species and subspecies of animals have already vanished from the face of the earth as a result of human activities. Obviously, it is difficult to attach a price tag to the extinction of some species of wildlife. "Since the extinct species is lost forever, any value at all, if calculated to infinity, would necessarily exceed any short-term gain from the activities causing the extinction" (Brown, 1974:67).

Soil Erosion

The social costs of soil erosion, soil depletion, and deforestation are abundant. "In particular, they may give rise to social damages such as floods, the silting of streams and reservoirs, the diminution of ground-water stores, the pollution of rivers, the destruction of irrigation schemes, the harmful effects of dust storms and the disappearance of wildlife" (Kapp, 1971:127–128). For instance, despite improved conservation techniques, more acreage in the Great Plains was damaged by wind erosion in the 1950s than during the 1930s. And again, in 1976/1977, wind erosion damage reached comparable levels to the 1930s. Why? Sharply higher wheat prices, fostered by world food shortages, brought a rapid expansion of crop production on acreage that should have been left uncultivated as grassland (Lockeretz, cited in *The Wilson Quarterly*, 1979:41–42).

There are many other illustrations of human beings' abuse of the soil that sustains them. For example, North Africa, once the fertile granary of the Roman Empire, is now largely a desert, or near desert, sustained by food imports. Even the "decline of whole civilizations can in fact be traced to an overutilization of land" (Kapp, 1971:128). In the United States, deforestation frequently left entire industries and whole communities stranded. For example:

> In the Pacific Northwest 76 ghost towns have resulted from disorderly forest liquidation; and in another 77 communities decline of population has kept steady pace with the closing of mills due to dwindling timber supply. . . . Millions of acres of cutover land have become tax delinquent and abandoned. . . .
>
> The Ozark region of Missouri contains 35 counties originally covered with splendid stands of pine, oak, and hickory. With the cutting out of timber, forest industries moved out, leaving a large dependent population unable to support itself in decent fashion. The farmers lost both nearby markets for farm produce and the opportunity for profitable winter employment. More than 20 percent of the rural families went on relief, with the remainder eking out a sorry existence. . . . (Kapp, 1971:144)

In developing countries, 90 percent of the population depend on wood for cooking and heating. In the tropics, 80 percent of all wood harvested is used for fuel (Hillary, 1984:67–68). In these areas, firewood is as vital to the local economy as oil is to the global economy. The depletion of forests has dramatically increased the price of wood in many regions. The high cost of firewood, in turn, diminishes the prospects for improved livelihood among the poor, who are forced to spend more of their small incomes on cooking fuel. It often reduces families to one hot meal a day. In India, for example, this is becoming a chronic problem (Brown & Postel, 1987:13). The combined effects of fuelwood need and the conversion of forests into farmlands threaten to destroy entire forest systems in some developing areas.

Ecological Undermining of the Food Economy

The growing pressure for food is beginning to undermine local food-producing systems in a number of widely separated areas around the world with increasing frequency. For example, evidence now shows that the heavy offtake from the anchovy fishery, off the western coast of Latin America, ranging from 10 to 12 million tons in the later 1960s and early 1970s may have exceeded the capacity of the fishery to regenerate itself, resulting in its collapse (Brown, 1974:71). Ecological overstress is also evident in much of the Indian subcontinent. During the last generation, as human and livestock populations have expanded, the subcontinent has been progressively deforested. Deforestation, in turn, may undermine the food-producing capability by contributing to the incidence and severity of flooding. This is what happened in 1973 when the worst flood in Pakistan's history destroyed a large share of the spring wheat crop in storage on farms as well as much of the standing crops. "Entire communities were washed away. Since the deforestation is continuing, the incidence and severity of flooding in Pakistan, India, and Bangladesh seems certain to worsen in the future" (Brown, 1974:73). Lester Brown's prediction was correct. Over a period of two months, in September and October 1978, four successive floods affected much of northern India. In West Bengal, the worst-hit state, an area of about 21,000 square miles (more than four times the area of Connecticut) has been ravaged. Some 15 million Bengalis had to leave their homes, and the floods ruined 6.5 million tons of wheat and rice in the fields and godowns, and killed 1.5 million cattle. There is considerable evidence that humans must bear some of the responsibility for the severity of the floods (*New Yorker*, 1978:37–39). In Bangladesh, tens of thousands of people are swept away by floods each year (Mydans, 1987).

Reduction of Options

Another way of looking at the social costs is in terms of the reduction of options open to individuals. As a result of resource limits and abuses, Lester Brown points out that the need to regulate human activity increases exponentially (Brown, 1974:139). The regulation of options, in turn, affects life-styles, including what we eat, where we live, and where we travel.

Generally, economic development brings about dietary changes. The trend during the course of development is from a diet heavily dependent on a few starchy staples to one greatly enriched with high-protein livestock products. However, this trend may be arrested by the growing pressures on food resources. Already, as Brown (1974: 139) points out, some nations are experiencing at least a temporary downturn in per capita intake of livestock products. In Argentina, for example, per capita consumption of beef has declined from nearly 200 pounds to less than 140 pounds in recent years. In the United States, "beef consumption declined from 116 pounds in 1972 to 112 pounds in 1973" (Brown, 1974:139). Whether or not less beef consumption can be construed as a social cost is secondary. The cost comes about in terms of the reduction of options.

The choice of where one lives is also beginning to diminish throughout the world. Not too long ago opportunities for migrating from one country to another were quite prevalent. In recent years, however, migration has become increasingly subject to various restrictions as nations become concerned with overcrowding and more selective about immigrants they consider as economically and socially unacceptable. In some areas even the movement from rural to urban communities is becoming more difficult. Even in the United States there are calls for measures to stem the growth of big cities, to check and reverse the decades-old trend of migration from rural areas to the cities and from smaller cities to larger ones. In policy-making circles there are more and more references to the terms "national population dispersal policy" and "population distribution policy" (Sundquist, 1975:6–12).

Social costs incur also from the restrictions on human mobility—how frequently and how far we are able to travel from home. The restrictions on the automobile already impinge on mobility. In terms of international travel, some countries are already unwilling or unable to accommodate the large influx of people that unrestricted international travel brings them. Even in the United States, in terms of domestic travel, some states, such as Oregon, have stepped up psychological campaigns to discourage visitors from lingering too long. Those having a second home at a lake, the seashore, or in the mountains face problems and difficulties that did not exist a few years ago. There is also a decrease in the opportunity to own land, and the freedom to utilize it in a way one desires. Inevitably, as Brown (1974:141) observes, "there will be little choice but increasingly to restrict various individual freedoms."

Trade-Offs

There are also social costs involved in the choices and trade-offs stemming from emerging pressures on resources of various kinds. At the community level, it is increasingly necessary to make choices as to how freshwater lakes are used. In many instances the choice is between recreation, irrigation, waste absorption, or the production of fish. Obviously not all of these uses are compatible. If a lake is used for waste absorption, it is not suitable for fish production or recreation purposes.

There is a trade-off that must be taken into consideration between air pollution and rising energy costs. As a result of the energy shortage, there is growing pressure to use high-sulfur fuels for the production of power and heat. "In effect, the choice is between a rising incidence of respiratory illnesses such as emphysema and lung cancer on the one hand, and a more abundant supply of energy for heating, transportation, and industry on the other" (Brown, 1974:142). Similarly, strip-mining coal desolates the countryside and is an abomination, but strip mining is four times safer for the miner than shaft mining; hence its direct cost in human life is only one quarter that of shaft mining. Macklin Fleming (1974:7) raises the question, "Do we outlaw strip mining at the cost of the extra expenditure of human life that shaft mining entails?" This is only one of the questions involved in the trade-off between the destruction of the natural topography and the desire for cheap energy. Such balancing of relative values and weighing of the costs of alternatives takes place in all human activity. Obviously the decisions are hard, and in many instances judgmental righteousness does not coincide with the exigencies of a situation.

The trade-offs can also result in conflicts between local and national governments and between national and international interests. Brown (1974:142) poses the question: "Should land in East Africa that is now in game preserves be maintained for that purpose, or should it gradually be shifted to food production to meet the needs of the rapidly growing populations in the nations where the reserves are located?" In the United States, water resources in the northern Great Plains may be used either for agricultural purposes, as is now the case, or for coal gasification and restoration of strip-mined areas. Because there is not enough water for both purposes, a choice will have to be made. Regardless of the level at which a decision will be made in both instances, the choice will result in additional social costs.

There are no easy answers to this dilemma. In a now-classic essay, "The Tragedy of the Commons," Garrett Hardin (1975:250–264) captures the essence of the problem. According to Hardin, humankind is caught in a situation akin to a classic tragedy. Although each individual apparently has no ill will toward others, all humans acting in self-interest move inexorably toward self-destruction. Hardin uses the example of animals being kept on a commons, an area open to all villagers for pasturing their stock. There are no problems on the commons as long as the number of animals is small in relation to the size of the pasture. From the perspective of each herder, however, the optimal strategy is to enlarge one's herd as much as possible. If one herder's animals do not eat the grass, someone else's will. Thus, the size of each herd grows and the density of stock increases until it exceeds the carrying capacity of the commons. The result is that everyone eventually loses as the animals die of starvation. The sum of a set of apparently rational individual strategies equals social irresponsibility, leading to disaster. The tragedy is that even though the eventual result should be perfectly evident, no one acts to avert disaster. As yet there are no socially acceptable ways to keep the size of the herd in line.

Urban Living

Although the social costs are more pronounced in the domain of changes brought about in the environment as a result of increased size, affluence, and energy requirements, there are many other areas of social life that have been also affected. For example, most urban areas in the United States are faced with a high crime rate, vandalism, relatively poor-quality public schools, lack of adequate mass-transportation, and the already mentioned serious traffic congestion. As a result of the dismal state of many cities' finances (due in large part to the mass exodus of large employers that reduces the tax base), public services such as street cleaning, garbage removal, street repair and maintenance, and fire and police protection are being reduced (Spates & Macionis, 1987:359–400). The plight of urban areas is further compounded by the presence of abandoned cars and buildings not yet demolished, and the poor property maintenance and upkeep of many occupied structures. For many people, housing is at a premium, and there is a high concentration of households on welfare, and what may be called a non-child-oriented environment that lacks open space suitable for playgounds because of the high-rise dwellings that make watching over children difficult. Such an environment is generally more oriented to adult activities than those of children. There is tension between whites and ethnic and minority groups (Takaki, 1987). The proportion of ethnic and minority groups, fueled by large waves of Asian and Latin American immigrants, is increasing in urban areas, accompanied by a downward shift in average incomes, which is most pronounced when neighborhoods undergo a transition from middle-income to low-income residents. At the same time, selected urban areas are being revived through the process of "gentrification" (the movement of more affluent Americans back into older, often decaying, parts of the city). This increases property values, which in turn often forces poorer residents in the area to relocate. Urban dwellers, regardless of where they live, pay higher insurance rates than do their suburban or rural counterparts, as well as higher security costs stemming from the use of burglary systems and other crime-control devices.

A balance sheet of costs and benefits to individuals, families, and society resulting from changing conditions in urban areas would be exceedingly complex even if all the factors could be identified and measured. The calculation is further complicated by the presence of many factors that defy quantification. For example, no figure has been placed on many important costs, including the time lost by millions of workers in their daily commutation journeys, limited access to outdoor recreation, high air and noise pollution, and the consequences of crowding. The social costs of these conditions have yet to be measured by social scientists. As Claude S. Fischer (1976:201) observes, "Perhaps the psychic or social pains of city life are too subtle, too camouflaged, or too spiritual in character to be measured by the crude instruments of social science. Plausible arguments along this line can be constructed. But plausibility is promiscuous, and will couple readily with most theories that come by, no matter how incompatible the theories are with one another."

Reasonable arguments about social costs could be made about the consequences of the lack of social ties, the prevalence of fear that was previously noted, isolation, and the friction among heterogeneous populations in urban areas. Urban living adversely affects social well-being by undermining traditional primary group relations, especially those based on the family, extended kinship ties, and the neighborhood (Milgram, 1970; Wirth, 1938). Urbanism as a way of life is characterized by anomie and an absence of both moral consensus and social responsibility. Louis Wirth (1938) suggests that such conditions of social disorganization give rise to individual psychological disturbances and increased crime, delinquency, and corruption. Urbanites have contact with many people, most of them strangers, and public encounters are usually formal, brief, and superficial. By way of protecting themselves from becoming involved, city dwellers often discourage interaction by being formal, unfriendly, and brusque. But the cost of this disengagement from others is high. It results in a tendency to disregard the personal needs of people encountered in public places, especially when the burden of social responsibility is shifted to formal agencies. For example, the police are expected to respond to the injured in a traffic accident, and welfare agencies are expected to deal with the poor and the homeless. Two highly publicized examples of the absence of social responsibility and the tendency of most city dwellers to not involve themselves in the affairs of others will illustrate this point. The first involves the murder of Catherine Genovese in Queens, New York, in 1964. She was repeatedly stabbed for an extended period of time. Investigators discovered that 38 neighbors either heard her screams or actually witnessed the attack. But no one did anything to help her. The second involves the gang-rape of a woman in a bar in New Bedford, Massachusetts, in 1983. Again, no one came to the woman's aid, although many customers witnessed the attack. Only when she ran out naked into the street did a motorist call the police. There are, of course, many similar examples.

Underutilization of College-Educated People

Social costs stemming from changes in the domain of education are becoming more pronounced. During the past two decades in particular, the educational system in the United States has continued to expand and diversify, with a number of consequences. Most important is the fact that a consistently increasing proportion of the population has had the opportunity to pursue higher education. These educational experiences have significantly influenced levels of aspiration and expectation in a number of areas, including life-styles and satisfaction derived from work. Although the educational system has expanded and diversified, the occupational pyramid has remained relatively rigid in terms of the capability of offering the range of options that could effectively provide "interesting work" to all. There are now more qualified people looking for jobs in the upper echelons than the present occupational pyramid could possibly accommodate. While aspirations and expectations about work have been generally rising, it is obvious that ongoing technological change has served to imbue much work with routine and repetitive qualities. The price of this is work dissatisfaction and alienation.

Greater social costs result, however, from the underutilization of the educated population. As Ivar Berg and Marcia Freedman (1977:30) comment: "A significant degree of underutilization is undoubtedly inevitable in a society in which the occupational structure has stabilized while educational achievements have bounded upward; neither the occupational structure's shape nor the educational achievements of the work force are realistically amenable, at this late date, to much amelioration by the nation's employers." For 1975, they found that approximately 45 percent of the almost 14 million employed college graduates were underutilized (48 percent of the men and 40 percent of the women), and "Depending . . . on the assumptions and standards used, underutilization at the present time ranges between a quarter and one half of the college graduate labor force" (1977:26). The plausible social costs of this underutilization of educated people include "alienation and political cynicism" and a "kind of intellectual atrophy in which people whose education is underutilized, who are not challenged by the work they do, fall to the level of their jobs" (1977:28). Berg and Freedman consider the problems stemming from this underutilization as "mind-boggling" and anticipate no major change at the workplace to accommodate the growing number of college-educated workers.

The Dilemmas of Scientific Specialization

Even those college-educated workers who are not underutilized are confronted with a series of dilemmas. In general, more education is associated with greater specialization. Scientists, in particular, whether they are employed in institutes, research establishments, or universities, are subjected to a growing pressure on their time and on their "innate capacity in consequence of the sheer output of the current research, theoretical and applied" (Mishan, 1967:139). Not only are they expected to keep abreast of the avalanche of journal literature, in which inevitably the writing is increasingly concentrated and increasingly technical, but in most instances they are expected also to contribute an article or two from time to time to "the accumulating weight that is bearing down on them." Perhaps more than other professions, "the ordinary academic tends to become overextended, his faculties too polarized to respond fully to other aspects of life, be they intellectual, aesthetic or emotional. Like all too many of us today, he may seek gaiety but is hard put to generate any" (Mishan, 1967:139). We recall from an earlier chapter that contemporary academics are expected to contribute to their discipline in the form of research or publication as a condition for advancement. Consequently, they count their published works "as a miser counts his goal. They are his kudos, his claims to recognition. Above all, they are his certificates encashable in the world he moves in" (Mishan, 1967:140–141).

The pressure for research and publication further reinforces specialization and has the unsurprising consequences that only a handful of people know more than a fraction of the broader discipline in which they work, or are competent to judge the work of their colleagues over a wide field. Editors of scholarly journals already find it difficult to find scholars able to appraise the quality of some of the highly specialized papers submitted to them. Moreover, because of the demands upon one's time and capacity, no scholar is able to read more than a fraction of the output of professional papers in one's own field. Mishan (1967:140) mentions an estimate that "the average scientific paper is read by about 1.3 people— while many are read by several people and a few by hundreds, a large number are read by nobody but their authors (if we exclude the editors)." Uncoordinated knowledge is growing at a rapid rate. The number of technical journals in the world exceeds 100,000, and the annual output of books is rapidly approaching that number. In a sense, we are faced with an overload of information (Klapp, 1986). Some 142 periodicals are now available in the United States on the subject of sociology alone (*The New Republic*, 1987:7). In sociology *and* related fields, there are more than 350 journals in English (Sussman, 1978). One could indulge in a bit of rough calculation assuming that each of these 350 journals appears four times a year containing on the average a dozen articles annually. That would come to 16,800 articles a year, averaging about 46 articles a day. Obviously, Professor Mishan's observation is not too farfetched. Even dedicated graduate students preparing for their Ph.D. qualifying examinations would find the digestion (or even the reading) of that many possibly "relevant" articles a task beyond their endurance. In the next section, the psychological costs of change will be considered.

PSYCHOLOGICAL COSTS

In addition to the economic and social costs, change also entails a series of psychological costs. Perhaps most noticeable is the loss of the individual's ability to understand and control his or her environment. People have become utterly dependent upon the operation of complex technological and social organizations that they can neither understand nor control. Generalized knowledge and practical problem-solving abilities are being undermined, leaving in their absence the specialists and experts with their set of instructions and push-button solutions. "We may use many materials of whose provenance we know next to nothing; we are surrounded by household implements we know how to operate but whose working principles we ignore; and we are more and more at a loss when trying to answer the simplest questions of our children concerning the nature of the everyday objects around them. This applies not only to the atom but even to the shirts on our backs. Hence man's feeling today of the utter dependence of his everyday life on a complex technical and social organization about whose working, outside his own narrow sphere, he is largely in the dark; and this, too, contributes to his feeling of impotence in relation to organized society" (Scitovsky, 1964:227). As a result of people's loss of control and utter dependence, Samar Amin (1974:1) offers an extreme view, which is nevertheless worth noting, of the personality in the making: "These beings no longer speak—they have nothing to say, since they have nothing to think or feel. They no longer produce anything, neither objects nor emotions. No more arts. No more anything. The electronic machine produces—the word itself has lost all meaning—everything, these beings included."

Although Amin's description of the personality in the making is a bit farfetched, there are many other "psychological victimization syndromes" of social change in the literature. Theodore Roszak (1973) talks about the "automatization of personality" as a result of technological changes. Jacques Ellul (1964) argues that technological changes lead to the "systematization" of all aspects of social life, and humans will be alienated not only from their work but from their recreation as well, as that is also becoming increasingly technical. These voices are merely the latest additions to a tradition that in some ways includes such names as Herbert Marcuse and even Sigmund Freud, the general point being that modern technological civilization fragments human personality, forces people to repress essential needs, deprives people of the experiential gestalt enjoyed by primitive beings, and thus reduces individuals to a mechanized and dehumanized entity. Anton C. Zijderveld's (1971:64–68) concept of "intellectual Taylorism" eloquently summarizes the modern individual's intellectual predicament as perceived by many authors. He posits that automation is taking place not only in industry, but also in thought. It is a characteristic of modern science. As Western societies become automated, bureaucratized, and pluralized (that is, fragmented), Zijderveld argues, they move away from "the common human pattern." As a consequence, human experience in Western societies is becoming increasingly unnatural or *abstract*.

Robopathology

An image of the ideal type of humanistic personality is what psychologist Abraham Maslow calls a *self-actualized* person. Such a person, Maslow suggests (1959:127), has the following attributes: clear and efficient perception of reality; an openness to new experience; integration; wholeness and unity of the person; spontaneity; expressiveness; aliveness; a firm identity; autonomy; uniqueness; objectivity; detachment; creativeness; ability to fuse concreteness and abstractness; a democratic character structure;

and ability to love. The attainment of these ideal characteristics are, however, hampered by the conditions created by accelerated technological and
social changes. Instead of self-actualization, Lewis Yablonsky (1972:16) argues that we have *robopathology*, which emerges when people *"cop out* or *sell
out* their humanistic drives of excitement, joy, and courage to the cultural
press of social machines because of fear and often an instilled sense of
inadequacy. They often trade their more spontaneous creative potentials
for familiar regularized rituals. . . . In the process of a dehumanized society
they live in familiar, routine, and predictable patterns of behavior. Thus
they *cop out* on their humanistic motivations and become part of the social
machine."

Robopathic behavior, Yablonsky contends, is found in many aspects
of life. Many creative people are often corrupted "by the rewards of the
plastic society. They find a groove and freeze in it" (1972:18). Many writers,
teachers, and artists, after an initially courageous and creative productive
life, "cop out and become robopathic in their later creative attempts. They
find a successful mold, receive their rewards, and ritualistically stick to it
for the rest of their lives. . . . Their fears and lack of courage freezes them
into static, uncreative roles, where they lock into a robopathic existence"
(1972:18).

Many social roles in contemporary society lack opportunities for humanistic expression, spontaneity, creativity, and compassionate action. These
include such roles as file clerk, assembly line worker, and the like. Yablonsky
calls these "robot roles" whose monotony, boredom, and dehumanizing
qualities are exemplified "by the daily monotony of work on an assembly
line in a factory. The *robot role* occupants rise at the same time, go through
their ritualized breakfast, turn the screws at work, watch TV, make ritualistic love on a prescribed night, take their two-week vacation—and become
increasingly frustrated and bored by their routinized life style. Increasingly
their zest for life, and capacity for spontaneity and creativity, is reduced
to zero. One common consequence of this malaise is a simmering, underlying feeling of hostility and aggression toward others." (1972:19).

Yablonsky concedes that modern societies have produced enormous
advantages for people. "It would appear that time and space dimensions
have been changed for their benefit; leisure time possibilities have increased
through automation; the health, wealth, and welfare of many people has
apparently been grossly improved by technocratic systems; and this is reflected in a longer life span." But, "Despite these and other apparent gains
from modern technology, a chorus of questions and issues have been posed
and amplified about the price paid for 'technological' progress" (1972:57).

Yablonsky contends that the psychological costs of progress are indeed
high. Individuals' coherent self-identities have been fragmented or rendered anonymous by their work roles in modern society. Their relationship
to nature, their natural state of existence, and their enjoyment of nature's

beauty have been seriously impaired by the overdeveloped machine society. The dehumanizing aspects of contemporary life have escalated crime and various forms of alienation. Current conditions are largely responsible for the acceleration of various routes of escape from self though drugs, alcohol, mysticism, superreligions, and growing fantasy states of existence. Finally, the mass media have confused people's sense of reality and personal identity, and there is a confused blur between mass media news, drama, and live experience. "Existence has increasingly become a spectator sport" (1972:58).

Anxiety and Insecurity

To what extent people's emotions, spontaneity, creativity, personal identity, and ability to become compassionate are reduced to a set of robopathic responses is hard to tell. Much of the literature supports these impressions and indeed there *seems* to be an escalation of tension, discontent, and anxiety in the face of social change. For example, Robert H. Lauer and Rance Thomas (1976) investigated the relationships among change in individual life circumstances, perceived rate of social change, and anxiety level in England and in the United States. In both societies the authors found a positive correlation between both kinds of change and anxiety level, with the perceived rate of social change being more significant as a predictor of anxiety level than change in life circumstances. In particular, the greater the number of changes in life circumstances in a year and the greater the perceived rate of change, the greater the likelihood of a high anxiety level. The data in general support the argument that a high rate of change generates psychological reactions, which in turn require adjustment on the part of individuals. They point out, however, that when the changes are defined as desirable, the deleterious effects are minimized.

At times anxieties produced by change may carry over into group relations and when there are no agreed-upon measures to mediate the stress, there is a possibility that hostility will erupt within or among groups. Cyril E. Black (1966:24) observes, for example, that insecurity and anxiety may also interfere in the relationship between countries: ". . . the growing sense of insecurity . . . can be traced to the tensions resulting from the simultaneous development of nationalism and interdependence. Indeed, this sense of insecurity has been such a pervading force that one may venture to interpret the various forms of imperialism, alliance relationships, wars, and experiments in political integration that have characterized international relations in modern times as a search for security that is significantly more urgent than in earlier times."

The rise of anxiety and insecurity in modern society is generally attributed to the increased emphasis upon competition and achievement; the sacrifice of individuality to organizational purposes; to the demand for emotional constraint and self-control; and to the inability of comprehending one's material surroundings. As a consequence, Tibor Scitovsky (1964:228) points to "man's need to compensate for his increasing remoteness from the material world around him." This compensation may take several forms. For example, there is a renewed interest in the United States in handicrafts, in a country where they have become the most obsolete and unprofitable. He notes that schools put the greatest stress on the teaching of handicrafts, and handicrafts as a hobby are becoming the most popular. He remarks: "Let us hope that making one's own ashtrays, finishing one's own furniture, and doing one's own plumbing, painting and papering accomplish this. But even if they do, they do it at the cost of time—and a lot of time— being diverted from more intellectual pursuits. This is especially true of school, where pottery, weaving, glove making, etc., divert time and energy not only from the humanities but probably also from the three Rs" (1964:228).

There are other signs of compensation for the increased sameness and homogeneity of contemporary life. For example, the notion that a house reflects the personality of its occupant is new to this century. Traditionally, houses reflected the *class* of their occupants. With all the utensils, artifacts, and folk art we put in our homes, we cannot hide the fact that we are living not in a farm house, or Greek peasant huts, or potty Victorian collectors' parlors, but in a technologically developed society where things do seem to be getting more and more the same. As our habitations grow more and more alike (our clothes already are alike) does it necessarily follow that we ourselves will be less individual and distinguishable from one another? Most authors discussed in this section would tend to agree that the answer is yes. One, of course, can always question this interpretation.

Mental Illness

Thus far it has been noted that social change is associated with a number of psychological costs such as anxiety, insecurity, stress, a reduction in spontaneity, creativity, personal identity, and the ability to be compassionate. It is now appropriate to raise the question: Does social change lead to a variety of debilitating kinds of states and of behavior and does it extract a cost in terms of mental health? Marc Fried (1972:451) notes that only a few epidemiological studies dealt directly with the effects of social change on mental illness. He describes one important group of studies that investigated the changes over periods of time in rates of psychiatric hospitalization. The studies considered admissions between 1840 and 1940 and showed that, with appropriate adjustments, age-specific first admission rates for ages under 50 were just as high during the last half of the nineteenth century as they are today. There were some short-term fluctuations associated with wars and depressions, but the long-term trends revealed no marked increase that might correspond to this century of urbanization and industrialization in Massachusetts. He points out that other longitudinal studies draw a similar conclusion. The frequency of hospitalization for psychosis, for example, has remained strikingly constant over time. Although in spite of the evidence that rates of psychiatric hospitalization have not risen substantially in the United States over long periods of time, Fried notes that there are suggestions of increased rates of other forms of emotional disturbances (1972:453). Fried refers to studies that make an excellent case for both the rise of psychosomatic disorders and changing distributions of physical illness according to age and sex which "suggest the increasing importance of stress in impaired functioning" (1972:453). He further observes, however, that "A rise in rates for any one sign of disturbed reactions to stress of social change may be, hypothetically, offset or compensated by a decline in other disordered reactions" (1972:453). It is worth noting in this connection that recent studies on mental health indicate that in the United States there is no difference between rural and urban residence in terms of mental disorders (Fischer, 1976:178).

Fried also refers to several comprehensive reviews of the literature on mental illness in developing societies that support the view that acculturation to Western patterns leads to increased rates of psychopathology, and suggests that "we cannot dismiss the possibility that acculturation experiences, particularly those entailing a very rapid and uncoordinated change only for some members of a society, may lead to increased impairments in functioning" (1972:453). This possibility indeed exists and accelerated change conceivably disrupts basic social ties, breaks down social controls, and thus produces a train of personal disorientation, confusion, and uncertainty, which ultimately leads to misery and could produce mental breakdown among some individuals.

On the other hand, there is evidence in the literature that modernization does not produce mental disorders and does not lead to mental breakdowns. Alex Inkeles and David H. Smith (1974:262), in a study of modernization in six countries, found: "Of the modernizing experiences frequently identified as likely to induce individual disorganization by disrupting personality, creating strain, introducing disturbed stimuli, and the like, none consistently and significantly produced increased maladjustment as measured by the Psychosomatic Symptoms Test. In contrast to our experience in studying the impact of the same independent variables on other psychological scales, such as our measures of modern attitudes, the patterns observed in relation to adjustment were not only weak but decidedly lacking in consistency across six countries." And "Whatever may cause psychosomatic symptoms in younger men in developing countries, *it is apparently something other than the exposure to the modernizing institutions such as the school, factory, the city and the mass media*" (1974:263). They have, furthermore, found no evidence that migration itself brings about psychic distress in developing countries.

The modernization experience may cause some emotional problems, but, based on the Inkeles and Smith study at least, it can safely be assumed that the experience is not associated with mental disorders or breakdowns. In some instances, as in the case with India, increased exposure to modernizing influences actually brought with it a *decrease* in the number of psychosomatic symptoms. In this sense, one may even argue that modernizing influences actually improved personal adjustment. As the authors say, "Quite contrary to popular expectation, therefore, one is forced to conclude that, if anything holds in this realm, it is that the more modern the individual, the better his psychic adjustment as measured by the Psychosomatic Symptoms Test" (Inkeles & Smith, 1974:264).

SUMMARY

This chapter examined the economic, social, and psychological costs of change. It was noted that the costs of social change are never evenly distributed and that it is very difficult to determine the "net" pains and pleasures for widely differing groups. There are, however, several broad societal changes that extract a toll from most of us.

The proponents of economic development argue that growth is an essential condition for social advance and for improving the standard of living. The realization of economic benefits is a major preoccupation of the literature dealing with the problems of underdeveloped societies. However, too little has been said about the costs of growing pains associated with rapid growth rates. It has been noted that continued pursuit of economic development is more likely to reduce than to increase social welfare, and development in many instances entails ecologically faulty and socially wasteful types of production. Progress comes about at the costs of environment deterioration and an increase in air and water pollution. However, as Irving Louis Horowitz (1972) asserts, there are few individuals who would give up a single jetport, and even fewer still who would give up their family automobile for the sake of cleaning the atmosphere. He comments that it is well known that no people will endure for long a decrease in standards of income or return to more primitive economic forms in exchange for either a clean atmosphere or clean water. In addition to environmental considerations, there are economic costs incurred in the transition from traditional to a more modern society, and such a transition invariably entails a number of trade-offs.

The notion of social costs is essentially a normative concept and it cannot be satisfactorily measured. Many authors single out the automobile in their illustrations of social costs. More pronounced, however, is the decline in the quality of life as evidenced by a number of indicators and poll data. Social costs are also brought about by the rising incidence of environmentally induced illnesses, the lengthening list of endangered species, the progressive pollution and depleting of lakes and streams, and the ecological undermining of the world food economy. In addition, environmental changes also result in the reduction of options in terms of what we eat, where we live, and where we travel, and pose difficult dilemmas of choices and trade-offs. It was noted also that social costs incur from urban living, the increased underutilization of college-educated people, and scientific specialization.

There are many psychological costs of change in addition to economic and social costs. Perhaps most noticeable is the loss of the individual's ability to comprehend and control his or her own environment. Dehumanization, automatization of personality, and systematization of all aspects of social life are recurrent themes in the literature. The symptoms of "robopathology" are becoming more pronounced as many social roles lack opportunities for humanistic expression, spontaneity, creativity, and compassionate action. The psychological costs of change are also evidenced in increased anxiety and insecurity, and at times they may carry over into group relations, increasing the possibility of hostility. Finally, it was noted that change is not associated with an increase in mental disorders, although there are good possibilities for other forms of emotional disturbances. The experience of modernization does not lead to mental breakdowns, and in some instances modernizing influences actually result in a decrease in the number of psychosomatic symptoms. In the final chapter, the assessment of change will be considered.

SUGGESTED FURTHER READINGS

ANDREWS, FRANK M., ed. *Research on the Quality of Life*. Ann Arbor: Survey Research Center, Institute for Social Research, The University of Michigan, 1986. A series of articles on cross-cultural changes in the quality of life.

BROWN, LESTER R., ed. *State of the World 1987*. New York: W. W. Norton & Co., Inc., 1987. A Worldwatch Institute report on the various costs associated with economic development.

FISCHER, CLAUDE S. *The Urban Experience*. New York: Harcourt, 1976. A highly readable summary of existing knowledge of the social and psychological consequences of urban life.

KAPP, K. WILLIAM. *The Social Costs of Private Enterprise*. New York: Schocken Books, 1971. A most comprehensive account of social costs stemming from people's diverse activities.

LAUER, ROBERT H., and RANCE THOMAS. "A Comparative Analysis of the Psychological Consequences of Change." *Human Relations*, 29(3), 1976, pp. 239–248. A cross-cultural study on the relationship between anxiety and social change.

MISHAN, E. J. *The Economic Growth Debate: An Assessment*. London: George Allen & Unwin, 1977. A widely cited source on the costs of economic growth.

YABLONSKY, LEWIS. *Robopaths*. Indianapolis: Bobbs-Merrill, 1972. A readable, if somewhat pessimistic, account of the psychological costs of progress.

REFERENCES

AMIN, SAMAR. "In Praise of Socialism." *Monthly Review*, 26, September 1974, pp. 1–16.

ANDREWS, FRANK M., ed. *Research on the Quality of Life*. Ann Arbor: Survey Research Center, Institute for Social Research, The University of Michigan, 1986.

BENSMAN, JOSEPH, and ARTHUR J. VIDICH. *American Society: The Welfare State & Beyond, Revised*. South Hadley, Mass: Bergin & Garvey, 1987.

BERG, IVAR, and MARCIA FREEDMAN. "The American Work Place: Illusions and Realities." *Change*, November 1977, pp. 24–30.

BERGER, PETER L. *Pyramids of Sacrifice, Political Ethics, and Social Change*. New York: Basic Books, 1974.

BLACK, CYRIL EDWIN. "Change as a Condition of Modern Life." In Myron Weiner (ed.), *Modernization: The Dynamics of Growth*. New York: Basic Books, 1966, pp. 17–27.

BROWN, LESTER R. *In the Human Interest: A Strategy to Stabilize World Population*. New York: W.W. Norton & Co., Inc., 1974.

BROWN, LESTER R., and SANDRA POSTEL. "Thresholds of Change." In Lester R. Brown (ed.), *State of the World 1987*. New York: W.W. Norton & Co., Inc., 1987, pp. 4–19.

BROWNE, MALCOLM W. "World Threat of Plastic Trash Defies Technological Solution." *The New York Times*, September 6, 1987, p. 16E.

CAMPBELL, ANGUS, PHILIP E. CONVERSE, and WILLARD L. RODGERS. *The Quality of American Life: Perceptions, Evaluations, and Satisfactions*. New York: Russell Sage, 1976.

COMMONER, BARRY A. *The Closing Circle*. New York: Knopf, 1971.

Development and Environment. The Hague: Mouton, 1972.

EHRLICH, PAUL R., and ANNE H. EHRLICH. *Population, Resources, Environment: Issues in Human Ecology*. 2nd ed. San Francisco: Freeman, 1972.

EHRLICH, PAUL R., ANNE H. EHRLICH, and JOHN P. HOLDREN. *Human Ecology*. San Francisco: Freeman, 1973.

ELLUL, JACQUES. *The Technological Society*. New York: Knopf, 1964.

FISCHER, CLAUDE S. *The Urban Experience*. New York: Harcourt, 1970.

FLAVIN, CHRISTOPHER, "Reassessing Nuclear Power." In Lester R. Brown (ed.), *State of the World 1987*. New York: W.W. Norton & Co., Inc., 1987, pp. 57–80.

FLEMING, MACKLIN. *The Price of Perfect Justice*. New York: Basic Books, 1974.

Forbes. "The High Cost of Stress," July 27, 1987, p. 12.

FRANKEL, CHARLES. "The New Egalitarianism and the Old." *Commentary*, September 1973, pp. 54–61.

FRIED, MARC. "Effects of Social Change on Mental Health." In David R. Heise (ed.), *Personality and Socialization*. Chicago: Rand McNally 1972, pp. 451–468.

GABOR, DENNIS, *Innovations: Scientific, Technological, and Social*. New York: Oxford, 1970.

GOULET, DENIS. *The Cruel Choice: A New Concept in the Theory of Development*. New York: Atheneum, 1973.

GREENHOUSE, STEVEN. "Comparing Wealth as Money Fluctuates," *The New York Times*, August 23, 1987, p. 3E.

HACKER, LOUIS. *The Course of American Economic Growth and Development*. New York: Wiley, 1970.

HAMILTON, RICHARD F., and JAMES D. WRIGHT. *The State of the Masses*. New York: Aldine Publishing Co., 1986.

HARDIN, GARRETT. *Exploring New Ethics for Survival: The Voyage of the Spaceship Beagle*. Baltimore: Penguin, 1975.

HARF, JAMES E., and B. THOMAS TROUT. *The Politics of Global Resources: Population, Food, Energy, and Environment*. Durham, N.C.: Duke University Press, 1986.

HARRIS, LOUIS. *The Anguish of Change*. New York: W.W. Norton & Co., Inc., 1973.

HELLER, WALTER W. "Coming to Terms with Growth and the Environment." In Sam H. Schurr (ed.), *Energy, Economic Growth, and the Environment*. Baltimore: Johns Hopkins University Press, 1972, pp. 3–29.

HERMAN, EDWARD S., and RICHARD B. DU BOFF. "How Not to Eliminate Poverty." *Monthly Review*, 25, February 1974, pp. 51–62.

HILLARY, EDMUND, ed. *Ecology 2000: The Changing Face of Earth*. New York: Beaufort Books, 1984.

HOROWITZ, IRVING LOUIS. "The Environmental Cleavage: Social Ecology versus Political Economy. *Social Theory and Practice,* 2, Spring 1972, pp. 125–234.

INGLEHART, RONALD, and JACQUES-RENE RABIER. "Aspirations Adapt to Situations—But Why Are the Belgians So Much Happier Than the French? A Cross-Cultural Analysis of the Subjective Quality of Life." In Frank M. Andrews (ed.), *Research on the Quality of Life.* Ann Arbor: Survey Research Center, Institute for Social Research, The University of Michigan, 1986, pp. 1–56.

INKELES, ALEX, and DAVID H. SMITH. *Becoming Modern: Individual Change in Six Developing Countries.* Cambridge, Mass.: Harvard University Press, 1974.

KAPP, WILLIAM K. *The Social Costs of Private Enterprise.* New York: Schocken Books, 1971.

KENNEDY, PAUL. "The (Relative) Decline of America." *The Atlantic,* August 1987, pp. 29–38.

KLAPP, ORRIN E. *Overload and Boredom: Essays on the Quality of Life in the Information Society.* Westport, Conn.: Greenwood Press, 1986.

LAMPMAN, ROBERT. "Recent U.S. Economic Growth and the Gain in Human Welfare." In Walter W. Heller (ed.), *Perspectives on Economic Growth.* New York: Random House, 1968, pp. 143–162.

LAUER, ROBERT H., and RANCE THOMAS. "A Comparative Analysis of Psychological Consequences of Change." *Human Relations,* 29(3), 1976, pp. 239–248.

LENSKI, GERHARD, and JEAN LENSKI. *Human Societies: An Introduction to Macrosociology,* 5th ed. New York: McGraw-Hill Book Company, 1987.

LEWIS, DAN A., and GRETA SALEM. *Fear of Crime: Incivility and the Production of a Social Problem.* New Brunswick, N.J.: Transaction Books, 1986.

LEWIS, W. ARTHUR. *The Theory of Economic Growth.* London: Allen & Unwin, 1956.

MASLOW, ABRAHAM. "Psychological Data and Value Theory." In Abraham Maslow (ed.), *New Knowledge in Human Values.* New York: Harper & Row, 1959, pp. 119–136.

McGARRELL, EDMUND F., and TIMOTHY J. FLANAGAN, eds. *Sourcebook of Criminal Justice Statistics—1984.* U.S. Department of Justice, Bureau of Justice Statistics. Washington, D.C.: U.S. Government Printing Office, 1985.

McHALE, JOHN. *The Ecological Context.* New York: Braziller, 1970.

MILGRAM, STANLEY. "The Experience of Living in Cities." *Science,* 167, March 13, 1970, pp. 1461–1468.

MISHAN, EZRA J. *The Costs of Economic Growth.* New York: Praeger, 1967.

MISHAN, EZRA J. *The Economic Growth Debate: An Assessment.* London: G. Allen, 1977.

MYDANS, SETH. "Life in Bangladesh Delta: A Race Bred by Disaster," *The New York Times,* June 21, 1987, p. 6Y.

New Yorker. "Notes and Comment," 54, November 20, 1978, pp. 37–39.

PARETO, VILFREDO. *The Mind and Society,* vol. 4, Andrew Bongiorno (trans.) and Arthur Livingston (ed.). New York: Harcourt, 1935.

POLLOCK, CYNTHIA. "Realizing Recycling's Potential." In Lester R. Brown (ed.),*State of the World 1987.* New York: W.W. Norton & Co., Inc., 1987, pp. 101–121.

POSTEL, SANDRA. "Stabilizing Chemical Cycles." In Lester R. Brown (ed.), *State of the World 1987.* New York: W.W. Norton & Co., Inc., 1987, pp. 157–176.

POWERS, CHARLES H. *Vilfredo Pareto.* Beverly Hills, Calif.: Sage Publications, Inc., 1987.

ROSZAK, THEODORE. *Politics and Transcendence in Postindustrial Society.* New York: Doubleday (Anchor Books), 1973.

SCITOVSKY, TIBOR. *Papers on Welfare and Growth.* Stanford, Calif.: Stanford University Press, 1964.

SHABECOFF, PHILIP. "Toxic Waste Threat Termed Greater Than U.S. Estimate," *The New York Times,* March 10, 1985, pp 1, 31.

SPATES, JAMES L., and JOHN J. MACIONIS. *The Sociology of Cities,* 2nd ed. Belmont, Calif.: Wadsworth, 1987.

St. Louis Post-Dispatch. "Changing Rainfall Patterns May Signal Agriculture Shift," July 12, 1987a, p. 9B.

St. Louis Post-Dispatch. "Study Calls Mining Riskiest Job In U.S.," July 24, 1987b, p. 4B.

SUNDQUIST, JAMES L. *Dispersing Population: What America Can Learn from Europe.* Washington, D.C.: Brookings, 1975.

SUSSMAN, MARVIN B., ed. *Author's Guide to Journals in Sociology and Related Fields.* New York: Haworth Press, 1978.

TAKAKI, RONALD, ed.   *From Different Shores: Perspectives on Race and Ethnicity in America.* New York: Oxford, 1987.

The New Republic.   "The Case for Book Burning," September 14/21, 1987, pp. 7–8.

U.S. News & World Report.   "Square One Again in the Gulf," September 14, 1987a, pp. 35–36.

U.S. News & World Report.   "Jam Sessions," September 7, 1987b, pp. 20–27.

WARD, BARBARA, and RENE DUBOIS.   *Only One Earth.* London: Andre Deutsch, 1972.

WEISBERG, BARRY.   *Beyond Repair: The Ecology of Capitalism.* Boston: Beacon Press, 1971.

Wilson Quarterly.   "Eroding the Great Plains." 3(1), Winter 1979, pp. 41–42.

WIRTH, LOUIS.   "Urbanism as a Way of Life." *American Journal of Sociology,* 44, July 1938, pp. 1–24.

Work in America.   Cambridge, Mass.: MIT Press, 1973.

YABLONSKY, LEWIS.   *Robopaths.* Indianapolis: Bobbs-Merrill, 1972.

ZIJDERVELD, ANTON C.   *The Abstract Society: A Cultural Analysis of Our Time.* New York: Doubleday (Anchor Books), 1971.

12 Assessment of Change

This chapter is concerned with the various measurements and methodologies used in the study of social change. It is organized around five themes: technology assessment, methodologies for change evaluation, use of social indicators, methodologies for forecasting change, and policy implications of change assessment. Prior to the discussion of these topics, let us briefly consider some of the more general ways sociologists go about studying change, such as the use of various surveys, and the employment of historical data, personal documents, and records.

The repertoire of social science methodology enables us to assess change at various levels. Although the majority of the studies in sociology deal with events at only one point in time, survey methods exist that can be used to measure change over time. They are employed in longitudinal studies (Babbie, 1986:81) designed to permit observations over an extended period and include panel, recall, and trend surveys.

ASSESSMENT TECHNIQUES

Panel Surveys

Panel surveys are often used to compare the same measurements for the same sample at several different points in time. The sample in this case is called the "panel." Panel analysis is useful in the study of the processes of change in a person's life. A classic example of this type of survey design is found in *The People's Choice* by Paul Lazarsfeld and associates (1944). The researchers interviewed a panel of 600 residents of Erie County, Ohio, once a month between May and November of 1940 with respect to how they intended to vote in the presidential election of 1940. Of particular interest to these investigators was the process by which panel members decided to vote in the way they eventually did. A more recent illustration of such a study is the Survey Research Center's (1972) *A Panel Study of Income Dynamics.* In this survey, approximately 5,000 households throughout the United States were personally interviewed during the spring of each year from 1968 to 1972. The survey obtained detailed information about various sources of income. It has been used to study, among other topics, the changes in the characteristics of those moving into and out of poverty during the five-year period.

A special type of panel analysis is called *cohort analysis.* Such a study deals with more specific subpopulations (cohorts) as they change over time. Generally, a cohort is an age group, such as those born during the 1930s, but it can also be based on some other time grouping, such as people attending college during the Vietnam War, people who got married in 1969, and so on. An example of cohort analysis would be a series of national surveys, at ten-year intervals, to study the changes in economic attitudes of the cohort born during the Great Depression of the early 1930s. A sample of individuals 20 to 25 years of age would be surveyed in 1950; another sample of those 30 to 35 years of age in 1960; up to the age group 60 to 65 years in 1990. Although the people studied in each of the surveys would be different, each sample would represent the survivors of the cohort born between 1930 and 1935 (Babbie, 1986:81).

Roberta Ash Garner (1977) notes that a well-designed panel study allows the researcher to draw conclusions about causality. Thus, one can study change in terms of cause and effect if a study has the following design: "(1) There should be two groups, initially similar (for instance, both selected by random sampling from the same population); (2) one group only is exposed to the possible causal factor; (3) the groups are then compared with the expectation that the one exposed to the factor ('the cause') will be in some way different from the other group" (1977:71). But she also points out that it is difficult and often unethical to establish an experimental situation of this nature for studying human beings. At times, however, such a situation is approximated. For example, in the well-known study of how the political and economic attitudes of young women changed as a result of their attendance at Bennington College would be an illustration of this design (Newcomb, 1943). In this study the similar political attitudes of women was the dependent variable and the four years at Bennington College was the independent variable. As a control, data were also gathered from students of similar background who attended two other colleges. It was found that women at Bennington College developed liberal and radical political and economic views more than did the students from the other two colleges. It can thus be concluded that something about the Bennington experience caused the changes in the attitude.

There are both advantages and limitations to panel studies. Many of the advantages relate to being able to interview the same subjects repeatedly over a period of months or years. If the researcher finds shifts in attitudes or reported behavior, he or she is in a better position to argue that there has been a real change in the population of interest than a researcher who undertakes a different kind of approach, such as the "one-shot" or *cross-sectional* analysis (that is, obtaining data at only one point in time). In cross-sectional surveys researchers know that any difference they find can be attributed either to a real change in attitude or behavior in the population of interest or to a difference due to *sampling error* (that is, even if two samples are drawn from the same population, there will be some differences in observed values due to random fluctuation). This sampling error difference can be ruled out when a panel design is used. Another advantage of panel studies is that they permit much more information to be collected about each respondent than is feasible with a cross-sectional survey design. They also avoid a heavy dependence on the memory of respondents for information about the time period covered by the panel; however, they may still rely on memory for questions about subjects' past.

Panel studies, like all research techniques utilized in social science, are obviously not without their limitations. One difficulty is that over a period of time there is bound to be some sample mortality; that is, there will be a loss of panel members due to the difficulty in reaching them, lack of cooperation, or death. It was pointed out elsewhere in the text, for example, that approximately one out of every five Americans change residence every year. The record-keeping problems caused by such mobility for a panel study are substantial. For example, in a panel study of income dynamics a substantial effort went into minimizing sample loss, but still only 62 percent of those in the original sample remained at the end of five years. Another limitation of panel analysis is that it takes a long time to collect data. It is also more expensive than other types of designs. Still another problem with repeated interviews with the same group is *panel conditioning*, that is, the risk of repeated contacts may sensitize the subjects. For instance, members of a panel may want to be consistent with the views they express on con-secutive occasions. If this happens, the panel becomes atypical of the population it was selected to represent (Nachmias & Nachmias, 1987:142).

Recall Surveys

Another form of quasi-longitudinal design is the *recall survey*. Such a survey conducts an observation at one point in time and has respondents remember information to establish a prior observation. Such an approach is practically useless as evidence for inferring causality. Still, studies based on recall surveys occasionally appear in the literature. For example, after the United States recognized China, an investigator may want to study the impact of recognition on attitudes toward China. The investigator takes a survey of present attitudes and also asks respondents to recall their attitudes before recognition of China. He or she then compares the remembered attitudes with present attitudes to determine how much they have changed. The recall survey is the weakest kind of longitudinal design. It attempts to approximate the *pretest-posttest* one-group design by recalling the pretest observation. Obviously, lacking control over history, maturation, and experimental mortality, recall designs provide a very weak basis for causal inferences. In addition, memory decay and distortion are forms of the maturational factor that is particularly likely to contribute to survey invalidity.

Trend Surveys

Trend surveys are useful for describing changes. Trend surveys sample a population at two or more points in time. The population is the same but different samples are drawn for different observations. Examples would be a comparison of U.S. censuses over time, indicating growth in the national population, or a series of National Opinion Research Center polls showing trends in attitudes over time concerning, for instance, abortion, pornography, satisfaction with work and financial situation, or extramarital sex (*Public Opinion*, 1987:25–27). Trend surveys are also used to determine changes in income and wealth, work time required to buy certain consumer goods and services (*Fortune*, 1987), and in general to "monitor" social change in the form of social indicators (Moore & Sheldon, 1965; Harris, 1987), which will be discussed shortly.

Historical Analysis

In addition to panel, recall, and trend surveys, sociologists interested in the study of social change often use historical data to establish long-term trends or to test theories (Motz, 1983). For example, in an attempt to study long-term trends, Pitirim A. Sorokin (1957) used content analysis (a technique to determine the content of a recorded communication by systematic, objective, and quantitative analysis) of paintings. He classified paintings of the various historical periods into two categories, *religious* and *secular*, in an attempt to learn what changes had occurred in the world view. He found that 94.7 percent of the known European paintings of the tenth and eleventh centuries were of the religious nature and only 5.3 percent were secular. By the fourteenth and fifteenth centuries, the percentage of paintings of a religious nature had dropped to 85, by the seventeenth century to 50.2, by the nineteenth century to 10, and by the twentieth century to 3, with corresponding rises in the secular category.

Other illustrations of attempts to establish long-term historical trends include David Riesman and associates' (1961) study of changes in American national character, Karl Polanyi's (1957) description of the rise and fall of market economies, A. M. Carr-Saunders and P. A. Wilson's (1933) detailed treatment of the growth of professions in modern societies, and Seymour Martin Lipset's (1963) analysis of the development of democratic institutions in the United States.

At times historical case studies are used to test theories. In such instances the emphasis is not so much to document trends over time as to examine in detail one reasonably limited set of historical events. A good illustration of this is Kai Erikson's (1966) analysis of American puritanism. Ever since Emile Durkheim formulated the notion that deviance served certain social functions in a society, sociologists have looked for evidence to support this contention. Durkheim had in mind the idea that a society needed its deviants in order to reaffirm continually the boundaries of propriety in society. The arguments for the importance of deviants are intriguing. They provide a novel way of showing how certain institutions in a society, if not the society itself, continue to operate. Durkheim argues, for example, that without the existence of sinners, a church could not exist. The very existence of sin provides the opportunity for believers to reaffirm the faith that has been offended by the sinner. So the worst thing that can happen to a church is to eliminate sin completely from the world and completely propagate the faith to society.

By selecting a specific case, Erikson hoped to demonstrate how, to the extent that a common morality exists in a society, the society comes to depend on its deviants for the maintenance of its social boundaries. In *The Wayward Puritans* he shows how these theoretical notions can be applied to understand the witch hunts of colonial America. Relying primarily on secondary sources, he describes how the "moral entrepreneurs" of early Massachusetts colonial society, in their zeal to maintain religious purity, launched full-scale attacks on alleged Salem witches. This particular attack on "deviants" is only one of several that Erikson documents and analyzes. Although he does not draw these parallels himself, one could, on the basis of causal historical knowledge, assume that a number of historical cases might be used as additional historical illustrations of the functional view of deviance: the McCarthyism of the 1950s, the events leading up to the laws of discrimination against Jews in Nazi Germany, the internment of Japanese-Americans during World War II, and so on.

The use of personal documents, such as diaries, letters, and biographical statements, has long been considered useful in sociological research aimed at studying social change. Perhaps the best-known example of this form of primary data in sociological research is W. I. Thomas and Florian

Znaniecki's (1918) study, *The Polish Peasant in Europe and America*. In this investigation the authors were concerned with the adaptation of individuals to new forms of social organization. The Polish peasant in America provided an excellent opportunity for understanding the modes of adaptation of persons transplanted from a largely agrarian to a modern industrial society. Their research was based on letters that these immigrants sent to their families in the "the old country." The data obtained from these letters, in fact, provided a continuous history of their New World experience. These letters, constituting actual interaction between persons, allowed the researchers to assess dynamics of attitude change, changing relations within primary groups, and the development of community life.

Sociologists interested in historical experiences of large groups or population aggregates often turn to available records that provide systematic historical data on large numbers of individuals. For example, when demographers seek to document rates of fertility, patterns of immigration and migration, changing food resources in society, and birth and death rates, they utilize existing statistical records. These records enable them to examine trends of changes on a number of levels: for a selected part of society, for a whole society, for several societies—indeed, even for the world.

Of course, historical records can be used for other types of studies of change. For example, Frances Fox Piven and Richard Cloward (1971) traced the welfare system in the United States from the Great Depression to the present, revealing a distinctive pattern of relief policy—at certain times relief policy has been quite liberal and at other times highly restrictive. Their major thesis, which is convincingly documented through their historical investigation, is that the welfare system has been used to control and regulate the poor. "Historical evidence suggests that relief arrangements are initiated or expanded during occasional outbreaks of civil disorder produced by mass unemployment, and are then abolished or contracted when political stability is returned" (Piven & Cloward, 1971:xiii).

These general comments on methodological tools for social change research are not intended to replace the more detailed discussions found in books about methods of social research. They are simply intended to provide a brief exposure to some of the strategies utilized in the study of social change. Let us now consider the subject of technology assessment.

TECHNOLOGY ASSESSMENT

In Chapter 4 it was shown that technology is one of the principal sources of social change. Technological developments have certainly brought society to an unprecedented level of comfort and prosperity, but they also have all too often brought unanticipated and undesirable consequences.

From environmental pollution to urban congestion, many of the major problems in society are strongly influenced by modern technology. The concern with the growing impact of technology on society and some of its deleterious effects gave rise to *technology assessment*. It is defined by one of its most influential practitioners and spokesmen, Joseph F. Coates (quoted by Alan Porter and associates, 1986:208), as "a class of policy studies which systematically examine the effects on society that may occur when a technology is introduced, extended or modified. It emphasizes those consequences that are unintended, indirect, or delayed." Such studies should also offer alternative solutions to a problem based on their social costs, and make recommendations for policy changes or for new initiatives.

In a provocative book, *Technology and Society*, David M. Freeman (1974:2–3) posits five reasons for the necessity of increased technology assessment:

1. The new technologies advanced and diffused in recent times have shown enormous power to alter society and affect the environment on previously unknown scales. Supersonic aircraft, pesticides, nuclear wastes with half-lives of thousands of years, the decline and growth of industries relocating populations, transportation systems contributing to suburban sprawl, mind- and body-altering drugs, all these and many more produce effects felt over great space and time.

2. Nowadays there is a trend of diminishing lead times between initial technological invention and widespread diffusion and application leaving less time to make analysis and adjustment.

3. Various technologies are impacting on a human population of increasing size, diversity, and differentiation—developments that make technological impacts more diverse, uneven, and difficult to sort out.

4. Formerly, a small group of elites made strategic decisions unencumbered by interests of outsiders, peasants, and the urban poor. However, political revolutions of the last two centuries have all posited the ideal of participatory decision making on the part of the affected. The world is full of conflicting and cooperating groups who seek access to decisions that affect their lives and those of their children.

5. Both the beneficial and detrimental impacts of technologies are felt with increasing rapidity ever more powerfully and unevenly on diverse sectors of the population. Our technical powers, as in the past, exceed our capacity to make fully intelligent social choices with full awareness of the consequences.

In recent years the spread of concerns with technological impacts has led governments of industrialized nations to begin thinking about new modes of technological planning and decision making. In the United States, Emilio Q. Daddario, then a congressman from Connecticut, introduced a bill in 1967 calling on the federal government to establish a Technology Assessment Board in order "to provide a method for identifying, assessing, publicizing, and dealing with the implications and effects of applied research and technology (Teich, 1986:137). His initiative resulted in the passage of the Technology Assessment Act of 1972, establishing within the legislative branch an Office of Technology Assessment (OTA)—a move that greatly enhanced the capacity of Congress to deal with technological issues. Over the years, OTA has grown increasingly influential as a policy advisory body to Congress, greatly expanded its scope, and gained increasing currency among executive agencies of the federal government, corporations, and academic researches (Teich, 1986:138).

The scope of technology assessment ranges from broad *problem-oriented* investigations, which may consider a major social problem (for example, energy shortage), through *technology-oriented* studies designed to anticipate the effects of a particular technology (videophone, for example), to the most specific form, the *project* assessment, which concentrates on a single application of technology (for instance, power-plant siting) (Porter and associates, 1986:210).

The approaches to technology assessment may be future-oriented, present-oriented, or past-oriented. There are two types of *future-oriented* approaches: anticipatory and responsive. The former entails forecasting new trends and their possible effects—for example, genetic engineering. The latter responds to already perceived problems—for example, new nuclear power plants. There are also two types of *present-oriented* assessments: reactive and corrective. The reactive deals with problems of unknown causes or disasters such as large-scale oil spills or earthquakes. The corrective is concerned with known problems whose effects are felt, their causes already traced, and for which corrective actions are possible, such as air or water pollution. *Past-oriented* assessments are retrospective in nature. They examine the circumstances and facts of why a project was successful (for example, sperm banks), rejected, or abandoned—for example, nuclear planes (Bartocha, 1973:341–342).

Common Steps in Technology Assessment

In five technology assessment studies (of automotive emissions, computers and communications, industrial enzymes, mariculture, and water pollution by domestic wastes), Gabor Strasser (1973:915) identified seven general steps that are comprehensive enough to fit many circumstances.

- **Step 1:** Define the assessment task—discuss relevant issues and any major problems; establish scope (breadth and depth) of inquiry; and develop project ground rules.
- **Step 2:** Describe relevant technologies—describe the major technology being assessed, other technologies supporting the major technology; and the ones that are competitive to the major and supporting technologies.
- **Step 3:** Develop state-of-society assumptions—identify and describe major nontechnological factors influencing the application of the relevant technologies.

- **Step 4:** Identify impact areas—ascertain those societal characteristics that will be most influenced by the application of the assessed technology.
- **Step 5:** Make preliminary impact analysis—trace and integrate the process by which the assessed technology makes its societal influence felt.
- **Step 6:** Identify possible action options—develop and analyze various programs for obtaining maximum public advantage from the assessed technologies.
- **Step 7:** Complete impact analysis—analyze the degree to which each action option would alter the specific societal impacts of the assessed technology discussed in Step 5.

Methods of Technology Assessment

Technology assessment has no defined set of tools to be applied in a definite predetermined way (Bartocha, 1973:345). The tools are borrowed from all fields—the econometrician, the statistician, the sociologist, and the operations research analyst. These techniques include qualitative and quantitative appraisal techniques such as those used for the selection of research projects; systems analysis; decision aids such as relevance trees and evaluation matrices; economic, technological, social, and if it were possible, political forecasts; simulation and operations research models, especially those that are able to cope with random phenomena; questionaires; public participation hearings; and finally, and not to be overlooked, sheer gut feeling and intuition.

As it may be expected, there are several deficiencies in the use of technology assessment. According to Bodo Bartocha (1973:347–348), the most critical voids in our knowledge regarding technology assessment are:

1. Criteria for choice and priorities
2. Reference standards and pacing parameters sensitive to end objectives
3. Indications and new values systems to express "worth" in other than just monetary terms
4. Better simulation techniques and dynamic models
5. Skilled interdisciplinary personnel and adequate resources
6. Popularization and public understanding of long-range risk, expected values, and uncertainty, and
7. Imagination

These limitations are further compounded by the high cost of technology assessment programs. Joseph F. Coates (1977:269–270) says that the costs of conducting the Alaska Pipeline study are alleged to have run about $9 million. Smaller assessment studies range from $125,000 to $300,000. A study conducted by the Department of Health, Education, and Welfare on "violence and television" cost $1.5 million.

Environmental Impact Statement

An independent examination of methods and techniques for assessing the impacts of technology stemmed from the requirements of the National Environmental Policy Act of 1969 for the preparation of environmental impact statements. According to Section 102 of the act, each agency "must include in every recommendation or report on proposals for legislation and other major Federal actions significantly affecting the quality of the human environment, a detailed statement by the responsible official on: (i) the environmental impact of the proposed action; (ii) any adverse environmental effects which cannot be avoided should the proposal be implemented; (iii) alternatives to the proposed action; (iv) the relationship between local short-term use of man's environment and the maintenance and enhancement of long-term productivity, and (v) any irreversible and irretrievable commitments of resources which would be involved if the proposed action should be implemented" (Coates, 1977:261).

This requirement to prepare environmental impact statements has created a general demand throughout the federal system for systematic exploration of the secondary impacts of projects, and a consequent demand for the development of methodology, techniques, approaches and procedures. During the first three years of the act, some 3,500 impact statements have been prepared, at an aggregate cost of about $65 million.

The 1972 World Environmental Conference in Stockholm was instrumental in creating an international awareness about the protection of environment and the conservation of natural resources. Following the model of the United States, many countries drafted legislation to create new departments on environmental protection and mandated environmental impact requirements (C. Porter, 1985:27–29). In the years since the conference, there has been a trend toward the gradual acceptance of thorough environmental investigation and evaluation of projects in most industrial countries of the world. There has also been a growing concern with social impacts. In Australia, for example, there were many instances in which white orkers were introduced into a remote or rural area with a small population. Aboriginal communities were particularly vulnerable to intrusions, and hostility often developed between an existing black community and the new white population. Even without racial conflicts, the introduction into a poorer settlement of a new highly paid work force, associated with, for instance, strip-mining ventures, can result in tensions resulting from envy of the more affluent life-style of the newcomers. In addition, when hundreds, if not thousands, of workers descend on a small isolated community, severe pressures are exerted on existing social organizations (schools, recreation facilities, hospitals), and conflict is likely to ensue between members of the community and the workers. Even with an urban environment, certain types of developments need attention. For instance, a major highway may geographically divide a community, as a lack of access across the highway would interfere with shopping patterns or children's movements to and from school. It is part of the environmental impact statement to consider the results of the development on the existing social environment and for the necessary commitments to be made to mitigate any adverse impacts.

Social Technology

It should be noted that the methods of technology assessment can also be used for the study of the effects of "social" technologies. The definition of technology assessment is capable of embracing changes in institutions and organizations—changes such as the invention of mass armies and the related invention of the military draft, the Land Grant Act establishing the state college system in the United States, the invention of pay-as-you-go income tax, and many others (Coates, 1977:268). One may consider legislation as a principal means of institutionalizing such social inventions and, therefore, clearly in need of continuing assessment. In fact, some assessments of this nature have been already carried out; for example, studies of the impact of marijuana on society, and the 1986 study by the Attorney General's Commission on Pornography (Vago, 1988:309).

Assessment Criteria

David M. Freeman (1974:125–137) provides some useful guidance for "good" technology assessment, which must at the same time be a good "learning system." He presents six criteria for judging the quality of the technology assessment effort:

1. *The criterion of externality.* Individuals and organizations try to project anticipated gains and losses to themselves of alternative courses of action. Such self-interested analysis ignores the implications of alternatives for others who are not represented in the action. For example, oil shale residues contain many salts that, if leached by water, could greatly raise salinity levels of the Colorado River. Such an increase in water salinity would represent a significant negative externality imposed on the peoples of Arizona and Mexico. Producers of petroleum could raise the prices of oil sufficiently to pay for controls on leaching and thus internalize the costs, but price competition in the industry creates an incentive to externalize as many of these costs as possible. Obviously, petroleum producers would find it "irrational" to pay the costs of maintaining the higher levels of water quality for the benefit of others.

2. *The criterion of allocating burdens of uncertainty.* Freeman notes that there has been an assumption that a technological trend should be permitted to continue as long as economically profitable, unless it can be con-

clusively proved that the technology causes or contributes to important social or environmental problems. Therefore, the burdens of uncertainty are on those groups who challenge the system of ongoing trends. It is left to the opponents to establish the presence of harm. Shouldn't manufacturers and promoters try to establish "harmlessness" of their products? A good planning system must collect evidence regarding a technology's impacts before it is allowed either to proliferate or stagnate. The important consideration now is how to allocate the costs of research among developers, opponents, and the public. Uncertainties can be converted to risk by grouping possible future events—beneficial and adverse—into probability distributions. Then the clusters of events can be analyzed as to their probabilities of occurrence. Freeman believes as a general principle that the burden of uncertainty should be upon the opponents and the general public in the early stages of innovation. However, in the interests of a more balanced assessment and before the technology proliferates and is "frozen" into potentially dangerous patterns, he feels that the burden of uncertainty should be shifted to the promoters.

3. *The criterion of constituency creation.* A key concern here is that present assessment systems fail to provide significantly impacted social interests with effective representation. There is a lack of organized efforts to challenge the interests of powerful groups coupled with a reluctance to challenge the tendency to assume that existing technological programs are harmless. Freeman notes that a public agency has already been proposed to act as a technological ombudsman to represent otherwise unrepresented interests in public forums. The agency, possibly acting as an arm of Congress, like the General Accounting Office, would be charged with investigating the negative factors associated with technological projects, identifying potentially impacted groups, and pressing their interests. The result would be to shift more of the burdens of uncertainty upon promoters of technology and it would give voice to unorganized interests before cumulated impacts become severely damaging.

4. *The criterion of preserving future options and reversibility of action.* Because planners engaged in technology assessments have no adequate means to balance social costs against benefits and because they are inevitably operating with low levels of understanding and control in highly complex and changing systems, they should value highly those courses of action that retain the greatest possible latitude for further action. Reversibility of action should be counted as a principal benefit, and irreversibility as a principal cost. For example, pollution of a lake tends to be more highly irreversible than pollution of a river because of the river's capacity to disperse the pollutants. Therefore, the penalties for polluting lakes should be greater than those imposed on parties polluting rivers. Four kinds of decisions are likely to entail long-term irreversibilities: (1) those requiring permanent

and costly physical structures such as San Francisco's Bay Area Rapid Transit System; (2) commitment to new technologies such as shale oil exploitation; (3) decisions about manpower outputs of educational institutions; and (4) when long sequences of decisions are highly interrelated, the frameworks are established, and it is easier to adopt successive decisions to them than to change them. The more planners learn to identify and analyze the problems associated with preserving options and reversibility of actions, the better the quality of technology assessment.

5. *The criterion of predicting cumulative effects of scale.* Impacts vary according to the amount of diffusion of a technology. Conceptual tools need to be developed to predict the impacts of technological proliferation. One approach might be to portend the multipliers of a technology within certain timeframes. Even if the estimates are incorrect, it is useful for policy purposes to have some notion as to what alternative multipliers would mean for the input demands of the technological programs on physical and social resources and the positive and negative impacts of their outputs on social systems. For example, only a few decades ago DDT was considered a miraculous insect killer, yet because of the cumulative effects of large applications, it became magnified in the biological food chain and has become a potential threat to humankind.

6. *The criterion of predicting impacts of converging technologies.* Multiple technologies tend to interact to produce outcomes different from that produced from any single one. For example, transportation, mining, and construction technologies have converged with farming technologies to produce unemployment of unskilled labor. Women's suffrage was greatly affected by the convergent technological impacts of the tin can, motion pictures, the typewriter, telephone, and contraceptive devices. To the extent that convergence problems can be analyzed, technology assessment is improved.

These recommendations by Freeman need to be taken into serious consideration for improving the art of technology assessment. Obviously, many constraints stand in the way of improvement, such as our ability to predict innovation and determine safe thresholds and our capability to predict new values of fundamental importance. Donald C. Blaisdell (1973:56–57) believes that perhaps the most serious handicap to all proposals for technology assessment is that it is entirely alien to the American ethos. He maintains that the philosophy and methods of technology assessment are grounded in the assumption that persons are both legally and naturally willing to face the consequences of their actions. Historically, risk taking, rather than consequence facing, characterized the American outlook. There is also a strong obsession that all our ills can be solved by applied science. So prevalent is this belief that Blaisdell believes that some means must be found for harnessing the dynamism of professionals and the fate of laypeople in the potential of research and development to improve the environment. In the next section the methodologies for change evaluation will be considered.

METHODOLOGIES FOR CHANGE EVALUATION

In recent years there has been a noticeable rise of interest in applying social science methodologies to the evaluation of change. This concern is reflected in the increasing use of social science methods under the heading of "evaluation research." Evaluation research is a form of applied research (as contrasted to "pure" research) whose objective is to assess the effectiveness of ongoing programs and activities intended to bring about some kind of planned change. The aim of evaluation research is to establish how successful a particular planned change effort is in achieving its goals of improving conditions for some groups or individuals (Rossi & Freeman, 1985:19–20). There have been many attempts for planned change to eliminate some negative condition or create some positive condition that affects the lives of people by instituting various programs. The federal government, for instance, initiated a large variety of programs during the 1960s with the purpose of eventually eliminating poverty. Similar examples of planned change efforts can be cited in the areas of corrections, mental health, and fertility control. A basic objective of evaluation research is to answer the question of whether or not such improvement-oriented programs achieve what they set out to achieve. The outcome of such research can be used in policy-making to determine which programs should be changed in what way, which programs should be eliminated, and so on.

Technically speaking, there are no formal methodological differences between evaluation and nonevaluation research. Both have in common the techniques and the basic steps that must be followed in the research process. The difference is in the intent and purpose of the investigator (Smith & Glass, 1987:33). Evaluation research uses the deliberately planned introduction of some independent variable. Unlike nonevaluation research, evaluation research assumes that program goals and objectives are desirable and its purpose is to determine the extent to which these objectives have been attained. Essentially, "evaluative research asks about the *kind* of change the program views as desirable, the *means* by which this change is to be brought about, and the signs according to which such change can be recognized" (Suchman, 1967:15).

Carol Weiss (1972:6–8) identifies several additional specific criteria that distinguish evaluation research from other types of research: (1) evaluation research is generally conducted for a client who intends to use the research as a basis for decision making; (2) the investigator deals with his or her client's questions as to whether the client's program is accomplishing what the client wishes it to accomplish; (3) the objective of evaluation research is to ascertain whether the program goals are being reached; (4) the investigator works in a situation where priority goes to the program as opposed to the evaluation; (5) there is always a possibility of conflicts between the researcher and program staff because of the divergences of loyalties and objectives; and (6) in evaluation research there is an emphasis on results that are useful for policy decisions. Consequently, some special problems are associated with evaluation research. There might be resistance to it by administrators of programs who feel that negative results might terminate their programs. The investigator might also be subjected to time constraints because he or she must deal within the time structure of the program being studied.

Identifying Evaluation Goals

In evaluating change, a number of areas must be taken into consideration. For ascertaining the program objectives, Suchman (1967:39–41) provides a guideline for questions that should be raised:

1. *What* is the nature of the content of the objective? Are we interested in changing knowledge, attitudes or behavior? Are we concerned with producing exposure, awareness, interest, or action?
2. *Who* is the target of the program? At which groups in the population is the program aimed?
3. *When* is the desired change to take place? Are we seeking an immediate effect or are we gradually building toward some postponed effect?
4. Are the objectives *unitary* or *multiple*? Is the program aimed at a single change or at a series of changes?
5. What is the desired *magnitude* of effect? What is the extent of anticipated results?
6. *How* is the objective to be attained? What methods, procedures, and techniques will be used in realizing program objectives?

To this list, one should add: What are the unintended effects of the program objectives? How much does it cost? And what are its costs relative to its effectiveness and benefits? (Rossi & Freeman, 1985:18).

Design Considerations

Many possible research approaches can be used for evaluating the effectiveness of a program. One approach might be the study of a group of individuals from the target population after it has been exposed to a program that had been developed to cause change. This approach is referred to as the *one-shot study*. Another possible approach is to study a group of individuals both *before and after* exposure to a particular program. Still another possibility would be the use of some kind of *controlled experiment*.

There are many different kinds of controlled experiments, and the simplest kind for evaluation research may be set up in the following way: A number of individuals are selected from the target population with the use of probability sampling. The object is to create two groups as nearly similar as possible. The usual way to do this is through the random assignment of half the selected individuals to one group and the other half to the second group.

The key aspect of experimentation is that one group, the experimental group, participates in the program under consideration while the second group, the control group, does not. Measurements of the desired goals and outcomes of the program are made both before and after the program is conducted to see whether the program produces its desired changes. This is done for both the experimental and the control group. Ideally, the measurements should show no difference between the two groups before the program commences. If, however, the program is effective, the "after" measurements should show that the experimental group has experienced a change in the desired direction, which is noticeably greater than any change registered for the control group. The "after" measurement for the control group is the means by which we take into account any of the "other changes" related to the desired outcome of the program, which may be occurring for both the experimental and control groups. If we subtract the change experienced by the control group from the change evidenced in the experimental group, the result is a measure of the program's impact.

At this point it should be obvious that an experiment is clearly superior to either a one-shot study or a before-and-after study. The control group in an experiment eliminates the possible interpretation that "other changes" are not accounted for in the one-shot and before-and-after approaches. However, in actual situations, the use of control groups is not always feasible. In some instances, the use of control would involve the denial of certain program treatments (for example, clinical) or benefits (for instance, welfare) to individuals.

At times, these research designs are supplemented by *cost-benefit analysis* and *social audits*. Cost-benefit analysis is basically a method for discovering the value of a good for which no market price exists. In social research, the difficulty with cost-benefit analysis is that there are no objective criteria with which to measure costs and benefits. More important, no provisions exist for incorporating nonmonetary elements into the calculations of cost-benefit analysis. For example, how does one assign a value to "marital happiness" or "work satisfaction"? Moreover, because a change in one part of the social system will affect other parts in the same system, it is essential to make decisions about which effects are the important ones. For example, a program for reducing speech problems may in turn create the need to retrain speech therapists for other occupations. Although there are limitations to cost-benefit analysis, at times it has proved to be a useful supplemental method in evaluation studies.

Perhaps the easiest types of costs to estimate are "extra expenditures needed to add a particular supplemental service to an ongoing program" (Glaser, 1973:25). For example, the cost per client can be determined by adding up the costs of operating the entire supplemental services needed and dividing by the number of clients per year. Benefits may be measured by "estimated reductions in social costs" (Glaser, 1973:27). But Daniel Glaser (1973:36–39) also notes that many social costs are purely speculative. For example, there is no way of expressing the anguishes of rape or the emotional costs of mugging. Still, some social costs can be rationally dealt with. For instance, the costs of heavy drug usage may be viewed from the point of view of society's loss of the drug user's work power and the loss of his or her potential tax dollars.

Social audits are also used to supplement other forms of research design and are helpful in determining the efficiency of a program. In the social audit "resource inputs initiated by policy are traced from the point at which they are disbursed to the point at which they are experienced by the ultimate intended recipient of those resources" (Coleman, 1972:18). Social audit is obviously related to research outcomes. Lack of social change may be due to two factors: (1) The resource inputs may have been ineffective, or (2) they may never have reached their intended recipients. As an illustration of social audits, one may consider the tracing of resource inputs from the point of dispersement in voluntary organizations such as the United Fund to the point at which those inputs are experienced by the intended recipients.

Data Collection

In addition to considerations of objectives and research designs, evaluation research also includes plans for data collection, sampling, and measurement. Concerning data collection sources for evaluation research, Weiss (1972:53) compiled the following list:

> Interviews, questionnaires, observation, ratings (by peers, staff, experts), psychometric tests (of attitudes, values, personality preferences, norms, beliefs), institutional records, government statistics, tests (of information, interpretation, skills, application of knowledge), projective tests, situational tests (presenting the respondent with simulated life situations), diary records, physical evidence, clinical examinations, financial records, and documents (minutes of board meetings, newspaper accounts of policy actions, transcripts of trials).

As far as sampling is concerned, probability sampling plans are generally preferred for choosing people from the target population, but they are not always possible in evaluation research (Rossi & Freeman, 1985:235–263). In reality, more often than not a sample will consist of self-selected volunteers. The purpose of measurement in evaluation research is to develop measures of variables that validly and reliably reflect what the investigator is trying to measure. It is important for a program to have clear and explicitly stated goals if it is to permit valid and reliable measurements.

Problems of Research Implementation

It is important to note that the effectiveness of a program is often considered by administrators and program personnel to be secondary to the implementation of the program. Clearly, conflicts exist between the two goals. For example, as a program is being carried out, the strategies for dealing with the problem area may change because of the decisions of program administrators. It is also possible that program personnel may change or participants may drop out during the program. To cope with these and similar problems, Weiss (1972:98) makes the following suggestions:

1. Take frequent periodic measures of program effect (for example, monthly assessments in programs of education, training, therapy) rather than limiting collection of outcome data to one point in time.
2. Encourage a clear transition from one program approach to another. If changes are going to be made, attempt to see that A is done for a set period, then B, then C.
3. Clarify the assumptions and procedures of each phase and classify them systematically.
4. Keep careful records of the persons who participated in each phase. Rather than lumping all participants together, analyze outcomes in terms of the phase(s) of the program in which each person participated.

Utilization of Results

The final consideration of evaluation research involves the utilization of results. As James Coleman (1972:6) states, "the ultimate product is not a 'contribution to existing knowledge' in the literature, but a social policy modified by the research results." In many instances, however, the clients fail to utilize results of evaluation research, or the results have no visible impact on subsequent policy decisions (Weiss, 1986:216). They may feel committed to particular ways of doing things despite evidence that the program is ineffective. (This is particularly true in instances when programs were instigated by political pressures such as the various endeavors in model city programs, war against poverty, drug and alcohol rehabilitation, and corrections. As public interest waned in the later stages of these programs, there was no pressure to incorporate the results of evaluation studies into the ongoing activities.) The utilization of results could also bring about changes in relationships with funding agencies, clients, or other organizations. It is also plausible that the recommendations are economically unfeasible for the organization, and as a result, it cannot change its practices.

Obviously, there are a number of ways an organization can respond to the results of evaluation research. If the results are negative or anticipated to be so, an organization can attempt to use evaluation research in the following ways:

1. *Eyewash:* an attempt to justify a weak or bad program by deliberately selecting only those aspects that "look good." The objective of the evaluation is limited to those parts of the program evaluation that appear successful.
2. *Whitewash:* an attempt to cover up program failure or errors by avoiding any objective appraisal. A favorite device here is to solicit "testimonials" which divert attention from the failure.
3. *Posture:* an attempt to use evaluation as a "gesture" of objectivity and to assume the pose of "scientific" research. This "looks good" to the public and is a sign of "professional" status.
4. *Postponement:* an attempt to delay needed action by pretending to seek the "facts." Evaluative research takes time and hopefully the storm will blow over by the time the study is completed. (Suchman, 1967:143)

The common feature of all these techniques is the attempt by the organization to manipulate evaluation research for its own interests. Evaluation researchers must be aware of this possibility and act accordingly.

In some instances where the results of evaluation research are negative, the clients can discard the negative findings. In the field of corrections, for example, the following list of rationalizations of negative results has been used by professionals (Ward & Kassebaum, 1972:302):

The therapeutic relationships examined or the impact of the program is "too subtle to measure with statistics."

Even though they may come back to prison, they are better or happier or more emotionally stable people for having participated in the program.

The effects of the program can only be measured in the long run, not just during the first six months or year after release.

The program or the technique is OK but it is not designed for this particular individual.

The reason that the program failed was that it wasn't extensive enough or long enough or applied by the right people.

The program is worth it if it saved one person.

It is not too surprising to see such rationalizations from individuals and organizations whose programs are subjected to criticism as a result of evaluation research. On the other hand, dismissing the findings of evaluation research may be the result of methodological weaknesses and design irrelevance because policymakers are more likely to rely on their own experience rather than trust results of poorly executed studies. Finally, even if the study is methodologically sound and well carried out, it may not bear on the "critical issues." In spite of these limitations, evaluation research should be perceived as an important way of making the knowledge of the social sciences relevant to the study of social change, and social scientists need to be encouraged to devote more attention to it (Rossi & Freeman, 1985:389–398). In the next section the use of social indicators in the study of change will be examined.

SOCIAL INDICATORS

Social scientists have long felt the need to develop valid statistical measures to monitor levels and changes over time in fundamental social concerns. In the 1960s there was a growing interest in the United States in measures of social conditions to supplement economic indicators with information on the quality of life. This interest resulted in proposals for social indicators that allow researchers to assess changes in the condition of a nation over time from some point in the past to the present. Measures of social indicators basically involve the identification of certain key aspects of social life such as health, crime, housing, satisfaction, use of time, etc. These categories, in turn, are broken down into specific contents for which data are gathered over time. Generally, social indicators are conceived of as long-term measures in that the same data are gathered consistently at specific intervals to allow for an analysis of changes which have taken place.

The social indicators "movement" is relatively recent, although there were earlier attempts. For example, in 1929 a presidential committee was appointed to undertake a quantitative analysis of American society and the changes that were occurring. It resulted in the publication of *Recent Social Trends* in 1933 (de Neufville, 1975:40). Much of the resurgence of interest in social indicators was due to the success of economists using economic indicators to predict the advantages of a tax cut upon the economy in the early 1960s. The question was posed by Raymond A. Bauer: "If we have highly organized *economic* indicators, why can't we set up a system of social indicators as well?" (quoted by Gross & Springer, 1969:18). The same question was in the minds of the President's Science Advisory Committee when, in 1962, it called for "the systematic collection of basic behavioral data for the United States . . . data that are comparable, systematic and periodically gathered" (Gross & Springer, 1969:18). By 1972 more than a thousand books and articles on social indicators had appeared. In the early 1980s, there was widespread reduction of funding for social research, which included social indicator work, and an apparent decline in interest by government officials in monitoring perceptions of well-being. By the mid-1980s, funding for social indicators research was partially restored by both the government and private organizations, and the major journal of the social indicators movement, *Social Indicators Research*, remains vigorous, and important conceptual and empirical contributions continue to be made (Andrews, 1986). Social indicators research concentrates on attempts to develop and refine measures of the *quality of life*, on indicator systems for *monitoring* an existing situation in society at a particular administrative or geographic level (for example, housing needs of low income people), and on the development of *performance measures* of public service delivery (for instance, health care for the elderly) (Carley, 1983:153).

Approaches to Social Indicators

Various approaches and emphases have been adopted by the adherents of the social indicators movement. They all have in common attempts to provide guidelines for the development of measures to fill the gaps in existing knowledge about social conditions; to try to link various measures so as to provide a picture not only of relevant phenomena but also of the relationships between them; and they all try to reduce information overload through concentration on relevant indicators and supporting data. It is obvious that whatever merit these various approaches have is determined by the criteria used to establish "relevance," what should be measured, what should be related to what, and how it should be presented. Let us now consider some of the more widely used approaches to social indicators.

One mode is to "regard the problem as one of choosing or designing the best set of measures for a society" (de Neufville, 1975:45). The uses for the measures are not indicated, and the principal effort is limited to the determination of problem areas in society and to their best measurement. For example, the Russell Sage Foundation sponsored two important compendia of essays on various aspects of social change in the United States: *Indicators of Social Change* (Sheldon & Moore, 1968), dealing with structural and institutional changes in topics like knowledge, labor force, population, and leisure; and *The Human Meaning of Social Change* (Campbell & Converse, 1972), dealing with similar topics, but focusing on subjective measures. The essays, however, "contained no common methodology or approach, and anyone reading them for guidelines about how a social indicator should be designed would be mystified" (de Neufville, 1975:46–47).

A second approach to social indicators is to work on new methods for measuring hard-to-quantify aspects (de Neufville, 1975:49). Illustrations for this approach would entail the search for new ways to measure socioeconomic status, underemployment, or poverty. Experimental work is also under way in attempts to measure things such as work and housing satisfaction, housing and neighborhood quality, and inequality.

In the third approach, the emphasis is placed on the design of theoretical frameworks for social indicators. A best-known illustration of a kind of framework is that of the social accounts suggested by Bertram M. Gross in a now-classic essay, "The State of the Nation: Social Systems Accounting." In this essay he delineated in a broad scheme what an ideal system of social statistics would look like. Specifically, he takes national income accounting as his model, extending it to a system of social accounting. This extension, in turn, is based upon a conception of society that he terms a "structure-performance model":

> The structure of any social system consists of (1) people and (2) nonhuman resources (3) grouped together into subsystems that (4) interrelate among themselves and (5) with the external environment, and are subject to (6) certain values and (7) a central guidance system that may help provide the capacity for future performance. . . .
>
> The performance of any social system consists of activities (1) to satisfy the interests of various "interesteds" by (2) producing various kinds, qualities, and quantities of output, (3) investing in the system's capacity for future output, (4) using inputs efficiently, (5) acquiring inputs, and doing all the above in a manner that conforms with (6) various codes of behavior and (7) varying conceptions of technical and administrative (or guidance) rationality. (quoted by Land, 1975:8)

Vastly oversimplified, Gross's idea is that the inputs and outputs of social programs can be measured and laid out in a matrix showing their interactions to help determine how best to allocate scarce resources. Unfortunately, his framework puts an unrealistic strain on existing data production capacity.

The fourth approach to social indicators entails replication studies (de Neufville, 1975:51). In this approach the argument is that social indicators are supposed to measure social change but in reality very little is known about how to do that. Here the emphasis is on one-time surveys, not on longitudinal time-series data. What is required is a set of measures taken in a carefully controlled way over time. To save time, the effort is to replicate studies that have already been done at least once. The objective is both to learn more about ways of collecting and interpreting indicators over time and more about the social processes themselves. Studies of social change in communities would be illustrative of this approach.

In the final approach, the emphasis is on indicators in their specific political and organizational context (de Neufville, 1975:54). The accent is on how information can be used in a decision-making process. For example, some United Nations agencies are searching for indicators that will help redirect particular policies of developing countries and the international organizations that influence them. Some organizations such as the World Bank and the United Nations Commissions for Trade and Development provide loans and aid to nations at least in part in relation to their performance on certain indicators. For instance, nations in the lowest quartile of the gross domestic product, literacy levels, and percentage urban population are eligible for special aid. International loans are generally given for projects perceived to increase the gross domestic product (Lengyel, 1986).

The discussion on these five approaches, although oversimplified, attempted to provide a perspective on social indicators. They highlighted some of the different problems, definitions, objectives, and methodological inclinations in social indicator studies. The next question is: What makes a good indicator? De Neufville (1975:58) suggests some general criteria for the construction of "good" indicators:

The measure must be pertinent to the question of concern.

The concepts underlying the measures must be clear and agreed upon.

The measure must relate to the concept which it is assumed to, and do so in a well-understood way.

The methods to produce the measure must provide reliable results, measuring what they purport to without hidden or unexpected bias.

The measure must be understandable and understood in its concept and limitations.

It must be known to essential participants.

Major parties to discussion on opposite sides must accept the measure.

It must be appropriate to its uses.

It should relate to more complex analytical models.

Data Collection

The principal methods of data collection for social indicators include interviews, self-reports, observations, and archives research.

The *interview* is the dominant technique because it is the most flexible. However, it is also the most expensive way of gathering data. *Self-reports,* where individuals or organizations provide information on themselves according to certain established formats, provide a less expensive means of getting some of the information otherwise obtainable only through interviews. It has obvious limitations, however, such as incomplete answers to questions, or failure to return the forms. *Observation* means getting information through watching, hearing, or otherwise directly sensing something. Its disadvantages include difficulties in interpretation and possible reactions in the observed. Finally, using *existing documents* is probably the easiest and least expensive way of collecting data. However, it should be noted that "the birth and death rates, most crime rates, and welfare case closings are all common indicators that depend heavily on documents that are filled out primarily for other purposes" (de Neufville, 1975:149). Documentary information is generally more useful in performing the activity it was designed for rather than analyzing it for other purposes.

Social Indicators in Use

There are many social indicators in use both internationally and nationally. International organizations, in particular the Organization for Economic Cooperation and Development (OECD), have been active in developing social indicators to measure the quality of life among its member countries. The OECD social indicators concentrate on general social concerns common to the 24 member nations (Organization for Economic Cooperation and Development, 1976). These concerns include health; individual development through learning; employment and quality of working life; time and leisure; commands over goods and services; physical environment; personal safety and the administration of justice; and social opportunity and participation. Let us briefly consider the content of these eight broad categories as they are illustrative of current emphases on social indicators.

In the context of *health*, measurements are being used to ascertain the probability of a healthy life through all stages of the life cycle and to measure the impact of health impairments on individuals.

The second category, *individual development through learning*, includes concerns such as attainment, maintenance, and development by individuals of basic and further knowledge; skills and values necessary for their individual development and their successful functioning as citizens in their society; the organized opportunities available to individuals to acquire, maintain, and develop the knowledge and skills necessary for their individual development and their successful functioning as citizens, and the propensity of individuals to use these organized opportunities; the individual's satisfaction with the process of individual development through learning; and the maintenance and development of a cultural heritage relative to its positive contribution to the well-being of the members of various social groups.

The third broad area of concern is devoted to *employment and the quality of working life*. It includes measures of the availability for gainful employment for those who desire it; the quality of working life in terms of working conditions, earnings, fringe benefits, employment time, employment-related time, and paid holidays; and individual satisfaction with the experience of working life such as conditions, earnings, fringe benefits, relations among and participation by employers and supervision, autonomy, and job challenge.

The fourth category, *time and leisure*, is devoted to indicators on the flexibility of patterns of working time; accessibility and quality of leisure-time opportunities; and time available for personal development, family and social obligations, and social participation.

The fifth category, *personal economic situation,* or command over goods and services, is intended to measure personal income and wealth in terms of the level and distribution of income and wealth; number of individuals experiencing material deprivation; the consumer's position in society and the availability of information on which to base effective consumer choices, and safety and quality of goods and services; the protection of individuals and families against economic hazards in terms of the extent to which individuals and families obtain insurance or other compensation for adverse change in their economic status; and the extent to which individuals and families perceive themselves as secure against adverse changes in their economic status.

The sixth area, *physical environment,* is considered for social indicators in housing conditions, including measures on the cost and availability of suitable dwellings, living space and utilities of dwellings, accessibility to neighborhood shops and services, workplaces, and neighborhood and environmental amenities; population exposure to harmful and/or unpleasant pollutants such as air, noise, water, and land; and the benefit derived by the population from the use and management of their environment in terms of land and water management, management of the urban and rural landscape, housing conditions, control of pollution, reduction of congestion, accessibility among social services and functions, and environmental contribution to recreation and amenities.

The seventh category, *personal safety and the administration of justice,* includes indicators on violence, victimization, and harassment suffered by individuals; fairness and humanity of the administration of justice; and the extent of confidence in the administration of justice.

The final category deals with *social opportunity and participation* in terms of the degree of social inequality, including measures on inequality among social strata; the extent of opportunity for social mobility and the position of disadvantaged groups; and the extent of opportunity for participation in community life, institutions, and decision making.

These indicators provide opportunities for intergroup, intertemporal, and international comparisons. Intergroup comparisons reveal relative levels of well-being of various population categories and thus provide guidance with regard to priorities for policy attention. Intertemporal comparisons give indications of changes that have taken place and show the quality of past government interventions. Finally, in addition to their inherent normative interests, international comparisons can throw light on how alternative schemes and institutional frameworks can effectively contribute to improve levels of quality of life in a society. The next section will consider the methodologies for forecasting change.

Methodologies for Forecasting Change

The future has always had a fascination for humankind. From the earliest times, humans have sought means for predicting the future. The tools they have used range "from chicken entrails to computers, while the range in success they have achieved has been similarly broad—and not necessarily related to the sophistication of the tools" (Teich, 1986:133). To a great extent, the ability to control the affects of change depends on being able to forecast the likely course of its development.

Current interest in forecasting methodologies can be attributed to the confluence of a number of factors. Rapid changes in population, depletion of natural resources, and overproduction of scientific manpower have created an awareness of the importance of ascertaining optimal rates for consumption and technological growth and anticipating supply and demand levels in the advanced skills provided for youth. Forecasting of changes is also needed in social planning, in the setting of national goals, and in establishing priorities for governmental intervention and manipulation. For planning purposes, for example, it is important to estimate with some degree of accuracy what the population of a society will be 10, 20, or 30 years later. Casual reading of newspapers also suggests the importance of knowing what energy needs and natural resources will be in the future. We might also want to know whether significant changes will occur in employment opportunities in the future or whether welfare case loads will increase or decrease.

There is no shortage of forecasting methods. In an Organization for Economic Cooperation and Development survey, Erich Jantsch (1967) identified more than 100 distinguishable techniques—although many of these are only variations in the choice of certain statistical or mathematical methods. For the present purposes, only a few of the more common (and not too mathematical) methods will be considered to illustrate briefly some of the ways in which change may be forecasted.

Extrapolative Forecasting

The foundation of all forecasting is some form of *extrapolation*, namely the effort to read some continuing tendency from the past into a determinant future. The most common, and deceptive, technique is the straight projection of a past trend plotted on a line or curve. Linear projections represent the extension of a regular time series—productivity or expenditures—at a constant rate. Most of economic forecasting is still based on linear projections because the rates of change in the economy seem to be of that order. In other areas, such as population, one cannot make simple predictions based on past trends. Instead, those interested in population changes talk about ranges of growth or decline that are based on a number of forecasts, and each forecast is based on a different assumption about future fertility rates. For example, a demographer might say, "If the fertility rate is 2.9 births per woman, we can expect the population to grow this way; if the rate is 2.4 births, population growth will assume a different direction," and so on. In other words, demographers will not make one flat prediction but, instead, will present a number of forecasts based on alternative assumptions about key rates.

Intuitive Forecasting

There are two popular forms of intuitive forecasting: scenario writing and the Delphi technique. The technique of *scenario writing*, popularized by Herman Kahn and Anthony Wiener (1967) and the Hudson Institute, is used widely for sociological, political, and environmental forecasting. A scenario attempts to describe, in systematic but hypothetical and largely qualitative terms, the future sequence of events that would appear logically to evolve, step by step and through cause-and-effect relationships, from any given set of conditions or recognized trends. Emphasis is placed on those critical decision points from which alternative chains of events might arise and on the simultaneous interactions between events and their environment. A single set of assumed initial circumstances can generate an entire family of related scenarios (or alternative futures), any one of which may be plausible. Military strategists in the Pentagon, medical researchers, business persons, demographers, and many others rely on the technique of scenario writing. For example, the Pentagon continuously prepares, revises, and updates scenarios for nuclear attack in view of the changing nature of weapons technology. Medical research and planners concerned with the AIDS epidemic use scenarios of the future based on different assumptions about the spread of the disease.

The *Delphi technique* was developed by Olaf Helmer (1966), a mathematician at the RAND Corporation. It is designed to apply the collective expertise and intuition of a panel of experts by developing a consensus through several steps of systematic questioning and polling about future events. The polling process is carefully organized so as to minimize the biases that might otherwise arise from interacting personalities or other psychological influences within the expert panel. A feedback system is used to sharpen or narrow the forecast through successive rounds of polling that are designed to call the attention of the panelists to factors they might have initially overlooked or dismissed and to force them to rethink or defend responses that differ markedly from the panel's overall views. The outcome typically is an approximate schedule of future occurrences. Delphi exercises can be particularly useful for exploring the future when adequate historic data are unavailable or when future developments are likely to be strongly influenced by such considerations as changing social values or political feasibility. Scenario writing and the Delphi technique have been applied to a variety of topics such as automation, space progress, probability and prevention of war, and population growth.

Modeling Forecasting

In *modeling forecasting,* researchers increasingly use computer technology to simulate future social trends. It is one of the most difficult forecasting techniques, and the outcomes usually tend to be controversial. One of the most publicized debates is the controversy precipitated by the publication of *The Limits of Growth*, in 1972, by Donella Meadows and her colleagues (1972). In their book they raised the question: What will happen to the world if current economic and demographic trends continue to increase at present rates? On the basis of data from 1900 to 1970, Meadows and her associates constructed a model composed of five key variables central to the world's ecological system—population, food supply, natural resources, industrial production, and pollution. They then constructed a set of mathematical equations detailing the processes through which the five variables interact with each other. These equations, constructed from available data, describe a *feedback* system in which a change in any one of the variables effects changes in the other variables, which in turn modify the variable that started the change process. One of the several equations describing the dynamic interactions between the variables might, for example, detail a feedback process that is set in motion by a change in population growth rates resulting in changes in demands for natural resources. This produces changes in productivity; these changes in turn affect the food supply, resulting in changes in population growth. After describing mathematically how the variables have interacted with each other in the past, they were prepared to simulate that same process into the future. The results are quite gloomy. They have predicted that the limits to growth on earth will be reached within the next 100 years and most likely will result in a rather sudden and uncontrollable decline in both population and industrial capacity (Meadows and others, 1972:23).

A more recent attempt in global forecasting was the *Global 2000 Report to the President*. It was commissioned by the Carter administration as an attempt to employ the huge amount of data and modeling techniques available to the federal government to develop a comprehensive and authoritative series of projections concerning the world's population, environment, and resources. It was a massive three-year study with rather gloomy conclusions. In the dramatic words of the study's summary:

> If the present trends continue, the world in 2000 will be more crowded, more polluted, less stable ecologically, and more vulnerable to disruption than the world we live in now. Serious stresses involving population, resources, and environment are clearly visible ahead. Despite greater material output, the world's people will be poorer in many ways than they are today. (Teich, 1986:136)

Survey Forecasting

Survey forecasting entails the use of survey instruments in either a panel design (using the same respondents in successive surveys) or in a cross-sectional design (using samples of individuals drawn at successive points in time), both with a view to identifying emerging trends in or estimates of attitudes. It is used primarily to forecast for a limited time horizon in areas such as political campaigns (Whom would you vote for?) and consumer behavior (Do you plan to buy . . . ?). As a rule, political pollsters do not consider their polls to be valid for more than a week or so, and, similarly, consumer buying and economic confidence forecasts tend to have a rather short time horizon.

Clinical Prediction

In this method of forecasting the emphasis is on what individuals, groups, or societies will do, given information about attitudes, beliefs, past experiences, and so on, and observations on their or its behavior. "The transfer of this procedure from the clinic to the society at large is referred to as 'social psychiatry'—an enterprise that is generally subject to severe criticism as being too superficial and anthropomorphic" (Harrison, 1976:7). On the individual level, fairly accurate predictions may be made based on performances on intelligence tests, standardized personality tests, other measurements and instruments (such as the various college and professional school entrance examinations), and the analysis of existing biographical information. The usefulness of this method is, however, highly questionable for the prediction of social events.

Intuitive Planning

Technically speaking, *intuitive planning* is not a method of forecasting; rather, it is a subjective, nonexplicit, nonreproducible estimation of a likely course of events in a plan (Harrison, 1976:8). It is based on a combination of past experience, common sense, and a touch of self-attributed clairvoyance and is mentioned here simply because some policymakers use this fast, inexpensive, and methodologically sloppy approach in their work.

Multimethod Forecasting

Quite frequently one finds a number of the preceding types of forecasting methods combined in various ways to produce a forecast. Obviously, it is very difficult to formulate guidelines for the best mix of methods to use for a given social forecasting problem. One may assume that if several different forecasting methods are used with the same set of data it may be more accurate than if only one method is used. However, there is no information on how much more accurate a forecast will be as to the use of combination or multitude methods.

Accuracy of Forecasts

Those doing most of the forecasting research—the think tanks, corporate planning offices, government agencies, and the like—are subjected to strong economic, time, and professional prestige motivations to produce social forecasting studies that look good. Daniel P. Harrison (1976:56) notes that with the various kinds of forecasting methods, the amount of error ranged between just a few percentage points (for example, with econometric models, survey forecasting) to over 40 percent (clinical prediction), depending on the method and time horizon used. He comments that "In almost every instance where forecast accuracy was assessed in terms of estimated user needs in particular contexts of use *none* of the methods could be said to perform at an adequate level; this may help to account for the modest impact forecasts have had on decision making" (1976:57). The state of the art of forecasting change clearly provides vast opportunity and need for research on forecasting methods in addition to the substantial amount of work that has been done on forecasting methodology to date. In the final section, policy implications of change assessment will be considered.

POLICY IMPLICATIONS

In the preceding sections several methodologies have been discussed that are used in the assessment of social change. In a sense, the development of these methodologies can be seen as a response to the growing demand for the quantification of social phenomena for decision-making purposes. Many of these methodologies are capable of generating information that can have policy or applied implications. Such information is helpful in transferring the basic knowledge and techniques for use in policy decisions or in evaluating current policies or proposed policy alternatives. Data generated through research provide policymakers with means for identifying problems and grounds for their discussion. Availability of hard data also helps in reducing the judgmental elements in decision making and thus the personal responsibility of decision makers.

Research findings also filter through to policymakers indirectly. Often, they hear about generalizations and ideas in the mass media or pick up information during conversations with colleagues and consultants. In this sense, research enlightens them and modifies the definition of problems they face (Weiss, 1986:218–219). This does not mean, it should be noted, that policymakers always rely directly or indirectly on data in making decisions. Often political considerations, personal experience, interest-group pressures, and a host of other phenomena enter into the picture.

Still, the methods of technology assessment are being increasingly used in policy-making. Technology assessment is policy- and action-oriented, and the results are being used to change or influence policy decisions. This orientation stems from the milestone events that have contributed to the establishment of technology assessments as legitimate and substantive programs within the realm of governmental activities, both in the United States and elsewhere. As it was pointed out, the recognition of the need for technology assessment resulted in the formal establishment of the Office of Technology Assessment in the United States Congress.

Technology assessment may be seen as part of a rational process of policy-making with four steps: (1) identification of possible outcomes of policy alternatives; (2) estimation of the valency or probability of each of the possible outcomes; (3) estimation of the utility or disutility of each of the outcomes to the interested parties; and (4) weighing the utilities and disutilities to the interested parties and deciding whether the policy alternative is better than other alternatives (Folk, 1977:243). The importance of the methods and techniques of technology assessment for decision making is also reflected in the requirements of the National Environmental Policy Act of 1969 for the preparation of environmental impact statements for federally sponsored projects.

The use of quantitative information is increasingly built into legislation, and there are specific requirements for the evaluation of many federal programs and activities designed to induce change in some area. As it was noted, evaluation research is characterized by explicitness of policy implications in the design and execution of the research plan and the incorporation of variables specifically relevant to the problem at hand. Evaluation research allows policymakers to determine the effectiveness of a program, whether or not it should be continued or phased out, and what in-course adjustments, if any, are needed to make it more effective (Salasin, 1978).

Social indicators for some time now have been used for measuring and reporting changes in the quality of life and related social concerns. Lately there has been a growing reliance on social indicators in decision making, both at the national and international levels. Policymakers increasingly find it desirable to issue information designed to estimate or evaluate the state of society and in varying degrees to assess alternative courses of action. Social indicators are also used as a vehicle to focus on public discussion on changes in the quality of life, increasing the level of awareness of the public, who in turn can exert some pressure on decision makers to engage in alternative courses of action.

For those who want to improve the information content of social indicators for public decision making, de Neufville (1975:243–246) offers the following advice:

1. Planning should take place in terms of *systems* of production and use of data that should take into account the way decisions are made and should include strategies for changing processes.

2. The creation of a new indicator takes time. Since time has to be allowed for trial and error even with background information and consensus on the problem, it is likely to take at least ten years between the desire to have a measure and its actual production.

3. The development of a new indicator requires a massive effort and a great deal of money, which may not seem rational in terms of immediate results. In view of the scope of the effort, it is recommended to link the development of systems for indicator production and use to the implementation of new policies and programs.

4. The impetus for the development for a new indicator usually comes from Congress or from a new administration during its initial wave of activity. An existing administration may be reluctant to develop new indicators because they might be used as weapons against them.

5. The development and maintenance of a set of measures should be related to important public policy concepts. This way each will upset bias or errors in the others and the interpretation of all as a group is more dependable than any one alone.

6. The production and use of social indicators need to be institutionalized so they cannot be arbitrarily stopped or ignored by those in power. Good public relations are also helpful since consensus is important to assure that an indicator can have an impact, and use itself tends to improve and legitimize a social indicator. Finally, regular communication and consultation between users or potential users and producers of the data for social indicators is essential if policymakers are to incorporate the results of indicators in decision-making activities.

Forecasting methodologies are essential for long-term planning and decision-making efforts. As with other methodologies of change assessment, governmental and nongovernmental policymakers at various levels are increasingly relying on the use of estimates and projections for future trends. With improvements in forecasting technologies, this reliance is anticipated to grow.

It should be noted, however, that once these various social science methodologies become relevant to and influential on policy, they become part of politics by definition. In such a situation, data can become tools for immediate political ends, and politicizers of data are not interested in them for their information content, but for propaganda. Ideally, the objective should be to insulate, but not isolate, the statistics from the immediate vagaries of day-to-day politics and to strike some sort of balance between political and technical considerations, permitting neither to dominate.

In contributing to decisions of technological, economic, administrative, and social welfare policy, social scientists can provide skills and perspectives related to an enriched appreciation of human needs, a fuller anticipation of the consequences of new technological inventions or new policies, and a greater respect for basic human values. In order to do so, however, there is a need for a greater dialogue between social scientists and decision-making bodies.

SUMMARY

This chapter examined the various measurements and methodologies used in the assessment of change. Longitudinal designs conduct observations at two or more points in time. There are two major types: panel and cohort. Panel analysis involves the observation of the same sample at two or more points in time. Cohort analysis is the observation of a specific cohort (age group) at two or more points in time. A form of quasi-longitudinal design is the recall survey, which conducts an observation at one point in time and has respondents remember information to establish a prior observation. Trend surveys also sample a population at two or more points in time. In addition to these types of analyses, sociologists interested in the study of change often use historical data to establish long-term trends or to test theories. The use of personal documents such as diaries, letters, and biographical statements have long been considered useful in the study of change. Researchers interested in historical experiences of large groups often turn to the use of available documents and records, which provide systematic data on large numbers of individuals.

The concern with the growing impact of technology on society gave rise to technology assessment to provide methods for identifying the implications and effects of technology on society. The methods of technology assessment may be future-, present-, or past-oriented. The common steps in assessment entail the definition of assessment task, description of relevant technology, development of state of society assumptions, identification of impact areas, preliminary impact analysis, identification of possible action options, and impact analysis. The methods of assessment are borrowed from different fields, for technology assessment has no defined set of tools. Comprehensive technology assessment programs can be very expensive. Methods of technology assessment are used also for the preparation of environmental impact statements and in the study of social technologies. The criteria for judging the quality of technology assessment efforts include the analysis of externalities, the burdens of uncertainty, the creation of constituencies, preservation of options, cumulative effects of scale, and technological convergence.

In recent years there has been a considerable rise of interest in applying social science methodologies to the evaluation of change. This interest is reflected in the growing emphasis on evaluation research. The object of evaluation research is to establish how successful a particular planned change effort is in achieving its goals. The designs of evaluative research include one-shot studies, before-and-after studies, and controlled experiments supplemented by cost-benefit analysis and social audits. It also includes plans for data collection, sampling, and measurement. The differences in emphases between program administrators and researchers is a potential source of problems. If the results of the evaluation program are negative, the client might attempt to dismiss the findings or rationalize the conclusions.

The social indicator "movement" is relatively recent. Three rationales for social indicators have been described: social policy, social change, and social reporting. The approaches to social indicators include the design of "the best set of measures for a society," devising new methods for measuring the hard-to-quantify, the design of theoretical frameworks, replication studies, and the use of indicators in their specific political and organizational contexts. After a brief review of the social indicator model proposed by Land, methods of data collection for indicators were considered, which include interviews, self-reports, observations, and the use of existing documents. The section concluded with a description of the use of social indicators by the Organization for Economic Cooperation and Development.

The methodologies discussed for forecasting change included extrapolative, intuitive, modeling, and survey forecastings, clinical prediction, intuitive planning, and the use of multimethod forecasting. In spite of the considerable amount of research that has been done on social forecasting methodology to date, the state of the art of forecasting warrants additional research to increase the accuracy of both short- and long-time horizon forecasts.

The methodologies discussed in this chapter have important policy implications. Technology assessment is policy- and action-oriented, and the results are being used to alter or influence policy decisions. Evaluation research is increasingly built into legislation, and there are specific requirements for the evaluation of federal programs and activities dealing with deliberate social change. There seems to be a growing reliance on social indicators in decision making, both at the national and international levels. Forecasting methodologies are essential for long-term policy planning and decision-making activities. Policymakers at various levels are increasingly relying on the methods of change assessment, and this reliance can only expand in the future as the government undertakes more responsibility and wants more information.

SUGGESTED FURTHER READINGS

DE NEUFVILLE, JUDITH INNES. *Social Indicators and Public Policy: Interactive Processes of Design and Application.* New York: Elsevier, 1975.   A readable and nontechnical book on social indicators and their usefulness to policy.

FREEMAN, DAVID M. *Technology and Society: Issues in Assessment, Conflict, and Choice.* Chicago: Rand McNally, 1974.   A provocative discussion of assessment of technological impacts on social life.

HARRISON, DANIEL P. *Social Forecasting Methodology: Suggestions for Research.* New York: Russell Sage, 1976.   A short review and evaluation of the methods used in social forecasting.

HELLER, FRANK, ed. *The Use and Abuse of Social Science.* London: Sage Publications, Ltd. 1986.   A collection of articles by noted international authors on the utilization of social research.

Porter, Colin F. *Environmental Impact Assessment: A Practical Guide*. St. Lucia, Australia: University of Queensland Press, 1985. A cross-cultural review of environmental assessments and concerns.

Rossi, Peter H., and Howard E. Freeman. *Evaluation: A Systematic Approach*, 3rd ed. Beverly Hills, Calif.: Sage Publications, Inc., 1985. A sophisticated discussion of the various facets of evaluation research with a minimal of technical jargon.

Singleton, Royce, Jr., Bruce C. Straits, Margaret M. Straits, and Ronald J. McAllister. *Approaches to Social Research*. New York: Oxford, 1988. A lucidly written survey of social science methodologies.

Teich, Albert H., ed. *Technology and the Future*, 4th ed. New York: St. Martin's Press, 1986. See, in particular, Part II on forecasting, assessing, and controlling technology.

REFERENCES

Andrews, Frank M., ed., *Research on the Quality of Life*. Ann Arbor: Survey Research Center, Institute for Social Research, The University of Michigan, 1986.

Babbie, Earl. *The Practice of Social Research*, 4th ed. Belmont, Calif.: Wadsworth, 1986.

Baram, Michael S. "Technology Assessment and Social Control." In Albert H. Teich (ed.), *Technology and Man's Future*, 2nd ed. New York: St. Martin's Press, 1977, pp. 311–335.

Bartocha, Bodo. "Technology Assessment: An Instrument for Goal Formulation and the Selection of Problem Areas." In Marvin J. Cetron and Bodo Bartocha (eds.), *Technology Assessment in a Dynamic Environment*. New York: Gordon and Breach, 1973, pp. 337–356.

Blaisdell, Donald C. *Technology—The Key to Better Environment?* New York: Exposition Press, 1973.

Campbell, Angus, and Philip E. Converse, eds. *The Human Meaning of Social Change*. New York: Russell Sage, 1972.

Carley, Michael J. "Social Indicators Research." In Kurt Finsterbusch, Lynn G. Llewellyn, and C.P. Wolf (eds.), *Social Impact Assessment Methods*. Beverly Hills, Calif.: Sage Publications, Inc., 1983, pp. 151–167.

Carr-Saunders, A.M., and P.A. Wilson. *The Professions*. New York: Oxford, 1933.

Coates, Joseph F. "Interdisciplinary Considerations in Sponsoring Technology Assessment." In Marvin J. Cetron and Bodo Bartocha (eds.), *Technology Assessment in a Dynamic Environment*. New York: Gordon and Breach, 1973, pp. 271–324.

Coates, Joseph F. "Technology Assessment." In Albert H. Teich (ed.), *Technology and Man's Future*, 2nd ed. New York: St. Martin's Press, 1977, pp. 251–270.

Coleman, James S. *Policy Research in Social Science*. Morristown, N.J.: General Learning Press, 1972.

de Neufville, Judith Innes. *Social Indicators and Public Policy: Interactive Processes of Design and Application*. New York: Elsevier, 1975.

Erikson, Kai. *The Wayward Puritans: A Study in the Sociology of Deviance*. New York: Wiley, 1966.

Folk, Hugh. "The Role of Technology Assessment in Public Policy." In Albert H. Teich (ed.), *Technology and Man's Future*, 2nd ed. New York: St. Martin's Press, 1977, pp. 243–251.

Fortune. "Do We Live As Well As We Used To?" September 14, 1987, pp. 32–46.

Freeman, David M. *Technology and Society: Issues in Assessment, Conflict, and Choice*. Chicago: Rand McNally, 1974.

Garner, Roberta Ash. *Social Change*. Chicago: Rand McNally, 1977.

Glaser, Daniel. *Routinizing Evaluations: Getting Feedback on Effectiveness of Crime and Delinquency Programs*. Washington, D.C.: Government Printing Office, 1973.

Gross, Bertram M., and Michael Springer. "Developing Social Intelligence." In Bertram M. Gross (ed.), *Social Intelligence for America's Future: Exploration in Societal Problems*. Boston: Allyn & Bacon, 1969, pp. 3–44.

Harris, Louis. *Inside America*. New York: Vintage, 1987.

Harrison, Daniel P. *Social Forecasting Methodology: Suggestions for Research*. New York: Russell Sage, 1976.

HELMER, OLAF. *Social Technology*. New York: Basic Books, 1966.

JANTSCH, ERICH. *Technology Forecasting in Perspective*. Paris: Organization for Economic Co-operation and Development, July 1967.

KAHN, HERMAN, and ANTHONY WIENER. *The Year 2000: A Framework for the Next Thirty-Three Years*. New York: Macmillan, 1967.

LAND, KENNETH C. "Social Indicator Models: An Overview." In Kenneth C. Land and Seymour Spilerman (eds.), *Social Indicator Models*. New York: Russell Sage, 1975, pp. 5–36.

LAZARSFELD, PAUL, BERNARD BERELSON, and HAZEL GAUDET. *The People's Choice*. New York: Columbia University Press, 1944.

LENGYEL, PETER. "The Misapplication of Social Science at Unesco." In Frank Heller (ed.), *The Use and Abuse of Social Science*. London: Sage Publications, Ltd., 1986, pp. 54–63.

LIPSET, SEYMOUR MARTIN. *The First New Nation*. New York: Basic Books, 1963.

MEADOWS, DONELLA H., DENNIS L. MEADOWS, JORGEN RANDERS, and WILLIAM W. BEHRENS, III. *The Limits to Growth*. New York: Universe Books, 1972.

MOORE, WILBERT E., and ELEANOR BERNERT SHELDON. "Monitoring Social Change: A Conceptual and Programmatic Statement." *Social Statistical Proceedings of the American Statistical Association*, 1965, pp. 144–149. Washington, D.C.: American Statistical Association.

MOTZ, ANNABELLE BENDER. "Historical Documents." In Kurt Finsterbusch, Lynn G. Llewellyn, and C.P. Wolf (eds.), *Social Impact Assessment Methods*. Beverley Hills, Calif.: Sage Publications, Inc., 1983, pp. 111–125.

NACHMIAS, DAVID, and CHAVA NACHMIAS. *Research Methods in the Social Sciences*, 3rd ed. New York: St. Martin's Press, 1987.

NEWCOMB, THEODORE M. *Personality and Social Change*. New York: Dryden Press, 1943.

Organization for Economic Cooperation and Development. *Measuring Social Well-Being*. Paris: Organization for Economic Cooperation and Development, 1976.

PIVEN, FRANCES FOX, and RICHARD CLOWARD. *Regulating the Poor: The Function of Public Welfare*. New York: Random House, 1971.

POLANYI, KARL. *The Great Transformation*. Boston: Beacon Press, 1957.

PORTER, ALAN L, FREDERICK A. ROSSINI, STANLEY R. CARPENTER, and A.T. ROPER. "An Introduction to Technology Assessment and Impact Analysis." In Albert H. Teich (ed.), *Technology and the Future*, 4th ed. New York: St. Martin's Press, 1986, pp. 208–213.

PORTER, COLIN F. *Environmental Impact Assessment: A Practical Guide*. St. Lucia, Australia: University of Queensland Press, 1985.

Public Opinion. "Public Opinion Potpourri," 10(3), September/October 1987, pp. 25–27.

RIESMAN, DAVID, NATHAN GLAZER, and REVEL DENNEY. *The Lonely Crowd*. New York: Doubleday (Anchor Books), 1961.

ROSSI, PETER H., and HOWARD E. FREEMAN. *Evaluation: A Systematic Approach*, 3rd ed. Beverly Hills, Calif.: Sage Publications, Inc., 1985.

SALASIN, SUSAN. "Linking Knowledge to Social Policy-Making: An Interview with Amitai Etzioni." *Evaluation*, 4, 1978 (special issue), pp. 54–62.

SHELDON, ELEANOR BERNERT, and WILBERT E. MOORE, eds. *Indicators of Social Change: Concepts and Measurements*. New York: Russell Sage, 1968.

SMITH, MARY LEE, and GENE V. GLASS. *Research and Evaluation in Education and the Social Sciences*. Englewood Cliffs, N.J.: Prentice-Hall, 1987.

SOROKIN, PITIRIM A. *Social and Cultural Dynamics*, one-volume ed. Boston: Porter Sargent, 1957.

STRASSER, GABOR. "Methodology for Technology Assessment, Case Study Experience in the United States." In Marvin J. Cetron and Bodo Bartocha (eds.), *Technology Assessment in a Dynamic Environment*. New York: Gordon and Breach, 1973, pp. 905–937.

SUCHMAN, EDWARD A. *Evaluative Research: Principles and Practice in Public Service and Social Action Programs*. New York: Russell Sage, 1967.

Survey Research Center. *A Panel Study of Income Dynamics*. Ann Arbor, Mich.: Institute for Social Research, 1972.

TEICH, ALBERT H., ed. *Technology and the Future*, 4th ed. New York: St. Martin's Press, 1986.

THOMAS, W.I., and FLORIAN ZNANIECKI. *The Polish Peasant in Europe and America*. Chicago: University of Chicago Press, 1918.

VAGO, STEVEN. *Law and Society*, 2nd ed. Englewood Cliffs, N.J.: Prentice-Hall, 1988.

WARD, DAVID, and GENE KASSEBAUM. "On Biting the Hand That Feeds: Some Implications of Sociological Evaluations of Correctional Effectiveness." In Carol Weiss (ed.), *Evaluating Action Programs.* Boston: Allyn & Bacon, 1972, pp. 300–310.

WEISS, CAROL. *Evaluation Research: Methods of Assessing Program Effectiveness.* Englewood-Cliffs, N.J.: Prentice-Hall, 1972.

WEISS, CAROL HIRSCHON. "Research and Policy-Making: A Limited Partnership." In Frank Heller (ed.), *The Use and Abuse of Social Science.* London: Sage Publications, Ltd., 1986, pp. 214–235.

*Index

*Page numbers in italics refer to suggested additional readings.

420